The Crown of Arsinoë II

The Creation of an Imagery of Authority

Maria Nilsson

Published by
Oxbow Books, Oxford, UK

ISBN 978-1-84217-492-0

A CIP record for this book is available from the British Library

This book is available direct from:

Oxbow Books, Oxford, UK
(Phone: 01865-241249; Fax: 01865-794449)

and

The David Brown Book Company
PO Box 511, Oakville, CT 06779, USA
(Phone: 860-945-9329; Fax: 860-945-9468)

or from our website

www.oxbowbooks.com

Library of Congress Cataloging-in-Publication Data

Nilsson, Maria, 1979-
The crown of Arsino? II : the creation of an imagery of authority / Maria Nilsson.
p. cm.
Includes bibliographical references and index.
ISBN 978-1-84217-492-0
1. Arsinoe II, Queen, consort of Ptolemy II, King of Egypt, ca. 316-270 B.C. 2. Crowns--Egypt. 3. Crowns in art. 4. Clothing and dress--Symbolic aspects--Egypt. 5. Egypt--History--332-30 B.C. 6. Egypt--Kings and rulers--Biography. 7. Queens--Egypt--Biography. 8. Bas-relief--Egypt. 9. Statues--Egypt. I. Title.
DT92.N55 2012
932'.021092--dc23
[B]
2012022307

Front cover image: Philae, inner sanctuary (chamber X), eastern partition, lower register. Photo: Maria Nilsson
Back cover image: Philae, inner part (outer wall of the sanctuary)(chamber VII), northern partition, eastern side of the door, lower main register. Photo: Maria Nilsson.

Printed in Great Britain by
Short Run Press
Exeter

Contents

Illustrations

NB: All photographs are by the author unless otherwise stated

Tables

Abbreviations

Abbreviations related to the citations are listed in the Bibliography

AC – crown of Arsinoë type
CS – cow horns and solar disc
DFP – double feather plume
RC – red crown
RH – ram horns
SFU – single forehead uraeus
TFC – traditional female crown
TW – tripartite wig
UR – uraeus

Preface and acknowledgements

The historical figure of Arsinoë II Philadelphos has received various degrees of scholarly attention over the years. Debates have concerned her political position and actual influence in the society during her lifetime, as well as her deification in connection with her death. Archaeological material referring to Arsinoë incorporates records of both Greek and Egyptian origin, textual as well as pictorial, but, while her name and actions survive into modern times, her tomb, along with those of Alexander the Great and the Ptolemies, so far remains undiscovered. This book deals with archaeological records in the form of Egyptian reliefs – as free-standing stelai or as part of preserved Ptolemaic temples – and focuses on pictorial depiction while including also hieroglyphic texts. While some artistic media incorporate descriptive titles enabling an absolute identification of the figure depicted, others are left to interpretation based on style, general appearance and, most importantly, personal attributes. Such a personal attribute was provided for Queen Arsinoë, and consisted of a pictorial composition of five main details. Together the ram horns, double feather plume, red crown, cow horns and solar disc composed an item that thereafter would identify its wearer: a crown here referred to as the crown of Arsinoë.

Ptolemaic art and socio-religious history offer the modern interpreter possibilities and difficulties alike owing to the dynasty's Macedonian origin. This dynasty was strongly anchored in Greek traditions, while ruling and reaching out to the people of one of the most ancient of societies, Egypt, with its own set of customs and regulations. The present investigation thus deals with not only the modern (hermeneutic) interpretation of ancient material but also Greek illumination of ancient Egyptian norms, and focuses on a comprehensive analysis of the crown of Arsinoë not as a means of identifying the person wearing it but to understand the wearer's religious and political role within her contemporary society.

Throughout the years that I worked with this material, I have been privileged with the support and encouragement of numerous people. Here I wish to express my gratitude to those who have assisted in making the completion of my research possible, as well as those who have encouraged me to produce this book from my original thesis (Nilsson 2010). I would like to begin by expressing my deepest appreciation towards Ch. Wikander, who as a mentor in my early career introduced me to and evoked my interest in the subject of the Ptolemaic Period, and who inspired me to complete my two previous scholarly dissertations. Her recent death is a great loss not only to her family and friends but also to the academic world. Assoc. Prof. I. Wiman was my main advisor during my work on my doctoral dissertation, and I have her to thank not only for her support and encouragement but, primarily, for widening my perspectives on the study of ancient art. Without her guidance, this study would have lost its theoretical anchor. I have Dr I. Östenberg to thank for her honesty, clear directives, sense of structure and valuable communication. Prof. R. Hägg has been a great inspiration throughout my education and will remain a role model of scholarly dedication and professionalism throughout my career. I also owe my deepest thankfulness to Assoc. Prof. C. Gillis, who guided me clearly and with constructive criticism onto the scholarly path that follows doctoral research while during the latter part of my doctoral education becoming a close friend and trusted advisor.

I owe Assoc. Prof. I. Wiman and Prof. R. Hägg thanks for introducing me to my 'Alexandrian family', headed by Prof. M. el-Abbadi, who welcomed me with friendly and open arms into Egypt's amazing cultural environment. He introduced me to Prof. M. Haggag, who became not only a great mentor, advisor and inspiration but also a trusted and lifelong friend. I will always cherish our lengthy, constructive dialogues. Their scholarly and professional support has enabled me to study the ancient material *in situ* with ease and to feel comfortable in the foreign country, Egypt, which eventually became my home. These friends and associates will forever remain close to my heart and I hope that I will have the opportunity to prove my deepest respect and appreciation for their invaluable support and trust.

During the course of my research I received funding from a number of foundations, without which help my doctoral dissertation and subsequently this work would not have been completed. Thus, I express my deepest gratitude to the following foundations: 'Kungl. & Hvitfeldska Stiftelsen'; foundations connected to the Humanities Faculty of the University of Gothenburg, Sweden; Wilhelm & Martina Lundgrens Stiftelse; Helge Ax:son Johnsons Stiftelse; Kungl. Vitterhetsakademin; Halmstad kommun; Herbert och Karin Jacobssons Stiftelse; Gertrude och Ivar Philipsons Stiftelse; and Knut och Alice Wallenbergs Stiftelse.

I am grateful also for the support I have received from various organisations throughout the years. Among my Swedish associates, I have the Friends of Alexandria to thank. I would also like to express my gratitude to the Archaeological Society of Alexandria and all associates who, as part of my Alexandrian family, have enriched my work through discussions, lectures and other activities;

to the numerous interdisciplinary intellectuals who are involved in the Sirius Project; and to the many museum personnel who have assisted me with photographs and information. Special thanks go to the Egyptian Museum, Cairo; Musées Royaux d'Art et d'Historie, Brussels Archäologisches Institut der Universität Trier; Pelizaeus Museum, Hildesheim; Royal Ontario Museum, Toronto, Harvard Art Museum; Medelhavsmuseet, Stockholm. I owe the staff at Oxbow Books my deepest appreciation, with special thanks to Clare Litt, Lizzie Holiday, Sam McLeod and Sarah Harrison

Among the postgraduate students at the Department of Historical Studies in Gothenburg who have commented on my work, given me advice and supported me in various ways, I am grateful to A. Lindqvist, K. Ciambella Berggren, K. Johansson and S. Karlsson, who, in spite of our geographical distance, have inspired this work. As a very important step in any academic work, communication with scholars who are familiar with the material (as well as the psychological rollercoaster that comes with the process) is essential. Among others, I would like to thank Dr B. van Oppen, F. Hellander, U. Bornestaf, M. Saad and S. Montazer for sharing their thoughts and guidance.

I am forever grateful for the support, inspiration, vivid discussions and constructive criticism that I have received from my greatly beloved friend and scholarly associate L. Lundberg, MA. Her belief in me has enabled me to continue this research and to develop as a person on so many levels. My mother believed in me from the very beginning and encouraged me to fulfil my childhood dream of becoming an archaeologist; I thank her and my father and siblings for their never-failing support, patience and understanding. Finally, I would like to express my deepest thanks for all discussions, comments, questions and advice that have enabled me to develop in my scholarly thought processes; and my eternal respect and admiration for my life companion and research partner in the Sirius Project, Dr J. Ward, to whom I dedicate this work.

Chapter 1

Introduction and historical background

The historical figure of Queen Arsinoë II[1] has long been a topic of discussion. Her involvement in political affairs has interested a broad range of scholars over the years, engaging dedicated Egyptologists and classicists alike. However, in the eyes of modern scholars her political role has always surpassed her religious position in her contemporary society, while as a subject of study she has remained in the shadow of her more famous descendant Queen Cleopatra VII. These two queens are, however, connected through more than their royal status. They were both deified in their own right, receiving religious attention from Greeks and Egyptians alike. They were also closely involved in the established cult of the royal family, venerated as the daughters, sisters and mothers of their Macedonian dynasty.

This Ptolemaic queen and ruler cult was expressed in various ancient media, one of which consisted of reliefs. In a period when (hieroglyphic) writing was limited mainly to the highest social strata, including the priesthood and the royal court, the relief scenes, with their images, could address all levels of society, providing a strong and comprehensible message for literate and illiterate viewers alike. Each iconographic unit had an important place in a well-chosen composition, incorporating all parts of the figures as well as the full scene into a complete and structured setting. The pictorial elements represented in each figure of the scene allowed individualism, thus separating one figure from another, in an iconic context where one of the most important attributes was the crown.

Such an attribute – a unique crown – was created and developed for Queen Arsinoë. It was a crown composed of strategically chosen iconographic units intended to set this queen apart from other royal women as well as from female deities. This crown was reused by two later Ptolemaic queens, Cleopatra III and VII, both of whom held an official status equal to that of the king. The crowns and their position within the scene, as well as their relationship with surrounding pictorial units, provide the modern world with a key to the understanding of a period in which respect for ancient traditions was vital, and to which traditions a new foreign dynasty had to adjust. A study of this unique Ptolemaic crown and its later variations will throw light on both the creation and the development of an iconographic programme introduced by the royal court as a part of a conscious politico-religious agenda.

The reliefs, following an ancient Egyptian tradition, show a great assortment of iconographic manifestations, each unique in their own way. Seemingly, the Macedonian rulers further developed this ancient artistic programme in order to reach out to both the indigenous people of Egypt and the increasing Greek immigrant population by introducing a programme of assimilation. Two ancient civilisations, each one with its own strong conventional symbolic values, merged in this unstable political period, the Hellenistic era: thus ancient Egyptian mythological creatures, vividly illustrated in anthropomorphic forms or with features of the natural fauna, met a contemporary set of beliefs expressed in traditional Greek religion. These two cultures combined to produce a powerful dynasty resting on established traditional dynastic conventions of politics in a country where royal events were carefully documented and distributed to the people.

The most obvious means of reaching the population was iconography, which offered the opportunity to manipulate size, position and time. In order to inform the population of the new dynasty the pre-existing iconographic programme was developed to include every aspect of the Ptolemaic queens' cultural context, Greek and Egyptian. The Ptolemaic kingdom, conscious of its dual cultural heritage, enabled the development of a means of artistic expression in which each pictorial element, resting on a highly individual symbolism, merged in a full composition. The crown, as a personal attribute and a symbol of hierarchic position, was one of the most important details in a scene, and it was thus unsurprising that a special crown was created for Queen Arsinoë in order to convey her rank and position in society. This attribute contained a statement so powerful that it remained an influential, recognisable symbol of queenship and divinity throughout the entire dynasty. Religion, power, politics and pictorial symbolism thus meet in one personal attribute, the crown of Arsinoë.

Queen Arsinoë

Images of Arsinoë appear in a broad spectrum of iconographic media, depicting this historical figure in a Greek as well as Egyptian cultural setting, and as queen and goddess alike. Although her descendant Cleopatra VII is better known to the modern world, the larger part of the iconographic material depicting a Ptolemaic queen does in fact represent Arsinoë. The daughter of Ptolemy I and Berenice I, Arsinoë was born in Alexandria *c.* 316 BC (traditionally calculated on the commentaries on her marriage in Plut. *Vit. Demetr.* 31). At the age of 16, *c.* 299 BC, she was married to Lysimachus of Thrace, an ally general of Ptolemy I, who was many years her senior. Soon after the marriage the couple parented three sons, Ptolemy (*c.* 298 BC), Philip (*c.* 297 BC) and Lysimachus (*c.* 294 BC) (Just. *Epit.* 24.3). During her time as the Lysimachus' spouse she received great honours, among other things the cities of Heraclea, Amastris and Dium, all given to Arsinoë by her husband (Plut. *Vit. Demetr.* 31; Paus. 1. 10). She also received the city of Ephesus, changing its name to Arsinoë *c.* 293 BC (contemporary coins bear witness to this: Svoronos 1904, nos 875–892; Mørkholm 1991; Troxell 1983). After disputed circumstances surrounding the death of Agathocles, the son of Lysimachus from his previous marriage, Lysandra, Arsinoë's half-sister and wife of Agathocles fled to Seleucus at Babylon, seeking support. Seleucus supported Lysandra and fought Lysimachus, resulting in the death of the latter in the battle of Corupedium in 281 BC (for a discussion concerning the political role of Arsinoë in the murder of Agathocles and Lysimachus' death see Sviatoslav 2007). According to Justin, Arsinoë temporarily fled to Ephesus to regain strength and with the help of her sons she continued to Cassandrea, where she commanded a garrison to defend the territory (Just. *Epit.* 24.2).

While defending the remaining territories Arsinoë's half-brother, Ptolemy Keraunus, defeated Seleucus and became the ruler of Macedonia. Keraunus persuaded Arsinoë to marry him, his aim being the annexation of the power held by her and her children. This marriage ended shortly thereafter when Keraunus killed two of Arsinoë's three sons (Just. *Epit.* 24.3). Arsinoë fled from Cassandrea to the island of Samothrace, where she later erected a temple in honour of the gods who helped her on the island (Just. *Epit.* 24.3). From Samothrace Arsinoë returned to Egypt. The sources describing the period between Arsinoë's time at Samothrace and her marriage with Ptolemy II are fragmentary, and no absolute information is yet available (*e.g.* Theoc. *Id.* 17,128; Paus. 1.7.1; Ath. 621A; Plut. *Mor.* 736F; *cf.* Cameron 1995, 18–22). During her period as queen of Egypt she was involved with the royal fleet and is recorded participating with her brother in battles. She is also described by the text of Theocritus as a queen of the people when arranging a play honouring Adonis and Aphrodite (Theocr. *Id.* XV). She participated in the Olympics, where she won three events for harnessed horses during the summer of 272 (or 276) BC (*P. Mil. Vogl.* VIII 309, AB 78; *cf.* Grzybek 1990). She received queenly status during her lifetime but also a divine position when the cult of the *theoi Adelphoi* was instituted.

The cultic roles of Arsinoë

Owing to the lack of archaeological evidence for the crown of Arsinoë, modern scholars are limited to the information provided in the artistic and textual forums. Her depictions have been presented and studied by various scholars over the years: thus her portrait on coins was studied initially in the grand volumes of Svoronos (1904, nos 875–892) and her Greek queenly position on the faience *oinochoai* by Thompson (1973), while her representations on sculptures in the round, terracottas, cameos, figurines and, of course, reliefs, have also been the subjects of study (Figure 1). Although there are a few three-dimensional representations of Arsinoë wearing her personal crown, the main material is found in reliefs (*cf.* Ashton 2001a; Albersmeier 2002), all of which are of a religious type. Although Arsinoë is illustrated as a queen, the scenes and full pictorial settings in which she appears have highly cultic connotations.

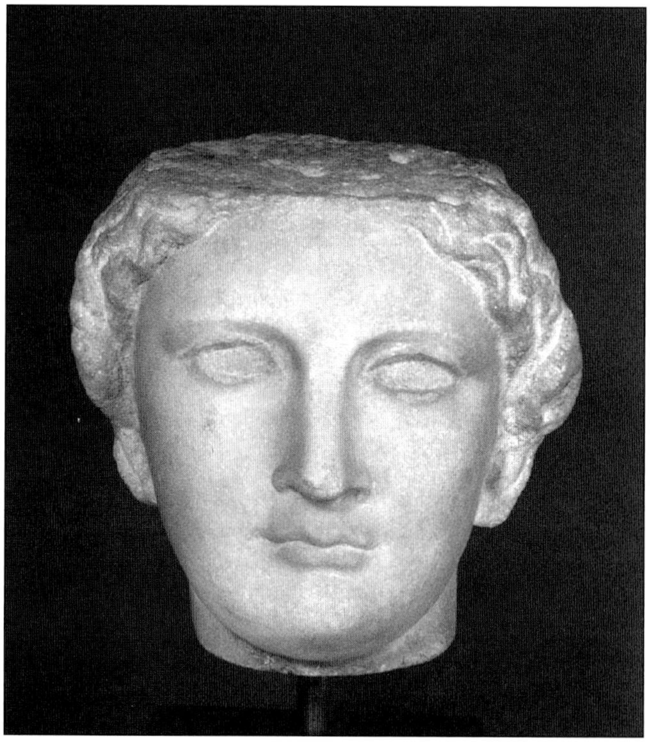

Figure 1. Greek-style portrait of Queen Arsinoë II, Bonn, Akademisches Kunstmuseum der Universität, B 284: photo by J. Schubert © Antiquities Museum, Bonn.

The cult of Arsinoë was multi-faceted and covered a great time span, from the reign of Ptolemy II throughout the Ptolemaic dynasty and into the Roman period (*P. Mil. Vogl.* 2, I.IV, dated 2nd century AD, describes Arsinoë in direct association with Aphrodite/Hathor). (One could argue that the cultic position of Arsinoë survived also into medieval times, since her name was still actively in use as designating several cities and the entire Fayyum province.) She received her divine status during her lifetime, initially together with Ptolemy II as the *theoi Adelphoi*, the sibling gods. Her individual cultic status as *thea Philadelphos*, the divine sibling-lover (brother-lover), is still today a contentious topic over which scholars remain in dispute (*e.g.* Quaegebeur 1971a; 1971b; 1978; 1988; 1989; Hazzard 2000, esp. chapter 5). The cult of Arsinoë also assimilated the queen with the Greek goddess Aphrodite, to whom pious worshippers dedicated much devotion. Her connection with other Greek deities is attested in more private forms throughout the Alexandrian area. It is, however, important to introduce at this point the religious role Arsinoë had in Egyptian society, where she was venerated not only in her queenly position as the earthly manifestation of Hathor but also in her own right. The cultic roles of Arsinoë should be considered individually, as each had its own priesthood, its own religious practices and its individual official as well as private meanings. A summary of these roles – the eponymous cult of *theoi Adelphoi*; the individual eponymous cult of Arsinoë; private cults of Arsinoë; the dynastic Egyptian ancestor cult of the *mr-sn*; and the native Egyptian cult of Arsinoë Philadelphos – will be provided here, while a more detailed account is provided in later chapters.

The eponymous cult of theoi Adelphoi

Although the material focuses on the Egyptian cult of Arsinoë, an introduction to the Greek counterparts is still important, as some cultic aspects of Arsinoë bridged cultural boundaries in this regard. The eponymous cult was Greek in its essence but, as will be further clarified below, it also had a strong similarity with the dynastic cult anchored in ancient Egyptian society. While all the scenes considered here are Egyptian in their artistic style, there is a thread linking the two cultures together: although the scenes are Egyptian in their setting, the official designations of the Ptolemaic couples are Greek in origin. The debate over whether these official cultic titles were translated from one language to the other or created from scratch contemporaneously (*e.g.* Winter 1978, 153f) is not addressed here. Regardless of chronological development or linguistic influence, the scenes at hand here describe the couple, Arsinoë and Ptolemy II, as the sibling gods. There is only scanty and fragmentary evidence that the Greek eponymous cult of the second Ptolemaic couple functioned in actuality as a cult in the truest sense. The main extant evidence comes from the dating formula, preserved in thousands of papyri dating to the entire Ptolemaic dynastic period (Clarysse and Van der Veken 1983; Fraser 1972, 219; *P. Mil. Vogl.* 309, 74 A–B; Bastianini *et al.* 2001, 200–202; Bingen 2002, 185–90; Barbantani 2005, 148; *cf.* Gutzwiller 2005). In the main these are documents which list the names of the serving priests of the eponymous couple (mainly associated with dates, names and geographic areas); only rarely do they refer to an existing sacred liturgy.

Arsinoë and Ptolemy II were deified as *theoi Adelphoi*, the sibling gods, in the year 272/271 BC (*P. Hib.*, 199, II. 11–17; Hauben 1970; Mooren 1975, 58–60; Hölbl 2001, 94f.). They were included in the official eponymous cult and were given their own priesthood, which designated each year. The cult of the *theoi Adelphoi* was placed immediately after the already established cult of Alexander the Great in the official records. The deification of the second Ptolemaic couple established a regal link with Alexander not only as his royal successors but, possibly more importantly, as his divine descendants. They were venerated in the chthonic centre of Alexandrian worship, the *Sema*, side by side with the immortalised Alexander (Fraser 1972, 215). This reconnection to previous rulers was a socio-religious phenomenon that already existed in ancient Egyptian culture and was mainly expressed through the ruler cult. The closest comparison that can be found in Greek society is the Hero cult (including the cult of famous athletes).[2] The decision to establish the cult of the *theoi Adelphoi* was clearly a strategic political act which placed the siblings in the same tradition as previous Egyptian pharaohs while also stating their Macedonian origin. Their deification also followed a contemporary trendrulers of the surrounding Hellenistic kingdoms. It was a cult in which the ruling couple was central and where the true royal bloodline was crucial. The cultic role as the female part of the sibling gods placed Arsinoë as the rightful queen in the eyes of the Egyptian people and acknowledged her true royal bloodline, thus clarifying her hierarchic status and sealing her position at the court. Through this role, Arsinoë prevented the intrusion of any contemporary woman aiming at the queenly position: she was the female member of a divine couple who were regarded as the founders of the dynasty throughout most of the Ptolemaic period (*cf. SB* 5680 = *P.Eleph.Dem.* VII 22, 26; Bricault 1999, 334–43; Barbantani 2005, 151; Fraser 1972, 219).

The individual eponymous cult of Arsinoë

The individual eponymous cult of Arsinoë is similar to the above: Greek in its essence. Arsinoë's official cultic designation was *thea Arsinoë Philadelphos*, the divine Arsinoë who loves her brother (sibling-lover). This title, chiming with the designation of the sibling gods, is identical to the Egyptian title present in the relief scenes investigated here. Although the cultic role of the divine Arsinoë Philadelphos is included in the general official eponymous cult (above), it can also be considered as an individual cult.

As stated above, Arsinoë's individual deification has been a contentious topic throughout modern times. As regards its date, most scholars can at least agree that this cult was established in relation to Arsinoë's death (*e.g.* Quaegebeur 1971b, 242). The ancient writer Satyrus is our main source of information in regard to the cult's practice (*e.g.* Momigliano 1993; McKenzie 2007).[3] This now fragmentary text, preserved from a work titled *On the demes of Alexandria*, describes a procession leading through the city in honour of the queen (*P.Oxy.* 2465, fr. 2, col. I). Satyrus states that the altar on which the offering was to be made should be made of sand, and, if not, then sand should be placed on top of pre-existing altars.[4] He further describes how any given object (except for a goat) was to be sacrificed at any location along the processional route. The procession was headed by a priestess officially designated *canephoros*, the basket-bearer. These were young women from the upper hierarchy, daughters of high officials or admirals, and they held this religious position for a period of one year (Clarysse and Van der Veken 1983; Fraser 1972, 222f). The priestess served in Alexandria as well as Ptolemaïs, and a *canephoros* has also been documented on Cyprus (Michaelidou-Nicolaou 1976; Barbantani 2005, 156; *cf.* Minas 1995). The procession was one of the crucial parts of a festival, honouring Arsinoë, called *Arsinoeia*. This is documented in both Alexandria and the Fayyum, and the textual sources describe a festival celebrated in the Egyptian month of *Mesore* (*P.Cair.Zen.* I, 59096; II, 59185; 59217; III, 59298; 59305; 59326; 59328; 59379; 59398; 59452; 59501; IV, 59690; 59710; *P.Col. Zen.* I, 56; *P.Lond.* VII 2000; *PSI* IV 364, *P. L. Bat.* XXI). The procession had its final destination at the centre of the worship of Arsinoë – a temple called *Arsinoeion* located by the sea in the Emporion area of Alexandria.[5] A famous passage from Pliny describes how the architect Timochares built the temple roof of a magnetic substance in order to lift an iron effigy of the queen into its place (Pliny *NH* 34, 148; Auson. *Mos.*, 311–17). An obelisk, an ancient Egyptian symbol, was placed outside the temple, connecting the queen to already ancient Egyptian customs. The obelisk had been transported to Alexandria from Heliopolis, where it had originally been placed undecorated by Nectanebo (Pliny *NH* 36, 67–9). The temple was probably totally destroyed during Augustus' building of the Caesareum near the area of the *Arsinoeion* (Pliny *NH* 36, 67–9; Fraser 1972, 25).

Although Berenice I was individually deified within this Greek cultural setting (supposedly) before Arsinoë, it was the latter who functioned as an ideological matrix for later Ptolemaic queens. The iconographic representations of Arsinoë in this Greek setting occur chiefly but not exclusively on coins. The main personal attribute accredited to Arsinoë in this cultural setting was the double cornucopia, which is illustrated on the reverse of each minted coin depicting Arsinoë (Svoronos 1904, 460, 475, 477, 938, 947, etc.; Troxell 1983). She is portrayed in profile on the coins, wearing a veil and other traditional Greek female attributes rather than the personal crown which is present in the Egyptian iconographic setting. There are no known examples of Greek artistic items illustrating Arsinoë where she is wearing the crown under consideration here (*cf.* Ashton 2001a).

Private cults

Connected with the officially recognised cultic roles of Arsinoë was also her position as an individual goddess assimilated with Greek Aphrodite. The ancient sources in which this cult is documented are all centred on the temple structure in which the goddess was venerated, the Temple of Arsinoë Aphrodite Zephyritis, situated on Cape Zephyrion between Kanopus and Nikopolis (Fraser 1972, 239; *cf.* Mattingly 1950) and dedicated to the queen by the admiral Callicrates of Samos. Court poets contemporary with Queen Arsinoë describe her as the goddess who calms the sea for sailors and gives them a safe journey. Poseidippus, Hedylus and Callimachus attest that the temple was open for everyone and that the devotees could perform their offerings on sea and land alike (Ath. 318D; Fraser 1972, 568f.; II 810 (chapter 10 iii), n. 129f.; Hauben 1970). They describe her as a queen with a divine epithet (*cf.* Fraser 1972, 569). Arsinoë supported the cult of Aphrodite in person during her lifetime, as is demonstrated by the play of Adonis and Aphrodite which was put on on the queen's behalf (Theoc. *Id.* 15; *cf.* Reed 2000). This festivity was celebrated after the death of Berenice I and is traditionally interpreted as representing Arsinoë's gratitude to Aphrodite for deifying the queen mother (Reed 2000, 320). Arsinoë was thereby also celebrating her royal descent in the female family line.

The worship of the divine Arsinoë also spread beyond the borders of Egypt. There are archaeological indications of an *Arsinoeion* in Idalion and *canephoroi* are documented on the island from at least 267/6 BC (Barbantani 2005, 156). The cult of Arsinoë on Cyprus was that of the deified queen, not in a full assimilation with Aphrodite (Michaelidou-Nicolaou 1976, A105; Mitford 1950; Friis Johansen 1953; *cf.* Barbantani 2005 156, n. 80; Stephens 2004, 161–76; Kyrieleis 1975, 78–80; Liphocka 1986, 311–22; Parente 2002). She was venerated also in association with goddesses other than Aphrodite. The famous faience vases, which are depicted with Arsinoë positioned in an offering act, connect the queen with Isis as well as Agatha Tyche (Thompson 1973; *cf.* *SB* 601, 602; *OGIS* 31; *PSI* 539.3; *P. Petrie*, I, 1; Fraser 1972, I, 241–3; Barbantani 2005, 150). Sources also attest a Delian Temple of Arsinoë-Agatha Tyche, called the Philadelpheion, where the worshippers offered shells. The inhabitants of Delos further celebrated a festival called Philadelpheia, most probably connected with this temple

(Vallois 1929, 32–40; Barbantani 2005, 147 n. 42). These are all examples of the wide-ranging nature of the individual cult of Arsinoë. This is, however, not the place to list all existing variations of the private cultic aspects of the queen. The reader is instead directed to the analytical chapters below, where parallels will be drawn between the Greek and Egyptian cultic roles of Arsinoë and the expressions these could take in her personal iconography – that is, the crown of Arsinoë.

The dynastic Egyptian ancestor cult of the *mr-sn*

It has already been stated above that one of the iconographic themes of the material under consideration here is the dynastic cult and ancestor worship, themes apparent in several scenes associated with Arsinoë. Such scenes concern the transfer of power from the dynastic ancestors to the ruling king. This theme is a religious continuation of ancient pharaonic ceremonies, which in the relief scenes are purely Egyptian in their settings. This religious depiction was practised by the Ptolemies at least from the time of Ptolemy II, although it is only absolutely documented from the reign of Ptolemy III, who is illustrated offering to his parents, Arsinoë and Ptolemy II. Arsinoë is once again referred to as the female part of the dynastic founders, as she was in the Greek eponymous cult described above. She is described in this setting as the divine mother or the great mother of the mothers, while also designated together with Ptolemy II as the *mr-sn*, the sibling gods. The ancestor cult, as practised by the Ptolemies, functioned as a means of reconnecting to and reclaiming the power of previous Ptolemaic ruler (couples), linking themselves back finally to the *theoi Adelphoi* (*e.g.* Winter 1978; Quaegebeur 1989). This dynastic ancestor cult did not, as far as archaeology has revealed, receive any centre of worship of its own, such as the *Sema* of the Alexandrian eponymous cult. Instead, the royal couples should be seen as temple-sharing deities when illustrated on the temple reliefs of the sanctuaries of the prominent Egyptian deities.

The native Egyptian cult of Arsinoë Philadelphos

Arsinoë was the first royal woman to receive a cult equivalent to those of the traditional Egyptian gods.[6] Furthermore, the cult of Arsinoë was, together with that of Cleopatra VII, the only cult of an individual queen to receive its own Egyptian priesthood in full ministration (*e.g.* Quaegebeur 1988, 42). The introduction of the divine Arsinoë was made by the court in close connection to and with respect and understanding towards the Egyptian priesthood. They, in their turn, accepted and acknowledged the importance of creating this bridge between the two strong cultures. Arsinoë's cult grew stronger in the Egyptian native religious sphere than any of those of the male rulers did. In many ways, the cult of Arsinoë was the initial point of introduction of the ruler cult in the Egyptian traditional temples and sanctuaries. Once the cult of Arsinoë and her younger sister Philotera had been introduced in the temples, and thereby approved by the powerful priesthood, the Ptolemaic ruler cult as a whole could develop. Arsinoë is, in this setting, equivalent to the *mr-sn*, the sibling gods, and is mainly depicted wearing the crown of Arsinoë. The only two existing exceptions, here listed as cat. nos 21 and 36, illustrate the queen wearing the traditional female crown.

The divine Philadelphos was introduced to the Egyptian people in Memphis as a temple-sharing goddess of Ptah sometime during the 3rd century BC and then took the place as the Great Wife of Ptah. Once the image of Arsinoë had been placed in the Temple of Memphis her cult was also incorporated under the supervision of the priests and scribes of Ptah. Philotera was initially also incorporated as a temple-sharing goddess in this temple, but disappeared from the official cult when the priestly office was given over to another, closely related, family, while the cult of Arsinoë only grew stronger and more influential (Crawford 1980, 26; Quaegebeur 1971b, 239–70). Written documents demonstrate that there was an individual Temple of Arsinoë in Memphis (Crawford 1980, 26; Quaegebeur 1971b, 250; Rundle Clark 1959, 60f.).[7] The priests of Arsinoë were servants of the old Pharaonic cult, following traditions that were sustained during the Ptolemaic period. Arsinoë's deification and acceptance into the ancient Egyptian pantheon was officially approved when she entered the sacred enclosures of Memphis: as one of the most important religious centres of Egypt, this was a great act of Ptolemaic propaganda. Here, Arsinoë dressed herself in the same divine attributes and designations as any of the legendary Egyptian goddesses. She became the eternally venerated queen, to whom the Egyptian people could turn when they were in need of divine intervention. However, the material cannot provide evidence that corroborates the priestly documentation in Memphis, primarily because of the lack of preserved temple structures in Memphis. Instead, it demonstrates a concentration of temple reliefs in Upper Egypt, with a few stelai bearing witness to a cult also in Lower Egypt.

Egyptian crowns

The crown was associated with royal political iconography. Each individual pictorial and architectonic unit was carefully selected in order to communicate a comprehensive message. In art, the Predynastic Egyptians, including queens, princes and princesses, showed themselves, in line with their gods, wearing different crowns which were reused and developed throughout the centuries. Ancient Egyptian sources provide us with six early forms of crown documented from at least the early dynastic period: the *khepresh*, the white crown, the red crown, the double crown, the double feather plume and the *atef* crown. All were still regularly depicted a couple of millennia later in the Ptolemaic and Roman periods (*cf.* Goebs 2008), and were stylistically elaborated and developed during later periods, forming a range of new variants of headdress symbol (Goebs 2001, 323–5).

The crowns were included in daily temple ritual from at least the Middle Kingdom, being associated with the rejuvenation theme of the constant rebirth of the solar disc through the cosmic cycle (*cf.* the hymns to the Diadem published by Erman 1911), as is documented in various Ptolemaic temples. Crowns are described as being carried in procession by priests and religious participants, who were illustrated on the walls of stairways and the roof structure (*cf.* a cultic crown made of wood depicting the white crown decorated with a set of outstretched arms in Cairo Museum, JE 91110; Goebs 2008, 28, n. 43).

As yet, no physical remains of a royal crown have been discovered, and pictorial representations of these objects sometimes provoke more questions than they provide answers. Owing to the lack of the objects themselves, it is difficult to reach any conclusions about the probable size, weight or makeup of the crowns. Ancient Egyptian textual and iconographic sources do not identify the materials employed in the composition of a crown. So, while the double feather plume appears to have a very light, naturalistic, physical form, it may have been made of, for example, (a grid of) gold or any other metal, and it would thus have been correspondingly heavier.

Iconography could arguably provide answers to questions about the crowns' original, physical forms. However, Egyptian art repeatedly provides examples of intentional adjustment of size, form and proportion, and may serve rather to confuse the viewer than to offer any guidance. It will be demonstrated below how the adjustment of images in artistic work was intended to emphasise one aspect or unit over another.

Pharaohs were depicted with individual crowns throughout ancient Egyptian history, each of which could symbolise a certain feature of kingship or divinity. These individual crowns were developed and presented in a great variation of compositions. Any modern observer can witness how the original crowns explode stylistically into new elaborated compositions, arranged structurally by a great variety of pictorial units and with a colourful palette. The crown of Arsinoë demonstrates this stylistic development, as do several other crowns worn by surrounding figures in the relief scenes investigated here.

The compositions of royal crowns followed certain conventions throughout the main dynastic periods, which limited the number of pictorial units used and ensured that the meaning of the message projected was clear. Prior to the Ptolemaic period, the double crown was the most important and powerful royal crown, and rarely received any pictorial additions. While retaining its clear symbolic value, it was also accompanied by additional crowns which were compiled from numerous units in an elaborated style, while still communicating a message of kingship and superiority. The crowns investigated here include elements of various traditional crowns with details originating in the natural fauna. By wearing a traditional crown, the Ptolemaic queens immediately associated themselves with the previous ruling couples as well as the divine world of Egypt. However, when combining existing pictorial units and developing them into new compositions, as represented in the crown of Arsinoë, they could reach a comprehensive symbolic individualism. The development of new individual compositions has ideological similarities with the socio-religious philosophy focusing on the individual, which was one trait of the Hellenistic period and was manifested and advocated by the scientific elite in Museion in Alexandria.

Egyptian crowns were used as personal attributes of deities: examples include the *atef* crown of Osiris, the fish-dolphin of Hat-Mehit and the flower of Seshat. However, in a majority of cases crowns contain or comprise elements temporarily borrowed or fully usurped from other deities. This is unmistakably demonstrated in images of Isis wearing the traditional Hathoric crown composed of cow horns and solar disc. Gods' temporary borrowing of full crown compositions or pictorial units of other crowns is sometimes associated with temple symbolism, in that a specific crown might be preferred owing to the figure's position in the scene, structural part of the temple or geographical location (Cauville 1987, 217; Goebs 2001, 323f.).[8]

The hieroglyphic sign for crown, 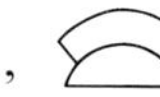 – *ḫʿw*, symbolises the crown itself, but can be translated also as 'manifestation', 'form of appearance', or as representing the rise of Atum from the primeval mound (Gardiner's sign-list (1957) N28; *cf.* Goebs 2008, 24f). In addition to the crown's clear link between royalty and divinity, it has been suggested recently to have a strong association with the Underworld and funerary iconography, in which royalty and common people alike were depicted wearing these headdress elements (Goebs 2008). Crowns could also have a cosmological connotation in which they were associated with cosmic events and stars constellations (Goebs 2008, 24f). Such connotations will be dealt with in following chapters.

Notes

1 This queen will be referred to here simply as Arsinoë, while Arsinoë I and III will retain their regnal numbers.

2 The main difference between the Alexandrian ruler cult and the native Egyptian ruler cult is based on the priesthood. In their roles as the divine pharaoh, the Egyptian kings were worshipped in temples with well-established hierarchical and hereditary priesthoods. Only a few pharaohs, including Menes, Snofru, Teti, Ramesses II, Merenptah, Amasis and Nectanebo II (*e.g.*

Crawford 1980, 26f.; Thompson 1988, 127 note 116; Hölbl 2001, 101f.), enjoyed a fully developed posthumous cult before the Ptolemies. The Alexandrian ruler cult, on the other hand, had eponymous priests who changed office every year. For a list of the priests and priestesses of the royal cult see Clarysse and Van der Veken 1983.

3 One part of the available information concerning this cult is the different forms of dedications made by private people in honour of the queen and goddess. These dedications, usually in the form of small stone plaques, were dedicated to a deity in honour of or on behalf of Arsinoë. They were often written in a simple form, usually just mentioning the name of the one performing the dedication and the one which it is dedicated on behalf of, in a grammatical dative form. They are one person's expression of gratefulness and loyalty towards the royal house, to the queen. The objects vary in form and size, from small plaques to entire sanctuaries and temples. Although the objects do not give any absolute information about the cult, they do indicate its existence (*e.g.* Fraser 1972, 226f.).

4 This passage may include a misinterpretation of the Greek word: rather than the altar being made of sand, it is possible that it was to be made of sandstone and that, if this was not possible, sand should be placed on top of the already existing altar to give the correct appearance. The explanation Fraser (1972, II chapter 5 n. 318) gives concerning the sand – that it was placed there to absorb any spilled blood from the offering – is unlikely to be correct, as there are no other known references to sand being placed on altars to serve this purpose. The sand must have been used for a very specific religious reason. Robert (1966, 199–203) connects the sand with Arsinoë's role as the patroness of sailors.

5 The exact location of the temple is still debated owing to inconsistent textual sources combined with the lack of archaeological material. Callimachus, in a fragment of *Apotheosis of Arsinoe* (Fr. 228, *Diegesis* X.10), places the *Arsinoeion* in the Emporion area. Strabo does not mention any temple of Arsinoë in his account of Alexandria. It has been suggested that it was a temple in which not only Arsinoë but also her sister, Philotera, who died when Arsinoë was still alive, was worshipped. If this is the case the *Arsinoeion* might already have existed during Arsinoë's lifetime, thereby supporting the theory put forward here regarding Arsinoë's deification in her own right when still alive (*cf. FGrH* 570, F16).

6 Compare, however, the cult of 18th-dynasty queens, which are occasionally reminiscent of the cult of Arsinoë.

7 Could this *Arsinoeion* possibly be the temple referred to in *P.Petrie* II 16, 13? For the papyrus see Milligan (1927, 7), Witwowski (1911, 6), Perpillou-Thomas (1993, 155–8) and Barbantani (2005, 147 n. 42). Owing to poor site preservation there are no archaeological remains that can support this. Neither can the archaeological remains reveal whether the *Arsinoeion* was a free-standing building or whether it was directly connected to the main temple of Ptah. See the full publication of *Studia Hellenistica* 24 (Crawford *et al.* 1980).

8 In previous publications, the crowns have in the main been divided into three principal groups, including one group of royal crowns limited to the pharaoh himself, the female royal crowns and the divine crowns. However, this categorisation is inadequate, since there are so many examples of the same crown being used by not only kings but also queens and deities. Goebs (2008) underlines also the interdependency between the king and deities, although she does not include any examples of queens except for Hatshepsut. The main examples from the first group, which is supposed to be limited to the pharaoh himself, are the red crown and the white crown, as well as a further one, the double crown, created by a combination of these. There are also other examples, as when a queen is wearing the traditional double crown of kingship, one of which is documented in Karnak, worn by Queen Amenirdis I. Each element of the Egyptian crowns included in the present study could be worn by all three groups and act as a direct link between them all.

Chapter 2

Methods and theory

Objectives

The crown of Arsinoë was composed of a carefully selected compilation of pictorial units, created exclusively for the second Ptolemaic queen. In this book thirty-six relief scenes illustrating Arsinoë (Table 1), encompassing all preserved Egyptian relief scenes depicting the queen, will be morphologically and contextually analysed, and the iconographic meaning communicated by the crown, as well as its political and socio-religious connotations, will be discussed.

It is necessary to deconstruct the crown of Arsinoë in order to comprehend the form and symbolic value of each iconic component (*cf.* D'Alleva 2009, esp. 131–8), examining the size and position of each pictorial unit in association with its contextual setting and in accordance with an iconographic and semiotic approach. Central questions concern the significance and intention of the messages conveyed by each individual pictorial unit, which may be comprehended via the examination detailed above.

A hermeneutic approach to the material will allow an exploration of the initial meaning of the crown of Arsinoë and the ways in which it was viewed by contemporary beholders. In addition, it will assist in an engagement with questions related to the socio-religious role of the original wearer of the crown of Arsinoë, the queen herself. Issues which are central in this regard concern Arsinoë's deification, particularly as regards the current debate over the temporal aspect – that is, whether her deification occurred during her lifetime or after her death; her possible role as pharaoh; and her religious role as high priestess within Egyptian religion. Together with the investigation of the meaning and message embedded in the crown of Arsinoë, these three topics (deification, possible kingship, religious role) form the foundation of the analysis within chapters 3–9 and are explicitly addressed in the discussion and iconological interpretation contained in Chapters 10–12.

It is of great importance that any investigation of Egyptian crowns includes an analysis of the full context of any given scene, as intimated above. Once the identity of the crown and its wearer has been ascertained, it becomes possible to recognise potential relationships with surrounding pictorial units and to examine the associations between the crown and these varying elements. Through contextual study of the iconographic units of the crown of Arsinoë comparison may be made with the pictorial details of crowns worn by previous queens as well as by priestesses. The resulting discussion of potential iconographic differentiation in the crowns worn by Egyptian women in their roles as queens and as priestesses adds to our understanding of the historical context of crown-wearing by Egyptian female figures, thus facilitating a further step in the hermeneutics of Egyptian iconography.

Moreover, the hieroglyphic titles of Arsinoë, which will, including epithets, be translated and listed individually, may be employed in order to amplify iconological interpretations, stressing potential pictorial associations. They can also demonstrate possible local variations of the roles of the queen when depicted wearing the currently investigated crown.

The present study is thus both a comprehensive analysis of this crown and its symbolic meaning and an endeavour to date the crown's introduction and pictorial development and variations. In analysing the crown of Arsinoë this book also deals with how reliefs and religious iconography were called upon by the royal family in order to reach out to the population of the kingdom and, more importantly, to establish full collaboration with the Egyptian priesthood. It is an inquiry intended to bridge the modern disciplines of classical archaeology, art history and Egyptology in order to more closely understand the multi-faceted intentions behind the reliefs of an Egyptian dynasty originating in a Greek culture.

Definitions

Ancient Egyptian crowns composed of several pictorial units, such as that presented here, are traditionally designated as composition crowns, a term which will be used here when describing multi-faceted crowns in general (*cf.* Abubakr

1937; Derchain-Urtel 1994; Quaegebeur 1988; Dils 1998). The iconographic and semiotic premises applied here include a stage of classification which consequently demands a clarified terminology. Previous scholarship has not given an adequate official name to Arsinoë's crown, instead vaguely referring to it as 'the crown originally worn by Arsinoë' (*cf.* Bianchi 1988, 103f.: 'the distinct crown'; Quaegebeur 1988, 47: 'crown of Arsinoë II'). Nor is there a recognised

SCENES CAT. NOS	CROWN	FEMALE FIGURE	MAIN FIGURES IN THE SCENE	LOCATION INCL. MUSEUM[1] AND INV. NO.
1	AC 1; AC2	Arsinoë × 2	8	CG 22181
2	AC 3	Arsinoë × 2	12	CG 22183
3	AC 4	Arsinoë	10	CG 22188
4	AC 5	Arsinoë	15	CG 22186
5	AC 5	Arsinoë	5	Zagazig 228 = Herriat Raznah Museum No. H 854
6	AC 6	Arsinoë	4	Brussels MRAH E. 8387
7	AC 7	Arsinoë	2	Moscow I.i. 5375
8	AC 8	Arsinoë	2	Relief of Arsinoë, University of Trier[2]
9	AC 9	Arsinoë	1	Hildesheim, Pelizaeus-Museum 1025
10	AC 4	Arsinoë	2	ROM 979.63[3]
11	AC 6	Arsinoë	6	CG 31104
12	AC 10	Arsinoë	1	Relief of Queen Arsinoë II as Hathor, Harvard Art Museum[4]
13	AC 12	Arsinoë	2	British Museum EA 1056
14	AC 11	Arsinoë	6	British Museum, EA 1057
15	AC 6	Arsinoë × 2	8	MM 10026
16	AC 11	Arsinoë	3	Edfu
17	AC 11	Arsinoë	3	Edfu
18	AC 12	Arsinoë	10	Edfu
19	AC 5	Arsinoë	3	Edfu
20	AC 12	Arsinoë	6	Edfu
21	TFC	Arsinoë	3	Edfu
22	AC 11	Arsinoë	3	Edfu
23	AC 13	Arsinoë	3	Karnak
24	AC 13	Arsinoë	3	Karnak
25	AC 6	Arsinoë	46	Karnak
26	AC 13	Arsinoë × 2 (× 4)	8 (10)	Karnak
27	AC 14	Arsinoë	3	Philae
28	AC 15	Arsinoë	3	Philae
29	AC 14	Arsinoë	3	Philae
30	AC 16	Arsinoë	3	Philae
31	AC 17	Arsinoë	3	Philae
32	AC 14	Arsinoë	4	Philae
33	AC 18	Arsinoë	2	Philae
34	AC 19	Arsinoë	3	Qasr el-Aguz
35	AC 20	Arsinoë	12	Tod
36	TFC	Arsinoë	3	Medamoud

Key: AC = Crown of Arsinoë; TFC = Traditional female crown. A name followed by ×2 indicates that the figure is depicted twice in the scene. The +sign is used when the scene includes additional figures such as in a procession.

Notes
1. CG – Egyptian Museum in Cairo; MM – Medelhavsmuseet in Stockholm.
2. Archäologisches Institut der Universität Trier.
3. Royal Ontario Museum, Toronto 979.63.
4. Harvard Art Museum, Arthur M. Sackler Museum, gift of Mr. and Mrs. Samuel H. Lindenbaum, 1983.96.

Table 1. The scenes: The table lists each individual scene, its crown-type, the identity of the female figure, the total amount of main figures in the scene, and the location of the image.

sufficiently descriptive ancient title of the queen's crown. The currently applied title, the 'crown of Arsinoë', is here regarded as the most applicable designation, given its original wearer, although the crown is attested also as a head attribute of the two later Ptolemaic queens Cleopatra III and Cleopatra VII (Dils 1998, 1302: 'la couronne portée par Arsinoé II ou Cléopâtre VII'). For current purposes it is a satisfactory title for a group of crowns composed of five basic pictorial details: the red crown, ram horns, double feather plume, cow horns and solar disc.

The crowns will be described below in accordance with the composition, size and position of each pictorial unit. The classification of each crown type also considers the individual headdress units, represented as wigs and additional ornaments. On the basis of the differentiations in size and placement, the crown is divided into twenty individual variations, abbreviated as AC 1–AC 20. When merely describing, analysing or discussing each crown, it will be referred to by its type name. When the discussion also includes a contextual demonstration of the interaction of the pictorial units of the full figure or scene, the reader will be directed to the title of the figure and the number of the scene given in the catalogue, abbreviated as 'cat. no(s)'. All individual pictorial units listed in the analysis are designated in conformity with a generally accepted terminology. The titles of the individual headdress and crown units/elements are accompanied by an abbreviation, which is placed within brackets following each title; for example, the tripartite wig is abbreviated TW. These abbreviations are confined in the main to the tables, but they also appear elsewhere throughout the work.

All ancient names used in the present publication will be given in their most recognisable form, so that Greek names appear in accordance with the modern English spelling rather than the ancient Greek form (thus Ptolemy instead of Ptolemaios); likewise, Latin names have their modern form (so Trajan rather than Trajanus). The main historical figure of this investigation, however, will be referred to as Arsinoë Philadelphos, indicating the pronunciation of the full designation in agreement with its Greek original form; this form of the queen's name is today generally preferred among established contemporary scholars. In the absence of a generally accepted up-to-date publication on the traditional full pharaonic names and titles it is necessary to combine *Livre des Rois* (Gauthier 1907; 1912; 1914; 1916; 1917), *Handbuch der ägyptischen Königsnamen* (Beckerath 1984), *Lexicon der Ägyptologie* (*LÄ* I–VII), *Encyclopedia of the Archaeology of Ancient Egypt* (*EAAE*) and the lists given in *Chronicle of the Pharaohs* (Clayton 2006) and *Chronicle of the Queens of Egypt: from early dynastic times to the death of Cleopatra* (Tyldesley 2006). Unless otherwise stated, geographic names given below follow the list published in *Atlas of Ancient Egypt* (Baines and Malek 2002) and will be given in accordance with their currently most familiar name, mainly using their ancient Greek forms, although when the modern name is more widespread, like Dendera, it will be used.

Theoretical and methodological approaches

Comprehensive iconographic studies of Egyptian crowns illustrated in relief are rare, almost deficient, largely owing to the great variation and complexity in Egyptian crown composition. The crowns have, likewise, not been systematically studied for their symbolic and mythological value. No adequately established methodology exists, therefore, for dealing with this material, leaving large areas of research unexploited.[1] However, theories and methods of communication sciences, such as semiotics, hermeneutics, contextualism and structuralism, facilitate attempts to methodologically analyse each sign of the crown and its correlation with surrounding pictorial details. All artistic work is anchored in some way in images reflecting the human psyche or the contemporary society in which the artists live. Such images can also express the ideological foundation upon which an entire society rests. Each society, in turn, contains encoded statements of politico-religious principles which are communicated through a language of man-made codes. In ancient Egypt, as in any culture, these codes were manifested in a textual, a verbal and a pictorial language. Here, the written language, consisting of hieroglyphs, is essentially associated with the conventional images represented in reliefs and sculpture.

Ancient Egyptian culture partly manifested itself in rich and colourful religious representations visible in all parts of the country. Regardless of access to the inner parts of the temples, Egyptian inhabitants could view each pictorial sign forming the full relief scene, which were depicted in strong colours and often in great size on the enclosure walls. Like any other society, whatever its time and geographic location, Egyptian culture created a system of conventions applied in the construction of imagery (*cf.* Morgan 1985, 7f.). These structural principles, which together form the full image, require an individual morphological examination, innately on the part of contemporaries and consciously on the part of modern scholars, prior to identification. It is only through an awareness of the morphology of each sign and the full syntax that we are able to approach any image regardless of the cultural setting.

The first step in any iconographic interpretation involves the transformation of an image into a verbal or written language in which each detail is described in words (Morgan 1985, 6f.). This process is essentially a practical one and can be combined with statistical information about, for example, how many times a certain scene occurs, how often it appears in a specific orientation within the temple and its relationship to surrounding scenes and registers (Walsem

2005, 21). The translation of the image into a verbal and descriptive language can be formulated through the application of semiotics, the theory of signs (D'Alleva 2009, 28f.). Semiotics, when applied to art, most often functions as an interdisciplinary complement of iconography, a method of investigating the meaning of any art work. It provides a practical and intelligible framework for interpreting the various associations between image and culture as well as between artist and viewer (D'Alleva 2009, 29). In a culture in which images are also used to express words – as in the case of Egyptian hieroglyphs – this semiotic correlation becomes most evident. Thus, information provided by Egyptian images has equivalence in value to the information provided by hieroglyphic texts.

The meaning of any image lies in the association between the form and the idea, and it is absolutely necessary to conduct a structural analysis of the form prior to any iconographic interpretation.[2] This means that each image must be deconstructed to its smallest definable pictorial unit, one defined as an individual form which can be understood on its own and from which nothing further can be extracted. For example, the Wadjet eye is composed of an eye, an eyeball, a tear, a curl and an eyebrow. The smallest iconographic detail is labelled here as a 'unit', each of which has an individual significance, but when placed together they make up one of Egypt's most renowned religious symbols. Similarly, a feather, composed of outline, rachis and barbs, is a full unit. The extraction of the outlines from the image leaves the rachis (the centre line) and the barbs, reminiscent more of a leafless tree than the core of a feather. However, if one instead removes the inner details of a feather, leaving only the outlines, the sign could still be recognised as a feather. The unit of a feather can thus be seen either in a simple form, without its inner structure, or in a more elaborated form, including the rachis and barbs, examples of which will be demonstrated below. Such a deconstructing process will eventually enable an identification of the full image.

The present study adopts a so-called paradigmatic analysis, which focuses on details with a similar significance that, regardless of their form, convey a comparable message (such as 'sun disc' and 'Aten' or 'Ra'). Thus, each unit has a symbolic value expressing certain cultural aspects or religious associations (Chandler 2002, 79–81; Olsson 2006, 44). These socio-religious connotations are considered here, as are possible existing associations in the natural surroundings and any political connections, which are also of great importance.

Once each pictorial unit has been determined, the image can be rebuilt via a process of observing the association of these units. This association is what de Saussure and Peirce refer to as a code: a larger system of units together constructed to demonstrate a message which is the full context of the units, and without which any unit would be individually meaningless (Saussure 1974; 2006; Peirce 1870; 1883; 1983; 1994). The meaning of the unit is based on the creation of a framework by the code, within which the unit exists. Thus a semiotic interpretation of iconography creates a relation between an image, its code and its individual units (D'Alleva 2009, 32).

The post-structuralistic theory of direct and indirect indications, described as denotation and connotation, is also significant. 'Denotation' refers to a meaning which is explicit, while 'connotation' refers to a less obvious (implicit) meaning which demands an interpretation (Kristeva 1980; D'Alleva 2009, 34f. with n. 32). Hathor, for example, is clearly denoted to have a maternal role when breast-feeding a young child. However, it is only through the connotations of her persona as royalty that the viewer can assume that the child signifies the pharaoh.

The analysis of the morphology and syntax of an image (the code of the iconographic language), and the evaluation of the full contextual setting, including the associations of each pictorial unit, combine to form for the viewer a full, self-supporting image in which the unit is included. The study of these associations is traditionally referred to as syntagmatic analysis (Morgan 1985, 14; Olsson 2006, 44). The solar disc is one of the essential pictorial units in the crown of Arsinoë. It holds an individual symbolic value. However, it might simultaneously function as an indicator of a greater message when combined with other units. This is demonstrated in the traditional Hathoric crown, where the solar disc is surrounded by large cow horns, together symbolising the goddess Hathor (and, later, other goddesses too). Therefore, two units have together structured and created a full crown composition which can function as a direct attribute of a goddess. Such a composition (although it may comprise only one unit in certain circumstances) is here referred to as an 'element': a composition which on its own constitutes a full form, the crown, but which can also function as part of a greater image, the full relief scene, when, for example, placed on a head or offered to the gods.

Such elements do not necessarily enjoy universal application or recognition. A viewer could possibly distinguish an Egyptian crown no less readily than any other crown, but it would be harder to interpret its particular meaning without a familiarity with the cultural code which structured the individual units. Within its cultural context, as discussed above, an element may also develop over time into an attribute: a pictorial component connected with a specific figure, where it forms a personal indication of identification, or a certain cultural aspect. An element is generally too influenced by its contemporary cultural setting to be universally identifiable. For example, the Egyptian *ankh* is an element commonly depicted in all Egyptian artistic settings. This element symbolised life in any form and was later adopted, with a very similar meaning, by Christian iconography. It is, however, not a universally acknowledged symbol. The crown of Arsinoë is an element and an attribute. It was created for and worn by Arsinoë to indicate a particular position. It was, however, also worn by the two later Ptolemaic queens, Cleopatra III and VII. Thus, it changed from being an element which was also a personal attribute to being an element which evoked certain cultural associations and possibly religious connotations.

Together, the paradigmatic and the syntagmatic analyses form the foundation of an iconographic study, translating an image into words so that an iconographic interpretation may be reached. In this context hermeneutics is employed to bridge the distance between recognised and unrecognised significances of an image, as well as between the pictorial units and the full figure (*cf.* Mikics 2007, 142f.). This study deals with an assortment of religious representations which incorporate the crown of Arsinoë and others, in which the crowns are considered to be vital in establishing the socio-religious position of the figures wearing them, and are also approached as key holders of information in relation to the contextual setting of the full scenes in which they appear, with the intention of reaching a deeper comprehension of their symbolic value within the full image.

The classification and cataloguing of the material is one of the most fundamental and cognitive matters in any scientific discipline. The methodological step of categorisation is only achieved once the stage of description is finalised and thus follows the previously described semiotic process of translating the coded language of units. The categorisation here, in which each crown is classified in accordance with its individual pictorial components, constitutes the main analysis. The iconological interpretation will thus constitute the last stage of this investigation (*cf.* Walsem 2005, 26).

The iconography under consideration here is associated with highly conventional religious settings unknown to the modern world. Previous textual translations have revealed that temple architecture and its decoration had a cosmological connotation with which cult and ceremonies were connected. The reliefs included in this study demonstrate various religious acts and positions, illustrating the pharaoh or ruling couple in an offering position before the gods. These scenes also represent ancient political propaganda, here mainly documented in scenes where the pharaoh is reconnecting to his deceased ancestors in order to gain their divine blessing and dynastic power. There are also scenes with a magical connotation, expressed in rites and cultic objects, which will be further examined below. This book will demonstrate how certain pictorial elements were considered to invoke the spirit of the illustrated deity, and might also signify how deities could act as benefactors when actively returning a divine blessing. These statements are based on an initial interpretation which is only possible through an experienced comprehension of the code embedded in the images, and as a modern interpreter of ancient material held in high cultic value by its contemporaries it is essential to approach these images sensitively, being aware that any result will always remain a hermeneutic interpretation.

Contextual setting

The relief scenes include one or several figures, royal as well as divine. The main focus will be on Arsinoë, while the other figures will be analysed and presented briefly in order to establish correlations between them. Arsinoë is found in the scenes as both benefactor and beneficiary in regards to offerings or religious performance, and is depicted either in a standing position or seated on a throne.

The relief material can be arranged in the following groups: Arsinoë unaccompanied; Arsinoë as a benefactor accompanied by Ptolemy II; Arsinoë receiving offerings from Ptolemy II; and Arsinoë as a beneficiary in a dynastic setting, accompanied by Ptolemy II as the *theoi Adelphoi*. The full scenes include, besides the iconographic elements and figures, hieroglyphic texts, of which *only* the designations of the figures and, if available, the epithets, will be referred to and analysed via a combination of personal and up-to-date translations (*e.g. WB*; Gardiner 1957; Faulkner 1962; Allen 2001; *Edfu*, vols I–VIII). The use of these texts allows a further step in the modern interpretation of iconography, although they rarely give the full meaning of the individual iconographic signs; rather, the hieroglyphic and sometimes Greek texts of the stelai and decrees can present a variety of possibilities in connection with the interpretation of the full scene, as will be further discussed below. Here, the iconographic material will be studied via, firstly, the morphology and the syntax of the crowns and, secondly, all the elements of the scene and their associations; and only then will these be compared with the titles and information given in the hieroglyphic and/or Greek text. The hieroglyphic, Greek and demotic texts of the decrees and stelai will not be fully translated and there will be no comparison between the different linguistic styles or languages. The texts will, however, be summarised and sections which directly refer to Arsinoë will be described in detail prior to their analysis in connection with the pictorial scenes and their comparison with one another in order to trace possible associations with their iconographic appearance. While the images can stand alone in providing an understanding of the artist and the pictorial contents, inscriptions surrounding a relief scene can communicate the general message, giving the relief scene its 'historical' setting. The complementary information provided by the texts can thus improve our comprehension of the original intention of the crowns.

Discussion relating to the dating of the relief scenes will be presented only in connection with scenes whose traditional dating is considered questionable (see Table 18).

Dates applied here are based on the reliefs in their present iconographic state rather than the dating of the architectural elements. If the traditional dating is undisputed, the reader is directed to the dates presented in the catalogue description. Where the date is unknown, mainly owing to damaged cartouches, a question mark is appended to the dating in the catalogue.

Descriptions of a type of later eradications – cut marks – will also be presented. These were caused mainly by (small) chisels, the use of which has damaged and sometimes totally erased certain parts of the figures. They are mostly documented relating to the face, hands and feet, occasionally the breasts and sporadically also hieroglyphs. When cut marks have damaged or destroyed a figure explicit pictorial elements have been left intact, including the crowns, as well as thrones and some hand-held objects. This indicates knowledge of the iconographic symbolism on the part of the person erasing the details and, since this is a study focusing on the crowns, the inclusion of these features is of great importance.

Relative scaling and relative placing as analytical instruments

A further approach to the material is the application of an ancient Egyptian artistic convention in a new way, to gain insight into the underlying messages transmitted through artistic visual representations. In general, Egyptian art can be approached as any other cultural iconography, in which the thoughts and aspirations of people were expressed as a narrative of their contemporary social ideology and religious principles; the ancient Egyptians thus established artistic principles to encode the world view which they wished to communicate. A fundamental convention in Egyptian art was the immediately identifiable shape of the object depicted (Robins and Fowler 1994, 3), a convention limited in the medium of reliefs by the flat surface of the stone. In this regard Egyptian iconographic representation differs from that of many other cultures, especially modern ones. Egyptian artists did not attempt to reproduce three-dimensional objects on a flat surface. Instead, the varied objects they depicted within their scenes were represented in their simplest, most essential forms (Robins and Fowler 1994, 6), either as a front or a profile view, or in a combination of both. Each unit, element or fully composed image was organised according to a geometrical arrangement of space and within a system of scale which could easily be manipulated to encode the relative importance of the figures. Along with the harmonious arrangement of space and scale adjustment, balance between each pictorial unit was considered essential in Egyptian art (Robins and Fowler 1994, 8–11 – although they do not deal with relative scaling).

This active and deliberate arrangement (and rearrangement) of individual pictorial units, elements and images conveys the most important principles underlying the scenes, commonly referred to as 'relative scaling' and 'relative placement', which are closely related to the relative importance of individual figures or the message intended to be communicated by the scene. A principle of relative placement firmly accepted by scholars, for instance, is that a right orientation (*i.e.*, looking to the right) expresses dominance (Robins and Fowler 1994, 21f.).[3] This and other principles function together as an analytical method in the present study, in which the crown is approached as a stylistic element expressing importance not only through its arrangement, composed of various individual pictorial signs, but also by adjustments in its size and height.

Ancient Egyptian society was based upon a geometrical order in which all things were related to one another in one way or another, especially as manifested in art. The symmetrical placement of the figures depicted in the relief scenes are fundamentally conventional. However, the size and position of each pictorial unit within every complete element and image might differ greatly. These varying proportions were deeply anchored in the religious belief system, meaning that the artist, in any medium, had to be sensitive to and aware of the dictates of religion as regards artistic expression (*cf.* Lurker 2002, 7–9; for a mathematical stand point, see *P.Brit.Mus.* 10057 and 10058; Peet 1923; Chace 1927–9; Robins and Shute 1987; the Moscow Mathematical Papyrus: Struwe 1930; Clagett 1995; the Kahun Papyrus: Legon 1992; Robins and Shute 1987, 41–3).

The most basic ancient geometrical order is a grid system composed of squares, each corresponding to a specific element represented in accordance with its correct mathematical position and in relation to its context (*e.g.* Kjelland 1955, 8f.).[4] The first scholar to investigate the convention of these ancient grids and lines was K. R. Lepsius (1897, 233–8), who undertook this work after finding several tombs in the Saqqara area many of which had grids still visible on the reliefs. The system was later referred to as 'Lepsius' Canon' and it was clarified that the principles were based on the proportions of the human figure (*cf.* Schwaller de Lubicz 1998, 323–8). The grid system was originally (Old Kingdom) based on a clearly marked vertical mid-line which centred and connected the figure from the top of the head (in profile) through the ear, abdomen, and hips down to the front part of the back foot (*e.g.* Lepsius 1897 on the Saqqara tombs; *LÄ* II, 1201, figs on 1202; Kjelland 1955, 14–17; Schwaller de Lubicz 1998, 328). Besides this most important vertical line, there were eight horizontal lines which followed individual mathematical calculations of position: that is, they were not spatially interrelated. The ancient lines, as referred to by Lepsius (1897, 234), relate to the highest point of the head, the fringe, the neck, the armpits, the elbows, the hips, the knee and, finally, the lowest line on which the figure stands, the base line. In addition to these lines there was also a series of markers or points in red or black which governed the placement of minor elements of decoration. The line which Lepsius refers to as the neck corresponds to the top of the shoulders.

The cultic conventions of geometrical harmony were applied to the decorative relief scenes with the use of a system of grids. Each grid or horizontal line was systematically placed upon the stone surface according to carefully calculated mathematical orders (*LÄ* II, 1201–3; Kjelland 1955, 22; Schwaller de Lubicz 1998, chapter 11, esp. figs 140, 142). They provided the artist with a drawn preview, a preliminary sketch, of the scene. The association of geometrical shapes could be refined when the artist was dealing with more detailed images. This system of grids or horizontal lines has been applied to the present material as an analytical instrument to measure height and correlation between, firstly, the pictorial units, secondly, the elements and, thirdly, the figures represented within the scene, focusing only on the practical application of the system to determine each individual's hierarchic position within the scenes in order to fully analyse and discuss the crowns and their physical positions as indicators of status.

As might be expected from the foregoing discussion, height is generally accepted as an indicator of importance in this context; together with a right-facing orientation, the most significant figure in a scene is the tallest. This is an artistic convention often used in Egyptian art and is, as noted, referred to as relative scaling (*e.g.* Bianchi 2004, 117; Robins 2008, 21f.).[5] The main figure of a scene was either enlarged in its entirety or, with the help of pictorial elements, increased in height (*cf.* the motif of the famous Narmer Palette: *LÄ* IV, 348–50). Traditionally the figures of a relief scene are measured from the feet up to the top of the head, occasionally using the fringe or the tip of the nose as the higher point, a method referred to by its authors as isocephaly (Wilkinson 1994, chapter 2; Vassilika 1989, 14, n. 74). True isocephaly – that is, heads drawn along the same horizontal line, sometimes called the classic mode of relief – refers to a position of equality between two or more figures (Wilkinson 1994, 46). The purpose of isocephaly in Egyptian art is traditionally interpreted as being to ensure that no figure is looking down on another, thereby securing the hierarchic order between the gods and the pharaoh (or equivalent figures) (Wilkinson 1994, 46f.). In order to ensure parity in height between figures in a relief scene, the artist, when creating the figures, needs to use the grid system as described above.

The only pictorial element which did not follow any specified convention within the system was the crown, for which there were never any indicating lines or points, leaving the artist the freedom to adjust the crown in accordance with the figure wearing it (*LÄ* II, 1201–3; Lepsius 1897, 233–8; Kjelland 1955, 18; *cf.* Perrot and Chipiez 1882; Edgar 1906). The material thus shows a great diversity of crowns, illustrated in various sizes and styles. When analysing the Egyptian relief scene using the paradigmatic and syntagmatic methods applied here, the crown is included as an integral part of the full figure: it is one of the most important elements of both divine and royal figures, expressing both individualism and hierarchy, and its presence raises the figure to a higher level. The crown is the *only* pictorial element that reveals individualism and differences in height, and as such it becomes a fundamental factor in determining the hierarchic order of the figures in a scene. Since Egyptian images were unities built up by units and elements carefully placed in a certain relationship to each other, based on sacred geometry, it is of great importance that the crown should be seen as an element equal to other pictorial details of the full figure and thereby should be included when measuring the image (*cf.* Schwaller de Lubicz 1998, 330–36, with fig. 136).

In order to measure the figures of a scene, the ancient grid system has thus been employed here in a modernised form by the superimposing of a series of horizontal lines over a photographic reproduction of a scene,[6] the ancient grids and horizontal lines thus being used mainly as a means to compare the height and spacing of the figures. For the purposes of this study, four of these ancient lines have been used, delineating (from the top) the top of the head, the shoulders, the knees and the base upon which the figures stand. The head line is included because of its traditional scholarly value, allowing comparisons to be drawn, whereas the lower lines are related to contextual elements in the present study. Where necessary, their use will be supplemented with that of additional lines, following the breast, navel and calf, when a certain relationship between the pictorial elements of the scene needs to be further clarified; and by that of a new one, the crown line (see pp. 79–90). This last line is not present in ancient images since crowns were depicted as varying in height. Whereas all of the *traditional* horizontal lines regulate the height of the figures correspondingly, the crown line is employed as the only horizontal line establishing individuality among figures otherwise of the same height.

A wide variety of studies has shown that Egyptian artists used a system of grids in creating both relief and sculpture and, although the system used in the present study is perhaps simple when compared with the advanced geometrical calculations upon which the original version was based, it still follows the basic premise of positioning the elements and figures of the scenes (*e.g.* Tomoum 2005). In using crowns of varying heights as a tool in establishing a hierarchic order, the eyes of the scene's figures can still remain on an equal level, so that no figure looks down at another, thus leaving unaffected the integrity of the head line.

Notes

1 Dils' article (1998) on the crown of Arsinoë, however, follows an approach similar to that taken here, in which the crown composition is deconstructed down to each individual element.

2 The form is what Morgan (1985, 7–9) refers to as an idiom.

3 Relative placement also includes a series of recognised poses, here represented as seated (on a throne), standing, running, kneeling or leaning over the enemies in a smiting position.

4 The use of geometrical patterns can be found not only in the aesthetic sphere but also in the religious rituals, since, with only a few exceptions, most of Egyptian art derives from either the temples or tombs. These grids, painted in red or black, can be traced back to at least the Old Kingdom and have been found in several tombs from this period.

5 The active administration of art was introduced together with the other major iconographic settings during the Early Dynastic period and developed during the Old Kingdom, when it was mainly represented in funerary art. The use of relative scaling is clearly documented in the famous sculpture of the male dwarf depicted as equal in size to his wife through the adjustment of the elements. In this case the dwarf has been placed on a podium next to his standing wife, enabling him to reach up to the same level as her. See Russmann (1989, 40f., fig. 14) and Schäfer (1974 [1919], 234).

6 There are occasions when scenes, especially those located in top registers, cannot be photographed directly from the front. Those scenes have, however, been carefully photographed so that all figures remain on a fully horizontal level.

Chapter 3

The elements of the crown

In this chapter each pictorial detail of the crowns is analysed in order to study their relation to the crowns' historical and iconographic applications and associations.

Ram horns (RH)

The ram horns are a fundamental component of the crown of Arsinoë. They are placed horizontally and appear in different sizes and styles, with or without decorated inner details. Their structural position in the overall crown composition varies in relation to their context. The ram horns are divided here into three types based on this variation of style, position and size.

Type RH 1 is the style most frequently seen (Table 2). The horns are positioned on top of the flat part of the red crown – that is, the platform – therefore forming a structural foundation for the double feather plume and additional crown units. This type is documented in temple reliefs and stelai alike. The horns illustrated in the stelai (cat. nos 2L–7, 10–11, 13–15) have a basic style with clear outlines, but without any detailed inner pattern (in cat. no. 3 only the right-hand horn is completely visible). These rather simple stylised horns, which are documented exclusively in crown compositions illustrated on the stelai, are placed in a horizontal position, with each side symmetrically arranged in terms of width. In comparison, the horns in the temple scenes are more decorated, showing clear outlines and a defined inner twined pattern. The two horns (left and right) are recurrently placed in an asymmetrical order in terms of their size and width. The horns in cat. no. 16, for example, spring up from an off-centre location (to the left), the twined pattern varies from side to side and the left-hand horn is more elongated than the right. All horns included in type RH 1 are fully visible; however, the outlines of the horns are rather vague in cat. no. 3 and the possibility that they might have had a different form originally cannot be dismissed.

The second most frequent type, RH 2, is found mainly in the Philae scenes. The type also appears in cat. no. 9, a scene which is fragmentarily preserved and has an unknown provenance. The horns are stylised, being illustrated with only the most important outlines. Cat. nos 31–32, which show some degree of decorative inner lines, are two exceptions. Type RH 2 horns are placed above the vulture cap and thus below the red crown. The two horns are not joined at their centre (compare RH 1) and instead show one fully visible side and one partially hidden one. Only cat. no. 33 shows a fully visible front horn, partially hiding the back horn behind the red crown. Remaining crowns have a fully visible back horn, whereas the front is partly hidden. E. Vassilika (1989, 86) suggests that the partial visibility of the horns was meant to communicate their physical reality and practical application, thus making the assumption that the crowns did indeed exist in a physical form. She suggests that the physical actuality of these horns is demonstrated on a two-dimensional surface through the rotation of the horn of the far ear allowing it to be shown over the forehead. The opposing direction of the horns in cat. no. 33, however, suggests that such a stylistic convention did not exist.

RH 3 is documented in three scenes. The horns, which are fully visible and positioned between the vulture cap and the red crown, are placed symmetrically, fully outlined and decorated only sparsely with inner patterns.

In Egyptian art there are two basic variations of ram horns: the twined, horizontal horns and the downward-curled horns (see Figure 2). Ptolemaic temple texts describe the horns as '*hnwtj pḏ*' and '*ʿbwj pḏ*' (*e.g.* Derchain-Urtel 1994, 30, n. 18). Ancient texts do not describe the symbolism and message of the ram horns as a part of crowns. Edfu and Dendera texts generally describe them as additional ornaments. It is possible that their symbolism was so obvious to contemporaries that it required no explanation. Downward-curled horns, together with the double cornucopia, frequently identify Arsinoë on Greek-styled coins (*e.g.* Mørkholm 1991, 63–70; Svoronos 1904, nos 875–892). Prior to Arsinoë, Alexander the Great was depicted wearing the downward-curled horns on coins and

ILLUSTRATION[1]	ABBREVIATION	DESCRIPTION	SCENES CAT. NOS	TOTAL NO. CROWNS
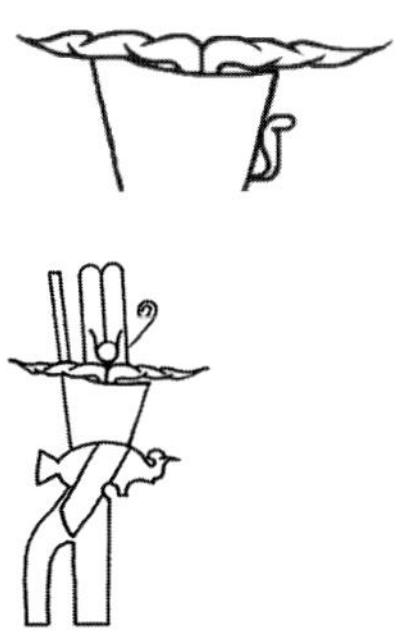	RH 1	The horns are placed on top of the platform of the red crown, forming a base for the cow horns and solar disc. The horns are joined and shown in front of the crown. Both sides are fully visible	2L–7, 10–11, 13–20, 22–26R, 34–35	27
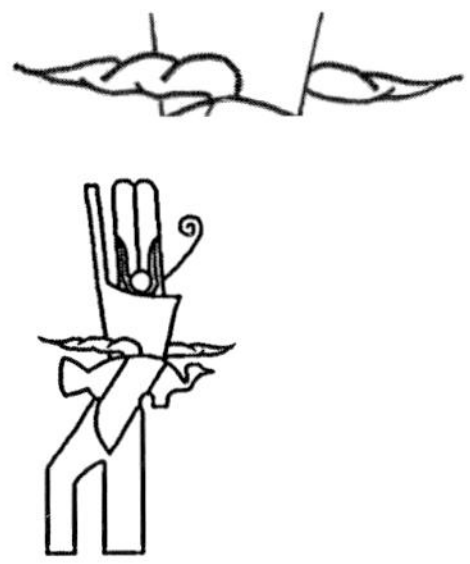	RH 2	The horns are placed at the base of the red crown, on top of a wig or cap. One horn is fully visible whereas the other is partially hidden, separated by the red crown (cat. nos 9, 27, 30–32 show a fully visible horn at the back part of the crown, whereas cat. no. 33 shows the horn on the front part instead. Cat. no. 29 is badly preserved)	9, 27, 29–33	7
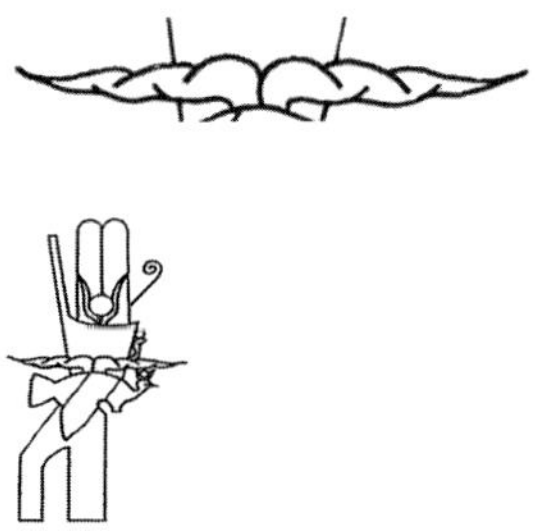	RH 3	The horns are placed at the base of the red crown, on top of a wig or cap, joined in the middle, both sides fully visible	1L, 8, 12	3

Note
1. This column shows a detailed illustration of the horns' structure followed by an overall representation of their contextual association

Table 2. Variants of the ram horns.

in other media, and this was probably one of the main reasons why Arsinoë choose the curled horn as an attribute. In Egyptian religion these horns were used as attributes of masculine deities such as Amun, Osiris and Khnum.[1] However, these horns are not the same as those illustrated in the crown of Arsinoë, which are those of the former type, shown in a horizontal position and more or less twined. At first sight they are similar to the horns of a Kudu antelope, or possibly a goat, rather than those of a ram/sheep. The horns in the crown are, however, identified with those of an ancient breed of sheep characterised by long, horizontally twined horns (Houlihan 1996, 22). Although this breed disappeared from Egypt during the New Kingdom, the sheep, or sometimes only their horizontal horns, kept a symbolic position in Egyptian iconography.

The horizontal horns are used as attributes for several deities, mainly as a component of larger compositions. Among others, Khnum, Mandulis, Ptah, Thoth, Ihy, Osiris, Sobek, Harpocrates, Khonsu, Geb, and Amun are illustrated wearing these horns (Figure 3). However, only a few deities, including the ram gods Amun and Khnum, used the ram horns as an individual attribute. Therefore, it might be assumed that the ram horn was originally an attribute of the ram gods in any local form, including Banebdjedet, who was a local form of Amun. J. Quaegebeur (1988, 43), as an advocate of the hypothesis of Arsinoë as a God's wife (see pp. 115–117), was one of many to argue that the horizontal horns of the crown of Arsinoë could be connected with Amun (*cf.* Winter 1978). P. Dils (1998, 1308f.) questions such an association, and argues instead that Amun frequently wore curled horns, using the horizontal horns only as a structural support for a solar disc or double feather plume. This argument is not completely convincing, however, as Amun is sometimes depicted wearing horizontal ram horns under an *atef* crown, which has no need for structural support. So far, the only explanation which seems convincing to me is Quaegebeur's.

What historical or mythological factors lay behind Arsinoë's decoration with these horns? Arsinoë's historical socio-political position was one in which she was deified in her own right (as well as with her brother-husband) and incorporated in the official Alexandrian eponymous cult. As such she was directly associated with the chthonic cult of Alexander. Her official cultic name (and the official designation of the sibling gods) followed Alexander's in official dating formulas and, as will be demonstrated below, Arsinoë was associated with Alexander by her official designations. For example, she used the title 'Daughter of Amun', which is comparable to Alexander's 'son of Zeus-Amun'. Arsinoë's cultic connection with Alexander is also demonstrated in iconography. Following Alexander's deification as the son of Zeus-Amun in the Temple of Siwa he was depicted with a ram's horn curling behind his ear. An iconographic association with Alexander, expressed in coins portraying Arsinoë, would be a plausible political motive for the selection of the ram horns also as a component of her personal crown. However, as noted above (pp. 16–17), it was not these curled horns of Amun, those illustrated on the Alexander portraits, that were chosen for use in the Egyptian crown of Arsinoë.[2]

Alexander's role as the son of Zeus-Amun appealed to both Egyptians and Greeks alike. For the Egyptians, Alexander was the son of Amun, the main god of the time, generally recognised as a ram. The Greeks regarded Alexander as the son of their most important deity, Zeus, and likened him with Dionysus. Therefore, Alexander, in his royal persona and cultic appearance, bridged the two cultures. The illustrated horns of Alexander link him with the Egyptian ram; however, it is arguable that there may also be an association with the Greek goat, based on Alexander's identification with Dionysus. In the Greek material, and subsequently in Egyptian sculptures, Arsinoë was attributed with an item associated with the goat, the *dikeras* – the double cornucopia. In Greek mythology, this was connected with the she-goat Amalthea, who is described as the nurturer of the infant Zeus at Crete. After her death her horns were made into a symbol of fruitfulness and she was remembered and venerated by the Greeks in this form throughout the ages (Dixon-Kennedy 1998, 93). This attribute was illustrated individually on the reverse of coins, or held by the queen when depicted on *oinochoai*, terracottas, figurines and sculpture in the round.

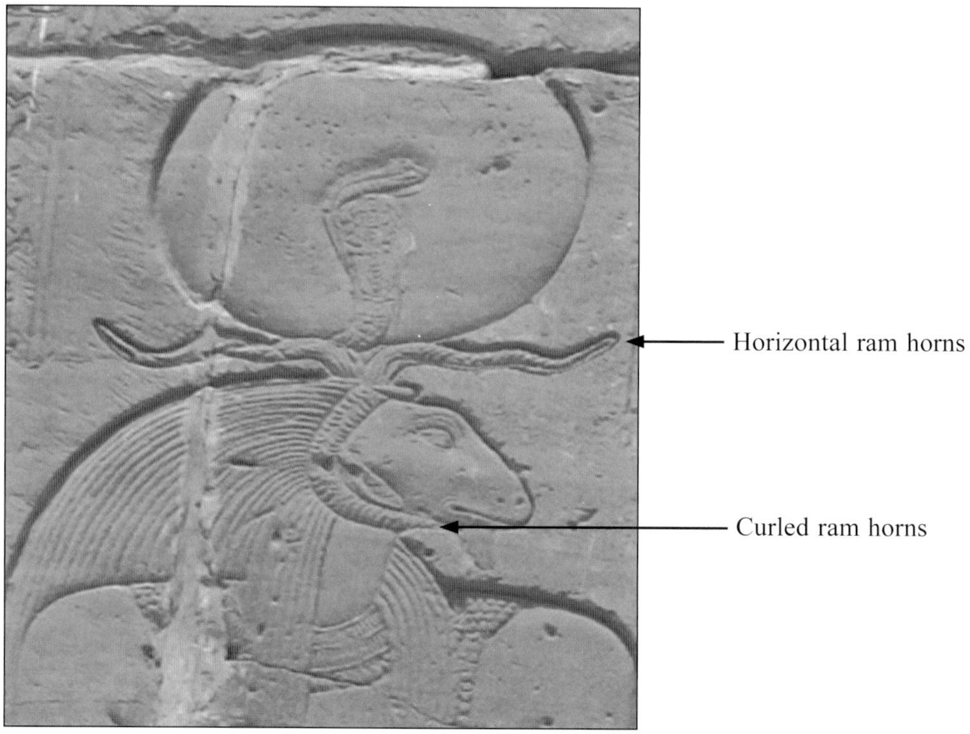

Figure 2. Amun-Ra decorated with horizontal as well as curled horns, Hibis Temple.

Another myth, recorded by Diodorus, describes further connections between Amalthea and Zeus. With reference to an ancient Egyptian tradition, he says that the Libyan Zeus-Amun returned to his nurturer and impregnated her, later parenting a young Dionysus (Diod. Sic. 3, 68). The myth records an Egyptian influence in an otherwise Greek setting; a coming together of two ancient cultures resulting in a divine being, Dionysus, from whom the female bloodline of the Ptolemies counted their descent. This divine association is discussed further in a passage of Callixeinus, preserved in Athenaeus, describing the grand procession of Ptolemy II in Alexandria, in which a *dikeras* was carried by a figure of Dionysus (Ath. 197a; *cf.* Fraser 1972, 233). The double cornucopia was created particularly for Arsinoë during the reign of Ptolemy II, and is traditionally considered to symbolise Arsinoë's close connection either with her husband-brother or with the Two Lands of Egypt (*e.g.* Ashton 2001b, 83; *cf.* Troxell 1983, 35–70; Reden 2007, 59). Although the double cornucopia is documented mainly in Greek visual arts, it is also an attribute of the Queen on Egyptian statues (*cf.* a limestone statue of Arsinoë, today located in New York, the Metropolitan Museum of Art 20.2.21). The cornucopia, therefore, associates Arsinoë with the goat.

A final point worthy of note is Satyrus' description of the cult of Arsinoë, which mentions a prohibition concerning sacrificing goats (*P.Oxy.* 2465, fr. 2, col. I.; *cf.* Fraser 1972, 229; Stephens 2005, 245).[3] This statement is identical with Herodotus' account of the Mendesian veneration of the ram god, describing it as the only cult disallowing a goat as an offering and instead sacrificing a sheep (Hdt. 2, 42). Later chapters will demonstrate Arsinoë's religious responsibilities as high priestess of Banebdjedet, the ram god of Mendes. The horns in the crown of Arsinoë thus indicate an assimilation of two very similar cults, accepted and practised by Greeks as well as Egyptians.

Arsinoë's association with the goat suggests an aspect of intercultural symbolism. Alexander was able to bridge the Egyptian and Macedonian cultures by claiming his descent from Zeus-Amun. Pictorially, Alexander's horns connect him with the ram and goat alike. Similar aesthetic aspects merged, but simultaneously kept their original frames of reference. Arsinoë was able to use the horns in a similar way, combining her cultic associations with Aphrodite and Amun

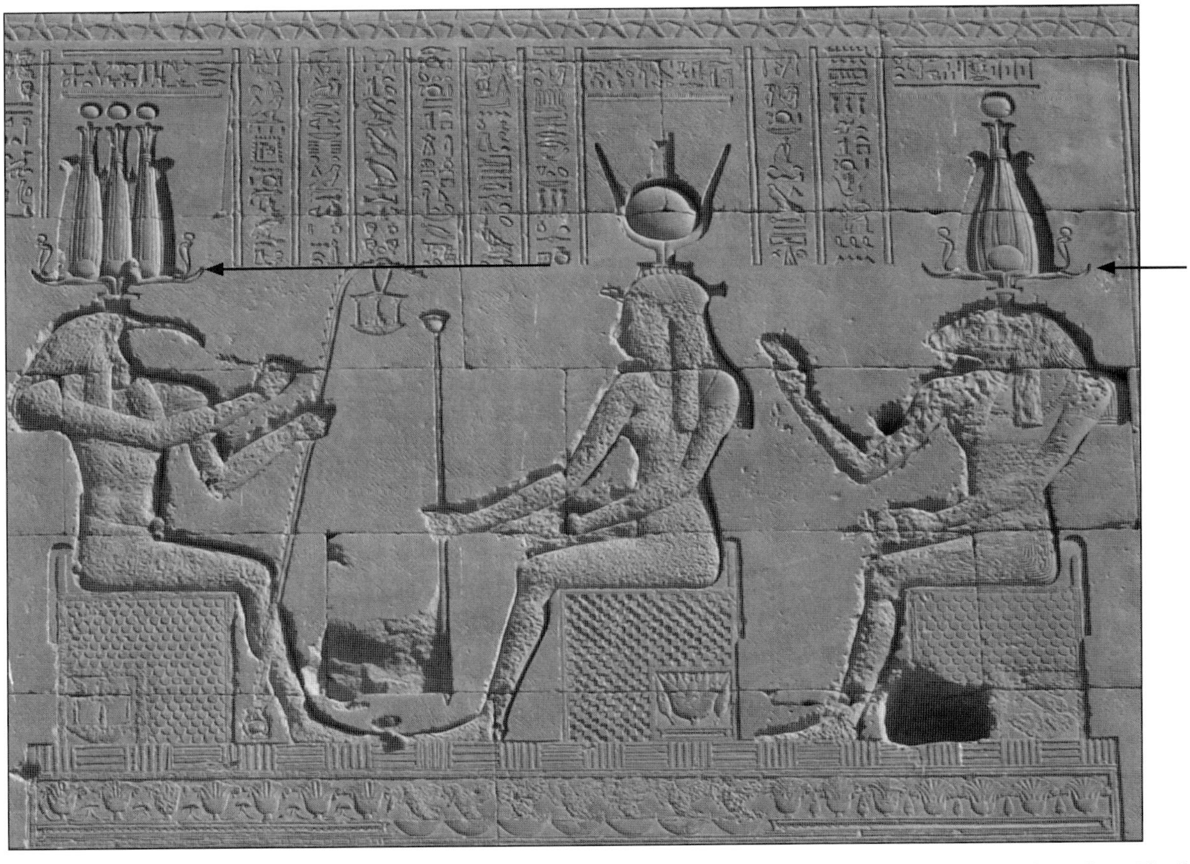

Figure 3. Thoth and Khnum with the horizontal horns as a component of larger crown compositions at the Temple of Dendera. The female figure is identified with Isis.

and her dynastic link with Alexander. Such an intercultural symbolism is communicated in the Egyptian sculptures of Arsinoë holding the cornucopia.[4]

Arsinoë's socio-religious roles during her adult life in Alexandria are only sparsely and often vaguely documented, much like her role in Egyptian society. However, cat. no. 1 might shed some light here. The figures illustrated in this scene are divided into two sections, a left and a right side, with figures who face each other. The left side represents the royal family and incorporates Ptolemy II, Arsinoë and a male figure designated 'Ptolemy, son of Ptolemy'. Facing them, on the right side, is a newly incarnated ram on a podium receiving offerings from the royal family. Behind him, also on a podium, stands a smaller figure of Harpocrates. Thereafter follows an anthropomorphic figure of Banebdjedet, representing the deceased ram god, after which stands his divine spouse Hat-Mehit. The last figure of the right side is Arsinoë. Arsinoë is thus depicted twice in the scene. She stands in an active position as a benefactor in the left side, together with the ruling royal family, and as a beneficiary together with the local divine triad in the right. The central theme in this scene (also expressed in the text) is the commemoration of the deceased ram god Banebdjedet and the celebrations of the transference of his incarnated soul into a new physical ram-body. One of many topics presented in this stele is Arsinoë's role, when alive, as high priestess of Banebdjedet. Banebdjedet was a local form of Amun, and thus connected Arsinoë with this main Egyptian deity previously suggested as a fundamental source of the symbolic association expressed in the ram horns of Arsinoë.

As argued above (pp. 16–17), these horizontal horns are mainly recorded in crowns worn by male deities prior to the composition of the crown of Arsinoë. Hieroglyphic texts designate Horus, Amun and Osiris, along with various pharaohs, as 'Lord of the Horns' (*WB* I, 173f.; III, 109; *cf.* Faulkner 1958 (*P.Brit.Mus.* 10569); *P.Chester Beatt*, I, 3,6). This title conveys the symbolic value of the horns, which are associated with kingship and express power, authority, control, prominence and even divinity (*LÄ* III, 9f.). A connection with the Two Lands, based on the dualistic nature of the horns, may also be suggested. Traditionally, these horns have been interpreted as symbolising the inundation and its fertility (Desroches-Noblecourt 1968, 40, n. 425). Vassilika (1989, 86, n. 15) suggests, in her study of Ptolemaic Philae, that the horizontal horns represent a trophy of war or hunt, and that they symbolised royal deification from the time of Amenhotep II (*cf.* Leclant 1956, 128–45). In her study on the *ḥptj* crown, Derchain-Urtel (1994), on the other hand, more or less omits any reference to the symbolic importance of the ram horns.

The ram itself symbolised respect and power and was strongly connected with kingship (Lurker 2002, 65). During the Ptolemaic period, and when worn by royals other than Arsinoë (and Cleopatra III and VII, who reused the crown of Arsinoë) the horns are frequently incorporated as a pictorial component of the *anedjti* crown or the triple crown, or as an additional unit in the composition when combined with the red crown and the *atef.* Most Ptolemaic kings were depicted with horizontal twined ram horns, thus continuing an iconographic convention applied by so many previous Egyptian rulers (*cf.* Dils 1998, 1315–25). Generally, the ram horns were seen as an addition to the royal regalia, connecting the person wearing it with the deities decorated with them (*LÄ* III, 814f.; Stanwick 2002, 35).

The symbolic significance of the ram horns in the crown of Arsinoë is thus entwined with various cultural events and individuals: Amun and his depiction as a ram God; and the solar cult, based on the assimilation of Amun, Ra and Horus (manifestations of Ra). The association with the solar cult explains the presence of the horns in crown compositions worn by Harpocrates/Horus, since he represented a certain aspect of the daily journey of the solar disc. The combination of a divine kinship and the eternal journey of the sun disc suggests that the horns were connected with rejuvenation, fertility and eternal life. This aspect merges with the message communicated in the Mendes stele, which describes a divine priestess-queen who entered heaven to join her divine family.

Red crown (RC)

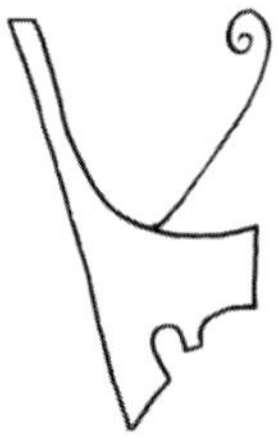

The red crown has a straight back and, usually, a crown spiral (*ḫ3bt*). Traditionally, both body and spiral are painted red. The red crown is documented in two styles in the material (including also crowns worn by figures other than Arsinoë), which vary according to the form of its lower end and how it sits on the head of the figure wearing it. The more frequently occurring style is worn mainly by male figures and by goddesses without a vulture cap. The crown follows the shape of the head, resting on the ears and the neck (Figure 4). The second style, mostly worn by females, sits directly on the top of the head or the vulture cap, and is illustrated with a flat bottom (Figure 5). The red crown is always placed directly on the head, in the latter style, when it is illustrated as a component of the crown of Arsinoë.

The red crown as an individual pictorial unit illustrates the difficulties of interpretation caused by the lack of archaeological evidence. The available material, despite its relatively limited nature, suggests varying hypotheses about the two styles of red crown relating either to the limitations posed by the artistic medium in which they are depicted or to the actual physical existence of the crown. As mentioned above, the red crown on female figures has a flat bottom and is positioned on top of the head when the figure wears a wig or cap. Most goddesses and queens wear a tripartite wig and/or a vulture cap, and thus the crown appears on top of the headdress. Goddesses without a tripartite wig or cap instead wear a red crown of the first type, resting on the neck and ears, as in the cases of Neith, Amaunet, Wadjet and Buto. Kings and male deities are almost always depicted in this way, with the crown resting on the neck and ears. However, the crown is placed flat on top of the head when they wear a *nemes* or *khat* wig, or when illustrated in an anthropomorphic style with a falcon head. Firstly, therefore, it is plausible that the two styles indicate an Egyptian artistic convention related to Egyptian workmanship and artistic approach to dimensions and position, including the systematic depiction of figures in profile in relief scenes. In such a scene, each iconographic element was illustrated in accordance with its most obvious features. A convention whereby the artist depicted the crown with a flat bottom and on top of the head would enable him to include a fully portrayed wig and/or cap which otherwise would be fully or partially hidden under the crown. This assumes that each pictorial detail was regarded as important and as a keeper of individual symbolism. Secondly, there is the matter of how these crown types would have functioned if they existed in a physical form. A wig alone would not be able to support a crown resting immediately on top of the head unless it was equipped with a metal or wooden instrument or structural 'ramp'.[5] However, archaeological records of wigs do not support such a suggestion. Preserved kerchiefs and wigs were mainly made of, respectively, fabric and natural hair, with no indications of a structural support built into them (*e.g.* Fletcher 1994); thus neither would have been able to independently support a heavy crown.

Although other possible explanations for the red crown's stylistic variations may exist, they will not be pursued here; rather, the focus is on the particular types of red crown as it is recorded in the crown of Arsinoë (*cf.* Goebs 2008, esp. p. 155). These are classified in accordance with the position (if any) of the crown spiral, as the only differentiating item (see Table 3).[6]

RC 1 is the most common type, in which the crown has a spiral rising up behind the double feather plume. The spiral is only partially visible as a result and it is thus impossible to establish its location definitively. This type of crown is documented equally in stelai and temple reliefs.

RC 2–3 are separated from RC 1 purely on the basis of the location of the spiral base: springing from the ram horns

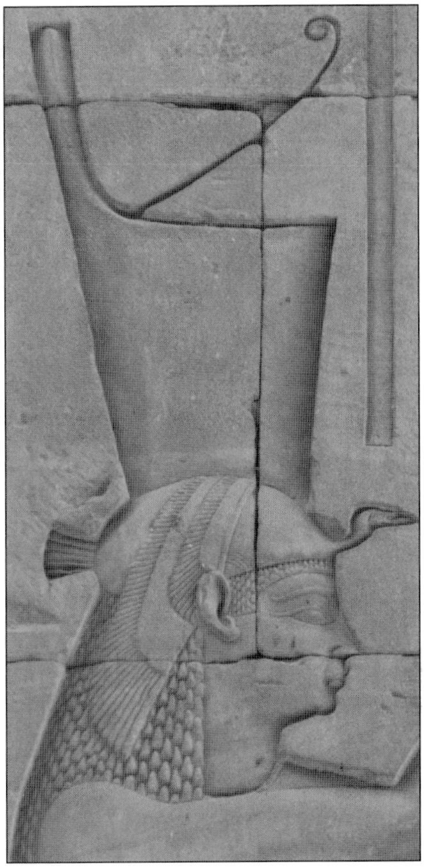

Figure 4. Example of red crown: Wadjet wearing a red crown with a flat bottom, resting directly on the top of the head, Edfu Temple.

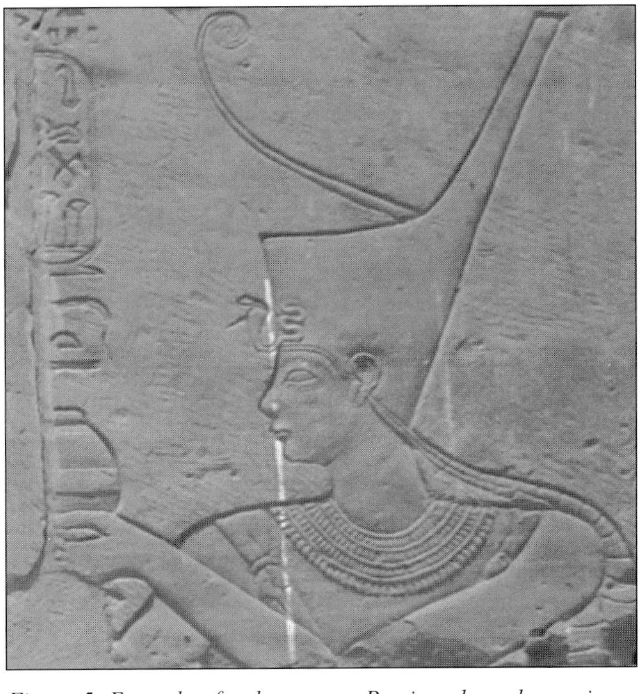

Figure 5. Example of red crown: a Persian pharaoh wearing a crown resting on the ears and neck, Hibis Temple.

ILLUSTRATION[1]	ABBREVIATION	DESCRIPTION	SCENES	TOTAL NO. CROWNS
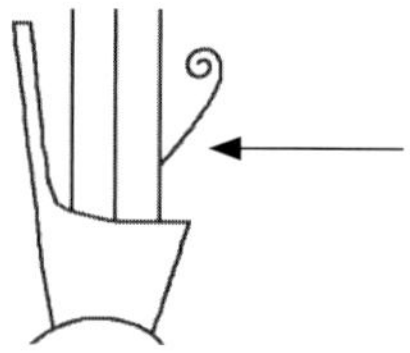	RC 1	The base of the crown spiral is placed behind the double feather plume	1R–2R, 6–8, 11, 15L–R, 23–30, 32–35	22
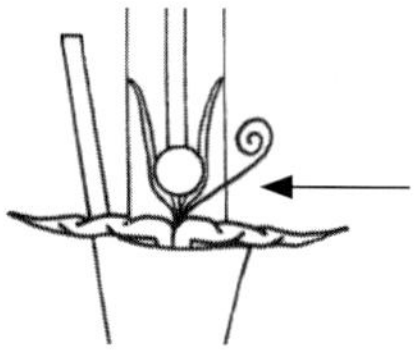	RC 2	The crown spiral rises from the ram horns, in front of the double feather plume and cow horns	4–5, 19	3
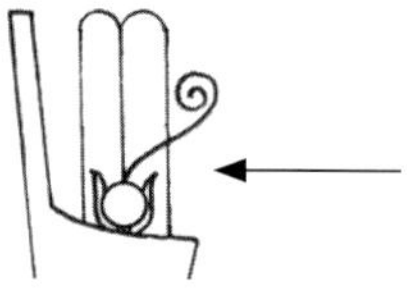	RC 3	The base of the crown spiral is placed behind the cow horns but in front of the double feather plume	31 (possibly also including 1L)	1 (2)
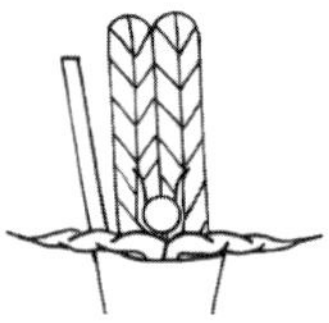	RC 4	No spiral	3, 10, 13–14, 16–18, 20, 22	9

Note
1. The arrows in the illustrations point to the position of the crown spiral.

Table 3. Variations of the red crown.

(RC 2) and from behind the cow horns (RC 3). There is only one example of RC 3 in the material, that worn by Arsinoë in the Philae Temple. Arguably, the two latter types could be the result of contemporary fashions, but they could also depend on the vagaries of local artists; the latter seems more likely given that there appear to be no socio-religious or cultural associations attached to the differentiation.

RC 4 is intriguing because of the seeming absence of a crown spiral, although this may simply be the result of poor preservation. All the stelai recorded with this type are more poorly preserved than others, owing to natural erosion. The area surrounding the crown is often uneven and sometimes rough and scratched, perhaps indicating deliberate interference and suggesting the possibility that the crown spiral once existed. The crowns of cat. nos 3 and 13 demonstrate well-defined outlines and, although the surrounding surface of both scenes is slightly roughened, there are no pictorial details, lines, or irregularities in the area of the red crown's platform that could support an original spiral. Therefore, it is argued that these crowns were created intentionally without a spiral. In another example, the crown of cat. no. 10 is generally well preserved but its colours have deteriorated. The crown is surrounded by a light yellow colour which has faded in several areas, bringing forward the natural colour of the sandstone. The crown was originally painted red, which has smudged surrounding details. The strong colours of this crown composition may suggest that the finer details were painted instead of engraved in relief and have disappeared over time. In terms of temple reliefs, cat. nos 16, 18 and 20 also show no indications of an original spiral (Figure 6), and it thus appears that the spiral was not an essential part of the red crown in every case.[7] These examples, rather, demonstrate an exception to a convention.

In art, the red crown was one of the oldest Egyptian crowns, documented as early as the Predynastic Period (Goebs 2001, 323f.). It is recognised as symbolising Lower Egypt, and is referred to mainly by the name *Deshret* (*dšrt*), meaning the 'Red One'. It is also known as *jnj*, *w3ḏt*, *mḥ*, *nt*, *nbt*, *ẖ3btt* (*LÄ* III, 812; Vassilika 1989, 85; Goebs 2001, 323). The crown was an attribute of Wadjet (among others), who was considered to be the goddess of Lower Egypt.[8] It was a part of the double crown (the *sḫmty* – 'the two powerful ones'), which symbolised the unification of the Two Lands. Generally in art the pharaoh wore the red crown on one side of a pylon, gate or door, while wearing the white crown on the opposite side. Such a display emphasised his power over the Two Lands. A few queens, including Hatshepsut, Amenirdis II, Arsinoë (II), Cleopatra III and Cleopatra VII, used the red crown, but always as a component in larger compositions. To my knowledge, no queen was depicted with a red crown as an individual/exclusive crown element.[9]

The red crown was frequently depicted in temple reliefs and stelai, but is rarely documented as royal insignia in pyramid or funerary texts (*cf.* Goebs 2008, 164f). In addition to the royal usage of the crown, it was attributed to several deities throughout the pharaonic ages. A pyramid text attributes the red crown to Ra in his association with Horus, and the crown functioned as a symbolic identification of Wadjet (PT 404 §702b). In addition, it is associated with Geb. Further, the text connects the crown with a cosmic feature represented by the morning star (Goebs 2008, 169; *cf.* Nilsson 2010, 433–51), a link which stresses themes of rejuvenation, fertility and rebirth (Goebs 2008, 173). Apart from Wadjet, already mentioned, other goddesses documented wearing the red crown include Neith, Amaunet and Buto.

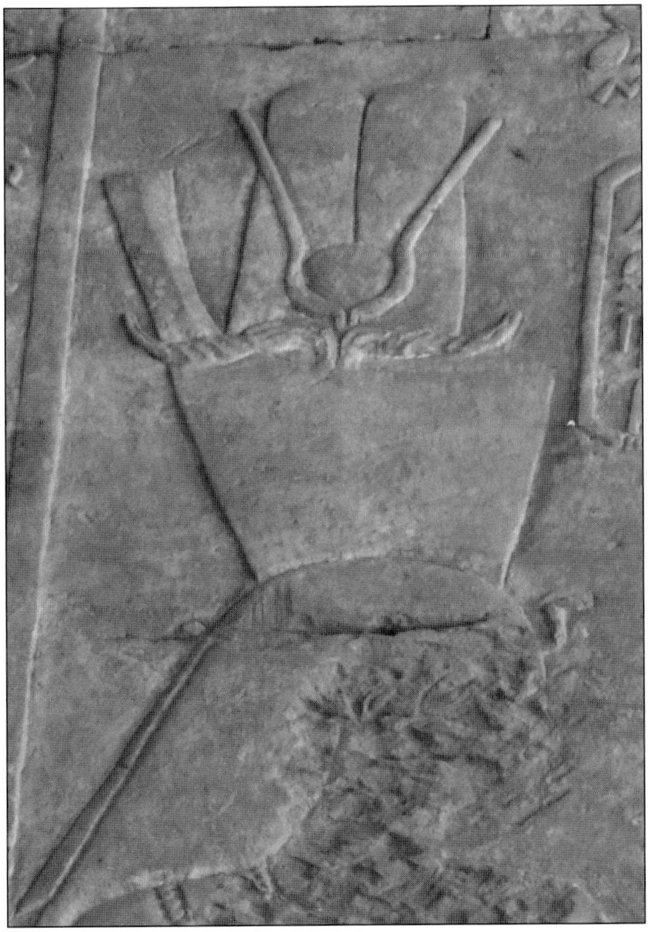

Figure 6. Detail of cat. no. 16, demonstrating a crown of Arsinoë without a crown spiral.

The message communicated by the red crown is connected with male royal power and with female deities of Lower Egypt. It is associated with the Hathoric daughter role because Wadjet, the eye of Ra, is identified in its shape. An alternative connotation will also be proposed here, however. When combined with the white crown, the red crown forms the outer structure of a complete composition. This symbolic structure seems to have a religious symbolism comparable to that of the Hathoric cow horns and solar disc (the traditional Hathoric crown), in which the solar disc rests inside the horns. Hathor's crown symbolises her protection of the divine king, while a Hathoric textual designation listed in Dendera Temple describes her as 'the nest of the cobra' (Nilsson 2010, cat. no. 89). It is arguable that this title refers not only to the maternal role of Hathor but also to Wadjet as the personification of the cobra, and could, therefore, describe a Hathoric maternal role manifested in Wadjet as the cobra, protecting her offspring in the nest. Such a complex string of associations comes full circle with Wadjet's connection with the red crown. The hypothesis put forward here, therefore, is that the red crown also functioned as a sign of protection, similar to the *uraeus*. A combination of the red and the white crowns in the double crown thus becomes a symbol of male and female, the fundamental components of Egyptian dualism: the red crown expresses the female aspect, connoting the maternal role as she protects the child within her womb, while the white crown communicates masculinity, and is identified (in this aspect) with Harsomtus as he rises from the horizon (Nilsson 2010, 445–7). As a symbol of the birth of Harsomtus, the white crown can be associated with the primeval golden egg, which could explain its peculiar form. While the hypothesis put forward here relates mainly to the combined form of the crown, the maternal association of the red crown could be applied also to the crown of Arsinoë and the queen's dynastic maternal role. The presence of a red crown in the crown of Arsinoë suggestively places the queen as a Hathoric mother of all descendants in the name of Ptolemy.

Double feather plume (DFP)

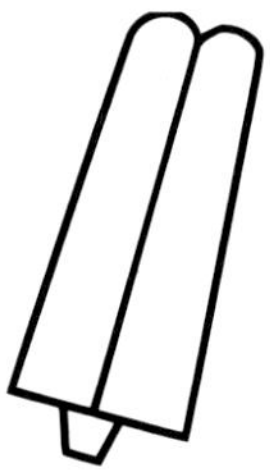

The double feather plume in the crown of Arsinoë is identical to those incorporated in the traditional female crown worn by queens, goddesses and the Divine Adoratrices of Amun. It is documented in two variants in the material according to its size and position (Table 4). Only one type is represented in the crown of Arsinoë.

The feathers of the crown of Arsinoë always rise up from the platform of the red crown, pointing either straight or slightly towards the back. All figures wearing a fully visible crown of Arsinoë are classified as DFP 1, within which type the feathers vary slightly.[10]

The double feather plume of cat. nos 21 and 36, which is contextually differentiated from the crown of Arsinoë, as shown in Table 4, is DFP 2. It occurs in the traditional female crown, where the feathers are always accompanied by cow horns and a solar disc.

The double feather plume is traditionally associated with Min, Amun and Ra (sometimes assimilated as Amun-Min, Amun-Ra and so on) (Figure 7). Montu and Horus use the crown when illustrated in an anthropomorphic form with a falcon-head. The two latter deities, however, wear the feathers chiefly as an iconographic component of a larger crown composition.

Kings never wore the double feather plume as an attribute. Instead, the pharaohs incorporated the feathers into the *anedjti* crown, or used them as a unit of other, larger, compositions (*cf.* Abubakr 1937, 40–46). The double feather plume was worn by female deities such as Hathor and Isis from at least the 18th Dynasty (*e.g.* Vassilika 1989, 91). It was implemented as an additional element in the traditional Hathoric crown, thus creating a new variant, the traditional female crown (Troy 1986, 126). The Divine Adoratrices are occasionally depicted with a plume resting on a low modus without any further pictorial additions. Such a crown is more connected with the original, individual crown element of the double feather plume (Figures 8–11). There is also a symbolic correlation, stressing male and female connotations, between the plume and the Holy Wedding, in which, in accordance with Egyptian religious practice, the god's wife entered into holy matrimony with Amun (a tradition which is documented from at least the New Kingdom).[11]

Egyptian texts describe the double feather plume as a symbol of the two eyes of Horus (or the two eyes of Ra) (*Edfou* VII, 109; *Edfou* VIII, 141; *Edfou* I, 425; *cf.* Derchain-Urtel 1994, 35, 38, 56; *Edfou* II, 295; *Edfou* VI, 271). In accordance with the Egyptian convention, the double feathers express dualism. Male and female also join in the symbolism of this unit, as noted above, as the two eyes of Ra/Horus emphasise the Hathoric daughter role.

ILLUSTRATION[1]	ABBREVIATION	DESCRIPTION	SCENES	TOTAL NO. CROWNS
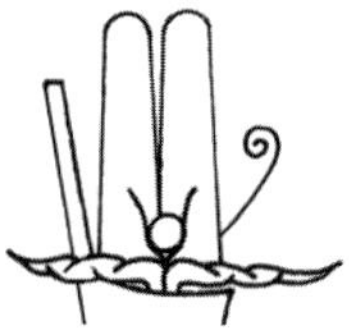	DFP 1	Large straight feathers rise from the platform of the red crown, straight or slightly curved towards the back of the crown	1R–8, 10–11, 13–20, 22–35	36
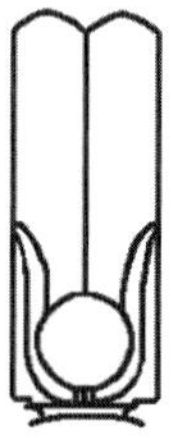	DFP 2	Tall, straight feathers rest on a low modus	21, 36	2

Note
1. This column shows an illustration of the feathers as they connect with contextual details.

Table 4. Variations of the double feather plume.

A further indication of a male and female association is expressed by the occasional identification with the divine siblings Shu and Tefnut, the children of Atum (Troy 1986, 128). This connection emphasises a cultic association with the sun and stresses, moreover, a Hathoric connection when the cow horns and solar disc, or just the disc, are placed at the base of the double feather plume, bringing to mind the myth in which Hathor lights up in the primeval darkness in her search for the lost siblings Shu and Tefnut, who can be compared with the deification of Arsinoë and Ptolemy II as the *theoi Adelphoi*.

Written sources, documented in the Temples of Dendera and Edfu, describe the plume as the crown of Amun-Ra, with its feathers stretching all the way to the sky (*Dendara* IV, 100; *Edfou* IV, 89; *Edfou* VII, 109; Derchain-Urtel 1994, 34f.). These texts refer to the double feather plume as a pictorial unit in larger crown compositions.[12] Again, the feathers are associated with the two eyes of Horus (*wḏ3tj* and *3ḫtj*), which symbolise the sun and the moon, and, therefore, connect with Shu and Tefnut once more (*e.g. LÄ* III, 48–51).

In summary, therefore, the plume represents male and female, heaven and earth, brother and sister, man and wife, and the two wings of the sun (wings of Horus). It conveys a clear statement of dualism, with themes connecting with the solar cult. The feathers also provide a link with the divine trinity (the sun and its children) and the divine (dynastic) lineage.

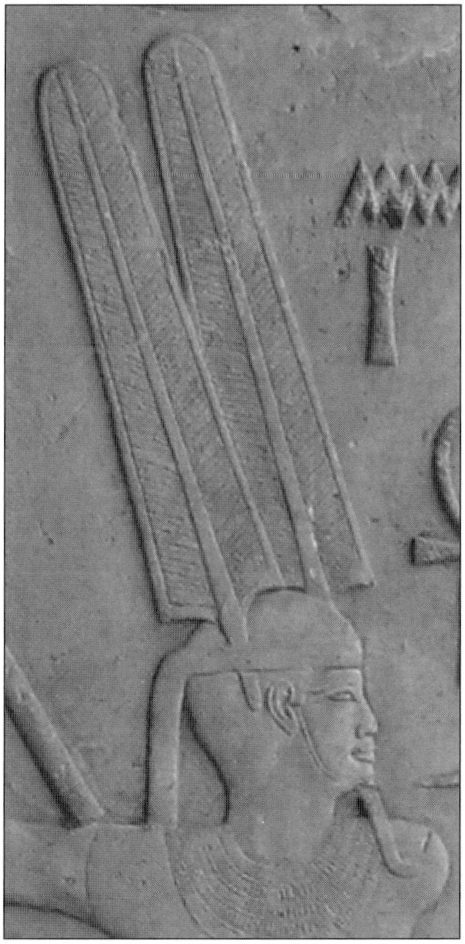

Figure 7. Detail of the figure of Amun, Karnak, showing how feathers could be tied to the head.

The physical origin of the feathers

For the ancient Egyptians, the two feathers were designated as *šwt* or *šwtj*. They are documented as a pictorial crown unit from the reign of Pharaoh Sneferu of the 4th Dynasty.[13] The feathers retained their iconographic importance in art throughout Egyptian history, including the Roman period. The physical origin, or species identification, of the double feather plume is an issue of continuous debate among modern scholars. The problem chiefly relates to the original physical form of the feathers, as the iconographic interpretation of the symbolic meaning is associated with the physical origin. As the Egyptian religion includes several birds with distinguished cultic roles and features, the debate continues.

Scholarly publications generally provide two options: falcon or ostrich feathers. The straight feathers are primarily interpreted as the tail feathers of a falcon, whereas the slightly curved plume is considered to be an ostrich feather.[14] The physical appearance and structure of the two types support such interpretations (Figures 12–13). The feathers of Arsinoë and the traditional female crown, however, cause great perplexity. These crowns have straight feathers. S. Albersmeier (2002, 54f.) and E. Vassilika (1989, 94f.) consider that the feathers resemble falcon feathers, and this belief structures their interpretations accordingly. L. Troy (1986, chapter II.6.3.1) share their opinion, arguing that the falcon feathers were feminine attributes, while the ostrich feathers were more masculine ones. However, this does not explain why the ostrich feather is the personal attribute of Ma'at, who is feminine, or why falcon feathers are worn by Amun, among other male deities. P. Dils (1998, 1305–9), in contrast, argues that the 'Arsinoë feathers' should be interpreted as those of an ostrich, based on the inner physical structure of the feathers.

Although many reliefs are preserved with details, it cannot be assumed that the ancients worried about biological exactitude. Instead, the way the feather appeared in the scene as a symbolic representation was more important than the presentation of an exact replica of the physical object. Figures 14–15, which show a falcon feather and an ostrich feather, demonstrate the resemblance (or lack of) between the feathers of the crown of Arsinoë (Figures 16–18) and the physical specimens. Based on the structural resemblance,

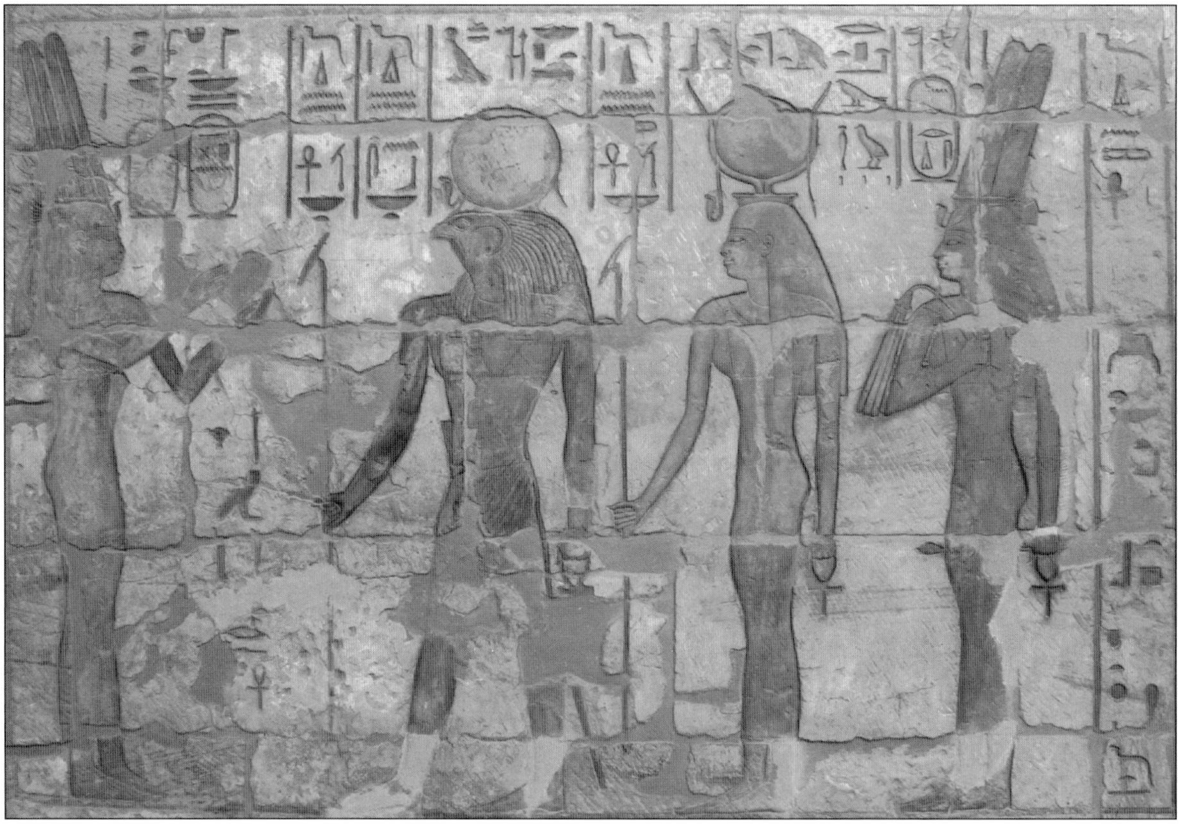

Figure 8. Example of the double feather plume: Queen Shepenwepet offering to three figures, including Queen Amenirdis, Medinat Habu.

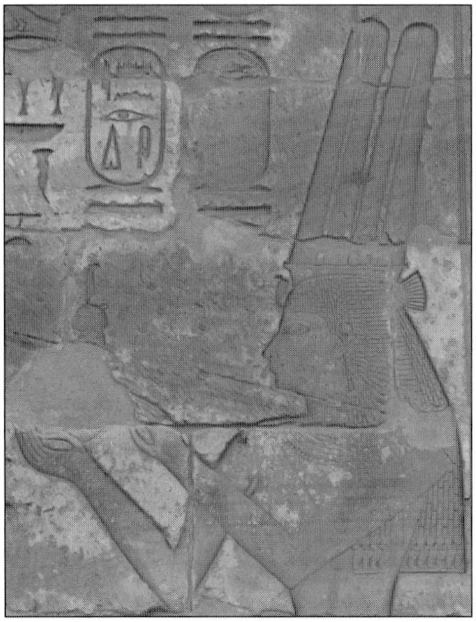

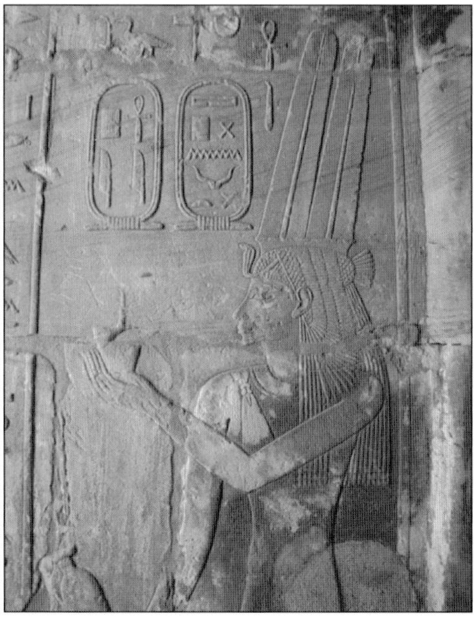

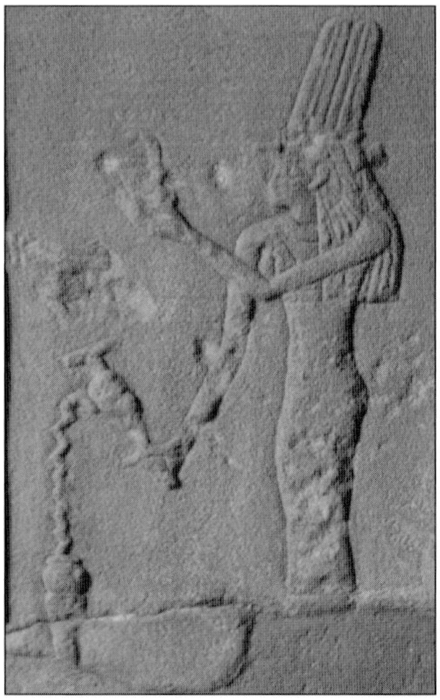

Figures 9 and 10. (Left and centre) Example of the double feather plume. Two generations of wives of the god: Queen Amenirdis and Queen Shepenwepet, Medinat Habu.
Figure 11. (Right) Example of the double feather plume: hieroglyphic sign, Medinat Habu.

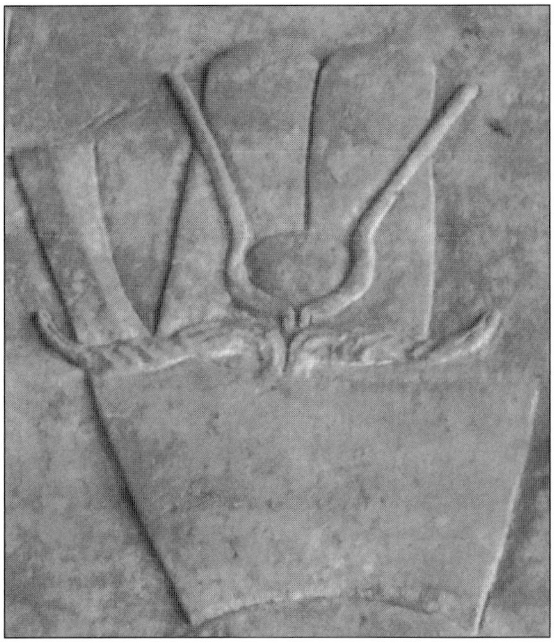

Figure 12. Detail of feathers: cat. no. 16, the straight feathers of the crown of Arsinoë, Temple of Edfu. Compare with Figure 13.

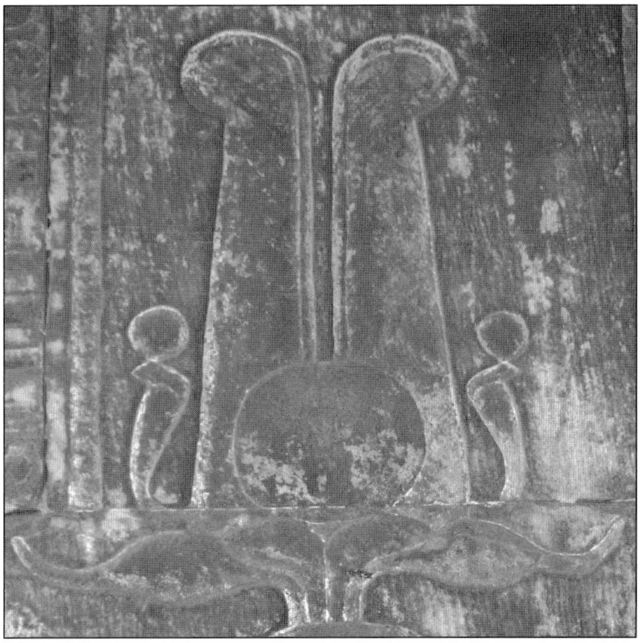

Figure 13. Detail of feathers: ostrich feathers of the anedjti crown, Temple of Edfu. Compare with Figure 12.

either type of feather may represent the physical original. There is, however, another possible candidate for the subject of the feather depictions. Although its feathers are rarely illustrated in art, the goose is regarded here as a plausible alternative to the birds already presented (Figure 19). The images shown as Figures 16–18 and 19 have been adjusted in size to allow the feathers' structure to be more easily compared. Their actual sizes vary greatly, and this, therefore, has an impact as regards the issue of the real physical existence of the crown and its individual units. The symbolism of the falcon has been studied and discussed at great length, whereas specific studies focusing on Egyptian ostriches and geese, and their symbolic meanings, are few and insufficient (*LÄ* IV, 72–82; Laufer 1926; Darby *et al.* 1977).[15]

As a natural sun worshipper, the ostrich was venerated and associated with Ra throughout the dynasties, although it never gained a clarified cultic status in Egyptian mythology or a pure form in iconography (*e.g. LÄ* VI, 72–5; *cf.* Vassilika 1989, 87; Phillips 2009). The ostrich feather was introduced as a crown unit during the Old Kingdom and worn by deities from the 2nd Dynasty and by pharaohs from the 4th Dynasty (*LÄ* VI, 77–81). It was worn initially by the god Ash, but is chiefly connected with the deities Ma'at and Shu (*LÄ* VI, 78; Vassilika 1989, 87). As an attribute of Ma'at, the ostrich feather symbolises universal truth. Tomb iconography, particularly scenes in which the soul of the deceased is weighed on the scales against the feather of Ma'at, demonstrates the association between the goddess

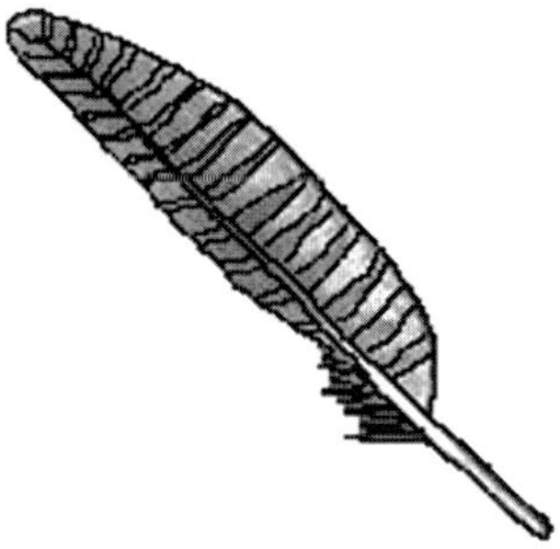

Figure 14. Falcon feather. Note similarity with Figure 17. The feathers in Figures 12–14 have been edited in order to highlight the outlines. For the original pictures see: http://www.themodernapprentice.com/feathers.htm (2010-01-23); http://www.continentalfeathers.com/images/ostrichwingblackbig.jpg (2010-01-23); http://www.friendsofjamaicapond.org/images/EmeraldBird/GreatHornedOwls/GooseFeather5463s.jpg (2010-01-23).

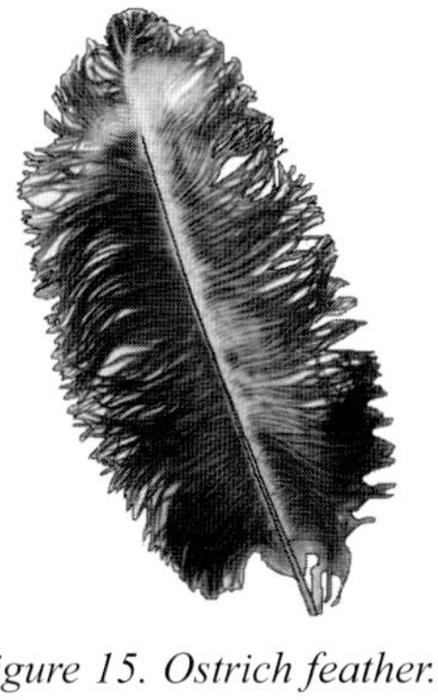

Figure 15. Ostrich feather.

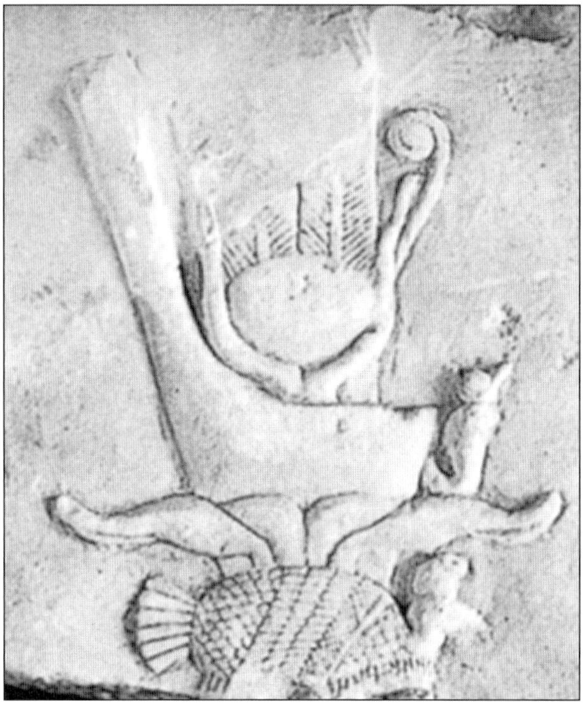

Figure 16. Detail of feathers: cat. no. 8.

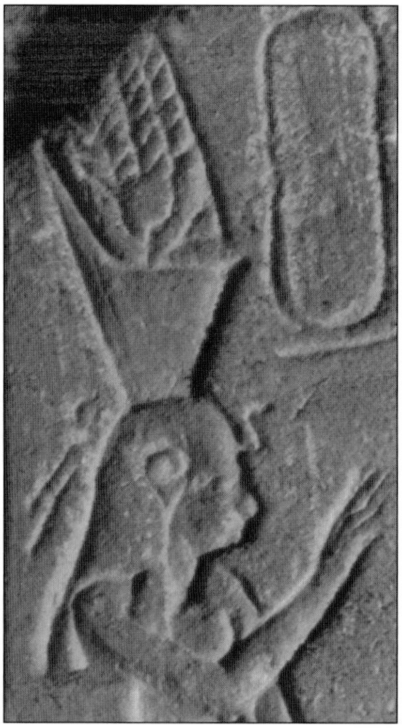

Figure 17. Detail of feathers: cat. no. 3.

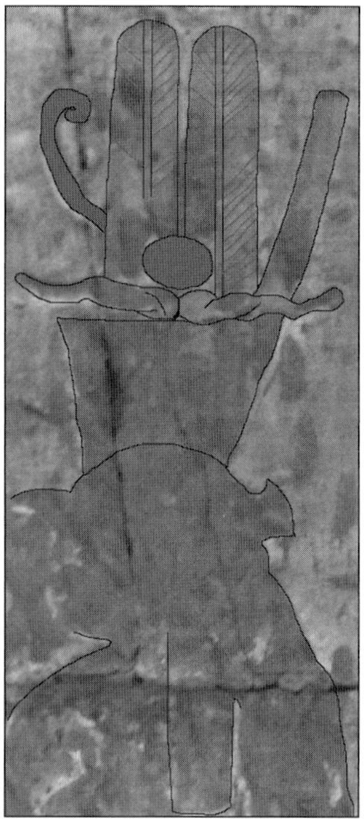

Figure 18. Detail of feathers: cat. no. 34.

and the feather. This goddess of truth was regarded as the personification of the divine balance and universal harmony, and she is one of the most ancient of Egyptian goddesses (*cf. LÄ* III, 1110–20). This feather was also used by Geb, Osiris, Arensnuphis, Ptah (when associated with Tanen) and Tutu, but when worn by these deities it was applied mainly as an additional unit rather than an individual attribute.

While the ostrich was generally excluded from art relating to the main mythology, the falcon was given a prominent position in Egyptian religion. It was venerated by the early Egyptians and had been associated with kingship since the beginning of the historical period, appearing in iconography at least from the late Predynastic period of Naqada III. It was one of the most common avian hieroglyphs and a symbol of kingship (Houlihan 1996, 161). Textual sources dating to the Old Kingdom designate the falcon *ḥr* – Hor, or Horus, 'the distant one', 'the lofty one' (Houlihan 1996, 160; Meltzer 2001, 119; 2002, 164f.). Horus was the divine ruling king, and his main role was to protect Egypt against its enemies (*e.g. LÄ* III, 14–47). The falcon was closely connected with the sky and the sun, and could take many shapes and names. In addition to Horus, the falcon was also associated with Ra, Montu and Khonsu. It has been suggested, because of the location of Horus' cult centre at Heliopolis, that the feathers of the falcon tail symbolise Lower Egypt (Vassilika 1989, 87).

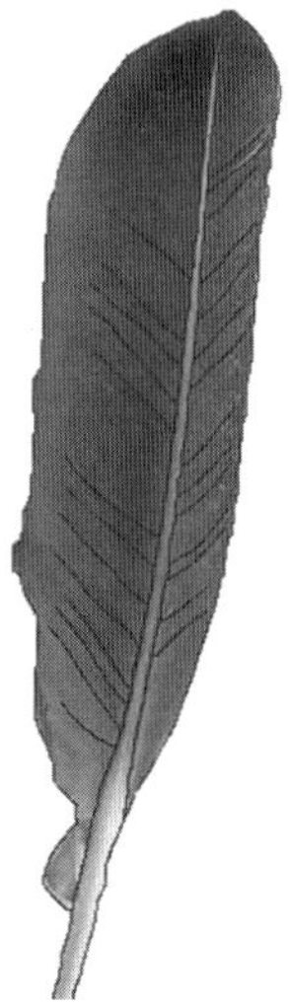

Figure 19. Goose feather. Note similarity with Figure 14.

However, Horus also had a cultic centre in Nekhen, in Upper Egypt, and there are several other temples dedicated to the falcon-god throughout Egypt. Therefore, it does not appear that the falcon feathers represent Lower Egypt exclusively.

No other scholar has considered the feathers to be those of a goose (or duck, a bird with very similar feathers), although the bird is clearly associated with some of the most prominent deities in Egyptian religion. Often, the goose is confused with the duck, and most scholars seem not to make an explicit distinction between them (Houlihan 1996, 139–44, esp. p. 139; Massey 2008 [1907], 21). The goose was initially an individual feature of Seb, the divine father of Osiris (Budge 2003 [1904], II, 94). As a hieroglyph, the goose symbolised a child, son or daughter, which, according to Horapollo (Horapollo, I, 53), signifies the goose's self-sacrifice on behalf of her young. Herodotus (Hdt. 2, 72) states that the goose was sacred in Egypt. According to the Hermopolitan cosmology, it was a goose that laid the golden egg, symbolising the soul of the sun, equivalent to the sun-god Ra (Massey 2008 [1907], 21f). According to the myth, the earth was imagined as a Mother Goose who laid a golden egg every morning (Pinch 2002, 120). The Mother Goose was identified with Hathor. A child who appeared from this egg and was mothered by Hathor was described as the vanquisher of Darkness (Massey 2008 [1907], 22). At Dendera and Edfu the reliefs often describe Hathor in her maternal role, as the mother of Harsomtus and Ihy (Nilsson 2010, 445–7). This story forms the basis for the interpretation given above of the double crown (red and white crowns) as a symbol of Hathor's protection of the golden egg. The golden egg is one of many descriptions of the rebirth of the sun in its daily journey.

Furthermore, the goose was an animal sacred to Amun, who was sometimes described as 'the Great Cackler', like Geb (Tobin 2002, 21). In his association with Ra, Amun is described as 'Amun-Ra, the beautiful Goose', or 'the beautiful Goose of Amun-Ra' (Budge 2003 [1904], II, 374). In one myth, Amun, in the shape of a ram-headed serpent (Kematef), is described as having created, or fertilised, the golden egg (Pinch 2002, 101). Possibly owing to its connections with Amun-Ra, the goose had erotic connotations which are traditionally considered to have alluded to female sexuality (Houlihan 1996, 143).

Clearly, all three types of feather have religious and symbolic significance. The falcon holds a prominent mythological position and is illustrated in realistic and anthropomorphic shapes. Although the ostrich and the goose are depicted in Egyptian iconography, they are excluded from anthropomorphic representation in the more religious sphere. So far, their most obvious connections are with the solar cult and Amun, regardless of the sort of feather. Their overall shared associations does raise a question of whether or not the actual variety of feather actually mattered. According to Troy (1986, 126), there was no distinction between feathers prior to the 18th Dynasty, and Egyptian art shows many inconsistencies in regard to the use of conventional feathers as divine attributes. Shu, who is generally depicted with the ostrich feather, occasionally wears four tall falcon tail feathers. Horus wears the four-feathered crown of falcon feathers, but he also wears the ostrich feathers as a structural part of other crown compositions. When associated with Shu, Osiris abandons his traditional ostrich feathers in favour of the tall falcon tail feathers (Vassilika 1989, 119). Mainly in his role as Harpocrates, Horus wears the triple crown, consisting of several ostrich feathers. In Speos Artemidos, Beni Hassan, lioness goddess Pakhet wears the traditional female crown with ostrich feathers instead of the conventional straight feather plume. Evidently, the choice of feathers varied, and thus the feather itself will be considered here regardless of type, a standpoint which concurs with the general views of many previous scholars, such as Vassilika, Troy and Albersmeier.[16]

A Greek counterpart?

In the Greek material there is no clear association with any of the birds mentioned above. However, Greek coins, including early casts depicting Arsinoë, frequently show the Ptolemaic eagle (Figure 20). Traditionally, the bird is assumed to be associated with Zeus-Amun, with eternity and, possibly, with apotheosis. Furthermore, it is connected with the mythic Phoenix bird, the *Benu* bird of the Egyptians, which was associated with solar cult, fertility and rejuvenation (Meyboom 1994, 129).

In a purely Greek forum the eagle was associated with Apollo and Zeus, deities who were connected with both the solar cult and fertility (Hunter 2003, 151). As depicted on Ptolemaic coins, the eagle is accompanied by a small

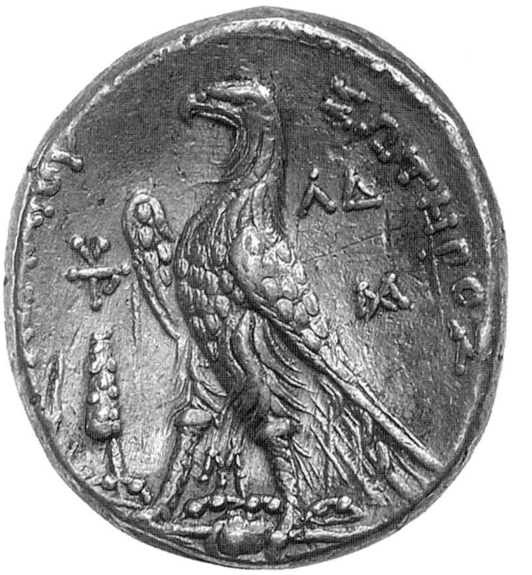

Figure 20. Coin depicting the Ptolemaic eagle: © Myntkabinettet, Stockholm.

cornucopia and/or a lotus, symbols referring to prosperity and fertility. The Greek material indicates cultural aspects and values similar to Egyptian ones, although the bird is different. Therefore, the Greek evidence supports the conclusion reached above that the feather in general had an individual symbolism, regardless of species.

Cow horns and solar disc (CS)

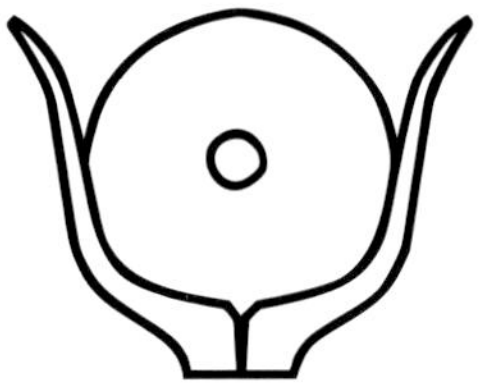

Two individual pictorial units, the cow horns and the solar disc, are combined here into one element, the classification of which is based on their joined position, size and style. The cow horns and solar disc are divided in six individual types (Table 5).

Five individual types of the crown of Arsinoë are recorded in the material. The sixth type relates to the traditional female crown worn by Arsinoë in cat. nos 21 and 36. The first four types comprise an element made up of the horns and disc. CS 1, the most frequent style, is a small element the size of an amulet and includes the Edfu scenes where Arsinoë and Ptolemy II are joined by other ancestral couples and deities (*cf.* CS 4). This type is mainly represented in the stelai.

The second most common style is CS 4, which is depicted mainly in temple reliefs. The cow horns stretch tall, with their tips tending to protrude slightly outside the outlines of the double feather plume. Arsinoë is illustrated alone or paired with Ptolemy II when she wears this type. She is identified as Arsinoë the divine Philadelphos and with Ptolemy as *theoi Adelphoi*. Consequently, the style cannot relate to a specific cultic role of Arsinoë. The Temple of Edfu has several examples of this type. These scenes illustrate Arsinoë and Ptolemy II as beneficiaries, receiving offerings as a couple from Ptolemy IV and VIII (the excluded Edfu scenes illustrate the *theoi Adelphoi* in a dynastic theme surrounded by additional Ptolemaic ancestral couples, or, as in cat. no. 20, by other deities). The prominent position of the horns may be interpreted as being associated with the Hathoric aspect of queenship.

Type CS 2, which is limited to the scenes from the Temple of Philae, is clearly differentiated from the rest of the material. The horns and the disc are identical in size to those of CS 4, but owing to the ram horns' position below the red crown, the CS-element is dissimilar to type CS 4 (where they are positioned on the platform instead).

Cat. nos 8 and 12, illustrated in the material in an exaggerated style, show two distinctive crown elements of the crown of Arsinoë forming CS 3. CS 5 denotes a unit which shows *only* the sun disc (Figure 21). This type is represented in two scenes. It may be misconceived owing to the current state of preservation of the scenes, and therefore the possibility that these crowns once included cow horns cannot be excluded. However, as has been stated previously, the analysis is based on the crowns' present pictorial structure. Cat. nos 34 and 35, which are included in this type, date to the reign of Ptolemy VIII and are thematically classified as dynastic.

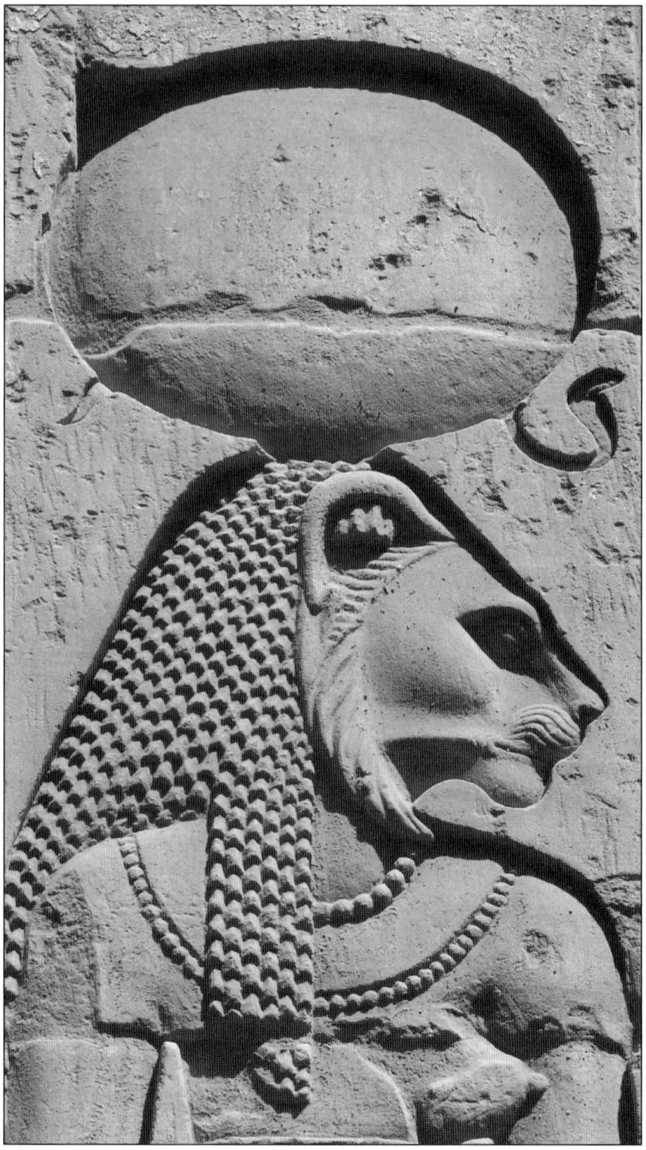

Figure 21. Sekhmet wearing the solar disc, Kom Ombo.

ILLUSTRATION[1]	ABBREVIATION	DESCRIPTION	SCENES	TOTAL NO. CROWNS
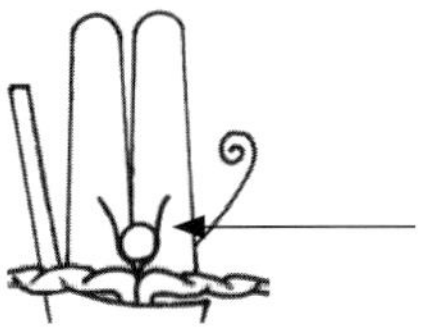	CS 1	The element is shown as a mere amulet above the platform and the ram horns	2L–3, 6–7, 10–11, 13, 15L–R, 18, 20, 25	13
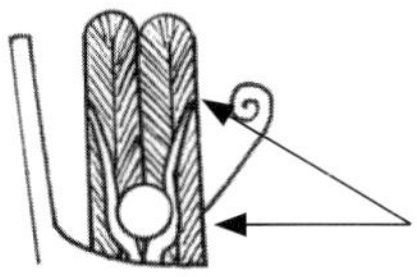	CS 2	The element is placed directly on the platform of the red crown. The horns are high, though remain within the dimensions of the feathers	27–32	6
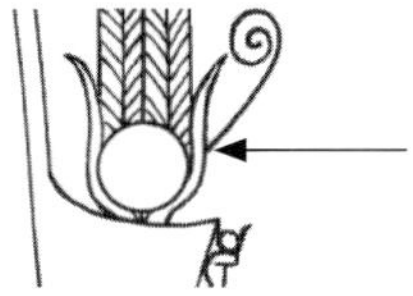	CS 3	The element is enlarged and rests directly on the platform of the red crown	8, 12	2
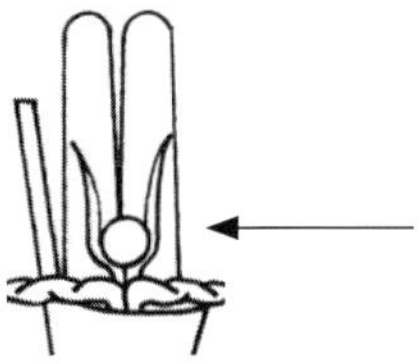	CS 4	The element sits on the ram horns and the platform. The horns are high, occasionally with their tips protruding outside the boundaries of the feathers	1R, 4–5, 14, 16–17, 19, 22–24, 26L–R (cat. no. 1R has been included in this group based on size, although (possibly) resting directly on the red crown)	12
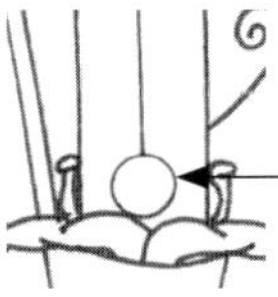	CS 5	Only the disc is depicted	34–35	2
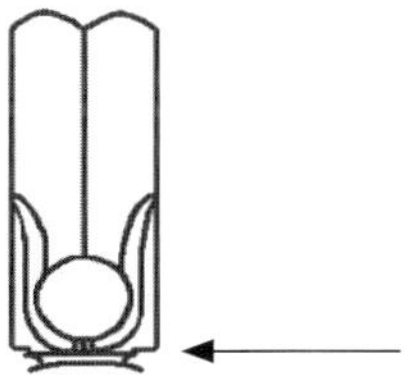	CS 6	The element rests on a modus and is enlarged	21, 36	2

Note
1. The arrows point to the position and irregularities of the element.

Table 5. Variations of the cow horns and solar disc

The cow horns

The sacred role of the cow, which is depicted as petroglyphs in Upper Egypt, dates back to the prehistoric period (*e.g. LÄ* V, 257f.; Brass 2003, 103; Stockstad 2002, *passim*; Hanotte *et al.* 2002, *passim*; *cf.* Brunton and Caton-Thompson 1928, 42, 91–4). Bovine deities include both male and female variants, all linked with fertility and rejuvenation. Cow horns are mainly associated with Apis and Hathor, but were also used by deities such as Bat, Buchis, Hesat, Mehet-Weret, Mnevis and Shentayet (*e.g. LÄ* V, 261). The horns are generally depicted in different styles depending on the sex of the bovine. Those of a cow either pointed straight up or were bent slightly outwards; those of a bull were (slightly or fully) rounded inwards. Often, bovine deities were depicted with a solar disc between their horns. The bull symbolised kingship primarily, whereas the cow connoted maternity and the queen in her role as the nurturer of the forthcoming pharaoh.[17]

The cow and bull were equally venerated in Egypt as sacred animals. Mainly connected with 'Hathor of Dendera, Lady of the Sky', the cow was also associated with Isis, Nut and other female deities (Nilsson 2010, 441f.). As the male bovine, the bull was venerated in three main forms: the Apis bull in Memphis; the Mnevis bull in Heliopolis; and the Buchis bull in Armant (*e.g.* Houlihan 1996, 11–21, esp. 19f.; *cf.* Crawford 1980).[18]

In Greek mythology the bull symbolised the sun, while the cow was the moon (Keightley 1866, 407). The cow was mainly associated with Hera, or with the infidelity myth of Io, a priestess of Hera (Keightley 1866, 361). The connection with Hera is similar to the symbolic connotations of Hathor and corresponds chiefly to fertility. Furthermore, bovines were common sacrificial animals, dedicated in Hera's honour (Petropoulou 2008, 96).

The solar disc

Primarily a symbol of Ra, the solar disc, Aten, was associated with fertility, rebirth, rejuvenation, reincarnation and so on. In the Egyptian myth the disc changed its shape, name and appearance in accordance with the three phases of the day: dawn, midday and evening (Roberts 1997, 20–22). Magical texts describe the disc as Khepri, the scarab-faced deity of the East, in the morning; as Ra, a falcon-headed anthropomorphic deity wearing the solar disc crown, at midday; and as the ram-headed god Atum in the evening, preparing for the nightly battles in the Underworld (Borghouts 1978, 54; Silverman 1991, 36; Roberts 1997, 20). However, in some myths Harpocrates/Harsomtus replaces Khepri. Ra is protected by his mother Hathor during the night from the evil serpent Apophis to once again be reborn as the youngster Khepri the following morning. This myth explained the continuation of life and gave worshippers hope that good might prevail over evil (Roberts 1997, 20–22; Nilsson 2010, 443–53).

As mentioned above, the Hermopolitan myth describes the solar disc as the light coming from the primeval egg laid at Medinet Habu and nurtured by Hathor in the shape of a goose (*cf.* Lesko 1991, 118). The solar disc was worshipped as the great creator who made heaven and earth and everything dwelling within them. In the name of Ra, the disc ruled deities and men equally, although in constant need of his daughter-wife-mother Hathor, in her role as his protectress. As the ultimate source of life, the solar disc was the King of the Gods, the true father of the pharaohs and the primeval true master (*e.g.* *LÄ* V, 156–80). Throughout the Egyptian ages the solar disc was associated with various deities other than Ra, including Amun and Horus and the goddesses Hathor, Isis and Ma'at.

In Greek religion, Apollo and Helios symbolised the sun primarily. In Greek poetry light and divinity, the personification and the god, were undivided. It is a myth similar to the Egyptian story in which Helios is described as travelling across the sky in a chariot drawn by horses (Parisinou 2005, 32, nn. 14f.). He used as his crown attribute a solar disc similar to that attributed to Ra and other Egyptian solar deities (Parisinou 2005, 32). Furthermore, the Greeks associated the sun with the all-seeing eye in a fashion again comparable with the Egyptian myths. In a parallel to the myth of Ra and his children Shu and Tefnut, the Greeks present Helios as the father of Eos and Selene (Hes. *Theog.*, 371–4).

The combined attribute

Many Egyptian bovine figures used the cow horns and solar disc as an attribute. As a complete crown, however, it was mainly used by Hathor (or aspects of her). Therefore, this crown is referred to here as the 'traditional Hathoric crown' (Figure 22). Hathor is illustrated in the Valley Temple of Mycerinus (Menkaure) during the Old Kingdom (Reisner 1931, 123f., pls 36–46), and the crown was attributed exclusively to Hathor until the New Kingdom, when Isis usurped the crown in order, it is suggested, to accentuate the maternal associations between the goddesses (*cf.* Meyboom 1994, 35). In order to clarify her individuality and her

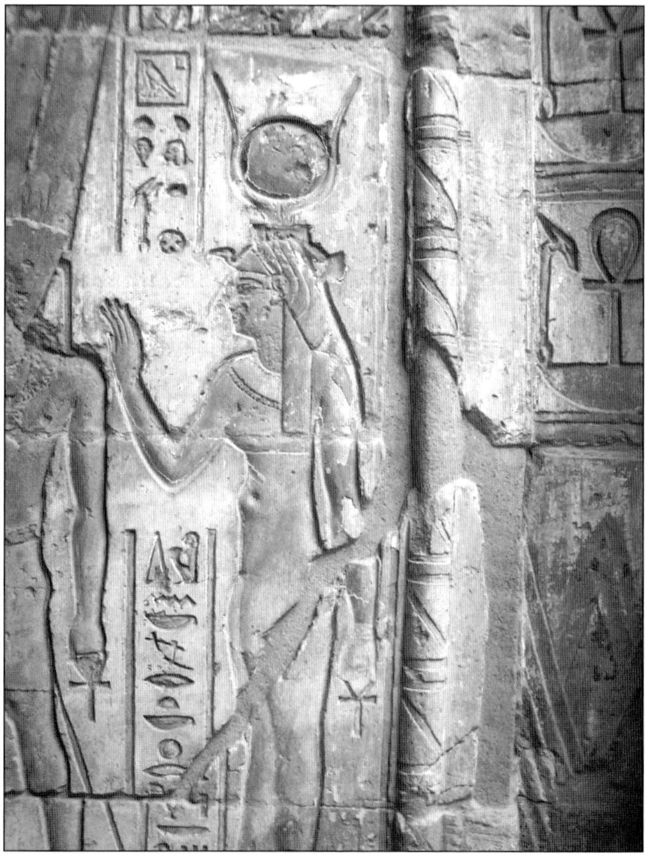

Figure 22. Hathor wearing her traditional crown, Deir el-Medina.

various alternative aspects, new and more elaborated crowns were developed for Hathor. Meanwhile, she also kept her traditional Hathoric crown.

The traditional Hathoric crown is generally regarded as symbolising the protective role of Hathor, within which the solar disc refers to Ra (*e.g. LÄ* II, 1024–33). Hathor, in her associations with Ra, was the mother and the daughter, the sister and the wife. She was entwined in Egypt's entire cosmology. Every day she gave birth to a new sun, and was, therefore, regarded as a goddess protecting women in childbirth (Nilsson 2010, 445–7). Hathor guided the deceased through the obstacles of the Underworld in order for them to be reborn (*e.g.* Pinch 2002, 137). Hathor and Ra, in a mutual symbiosis, were thus responsible for the continuation of the universe (*cf.* Delia 1998).

Deities other than Isis, including Mut, Wadjet and Mehnyt, used the traditional Hathoric crown (Nilsson 2010, 433–53). Such goddesses are described in texts as predominantly connected with Hathor. The traditional crown of Hathor indicates a feminine connotation.

Uraeus (UR)

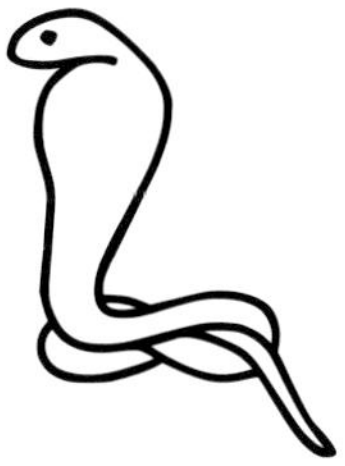

This pictorial unit communicates a symbolism fundamentally equivalent to that of the single forehead *uraeus* presented below. The main dissimilarity is their individual placements and their associations with surrounding pectorals. The unit labelled as *uraeus* (UR) is physically linked to the crown and is classified into three individual types based on position and additional pictorial details.

According to Table 6, UR 1 and UR 3 are applied equally frequently. UR 1 is illustrated on stelai that show Arsinoë as a goddess (cat. nos 2, 30) and as a living queen (cat. no. 8). Cat. nos 2 and 8 display Arsinoë in a Hathoric role, as will be noted below. UR 3 shows two cobras rising up along the outer sides of the double feather plume. Two of the scenes are located within the Edfu Temple, placing Arsinoë with Ptolemy II, where they are together referred to as *theoi Adelphoi*. These scenes date to the reign of Ptolemy IV and are classified here as dynastic. Cat. nos 7 and 13 show Arsinoë on stelai: she is individually deified, receiving offerings from her brother. The stelai scenes date to the reign of Ptolemy II. Any symbolism directly relating to Arsinoë's cultic roles can be excluded because of the dissimilarities between the scenes in which UR 3 appears.

UR 2, the most infrequently used type, is represented in only one scene (cat. no. 35). The scene is preserved in a bad state and the *uraeus* shown presumably belonged to type UR 3 originally. However, this is an assumption based on a plausible interpretation of the original depiction and not on the image as it is viewed today.

Conclusion

Each unit demonstrates associations with various gods, goddesses, kings and queens. The structural units comprising the crown of Arsinoë are each equally significant, and their many positions indicate that it was not the placement that mattered so much as their actual presence.

ILLUSTRATION	ABBREVIATION	DESCRIPTION	SCENES	TOTAL NO. CROWNS
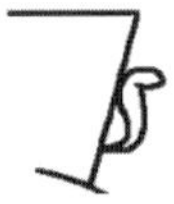	UR 1	A single *uraeus* is attached to the front of the red crown, sometimes wearing a solar disc. The *uraeus* of cat. no. 8 wears a traditional Hathoric crown	2L–R, 8, 30	4
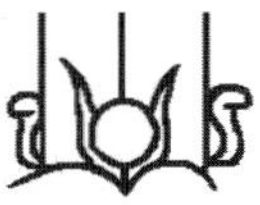	UR 2	Two uncrowned *uraei* rise from the sides of the double feather plume	35	1
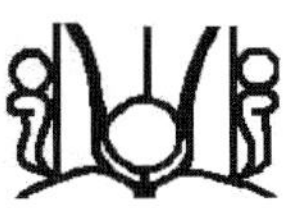	UR 3	Two *uraei* rise from the sides of the double feather plume, wearing a solar disc	7, 13, 18, 20	4

Table 6. Variations of the uraeus.

It is generally accepted that the red crown was associated with kingship and was an attribute of royal power. As an individual unit rather than a component in the double crown, it symbolised Lower Egypt. It was associated with Amun-Ra and Hathor (including Wadjet as the serpent-aspect of Hathor). Moreover, a symbolism has been suggested here which associates the red crown with the Hathoric maternal role, the female womb, as it protects the primeval egg (=the white crown). Prior to Arsinoë, the red crown was worn by two queens, Hatshepsut and Amenirdis, as a unit in larger compositions. These queens had great political and religious importance, and were both commemorated in various artistic media and with a designation placing them as the wife of God or daughter of Amun.

The ram horns, illustrated as twined, horizontal horns, have been identified as horns of the most ancient Egyptian breed of sheep. The material frequently places the horns on the platform of the red crown, either joined in the middle or separated in one visible and one partly hidden section. The Philae scenes stand apart from the others, placing the horns below the red crown. These horns are separated, with one side only partially visible. The horns have been established as associating Arsinoë and the later queens with, primarily, Amun.

The double feather plume is traditionally considered to be the tail feathers of a falcon or of an ostrich, but here an additional candidate is suggested: goose feathers. However, this interpretation of the plume is based on a stylised form of the feather rather than on the breed of the bird. The double feather plume is documented in both the crown of Arsinoë and the traditional female crown, and fundamentally symbolised the dualism of all Egyptian religious concepts, associating with the male and female, husband and wife, brother and sister, father and daughter/mother and son and so on.

As a pictorial component of the larger structure of the crown of Arsinoë and the traditional female crown, the cow horns and solar disc are regarded here as directly associated with Hathor and her various family-oriented aspects.

Each crown unit is interpreted as a manifestation of the divine world and its legacy. By wearing them, the royal couple distinguished themselves from commoners. The king and queen represented the sons and daughters of the gods, and manifested Horus and Hathor. Each crown, consequently, is an expression of kingship and divinity. The crown communicated a clear political and socio-religious statement of power and rightfulness.

Notes

1 Consider also the criosphinxes (ram-headed lions) decorating the avenues leading towards Karnak.

2 Based on the very limited Egyptian relief material depicting Alexander it is not possible to present any form of comparison between his crowns and the crown of Arsinoë.

3 His text describes a religious procession proceeding through the streets of Alexandria, incorporating the official priestess of Arsinoë, the *canephoros*. Satyrus describes how devoted worshippers of Arsinoë were told to place their sacrifice on an altar made of sand, or an altar with sand placed on top of it (see n. 4, and discussion in the text), and to sacrifice in front of their houses, on their roofs, or anywhere along the street where the procession passed. He says, moreover, that birds were a suitable offering, though he states that any offering would be accepted except goats. The goat was frequently sacrificed to the honour of fertility gods, and as a symbol of fruitfulness it was primarily associated with Aphrodite and Dionysus (*cf.* Pomeroy 1984, 33; Rosenzweig 2004, esp. 71).

4 Previous scholars have demonstrated that goats and sheep were regarded similarly by the Egyptians (*e.g.* Houlihan 1996, 22f.)

5 In his article, Dils (1998, 1315–25) states that a red crown of this second style would be impossible to wear in reality. Abubakr (1937, 48–50, n. 1 on p. 48) compares the red crown with a cap, and dismisses the flat-bottomed style that would rest directly on the head (which he includes on p. 52, Abb. 36).

6 Early scholars, such as Moret (1902, 285) and Abubakr (1937, 47), deconstructed the red crown in three parts based on the following hieroglyphic signs: 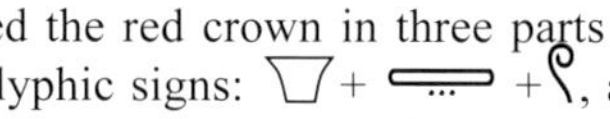, and the spiral was interpreted as a sunbeam or associated with the feather of Ma'at. In terms of material it has been compared to a metal wire, but unless archaeologists can provide a physical crown, all suggestions must be considered hypotheses.

7 Although cat. no. 22 lacks a spiral it is badly affected by soot and therefore remains questionable.

8 Thus, the above-listed hieroglyphic designation *w3dt*, meaning the 'Green One'. Another title of the red crown was *nsrt*, the 'Fiery One', referring to Wadjet.

9 Vassilika (1989, 94) suggests that Arsinoë's popularity made a representation of Upper Egypt – *i.e.* the white crown – unnecessary; this is, however, a 'missing' element which is regarded by the present author as a most important indication of the meaning of the crown. She describes the crown of Arsinoë as including 'Lower Egyptian crown, the Lower Egyptian falcon tail feathers and horizontal horns with sundisc on a vulture headdress'. Not only does she forget the cow horns of the crown, but she concludes that symbolism, both in general and in terms of these objects, was an unnecessary part of their interpretation.

10 Straight feathers with visible inner details (barbs) and joined in the middle: cat. nos 3, 8, 34; feathers with thin, straight and separated feathers: cat. nos 4–5; straight feathers, joined in the middle, no inner decoration: cat. nos 1–2, 6, 11, 13–14, 16–20, 22–26, 31–32; feathers slightly leaning backwards: cat. nos 15, 28–30, 33, 35; feathers slightly leaning inwards and joined in the middle: cat. nos 7, 10, 27.

11 The Holy Wedding between the priestess and Amun symbolised the divine lineage and the rightful heritage of the throne. The queen was believed to have been impregnated by the god in a ritual, in order to give birth to the next pharaoh (*e.g.* Troy 1986, chapter II, 4.3).

12 These crowns are traditionally referred to as *htpj*, but I use the terminology introduced in Nilsson 2010.

13 Traditionally, the feathers are described in their hieroglyphic form in the singular, in spite of their dualistic nature. I have applied this form when I refer to them as a plume (*cf.* Gardiner *et al.* 1952–5, pl. II no. 5; Troy 1986, 126; Derchain-Urtel 1994, 29 with n. 14).

14 Abubakr (1937, 38–42) describes the slightly rounded feathers of the *anedjti* crown as ostrich feathers. The crown which he refers to as 'die Horus-Feder-Krone' depicts straight feathers, and the plume is classified as being tail feathers of a falcon.

15 Hieroglyphic texts designate the ostrich *njw* (*e.g.* *LÄ* VI, 72).

16 Dils (1998), however, dismisses this interpretation, stating that the feathers of the traditional female crown and the crown of Arsinoë were those of an ostrich. He questions how the feathers could be those of Amun, when the Amarna queens are depicted wearing them. This is a clear paradox of Egyptian art and religious history. Although Akhenaton distanced himself culturally from the traditional cult of Amun, the royal family retained many previous customs and conventions. In iconography, the royal family of Akhenaton wore traditional headdress units, including the *uraeus*, the traditional female crown and the double crown. Female members are depicted shaking the sistrum, which was an established ceremonial instrument used to evoke the spirit of Hathor. In many illustrations, Queen Nefertiti wears the Two Ladies, the *uraeus* and vulture. As will be mentioned below (pp. 51–52), the Two Ladies were traditionally referred to as the earthly manifestations of Nekhbet and Wadjet, the goddesses of Upper and Lower Egypt. Furthermore, the figure of Ma'at was frequently depicted as an offering during the Amarna period. In fact, Nefertiti is one of only a few queens to be illustrated performing this offering. Although Akhenaton and his family worshipped the sun disc, Aton, primarily, while regarding the light as the only true divine source, other deities were clearly still incorporated in the religious agenda. In favouring the ostrich feathers for the female crowns, Dils bases his arguments on his conclusion that the crown of Arsinoë was male rather than female. He argues that the crown of Arsinoë includes only male elements except for the cow horns. However, one can argue that all the elements of the crown have also been worn by female deities. As listed by Dils, all figures, except for the later Ptolemaic queens, preceding and succeeding Arsinoë, wear the Ramesside crown and not the crown of Arsinoë. With such rich material for a crown which is not identical to the crown of Arsinoë, Dils' decision in masculinising the crown of Arsinoë seems incorrect. So far, there is nothing to support a conclusion that this crown was masculine, unless the scholar considers Arsinoë in a male role as the pharaoh of Egypt.

17 Compare the bull's ritualistic position in the Sed festival and the rejuvenation ceremonies of the pharaoh.

18 Cat. nos 12 and 26 describe Arsinoë as the mother of Hep (=Apis).

Chapter 4

The complete crown

The crown of Arsinoë is divided into twenty types which are classified in accordance with the individual details in the crown composition alone, thus excluding headdress elements (the classification thus proceeding differently from that in Nilsson 2010). As noted above, the crown of Arsinoë is composed of the red crown, ram horns, double feather plume, cow horns and solar disc. A type comprises those crowns (one or more) that are unique in their complete structural composition. Incomplete or fragmentary crowns are classified as individual types even if not all pictorial details are depicted: it will be assumed that the crown was complete in its original form, and it is categorised based on its current state of preservation, therefore preventing one type from being wrongly identified with another. In this chapter the crowns' structural composition, rather than their symbolic meaning, will be explained.

The categorisation of crown types is consistent with the method of classification used for the individual pictorial units, following contextual criteria of size, position and combination. Each type incorporates at least one example, though none includes more than five. The individual composition types of the crown of Arsinoë are shown in Table 7.

The composition type AC 6, which occurs most frequently, consists of a red crown (RC 1) with a spiral coming up behind the double feather plume (DFP 1). The ram horns (RH 1) rest on the platform of the red crown together with an amulet of cow horns and solar disc (CS 1). The four scenes (five figures) that show AC 6 differ significantly in their individual contexts. Cat. no. 25 is the only temple relief, while cat. nos 6, 11 and 15 (L–R) are stelai. In accordance with the crown line (discussed further below) Arsinoë is the tallest figure in cat. nos 5, 15 (L–R) and 25. She is positioned on the left side, facing right, in all scenes in accordance with the figural arrangement, though cat. no. 15 places her also on the right side. She is illustrated as a benefactor in cat. no. 15 (L–R), otherwise as a beneficiary. The scenes date to the reigns of Ptolemy II (cat. nos 6, 11, 15) and Ptolemy III (cat. no. 25).

Types AC 11 and 13 include four scenes each. All scenes in AC 11 are located in the Temple of Edfu except cat. no. 14, which is an individual stele. The crown is composed of a red crown without any spiral, horns placed on the platform, a straight double feather plume and a CS unit with long protruding horns. The Edfu scenes are categorised as dynastic, showing a Ptolemaic descendant (Ptolemy IV and VIII) offering to his deified ancestors, Ptolemy II and Arsinoë, depicted as the *theoi Adelphoi*. Cat. no. 14, however, is different: it dates to Ptolemy II, who sacrifices to his deified queen in addition to Amun-Min. Cat. no. 17 differs from the other figures as Arsinoë wears a simplified wig with a royal diadem and no vulture cap, which is present in all other scenes. Furthermore, there is no consistency when comparing the scenes in terms of relative scaling or relative placement.

All scenes incorporated in AC 13 are located in the larger Karnak Temple complex and date to the reigns of Ptolemy II and III. The crown is composed of a red crown with the spiral coming out from behind the double feather plume, ram horns sitting on top of the platform and a CS unit of increased size. Cat. nos 23 and 24 show a vulture cap with additional details (see pp. 50–51). Cat. no. 26, however, is damaged in this area, making an identification impossible. All scenes show Arsinoë as deified, although cat. no. 26L simultaneously depicts her as a living queen. All scenes describe the queen as 'Daughter of Amun'. The two scenes dating to Ptolemy II show the ruler offering to his deified queen, who is standing with the local deities, while cat. no. 24, dating to Ptolemy III, shows the king presenting offerings to his deified ancestors/parents as the *theoi Adelphoi*.

Among the more interesting types, AC 14 includes three scenes: cat. nos 27, 29 and 32. The crown consists of a red crown (RC 1) with its spiral coming up behind the double feather plume (DFP 1). The ram horns are divided and placed below the red crown (RH 2). While the solar disc remains an amulet, the cow horns are depicted tall, stretching far up (CS 2). All scenes are located in the Philae Temple, depicting Arsinoë and dating to the reign of Ptolemy II. Arsinoë is placed as a beneficiary, standing behind Isis, the great mother. She is the tallest figure in all these scenes.

ILLUSTRATION	TITLE AND ABBREVIATED UNITS	COMMENTARY	SCENES	TOTAL NO. CROWNS
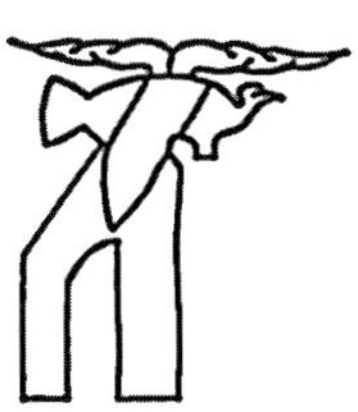	**AC 1** TW 1 + VC 1 + RH 3(?)	Only three individual details are visible, thus showing an incomplete crown of Arsinoë	1L	1
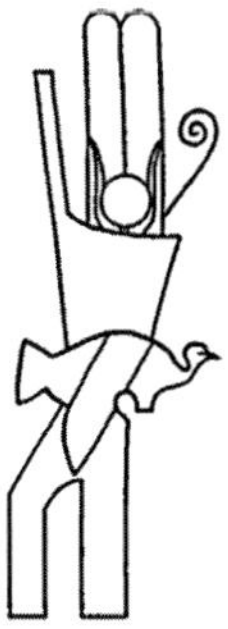	**AC 2** TW 1 + VC 1 + RC 1 + DFP 1 + CS 4	Not all details are visible, thus showing an incomplete crown of Arsinoë	1R	1
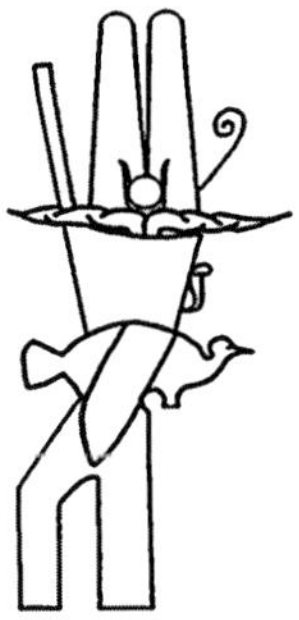	**AC 3** UR 1 + RC 1 + DFP 1 + CS 1 + RH 1	The crown is decorated with an additional crown *uraeus*	2L–R	2
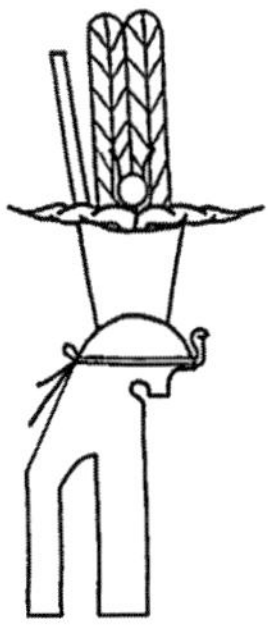	**AC 4** RC 4 + DFP 1 + CS 1 + RH 1		3, 10	2
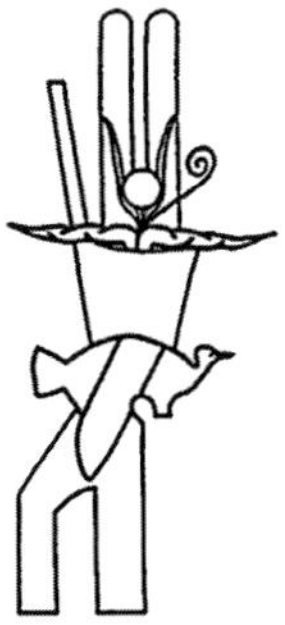	**AC5** RC 2 + DFP 1 + CS 4 + RH 1		4–5, 19	4

ILLUSTRATION	TITLE AND ABBREVIATED UNITS	COMMENTARY	SCENES	TOTAL NO. CROWNS
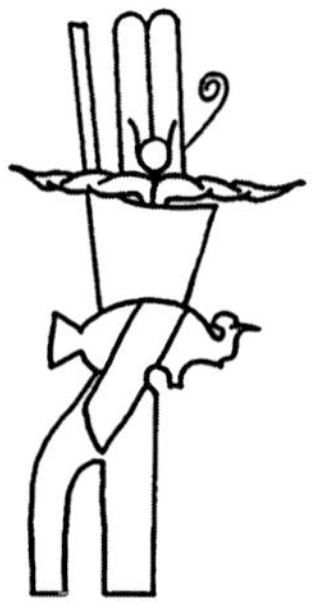	**AC 6** RC 1 + DFP 1 + CS 1 + RH 1		6, 11, 15L–R, 25	5
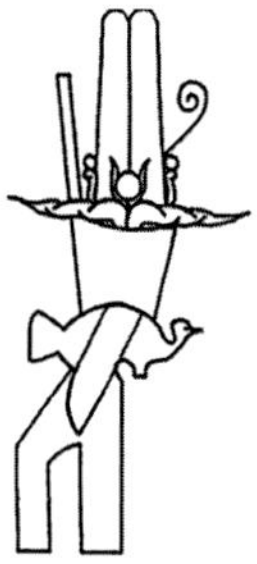	**AC 7** UR 3 + RC 1 + DFP 1 + CS 1 + RH 1	The crown is decorated with two crown *uraei*	7	1
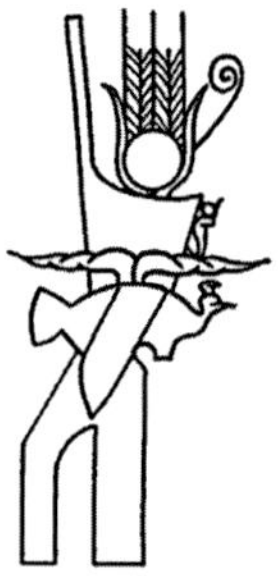	**AC 8** UR 1 + RC 1 + DFP 1 + CS 3 + RH 3	The cow horns and solar disc are enlarged. The crown is decorated with a crown *uraeus* wearing the traditional Hathoric crown	8	1
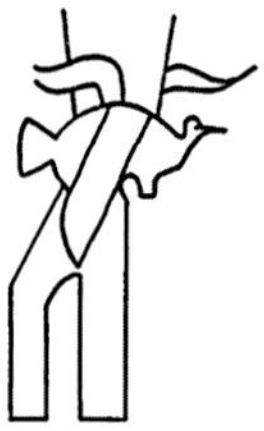	**AC 9** RC ? + RH 2	The crown is fragmentarily preserved	9	1
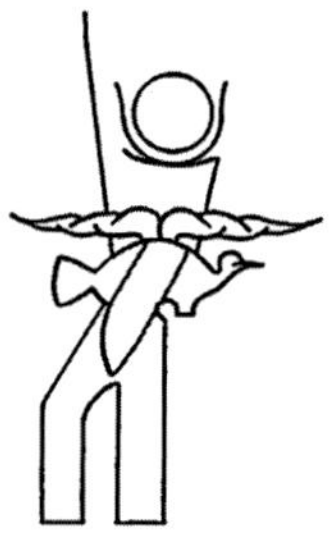	**AC 10** RC ? + CS 3 + RH 3	The crown is fragmentarily preserved	12	1

ILLUSTRATION	TITLE AND ABBREVIATED UNITS	COMMENTARY	SCENES	TOTAL NO. CROWNS
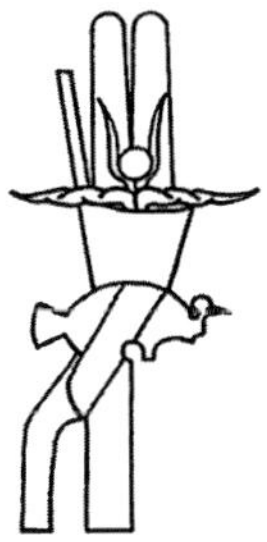	**AC 11** RC 4 + DFP 1 + CS 4 + RH 1		14, 16–17, 22	4
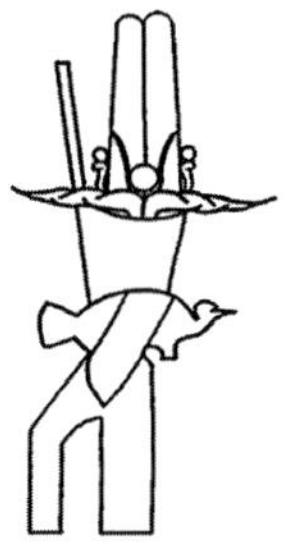	**AC 12** UR 3 + RC 4 + DFP 1 + CS 1 + RH 1	The crown is decorated with two *uraei*	13, 18, 20	2
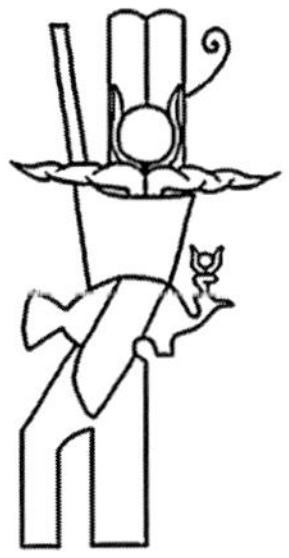	**AC 13** RC 1 + DFP 1 + CS 4 + RH 1		23–24, 26L–R	4
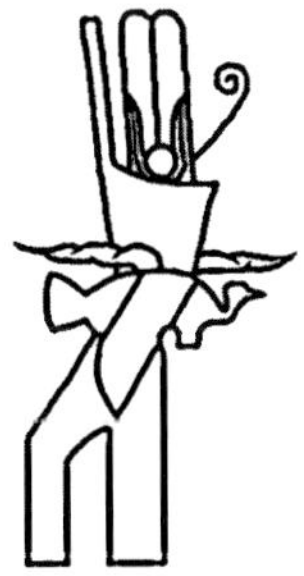	**AC 14** RC 1 + DFP 1 + CS 2 + RH 2		27, 29, 32	3
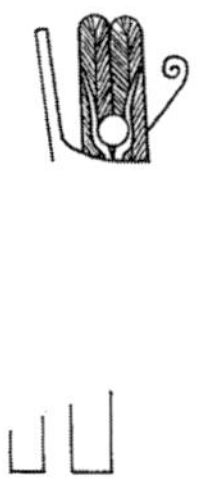	**AC 15** RC 1 + DFP 1 + CS 2	The crown is fragmentarily preserved	28	1

ILLUSTRATION	TITLE AND ABBREVIATED UNITS	COMMENTARY	SCENES	TOTAL NO. CROWNS
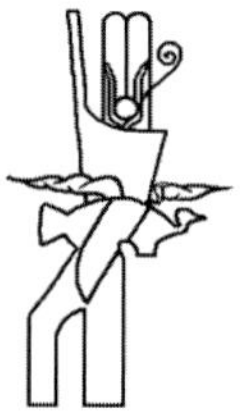	**AC 16** RC 1 + DFP 1 + CS 2 + RH 2 + UR1		30	1
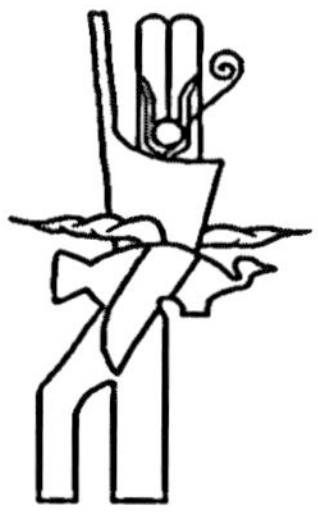	**AC 17** RC 3 + DFP 1 + CS 2 + RH 2		31	1
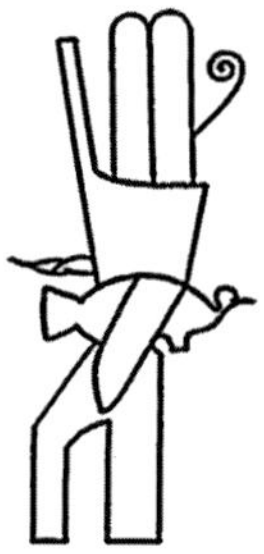	**AC 18** RC 1 + DFP 1 + RH 2	The crown is only partially visible, not showing all details	33	1
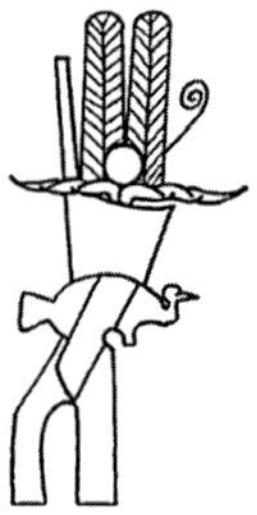	**AC 19** RC 1 + DFP 1 + CS 5 + RH 1		34	1
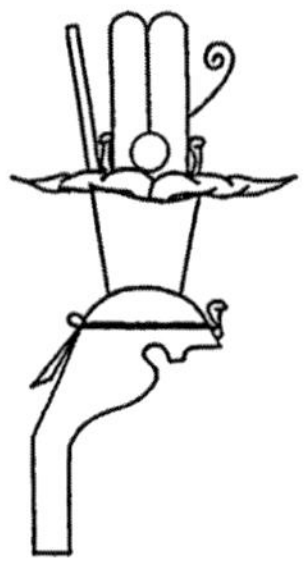	**AC 20** UR 2 + RC 1 + DFP 1 + CS 5 + RH 1	The crown is decorated with two *uraei*. The wig is decorated with a royal diadem	35	1

Table 7. Individual composition types of the crown of Arsinoë.

She stands on the very left in two scenes (cat. nos 29, 32) and at the right in the third (cat. no. 27). While separated from this group by its additional crown *uraeus*, cat. no. 30 clearly relates to this group.

AC 5 (cat. nos 4, 5, 19) shows a crown composed of a red crown (RC 2) with a spiral coming up from the ram horns (RH 1) in front of the double feather plume (DFP 1). The horns are placed on the platform of the red crown. The cow horns and solar disc are placed in a prominent position above the ram horns (CS 4). These scenes are dissimilar in their iconographic layout as well as their themes. Cat. no. 4 illustrates the *theoi Adelphoi* participating in the Egyptian ceremony of the annuals, the reckoning of time. It is a propagandistic dynastic scene, in which the ruling couple associate themselves with their deceased ancestors and the Egyptian deities. The scene dates to the reign of Ptolemy III, and illustrates Arsinoë as she accompanies her descendants on the left side. The scene is represented on a stele. Cat. no. 5 is a smaller copy of the better-known Mendes stele (cat. no. 1). It places Arsinoë as an individual goddess joined by Mendesian gods. Arsinoë is the tallest figure of the scene, and stands on the left side. The stele dates to the reign of Ptolemy II. Cat. no. 19 is located in the Edfu Temple, dates to Ptolemy IV and shows Arsinoë in a dynastic scene with her brother-husband as the *theoi Adelphoi*.

As shown in Table 7, the remaining type groups include one or possibly more crowns. On occasional, one small detail may be all the difference that separates one type from another, but is primarily a combination of factors that determines the division of types. Some crowns have been classified as individual types although some details are no longer visible and it is, therefore, possible that some types originally concurred with others. However, at this point no assumptions can be made based on personal interpretations regarding the original form of the crowns that are now damaged or incomplete.

A comparison of the individual types demonstrates that the main differentiation is based on minor pictorial dissimilarities. Evidently, such distinctions could have a significant effect on the symbolic message communicated by the specific crown type. For example, the cow horns and solar disc in AC 8 and 10 reveal a plausible association with Hathor. However, it does not seem likely that all minor differentiations expressed a certain symbolism: rather, they are probably the result of an 'artist's hand', thus expressing what could be termed a form of artistic freedom. For example, the red crown has been divided into types according to the position of the crown spiral: there are currently no known symbolic meanings for these types, although the possibility that they exist cannot be dismissed. And, as subsequent chapters will argue, there is no obvious socio-religious dissimilarity between the figures represented with the cow horns and solar disc in the size of an amulet and those with the same pictorial element with elongated cow horns. Rather, these differences suggest an artistic influence on the image.

The twenty types listed in Table 7 are classified in accordance with the placement and size of each pictorial unit. However, if the size is disregarded for the moment, a difference is immediately noticeable. The locations of the red crown, the double feather plume, the cow horns and the solar disc remain the same, but the position of the ram horns differs (Table 8). Therefore, it seems that the location of the ram horns marks the principal differentiation of the crown of Arsinoë, leading to yet another classification, in which the minor pictorial differentiations are disregarded and the location of the ram horns is taken as the significant factor.

AC 3–7, 11–13 and 19–20 consist of a crown with the ram horns positioned on top of the platform of the red crown, upon which the cow horns and solar disc rest, and from which the double feather plume rises. This style (RH 1) appears most frequently, and includes in its ten AC types twenty-six individual crowns. It is represented on stelai and temple reliefs equally, of which the latter are located in the Temples of Edfu, Karnak, Tod and Qasr el Aguz. The scenes date to Arsinoë's lifetime and those of Ptolemy II, Ptolemy III, Ptolemy IV, Ptolemy V and Ptolemy VIII. This suggestively 'standardised' style appears in all scenes with a dynastic theme (cat. nos 3–4, 16–22, 24), scenes that relate to a historical event (*e.g.* cat. no. 2) and and scenes depicting traditional divine veneration (cat. nos 2L–R, 5–7, 10–11, 13–15R, 23, 26L–R). Arsinoë is figurally established as both benefactor and beneficiary.

STYLE	DIFFERENTIATION	CROWN TYPE	TOTAL NO. TYPES	SCENES	TOTAL NO. CROWNS
1	Ram horns are placed on top of the platform of the red crown	AC 3–7, 11–13, 19–20	10	2L-7, 10–11, 13–20, 22–26R, 34–35	26
2	Ram horns are placed at the base of the red crown	AC 8–10, 14, 16–18	7	8–9, 12, 27–33	10

Table 8. Crown of Arsinoë according to the position of the ram horns.

In contrast, AC 8–10, 14 and 16–18 depict horns that are placed at the base of the red crown, thus resting immediately on the head (wig/cap) of Arsinoë. Within these seven AC types are included ten individual figures. This style is documented in stelai and temple reliefs (exclusively in the Temple of Philae), but is limited to the reign of Ptolemy II and Arsinoë's lifetime. The three scenes dating to her lifetime place Arsinoë in an active benefactor's position. However, these scenes are fragmentarily preserved and it is impossible to determine whether Arsinoë was depicted independently or accompanied by Ptolemy II in a complete original scene (cat. no. 8 probably excluded Ptolemy II, since Arsinoë stands closest to the deity). The Philae-scenes, cat. nos 27–33, describe Arsinoë with royal epithets plausibly dating to the period immediately following her death.

It appears, therefore, that the crown of Arsinoë existed in two main styles, regardless of any size variation in the individual units. These styles demonstrate one standardised (official) variant that was used throughout the Ptolemaic Dynasty, and one more personalised crown (which was overlooked by later Ptolemies until Cleopatra VII included it in her iconography once again). It is tempting to suggest that the first style relates to Arsinoë as the divine Philadelphos, whereas the second style corresponds to her queenly position.

The crown of Arsinoë was the first personalised crown to be composed and granted for an individual queen (previous queens were primarily depicted wearing the traditional female crown), and seems likely to have been created for Arsinoë's personal and cultural positions, incorporating her socio-religious and political roles. The crown underlined her position as a goddess and her role as a ruling queen. The symbolism incorporated in each unit of the crown placed the queen among the main deities of the Egyptian pantheon, and the complete composition signified eminence. In general, the crown made Arsinoë noticeable among previous and succeeding queens regardless of its individually communicated message, as will be discussed in subsequent chapters.

Pictorial precursors

Ramesside crown

A crown here referred to as the 'Ramesside crown' is almost identical to the crown of Arsinoë. As Figures 23–25 show, it displays a red crown, double feather plume, ram horns and a solar disc (regularly with additional minor units, such as the *uraeus*, in a manner similar to the crown of Arsinoë), corresponding to the units presented here as RC 1, RH 1, DFP 1 and CS 5. It is dissimilar to the crown of Arsinoë in that it lacks the cow horns. In its full composition, the Ramesside crown was used by male pharaohs exclusively.[1] The crown is firstly recorded as crowning the head of Seti I (Osing 1977, pl. 4) in his temple of modern Gourna, though most preserved examples decorate the heads of Ramses II and III.[2] Eventually, the Ramesside crown became a popular attribute for Graeco-Roman rulers (*e.g.* Dils 1998, 1316; and see pp. 139–140).

As a complete crown composition, the Ramesside crown has previously been considered, on the basis of the evidence, the only precursor of the crown of Arsinoë. It has been assumed to be a royal, rather than divine, crown (Dils 1998, 1315–25). The royal denotation is not disputed here, but its status as the only precursor of the crown of Arsinoë is, and an alternative proposed: a crown which only recently has come to the author's attention. This additional crown decorates a male figure depicted on a sarcophagus originating in the Asiut area and dated to the Late Period (27th Dynasty).[3] As Figures 26–27 show, the figure sits on a throne on the right side of the scene and wears a crown composed of a red crown (RC 1), double feather plume (DFP 1) and solar disc (CS 5). He is textually identified with the primeval god Atum. Figure 28 shows a second example of this crown in another scene of the sarcophagus. The ram horns and the cow horns are not depicted in this crown, but it still shows some fundamental structural similarities to the crown of Arsinoë and the Ramesside crown. Therefore, the crown of Atum may be a possible symbolic forerunner, an original model of inspiration for the crown of Arsinoë. Figures 29–31 demonstrate the stylistic similarity of the three crowns.

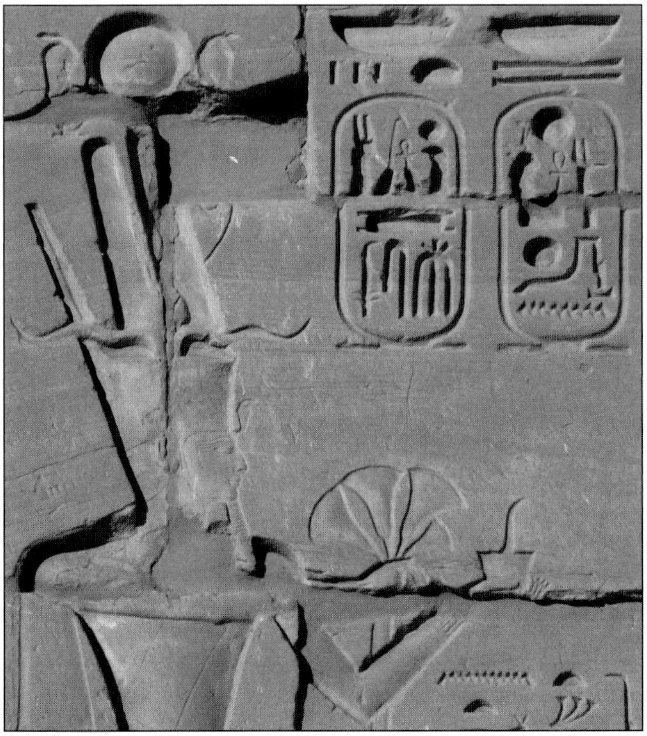

Figure 23. Ramses II wears the Ramesside crown, Karnak.

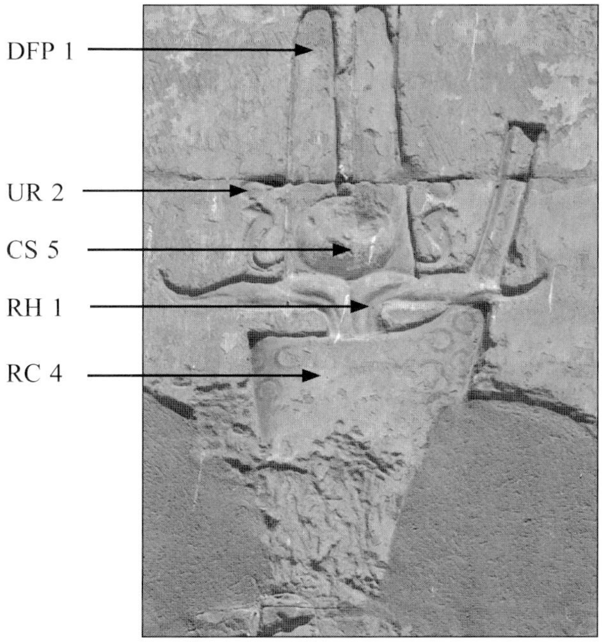

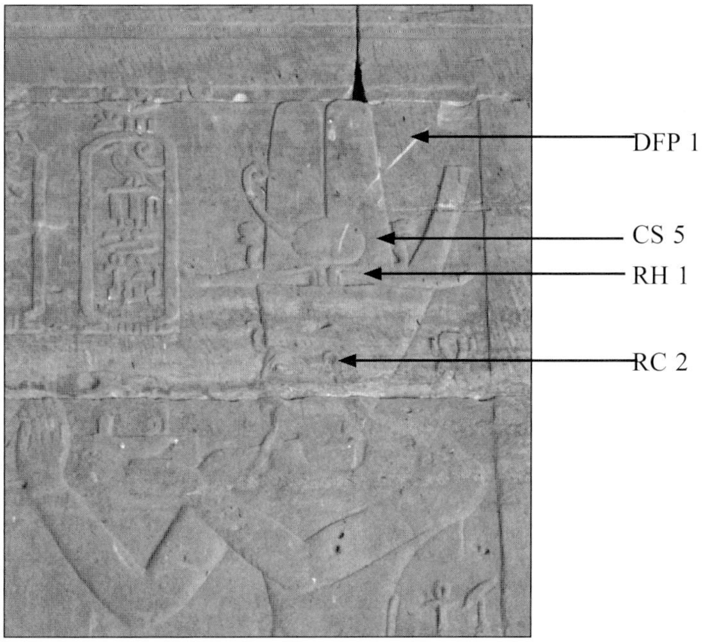

Figure 24. (Left) Later ruler wearing the Ramesside crown, Edfu Temple. For abbreviations see Chapter 3.
Figure 25. (Right) Later ruler wearing the Ramesside crown, Temple of Kalabsha. For abbreviations see Chapter 3.

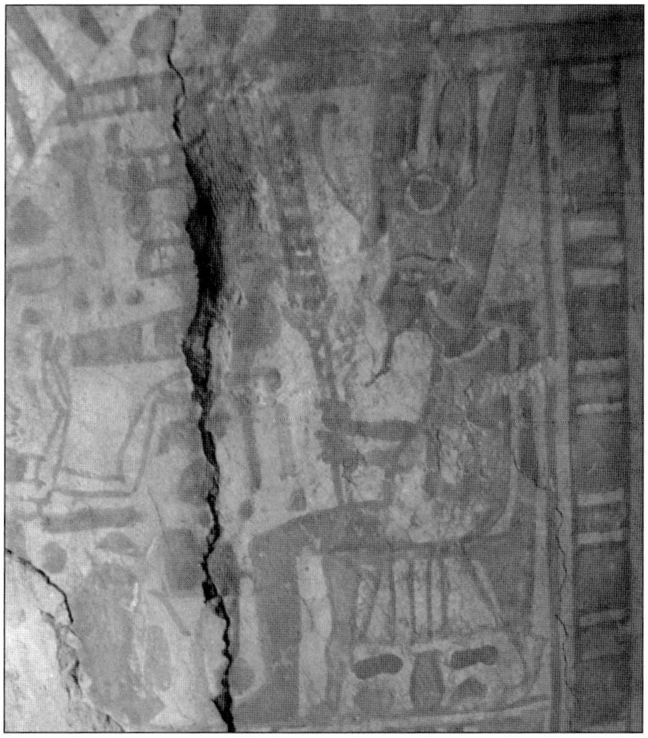

Figure 26. (Left) Scene of the Alexandria sarcophagus. Photo by J. Ward.

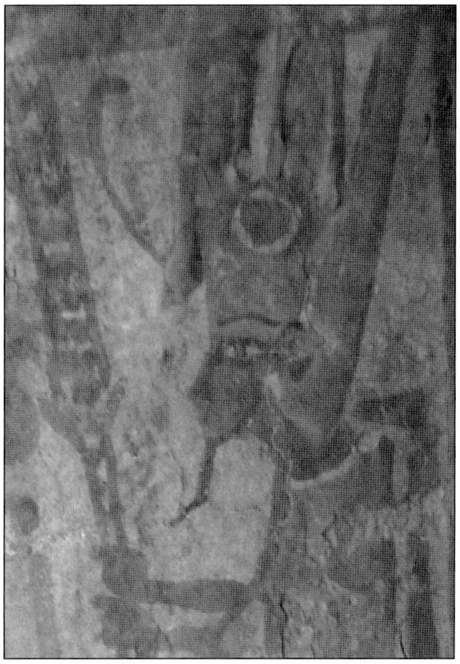

Figure 27. (Right) Detail of the Alexandria sarcophagus. Photo by J. Ward.

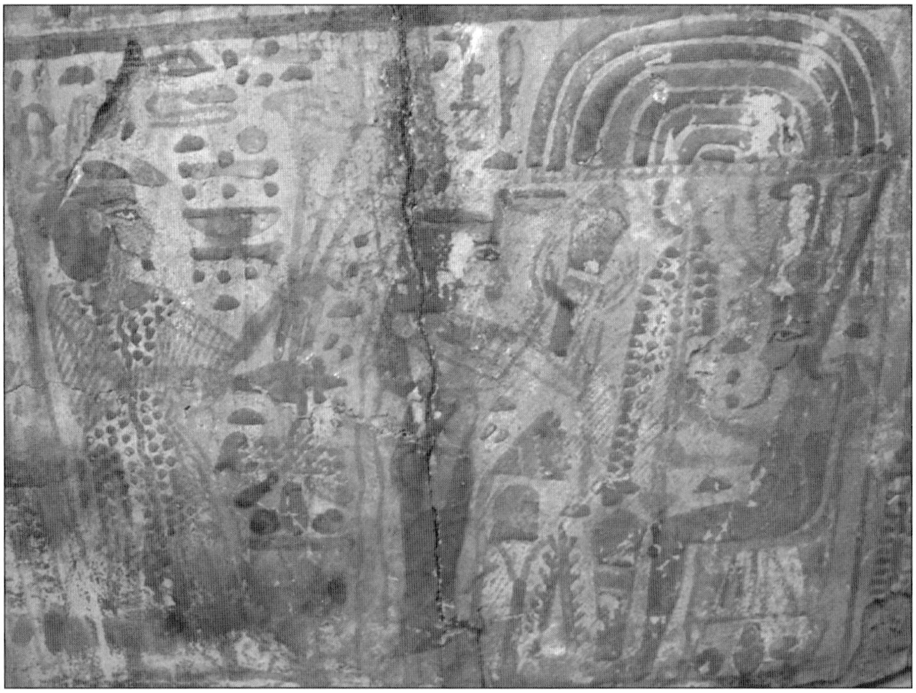

Figure 28. Scene of the Alexandria sarcophagus. Note the curled tops of the ostrich feathers. Photo by J. Ward.

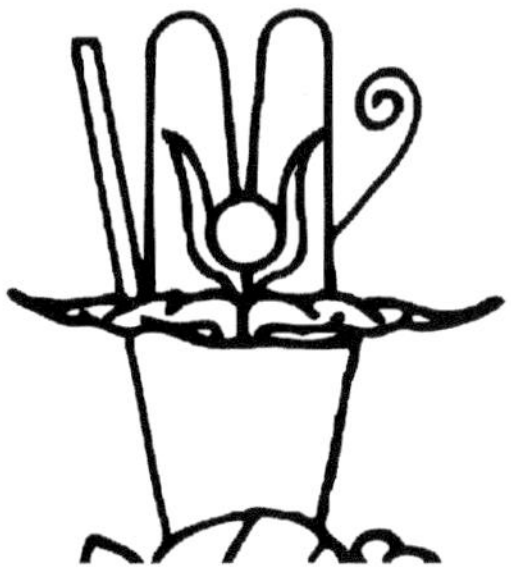

Figure 29. Crown of Arsinoë. Drawing by the author.

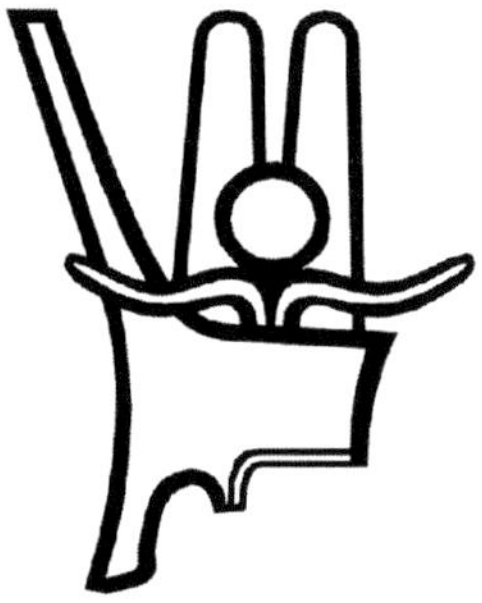

Figure 30. Ramesside crown: hieroglyphic signs JSesh S51A.

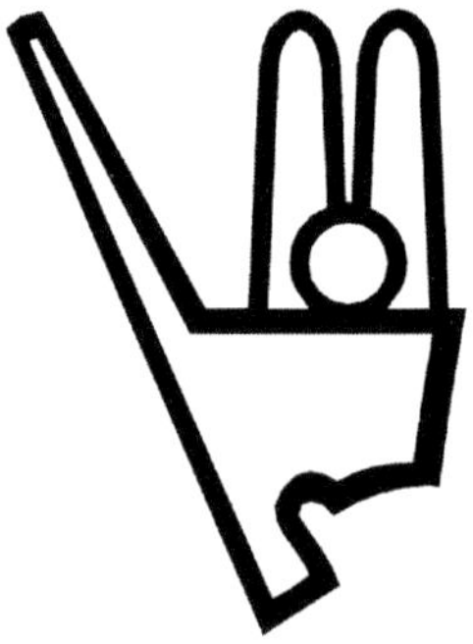

Figure 31. Atum's crown: hieroglyphic signs JSesh S52.

Traditional Female Crown

It has been demonstrated above that the crown of Arsinoë was created uniquely for the queen and that it emphasised her position among other royal women as she was the first among her peers to receive a personalised crown. Two relief scenes (cat. nos 21, 36) reveal that Arsinoë also used the traditional female crown (TFC), however, which has been included in the material under consideration here in order to present as complete a catalogue as possible of reliefs illustrating Arsinoë.

As exemplified in Figures 32–33, the traditional female crown is composed of a high and straight double feather plume and a joint element of cow horns and a solar disc. The traditional female crown was initially associated with Hathor, complementing her traditional large cow horns and solar disc. However, as with the traditional Hathoric crown, the traditional female crown was eventually usurped by Isis and by pharaonic queens. The crown functioned as a female equivalent to the male double crown in terms of a royal attribute, and from the 13th Dynasty the majority of queens used it (Robins 1993, 24). It was used by the Divine Adoratrices of Amun, where it was occasionally illustrated without cow horns and solar disc, and became a standardised pictorial head attribute of all Ptolemaic queens when depicted in an Egyptian setting. Obviously, Arsinoë was an exception, as she received a personalised crown, and although her crown was occasionally reused by Cleopatra III and VII their main crown attribute was the traditional female crown.

Cat. nos 21 and 36 are the only (preserved) relief scenes in which Arsinoë wears the traditional female crown. Cat. no. 21 shows three figures and is located on the top register of the corridor of the Edfu Temple. Arsinoë stands on the left side, behind a seated Ptolemy II, holding an *ankh* in her resting hand while the other hand is held in a protective manner. Ptolemy and Arsinoë, who receive incense and libation from Ptolemy VIII, are the beneficiaries of the scene. As will be further examined below, this scene is a part of a dynastic arrangement which in its entirety incorporates four individual scenes. Arsinoë is described in the text as 'Great wife, Arsinoë, Ptolemy's divine wife' and is, together with Ptolemy II, designated '*theoi Adelphoi*, the dwellers of Mesen [= Edfu]'. Arsinoë is the tallest figure of the scene. Cat. no. 36 was originally located on the right jamb of a gate in the Temple of Medamoud, but is now preserved as a block fragment. The scene shows two main figures and a third smaller one which is vaguely visible in a position of *proskynesis*. Arsinoë is placed on the right side, in a standing position, and holds a lotus flail. Ptolemy is placed in front of Arsinoë; he sits on a throne within a Sed festival pavilion and faces in the same direction as Arsinoë. The scene dates to the reign of Ptolemy II and is a part of a rejuvenation theme commemorating his celebration of a Sed festival. Arsinoë is described as 'Female King' and is depicted as the tallest figure in the scene.

There is no obvious connection between these two scenes. The geographical location, the date, Arsinoë's position in the scene, the hand-held objects, the titles and the theme of the scene: all are different. The only similarity is that both scenes depict Arsinoë in a standing position behind Ptolemy and as the tallest figure in the scene. These aspects are far from sufficient to explain why Arsinoë wears the traditional female crown in these scenes and no others.

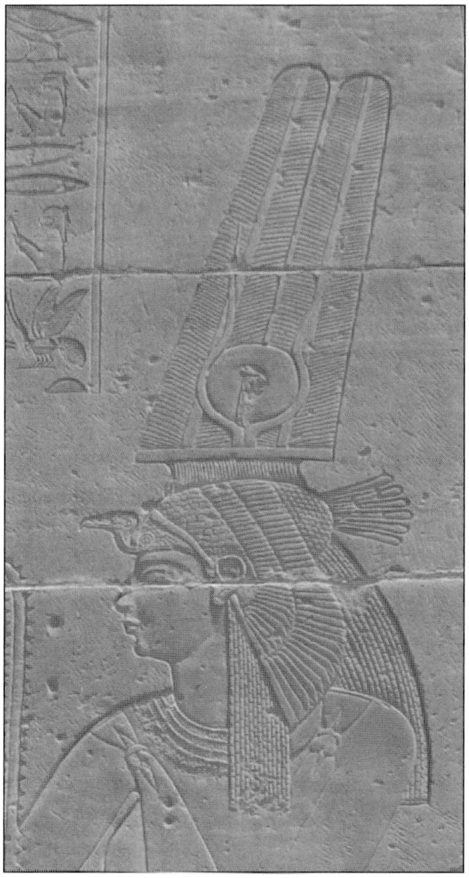

Figure 32. The traditional female crown: Hathor, Hibis Temple.

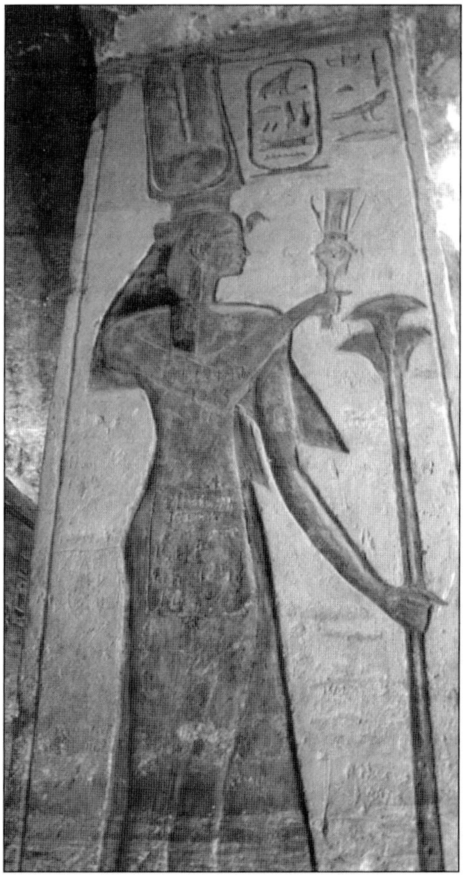

Figure 33. The traditional female crown: Nefertari, Abu Simbel.

The later Hathoric crown

A later crown similar to the crown of Arsinoë, here labelled 'the later Hathoric crown' (traditionally designated *ḥptj*), was recently introduced into scholarship as a composition crown reusing the symbolism of the crown of Arsinoë (Nilsson 2010, cat. nos 37–141, 143–155; *cf.* Derchain-Urtel 1994). The basic composition consists of a double crown, double feather plume, ram horns, cow horns and solar disc, and at times combined with an *atef* feather attached to the back of the crown and/or a single crown *uraeus* placed in the front of the red crown (Figures 34–37). A 'male' variant consists of the same details except for the cow horns. The crown symbolises divine kingship, rejuvenation and eternal life through its association with Ra, Horus/Harpocrates, Hathor and Amun (Nilsson 2010, 288–99; *cf. Edfou* I, 425; Derchain-Urtel 1994, 56). In terms of time, the original *ḥtpj* crown dates from the reign of Ptolemy IV to Trajan (Nilsson 2010, 392).

Conclusion

The crown of Arsinoë has been divided into twenty variants based on the size and position of each pictorial unit. The analysis, however, has demonstrated that such minor differentiations have little effect on the overall interpretation of a scene. Nevertheless, there does appear to be a cultural connotation to the location of ram horns. Two main types of crowns, divided in accordance with the horns' position on top or at the base of the red crown, indicate the existence of one official and one less recognised, private crown style respectively. The official crown was frequently used throughout the Ptolemaic period, and is documented in temples and sites throughout Egypt. It describes Arsinoë as the divine Philadelphos. The alternative crown is primarily limited to the Temple of Philae, where it dates to the reign of Ptolemy II and focuses on Arsinoë's role as a queen.

The crown of Arsinoë has traditionally been compared with that crown termed here the Ramesside crown. These two crowns are separated only by the cow horns present in the crown of Arsinoë. Both are acknowledged as royal crowns. This chapter, however, demonstrates that another crown, worn by the god Atum, might have functioned as a pictorial model at the time of the creation of the crown of Arsinoë. The crown of Atum is not identical with the crown of Arsinoë, but, structurally, demonstrates similarities. As a consequence, the crown of Arsinoë may also be compared with a divine crown that symbolises celestial royal power.

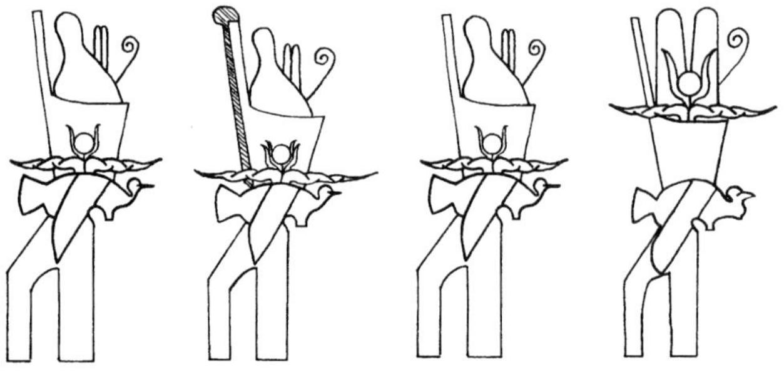

Figures 34–37. Variants of the later Hathoric crown. Drawings by the author.

The Ramesside crown and the crown worn by Atum are both male crowns. A female crown useful for comparison is the traditional female crown, which is composed of tall feathers, cow horns and a solar disc. This crown was originally created for Hathor, but was later usurped by Isis and royal queens. Arsinoë is recorded using such a crown twice, although the available evidence does not explain its use in place of her own crown. The two scenes representing Arsinoë with the traditional female crown are not comparable, and while it does not seem likely that such a depiction was due to an artistic mistake, as previous scholars have argued, without evidence to back up an alternative hypothesis, such a possibility must remain open.

The crown of Arsinoë was a prestigious attribute created for Arsinoë exclusively. It symbolised royal power while simultaneously emphasising the queen's divine lineage. The crown combined some of the most ancient Egyptian pictorial elements, all of which connoted her socio-religious importance. Her crown, as will be demonstrated below, would also provide Arsinoë with an iconographic means of showing individual importance. It was eventually reused by the later Ptolemaic queens Cleopatra III and VII.

A later crown, the Hathoric crown (ancient name *ḥptj*), is almost identical with the crown of Arsinoë. The most basic form shows a structure composed of a double crown, double feather plume, ram horns, cow horns and a solar disc, which is thus differentiated from the crown of Arsinoë by the addition of the white crown. The later Hathoric crown, which is limited to the Temples of Dendera and Edfu, with one example from the Temple of Kalabsha, was introduced during the reign of Ptolemy IV and is attested throughout the Ptolemaic and Roman periods.

Notes

1 No queens have been depicted with the Ramesside crown. See, however, AC 19–20, considering the possibility that the missing cow horns of the crowns have faded over the years.

2 Designations other than the Ramesside crown might be more suitable for the attribute, especially regarding gender, and also since it is worn by pharaohs other than Ramses II and III. However, an *initial* generalisation regarding gender issues has been consciously avoided here and, therefore, it would

be inappropriate to label the crown as a 'male variant of the crown of Arsinoë'. Furthermore, it would be incorrect to label it as such since the Ramesside crown was introduced far earlier than the crown of Arsinoë. Dils' (1998, 1327–30) generalisation regarding this crown and the crown of Arsinoë, as he lists both crowns in a table titled 'Liste des scènes où le roi officiant porte la couronne d'Arsinoé', is not one that will be followed here. The name used here, the 'Ramesside crown', instead corresponds to the two rulers most often seen wearing this head attribute prior to the introduction of the crown of Arsinoë.

3 Today, the sarcophagus is located in the museum of the faculty of Art in Alexandria, Egypt. The author is grateful to the personnel of the museum and the university for their assistance and for permission to publish this material.

Chapter 5

The crown of Arsinoë in context

A contextual study of the crown of Arsinoë, examining how it corresponds with other individual items as well as the more general theme of the scenes, will enable a greater understanding of the overall meaning of the crown. This chapter, therefore, deals with additional headdress elements, including the tripartite wig, the vulture cap, the single forehead *uraeus* and the royal diadem; hand-held objects, including the *ankh*, sceptres and staves, the sistrum, the hand held in a protective manner and the notched palm branch; and additional decoration, including the sheat dress, sandals, jewellery and thrones and corner boxes.

The Headdress

The individual headdress elements are classified here as additional units (attached to Arsinoë) because they communicate more general concepts, seldom relating to unique events or specific individuals, and they were used by a variety of divine and royal characters. However, each and every detail is part of the larger image and deserves, therefore, a morphological analysis that describes the unit and relates it to others.

Tripartite wig (TW)

The wig that is illustrated in the material is generally referred to as a tripartite wig. It consists of shoulder-length straight or braided hair divided into three sections, hence its name (*cf.* Green 2001, 73f.). The wearing of a wig was common practice in ancient Egypt and it could be worn in various lengths and styles. Royal persons and aristocrats wore wigs made of real hair, while people of lower classes, if they wore one at all, probably had wigs made of wool, reeds or animal hair (Wilkinson 1837, 355–7, 369–70; Lucas 2003, 42f.). Normally, the wig was styled with a combination of curled and plaited hair. Aristocratic women kept their hair and wig long, plaited and with the ends left loose. The long plaited hair was sometimes decorated with beads, coloured woollen strings or even jewellery (Wilkinson 1837, 369). In the material examined here the wig is represented in two styles (Table 9).

Arsinoë wears a wig in all forty figures. TW 1 is by far the more favoured style, and is the only one illustrated on the stelai, as well as occurring frequently in temple reliefs. TW 2, in contrast, appears in only three scenes located in the Edfu Temple (cat. nos 16, 18, 19) and one scene situated in Tod (cat. no. 35). In Edfu, TW 2 places Arsinoë in scenes where she is paired with her husband-brother, dating to later Ptolemaic periods. However, other scenes in the Edfu Temple depict Arsinoë wearing TW 1. The differences between types TW 1 and 2 are probably an indication of artistic freedom or fashion rather than a matter of symbolic importance.

Herodotus (Hdt. 2, 37) notes that it was customary for the Egyptians to shave their heads, leaving it to grow long only when in mourning, in contrast with the practice in other countries. They replaced their natural hair with wigs. Such a statement concerns mainly the elite, but it is documented as a custom also among commoners, as intimated above. Herodotus explains that cleanliness was highly valued in the Egyptian society, and that the priests bathed several times daily (Hdt. 2, 37). Thus, men shaved their heads for reasons of hygiene (Fletcher 1994, 32). Women, however, did not shave their heads, but kept their natural hair (Hdt. 2, 65). One must ask, therefore, if the ancient Egyptians differentiated men from women in regards to cleanliness. In her study on wigs, J. Fletcher concludes that the main reason for the Egyptians to shave their head and wear wigs was to keep parasites, such as lice, away. Moreover, the wig protected the person from the sun, and was considered a highly fashionable item to wear (Fletcher 1994, 32). In contrast to Herodotus, Fletcher argues, based on her modern studies of ancient Egyptian material, that it was mainly *women* (who did not shave) who wore wigs (*cf.* Juv. 6, 120). Is it still reasonable to assume, therefore, that they did this mainly as a sign of cleanliness? It seems more likely, in fact, that they wore wigs primarily as a statement of status, and they followed the various trends in fashion.

Initially, the tripartite wig was created as a pictorial headdress for Hathor, but soon thereafter it also decorated the heads of other goddesses and queens (Green 2001, 75). The wig is documented as mainly a female decoration, but gods and kings could also wear it. Osiris, for example, is frequently documented in both relief and sculpture as wearing the wig under his *atef* crown (*e.g.* Raven 1998, 232–6). The difference in male and female wigs is found in the arrangement of the ringlets (Figures 38–39).

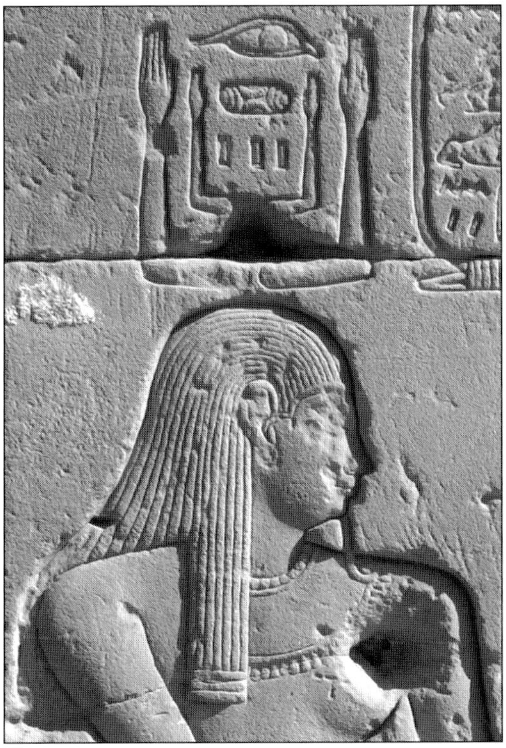

Figure 38. Detail of a male tripartite wig, Temple of Dendera.

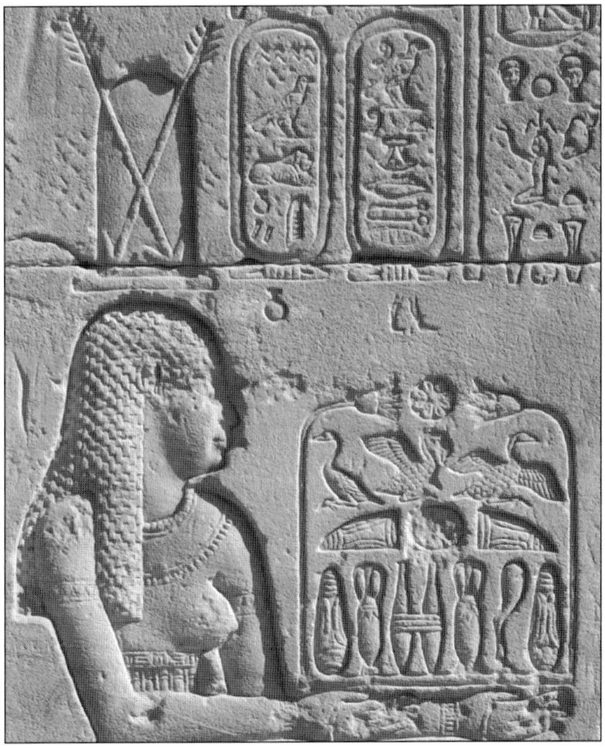

Figure 39. Detail of a female tripartite wig, Temple of Dendera.

ILLUSTRATION	ABBREVIATION	DESCRIPTION	SCENES	TOTAL NO. WIGS
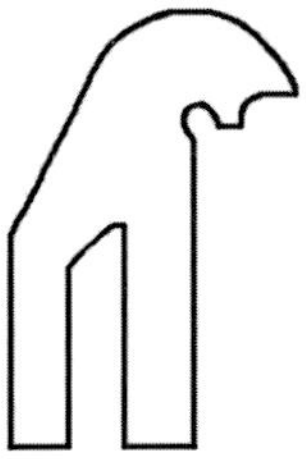	TW 1	The hair falls down on both shoulders and the back	1L–15R, 17, 20–34, 36	36
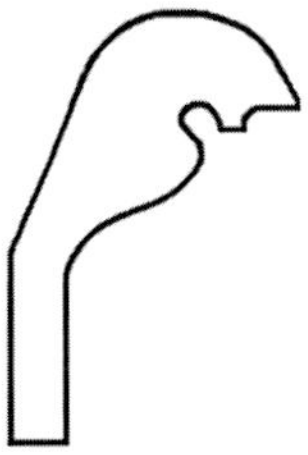	TW 2	The hair is hanging down the back (thus, a 'simpler' wig)	16, 18–19, 35	4

Table 9. Variations of the tripartite wig.

It is difficult to assess the cultural significance of the tripartite wig because it has no definite associations. Based on its frequent occurrence, it can plausibly be argued that it was an item of fashion and tradition. When Arsinoë was depicted with the tripartite wig, she reconnected with previous queens, traditional Egyptian goddesses and the cultural conventions of fashion.

Vulture cap (VC)

The vulture cap was worn by royal women and female deities from the Early Dynastic period, and the element associated the wearer primarily with the goddess Nekhbet and also, from the New Kingdom, with Mut, Hathor and Isis (Quibell 1904, pl. 66; Troy 1986, 117; Robins 2008, 67). The vulture and its hieroglyphic sign (𓅐 – *nrt*) denoted the (divine) maternal role, and has a connection to the divine sky (*e.g.* *LGG* III, 251f.; O'Neill 2003 [1897], 755). Therefore, it is not surprising that Nut wore the vulture cap in artistic representations.

The cap is generally illustrated as a vulture resting on its stomach above the female head, facing in the same direction as the figure wearing it. The wings of the bird are stretched out and smoothly follow the curves of the sides of the head. It is mainly depicted above, and complementing, the tripartite wig (Figures 40–41). In the material examined here the vulture cap is represented mainly in one original style with various degrees of detailed relief. However, the vulture cap has been divided here into two types in order to differentiate a style with additional pictorial details attached to the head of the vulture.

Table 10 shows that a clear majority of female figures wear this headdress. As with the tripartite wig, there does not appear to be any correlation between the cap and a specific time, locality or individual. The cap is documented in both stelai and temple reliefs dating to a period from Ptolemy II to Ptolemy VIII. Interestingly, most scenes that post-date Ptolemy IV illustrate Arsinoë without this headdress feature. All scenes dating to Ptolemy II (and Arsinoë's lifetime) show the vulture cap, except for cat. nos 10 and 36 (and cat. no. 28, in its present state, although it is plausible that Arsinoë also wore the cap in this scene, based on the surrounding scenes in the Philae temple). The scenes of the Edfu Temple demonstrate an artistic irregularity: two scenes include the cap, whereas the remaining four scenes illustrate Arsinoë without the cap.

Three images of Arsinoë provide exceptions in the material (VC 2). In this type, the vulture cap is accompanied by an additional *uraeus*. The serpent, moreover, wears a traditional Hathoric crown in the two latter scenes. These two latter figures, illustrated in cat. nos 23–24, are located within the Karnak Temple complex (the Khonsu Temple and the Gate of Euergetes) in close proximity to each other (the *uraeus* of cat. no. 23 rises higher than that of cat. no. 24, probably indicating a different artist). Cat. no. 23 depicts Arsinoë as a beneficiary, paired with Khonsu, to whom Ptolemy II expresses his piety. Arsinoë is positioned as an individual goddess, associated with the main deity of the temple in which the scene is located. Cat. no. 24 illustrates Arsinoë as a beneficiary, paired with Ptolemy II as the *theoi Adelphoi* and with Ptolemy III as the active benefactor. Arsinoë is no longer depicted as an individual goddess (*cf.* cat. no. 23), but instead as a member of the deified sibling gods. The two scenes that show VC 2 do not provide any indication that a message is intended to be communicated by the additional pictorial detail: they are not extraordinary in any respect compared with those which show VC 1 and cannot, therefore, be utilised as cultural indicators. Rather, they demonstrate a dissimilarity in regard to the cultic roles of Arsinoë, and, moreover, they date to different rulers. At this point, therefore, the stylistic dissimilarities between the two types cannot be attributed to anything other than artistic freedom or local fashion at the time.

ILLUSTRATION	ABBREVIATION	DESCRIPTION	SCENES	TOTAL NO. CAPS
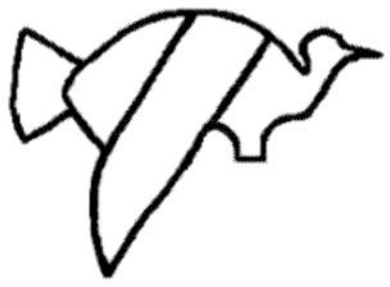	VC 1	Traditionally illustrated vulture cap without any extra details or ornaments	1L–2R, 4–7, 9, 11–15R, 17, 20, 25, 26L–27, 29–34	27
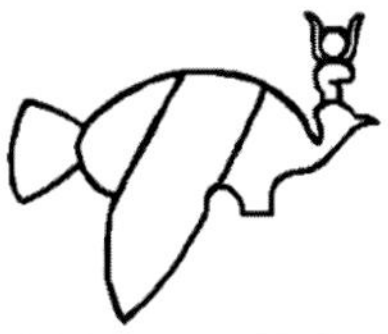	VC 2	The vulture head is accompanied by the head of a single *uraeus* (cat. no. 8) and two serpents are decorated also with the Hathoric cow horns and solar disc	8, 23–24	3

Table 10. Variations of the vulture cap.

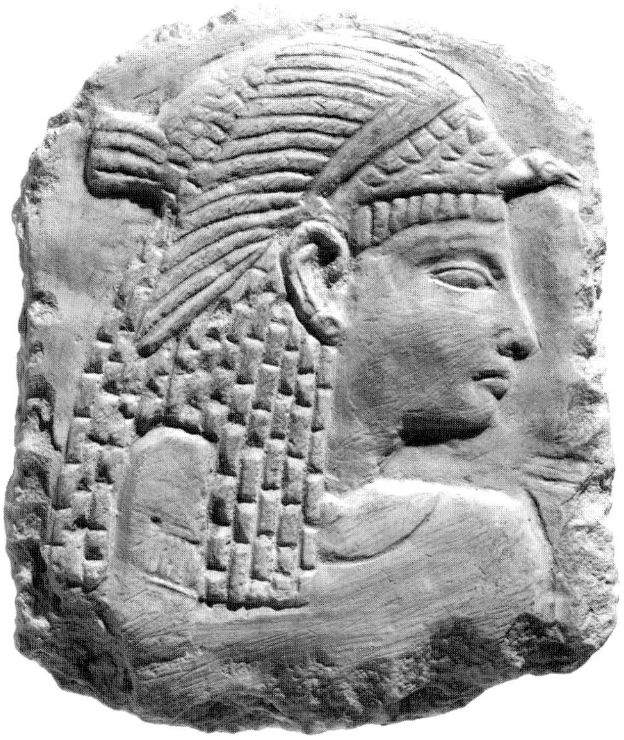

Figure 40. A so-called sculptor's model dating to the Ptolemaic period. It shows the combination of the wig and vulture cap. Medelhavsmuseet, Stockholm, inv. no. MM18579; © Medelhavsmuseet, photo Ove Kaneberg.

The vulture associates the wearer with the authority of Upper Egypt, with the maternal influence and with traditional Egyptian dualistic concepts when accompanied by the *uraeus*. The dualistic element is further attested in Nekhbet's role as one of the eyes of Horus (the other one is represented by Wadjet), connecting the deity (deities) with Hathor (Nilsson 2010, 437–40). The vulture was praised for its excellent sight and hearing, and was a symbol of Upper Egypt already during the Predynastic period. It became an emblem closely connected with kingship from the time of the unification of the Two Lands (*cf.* the wedding mace-head of Narmer, Ashmolean Museum, inv. no. E 3632; Emery 1961, 46; Troy 1986, 80, fig. 52; Lesko 1999, 65). The vulture was included in the female iconography at an early date, where it is documented as a headdress element exclusive to women (*e.g.* Robins 2008, 67f.; Troy 1986, 117f.), but when it became associated with royal women is debatable.

The vulture and cobra together (as in VC 2) formed the Two Ladies (*nbty*) of Egypt, symbolising aspects of femininity and control (Figure 42). The Two Ladies denote the unification of the Two Lands in the form of the goddesses Nekhbet of Upper Egypt and Wadjet of Lower Egypt (Figure 43); their union is artistically documented as early as the 1st Dynasty (Johnson 1990, 71). They symbolise dualism and unification, representing Upper and Lower Egypt, the sky and earth and the night sky and the solar eye, accompanied by their titles 'Lady of the Sky' and 'Lady of the Two Lands' (Troy 1986, 123–5). The Two Ladies were regarded as the defenders of not only the ruling pharaoh but kingship in general.

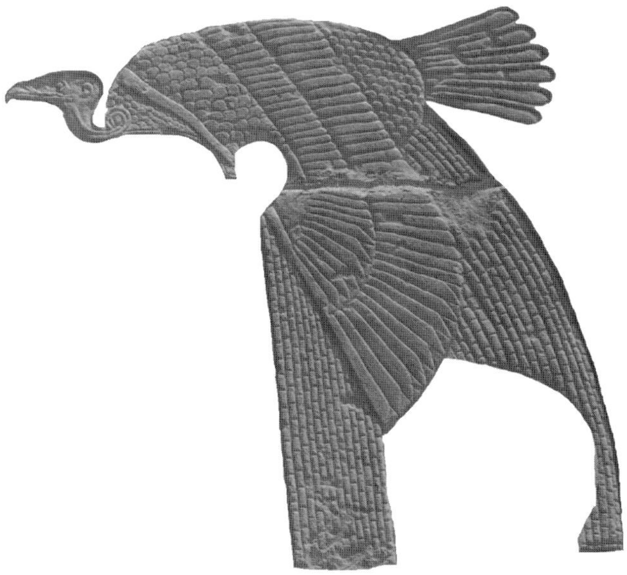

Figure 41. An edited female image from the Hibis Temple emphasising the tripartite wig and vulture cap. Photo and editing by the author.

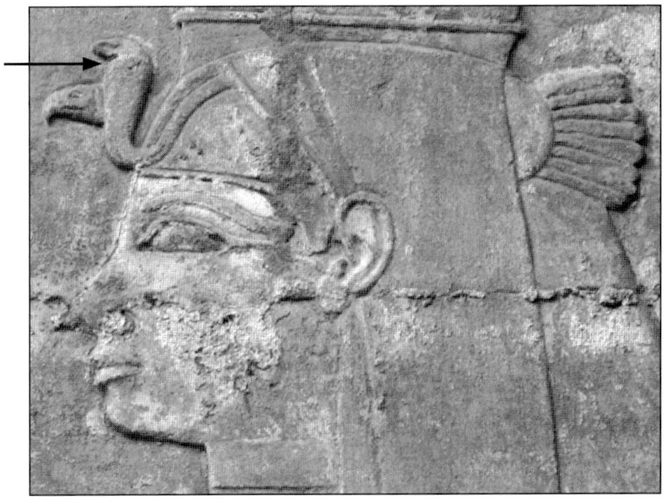

Figure 42. A detail of the Two Ladies, here worn as a crown element by Queen Amenirdis I at the Osirian Chapel, Karnak. The arrow points to the uraeus.

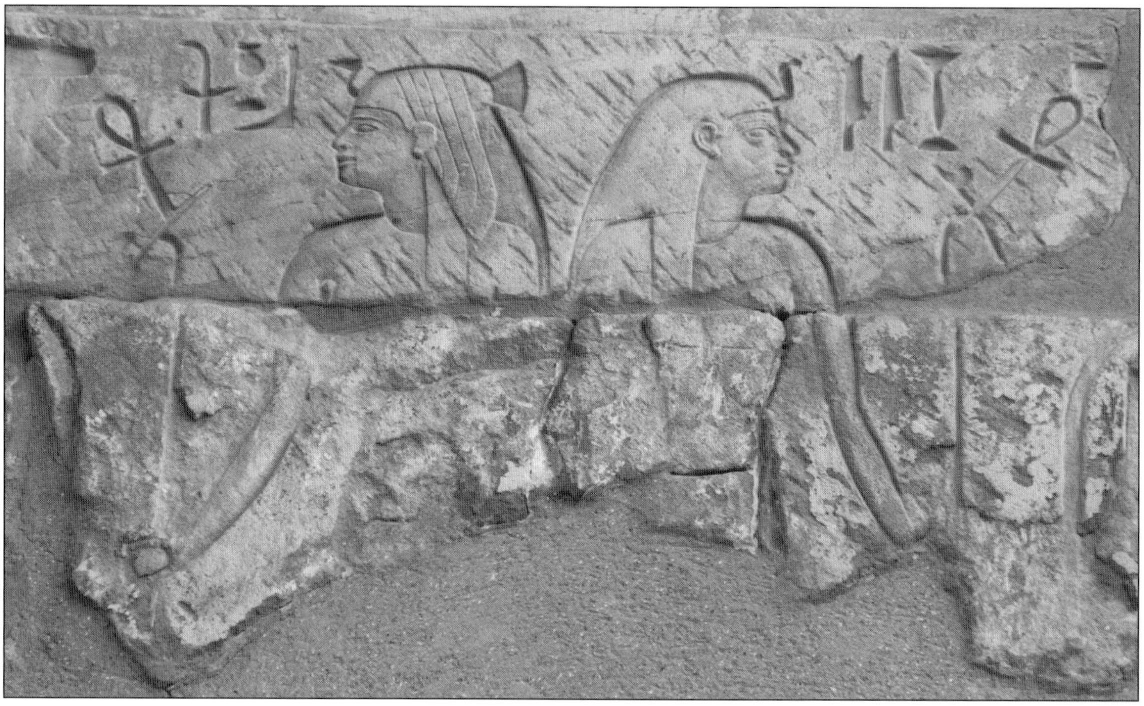

Figure 43. A Late Period scene of Nekhbet and Wadjet. They wear their personal attributes, the vulture and the cobra, represented in the vulture cap and the single forehead uraeus. From the Chapel of Amenirdis at Medinet Habu.

Single forehead uraeus *(SFU)*

The single forehead *uraeus* dates back to the Old Kingdom and the reign of Pharaoh Sneferu (Fakhry 1954, pl. XI A; Gardiner *et al.* 1952–5, pl. II no. 5; Troy 1986, 119; Albersmeier 2002, 42; *cf.* Hoffman 1984, fig. 64; Lesko 1999, 72). The Latinised Greek term *uraeus* probably derives from the Egyptian sign  – *iʿrt*, referring to 'the one who rears up' or 'the coiled one' (*LGG* I, 140f.; Andrews 1994, 75f.). As Table 11 shows, this headdress is represented in two types in the material. Like the vulture cap, the two types are separated by additional details rather than a differentiation in the item itself.

The single forehead *uraeus* was employed less frequently than the two pictorial details described above. SFU 1 is documented only once, dating to the reign of Ptolemy II. SFU 2 post-dates Arsinoë's and Ptolemy II's lifetimes, and its use is concentrated mainly in the Temple of Edfu. The figural arrangement of these scenes, together with cat. nos 3 and 35, are classed as dynastic. It is assumed here that type SFU 2 associates the queens with their dynastic role, rather than an individual divine position.

It seems probable that there was no difference between these two types; it is entirely plausible that SFU 1 also had a painted or narrowly carved diadem initially. The effects of natural erosion, sunlight and other potentially damaging factors could well have negatively affected the thin line of a diadem on a relief. However, it cannot be assumed that the diadem was attached to the *uraeus* at all times in a conventional manner because of its evident absence in some scenes and therefore, the distinction between the two styles as represented in Table 11 is retained.[1]

Ancient Egyptian myths describe the serpent as having lidless eyes, thereby being always able to protect the pharaoh (Houlihan 1996, 174f.). The *uraeus*, or the 'risen cobra' in common language, was closely connected with the Egyptian snake goddess Wadjet in her role as the protectress of Lower Egypt. Wadjet was worshipped throughout Egypt, but her cultic centre was located in the area of the two cities Pe and Dep, joined together as Buto (Modern Tell el-Fara'in), in Lower Egypt. The serpent was connected with the battle-stories of Horus and Seth, and is sometimes described as the eye of Ra, the one who protects the divine ruler against evil (Albersmeier 2002, 42). According to the myth, Shu and Tefnut, the children of Ra (Atum), were lost in the primeval dark waters. He sent his Sole Eye, Wadjet or Hathor, to light up the waters and to find and bring back the children. When Hathor/Wadjet, as the eye, returned with Shu and Tefnut to her father, she found that a new eye had taken her place as the eye of Ra. She raged against her father and wept many tears in despair, tears that created the first humans. Ra transformed Wadjet/Hathor into a risen cobra, the *uraeus*, and she became more powerful than any other deity. He placed her at his forehead so that she forever could watch out and protect him against any possible enemies (*e.g.* Pinch 2002, 199f).

Moreover, pyramid texts describe how the cobra was given to the pharaoh by the god Geb to legitimate the pharaoh's position as the monarch of the Two Lands (Hart 2005, 161). As the fearsome risen serpent on the brow of the pharaoh, Wadjet/Hathor protected him against evil and all enemies. Without her, the pharaoh would be lost. This is how the Hathoric goddess Wadjet became a frequent unit in the royal iconography (*cf.* Figure 42). By wearing the same attribute, the royal women were equally protected by a divine presence who no longer upheld the duality of male and female (as when placed on the pharaoh's head), but rather became a different aspect of the same myth (Figures 44–45).[2] The risen cobra symbolises Hathor (and other snake goddesses) as, primarily,

ILLUSTRATION	ABBREVIATION	DESCRIPTION	SCENES	TOTAL NO. URAEI
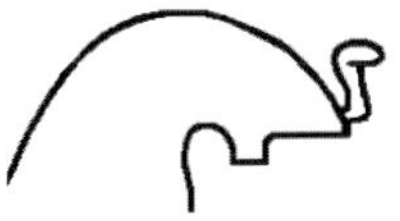	SFU 1	The single forehead *uraeus* is depicted without any visible connection to the royal diadem	36	1
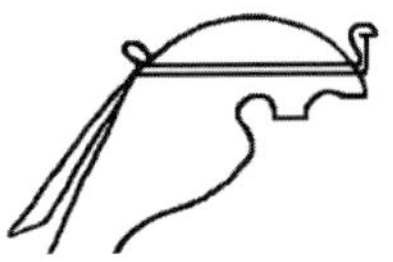	SFU 2	The single forehead *uraeus* is attached or connected to the royal diadem	3, 16, 18–19, 21–22, 35	7

Table 11. Variations of the single forehead uraeus.

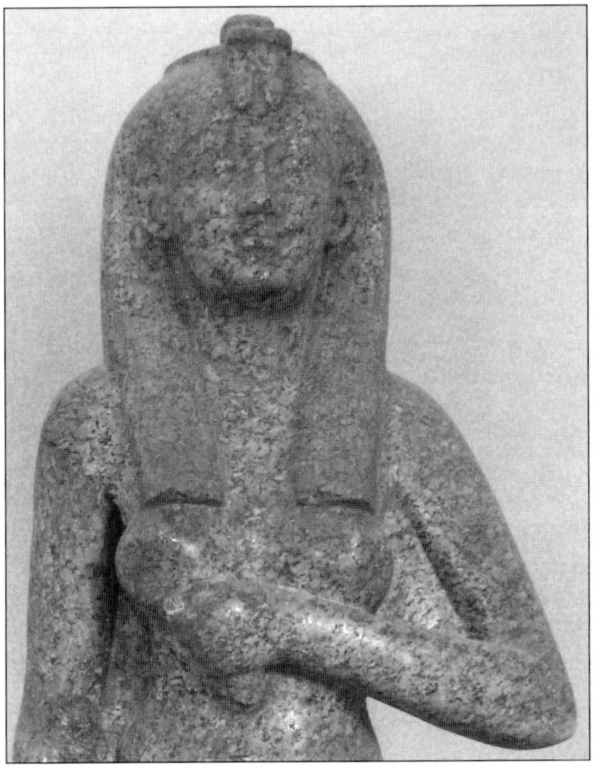

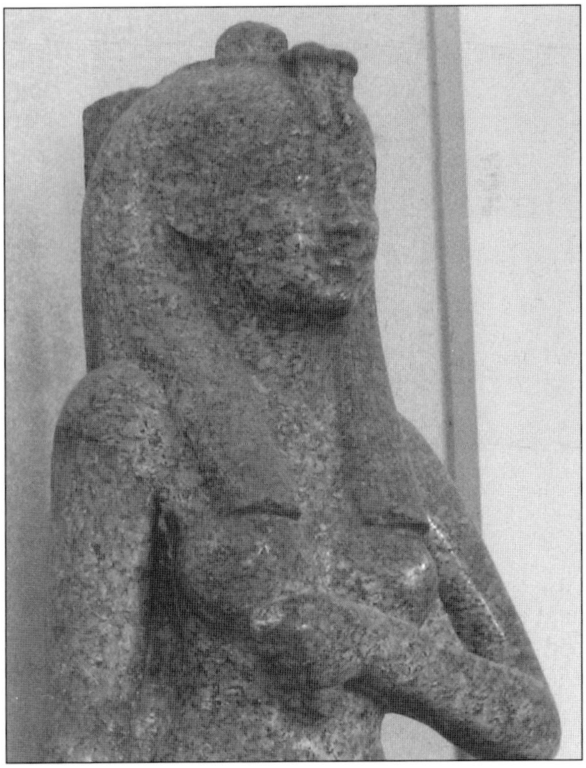

Figure 44. (Left) and Figure 45. (Right) 'Vatican Arsinoë' depicted with two forehead uraei. Arsinoë was the first, and debatably the only, Ptolemaic queen to wear the double uraeus. In order to explain their individual roles as the protectress of Upper and Lower Egypt individually, the two uraei frequently wear the white and the red crown, respectively denoting these areas (Calverley and Gardiner 1933, pl. 23; Smith and Redford 1976, pls 20:2, 23:9, and figs 35, 36, 41, 58). Photo by L. Lundberg; Museo Gregoriano Egizio, inv. no. 22681.

the daughter, wife and protectress of the primeval and most powerful deity. The pharaoh or queen would forever be safe from harm when the unit was placed on his or her forehead (*e.g.* Westendorf 1978; *LÄ* I, 562–7; *LÄ* III, 48–51).

Royal diadem

Six figures (cat. nos 3, 16, 18–19, 21, 35) are depicted with a royal diadem, which is shown as a thin ribbon tied in a knot at the back of the head with long streamers hanging down, following the outlines of the wig. The main thin band is seldom marked on the head or wig, but is illustrated instead as a knot or a bow-tie at the back of the head. It is attached to a single forehead *uraeus* resting on the brow. All figures documented with the diadem also wear a single forehead *uraeus* affixed to it.

The royal diadem is connected to the *uraeus* and sometimes the vulture as well. Egyptian terminology separated this headdress unit into headbands or fillets (*mḏḥ*, *sj3t*, *sšnn*, *sšd*) made of non-metallic materials and diadems (*3ḫt*, *j3bt*, *nfr-ḥ3t*) mainly produced in metal (*LÄ* VI, 45). As with many other iconographic details, the (cloth) headband served a practical function in keeping the hair in place. These functional and simple headbands, which were used by commoners, were most probably made of linen (*LÄ* VI, 46).[3] Apart from the more practical use of the headband, it was worn also as decoration, where it was elaborated with details and ornamental elements.

When decorating the head of a pharaoh or his queen, the practical function expanded to include acting as a holder of brow ornaments (*uraeus* and vulture) and the material changed from textiles to gold or some other precious metal. The unit thereby became a royal diadem, worn by kings and queens alike and sometimes by princes and princesses (*cf.* Albersmeier 2002, 38–40). The diadem is documented throughout Egyptian history from at least the Old Kingdom (Fakhry 1954, 584, pl. 11a).

Conclusion

The tripartite wig was a frequently used pictorial detail in the overall composition of female figures. It is difficult to attach any precise socio-religious interpretations or cultural connotations to the wig because it is shown so often in the material. Similarly, it was a headdress worn by queens and goddesses alike, without any identifiable individual connections. The tripartite wig was connected with mainly female figures, since the pharaohs and the male deities wore the *nemes* or the *khat*. However, the material shows that the tripartite wig was worn also by processional male deities, mainly the *ka*-figures,[4] and was therefore not an exclusively female attribute. Nor did the wig have any exclusive regional connections, since it was used by both Upper and Lower Egyptian deities.

The vulture cap was also a common pictorial element worn by Arsinoë. It is associated with Upper Egypt through the vulture goddess Nekhbet, and was an important part of the royal female iconography. The cap is, at the same time, connected with the Hathoric role (as Nekhbet represents a specific Hathoric aspect), in which the goddess protects the pharaoh. It was worn by women exclusively, and symbolises the divine power of protection given to the figure wearing it.

The single forehead *uraeus*, the risen cobra, symbolises Lower Egypt and is associated with Wadjet and Hathor in their roles as protector of the pharaoh. This element does not have any gender association, although the *uraeus* itself was feminine. The combination of the vulture and the cobra symbolises the Two Lands, Upper and Lower Egypt, the sky and earth, and the protection of the pharaoh, and is thus an excellent example of Egyptian dualistic symbolism.

The headdresses included in the material thus communicate an association with the Hathoric daughter role in which the goddess protects her father (or the individual wearing these elements). Generally, these units/elements are used too frequently throughout the Egyptian dynasties and are worn by too many individuals to allow any deeper interpretation. In general, the most frequently occurring headdresses communicate a message of royal and divine status, emphasising the unbroken lineage delivered from Ra through his divine children to include the royal family who secured the continuation of the divine Kingdom.

Hand-held objects

Arsinoë is associated with nine types of hand-held objects (including hands held in a protecting manner). These items are held equally by deities and royalties, usually without any direct association with the main theme of the scene. The objects analysed here are separated from items presented as offerings by a pharaoh or ruling couple.

Ankh

As the subject of much detailed investigation in the past, the *ankh* has previously been interpreted as a sandal strap, a phallic sheath – as associated with a bull's spine – or even a mirror (*e.g.* Sugi 2000, 103). The hieroglyphic sign of *ankh* – *ꜥnḫ*, literally translates as 'life', 'to live', 'living', 'alive', but also symbolises all living creatures in nature, signifying growth and fertility (*WB* I, 193). As the most frequently illustrated hand-held object in Egyptian art, it is not surprising to find the *ankh* as the most common item also here (Table 12). It occurs as an object held by Arsinoë thirty-two times (including double scenes) (cat. nos 1L–7, 10–11, 13–14, 16–24, 26L–34). The exceptions to the convention of holding an *ankh* are figures holding

ILLUSTRATION	DESIGNATION	SCENES	TOTAL NO. ITEMS
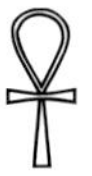	*Ankh*	1L–7, 10–11, 13–14, 16–24, 26L–34	32
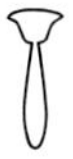	Papyrus sceptre	1R–2R, 4–7, 11, 13–14, 18, 23–24, 26L–R, 28, 30–34	21
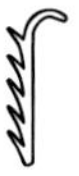	Notched palm branch	20	1
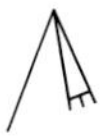	Flail	12, 27, 29, 36	4
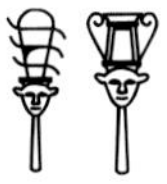	Sistra	9, 15L–R	4
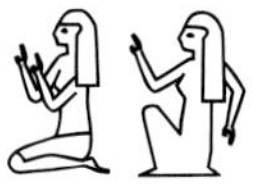	Hand held in protective or **blessing** manner	3, 16–17, 19, 21–22, 35; **25**	8

Table 12. Hand-held objects.

their hands in a protecting or praising manner, or, possibly, instances in which the hand-held object is undetectable owing to the state of preservation of the detail.

The *ankh* is held by royalties and deities equally. The general convention depicts standing figures with an *ankh* held in their inactive/resting arm behind the back; seated figures hold a fully horizontal or slightly diagonal *ankh*, with the lower end pointing away from them. When the figure is seated, the *ankh* is conventionally held in the hand placed lowest (Nilsson 2010, 302f.). It expresses a conventional message of life regardless of its holder. It is, however, also documented as a central element actively indicating the theme of a scene. As such, it is associated with crowning or rejuvenation ceremonies, rites of purification and the transference of ancestral dynastic power (for these variations see Figures 46–47). In cat. no. 20, for example, the *ankh* hangs from the top of a notched palm as it is handed over from the deceased ancestors (Ptolemy II and Arsinoë) to the ruling pharaoh (Ptolemy IV). The *ankh* is essential in Sed festivals, again emphasising a rejuvenation theme (Sugi 2000).[5] Similarly, Figure 48 shows *ankh*s in a stream, similar to water, poured over a pharaoh as a part of a cleansing ceremony.

Other pictorial elements occasionally fuse with and morph the original form of an *ankh*, while retaining its symbolism of life. The *hes* vessel, used for ritual libations, is based on the shape of an *ankh* and is generally interpreted as representing life-giving water (Sugi 2000, 103; *LÄ* III, 1014f.; Vassilika 1989, 100). At other times, the *ankh* assumes the shape of a flower, representing buds in a bouquet or individually placed on branches (*e.g. LÄ* III, 949–51; Sugi 2000, 103).

The material contains a few examples in which the *ankh* is depicted unconventionally as far as its physical position is concerned. Firstly, the *ankh* held by Arsinoë in cat. no. 3 is kept in front of her body rather than behind. Her arm is slightly raised as if holding a sceptre and the *ankh* is placed diagonally instead of, as is conventional, vertical. The scene shows Ptolemy V and Cleopatra I as the ruling couple, standing on the right side of the stele. Shu and Tefnut stand on the opposite side of the scene, accompanied by three deceased generations of Ptolemaic couples (excluding Ptolemy I and Berenice I). Shu, as the first divine figure of the scene, holds an *ankh* in a pose equivalent to Arsinoë's. Through his figural position and his sceptre, which symbolises divine kingship, Shu links the ruling royal couple with their deceased ancestors. The other figures of the scene keep a traditional position, holding a sceptre/stave in front of them and an *ankh* in the hand held behind the body. As the last figure of the scene, and with one hand raised in a protecting manner, Arsinoë usurps a Hathoric role, protecting the entire dynasty; she is also the tallest figure of the scene, emphasising her importance. This, combined with the presence of Shu and Tefnut (as the children of Ra and Hathor), establishes Arsinoë's Hathoric maternal aspect. As the first and last figure of the divine line, holding their *ankh*s in identical positions, Shu and Arsinoë establish a symbolic mother-and-child relationship. Arsinoë becomes a Hathoric wet nurse and caretaker of the entire dynasty, while Shu represents the divine child, the royal heir and the link to the ruling couple. At the same time, they represent the most fundamental aspect of Egyptian religion: as male and female, human and divine, Shu and Arsinoë display the concept of dualism.

Arsinoë holds the *ankh* in front of her body in cat. no. 21 in a way similar to that shown in cat. no. 3, but fully vertical. The scene illustrates Ptolemy VIII as the benefactor of the *theoi Adelphoi*. Arsinoë is, again, holding one hand in a protecting manner, and stands behind Ptolemy II. This scene may also be interpreted as a part of a dynastic setting where a ruling pharaoh takes upon himself the divine powers of his ancestors. The scene is the only one of the temple scenes where Arsinoë wears a traditional female crown instead of her personalised crown; apart from this, there is nothing distinguishing about the scene to suggest why this unconventional placement of Arsinoë's *ankh* should have been made.

In cat. no. 10 the scene places Arsinoë on the left side as Ptolemy II's beneficiary. The king and queen are separated by a horned altar located in the centre of the scene. Arsinoë keeps one hand in front of her body as she leans towards the altar; the other arm is bent upwards behind her head. There, behind her, is a vertical sceptre-like unidentified object. The *ankh* is placed above this vertical object, from which it is physically separated by Arsinoë's arm. The *ankh* is not connected with the unidentified object in terms of proportion and symmetry, nor is it physically attached to Arsinoë. Instead, the *ankh* sits on top of the back of Arsinoë's

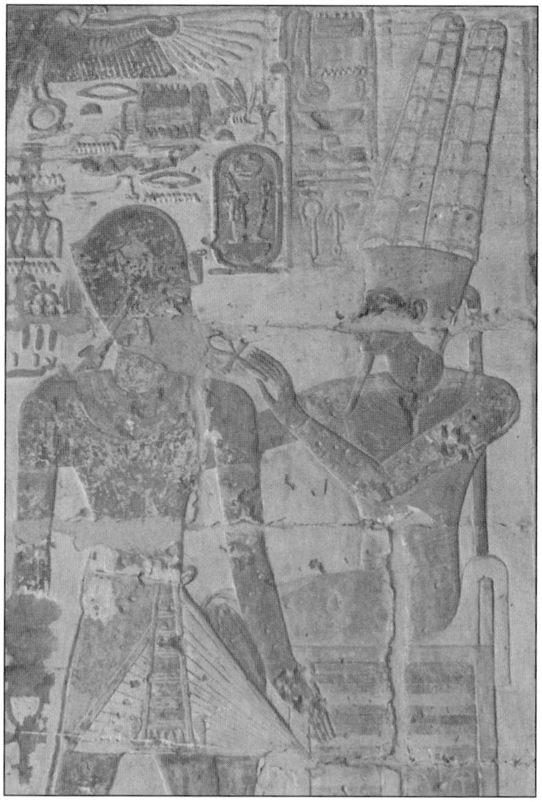

Figure 46. Dressed in the full kingship regalia, and wearing the war crown, Hatshepsut receives life from Amun while holding an ankh in her resting hand. Photo from el-Kab by J. Ward.

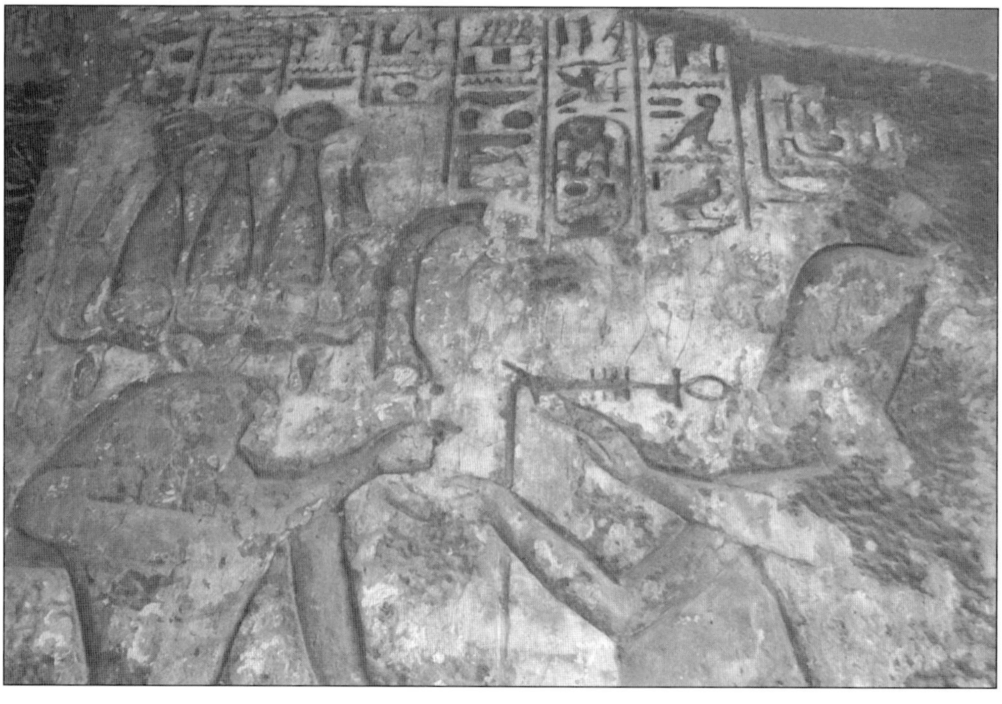

Figure 47. Ramses II receives strength, prosperity and life in the Temple of Wadi al-Sebua.

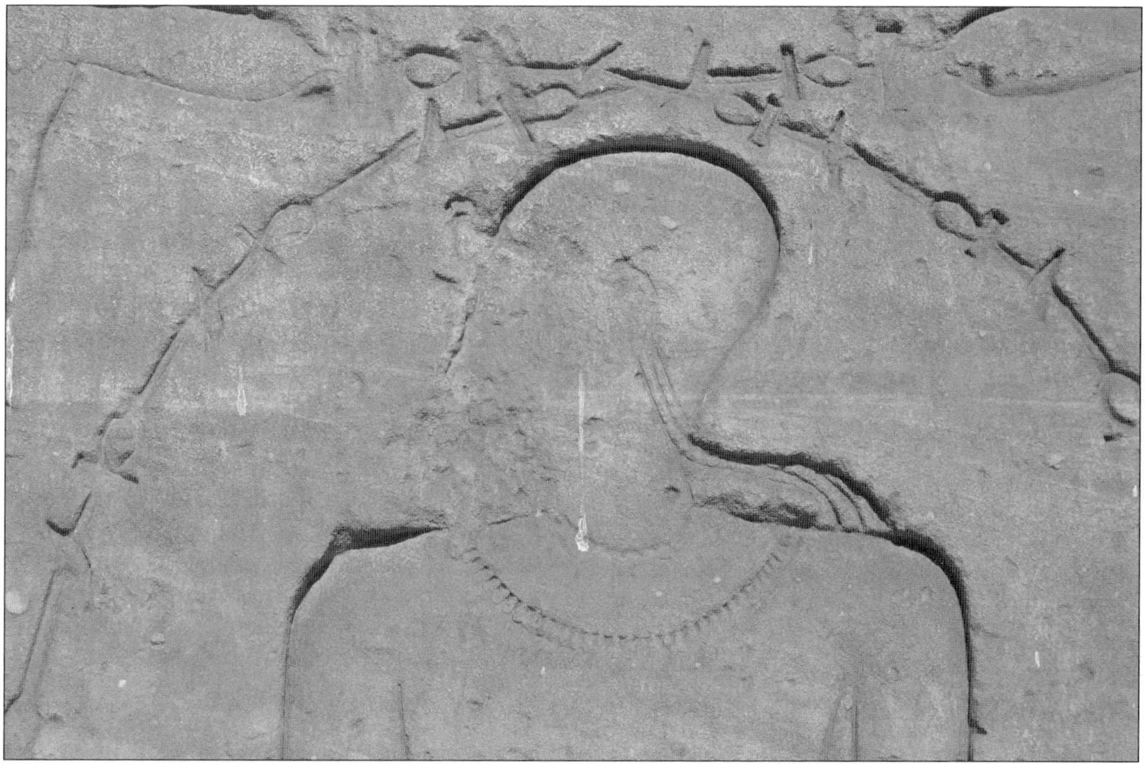

Figure 48. Detail from the Mammisi in Edfu illustrating the purifying stream of life.

hand. As a consequence of its very unusual placement, it is difficult to interpret its function and symbolic meaning.

The three scenes above exemplify exceptions to the conventional placement of the *ankh*. Their uniqueness, however, makes it difficult to determine any obvious meaning behind their differentiation. Consequently, additional comparative scenes are required if we are to gain an understanding of the socio-religious associations in these scenes, if any existed.

Sceptres and flails

Sceptres and staves are the second most common hand-held objects (Table 12). Twenty-one images of Arsinoë hold a papyrus sceptre (*w3ḏ*). Usually included in the group of insignia, sceptres and staves represent objects with a function more symbolic than practical.[6] The papyrus sceptre consists of a bloomed papyrus top, sometimes referred to as the bud of a lily, sitting on an elongated shaft or staff with a slightly thicker lower part. It symbolises protection, and is initially linked with Lower Egyptian deities and with goddesses sent out to protect the divine pharaoh (Graham 2001, 166; *LÄ* II, 1024–33).[7] In the material, sceptres and staves are always held in front of the figure. The uppermost part is generally level with the face of the figure when standing. The material examined here provides nothing to suggest a symbolic significance other than that already generally accepted.

Arsinoë's sceptre has some importance in the overall iconological interpretation of cat. no. 13. This scene illustrates Arsinoë as Ptolemy II's divine beneficiary. She holds a conventional papyrus sceptre in the usual position in front of her body. The issue of interest, however, is the poor quality of artistry in regard to the sceptre(s), which is asymmetrical and far from conventional. In accordance with artistic principles, all details should be fully symmetrical in a finished official relief. However, the lower section, separated from the upper by the hand holding it, does not agree with the upper part: they are (vertically) disorganised, as Figure 49 shows. Such a disarrangement of the details suggests an unfinished relief, possibly a practice piece, never intended for the public.

The flail is held by Arsinoë in four scenes (cat. nos 12, 27, 29, 36). It was originally a male attribute which, together with the crook, denoted kingship and superiority (Graham 2001, 166). The female version of the flail has a hieroglyphic and symbolic meaning of protection and is artistically separated from the male flail by a small supplementing detail of a lily or lotus-bud (*e.g. LÄ* VI, 1373–89). Apart from cat. no. 36, which depicts Arsinoë with the traditional female crown, these scenes show Arsinoë with her 'private' crown, which is limited to the reigns of Arsinoë and Ptolemy II.

Sistrum

The sistrum, or rattle (*sẖm*), was a musical instrument primarily associated with the cult of Hathor.[8] According to archaeological records, it was made of metal, generally bronze, and is recorded throughout all dynastic periods (including the Roman period) (Roberts 1997, 57f.). It is documented in the material in two variants referred to here as the 'looped sistrum' and the '*naos*-formed sistrum' (*sššt*) (*cf.* Roberts 1997, 57f.) (Figure 50). A looped sistrum consists of a handle with a top loop holding two to four horizontal bars or rods with small discs. These discs create the ceremonial tones believed to arouse the goddess: it was an instrument believed to have erotic connotations linked to Hathor's role as the hand of god when she masturbated Atum (Vassilika 1989). As its name suggests, the second type has a small *naos* placed on the handle instead of a pierced loop. The *naos* symbolised the temple, in which the goddess dwelt (*LÄ* V, 959–65).

Although not depicted in the material, the sistrum is occasionally combined with a phallus, when it is described as the sistrum of Nebet Hetepet and symbolises Hathor's role as the hand of Atum (Roberts 1997, 138; *cf.* cat. no. 2L). Apart from its association with Hathor, the sistrum was also connected with Ihy, the great son of Hathor. He is documented from the Old Kingdom, although his growth into a prominent youth deity dates primarily to the Ptolemaic and Roman periods (Roberts 1997, 29–32). His hieroglyphic name illustrates a youngster holding a sistrum in his outstretched arm. As the sistrum player personified, Ihy symbolised the rebirth of the solar disc (Roberts 1997, 29–32; Nilsson 2010, 445–7).

In the material, three images of Arsinoë (cat. nos 9, 15L–R) hold one or several sistra. In the first scene, cat. no. 9, Arsinoë's sistrum is *naos*-formed, with a long and narrow shaft leading up to a conventional Hathoric face with cow

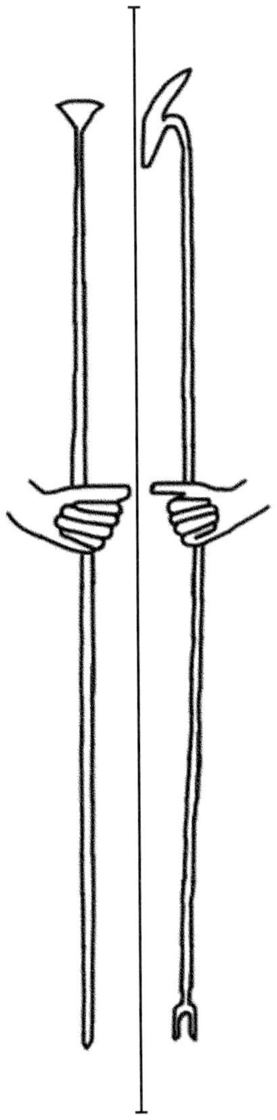

Figure 49. Detail of cat. no. 13, showing the asymmetry of the shafts. A vertical straight line has been added to the scene in order to emphasise the poor quality in terms of artistic accuracy.

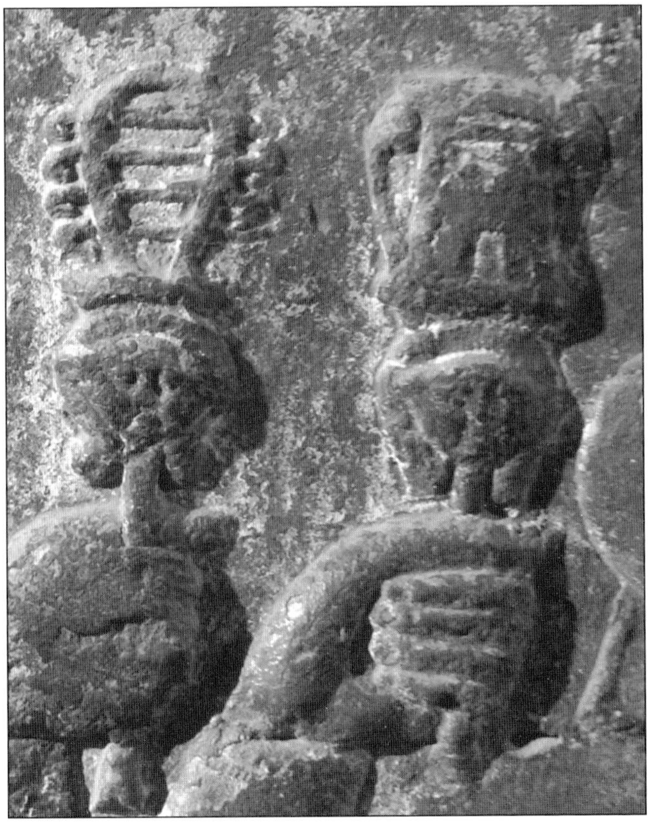

Figure 50. Detail showing looped and naos-formed sistra, Dendera Temple.

ears. The form of the *naos* is plain and traditional. The scene is fragmentary, making a contextual analysis to determine any unique symbolism of the sistrum or any associations with surrounding elements impossible.

The second scene shows Arsinoë holding two looped sistra on the left side (cat. no. 15L), and two *naos*-formed sistra on the right (cat. no. 15R). Arsinoë stands behind Ptolemy II; both are actively performing religious rituals to invoke the deities placed on their opposite side. The sistra in cat. no. 15 (L–R) have a traditional symbolism, demonstrating an active event in which the sistrum was held/rattled principally by priestesses (or priests) to invoke or arouse a divine spirit. The sacred ritual created an ecstatic bond between the worshipper (benefactor) and the deity (beneficiary). Owing to the cultic and ceremonial nature of the sistrum, it seems reasonable to interpret any given royal figure holding it as a person who is alive. An already deified royal figure, after all, did not need to invoke a divine spirit, as he/she was regarded as being on an equal cultic level with such spirits. Priest, priestess, king or queen, however, could use this instrument to actively express their piety and to come in contact with the god (Ihy, as a deity, has to be regarded as an exception, since he personifies the sistrum). The sistrum, therefore, is an instrument that indicates an active position/performance on the part of the figure holding it, and, in accordance with this interpretation, Arsinoë's role in cat. nos 9 and 15 (L–R) is that of a living priestess who performs a sacred religious ritual.

Hand held in a protective manner

This section deals with a figural pose rather than an object: the position referred to as 'hand held in a protective manner', which may also be referred to as 'blessings/praises'. Pictorially, one hand is raised in front of the body, with the palm facing forward. Female figures keeping their hands in this position generally stand behind a seated spouse, holding an *ankh* in the opposite hand. Arsinoë holds her hand in a protective manner in seven scenes (cat. nos 3, 16–17, 19, 21–22, 35). All these scenes show Arsinoë as the last figure, standing behind a seated Ptolemy II (except for cat. nos 3 and 35, in which Ptolemy II stands).[9] All these scenes describe the second Ptolemaic couple as the *theoi Adelphoi*, and each scene has a dynastic connection, emphasising ancestor cult. Any female figure who holds her hand(s) in this pose of protection stresses an association primarily with Hathor and her role as the eye of Ra (*e.g.* Nilsson 2010, 437–40; *cf.* Vassilika 1989, 100f.). It can be assumed, therefore, that Arsinoë possesses a position as a Hathoric mother protecting the entire dynasty.

Scenes that illustrate this gesture are far too scarce to provide strong evidence for any fundamental conclusions. However, based on the material, hands held in a protective manner indicate an association with ancestor cult and dynastic symbolism, emphasising a divine as well as a royal lineage. These scenes always depict Arsinoë in the official crown that places the ram horns on top of the red crown's platform.

A figure raising both hands (palm forward) is here described as blessing/praising. This position is documented only in cat. no. 25. All this scene's forty-six figures are positioned in this praising pose, together worshipping a centrally placed solar disc. The position expresses an active role of adoration.

Notched palm branch

As an object held by Arsinoë, the notched palm branch is documented only in cat. no. 20. The palm branch is held in front of the figure in a manner similar to that employed with sceptres and flails: it is held by seated (cat. no. 20) and also by standing contextual figures (cat. no. 4). In general, it is documented in scenes that describe the ceremony of reckoning of time (the annuals: *LÄ* I, 278–80), which is associated with the crowning of a new pharaoh and with the Sed festival in which the pharaoh renews his power and kingship. Stated also in textual records, the message communicated by any figure holding a palm branch is that he/she blesses the ruler with many years of rule and with many jubilees to come (Vassilika 1989, 99, 101; *cf.* cat. nos 1–2).

In art, the palm is documented since the Predynastic Period mainly in forms of ceramic decoration (Lurker 2002, 94). The palm was associated with Ra, and the crown of the tree was considered to manifest the solar deity. The tree was connected also with Thoth and Min, where it symbolised rejuvenation and fertility – that is, eternal life. As well as the hieroglyphic association with eternity, the palm branch or leaf signified the year (*WB* II, 429f.). The branch is occasionally decorated with additional pictorial elements, such as *ankh*s, cartouches or tadpoles/frogs. It could also be placed as a crown element attributing Heh, personifying eternity (*LÄ* II, 1082–5).

Like all other trees, the palm was also an attribute of Hathor (*LÄ* IV, 658f.); along with Min, she connects the palm branch with fertility and growth. It incorporates a dualistic structure in which male and female come together, laying the foundation of life. This observation is supported by the presence of Thoth and Seshat in scenes in which they write and record the annuals of the pharaoh (*e.g. LÄ* I, 278f.; *cf.* cat. no. 20).[10] As an attribute of Hathor, the palm branch may be interpreted as having a meaning and symbolic function related to lifecycle. Any figure holding a palm branch gives divine protection directly to the pharaoh, and links him with his divine primeval father, Ra. It is argued here that the palm branch is a symbol of life and of the life journey, an interpretation strengthened by the significance of the palm hieroglyph, which translates as eternity, and substantiated by the additional *ankh*s that hang from the top of the palm branches in cat. no. 20 (the dynastic legacy and the divine lineage are stressed also in cat. no. 4, where a circular cartouche is placed at the bottom end of the hand-held palm branch). When the divine or royal ancestors hold the palm branch before the pharaoh, therefore, they hold the key to the journey of life, directly guided and protected by Hathor.

Cat. no. 20 also includes a tree of life, which holds the primeval egg and the cartouche of the pharaoh. There, Pharaoh Ptolemy IV rises up from this tree, which is identified elsewhere with a sycamore, a species indigenous to the country that grows along the desert edge (Lesko 1999, 84). The sycamore was sacred to the Egyptians, being especially worshipped in the Memphite precinct of the temple complex of Ptah (Lesko 1999, 87). As the 'Lady of the Sycamore', Hathor was the main deity connected with the tree (*cf.* Lesko 1999, 83f.). It was planted in temple areas and around cemeteries across the country. Based on Hathor's association with burials and rebirth (fertility), this tree, like the palm (discussed above), can be seen as symbolising the full life journey of birth, growth, fertility, rejuvenation, and finally rebirth in the Underworld. The tree is consequently interpreted as another symbol of Ra, and describes the daily journey throughout the divine universe (Roberts 1997, 18–22).

Conclusion

All the hand-held objects described above are held either as personal attributes that indicate a religious act (sistrum); as objects indicating royalty (flail); or as a link between deity and royalty (*ankh*, sceptres). In addition, there are objects which are not direct attributes of the figure holding it, but instead an element indicating the theme of a scene (notched palm branch). A gesture indicating a theme, 'hand held in a protective [one hand] or praising [both hands] manner', has also been included here.

The objects linking royal persons with the deities are connected with life and protection, and include the notched palm branch as a symbol of the life journey. All these objects can be held by seated and standing figures, and by royal and divine figures equally. Most items are held by males and females, but the papyrus sceptre is considered as a female attribute exclusively.

The sistrum is an exceptional hand-held object that expresses an active position of religious worship, linking royal persons with the deities. It was an attribute of Hathor and was personified in her son Ihy. Here, the instrument has been interpreted as indicating a living royal person in the position of a benefactor, as the active role is one of someone who is alive.

The symbolism of the individual hand-held objects is too generic to establish any absolute association with the crown worn by Arsinoë. However, the flail, which symbolises royalty and power, is associated with the type of Arsinoë's crown that places the ram horns at the base of the red crown, and which relates to Arsinoë's royal position during her lifetime. Furthermore, when Arsinoë is illustrated in the gesture of holding the hand in a protective manner (associated with the dynastic ancestor cult), she always wears the more official and long-lived crown-type, which shows the ram horns on top of the red crown's platform.

Additional decoration

A number of items that are physically attached to the figure of Arsinoë are analysed here, including clothing, sandals and accessorising jewellery (Table 13). In addition to these decorative details, the throne, being the only furniture physically connected to Arsinoë, is discussed.

Sheat dress

Almost all female figures wear a traditional sheat dress. Of the exceptions, the figures are either too damaged or fragmentarily preserved for the dress to be visible. The

DECORATION	SCENES	TOTAL NO. FIGURES
Sheat dress	1L–7, 10–14,16–36	36
Elaborate sheat dress	8, 15L–R	3
Sandals	8, 15L–R	3
Necklace	9,12–13,16–19, 21, 24–25, 27–30, 32, 34–35	17
Bracelet	8, 12, 18, 23, 28	5
Upper arm bracelet	12, 18, 28	3
Ankle bracelet	8	1
Decorated corner box	20	1

Table 13. Decoration.

sheat is a tight dress without knots, seams or belt. As Figure 51 shows, the sheat usually has a relief pattern of long tail feathers, at times painted in red, blue and/or white. The shoulder straps, placed next to the breast in accordance with artistic convention, are occasionally decorated with a small pattern. This pattern also decorates the lower end of the dress. The figures occasionally wear an additional thin shawl placed over the shoulders. A more elaborate style of the sheat dress shows a curved lower part where the fabric folds in layers. As a necessary element in the full depiction of all female figures, the dress cannot be assumed to be the attribute of any specific deity or theme (*cf.* Witt 1997, 126 for the Isis dress).

Three images of Arsinoë, in the two scenes cat. nos 8 and 15L–R, wear an elaborated sheat. Figure 52 shows the lower part of this dress and exemplifies, at the same time, a pictorial combination with decorative sandals placed on Arsinoë's otherwise bare feet. The scenes place Arsinoë in an active position, where she either presents offerings or practises a religious ceremony. She is placed in an opposite position to the deity (deities) in both scenes. The three figures are textually described as 'King of Egypt'. These scenes are dated to Arsinoë's lifetime on the basis on her position and title (see pp. 90–93; 110–112). Other scenes that are redated here to Arsinoë's lifetime are preserved in fragments, making it impossible to establish whether or not the elaborated sheat dress denotes a living queen (the dress worn by Berenice II in cat. no. 4 is similarly elaborated, possibly indicating an association between the dress and a living queen).

Sandals

According to the general convention, most figures in the material are depicted barefooted, with only a few exceptions. Such exceptions are connected with the elaborated dress, as described above. The sandals show a low, flat sole; a thin strap runs over the ankle and is attached to another strap that comes up from between the toes. Arsinoë wears sandals in cat. nos 8 and 15.

Jewellery

Female figures in general are decorated with jewellery, including necklaces, bracelets and earrings. Jewellery is a decorative element relating to both males and females, however, and is primarily connected with hierarchic status. The necklace is pictorially associated with the *menit* collar of Hathor, although the latter is indicated by an additional back part. The necklace could also symbolise the arms of Atum, embracing any given figure wearing it, and as such it signified protection (Lurker 2002, 24). Jewellery is considered here to be pure decoration, primarily denoting status.

Thrones and corner-boxes

A traditional stylised Egyptian throne is illustrated in agreement with the hieroglyphic sign 𓊨. It is structured in three main sections: a backboard, a seat and a foundation. The seat of the throne is frequently decorated with a square, circular or feather pattern, as Figures 53–58 show. Occasionally the throne is decorated with a small framed quadrate located in the lower back corner of the throne. The quadrate is attached to the figure through its

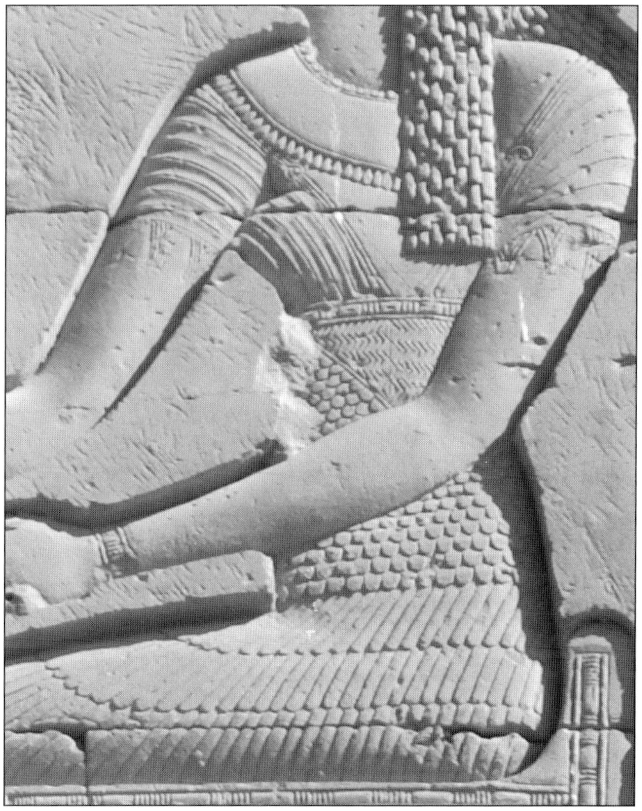

Figure 51. Detail of a decorated sheat dress, showing a combination of small and elongated tail feathers, Temple of Dendera.

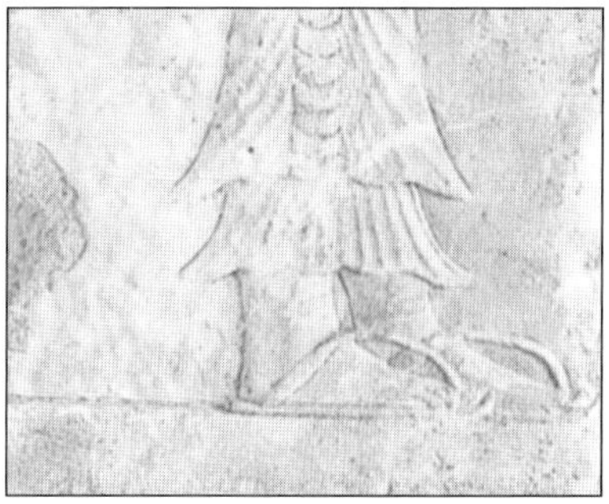

Figure 52. Detail of cat. no. 8, showing the lower part of an elaborated dress and feet decorated with sandals.

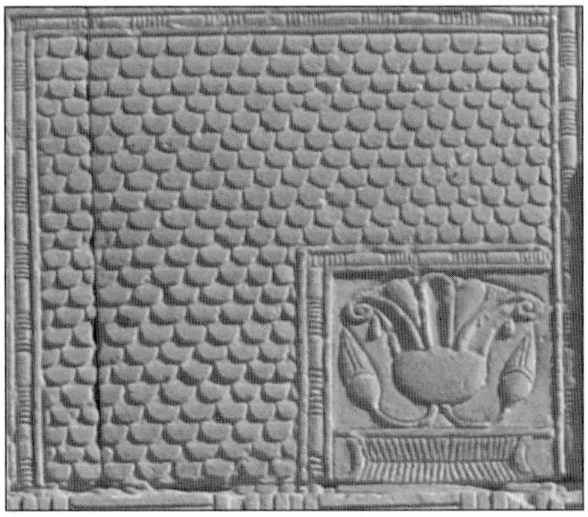

Figure 53. Corner box, showing lilies.

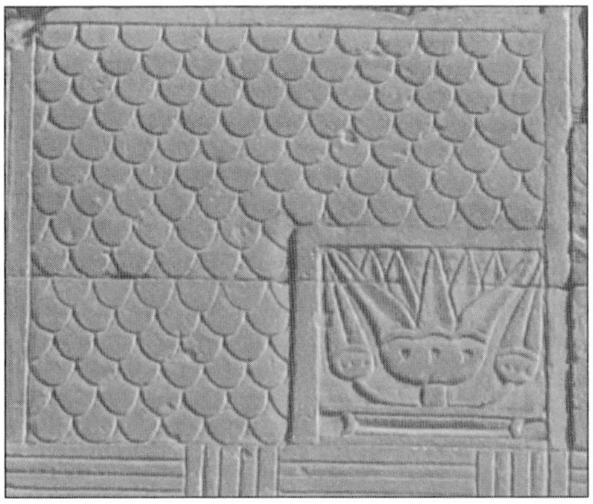

Figure 54. Corner box, showing lotuses.

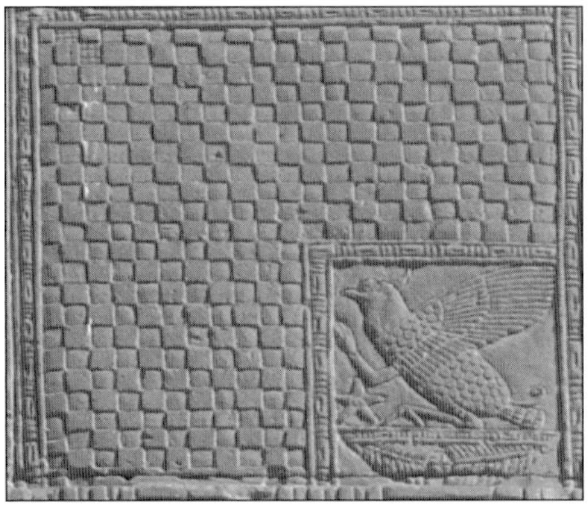

Figure 55. Corner box, showing Rekhtbird with star.

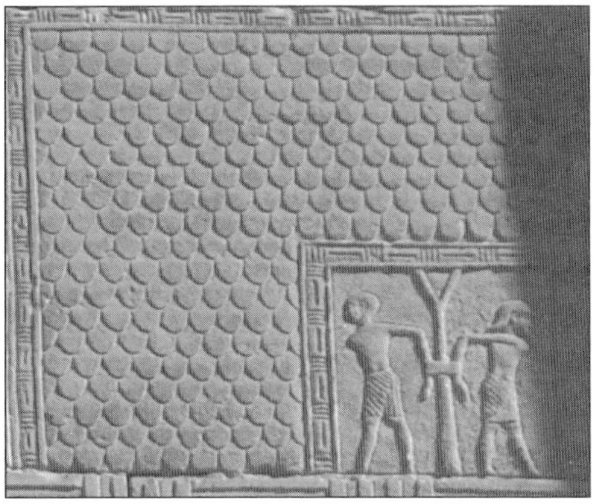

Figure 56. Corner box, showing captured enemies.

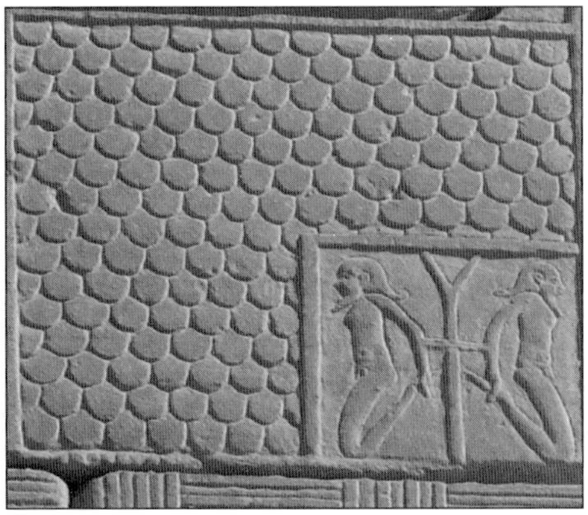

Figure 57. Corner box, showing captured enemies.

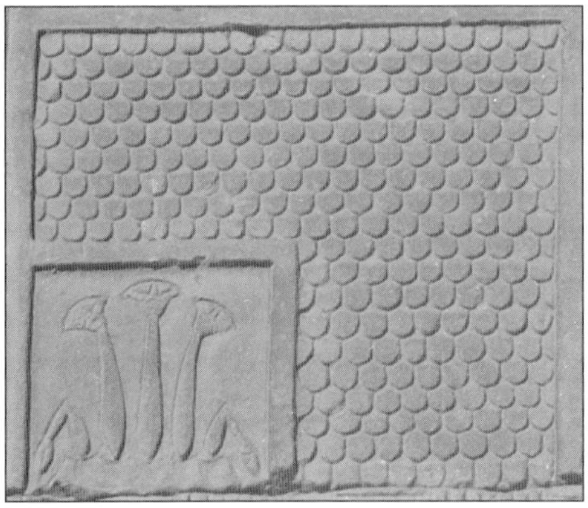

Figure 58. Corner box, showing papyrus cluster.

All figures are from the Dendera Temple.

physical contact with the throne, and is referred to as a 'corner box' on the basis of its location on the throne and its visual function. It is separated from the main pattern by one or several lines (horizontal and vertical) framing the square, and at times it displays one or several small relief or painted illustrations displaying very limited variation and mainly depicting a large lotus, a papyrus cluster with one flower and two buds, or the *sema* sign of unification (*cf.* Nilsson 2010, 315–17). Although this detail is dissimilar to the decorating items worn by the queen, it is nevertheless a decorating element owing to the presence of the illustrations.

In general, thrones shown on temple reliefs are illustrated with decorated corner boxes, although undecorated boxes occur on the stelai. This decoration is, however, rarely preserved. Cat. no. 20 is the only scene with Arsinoë that displays a corner box. In this scene, the thrones of Arsinoë and Ptolemy show indications of an original painted pattern, but they are too faint for any form to be established. The thrones of Hathor and Horus, however, reveal vague painted outlines indicating large lotuses.

Notes

1 Diadems are documented in archaeological sources, thus suggesting that the band of the diadem in the reliefs actually represents a realistic, physical headdress detail (*e.g.* Goebs 2001, 321f.)

2 Troy (1986, chapter II.6.2.3) goes further and explains this as being related to the generational roles of mother and daughter, in which Wadjet is interpreted as the youth and Nekhbet as the mother.

3 One can easily see the similarity with the diadem illustrated on the Greek-styled Ptolemaic coins, worn by queens and kings, as well as the two ribbons surrounding the double cornucopia on the coins of Arsinoë. The white, flat headband became a symbol of Hellenistic kingship connecting each individual ruler to Alexander as well as to Dionysus.

4 *Ka* and *Ba* figures personify two aspects of the pluralistic soul. The *Ka* signifies the social aspect, and incorporates the status and decorum of a person alive. The material emphasises male *Ka*-figures. The *Ba* represents the divine soul, which can move freely between the spheres and return on occasions to a bodily form. Isis and Osiris are generally believed to personify the female and male *Ba* (*e.g.* Karenga 2004, 180; Török 2009, 424).

5 In addition, the *ankh* is included in scenes illustrating the ceremony of opening the mouth, where the *ankh* is delivered to the deceased through the breath of the gods themselves (traditionally associated with Ptah or Amun). In these scenes the *ankh* represents eternal life. See cat. no. 1 and the description of Arsinoë's death.

6 Other than sceptres and staves, insignia include maces, spears, clubs, etc.: these additional objects are never held by any of the present female figures. All these items had a practical meaning originally, but the two types documented here had a more religious ritual significance.

7 Separated from the papyrus sceptre by a split lower end, the *was* stave has a form originating in a practical application to catch or control snakes. This item is never held by Arsinoë, but is recorded as a hand-held object of surrounding figures.

8 In early literature, the sistrum was associated with secret initiations performed in the temples. Such texts include the creation myth from Gebelein (*e.g.* Rundle Clark 1959, 88).

9 Overall, many scenes depict the *theoi Adelphoi* as the last couple of a standing dynastic line (including scenes other than those where Arsinoë is positioned in a protecting or prais-ing manner). Cat. nos 4 and 18, however, place an additional couple in the end of the dynastic setting. In such exceptional scenes, the *theoi Adelphoi* are not regarded as the original ancestors of the dynasty since Ptolemy I and Berenice I represent the last standing couple.

10 In these scenes, Thoth and Seshat are depicted on the same side as the pharaoh, surrounded by symbols of kingship. Hathor and Horus are placed on the opposite side handing over the signs of life. Divine ancestors, if any, are placed on the same side as Hathor and Horus. In cat. no. 20, Arsinoë and Ptolemy II, as the (deceased) dynastic ancestors, join Hathor and Horus. For a discussion about the placement of the pharaoh contra deities in dynastic scenes see below (pp. 90–93) (*cf.* Winter 1978).

Chapter 6

Religious rituals

The first part of this chapter studies the physical positions and gestures of the pharaoh, or the royal couple, in order to identify the religious ritual and how (or if) it is connected with the studied crowns. The positions and gestures generally express a symbolic message (*e.g.* Wilkinson 1994, chapters 8–9) and are represented and divided in the material in accordance with seven main themes: active sacrifice, adoration, smiting pose, rejuvenation/crowning ceremonies, dynastic settings and evocation. The aim is to understand these thematic religious and pictorial backgrounds in the complete relief scenes, which will function as a platform (together with additional contextual details) when subsequently discussing the crowns' function and meaning. Ritual gestures symbolise veneration, subservience, honour and respect in a manner similar to the way in which differentiations in height convey the hierarchic structure.[1]

Following this discussion, the analysis turns to individual offering objects. Documented in art since prehistory as part of traditional depictions of rituals and ceremonies, offerings can verify the theme of the scene in which they are represented, and as such they are an important indicator or determiner of the complete message communicated (*e.g.* Vassilika 1989; 1998; *cf.* Englund 2001; Leprohon 2001). In the material, offerings are documented as part of ritual ceremonies connecting a benefactor with beneficiaries, a central act in all forms of ancient Egyptian worship. The objects in the material include incense, the figure of Ma'at, libations and fluids, items of the natural flora, ointments, textiles, crowns, staves, collars and the slaying of an enemy. These are all connected with the dynastic ancestor cult, with the ruler cult of the pharaoh and with traditional veneration of deities.

Active sacrifice

The most frequently depicted theme in Egyptian relief scenes is the presentation of offerings directly to the gods by a king or queen (Table 14). Two main Egyptian formulas were used to describe the act of sacrifice: *ḥtp* – 'sacrifice', 'to satisfy', 'to be pleased', or *ḥnk* – 'to present', 'to give' (*WB* III, 118f., 186–96; *LÄ* IV, 584). The ancients utilised this religious act as an esoteric instrument to maintain universal order. They also believed that it would protect them against evil or possible enemies. It was an act of appreciation or a manifestation of prayer (Hornung 1996, 197).

Although the gods never asked for material offerings, they expected recognition and respect. Through the offerings, the benefactor entered the divine sphere, in which he or she represented humankind in general (Hornung 1996, 203). In such a meeting, the sacrificed object was regarded as a gift from the humans to the Gods, and the deity or deceased ancestor to whom the benefactor presented his offerings was regarded as the Lord/Lady or Father/Mother of the sacrificed objects. The humans were not supposed to expect the god to return the gift. However, many probably hoped that the gods would reciprocate and bless them similarly (Englund 2001, 564): if the god appreciated the gift he would offer more in return. Scholars frequently refer to this form of offering as *do ut des*, 'I give so that you may give' (*e.g.* Vassilika 1989, 98). However, as E. Hornung (1996, 204) points out, owing to the omniscient nature of the Gods they would have provided those things humans desired prior to their asking for them.

A sacrifice was an instrument of communication as it mediated royal persons' respect and thankfulness towards the gods. It was believed to increase the gods' presence, ensure divine protection, and keep the fearsome side of the gods suppressed. It also showed the that the pharaoh was capable of communicating and interacting with the divine world (Hornung 1996, 205). The illustrated theme on a relief was considered to be as efficient as an actual physical performance in achieving these outcomes (Teeter 1997, 154). Therefore, a scene depicting the pharaoh or ruling couple presented their offerings might not record the actual practice of the ceremony in real life, and it is plausible that the ritual existed *only* in the relief, which obtained an esoteric value equal to a physical ritual even though the pharaoh never personally attended the particular temple/site.

TYPE OF SCENE BY RITUAL ACT	SCENES	TOTAL NO. SCENES
Active sacrifice	1L, 2L–R, 5–11, 13–19, 21–24, 26–33, 35	32
Adoration	25, 34	2
Smiting scenes	3	1
Rejuvenation or crowning ceremonies	4, 20	2
Dynastic scene	3–4, 16–22, 24, 34–35	12
Evoking/arousing the god	9, 15L–R	3

Table 14. The setting of the scenes.

As a general and commonly occurring theme which corresponds to a vast number of scenes (and thus many different crown types), this active offering ritual requires additional clarification. It will be further explored below, in the analysis of the individual offering items.

Adoration

In scenes of adoration, a king or queen stands before the gods without any offerings. Their hands are raised in a praising manner or rest alongside their thighs. Since both modes express adoration they have been separated here in accordance with their physical positions, and are consequently referred to as 'adoration' (=raised hands) and 'standing before the god' (=resting hands) (*cf.* Hornung 1996, 203–5; Baines 1991, 125–7). The act of adoration was performed by the ruling couple when they entered the divine sphere and by the Egyptian people when they occasionally approached their king. The act demonstrates piety, respect and veneration (Gardiner's sign-list (1957), A30). This act has been separated from the scenes showing the ritual of sacrifice on the basis of the additional pictorial elements displayed in the latter type. As mentioned above, cat. no. 25 is the only scene in the material showing a pose of praise, as opposed to that of standing before the god. The act of adoration and standing before the god are exclusively documented as being expressed by male rulers in the material. As an example, Ptolemy VIII adores his deceased ancestors, the *theoi Adelphoi*, in cat. no. 34. No unique connection is evident between this act and the crown of Arsinoë.

Ritual of slaying the enemy

Elsewhere described as war scenes, the smiting scenes are here termed in agreement with the theme that they illustrate: a pharaoh slaying his enemies (*cf.* Vassilika 1989, 104). Cat. no. 3 shows a pharaoh (Ptolemy V) smiting a single captive enemy in a scene placed on the upper part of a stele. It has a dynastic association, in that the divine figures depicted are (deified) deceased ancestors, which is relevant for the overall interpretation of the crowns; but this association is far from limited to this theme.

Smiting scenes communicate and commemorate a pharaoh's victory or victories, documenting his strength and his power to uphold universal harmony (Hall 1986; Gilbert 2004, 88f.). Although some scholars consider these scenes to represent factual historical events, it seems more likely that the smiting scenes are instruments of propaganda in which the pharaoh demonstrates his authority (*cf.* Teeter 1997, 155f.).

Rejuvenation or crowning ceremonies

The theme of rejuvenation or crowning includes purification rites and jubilees, such as the Sed festival (*LÄ* IV, 579–84). Two scenes, cat. nos 4 and 20, express this theme. As noted previously, rejuvenation scenes frequently place the ruler in an passive position as he receives the attention of surrounding deities. The pharaoh encounters the protection and strength of the gods, and sometimes also of his deceased ancestors. As noted above, this type of scene includes pictorial elements such as notched palm branches, the tree of life and the writing instruments of Thoth and Seshat. Cat. no. 20 represents the pharaoh (Ptolemy IV) rising up from the tree of life, while Thoth and Seshat write his annuals and deliver his name. On Ptolemy IV's opposite side, Horus, Hathor and the divine ancestors witness the ceremony while they symbolically wish for him many years of rule, as expressed by their hand-held objects.

The royal couple represented all humans, at the same time being considered as divine through their royal legacy. As later chapters will demonstrate, some of the royal titles, including the designations 'son of Ra' and 'Daughter of Amun', reflect such a divine legacy for both kings and queens. When the royal persons entered their positions as kings and queens, they surpassed mortality and became earthly manifestations of Horus and Hathor (*e.g.* Troy 1986, chapter II.2.4; Silverman 1991, 70f.). In contrast to the gods, who remained in the divine sphere, the royal couple hovered between the human and divine and had to prove their right to enter the celestial universe (Silverman 1991, 62–4).

Initiated by the crowning ceremony, the royal accession was celebrated annually as a part of the official festivals (*e.g.* Spalinger 1998, 243). The rejuvenation rituals of the Sed festival were illustrated in a way similar to the crowning ceremony and the reckoning of time (however, each ceremony has its own set of pictorial indications and units). The Sed festival (literally *Heb-sed*) was principally celebrated when a pharaoh had ruled Egypt for thirty years (however, history contains many examples of Sed festivals that were celebrated prior to a thirty-year reign: *e.g.* Uphill 1965), and was a ceremony in which the pharaoh had to prove himself worthy of contining rule. Consequently, the ruler had to complete rituals connected with physical performance. Once he had passed the tests, the king was once more crowned with a double crown, and he was shown to the people as a rejuvenated ruler of Egypt (*e.g.* Najovits 2003, 155f.). The Sed festival is represented in cat. no. 36, but cat. nos 1–2 also allude to such an event, as will be discussed further below. The theme of rejuvenation/crowning relates primarily to dynastic propaganda, but as such a generic topic it is difficult to establish a precise association with the crown worn by Arsinoë.

Dynastic scenes

The Egyptian priesthood could comprehend and, therefore, incorporate the principles of the Alexandrian ruler cult in the conventional royal cult, consequently venerating the Ptolemies side by side with renowned pharaohs such as Ramses II and Nectanebo II (*cf.* Quaegebeur 1980 and Crawford 1980). As J. Quaegebeur (1988, 42) has argued, the main difference between the Greek ruler cult and the conventional Egyptian veneration of the Ptolemies was the latter's exclusion of Alexander the Great and Ptolemy I. This official native Egyptian ruler cult of the Ptolemaic couples has, however, received limited modern scholarly attention. As many scholars dedicate their research to the Alexandrian cult, which is well documented in various artistic and textual media, the Egyptian ruler cult of the Ptolemies remains undefined and possibly misunderstood (*e.g.* Otto 1905, I, 137–63; Fraser 1972, chapter 5; Clarysse and van der Veken 1983; Hölbl 2001, chapter 3).

Twelve individual scenes of Arsinoë are classified as dynastic (Table 14). All scenes where a ruling pharaoh faces his deceased ancestors are categorised thusly, regardless of additional themes. Although there are various examples of a divine dynastic association, the later material, that post-dating Ptolemy VIII, does not include any scenes in which the ruler connects himself/herself with his/her deceased (human) ancestors. This is an important factor when comparing the scenes with the individual types of the crown of Arsinoë. Regardless of the more detailed types presented initially, and instead focusing on varying placement of the ram horns (see Table 8), all the scenes that are here classified as dynastic show Arsinoë wearing her crown with ram horns located on top of the red crown's platform. As suggested above, this type was used as the more official and generally recognised crown throughout the Ptolemaic Dynasty, which naturally is emphasised by the dynastic theme.

Dynastic scenes in the material show a (later/descendant) Ptolemaic ruler presenting offerings to Ptolemy II and Arsinoë. Cat. nos 3–4, 16–22, 24 and 34–35 thematically associate a ruling pharaoh with Ptolemy II and Arsinoë as the *theoi Adelphoi*. The *theoi Adelphoi* are chiefly illustrated in individual scenes, some of which relate to surrounding scenes that depict succeeding dynastic couples in a similar style (such scenes are placed on a lower or an opposite relief register). The *theoi Adelphoi* are only occasionally placed in a larger dynastic scene, where they are depicted in a line with previous (*theoi Soteres*) or succeeding Ptolemaic couples (*theoi Euergetai*, *theoi Philopatores*, *theoi Epiphanes*).

Starting with the less frequent scenes, deceased Ptolemaic couples are placed in an ancestral line,[1] including two or more divine couples, in four of the dynastic scenes (cat. nos 3–4, 18, 35). These scenes vary in their contextual settings: all are associated with ancestral worship and the transfer of dynastic power, but there are no other direct pictorial aspects linking them to each other. Cat. no. 3 illustrates an act of handing over the mythological and royal power of kingship. It shows Ptolemy V and Cleopatra I as the royal benefactors associating themselves with the divine royal children Shu and Tefnut and three previous generations of Ptolemaic rulers (*theoi Adelphoi*, *theoi Euergetai*, *theoi Philopatores*). The second scene, cat. no. 4, shows the ceremony of reckoning of time, the crowning, and the ruler cult. This scene shows the ruling couple, Ptolemy III and Berenice II, standing on the same side as their deceased ancestors and deities associated with crowning ceremonies and on the opposite side to several national paired gods and goddesses. The third scene, cat. no. 18, shows a traditional act of sacrifice in which the new pharaoh (Ptolemy IV) worships his royal and divine ancestors (*theoi Soteres*, *theoi Adelphoi*, *theoi Euergetai*, together with Hathor, Horus and Harpocrates). The last scene, cat. no. 35, which is divided by two figural (horizontal) lines, is an offering scene, in which the ruling couple present incense to their ancestors.

The other and more frequently illustrated dynastic scenes (cat. nos 16–17, 19, 21–22, 24, 34) depict a ruling pharaoh who presents offerings to an individual ancestral couple (Cat. no. 25 is different from the other scenes because it illustrates gods and royal persons worshipping the solar disc. However, the scene remains connected with the dynastic setting through its structural position and surrounding context, as discussed above). These scenes, in contrast to the four scenes described above, are contextually comparable. All illustrate the *theoi Adelphoi* as beneficiaries, with Ptolemy IV, or Ptolemy VIII, as their benefactor. The ruler presents ointment and cloth in cat. no. 16 (Ptolemy VIII) and cat. no. 19 (Ptolemy IV), and incense and libation in cat. no. 17 (Ptolemy IV) and cat. no. 21 (Ptolemy VIII). The rulers keep other religious poses in cat. no. 22 (Ptolemy IV) and cat. no. 34 (Ptolemy VIII). These items – ointment, cloth and so on – might not demonstrate an immediate correlation between the scenes; in order to show this connection, the scenes have to be analysed in accordance with their structural placement and their association with surrounding scenes. All these individual scenes are structurally connected with one or three surrounding scenes, symmetrically placed with regard to one another's positions. Scenes dating to Ptolemy IV (cat. nos 17, 19, 22) structurally relate a scene with the *theoi Adelphoi* to another that shows the *theoi Euergetai*, while those that date to Ptolemy VIII (cat. nos 16, 21, 34) are also connected with scenes that show, individually, the *theoi Euergetai*, *theoi Philopatores* and *theoi Epiphanes*.

Thus cat. no. 16 is located in the top register in the eastern partition of the outer hypostyle hall of the Edfu Temple. The scene immediately below shows the same ruler, Ptolemy VIII, presenting incense and libation to the *theoi Epiphanes*. Two additional individual scenes are placed opposite – thus in the western partition – and show Ptolemy VIII venerating the *theoi Euergetai* and *theoi Philopatores* respectively. Similarly, cat. no. 17 is located in the middle register in the northern partition of the offering hall of the Edfu Temple. In the scene immediately below is shown the veneration of the *theoi Euergetai*. Cat. no. 19 is located in the middle register of the same temple, in the eastern partition of the inner sanctuary, while Ptolemy IV is shown presenting incense and libation to the *theoi Euergetai* in the scene located immediately below. Cat. no. 21 is one of four scenes, as Figures 59–60 show. It is located in the top register in the western partition of the corridor of the Edfu Temple. One of the three related scenes is located immediately beneath, and the other two are on the opposite side of the temple, in the eastern partition. The four scenes are placed in facing positions, with two on each side. Ptolemy VIII presents ointment and cloth to the *theoi Epiphanes* in the scene immediately below cat. no. 21 and corresponding items to the *theoi Euergetai* in the opposite scene in the eastern partition. And, corresponding to cat. no. 21, he presents incense and libation to the *theoi Philopatores* in the top eastern scene. Cat. nos 22 and 34 (the latter in the Temple of Qasr el Aguz) follow a similar pattern.

As noted above, a dynastic scene is classified in accordance with a figural arrangement that shows a pharaoh facing his deceased ancestors (thus acting as their benefactor), regardless of additional themes, but scenes that depict more dynastic couples/figures than actual ruler/rulers are also included. So, all scenes that illustrate one or several royal couples keeping a position as beneficiaries, incorporating also those that express a theme of rejuvenation or crowning, as recorded in cat. nos 4 and 20, are classified as dynastic. This categorisation agrees with J. Quaegebeur's (1989; 1998) identification of the dynastic scenes, rather than with that of E. Winter (1978), before him.

These dynastic themes are fundamentally based on a ruler's claim of divine ancestry, and pictorially identify or associate his ancestors with Horus and Hathor. The individual scenes always incorporate the *theoi Adelphoi*, but

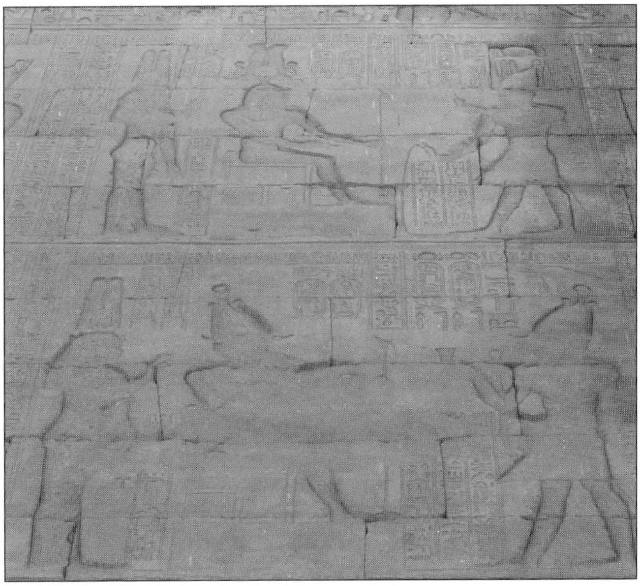

Figure 59. Dynastic scene related to cat. no. 21, Edfu Temple.

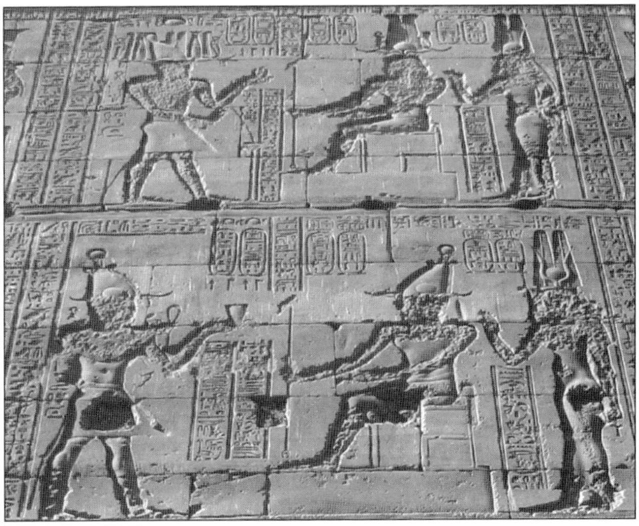

Figure 60. Dynastic scene related to cat. no. 21, Edfu Temple.

only occasionally their subsequent ruling couples (cat. nos 24–25 are exceptions that only include the *theoi Adelphoi*). The total number of dynastic couples varies according to the identity of the benefactor. The scenes incorporate seven ancestral couples or individuals at the most, from the *theoi Soteres* to Ptolemy VIII. Ptolemy VIII and Cleopatra III, who are always depicted as benefactors, mark the last dynastic ruling couple to venerate their ancestors.

The *theoi Soteres* appear only rarely in the pictorial dynastic scenes, but are occasionally mentioned in textual records in connection with the official dating formula. They are never included in scenes that date to Ptolemy VIII: the material reveals that this ruler claimed his ancestry from the *theoi Adelphoi* instead, and that he regarded them as the original founders of the dynasty. The scenes that incorporate the *theoi Soteres*, cat. nos 4 and 18 (they are textually mentioned in cat. no. 3), date to the reigns of Ptolemy III and IV. This is intriguing at first, as other scenes that date to the same periods exclude this first Ptolemaic couple. However, there may be a conventional differentiation based on the cultic aspects that are communicated in these scenes. The first scene, cat. no. 4, is classified here as a crowning/rejuvenation ceremony. The ruling couple stand on the same side as their deceased ancestors (*theoi Adelphoi* and *theoi Soteres*) and are accompanied by Thoth and Seshat. Ptolemy I and Berenice I are symbolically comparable to the divine couple Osiris and Isis, whereas Ptolemy II and Arsinoë are shown in a more individual style. These two couples are also textually differentiated: the *theoi Soteres* are (individually) described as the divine mother and father, while Ptolemy II and Arsinoë retain their royal names. This scene indicates that Ptolemy III acknowledged his grandparents in their role as the first Ptolemaic dynastic couple, as he provided them, as was usual for deceased pharaohs (fusing with Osiris), with divine positions. The scene designates them as the divine father and mother, reflecting their roles as Osiris and Isis. In contrast, Ptolemy II and Arsinoë are placed in figural religious positions equal to those of Horus and Hathor. The scene, consequently, shows two ruling royal couples, a depiction made possible by the iconographic sleight-of-hand pictorial temporal adjustment, in which the two time periods of the two ruling royal couples come together so that royal persons who were not active at the same time in life can be so in the scenes (pp. 93–103). Ptolemy III thus demonstrates his undeniable ancestry from the initial Ptolemaic couple and shows himself to be the rightful heir of his preceding rulers, Ptolemy II and Arsinoë, at the same time.

In cat. no. 4, the pharaoh obtains the divine royal soul at the time of coronation, which describes a direct entrustment of power commended by the living royal siblings to their successors. Ptolemy II and Arsinoë are portrayed as physically attending the ceremony and as personally transferring their rulership to Ptolemy III as their successor. This transference of kingship is emphasised by the presence of Thoth and Seshat. The scene accentuates not only dynastic power *per se* but also a direct continuation and pure lineage, authorising the king as the earthly manifestations of all divine rulers. Once he finished the coronation ceremonies, Ptolemy III completed the rituals necessary to become a ruler and could symbolically step out of the celestial zone of oblivion (to which he would return once more at the time of his death) and return to the human sphere to claim his kingship.

Ptolemy III's different approaches towards the ancestors (*theoi Adelphoi* and *theoi Soteres*) is emphasised in cat. nos 24–25. Previous chapters have identified the right-side Ptolemaic couple in cat. no. 25 with Ptolemy III and Berenice II at the time of their coronation ceremonies, contradicting previous identifications of the couple with Ptolemy I and Berenice I. To my knowledge, there are no textual or pictorial recognitions of the first Ptolemaic couple on the Gate of Euergetes. Instead, the ruling couple, Ptolemy III and Berenice II, connect themselves with their parents exclusively (in terms of royal ancestry). Scenes attached to cat. no. 24 emphasise this kinship even further, as Ptolemy III receives his Horus name only when he is associated with his parents. As mentioned previously, Berenice II stresses her kinship with the *theoi Adelphoi*, being described (together with Ptolemy III) as deified 'at the head of the gods' (also referring to the divine sibling gods) (*cf.* Quaegebeur 1988, 48, n. 44; 1989, 97). Ptolemy III and Berenice II stressed such an immediate kinship in various scenes of the Gate of Euergetes, accentuating the instant transfer of power from one generation to the next. At the time, the important matter was not that of determining a dynastic lineage from the initial Ptolemaic couple or Alexander the Great. Instead, Ptolemy III and Berenice II chose to validate their continuous rule through their ancestry from Ptolemy II and Arsinoë and the native pantheon.

The figural organisation in cat. no. 18 is completely dissimilar to that in cat. no. 4, as it presents the ruling pharaoh in an offering position facing his divine dynastic family: Horus, Hathor and Harsomtus, followed by his Ptolemaic ancestors. The theme is no longer that of a coronation, but instead is that of a king who performs his duties in sacrificing to his ancestors. The last couple of the scene is identified as the *theoi Soteres*: they are no longer comparable to Osiris and Isis, but with Ptolemaic ancestors in general as they wear the same attributes as the *theoi Euergetai*. The *theoi Adelphoi*, however, are pictorially separated from the others on the basis of their individual iconographic compositions. Whereas the other dynastic scenes express a conventional reconnection with ancestors, depicting the king as he claims his right to the throne, cat. no. 18 illustrates a traditional offering scene, lacking an immediate pictorial reconnection in terms of the object of offering.

In terms of figural arrangement, cat. nos 4 and 18 are distinguished from the other dynastic scenes by the position of the last female figure, Berenice I: she stands in a traditional pose holding an *ankh* and a sceptre, whereas other dynastic scenes show the deceased queen holding her hands in a protective manner. The latter position is interpreted, as suggested above, as Hathoric, corresponding with the protection of the entire dynasty. Cat. nos 4 and 18 refer to Berenice I as the last female figure of the dynastic line, but neither one of the scenes illustrate her as the dynasty's protectress, and her figural position is equivalent to all other female figures in the scenes. Her role as a Ptolemaic ancestor is acknowledged, but she is not entrusted with a Hathoric role.

The public eponymous records were modified during the reign of Ptolemy IV, which is traditionally regarded as the reason for the sporadic, limited reference to the *theoi Soteres* in dynastic scenes (*e.g.* Quaegebeur 1989, 94f.; *cf.* Ashton 2003, 124). The material, however, demonstrates that such a modification had only an indirect impact on the conventional Egyptian settings. Ptolemy IV includes the *theoi Soteres* in cat. no. 18, but prefers to emphasise his kinship with the *theoi Adelphoi* in his coronation scene, here cat. no. 20. Furthermore, Ptolemy I and Berenice I are excluded from all other dynastic scenes which date to Ptolemy IV.[2] This reflects the fundamental difference between the cults addressing the first and second Ptolemaic couples. The *theoi Soteres* are included as ancestors but never as founders, which is a significant distinction. Their successors venerated the first Ptolemaic couple in the same way as they acknowledged the importance of Ramses II and Nectanebo II in Memphis, and respected their divine royal souls as a part of the overall Osirian concept. However, these Egyptian reliefs never recognised them as the physical founders of the Ptolemaic dynasty.

All other dynastic scenes illustrate Arsinoë as the last figure of the scene (thus, contrasting with cat. nos 4 and 18) and thus identify her as the main protectress of the dynastic family. Her official designations describe her as the 'divine mother', 'divine mother of his mothers' and 'royal mother'. Similarly, Ptolemy II is described as the 'divine father' (most dynastic scenes refer to the couple as the *theoi Adelphoi*). They are always pictorially distinguished from additional couples: Arsinoë with her personal crown and Ptolemy with either the *anedjti* crown or the Osirian crown, always as an opposite to the other male ancestors. They are associated with Hathor and Horus, but the pictorial setting also shows a connection with Shu and Tefnut, as the children of Ra, in accordance with their designations as rulers. According to the material, the ancestor cult of the *theoi Adelphoi* followed traditional Egyptian principles of the royal cult, but had a more prominent continuation than most pharaonic forerunners. All scenes post-date the lifetimes of both Ptolemy II and Arsinoë: an important point, because this separates the native Egyptian ancestor cult from the Alexandrian eponymous cult, as Greek sources primarily document a ruler cult of *living* couples.[3] According to the material examined here, the conventional Egyptian iconographic records remained separate from the eponymous Alexandrian accounts throughout the dynasty.

Arsinoë's political importance, as shown in the material, cannot be denied: she is placed in a cultural position that is equivalent to that of her brother-husband. However, it is clear that Arsinoë was not venerated as an individual goddess by her descendants in the Egyptian temples after the reign of Ptolemy II: she was always worshipped as the dynastic mother, as a co-regent, and as the female counterpart to Ptolemy II. This conclusion has a profound significance when comparing the reliefs with other artistic media, such as Egyptian textual records. Arsinoë's individual cult in Memphis, where she was paired with Ptah, is generally acknowledged, and additional sources describe her personal association with a vast number of deities (Thompson 1988; *cf.* Crawford 1980; Quaegebeur 1980; Hölbl 2001, 102). In terms of the dynastic cult, however, Arsinoë did not gain a continuous divine status as an individually venerated goddess equal with the traditional Gods, as far as most public records demonstrate. Instead, the ancient sources that refer to her individual cult originate in a more private sphere. Certainly, this ties in with the interpretation suggested by Quaegebeur (1989, 108). In terms of the dynastic veneration of Arsinoë, she was worshipped in harmony with the native Egyptian conventions of ruler cult: as a co-founder of the true dynastic lineage.

Dynastic scenes validate the legitimacy of a ruling pharaoh. They simultaneously emphasise the importance of the deceased ancestors and their position in history as well as in the eternal celestial sphere. Overall, the dynastic scenes represent Ptolemy IV and Ptolemy VIII as sole benefactors, except for cat. no. 35, which also includes Cleopatra III.[4] The presented offerings are identified as either libation and incense or ointment and cloth. They do not seem to be regulated by an obvious individual positional organisation, although they are always placed conventionally in term of symmetry. Scenes illustrating the *theoi Adelphoi* are, furthermore, always positioned as the top (highest) scene.

The scenes show a continuation of the conventional Egyptian principles of the ruler cult, but fail to provide any detailed information in terms of the priesthood or any additional cultic practicalities. Such information must instead be sought outside the material, in evidence such as priestly burials, such as those of the Memphite priesthood, and the documentation of the cult of Arsinoë recorded on tomb stones.

Invoking/arousing the god

As seen above, the sistrum was an instrument used to invoke and arouse the deities, mainly Hathor. It was not a sacrifice object *per se* but instead an instrument inserted into a scene in order to indicate an active ritual. Consequently, it is included here since it regulates the theme of a scene.

Offerings

Offerings are presented as part of the most frequently illustrated theme of the scenes: an active sacrifice. As a part of the daily temple ritual, priests maintained the cult statues of the gods and presented them with various offerings. Throughout Egyptian history the king was depicted in this position, fulfilling his responsibilities. It was his duty to accomplish the daily rituals, but the pharaoh could delegate his tasks to priests acting on his behalf (Teeter 1997, 149). This section studies the sacrifice of ointment, incense, the figure of Ma'at, textile, wine and water, the field of reeds, the ceremonial collar, libation and *hes* vessel, the smiting of enemies, offering trays and the *sekhem* sceptre. As mentioned above, offering objects are differentiated from hand-held objects on the basis of their direct and indirect effects on the theme. While hand-held objects are rather impersonal, and thus common to all, offering items can express a direct message from the benefactor to the beneficiary. The benefactors that present offerings are almost always identified as royal persons: in cases where the benefactor is not royal, the scene reverses in theme, showing a god returning a gift or actively participating in a royal ceremony.

Incense

Incense is the most frequently depicted offering in the material, being documented in fifteen scenes (Table 15). It is subdivided into three variants, of which are indicative of an active position on the part of the benefactor. The first type is illustrated as a censer stand placed in front of the benefactor, usually reaching to the knees of a standing pharaoh (cat. nos 2L–R, 5, 14–15R, 17, 21, 23, 27–28, 30, 35). It is generally depicted with a long and narrow shaft, curved and widened at both top and bottom (Figure 61). This item is never held by Arsinoë, and is instead always connected with a male ruler/benefactor. The benefactor is physically connected with the censer stand by the occasional act of pouring a libation upon it. Scenes of this kind, in which the censer stand is central to the offering act, are categorised here as dynastic, as the act links the benefactor with his deceased ancestors. The censer stand itself does not seem to hold any deeper symbolic significance. The object connected with it, such as a lotus flower placed upon it, however, acts as a direct connection, determining the setting or the theme of a scene. Otherwise, the censer stand is disconnected from the benefactor, and as such regularly holds a *nemset* vessel and a flower. All scenes with a physically disconnected stand date to the reign of Ptolemy II, except for cat. no. 15, which dates to Arsinoë's lifetime. Arsinoë is always illustrated as a beneficiary, except for cat. no. 15, where she accompanies Ptolemy II as a benefactor.

The second type included in this group is shown as a small hand-held vessel illustrated with one or several flames or pellets (cat. nos 1L, 21) (Figure 62). The third type consists of a small incense cup held by a long and stylised arm (censer) (cat. nos 17, 24, 35). The arm is generally decorated with a falcon head (Figures 63–64). Archaeological evidence suggests that the censer arm was made of bronze and, in addition to its metal hand and falcon head, it was depicted with a cartouche in its centre holding the incense or pellets (Fischer 1963; Beinlich 1978; Vassilika 1989, 105). Vassilika (1989) suggests that the censer arm could be read as a rebus for the king, where the falcon head symbolises a pharaoh's Horus name.

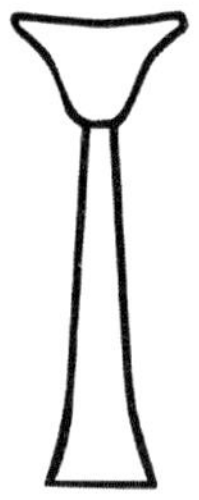
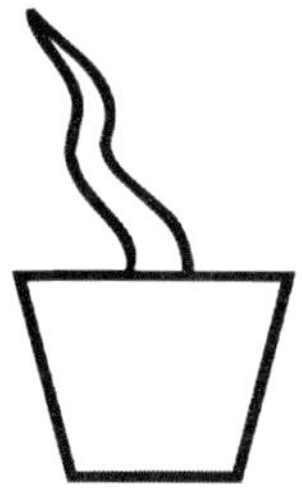
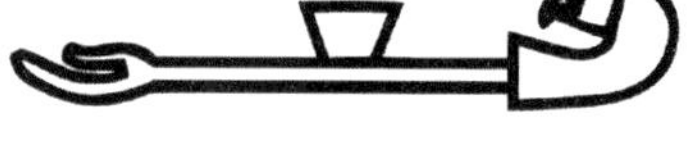
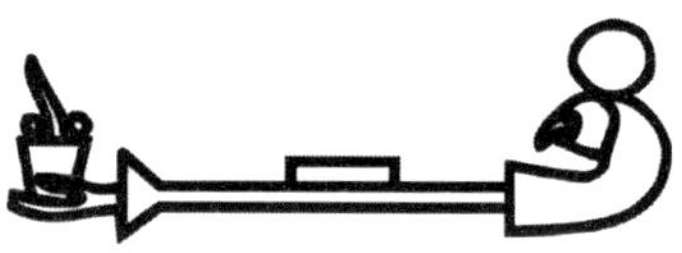

From left to right: Figure 61. Censing: Hieroglyphic sign R36; Figure 62. Censing: Hieroglyphic sign R7; Figure 63. Censing: Hieroglyphic sign Q 39; Figure 64. Censing: Hieroglyphic sign Q 6C.

ILLUSTRATION	DESIGNATION	SCENES	TOTAL NO. SCENES
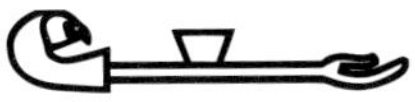	Incense	1L, 2L–R, 5, 14–15R, 17, 21, 23–24, 27–28, 30, 35	15
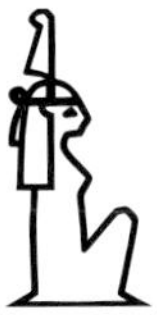	Figure of Ma'at	2R, 26L–R	3
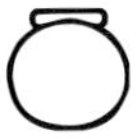	Wine and water	2L, 10–11, 31–33	6
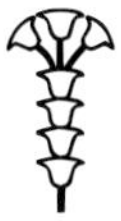	Flowers (includes the flowers that are placed above a censer stand)	1L, 2L–R, 5, 14–15R, 23, 27–28, 30, 35	12
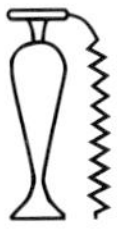	Libation and *hes* vessel	17, 21, 35	3
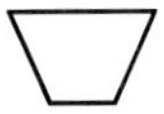	Ointment	1L, 16, 19	3
	Offering tray/table	18	1
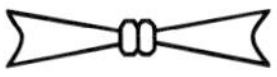	Textile band or clothing	1L, 8 (?), 16, 19	4
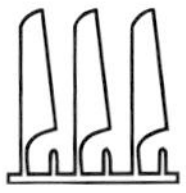	Field of reeds	5, 14, 27	3
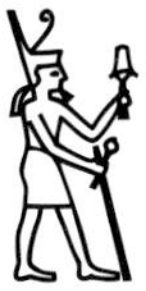	*Sekhem* sceptre	18	1
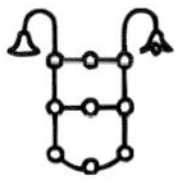	Ceremonial collar	15L–R	2
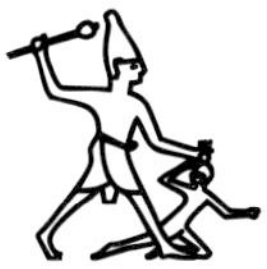	Slaying enemies	3	1
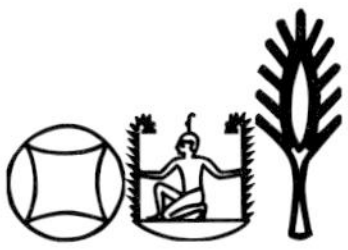	Other offerings, including unrecognisable and unidentified items	1L, 2L, 6–7, 13	5

Table 15. The most frequent offering objects.

It is generally acknowledged that incense offerings symbolised the ancestor cult, in which the benefactor justifies his divine and dynastic legitimacy and legacy (Bell 1985, 283; *cf.* Winter 1978; Quaegebeur 1989; Vassilika 1989, 104f.; *LÄ* V, 83–6). Censing had a primary meaning of purification closely connected with divine fragrance or sweat (Plut. *Alex.* 4. 4–5; *P. Mil. Vogl.* VIII 309, AB 36; *cf.* Lurker 2002, 39). Incense could symbolise the eye of Horus and was also used in funerary ceremonies and cultic activities (Vassilika 1989, 105). There is no unique connection between the incense and the crown of Arsinoë.

The figure of Ma'at

Three scenes of Arsinoë show the figure of Ma'at as an offering (cat. nos 2R and 26L–R). However, Arsinoë never holds this item personally, as it is always held by a male benefactor. Ma'at is depicted in a crouching/squatting position placed on a *nb* sign (⌓), and is held in the royal palm in all scenes. Cat. nos 2R and 26L illustrate Ma'at with an ostrich feather crowning her head as her only attribute; cat. no. 26R depicts the goddess with a crown feather and with an *ankh* in her hand.

The sacrifice of Ma'at is closely associated with royal and divine rulership, through which the benefactor is proven to uphold universal order or truth. The figure of Ma'at symbolises the transitory power of kingship, initially from Ra to Horus and subsequently to the pharaoh (Derchain-Urtel 1994, 44). Ma'at personified universal truth, justice, morality and order. She represented a true and pure way of living, and it is through her that the soul of the deceased can continue to the next life after the weighing of the soul against her feather (Roberts 1997, 32–7; Karenga 2004). It has been suggested elsewhere that the offering of Ma'at was meant to protect the pharaoh from evil (Fairman 1958; Vassilika 1989, 106).

An example of Ma'at as a figure of sacrifice is provided by cat. no. 26 (Figure 65). The scene is located on a lintel block on the eastern gate at Karnak, commonly referred to as the Gate of Nectanebo, leading into the (back part of the) temple complex. The two sections of the scene represent Upper and Lower Egypt, as demonstrated by the crowns worn by Ptolemy II. The right section (cat. no. 26R) shows Ptolemy II presenting the figure of Ma'at to Amun, Khonsu and Arsinoë. The left section (cat. no. 26L) depicts the same ruler accompanied by a female figure, again offering the figure of Ma'at, here to Amun, Mut and Arsinoë. In the overall scene, Arsinoë enters the roles of both mother and daughter as she replaces Mut on the right side and Khonsu on the left. Arsinoë's positions in the two sections show a goddess fully incorporated in the divine family, in a Hathoric mode as daughter (of Amun and Mut), wife (of Amun) and mother (of Khonsu).

The scene stresses an intentional dynastic and divine lineage expressed by the symbolism of Ma'at. Arsinoë functions as a link between the spheres. The scene has a dynastic association, but it does not describe the ancestor cult as it is recorded above. Instead, this scene is associated with a direct royal cult, establishing the personal cult of Arsinoë. Such a dynastic connection between a ruling king and his deified queen is supported by the presence of an additional female figure who stands behind Ptolemy in the left section, determined as Arsinoë in her queenly role. Cat. no. 26L, thereby, relates to cat. no. 1, which depicts Arsinoë as a queen presenting offerings to herself as a goddess (*cf.* Quaegebeur 1988, 46, and the scene of Ramses II where he is positioned as both benefactor and beneficiary). Her double appearance strengthens the dynastic theme in which the queen is fully incorporated in the Egyptian religious practice, acting as the manifestation of Hathor and as a god's wife at the same time.

There are no obvious associations between the figure of Ma'at and the crown of Arsinoë, nor with those worn by the male figures (both benefactor and beneficiary). For example, in scenes that include Ma'at, Ptolemy II wears a *khepresh* (war crown) in cat. no. 2R and the white and red crowns respectively in cat. nos 26L–R. Nor are there any evident connections between Ma'at and the figural arrangements in the scenes. The king is located on the right side as well as the left, and sometimes, but far from always, he is the tallest figure of the scene. The total number of figures differs in the scenes, with a minimum of three.

Wine and water

Wine, water or milk offerings (Figures 66–70) are documented in five scenes with Arsinoë (cat. nos 2L, 10–11, 31–32). Cat. no. 33 shows a single rounded vessel,

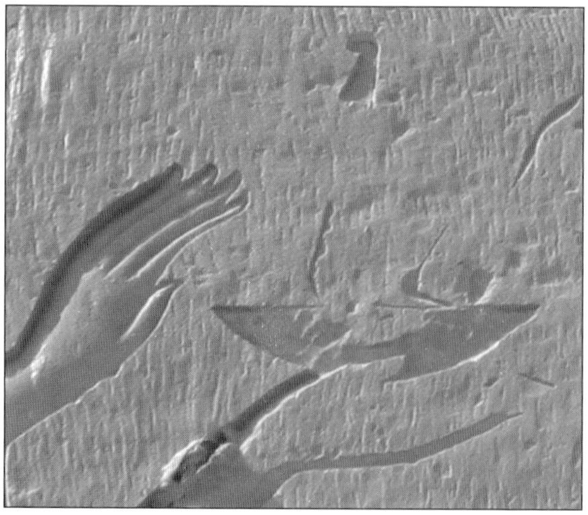

Figure 65. Unfinished figure of Ma'at in cat. no. 26L. Note her crown feather.

generally described as a water container (Vassilika 1989, 111). Cat. nos 2L, 10 and 11 illustrate a smaller circular wine vessel. Two of the Philae scenes, cat. nos 31–32, illustrate a pharaoh (Ptolemy II) holding a tray with four *nemset* vessels of water. As with many previous offering items, there seems to be no obvious or unique connection with the crowns worn by Arsinoë.

Wine is recorded in various offering lists as associated with fertility and life (Petrie 1923, 135; 1927, nos 393–400). It was used during festivals and official ceremonies, also favoured by aristocrats and royalty (*e.g.* Poo 1995; Murray 2000). Osiris is occasionally described as the 'Lord of wine' (Lurker 2002, 130), but the primary association is with Hathor. In the story of the *Destruction of Humanity*, Ra sends out Hathor in her role as the eye to punish his enemies (Vischak 2002, 159f.). The goddess changes character and becomes the savaging Sekhmet. She rages against all things possible. When Ra witnessed the destruction caused he regretted his decision and tried to stop Hathor. The goddess, however, was in a bloodthirsty mood and could not be stopped. Ra then flooded the land with beer and wine, coloured red in order to resemble blood, which attracted and intoxicated Hathor. As she drank the blood-red wine she became the 'Drunken One', and in this persona she was celebrated annually. Therefore, wine was in many ways connected with Hathor in her role as the drunken mistress, the goddess of love, music and dance, venerated in her cult centre in Dendera.

Water is considered to epitomise purity and was used in purifying ceremonies connected with crowning or the Sed festival. Like so many other offerings, water symbolised life and rebirth, referring to the wealth and fertility brought by the inundation (Kees 1953, 66; Vassilika 1989, 105). Osiris was the main god associated with annual flooding of the Nile, and was as such worshipped as 'Lord of the water' (Lurker 2002, 127f.). Water was the substance originating in the primeval matter from which all things alive were considered to derive. Through its primeval position as life-giver it was associated with the divine maternal role and femininity. Priests, royal persons and cult statues were purified with water believed to hold divine essence, bringing them closer to divine eternity.

Libation and hes vessels

As a continuation of the jugs described above, libations and *hes* vessels form a category on their own. The body of a *hes* vessel, as Figures 71–75 show, was originally based on the shape of an *ankh*, showing an elongated and narrow lower body, rounded shoulders, narrow neck and a wide mouth. It is primarily shown in the material as a vessel holding libations. A libation is characterised by one or several zigzag lines demonstrating the liquid poured from a *hes*, or occasionally a smaller circular vessel. Cat. nos 17, 21 and 35 show a libation being poured from a *hes* vessel upon a censer stand. The symbolism of libation has been clarified

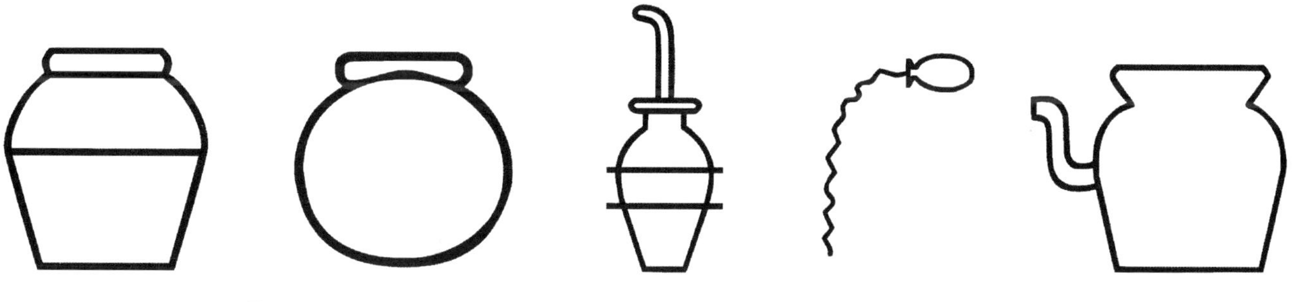

Figures 66–70. (From left to right) Water and wine vessels: Hieroglyphica W-list.

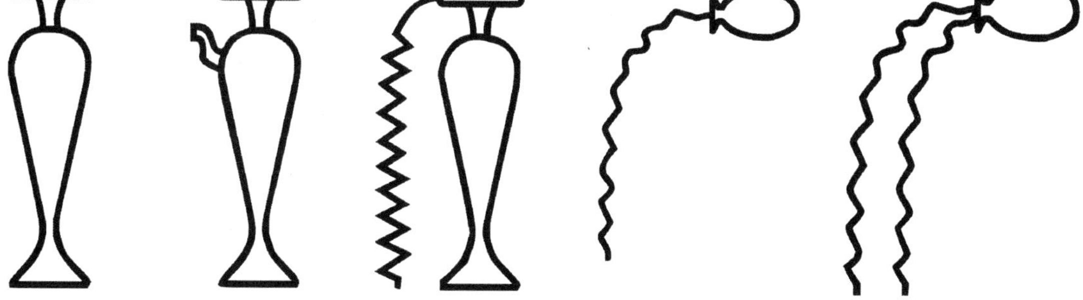

Figures 71–75. (From left to right) Libation vessels: Hieroglyphica W-list.

in the previous section (*cf.* Vassilika 1989, 105; Blackman 1912). There is no apparent association between these items and the crown worn by Arsinoë.

Flowers

Table 15 lists twelve scenes in which flowers form offerings (Figures 76–77). They occur as an individual hand-held plant (cat. no. 28), but the majority of the scenes illustrate flowers as an additional element placed on top of censer stands (cat. nos 2L–R, 5, 14–15R, 23, 27–28, 30). Cat. no. 35 illustrates hand-held flowers arranged in a slightly bent columned bouquet, while cat. no. 1 depicts a lotus in the shape of a columned vertical plant without a stalk. A lotus placed above a censer stand apparently indicates the nature of the incense. Similarly, those in cat. no. 1L may be interpreted as indicating the physical nature of the (scent of the) ointment which Ptolemy II strokes on the nose of Banebdjedet.

The lotus flower is traditionally associated with primeval mother goddesses – that is, Hathor/Nut, who gives birth to the sun each morning (*e.g.* Pinch 2002, 158). The blue lotus opens up into full bloom with the sunrise, closing again at sunset and withdrawing below the water's surface only to resurface and bloom once more the following morning (Lurker 2002, 77f.). Consequently, the ancient Egyptians associated the lotus with the daily journey of the solar disc, and as such it was designated as 'the redolent flower, the soul of Ra' (Armour 2001, 1). As the personification of the morning sun, symbolising rebirth and rejuvenation, Harsomtus is depicted as a naked child sitting inside a bloomed lotus (*LÄ* V, 1080f.; Pinch 2002, Lotus), while Ihy is described as 'the child who shines in the lotus' (Pinch 2002, 158).

In general, flowers were believed to contain divine fragrance, or godly essence.[5] As a bouquet, flowers could assume the shape of *ankh*s or stems crowned with *ankh*s. By offering this item, the pharaoh was seen as a benefactor of life (Vassilika 1989, 111; *LÄ* I, 837–40). There is no obvious connection between the flower and the crown of Arsinoë.

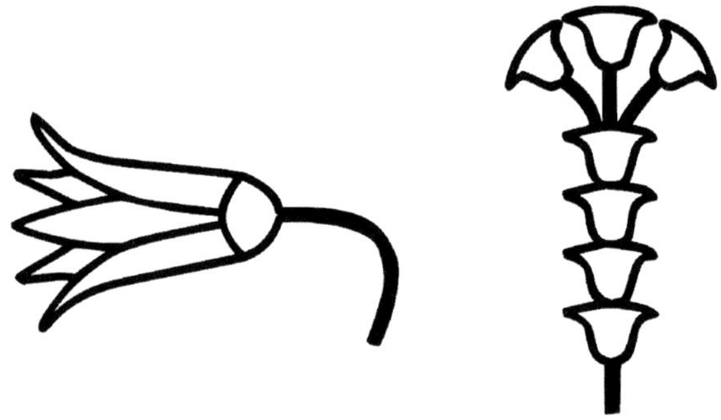

Figures 76 and 77. Variant of flower: Hieroglyphica M-list.

Ointment

Three scenes (cat. nos 1L, 16, 19) include as an offering a small cup containing ointment. Cat. no. 1L demonstrates that ointment could also be held immediately in the hand instead of in a cup; here it is described in the text as to be placed on the nose of Banebdjedet. Cat. nos 16 and 19 combine ointment with a piece of folded cloth, symbolising daily temple purifications. In these scenes, Arsinoë always wear her more official crown (the crown with ram horns located on top of the red crown's platform).

The ancient Egyptians used a broad spectrum of oils and waxes for religious ceremonies and personal body care. Ointment was mainly used in purification rites associated with temple or burial ceremonies, and was placed on cult statues after their daily cleansing (Lurker 2002, 27). It was based on oil or wax mixed with scents of flowers, herbs, aromatic wood, spices or myrrh (Serpico and White 2000, *passim*, esp. 390). It was considered magical as it was connected with Ra, who wept tears in the shape of bees (Lurker 2002, 32). The scent of oils and waxes was also interpreted as a divine fragrance through which any given benefactor shared the qualities of the god. As such, ointment is depicted as raised to the nose or, as in cat. no. 1, stroked on the nose of a deity.

Offering trays and tables

One scene includes a hand-held offering tray or an offering table upon which is placed an assortment of food, flowers and fluids. The reader is referred to each item analysed here.

Textile band or clothing

In the material examined here, cloth as a gift to the gods is rendered as a looped textile band. It is shown in three scenes (cat. nos 1L, 16, 19; possibly four if including cat. no. 8). Cloths (*mnḫt*) are mainly depicted as two folded bands of textile held in one or both hands of the worshipper, and were used in the daily rituals of dressing cultic statues (Blackman and Fairman 1943; Vassilika 1989, 110). The material occasionally shows folded cloth combined with ointment (cat. nos 16, 19).

Field of reeds

Three scenes (cat. nos 5, 14, 27) depict a field of reeds (*sḫt*) as a sacrifice. This signifies the growing fields in which Hathor protects the baby Horus, and is a symbol of fertility, rejuvenation and protection. The hieroglyphic sign for the field indicates an offer made in order to secure abundance and power (Gardiner's sign-list (1957): M20). In the material, and also in general, the field of reeds is illustrated as three fully grown reeds separated by three stubs representing incipient reeds. The traditional interpretation of this sign is associated with eternal life and rebirth. The presence of the field of reeds in cat. no. 5 is associated with the theme of the scene, showing Ptolemy II celebrating the newly incarnated ram god alongside the recently deceased Queen Arsinoë, who is reborn as a full divine character. There is no evident association between this item and the crown of Arsinoë.

Sekhem stave

The *sekhem* stave () is represented in one scene: cat. no. 18 illustrates Ptolemy IV holding a *sekhem* stave in his right hand and a mace and an additional small, straight sceptre in his left hand. A large offering table presented with various types of food and fluids is placed in front of him. The scene has a dynastic theme, as in it Ptolemy IV reconnects with his deceased ancestors. He wears an *atef* crown placed within the red crown. In general, the *sekhem* stave is held in the right hand, frequently in a horizontal position. Most rulers also grasp a mace and an additional sceptre/stave in the opposite hand. The stave was traditionally utilised in both temple and funerary rituals. It is described as being held in the right hand and waved four or five times over the offerings as the ritual was carried out (Gardiner 1957, 509).

Ceremonial collar

The presentation of a ceremonial collar is illustrated in one scene (two sections). Necklaces are depicted in a broad spectrum of variants which are differentiated mainly by the numbers and styles of beads or decorating pattern. The pectoral medallion symbolised the sun and the moon, and, as with jewellery in general, the necklace was believed to contain superhuman, magical powers. The collar is connected with the daily rituals of dressing the cult statues (*e.g.* Andrews 1994). The two sections of cat. no. 15(L–R) depict Ptolemy II wearing a double crown while presenting a ceremonial collar. In cat. no. 15L, the collar consists of five rows of beads, while 15R shows four. The collars have a rounded bottom part. The collars are shown as 'open', ready to be placed on the beneficiary's neck (). The two collars recorded here have undecorated terminals. There is no unique association between the sacrificed item and the crown of Arsinoë.

Smiting enemies

The theme of slaying one or several enemies by spear is illustrated in one scene (cat. no. 3). A single enemy is illustrated with his hands tied behind his back, and is positioned on his knees in front of Ptolemy V. He is a male, possibly fully naked (otherwise with only a thin strap around his waist), and is shown with shoulder-long hair and a beard. Ptolemy V wears a double crown and is accompanied by his spouse as they greet their deceased ancestors.

Conclusion

This chapter has discussed the various religious rituals, including offerings, that are shown in the thirty-six scenes examined here. Of the thematic settings, the most frequently illustrated is an active act of sacrifice, in which a pharaoh presents objects as an active benefactor facing the deities and/or his deceased ancestors. In addition to the act of presenting offerings, the discussion here documented scenes of a ruler adoring or standing inactively before the deities. Although these differ in their setting from the active offering, they are essentially of a similar nature, with an aimed direction from the ruler to the gods. The scenes presented in material of a pharaoh smiting captured enemies are dissimilar to the active offering scenes in that the pharaoh proves himself as a ruling king capable of bringing victory to Egypt, while simultaneously keeping the country safe.

A few scenes have been classified in accordance with a theme of rejuvenation and crowning. These scenes demonstrate a reversed setting, where the immediate focus is placed on the ruler rather than the deities. Generally, the divine figures of Thoth and Seshat are located on the same side as the king, whereas the divine royal couple, Horus and Hathor, and possibly also the deceased ancestors, are found on the opposite side.

The ancestors are also incorporated in scenes classified as dynastic. A ruling pharaoh addresses his deceased ancestors with or without the divine royal couple. These scenes primarily depict the pharaoh with individual previous ruling couples, directly or indirectly associated with surrounded scenes illustrating other ancestral couples. Other scenes show the ancestors in a line, where the founders of the family are located at the very back.

The sistrum was studied above (pp. 58–59) as a hand-held object used to invoke/arouse the deity. This chapter emphasises the earlier conclusion: that it was an object ruling an active act performed by the benefactor, indicating a living ruler.

Most importantly, the study of thematic settings confirms that there is a symbolic meaning to the varying placement of the ram horns in the crown of Arsinoë. All scenes that have been classified as dynastic in this chapter occur with the official variant of the crown of Arsinoë, which shows the ram horns on top of the red crown's platform. Other thematic settings seem to lack such an association.

The discussion subsequently moved on to a study of offerings indicating a theme of the scenes. The most frequently depicted offering is incense, which has been divided into three categories on the basis of shape. Regardless of its form, incense connects a ruler with his divine and royal lineage and, therefore, it is not surprising to find this object in most dynastic scenes. The censer stand itself appears to hold no greater symbolism, although it acts as a sign of what was intended by the scene; the communicated message is, rather, contained in the object placed upon it.

The figure of Ma'at is associated with kingship and the upholding of universal order, and has the most profound importance for Egyptian concepts of truth. It was utilised throughout Egyptian art as an indicator of divine royal continuation, linking the ruling couple with their deceased ancestors as well as with the divine solar force himself.

Further discussion here has focused on ointment, wine and water, libations, ceremonial collars, speared enemies, offering trays and the *sekhem* stave. Most importantly, it has been emphasised that these offerings are associated with the eternal cycle, incorporating rebirth, fertility and rejuvenation. All offerings included in the material have not only a profound mythic anchoring but also a more practical function, as they are parts of the daily temple rituals. The symbolic values of the offerings are fundamentally similar to each other and they function, primarily, to establish a bond between the benefactor and the beneficiary. The offerings very rarely show a unique connection with the crown of Arsinoë. Furthermore, it has been elucidated throughout that there are very few associations between the crowns worn by the benefactor and the offerings which he presents.

Notes

1 The term 'line' is used here to describe a position where the figures are placed as in a queue or row.

2 Compare the above-cited hieroglyphic text that describe Ptolemy IV as beloved of the local gods, the *theoi Adelphoi*, *theoi Euergetai*, and including also his own deified self as the *theoi Philopatores* together with Arsinoë III. Evidently, the *theoi Soteres* are excluded (*cf.* Quaegebeur 1989, 101 with n. 48).

3 It is generally accepted that the cult of the *theoi Adelphoi* was institutionalised already during Arsinoë's lifetime, *c.* 272 BC (*e.g. P. Hib.* II 199; Clarysse and van der Veken 1983, 4f.; Quaegebeur 1989, 95).

4 Owing to the poor state of cat. no. 35 it is difficult to absolutely identify all the figures. The ruling couple are identified as Ptolemy VIII and Cleopatra. Identified also are the *theoi Philopatores*, *theoi Euergetai* and *theoi Adelphoi*. The first male figure of the upper scene is described in the text as Ptolemy VI Philometor. The designation of the first male figure of the lower scene states only 'Ptolemy', relating to either Ptolemy I (if the couple behind him is the *theoi Epiphanes*), Ptolemy V (if the couple is the *theoi Soteres*) or Ptolemy Eupator, the brother of the ruling king. It is very unlikely that the figure represents Ptolemy I as Berenice I is absent. Instead, the most probable alternative identification is Ptolemy Eupator. The figure is depicted as a king, not as a prince, indicating a history of rule. Judging from the position of the *theoi Adelphoi*, as the last couple of the lower register, it is not likely that the fourth couple (on the upper part) represents the *theoi Soteres*. According to Egyptian conventions, the *theoi Soteres* would have been placed behind the *theoi Adelphoi*. With their position, as being the couple after the *theoi Philopatores*, it is most likely that the couple is the *theoi Epiphanes*.

5 Compare the hieroglyphic title of Arsinoë in cat. no. 1 (M) 'She who fills the palace with her beauty', corresponding to the divine fragrance (*cf.* Troy 1986, A4).

Chapter 7

Size, position and time

In Chapter 2, the historical background of the Egyptian geometric order, the artistic principles with which contemporary artists worked and the new analytical method to be applied to these principles here were presented. Chapter 6 analysed the thematic settings of the scenes. These ideas are further explored below in a study of the concepts of size, position and time using a new approach to the viewing of Egyptian reliefs by modern observers. 'Relative relations' in art refers to the adjustment of the size and placement of pictorial details in order to convey a specific cultural aspect or message to the viewer. The concepts of size and position have been investigated by other authors, where they were referred to as 'relative scaling' and 'relative placement'; these terms will also be used here (Wilkinson 1994, chapters 2–3 (including scale and position); Robins and Fowler 1994, 8 (scale); Bianchi 2004, 117 (scale); *cf.* Baines 1976, 14; 1991). While size is a frequently occurring topic of discussion in relation to Egyptian art, as is evident from these citations, examinations of position are less noticeable in modern publications. In this chapter, furthermore, a new approach will be introduced that develops the already established concepts of size and position and expands them with additional analytical instruments in order to enable a reassessment of ways in which to read Egyptian art. Most important is a new tool for measuring the importance and hierarchic order of the figures in a scene based on their complete structure, using the height of the crown as the uppermost level of comparison. In terms of Egyptian reliefs, the concept of time is a topic which is generally unexplored.[1]

Whereas relative scaling and placement are evident pictorially to even an untutored eye, the recognition of temporal adjustment can come only as the result of an iconographic interpretation.[2] The concepts of size and positional are applied as a theoretical foundation when approaching time: thus, all three aspects are interconnected and occasionally mutually dependent.

Relative relations in art, as approached here, are based on an ancient system of related horizontal lines, occasionally combined with a grid. Traditionally, the Egyptians used grids and horizontal lines when creating a scene in order to determine the correct measurements, size and position of each figure. At the same time, the grids enabled the artist to actively regulate individual details in order to emphasise a certain section or the overall message of the scene, following encoded principles recognised by contemporaries. As there were no obvious attempts to reproduce natural details in a three-dimensional scene, every pictorial detail was depicted in its most recognisable visual form (some being more recognisable than others) and placed in a harmonious arrangement following the grids or horizontal lines (the enhanced images of Figures 78–79 demonstrate traditional examples of the application of a grid system). Although the importance of the ancient mathematical and geometrical background of these grids/lines is clear, they are applied here entirely as an instrument for measuring the figural positions as indicators of status.

Egyptian art was in many ways different from modern ideas of art. Although sometimes applying realistic elements and proper proportions, the Egyptians often adjusted details of each figure. These adjustments occurred in all artistic media, from reliefs to small shabty figurines placed inside the tombs by commemorating family members. The two-dimensional figures of the material are structured in agreement with an assortment of associated pictorial elements. The particulars (and whole figures) could be adjusted in size and position in order to emphasise a specific cultural aspect, or to show a fusion between two individual gods (*e.g.* Amun-Min, Harakhte (Horus and Ra); *cf.* Arsinoë-Isis-Hathor). Horus, for example, wears the double feather plume with a solar disc when he appears as an adult Harsomtus, but the male Edfu crown (the double crown prior to the Ptolemaic period) in his royal position as Horus of Edfu (Nilsson 2010, cat. no. 74 for Harsomtus and cat. no. 56 for Horus of Edfu). As described in the Introduction, each image was carefully arranged in terms of space, scale and contextual composition in order to communicate a comprehensive message to the viewer. The (re)adjustment of such factors conveys the relative importance of each figure and the associations between the individual characters. The fundamental principles of administrating

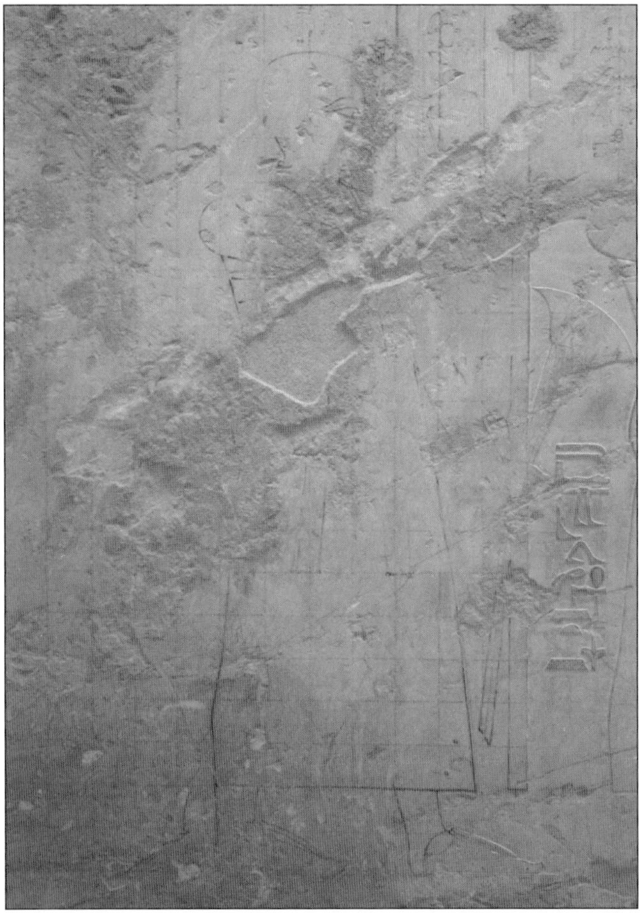

Figure 78. Detail of grid from the Tomb of Ramose, Valley of the Nobles. The image shows the remains of an original red-painted grid, in which the figures were placed in accordance with the artistic principles, and demonstrates how the lower outline of the kilt follows the horizontal line, and the figure's feet are placed along another horizontal line. Photo by J. Ward.

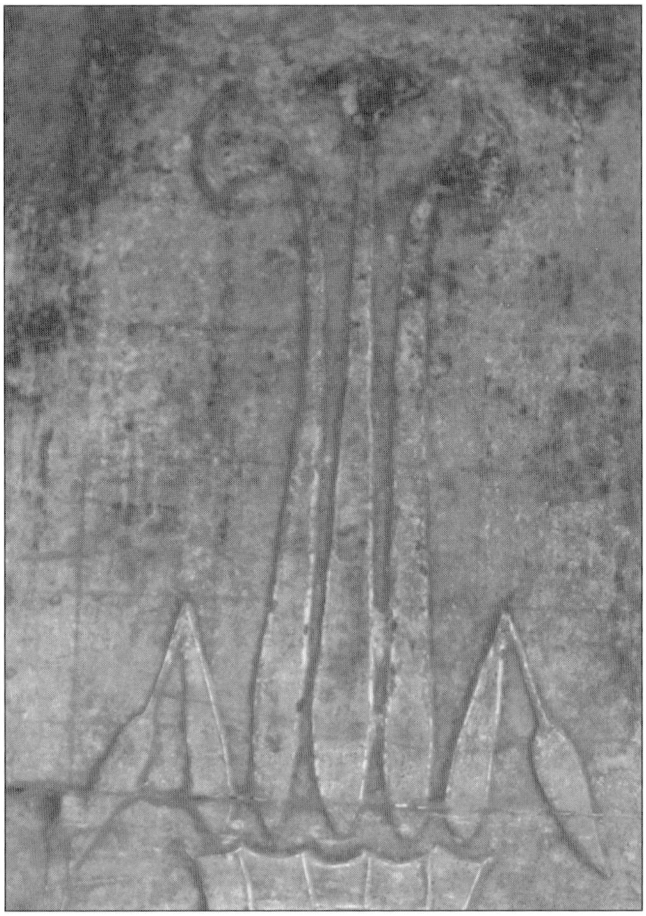

Figure 79. Example of grid: a Nile crown worn by the god Hapi, Temple of Edfu. The image shows the remains of an original red-painted grid, in which the figures were placed in accordance with the artistic principles, and shows how the horizontal lines regulate the upper and lower outlines of the plants.

elements make the tallest figure the most important: this concept will be reassessed here in terms of ways of measuring full figural size (Robins 2008, 21f.).

Relative scaling

Relative scaling refers to an adjustment of size of any given figure or pictorial element in order to emphasise a hierarchic order. This order determines the relative height of the figures, and can regulate all minor details as well. The cow horns of the crown of Arsinoë, for example, are occasionally scaled down to the size of an amulet or, alternatively, enlarged. It is generally accepted that the tallest figure of the scene has the greatest hierarchic status, a rank previously measured in accordance with a horizontal line following the top point of the head, the tip of the nose or the fringe (Bianchi 1988, cat. 14; Vassilika 1989, 14, n. 74; Wilkinson 1994, chapter 2).[3] Wilkinson (1994, 39) once stated that individual differences in height were the result of pure artistic freedom, but the modern viewer has to consider that the artist was heavily influenced by the intended message of the image, to which the figures included had to conform. By alterating the sizes of pictorial units within a scene the hierarchic structure was easier to recognise and the importance of each figure was clarified.

Relative scaling may also relate to age differentiation. Children and youths were distinguished from adults by their smaller size. Youngsters, generally represented by the gods Harpocrates, Ihy and Harsomtus, measure half the size of the adults in most scenes in which they appear. As an example, cat. no. 32 illustrates Ptolemy II sacrificing to

Isis, a child and Arsinoë. The youngster is smaller than the adults. However, his identity remains debatable because the text does not identify him: he could be interpreted as either Harpocrates, son of Isis, or the rejuvenated adolescent aspect of Ptolemy II. Similarly, a (human) wife could be reduced in size, being generally smaller when standing next to her husband – indeed, sometimes hardly reaching up to his knees. This diminution, while acknowledging a queen as the royal element expressing femininity in this dualistic culture, conveys the king's ultimate status as the more important figure.

As discussed in the Introduction, each pictorial element was ruled by the harmony of space and scale, and every individual grid-square and horizontal line was controlled by mathematical and geometrical orders (Lepsius 1897, 234; Kjelland 1955, 8f.). The order of the horizontal lines followed four main bodily particulars, and included a base line upon which the figures stand, a knee line, a shoulder line and a head line (measured more or less from the top of the head); additional lines were occasionally arranged in conformity with the breast, navel, hip and calf (*e.g. LÄ* II, 1201f.; the latter lines are referred to as supplementary rather than as direct references). These traditional orders, however, lack a horizontal line adequately binding all crowns together, as can be seen in the material, which contains a great variety of crown compositions in different styles and sizes. Therefore, a method has been developed here which incorporates the crown as an instrument and element of individualism, as the most obvious item that can determine a comprehensible and visible differentiation in terms of height. The ancient horizontal lines are thus used as tools to measure and determine the connections between individual pictorial elements, while the 'crown line' is applied in order to establish the hierarchic structure.

This study uses original photographic reproductions, over which the crown line and a series of horizontal lines are drawn, following the bodily elements mentioned, in order to present a basic correspondence between the particulars. A base line, drawn in accordance with the physical connection to the ground, follows the feet of the figures. Seated figures are measured by the lower outline of their thrones. Exceptions include youngsters or smaller figures (such as Harpocrates), who occasionally stand on a podium or another pictorial element, which are measured as the thrones. The lines of the base, calf, knee, hip, navel, breast, shoulder and head (the calf, hip, navel and breast according to their centred point, and the shoulders and head in agreement with their uppermost point) in general follow the adult figures of the scenes and are common for all, rarely showing any individual inconsistencies. If such do occur, the relevant horizontal line is based on the higher of the points/figures. However, minor differentiation between the figures in terms of any one of the bodily lines cannot be considered sufficient to indicate a hierarchic order.

The use of the head line as a traditional basis for measuring individual importance is commonly referred to as 'isocephaly', described as 'the characteristic of depicting heads of figures at the same level, as in a painting' (Wilkinson 1994, 46; Head 2008, 514f.; *cf.* Vassilika 1989, 14, n. 74). This regulation is generally believed to prevent figures from looking down at one another, an interpretation primarily based on modern conceptions of social behaviour (Wilkinson 1994, 46f.). The head line is not an appropriate instrument to utilise when establishing a hierarchic structure of a scene, however, as its main aim was to regulate the position of the head, in the same way that the other lines regulated other body parts. Here, the crown is not separated from the head of a complete figure and consequently the head line is employed as a supplementary guide rather than a fundamental demarcation of social or other significance, with the crown line finally denoting each figure's status relative to one another.

The crown line

The use of the crown line applies to Egyptian reliefs exclusively. It is based on the highest peak or detail of the highest crown(s) in a given scene and, from it, the intended structural figural hierarchy may be calculated according to the differences in height of surrounding crowns. In other words, the figure wearing the highest crown is the most important figure of the scene. As demonstrated above, each unit of a crown composition had an individual symbolic value; these communicated a joint message when placed together. As each figure received a personal crown, he/she obtained his/her hierarchic position in the full setting. A figure's size could be increased by the utilisation of the crown as a non-regulated element of scale. The crown of Arsinoë was created for the queen solely and explicitly. It distinguished her from any surrounding female figures and strengthened her position in the scene.

An example from the material will serve to demonstrate the importance of the crown line as an instrument. Cat. no. 26L (Figure 80) illustrates Ptolemy II facing Amun (-Ra), Mut and Arsinoë. In this relief the male figures are physically incomplete, but their crowns are completed and fully visible. Their identities are established in the hieroglyphic text. Amun was one of Egypt's most important deities, and it

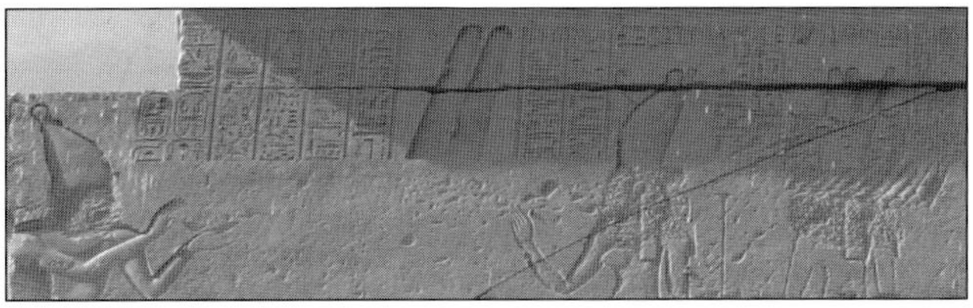

Figure 80. Detail of cat. no. 26L, showing the differentiation in height in terms of a crown line.

was essential to emphasise his prominence in illustrations. The scene shows him wearing his traditional crown – a tall double feather plume which is the tallest of all crowns in the scene: therefore, based on the evaluation of the crown line, Amun is the most important figure of the scene.

The crown line may also be invaluable in dealing with observed inconsistencies in the use of isocephaly in Egyptian art. As noted above, Wilkinson (1994, 46) states that isocephaly was applied in order to prevent figures from looking down at one another. However, the two uppermost horizontal lines of cat. no. 11 (Figure 81) show problems with isocephaly: the top of Ptolemy II's head is slightly higher than the heads of Arsinoë and Hathor, and far higher than those of Horus and Sarapis. In fact, the head of the pharaoh reaches the same level as the solar crown of Sarapis. Evidently, the head line fails to organise the figures adequately in accordance with a common horizontal line, although the shoulder line does. Such a discrepancy could indicate that the relief was created in haste. More importantly, it demonstrates that the theoretical foundation of isocephaly is inadequate and needs reconsideration. When the crown line is employed in order to address the discrepancy in the head line, however, it is clear that the figure of Horus is comparable in height to the king and that the king and Horus thus hold the highest rank within the scene, with Arsinoë third.

Cat. no. 13 (Figure 82) is a further example of a scene with a hierarchic structure on which the application of a crown line might shed new light. The scene depicts Ptolemy II and Arsinoë, and has been a topic of an ongoing scholarly debate regarding the placement of the figures and the indicated social positions. Quaegebeur (1971b, 239; 1971a) has argued that Arsinoë has a superior role based on her placement on the left side, where she stands in the position occupied by the 'beneficiary' and also faces right, symbolising dominance, as discussed in the Introduction. However, owing to Ptolemy's position as the higher figure according to the rules of isocephaly, Bianchi (1988, cat. 14) declared an equal status between the figures. According to the crown line, however, Arsinoë is identified as the superior figure, which agrees with Quaegebeur and her placement. As far as the other horizontal lines are concerned, Ptolemy's head line is hidden beneath his crown, although Arsinoë's head line indicates a level equal to Ptolemy's eyebrow (*cf.* Vassilika 1989, 14, n. 74). In terms of corresponding pictorial elements, Arsinoë's head line regulates the uppermost part of the vulture head (of the cap). Whereas Ptolemy's navel is placed somewhat the higher of the two, the shoulder

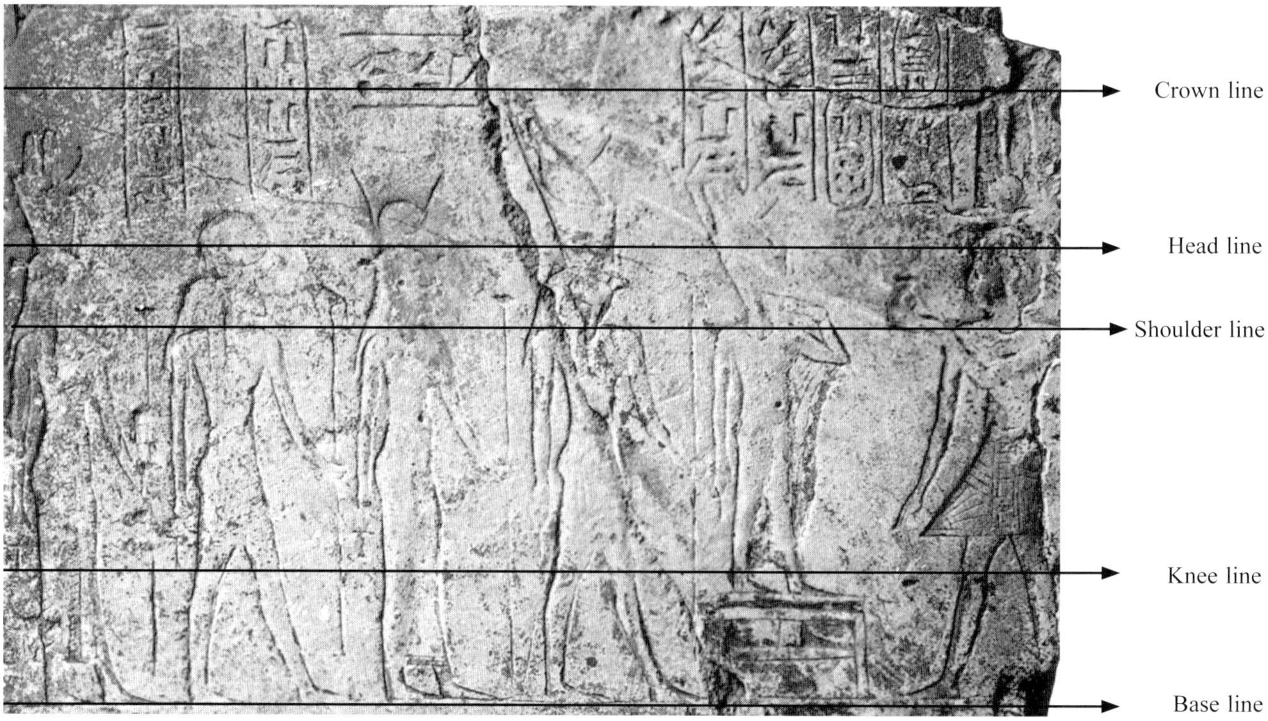

Figure 81. The scene shows Ptolemy II (far right) venerating (from right) Harsomtus on the podium, Horus, Hathor, Sarapis and Arsinoë. Five horizontal lines have been added to the original scene, showing Horus and Ptolemy II as the tallest figures according to the crown line, the head line is based on the figure on the figure of Arsinoë. The shoulder line is common for all, while the knee line is limited to the adults. Notice the variation in the head line between Arsinoë, Sarapis and Ptolemy II. The image is a detail of cat. no. 11.

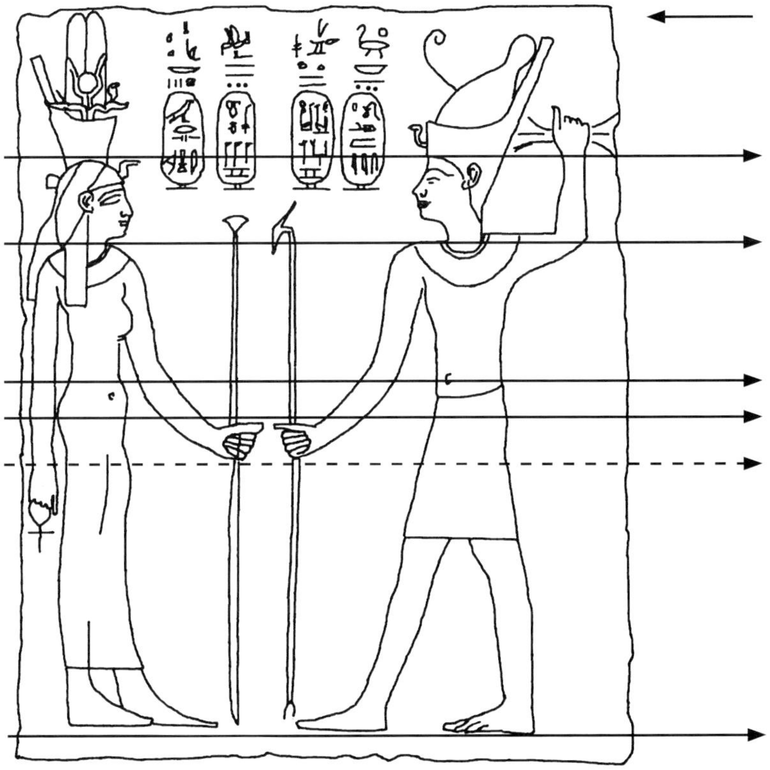

Figure 82. Horizontal lines have been added to this detail of cat. no. 13 showing Ptolemy II and Arsinoë. Ptolemy II can be interpreted as the taller figure according to the rules of isocephaly. However, according to the crown line, Arsinoë is the taller figure (feathers reaching to the top of the grid).

and hip lines are common for both figures. The shoulder line controls the position of Ptolemy's elbow, and the hip line corresponds with the upper outlines of the couple's hands. By adding another (imaginary) horizontal line following the lower outline of Arsinoë's hand, a further irregularity – in this case, one of size – is revealed, which is noticeable when comparing the couple's hands. In terms of general artistic administration, cat. no. 13 shows many discrepancies, a topic which is further discussed below in relation to relative placement.

The process of estimating the cultural status of each figure according to the crown line is combined here with a study of the correlation of other pictorial components via the conventional ancient Egyptian horizontal lines of measurement (Figures 83–86).[4] As a first example, two main lines, following the knee and base, join Ptolemy II and Arsinoë equally in cat. no. 10 (Figure 83). The knee line simultaneously agrees with the flat top surface of the altar placed between the couple. All other horizontal lines, however, fail to unite the corresponding elements of the king and queen. To demonstrate the physical difference in terms of space, the lines of the crown, head and shoulders are based on the image of Arsinoë, as she marks the higher points.[5] Arsinoë's left-side position combined with her height (slightly taller than Ptolemy II) demonstrates that she is the subject of the scene. All other differentiations, in terms of height and based on the horizontal lines, are interpreted here as indications of poor artistry rather than of a hierarchic order.

The lines added by the author to cat. no. 15R (Figure 84) govern the position of the head, shoulder, knee and base for all standing figures. The figural elements of the seated Osiris concur with the lines of the head and shoulders, and the lowest part of the throne follows the base line shared by all. The crown line clearly establishes Arsinoë as the more important figure, and it agrees with the upper outline of her cartouche (the head line corresponds with the lower line for the cartouche). Small insufficiencies in terms of corresponding pictorial elements in the figure of Osiris may suggest that the artist did not arrange the scene according to a grid, and/or that the work was carried out in haste. As will be demonstrated below, details of a seated figure generally share horizontal lines with standing adult figures: accordingly, Osiris' corner box should have been joined with the knee line.

The crown line in cat. no. 26R (Figure 85) authenticates Amun as the figure of highest rank, placing Arsinoë second.

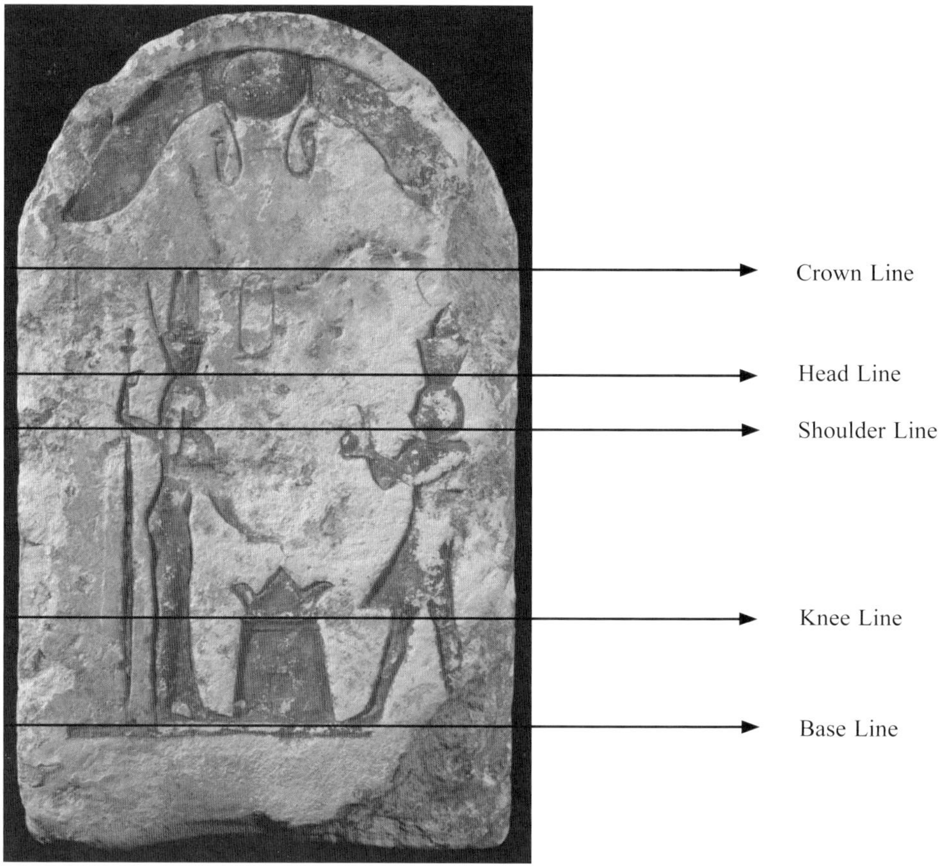

Figure 83. Cat. no. 10 shows Ptolemy II presenting sacrifices to Arsinoë. Five horizontal lines have been added to the original scene, all following Arsinoë's bodily elements.

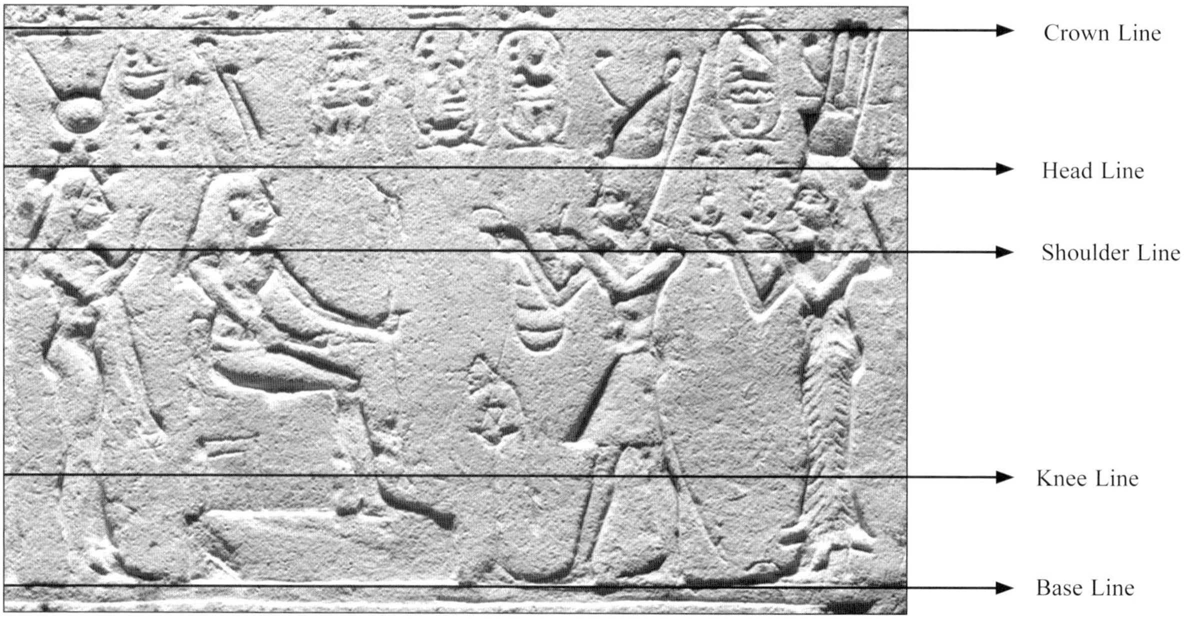

Figure 84. Cat. no. 15R shows Ptolemy II and Arsinoë (right) venerating the local deities of Athribis (left). Five horizontal lines have been added. Arsinoë's crown line is the highest, thereby making her the subject of the scene.

In terms of the traditional horizontal lines, only those of the head and shoulder join the figures accurately, as the male figures lack their lower bodies. The head line of the main characters creates a crown line for the offering figure of Ma'at (wearing her traditional *atef* feather as a crown), while the shoulder line functions as her base line (if excluding the *neb* basket in which she is seated). The crown line remains the only (visible) indication of a hierarchic differentiation.

As a comparative example from the Edfu Temple, Figure 86 shows Ptolemy VIII and Hathor of Dendera. The four lower lines accurately join the figures in terms of space and scale, and the crown line establishes Ptolemy as more important in terms of status. The shoulder line concurs with Ptolemy's hands and the tray holding a sacrifice, and the knee line agrees with the lowest point of Hathor's *ankh*. This scene evidently follows the ancient principles of geometrical symmetry.

This brief analysis shows that the temple reliefs illustrated here as Figures 85–86 were created in accordance with the ancient conventions of a geometrical system, as each pictorial element is regulated by traditional horizontal lines according to a clear level of symmetry. The scenes from the stelai (Figures 82–84), on the other hand, seem to lack any clear geometrical directives: it is plausible that they were created without a grid or system of horizontal lines, instead following the individual hand of the artist. If this was the case, then the figures and contextual elements were based on the artist's interpretation of iconography and the message to be communicated, and the sacred symbolism embedded in the traditional geometrical orders was apparently disregarded. All scenes consistently show, however, that the crown line indicates the highest hierarchic standing among the figures.

Further examples of the value of the crown line may be found in the Graeco-Roman temples. To these, more horizontal lines have been added once again in order to study the correspondence between contextual elements. Firstly, two supplementary horizontal lines relating to the navel and hip (nos 4 and 5) have been added to the scene shown as Figure 87, and are combined with the five lines used above. The scene thus incorporates seven horizontal lines. The supplementary lines demonstrate in more detail how all particulars are connected in a clear mathematical, symmetrical relationship. Once more, the crown line differentiates the figures and thus indicates rank. The head line (no. 2) joins the heads of Emperor Augustus and Hathor, whereas Horus's head is somewhat lower, on the basis of his anthropomorphic character (he is shown with an animal head). This line simultaneously marks, more or less, an individual crown line for the offering figure, Ma'at. The shoulder line (no. 3), which is common for all adults, regulates Ma'at's lower outlines and Augustus' right hand. The navel line (no. 4) again connects the adult figures and also incorporates the smaller figures of Ihy, forming their shoulder line. The hip line (no. 5) joins Augustus and Hathor, although it is placed slightly too high in regard to Horus. This line makes a navel line for the two youngsters and fixes the upper part of the adults' hands. The knee line (no. 6) binds together all adult figures and functions as a base line for the youngsters. The two figures of Ihy are placed on top of the Egyptian unification symbol, the *sema*, which connects them with the base line, which is common to all.

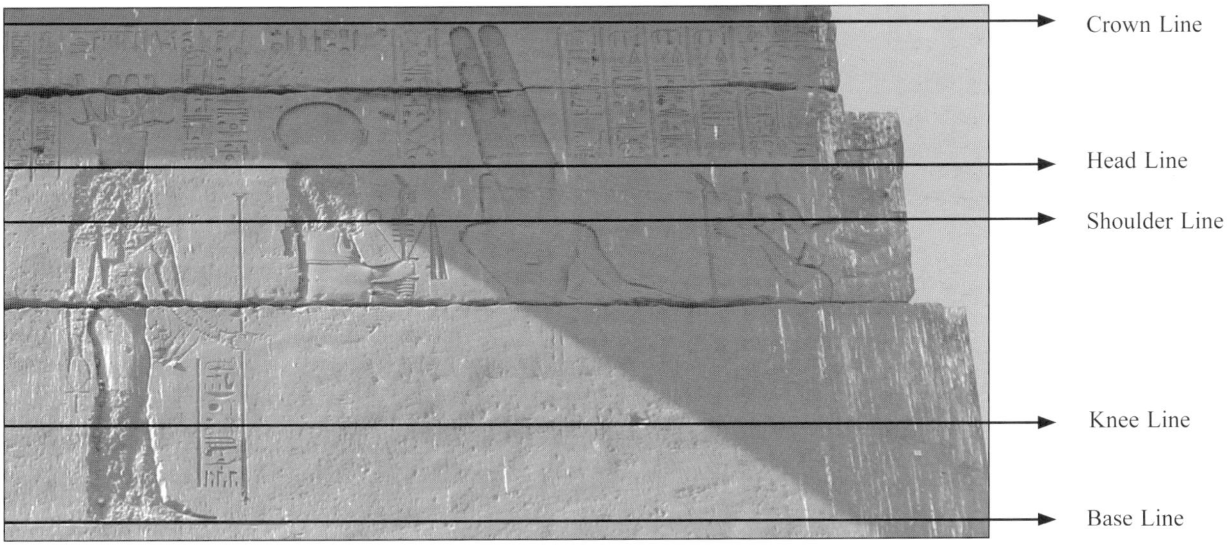

Figure 85. Cat. no. 26R shows Ptolemy II (far right) holding Ma'at before (from the right) Amun, Khonsu and Arsinoë at Karnak. The crown line establishes Amun as the most important figure of the scene. Note that all the other lines are equal for all the figures, as far as can be seen.

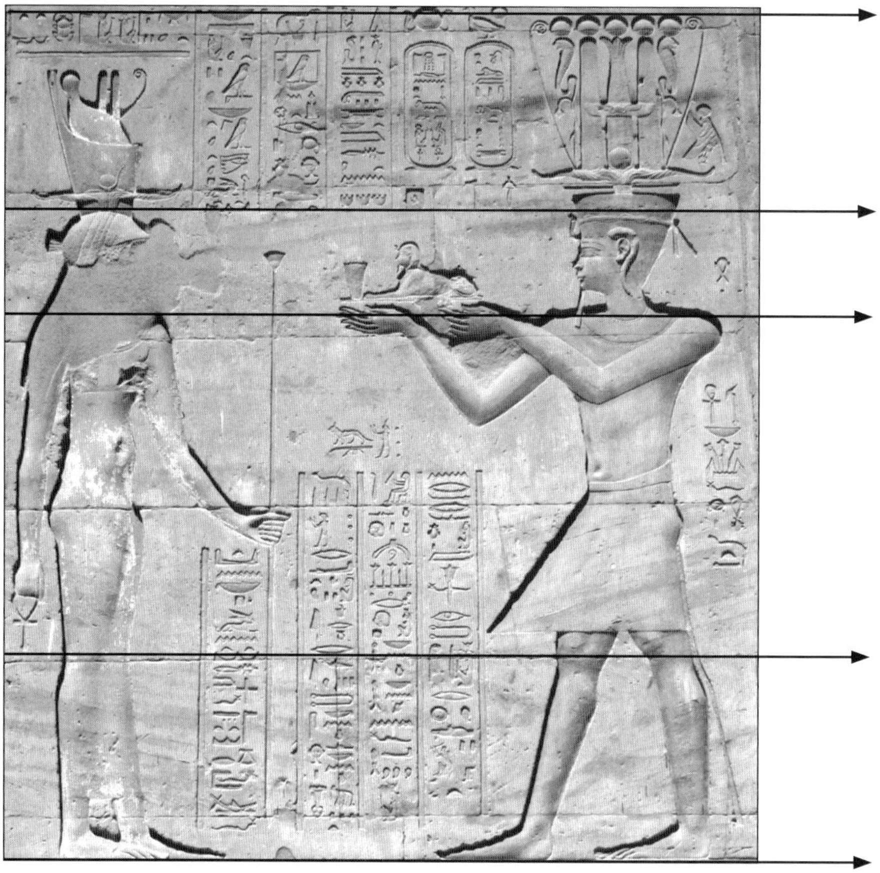

Figure 86. Ptolemy VIII and Hathor of Dendera in the Edfu Temple. The crown line establishes Ptolemy as the more important figure. The four lower lines are similar for both figures.

Overall, the scene displays highly calculated positions for each pictorial element.

In another example, the scene in Figure 88 shows a crown line that places Hathor as the more important figure based on only a minimal differentiation in height. Most horizontal lines below connect Augustus and Hathor, except for the navel and hip lines, which are slightly higher on Hathor. The head line functions as an individual crown line for the offering (figure of Ma'at wearing an *atef* feather), and the general shoulder line forms its base line. The knee line of the adults follows the lowest point of Ihy's outstretched arm. The navel line directs the lower point of the elbows of the adults, and the hip line becomes an individual crown line for Ihy, who stands on the common base line. The figure of Ihy is regulated here, therefore, by norms other than those regulating the youngsters in Figure 87.

When comparing Figures 87 and 88 it is evident that the lower horizontal lines lack an absolutely defined principle for regulating contextual particulars. In Figure 87 the shoulder line moderates the highest point of Augustus' hand (compare Ptolemy VIII's in Figure 86), whereas it pierces it in Figure 88. This can be compared with the hip line in Figure 82, which controls the upper outlines of the hands, whereas it pierces the centre of Hathor's hand in Figure 88. These irregularities indicate that the horizontal lines were arranged according to a fundamental principle, but that additional pictorial elements could be adjusted independently.

Figure 89 shows a scene with seated figures. The details of the scene enable the additional of further horizontal lines, including a breast line and a calf line, marked as *a* and *b* respectively. The head line is common for all except for Harsomtus, who is illustrated as an anthropomorphic figure with a falcon head (and who consequently has a lower head line than the others). The main head line guides the uppermost point of the sistrum (held by the emperor), which is bordered at its lower end by the shoulder line, no. 3, which also establishes the lower part of the wigs of Isis and Harsomtus. The navel line, no. 4, connects the figures, piercing all their elbows. No. 5, Nero's hip line, coincides with the seat of the thrones, representing a knee line for the deities. The main knee line, no. 6, agrees with the highest point of the corner box. Line *b* links Nero's calf with the

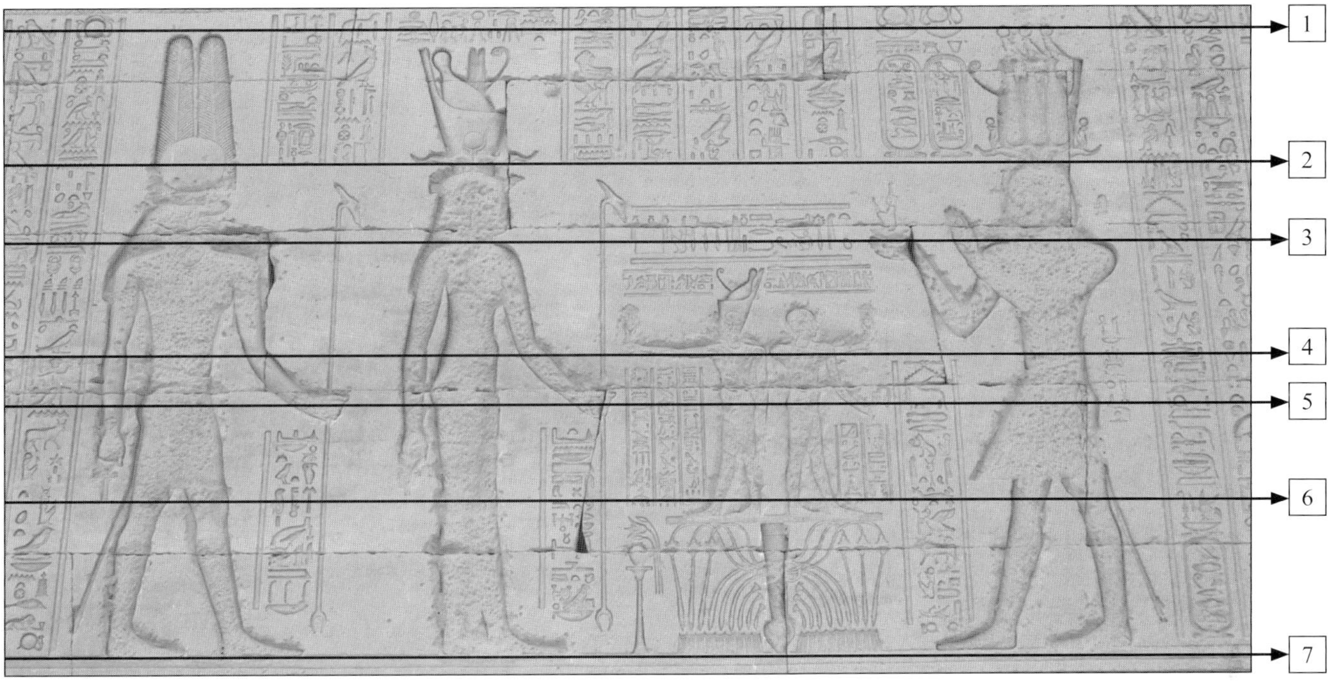

Figure 87. Emperor Augustus (to the right) presenting the figure of Ma'at to Hathor and Horus (left), accompanied by two figures of Ihy (middle), Dendera Temple. The scene has seven horizontal lines: 1. crown line; 2. head line; 3. shoulder line; 4. navel line; 5. hip line; 6. knee line; 7. base line.

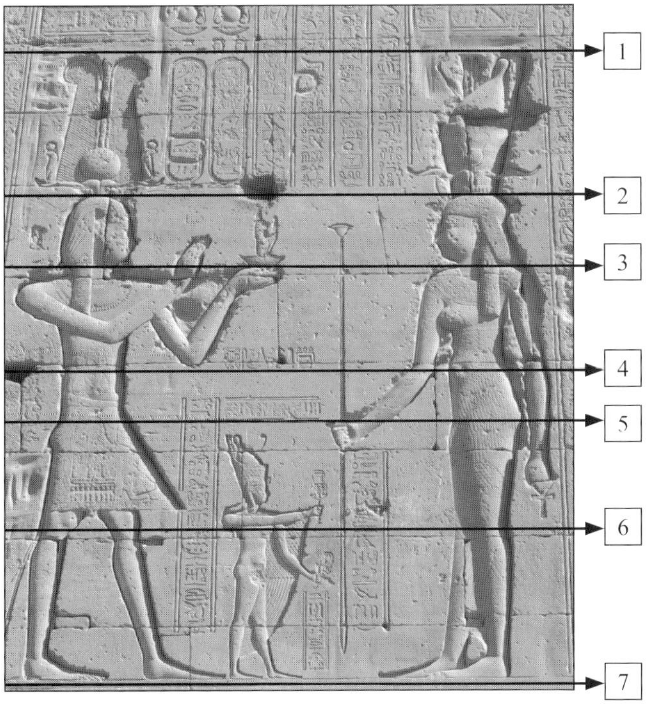

Figure 88. Emperor Augustus (to the left) with Ihy and Hathor, Dendera Temple. Seven horizontal lines are added to the photographed scene: 1. crown line; 2. head line; 3. shoulder line; 4. navel line; 5. hip line; 6. knee line; 7. base line.

base line of the deities and with the lower point of the seats and corner boxes. The emperor's base line connects him with the bases of the thrones of the deities. Again, the crown line separates the figures in height, establishing Nero as the most important, whereas all the lower lines follow symmetric regulations.

The scenes studied above confirm that temple reliefs were regulated and adjusted by a series of horizontal lines created to connect individual elements according to geometrical principles. The importance of applying a crown line as an instrument has been established and substantiated as the horizontal line which determines hierarchic order within a scene. In order to investigate all aspects of the scenes in relation to the horizontal lines, three scenes are examined below exclusively on the basis of the pictorial units of the crowns, which are excluded from the ancient geometrical system. A series of horizontal lines has been added to all three examples/scenes based on the integral structural parts of the crown of Arsinoë.

Figure 90 shows an enhanced detail of cat. no. 3, illustrating Ptolemy II and Arsinoë. Four horizontal lines are added to the photographed representation, including the crown and head lines described above and two additional lines based on individual details of the crown of Arsinoë. In this Figure the crown line establishes not only that Arsinoë is the more important figure but also that there is

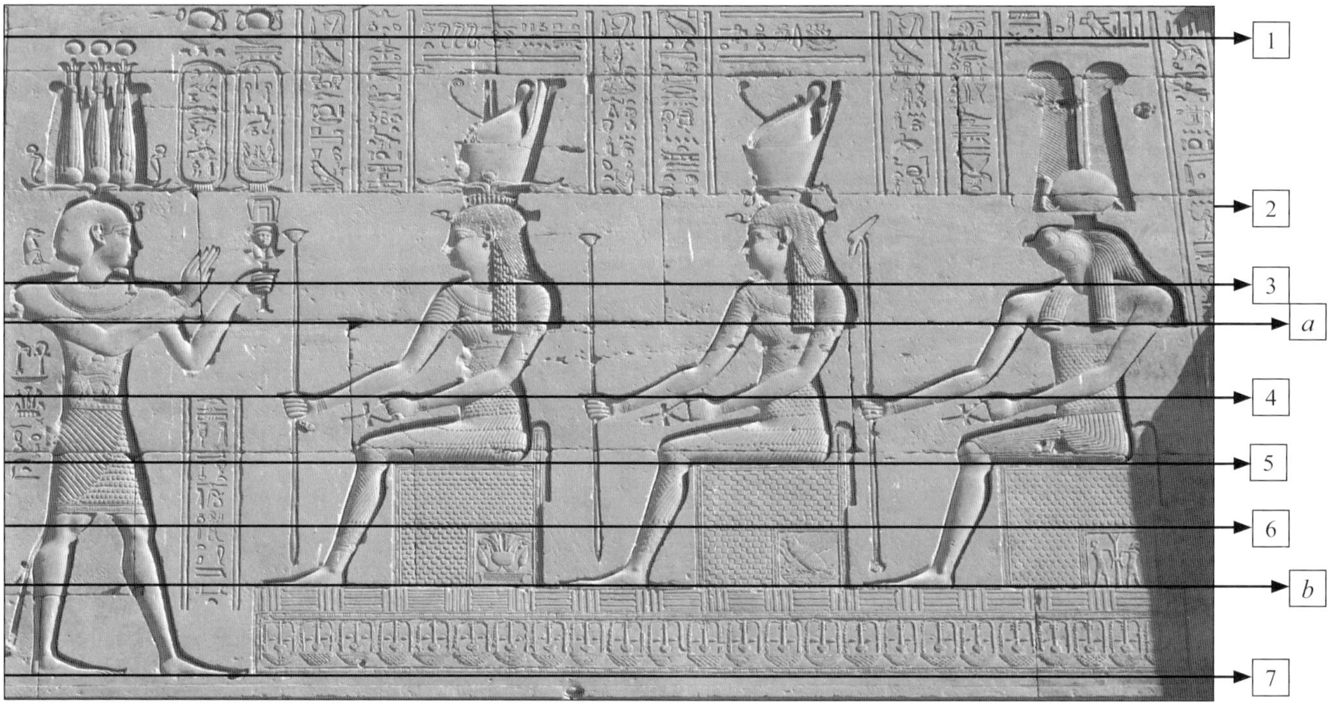

Figure 89. Emperor Nero (far left) before (from the left) Hathor, Isis and Harsomtus, Dendera Temple. Nine horizontal lines are added to this scene: 1. crown line; 2. head line; 3. shoulder line; 4. navel line; 5. hip line; 6. knee line; 7. base line; a. breast line; b. calf line.

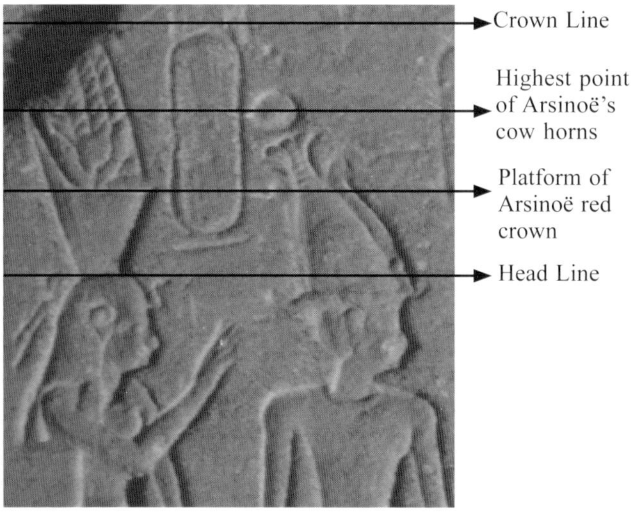

Figure 90. Detail of cat. no. 3, showing Ptolemy II and Arsinoë.

a linear relationship between the top of the double feathers of Arsinoë's crown and the highest point of her cartouche. The line marking the highest point of Arsinoë's cow horns relates to an upper part of Ptolemy II's *atef* crown, although excluding the small disc on top. The platform of the red crown does not match any of the individual pictorial details in Ptolemy's crown, although the head line connects the couple.

In cat. no. 4, shown in Figure 91, Arsinoë's superiority over Ptolemy II in terms of height is demonstrated by the crown line. The upper horizontal lines provided are based on the details of the crown of Arsinoë (nos 1–4), while the lower ones follow her facial features (5–8). The former show no obvious connection between the individual details of the crown of Arsinoë and the crown worn by Ptolemy II. On the other hand, the lower lines, following the head, the fringe/ear, the nose tip and the chin, generally concur. The uniqueness of each crown structure displayed in Figure 91 confirms the theory put forward here of the use of a crown line, based on an individual symbolism, to indicate status.

Figure 92, showing cat. no. 13, shows a scene with Ptolemy II and Arsinoë. Horizontal lines have been added in a similar manner to the two previous scenes. The crown line confirms Arsinoë as most important. Line no. 2 demonstrates a consistency between the highest points of the red crown and the cow horns in the crown of Arsinoë, but it does not correlate with any details in Ptolemy's crown. Line 3 follows the back of Ptolemy's hand but is unrelated to his crown details, although it correlates with the platform of Arsinoe's red crown.

The three examples together reveal that the crown was a very individual pictorial element, and that, if two or more

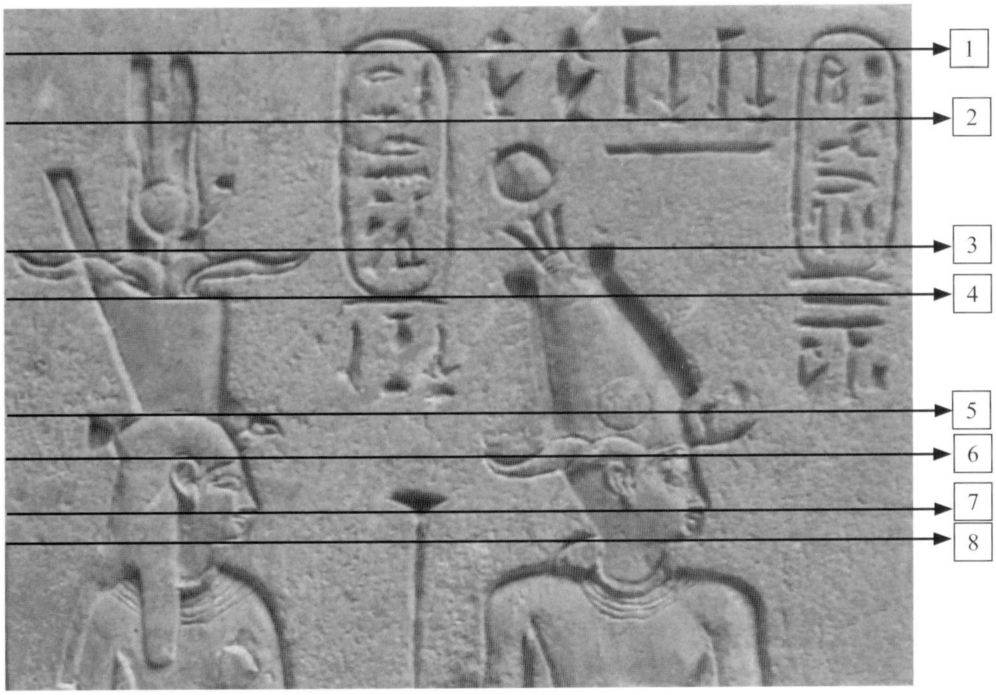

Figure 91. This detail of cat. no. 4 shows Ptolemy II and Arsinoë: 1. crown line; 2. highest point of Arsinoë's cow horns; 3. upper outlines of Arsinoë's ram horns (and lower outlines of cow horns); 4. platform of Arsinoë's red crown; 5. head line; 6. fringe/ear line; 7. line following the nose tip; 8. chin line.

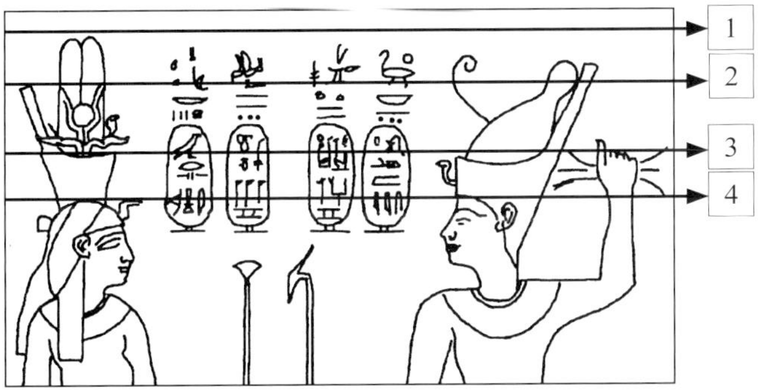

Figure 92. This detail of cat. no. 13 shows Ptolemy II and Arsinoë: 1. crown line; 2. highest point of Arsinoë's cow horns; 3. platform of Arsinoë's red crown; 4. head line.

were shown, they were not regulated externally by any corresponding lines. Although the units of a crown may show a general geometrical order within a crown composition, there is nothing to suggest a contextual correlation. This validates the crown line as the most obvious and direct instrument in understanding ancient Egyptian hierarchic structures as far as reliefs are concerned; used in this way, it demonstrates that Arsinoë is the tallest figure, and consequently the most important, in twenty-two scenes (twenty-three figures) and equal to the other figures in five scenes (Table 16).

Pictorial elements as tools of height (size) regulation

Figures 87 and 89 have revealed the utilisation of various details as instruments to increase the height of any given figure. The material frequently identifies a throne or a *sema* sign as such an instrument. Accordingly, Figure 93, the Mendes stele, illustrates on the right side a naturalistically represented ram standing on a podium. The artist manages to maintain the ram's realistic form and still correlate it with surrounding figures in accordance with a common head line by adding the plinth upon which the ram stands. The scene provides another example of relative scaling in order to express an age differentiation. Harpocrates, standing behind the naturalistic ram, is half the size of the adults. His importance, however, is indicated and increased by the addition of a podium of his own that enables him to reach a higher level, although remaining differentiated from the adults. Owing to the conventions of age representation in Egyptian art, Harpocrates would never be able to attain a position fully equal to the adult figures surrounding him.

As a non-biological part of the figure, the crown is an optional addition to each individual, but its direct attachment to the body enables it to be included as a status indicator. Similarly, any figure could be enhanced, or generally manipulated in size, by the inclusion of hand-held objects. In terms of the crown line, Figure 94 establishes Queen Cleopatra (I) as more important, as she reaches a higher level than her husband, Ptolemy V. However, through the utilisation of a hand-held object (a spear), Ptolemy V attains a height equal to his sister-wife. Consequently, the couple are hierarchically equal (this is of great interest owing to the theme of the scene, in which Ptolemy V and Cleopatra I reconnect with their ancestors and prove themselves capable of safeguarding the Kingdom, as demonstrated by Ptolemy's action of spearing an enemy, a traditional representation of Horus, the divine king).

A final example of relative scaling is provided by the cartouche, although its significance is more textual in nature (*cf.* Wilkinson 1994, 46f.). The text inside the cartouche has a linguistic value, but its shape has a symbolic essence, being a part of the overall scene. The cartouche reflected royalty and a divine legacy, while at the same time identifying the figure(s) illustrated. Cartouches generally follow certain principles of position: they are primarily located in a personal register of text, placed in front of the head of the figure they describe. However, the material reveals a few examples of scenes, exclusively located in the Philae Temple, in which Arsinoë's cartouches are unconventional (cat. nos 27–29). These probably date to the period immediately following Arsinoë's death, thus to the reign of Ptolemy II. The unusual placement of Arsinoë's designations may indicate an artist unaware of all conventions or, as is argued here, a transit period relating to Arsinoë's death, as she advanced from the status of a queen to that of full goddess. The irregularity of these cartouches, however, relates more to relative placement than scaling.

HEIGHT	SCENES	TOTAL NO. FIGURES
Tallest figure	2R, 3, 5–8, 10, 13, 15L–R, 17, 19–20, 22–25,[1] 28–29, 31, 33–34, 36	23
Equal height with one or several surrounding figures	4, 18, 27, 32, 35	5

Note

1. Arsinoë is illustrated as the tallest figure in her immediate surroundings in cat. no. 25. However, in the full scene, she is placed on an equal level with Montu.

Table 16. Height of Arsinoë according to the crown line.

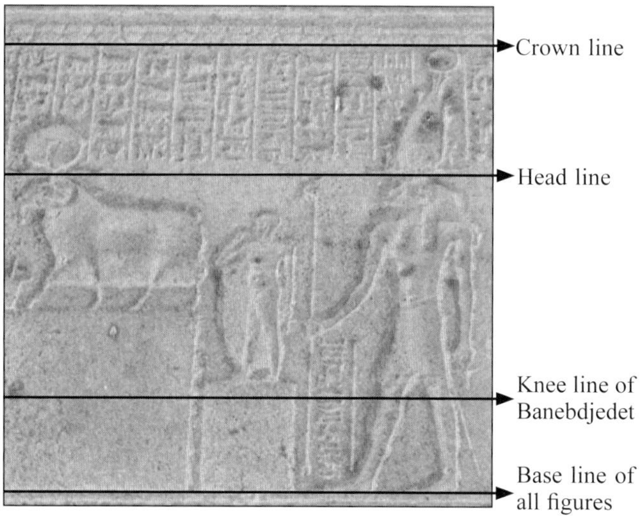

Figure 93. This detail of cat. no. 1 shows, from the left, the newborn, incarnated ram god, followed by Harpocrates and the deceased Banebdjedet, all identified in the hieroglyphic text. All horizontal lines are based on the adult Banebdjedet. The knee line concurs with the platform upon which Harpocrates stands. The head line unites the adult Banebdjedet with the newly incarnated ram.

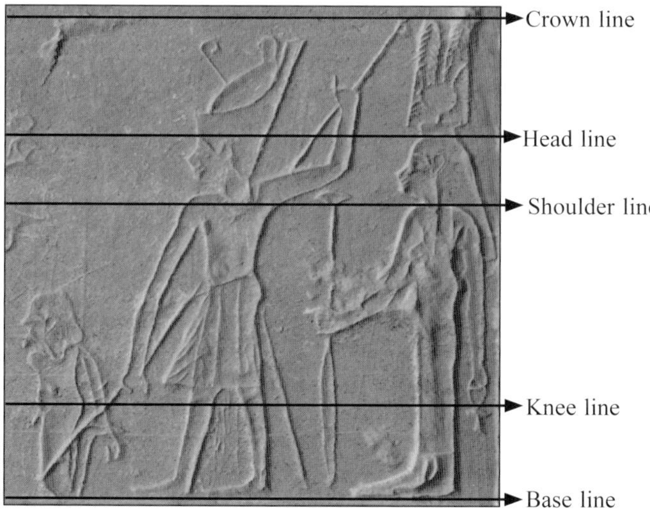

Figure 94. This detail of cat. no. 3 shows Ptolemy V, Cleopatra I and the captive enemy. The crown line establishes Cleopatra as the more important figure, but, owing to the height of the handheld object, Ptolemy V increases his size. Thus, the couple are made equal in size by an application of additional elements.

A few examples from the material will suffice in order to briefly study a possible arrangement of the cartouches in accordance with horizontal lines which could shed some light on the applied artistic conventions. Even if the hieroglyphic designations have faded over time, the royal figures in cat. no. 3 (Figure 95) are preserved with individual cartouches. These are dissimilar in size, width, position and symmetry. The two lines added in Figure 95 follow the uppermost and lowest points of Arsinoë's cartouche (far left); the others are placed on either a higher or lower level or are smaller. Some are deeply carved, other shallower. This dissimilarity indicates that the artist created the relief without using a conventional grid system. Consequently, it can be concluded that cat. no. 3 is not ruled by traditional principles of proportion, and that the asymmetric order indicates a relief probably created in haste.

Opposite cat. no. 3, cat. no. 4 (Figure 96) displays cartouches that, despite seemingly following an artistic grid, show an irregularity. A cartouche is, in general, surrounded by both preceding (prefix) and succeeding (suffix) hieroglyphic text, placing traditional royal titles as prefixes and more individual epithets as suffixes (p. 120). If a scene includes two or more royal figures, their titles are (visually) organised according to a common style, including corresponding prefixes and suffixes. The cartouches in cat. no. 4, however, are on some occasions placed above the epithets, sometimes below, although the complete text (incorporating both cartouches and epithets) always remains within a constant space (the differentiation relates to the character of the figure described: Ptolemy II's and Arsinoë's cartouches are documented above the epithets, opposing the cartouches of the *theoi Soteres*, which are placed below).

The structure of the cartouches shown in the material overall indicates that a grid or horizontal lines has been used. Although minor variations occur, most cartouches are equal in size (Figure 97).[6] This brief analysis, however, demonstrates that the placement of the hieroglyphic designations does not follow the same conventions as does iconography in general.

In his discussion on equality of size, Wilkinson (1994, 46f.) provides the reader with two examples of (what he interprets as) non-symbolic size representation. Firstly, he argues that seated and crouched figures do not fall within the limits defined by the common horizontal lines (based on surrounding standing figures); and, secondly, he compares

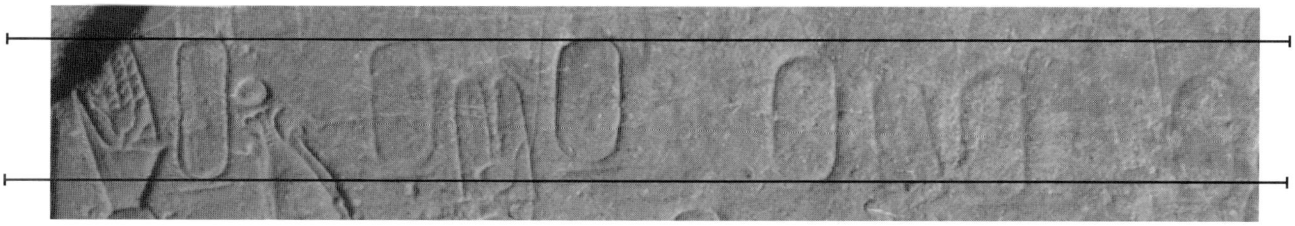

Figure 95. The image shows the six royal cartouches of cat. no. 3. Two indicating lines are added to the image based on the uppermost and lowest points of Arsinoë's cartouche.

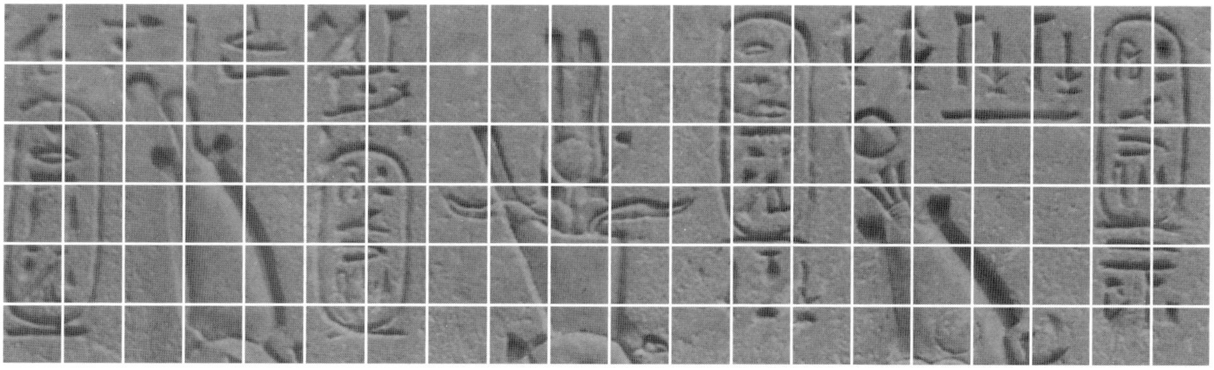

Figure 96. This detail of cat. no. 4 shows the personal register of text of two Ptolemaic couples. A grid system has been placed above the photographed original. The position of the cartouches and the epithets are dissimilar, but the overall text more or less follows an equal scale. The scene could not be photographed from directly in front owing to the reflection in the protecting glass. As a consequence, the reproduced photograph was taken slightly from the side, and is, therefore, not completely horizontally accurate.

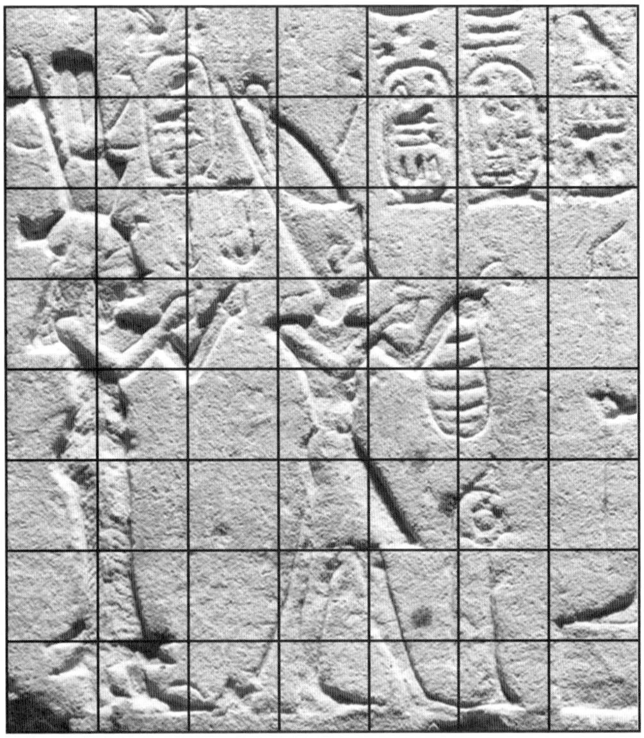

Figure 97. This detail of cat. no. 15L shows Ptolemy II and Arsinoë. The cartouches are dissimilar in their structural organisation, but are equal in size and position.

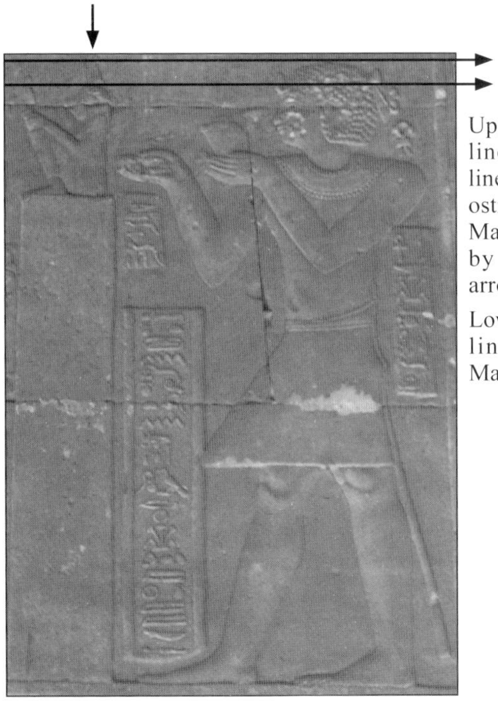

Figure 98. An unidentified Ptolemaic king standing behind the figure of Ma'at, Dendera Temple. The artist manages to increase the height of Ma'at by adding a plinth. Ma'at's head line concurs with the highest point of the king's eyebrow.

a pharaoh in a smiting pose to his equally sized captured enemies. His theory does not seem sustainable, however, given the conventional calculations applied in Egyptian art as documented above. The material makes it obvious that each pictorial unit was carefully chosen in order to stress a certain figural aspect or an overall relationship. The figure of Ma'at acts to disprove his first contention: she is illustrated in a squatting position in several scenes during the Graeco-Roman period, and is placed on a plinth in Figure 98 in order to increase her height, here becoming even taller than the ruler (Nilsson 2010, cat. no. 131). Wilkinson's second example, the pharaoh and the captured enemies, may have symbolic associations with social status. The size of the first-placed enemy reveals his individual cultural status and, while the scene establishes the importance of his enemy, the pharaoh simultaneously proves his own power, as he managed to defeat this foe. Consequently, the scene does not focus on the enemy, but can be interpreted instead as a reflection of a pharaoh upholding Ma'at – universal harmony – by defeating such a strong enemy. The triumph over evil, particularly when it was equal in rank to the pharaoh, was the greatest victory for any king and it placed him in his correct cultural position as the embodiment of the all-powerful Horus. The enemy in the material (cat. no. 3) is depicted, in contrast, in a smaller size.

Relative placement – benefactor and beneficiary

Relative placement refers to an (re)arrangement of the location of images within a scene. It encompasses the figures' directional positions and their associations with others. Relative placement also applies to the (re)location of pictorial details. The ram horns of the crown of Arsinoë, for example, are occasionally located below, sometimes above, the red crown. Here, an active position refers to a figure who worships, is in motion, or dynamically participates in a ceremony. Figures placed in an active position generally stand on the opposite side from the deities, symbolically separating themselves from the divine world. This position is frequently held by the pharaoh or the royal couple. Figures in this position are illustrated as performing a sacrifice (*e.g.* Baines 1976; Vassilika 1989), and they are the active benefactors.

The position of active adoration was exclusively occupied by the ruling pharaoh/queen (however, cat. no. 25, which expresses a similar theme, shows forty-six individual deities praising the sun disc). It is unlikely that a ruling pharaoh/queen would illustrate his/her father/mother or ancestor in this position: based on the Egyptian religious conventions, the deceased pharaoh was believed to enter the Underworld as a manifestation of Osiris. As such, he was no longer separated from the divine world. On the basis of this convention, and if not otherwise stated, all scenes with

Arsinoë in an active benefactor's position are dated to her lifetime. An inactive beneficiary's position correspondingly marks the figure as a deity or a deceased ancestor receiving the veneration of the ruling pharaoh.

As noted above, Egyptian temple reliefs generally follow certain conventions. For example, in his article about temple symbolism Baines (1976) states that field processions, depicted in the bottom register, always lead to the inner sanctuary. Additionally, in most scenes the king faces the *naos*, while deities face outwards (*cf.* Vassilika 1989, 14f.), in a type of correlating placement termed here a 'directional position'. These positions emphasise the symbolic traditions of the pharaoh as a visiting benefactor, piously honouring the deities, the beneficiaries and the dwellers of the temple. Although it was customary for the pharaoh to bring forward sacrifices, the material also includes scenes depicting him in a running, kneeling or smiting position. Pharaonic conventions furthermore dictate that all deities are in a standing pose when illustrated in a lower register, on dado decorations, jambs and pillars: otherwise, gods located in any other structural part of the temple should be seated on a throne (*cf.* Vassilika 1989, 17).

Table 17 documents the positional placement of Arsinoë. It can be seen that she is standing in all scenes except cat. no. 20. As noted above, the principles of directional position in reliefs frequently regulate the placement of the divine figures in accordance with the architectural location of the scene: all gods are supposed to be seated on thrones if the scene is located in any of the higher registers (Baines 1976; Vassilika 1989). Seven of Arsinoë's temple scenes are located in higher registers, indoors and outdoors: however, six of these scenes contradict the general convention, as Arsinoë, shown as the divine Philadelphos, is standing (cat. nos 16–17, 19, 21–22, 34).

Arsinoë is predominantly placed in a left-side position, looking right. Twenty-nine of the forty figures (thirty-six scenes) illustrate her on the left side, whereas twelve scenes place her in the opposite direction, looking left. A few scenes (cat. nos 1–2, 15, 26) place her on both sides simultaneously. Cat. nos 2 and 26, moreover, enhance Arsinoë's overall hierarchic position by placing her two images back to back (facing out) in the very centre of the scene. She becomes the immediate focal point.

The principles of directional position are directly associated with temple symbolism, where they apply also to the correlation of architectural parts. However, such connotations are irrelevant when analysing free-standing stelai, where it is the individual positions of the figures within the scene that are significant. Arsinoë keeps a left-side position in all stelai (including the double-scenes) except cat. no. 6, where she stands on the scene's right side. Clearly her position is of importance.[7]

Cat. no. 13, which shows Ptolemy II and Arsinoë, places Arsinoë on the left, where she is taller than Ptolemy II according to the crown line; together, these points indicate her superiority in the scene. One of the many irregularities displayed in the scene concerns Ptolemy's stance: he follows the conventional position of a male ruler in general, but his left arm is raised behind his body, indicating an active movement, and he holds a still-unidentified object. Previously, most scholars have interpreted Ptolemy's position as non-Egyptian, or as Hellenised Egyptian, and the scene has, as a consequence, been labelled in such terms. However, several individual hieroglyphic signs from the A-series (for example A59, A59a: 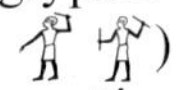) show male figures in positions similar to Ptolemy's, putting these suggestions in doubt. This relief may be a working piece, a draft or a practice object: the cartouches are shallowly

POSITION IN THE SCENE	SCENES	TOTAL NO. FIGURES
Benefactor	1L, 8–9, 12?, 15L–R, 26L	7
Beneficiary	1R-7, 10–11, 13–14, 16–19, 21–24, 26L-35[1]	31
Left side (facing right)	1L, 2R, 3–5, 7–15L, 16, 18–21, 23–26R, 28–30, 32, 35	29
Right side (facing left)	1R-2L, 6, 15R, 17, 22, 26L, 27, 31, 33–34, 36	12
Standing	1L-19, 21–36	39
Sitting	20	1

Note

1. Notice the scenes not included, cat. nos 20, 25 and 36. These scenes represent 'reversed' themes. The position of Arsinoë in cat. no. 20 could be referred to as a reversed benefactor: she participates in her divine role in the crowning/rejuvenation ceremony of Ptolemy IV. Cat. no. 25 illustrates all figures in a praising position, although all figures are divine. Cat. no. 36 depicts Arsinoë in a standing position behind Ptolemy II when he celebrates a Sed festival. Owing to its theme, cat. no. 36 cannot be labelled in accordance with the terminology of benefactor and beneficiary.

Table 17. Arsinoë's positions.

etched, the sceptre and stave are asymmetrical in their composition and Ptolemy's second hand-held object appears to be incomplete (rather than purely unconventional).

Cat. no. 14 (Figure 99) provided another example of traditional principles of hierarchy. The stele, which is in two sections, illustrates Arsinoë with Amun-Min and Ptolemy II on one side and Ptolemy II, Wadjet and Harsomtus on the other. Arsinoë is located in the right half, in a left-side position (looking right), standing behind Amun-Min. They are the inactive beneficiaries of Ptolemy II. In the left section of the scene, Ptolemy presents offerings to Wadjet and a smaller figure of Harsomtus. Based on the crown line, Amun-Min is the tallest figure of the overall scene, and he is accordingly established as the most important figure. Arsinoë reaches almost as high, which indicates her individual rank as the second most important figure. The positional relationship between Arsinoë and Amun-Min is stressed in the text, which describes them as father and daughter. It would be unacceptable, given the divine principles, to illustrate Arsinoë as taller than her divine father, which accounts for her rank in this scene. Cat. no. 14 shows a clear hierarchic ranking system, and the relative placement coincides with and is strengthened by the sacred words.

Arsinoë is represented as a benefactor in five, possibly six, scenes (encompassing six, possibly seven, figures) (cat. nos 1L, 8–9, 12, 15L–R and 26L(–R?)). This position concurs with her royal crown, documented in cat. nos 8–9 and 12, which places the ram horns at the base of the red crown and relates to her royal position as a living ruler. However, since the other scenes illustrate her with the 'official' and more long-lived crown, an absolute association cannot be established. She performs an active religious act in cat. nos 9 and 15, expressed by the shaking of the sistrum. Cat. no. 9 illustrates her unaccompanied. Cat. no. 15 depicts her in a double scene with the ruling pharaoh, Ptolemy II, and four local deities. Cat. no. 8 shows her holding an unrecognised object perhaps presented to an unidentified deity. The pictorial and textual information provided in cat. nos 12 and 26L is not sufficient to establish any connections. All these scenes (suggestively) show Arsinoë actively engaged in an event in a directional position opposite the deities, thus establishing her as an active benefactor. As such, she must be interpreted as a living queen and the scenes dated to her lifetime, which concurs with the suggested interpretation of her 'royal crown'.

All figures who are placed in an active position, acting as benefactors, are interpreted here as kings and queens shown during their lifetime. It is unlikely that a ruling king would order an artist to create a religious scene depicting a person other than the king himself.[8] Apart from the obvious socio-political reasons, such an act would oppose the conventions of Egyptian religion, according to which the deceased pharaoh became Osiris. The same socio-religious convention can be applied also to the queens, unless the scene in fact demonstrates a narrative element, as in the Mendes stele (cat. no. 1).

As argued above, the roles of benefactor and beneficiary are suggested to be regulated by the active or inactive position of the figure. However, as with all artistic principles there are exceptions, of which cat. no. 20 is an example. The scene shows Ptolemy IV with Thoth and Seshat, and

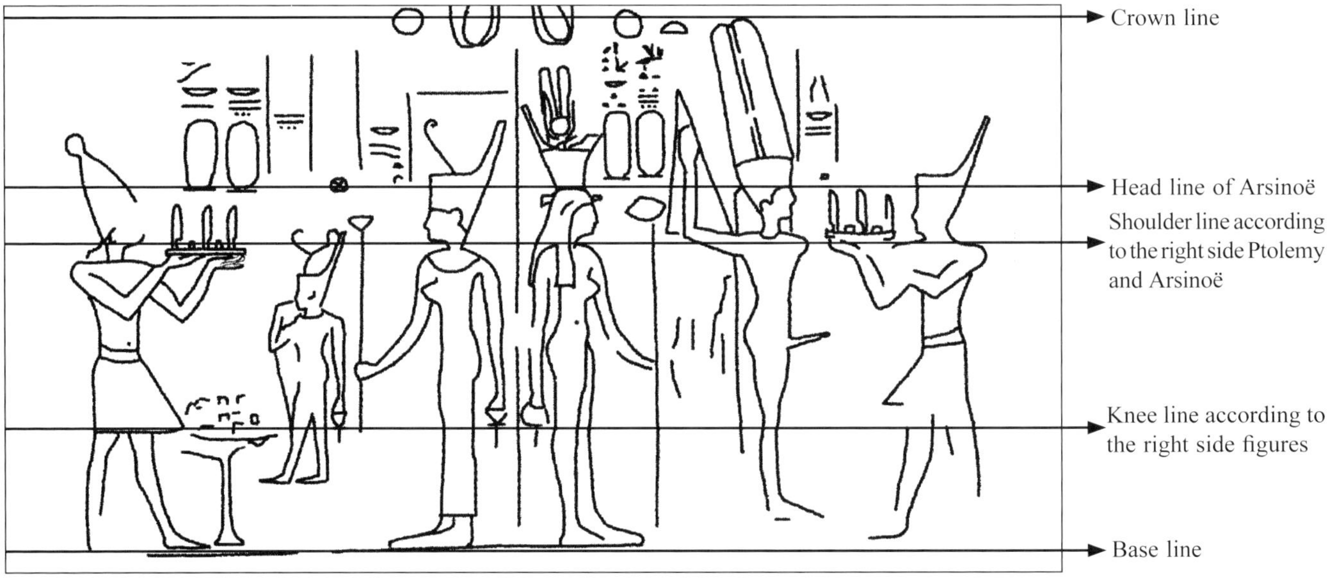

Figure 99. Detail of cat. no. 14, showing Ptolemy II far left and far right as a benefactor, with Amun-Min and Arsinoë on the right and Harsomtus and Wadjet on the left side. Horizontal lines are added to the photo in order to establish a hierarchic order.

Ptolemy II with Arsinoë, Hathor and Horus. The central theme is Ptolemy IV's crowning and rejuvenation, a rebirth of his royal soul: he ascends from the tree of life surrounded by symbols of kingship. Thoth and Seshat write his royal annuals and present him with his royal name. They break the positional principles, as they stand on the same side as the pharaoh and thus in a directional position opposite the other deities. Thoth and Seshat, as noted previously, are associated with kingship and the ruling pharaoh: they are connected with the human world regardless of their individual divinity, and they actively participate in the religious event, which accounts for their position with the human ruler. They give the king their blessing and guidance as he obtains their attention: symbolically, Ptolemy IV is the beneficiary and Thoth and Seshat his benefactors. Thus, the scene has a reversed theme. Ptolemy II, Arsinoë, Hathor and Horus, however, maintain a conventional inactive stance, monitoring the ceremony. They are separated from the king in terms of both space and posture.

Cat. no. 25 is another unique scene in the material. Including two royal couples, all the figures within it are divine. The object of their veneration is a large solar disc located in the centre of the scene. The forty-two deities and the two royal couples are divided equally on both sides of the solar disc. The *theoi Adelphoi* stands at the far left and the other royal pair (here identified as the *theoi Euergetai*) stands at the far right. All anthropomorphic figures praise the sun disc, thus placing them in the position of divine benefactors. The sun disc is identified as the scene's only beneficiary.

Concepts of time

This chapter has so far presented visual attestations of an active pictorial administration and the relativity of Egyptian art. The concepts of time, however, are dissimilar to those of size and position and have never been properly studied within the artistic field of Egyptian reliefs. Traditionally, time is presented as relative or absolute, and is invoked primarily in terms of providing a date for the object under study (Artioli 2010, chapter 2.5, esp. 130f.). Others approach the concept of time in accordance with the cultural differentiation of maker and viewer, when considering the linear, temporal development that separate them. However, time is studied here in accordance with the period(s) of time communicated in the iconographic composition of the relief, incorporating not only 'objective' time, but also the 'phenomenal, subjective' concept.[9] Thus, the modern viewer must decipher the ancient maker's pictorial code in order to understand his/her original, intended message in terms of relative time, which is unlimited when working outside traditional parameters of visual depiction.

The fundamental indications of temporal adjustments are embedded in the association of pictorial elements and defined in the combination of iconography and text. As mentioned in the Introduction, the concept of time depends on those of relative scaling and placement. It is made comprehensible only when reading between the lines (symbolically speaking), as it is manifested indirectly in a scene's figural arrangement.[10]

Temporal adjustment refers here to an artist's deliberate use of elements in order to express one or several time periods, including the present, thus signifying relative time. Normal Egyptian artistic conventions limit any depicted time period to a contemporary time or to the past, as each scene was believed to represent a human physical or divine event, and as such could not depict the future. This study of (relative) time is important when establishing the date of the crown of Arsinoë, primarily in order to understand its overall ideological significance. A scene that shows Arsinoë as a queen or high priestess would suggest that she had already received and used her crown as a symbol of authority during her lifetime.

The complex concept of relative time is approached here using three individual examples from the material (case studies 1–3, below). These are followed by an analysis of cat. no. 26, which provides an example of a scene where all aspects and concepts of size, position and time come together.

Case study 1: the Mendes stela

Cat. no. 1 depicts eight main and four minor figures. The scene is crowned by a winged solar disc and two pendant *uraei*. The main figures, illustrated on the lower section of the relief, are separated from the solar disc by a frieze of stars. On its left side, the scene illustrates three royal figures bringing offerings to the deities. The right side presents five divine figures. Arsinoë is depicted on both sides. The stele is named after its place of origin, Mendes, and the main deities are identified as its local triad: Banebdjedet (represented twice: as deceased and reborn), Hat-Mehit and Harpocrates. The following analysis will concentrate on an identification of the figures on its left side.

Here referred to as cat. no. 1L, the left side illustrates two male figures, positioned in front of and behind Arsinoë. In their personal registers of text, the two male figures are described with similar titles and epithets.[11] In the main text (below the relief scene), the second male figure is described as Ptolemy, son of the king. Traditionally, the two male figures are referred to vaguely as Ptolemy II and Ptolemy the son: such labels, however, raise further questions.

Owing to his age at the time, scholars generally agree that the second male figure cannot be identified with Ptolemy III (although *cf.* Clarysse 2007, 204f., who introduces an alternative date of 257 BC, which post-dates a possible identification with Ptolemy, son of Arsinoë and Lysimachus and enables an identification with Ptolemy III). Some scholars therefore suggest that this figure should be identified with Ptolemy, the son of Arsinoë and Lysimachus (Derchain 1985, 36; Bennet: http://www.tyndalehouse.com/egypt/ptolemies/nios_i_fr.htm). The circumstances surrounding the history of Arsinoë's son are uncertain, owing to inconclusive sources. Written sources describe Ptolemy II's co-regency with a man known to the modern world as Ptolemy the son. Lasting for around eight years, between 267 and 259 BC, this joint rule ended after Ptolemy the son's participation in a revolt in Miletus (*PP* VI 14542; *P.Sorb.* 2440; *P. Louvre* 2424; *Gr. Dem. Medinet Habu* 77; *P. Hib.* 1.100; *e.g.* Huss 1998, 229f.). Although his identity is inadequately substantiated, most scholars believe that this man was the son of Arsinoë and Lysimachus. The Mendes stele is frequently used to verify the identification of Ptolemy's co-regent as the son of Arsinoë. Here, however, the stele will be studied iconographically and semiotically prior to approaching the issue of identification. The pictorial elements associated with the two male figures respectively will be compared and their individual correlation to Arsinoë evaluated. To distinguish the two figures before their identification they will be referred to as the 'front figure' and the 'back figure', according to their positional correspondence with Arsinoë.

The front figure (Figure 100) wears a double crown including a single forehead *uraeus* and a royal diadem. Above his head is a small solar disc with two pendant *uraei* holding *ankh* signs, described in the text as the traditional Behutet. He wears the traditional kilt with a bull's tail. He stands in front of and looks at the newly incarnated ram god Banebdjedet. His posture suggests that he is about to stroke myrrh (from the hand-held cup) onto the ram's nose, which is a prominent and active action clearly stating his status as a ruler. This figure is depicted as independent, in a somewhat isolated position slightly apart from the figures behind him. No minor figures accompany him. His height, in accordance with the crown line, indicates a more prominent position than is accorded to the back figure. He is illustrated as a sole ruler of Egypt, personally performing the active offerings to the new ram, and is identified with the monarch of Egypt at the time of the creation of the stele: Ptolemy II. His social position as the living, ruling pharaoh is strengthened by the suggestion of imminent physical contact with the ram. His titles are associated with a ruling pharaoh. Furthermore, the plant placed in front of him, a lotus plant consisting of six levels of buds, is recognised for its symbolism of rejuvenation, new beginnings and the return of light from the dark waters of Nun, similar to a king's rejuvenated transformation after a Sed festival (Rundle Clark 1959, 66f.). Its symbolism connects well with the theme of the stele.

The back figure (Figure 101) wears a *khepresh* crown – the blue crown, commonly worn by pharaohs at war, but also during religious ceremonies – with an additional single forehead *uraeus* (*cf.* van Oppen 2007, 435f.). Above his head is a small solar disc with two pendant *uraei* holding *ankh* signs, identical to the composition above the front figure's head. He wears a leather kilt with a bull's tail, instead of the traditional kilt. Together, the blue crown and the leather kilt indicate a religious association, suggesting a placement of the ruler in his royal position as high priest (*cf.* Green 2001, 275, for the leopard-skin clothing found in Tutanchamun's tomb, which is associated with his position as a *sem*-priest). He holds folded cloth and a vessel in his hands. Neither size nor pictorial elements (the figure is depicted without a side or prince lock, the use of which would place him as a youngster or a prince) suggest that this back figure represents a youngster: he appears to be an adult. As mentioned above, the crown line indicates that he is less important than the front figure (a comparison with Arsinoë is not possible owing to the state of preservation of her crown).

This latter figure of Ptolemy is linked with Arsinoë in accordance with their associated surrounding elements. Therefore, they are analysed as a pair prior to a comparison of the back figure with the front figure of Ptolemy. Figure 102 shows that Arsinoë is illustrated with a cluster of papyrus, whereas the back Ptolemy's contextual setting shows a cluster of lotuses. These plants generally represent Lower and Upper Egypt respectively. Arsinoë and Ptolemy are accompanied and protected by the smaller-scale figures of the falcon – Horus – and the vulture – Nekhbet – respectively. These birds, like the plants, principally signify Lower and Upper Egypt (Harakhte, Heliopolis and Nekhbet, el-Kab). The falcon of Arsinoë is described as 'Horus of Behutet, he who spreads his wings, he who gives protection to his mother'. The text of the vulture states 'Nekhbet, the White One from Nekhen, Great vulture, she who will protect her son with her wings'.

This part of the scene associates Arsinoë with Hathor, as the mother of the falcon, and Ptolemy with Horus the son, which is indicated by the attached figures of the birds combined with their individual textual descriptions: the two birds can be read as indicators of personal aspects of the royal couple, thus presenting Arsinoë as the maternal vulture (as the mother of the falcon), and Ptolemy as Horus the son (nurtured by the vulture). In addition to such an identification, the complexity of Egyptian religion allows at the same time a matrimonial relationship between Hathor and Horus (Arsinoë and Ptolemy II), and as such they ruled the world. The pictorial association between Arsinoë and the back figure of Ptolemy, based on their immediate contextual surroundings, appears to represent Upper and Lower Egypt: Arsinoë's association with the back figure is similar to the multifaceted relation between Hathor and Horus: together they communicate the socio-religious dualism upon which everything in Egyptian culture rested.

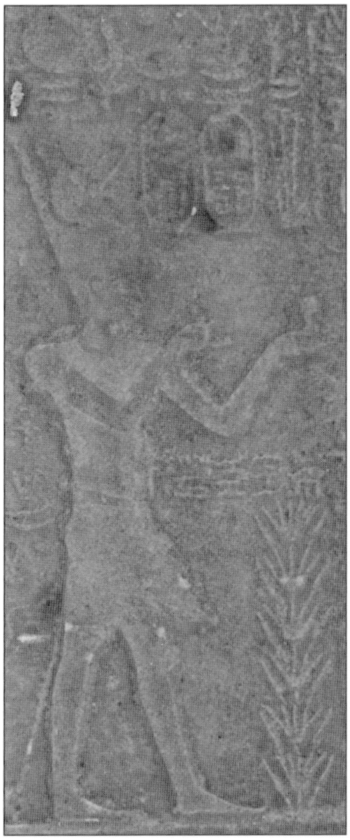

Figure 100. Detail of cat. no. 1L: front male figure.

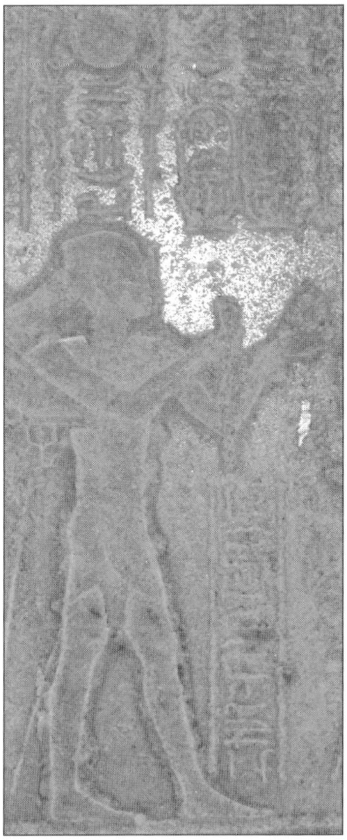

Figure 101. Detail of cat. no. 1L: back male figure.

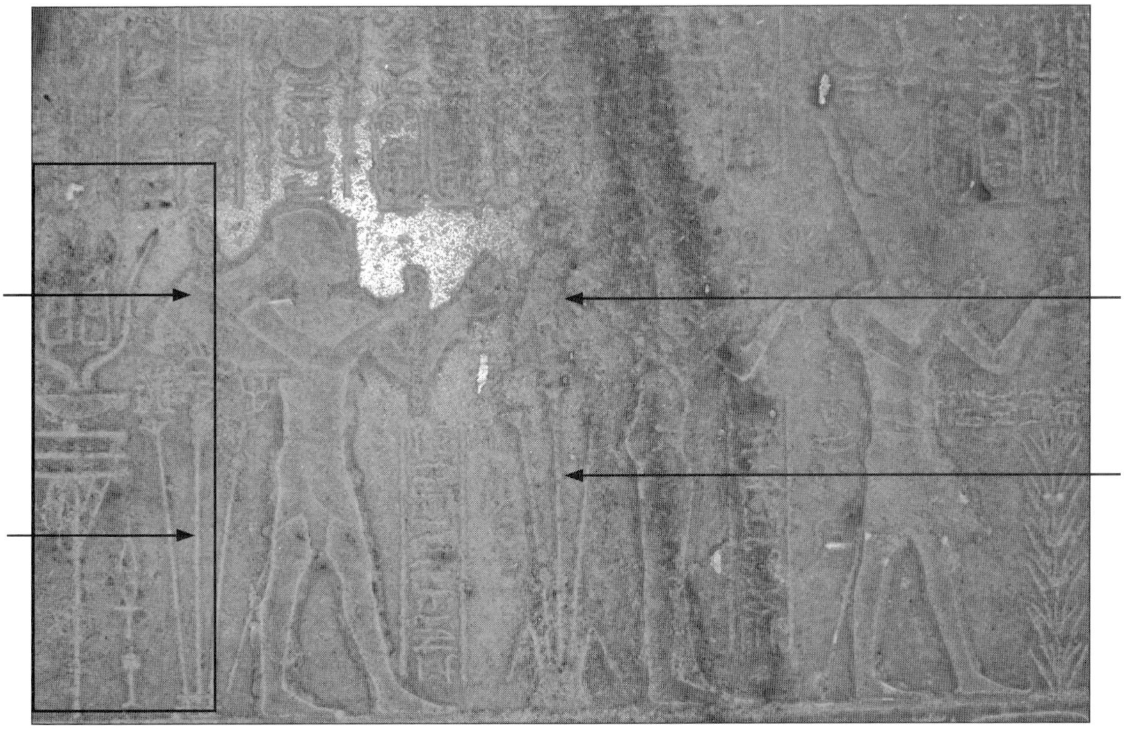

Figure 102. Detail of cat. no. 1. The left arrows show the two pictorial elements that correspond to Upper Egypt and the back figure of Ptolemy. The right arrows indicate the corresponding elements of Lower Egypt and Arsinoë. The rectangle shows the insignia. See also Figure 117.

Behind the back figure of Ptolemy and the vulture the scene shows a standard which appears to be unique (see Figure 102). The insignia is composed of two hieroglyphic signs, and (nb-*tꜣ*), traditionally translated as 'Lord/Lady of the Two Lands' (*cf.* Kamal 1905, 159–68, pls LIV, LV, where this sign is interpreted as (*mr*)). It also includes a set of large cow horns, within which are placed two empty 'Horus cartouches' crowned with two minor Horus figures. The first falcon wears the red crown and the second the white crown. The text connected with the insignia has previously been translated as 'King of Upper Egypt and King of Lower Egypt, the two Horuses, the 'brothers' are united… Lands' (; *cf. Urk.* II, 30 (Mendes stele C. 9); Roeder 1959, 174). Instead of translating the hieroglyphs – *sn-sn* (*sn.w*) as 'brothers' (as previously), they are interpreted here as 'siblings' (similarly, *mr-sn* – 'Philadelphos' is translated as the 'sibling-loving' and not just 'brother-loving', and – *nṯr.w-sn.w*, the '*theoi Adelphoi*', is translated as sibling-gods). This makes the latter part of the text 'the siblings are united': that is, Ptolemy II and Arsinoë, rather than the two male figures. As a result, this unique insignia describes two regents, based on the two individual Horus cartouches, who are protected by the nurturing Hathoric horns. The pictorial element thus describes a joint rule of two individuals.

The individual iconography of the back figure of Ptolemy indicates a ceremonial position, possibly high priest. Regulated by the symbolism of Upper Egypt, he is identified as the King of Egypt's southern part. Textually, he is described as 'Lord of the Two Lands (Strong is the soul of Ra, beloved of Amun)| the son of Ra, Lord of the crowns (Ptolemy)|'. This is Ptolemy II's official designation. In the main text, however, he is described as 'his [the king's] son, who carries the name of he who had sired him' (Mendes stele, l. 19), and is thus generally referred to as Ptolemy the son (*e.g.* Derchain 1985, 3). Importantly, there is no obvious indication that this textual description belongs to the figure depicted. Although this description – the king's son – could indicate a youngster, the pictorial representation is of an adult figure. As mentioned above, this title has caused a contentious debate regarding the identity of this figure which has focused on the various options of sons of Ptolemy II and/or Arsinoë. The listed title in the main text indeed describes a son of the ruling king. However, the epithet belongs to Ptolemy II, and the complexity of Ptolemaic epithets and royal titles is further described by C. Bennet (http://www.tyndalehouse.com/egypt/ptolemies/nios_i_fr.htm), who states 'there are plenty of examples showing that statements of royal relationships in Egyptian Ptolemaic documents have to be treated very carefully, starting with Ptolemy III as the "son" of Arsinoe II'. Furthermore, the title given in the main text cannot be determined beyond doubt as identifying the back figure. However, if it is accepted that the title belongs to the figure depicted behind Arsinoë, and that the complexity of textual titles and the manipulation of time within the general context produce a narrative depiction, it may be fitting to recall one of Ptolemy II's most common designations, establishing him as Ptolemy, the king's son: Ptolemy, son of Ptolemy.

An identification of these two male figures is thus suggested: Ptolemy II, the son of Ptolemy I, is represented twice within the left side of the Mendes stele, through an active and intentional temporal adjustment indicated by the contextual pictorial elements. The pictorial differentiation of the figures relates to two distinguishable time periods. The back figure represents Ptolemy II as the King of Upper Egypt, co-ruling Egypt with a living Arsinoë. According to the iconography and text, Arsinoë is the ruler of Lower Egypt. Therefore, the back part of the left side, which illustrate Arsinoë and Ptolemy together, shows a joint regency. Furthermore, on the basis of his ceremonial clothing and crown and her hieroglyphic titles, which will be analysed in greater detail below, they appear as high priest and high priestess, in accordance with their royal duties. The front figure of Ptolemy shows a sole ruler celebrating the rebirth and rejuvenation of a ram; here, the scene describes Ptolemy's rebirth as an individual ruler following the death of Arsinoë. This rebirth was made possible by the ceremonies of a Sed festival (*cf.* cat. no. 36). The death of Arsinoë, Ptolemy's co-regent, would have been a plausible reason for the king to have to prove himself worthy as Egypt's ruler. The lower hieroglyphic register of the divine Arsinoë, standing on the right side of the scene, supports this theory. She states 'I pray for you to the master of the Gods, so that he gives you numerous years as a king [*i.e.*, of rule]'. Cat. no. 1 documents Ptolemy's official commemoration of his deified sister-wife through his appearance in the same scene in two different time frames, as both her wife and her widower.[12]

Case study 2: the Sed festival Gate of Ptolemy II

Cat. no. 36 (Figure 103), from the Sed festival Gate of Ptolemy II, is rarely discussed elsewhere, although such debate that has taken place has provoked many questions (Sambin and Carlotti 1995; Quaegebeur 1998, no. 31). Sambin and Carlotti (1995) have analysed the gate, which is preserved only in fragments, with the present scene being only partially preserved. It depicts the upper parts of the second Ptolemaic royal couple and the head of a venerating unidentified figure facing them. Ptolemy II stands in a festival pavilion and is depicted with royal regalia, including the red crown, the flail and the crook. The queen stands behind him, outside the outlines of the pavilion. She wears the traditional female crown and holds a flail. The back part of the female figure is missing. The queen is much taller than Ptolemy according to the crown line, indicating her more prominent role. Ptolemy is described in the

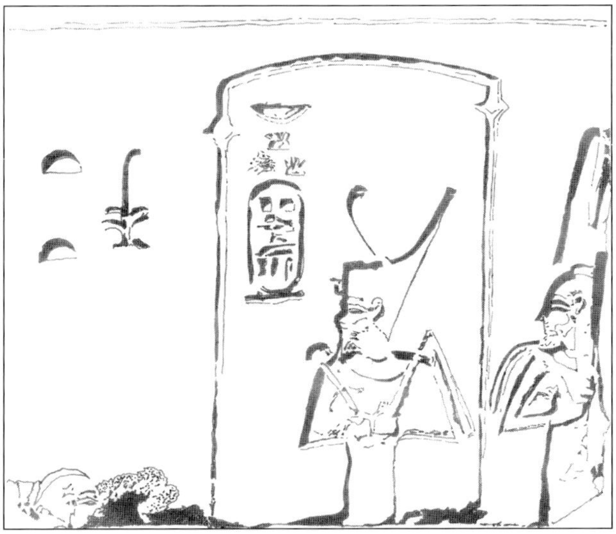

Figure 103. Cat. no. 36. Drawing by J. Ward.

cartouche as a living king, 'Lord of the crowns (Ptolemy)|' (*cf.* Sambin and Carlotti 1995, 391). His position within the festival pavilion underlines the rejuvenation theme of the gate. The topic of analysis here, however, is the identity of the female figure.

The queen is not identified in the traditional personal register of text; this space is blank. Instead, a female title is located in a position opposite the royal couple, above the head of the figure venerating them. The hieroglyphic signs are written at a scale much larger than Ptolemy's. In their present (fragmented) state they translate as 'female king (= Queen)'.[13] The designation alone does not provide an absolute identification of the queen, as it could refer to either Arsinoë I or Arsinoë II. However, a contextual dedication dating to Ptolemy III describes a renovation of the monument originally built by Ptolemy II and Arsinoë. Arsinoë is described as the daughter of Amun.[14] Thus, in terms of time and based on the contextual scenes, the figure is identified here as Arsinoë II. This conclusion corresponds with two fragmentary architectural blocks located in the vicinity which show Arsinoë's complete royal title, listing both Birth name and Throne name (Figures 104–105).

Cat. no. 36's theme is the Sed festival of Ptolemy. In such a ceremony, the queen was a most important element.[15] Traditionally, a Sed festival was celebrated after thirty years of rule and, subsequently, each third year (Troy 1986, 68–70). Other possible reasons for the celebration of the festival included civil unrest, war or any other situation which might have questioned the competence of the pharaoh. Ptolemy ruled Egypt for more than thirty years, but it seems more likely that this particular depiction of the ritual is dated closer to the lifetime of Arsinoë, as she is illustrated in the scene. There were some political affairs during the early years of Ptolemy's rule that might have triggered a need on his part to demonstrate his capability to continue ruling, five of which will be discussed below.

The first is Ptolemy I's death, when Ptolemy II became a sole ruler of Egypt. This Sed festival scene cannot refer to that time, however, as the queen has been identified as Arsinoë II. At the time of Ptolemy I's death Arsinoë was still married to Lysimachus and was not, therefore, a queen of Egypt. The First Syrian War is another plausible event. In terms of time, Arsinoë was at this point a ruling queen of Egypt. Her position as Ptolemy II's co-regent, managing and governing Egypt's civil affairs, made it possible for the king to actively participate in and win the war (*e.g.* Hölbl 2001, 37–40). However, a pharaoh who returned victorious after a war was certainly regarded as competent to continue his rule. Therefore, it seems unlikely that the First Syrian War was a plausible cause for a Sed festival. Arsinoë's death is a third possibility, given her socio-political position as Ptolemy's co-regent. As noted above, Arsinoë remained in Egypt when Ptolemy fought the First Syrian War. During this time she had an impact on Egypt's public domain and (as subsequent chapters show) a religious role as a high priestess, following in the footsteps of the renowned and politically powerful Divine Adoratrices. As a co-regent in control of internal affairs, to whom Ptolemy II turned for advice, Arsinoë was an important element in Egyptian society. In addition, Egypt was threatened immediately after Arsinoë's death by various international affairs which put the country and the new sole ruler in danger. Based on her socio-political importance combined with the following civil unrest, it seems likely that Arsinoë's death was the cause of Ptolemy's Sed festival. If this was the case it would have taken place when Ptolemy returned to the throne as a sole ruler in the face of political instability. Events subsequent to Arsinoë's death that might have precipitated a Sed festival were the Chremonidean War and the ending of Ptolemy's third co-regency after the dispute with Ptolemy the son. At this time, however, Ptolemy had no royal spouse and, had Arsinoë been depicted in the scene, it would have been as a goddess, rather than a queen, while Ptolemy himself would have been depicted alone. In addition, there are no obvious connections with Arsinoë to support the two last options.

In the scene Arsinoë is depicted standing outside the outlines of the festival pavilion. Her position is inactive, that of a beneficiary, and she is placed on the same side as the living ruler. Thus, the positional directions are reversed. In terms of comparison, Thoth and Seshat are placed on the same side as the ruling pharaoh in scenes with a theme of rejuvenation, crowning or purification (pp. 65–66). The Sed festival, too, is generally acknowledged as having a theme of rejuvenation. Ptolemy's and Arsinoë's positions demonstrate their close relationship, but it is possible that Arsinoë's role could be considered as similar to Seshat's given the rejuvenation theme. As such, she provided a divine

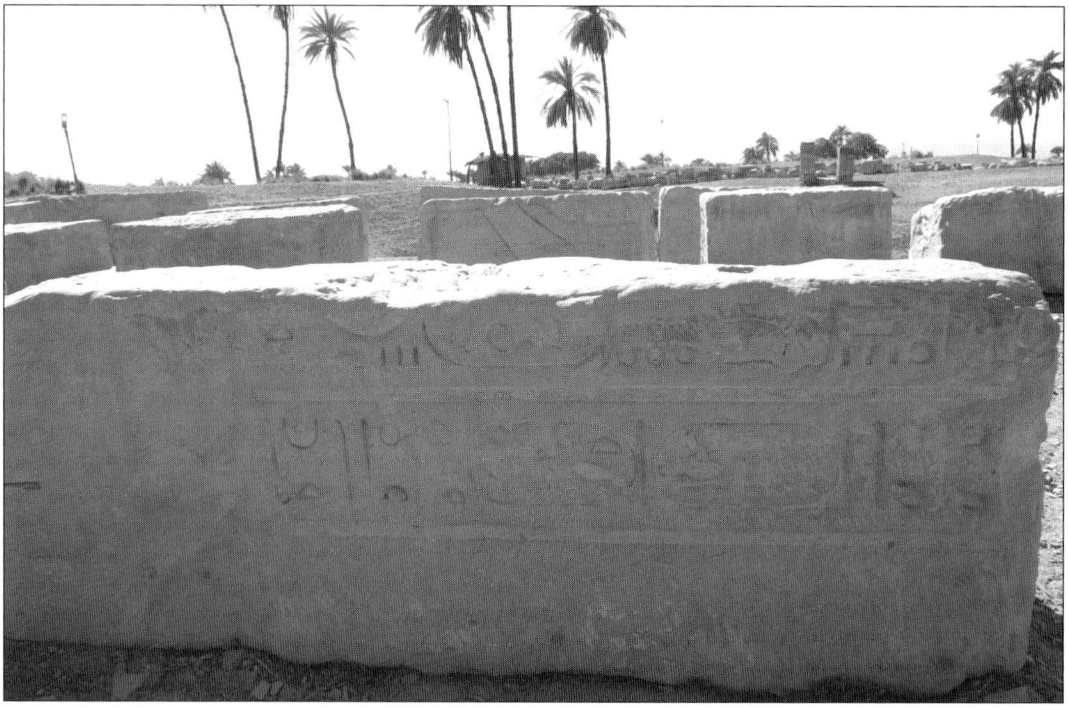

Figure 104. Full-size block of Arsinoë's designation, Temple of Medamoud.

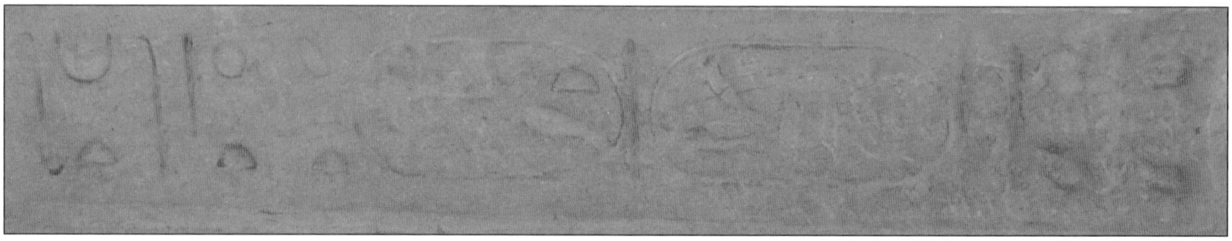

Figure 105. Detail of Arsinoë's designation, Temple of Medamoud. The title reads 'King's wife, sister, daughter (Daughter of Amun)| (Arsinoë)| the divine Philadelphos'.

link between the ruling pharaoh and the celestial universe. The position of her title opposite, and its magnified size, could suggest a twofold aspect of the queen. She is a royal queen, Ptolemy's co-regent, and the main cause of the event; but she is simultaneously a goddess, providing Ptolemy with divine protection in his rebirth as a sole ruler. Thus, this scene, cat. no. 36, can be interpreted as post-dating Arsinoë's lifetime. Her importance is stressed by the application of relative scaling, as she is the tallest figure of the scene, while the her title is enlarged in scale compared with the hieroglyphs of Ptolemy. It is suggested that her presence in cat. no. 36 is designed to explain the extraordinary circumstances that caused Ptolemy to celebrate the Sed festival; although she was no longer alive, her presence simultaneously with Ptolemy was thus of great importance. Cat. no. 36 demonstrates how the ancients applied temporal adjustments in art to stress certain aspects of time and events, in this case describing the cause of an event which would have taken place immediately *after* the death of a person depicted therein.[16]

Case study 3: the Pithom stela

Cat. no. 2, the Pithom stele, is divided into three individual sections (Figures 106–109).[17] Two of these, described as cat. nos 2L–R, illustrate Arsinoë. The third scene (without Arsinoë) commemorates the worship of Atum. This case study will investigate each section in order to understand its individual meaning and how each relates to temporal and general artistic adjustment.

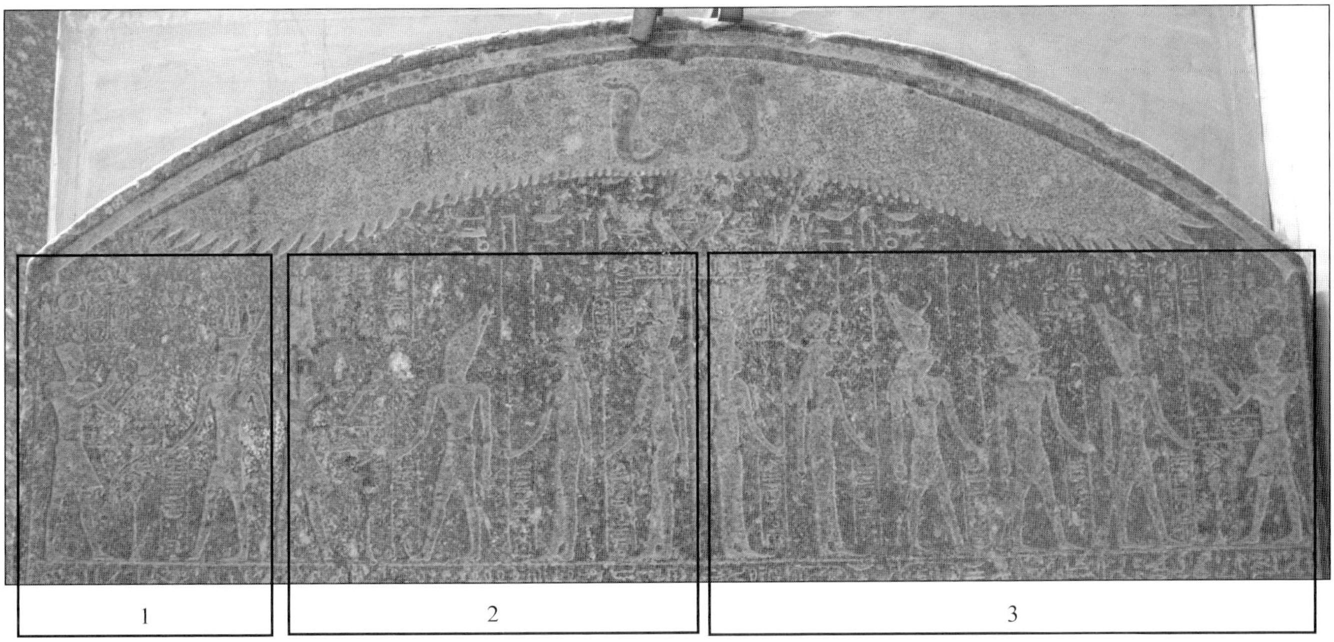

Figure 106. The full scene of cat. no. 2. Each section is marked by a rectangle (1–3) which concurs with enlarged details below: 1. Ptolemy II (far left) with a textually unidentified god; 2. Ptolemy II (left) with (from the left) Atum, a textually unidentified goddess, and Arsinoë; 3. Ptolemy II (far right) with (from the right) Atum, Osiris, Horus, a textually unidentified goddess and Arsinoë.

The scene on the extreme left (Figure 107) (unnumbered in the main catalogue, as Arsinoë is not depicted) shows Ptolemy II, wearing the blue crown (*khepresh*), sacrificing a Wadjet-eye to a textually unidentified god. The male deity holds the royal insignia, has a prince lock and wears a large composite crown (composed of a red crown and a triple crown); he is identified, on the basis of the overall message communicated in the text, as Atum. The prince lock, furthermore, establishes Atum as a youngster and, as such, his role is associated here with the morning sun, the first stage of the sun's daily journey (*cf.* Roeder 1998, 112, who suggests an association with Harakhte based on the main text. However, the main text also lists Khepri, who is generally accepted as symbolising the morning sun. It seems more likely, therefore, that the association is with Khepri, in accordance with line 3 in the main text.). This left-hand section is associated with the first main textual part, which describes Ptolemy as a sole ruler travelling to the city of Pithom. There he participated in the opening ceremonies at the Temple of Atum, a god who is textually described as Ptolemy's father. This first textual section also describes Ptolemy's journey to Asia, where he found, and subsequently returned to Egypt with, several cult statues of Egyptian deities. It describes a pharaoh dealing with official affairs on his own. Pictorially, the blue crown symbolises a pharaoh as a war lord, or may have a ceremonial meaning; in either case, it can be linked with Ptolemy's journey to Persia.

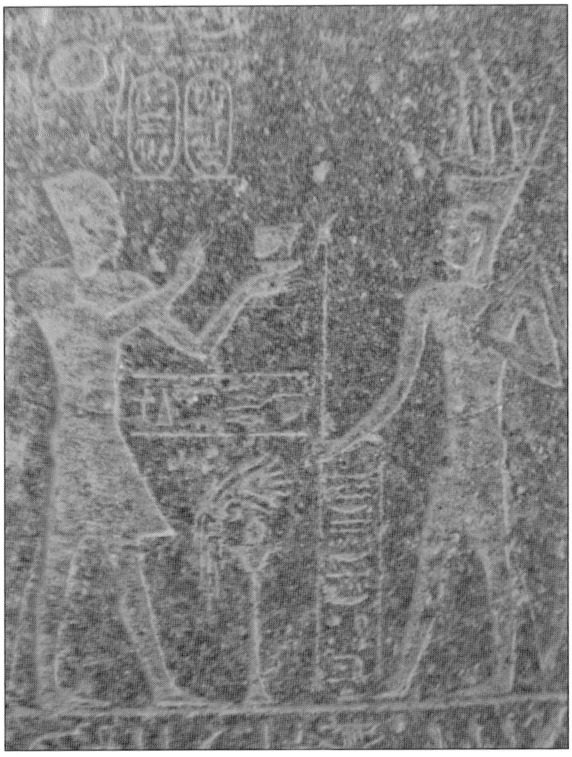

Figure 107. Detail of the third scene to the far left of cat. no. 2, showing Ptolemy II (left) with Atum as the newborn sun-god, protected by the Hathoric Wadjet-eye.

The object of sacrifice, the Wadjet-eye, is believed here to signify Ptolemy's gratefulness towards his divine father for receiving his protection while travelling in foreign countries. Moreover, Wadjet, with her fiery spirit, was believed to keep the pharaoh safe from his enemies. The Wadjet-eye may be further associated with Atum, who, according to his prince lock, is a youngster: the female cobra was responsible for keeping her newborn (rising sun) safe from harm.

In terms of a chronological order, the following scene should be cat. no. 2L. However, in order to identify the two unidentified goddesses in cat. no. 2R, the analysis here will begin with this scene. This section (Figure 108) shows Ptolemy wearing a war crown and presenting the figure of Ma'at to a group of deities. Ma'at, as noted above, symbolises the concept of universal order, and she establishes a link between the human and divine rulers. Held by the pharaoh, she encompasses the aspects of transferable royal power and kingship. The divinities in this section are identified in their personal registers of text as Atum, Osiris and Arsinoë. As noted above, Roeder (1998, 116) identifies the youngster in the far left scene with Harakhte on the basis of the main text (line 2), whereas he is identified here with Khepri, who possessed divine qualities equal to those of Harakhte, and who is also mentioned in the text. Rather, here the hieroglyphic name of Harakhte is connected with this figure of Atum (cat. no. 2R), which corresponds with the midday sun, the divine ruling king, often referred to as Harakhte (Horus-Ra). The third male figure and the female one that stand in front of Arsinoë, however, are textually unidentified. The male god is identified in the main text as Horus (in his role as the unifier – 'Harsomtus, Great God, Lord of Teku'), which can be combined with his conventional pictorial composition (falcon head, double crown). The goddess wears a traditional Hathoric crown – large cow horns and solar disc – and holds an *ankh* and a papyrus sceptre. The crown traditionally is attributed to Hathor, but, as detailed above, Isis usurped this crown and frequently used it in later dynastic times. Based on the figural arrangement of the associated deities this goddess appears to be Isis, as the mother of the Osirian triad (*cf.* Roeder 1998, 112). Isis is mentioned in the main text, supporting this identification.

The last section of the main hieroglyphic text, corresponding to cat. no. 2R, reads (in relation to Arsinoë):

> he founded a large royal city and gave it the great name of the daughter of King Ptolemy. A temple was built in honour of Queen Arsinoë Philadelphos. He placed images (*i.e.*, statues) of his divine sister in the temple. All the ceremonies were

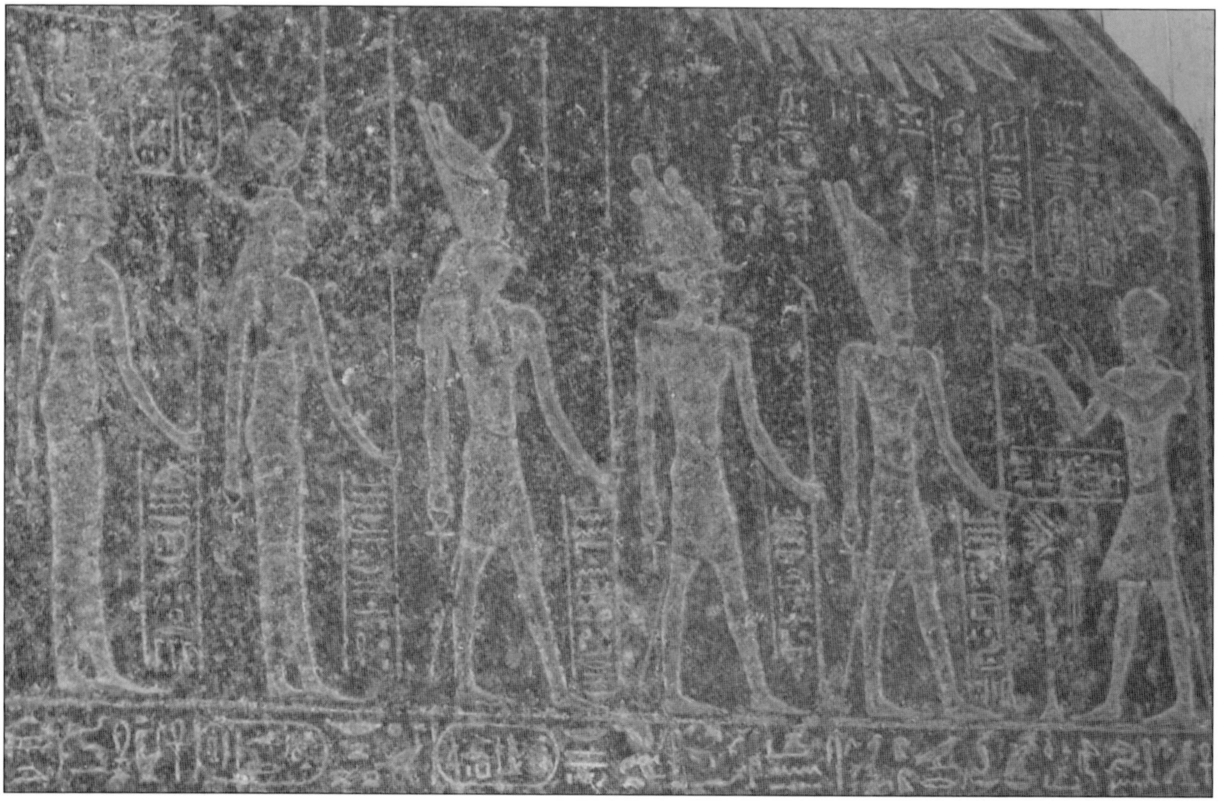

Figure 108. Detail of cat. no. 2R, showing (from the right) Ptolemy II with Atum, Osiris, Horus, Isis and Arsinoë. The presented figure of Maat emphasises a dynastic theme.

> practised by the priests in connection with the building of the Temple of their father Atum, the great god, who dwells in the city of Teku, like it is made in all the temples of Upper and Lower Egypt … .

The text describes Arsinoë entirely as a goddess. She receives the proper veneration in a temple built by Ptolemy. The siblings are described equally in terms of status, since they are both referred to as the children of Atum. Otherwise, they are separated according to the concepts of the human and divine. Cat. no. 2R places Arsinoë at the very left, protecting the divine family: a figural position that denotes importance. Her kinship with Atum, the first figure in the divine line, is stated in the main text: she is his divine daughter. Pictorially, such an association is only indirectly demonstrated, as they are separated spatially by the Osirian family. The connotations of the Osirian triad emphasise a dynastic continuation. Therefore, cat. no. 2R is interpreted as illustrating every ruler's immortality, which is personified in the figure of Osiris and relates to the death and divine rebirth of Arsinoë. It expresses the continuation of power through the descendants, manifested in the image of Horus. Atum is the main source of life and he is everyone's primeval father. Isis has to be interpreted as the great mother, nurturing and providing the royal heir with a safe haven. Indirectly, she is portrayed as Ptolemy's divine mother, since he is the earthly manifestation of Horus. Arsinoë is associated with all these deities, and establishes a comprehensible bridge between the divine royal house and the human. Ptolemy is associated with the divine legacy of kingship through the symbolism of Ma'at, his hand-held offering. He presents a symbol of transferable royal power, showing himself as Atum's son, the Osirian family's legitimate dynastic heir, and connects with Arsinoë in a clarification of an eternal royal kinship. Ptolemy is associated with his former co-regent while simultaneously emphasising that he now acts as a sole ruler, just as was seen in the case of the Mendes stele regarding Arsinoë. He assures the deities and his sister-wife that he retains universal order in accordance with the concepts of Ma'at.

The complexity of the scene is manifested in various contradictions, most of which relate to Arsinoë. Pictorially, Arsinoë is illustrated as the most prominent figure of the scene. She stands at the very left, protecting everybody, and is the tallest figure. The fact that she is taller than her divine father contradicts the fundamentals of religious artistic principles. Such a distinction must be understood as a indication of Arsinoë's great importance in the scene. This hierarchic anomaly may be interpreted as relating to the building of her temple and Ptolemy's active worship of his former queen. The scene stresses her individual divinity and her role as one who bridges the two worlds. Her divine kinship with Atum is recognised, but their positional distance reveals that other aspects have a greater meaning in the scene. Most importantly, her hierarchic position is related to her physical death, when she joins the primeval pantheon. Aiming at Ptolemy, she states in her lower hieroglyphic register 'I wish for you to celebrate numerous Sed festivals (with the blessing) of the gods.' Her statement relates the scene to cat. nos 1 and 36 (above), and supports the hypothesis put forward here that the cause of Ptolemy's festival was her death. Such a theme is strengthened by Ptolemy's hand-held figure of Ma'at, and her symbolism of transferable power. Consequently, cat. no. 2R is interpreted as relating to a period of time immediately following the death of Arsinoë. The theme of the section is the continuation of dynastic power and the rejuvenation of a sole regent of Egypt, Ptolemy II. Thus, cat. no. 2R is the only section that corresponds to the 'real' time (the time of creating the relief) and is, therefore, differentiated from the others. However, it is the combination of these three sections that forms the basis for the present hypothesis of temporal adjustment/relative time (temporal adjustment refers to a scene that corresponds to more than one period of time, and cat. no. 2R is the 'real' time section to which the others can be compared).

Reversing chronologically, cat. no. 2L (Figure 109) shows Ptolemy wearing an *anedjti* crown and holding two small cups. The deities of the scene include Atum, Arsinoë and a textually unidentified female figure. The goddess wears attributes identical to those of Isis in cat. no. 2R: a traditional Hathoric crown, an *ankh* and a papyrus sceptre. The second section of the main text reads

> Year 12, the first month of the flood, day three of His Majesty's rule, the King pronounced his wish and he travelled through Egypt together with the Queen who is Great of Praise, Lady of Loveliness, Sweet of Love, Wife of the King, Mistress of the Two Lands, Arsinoë, Daughter of the King, Lord of the Two

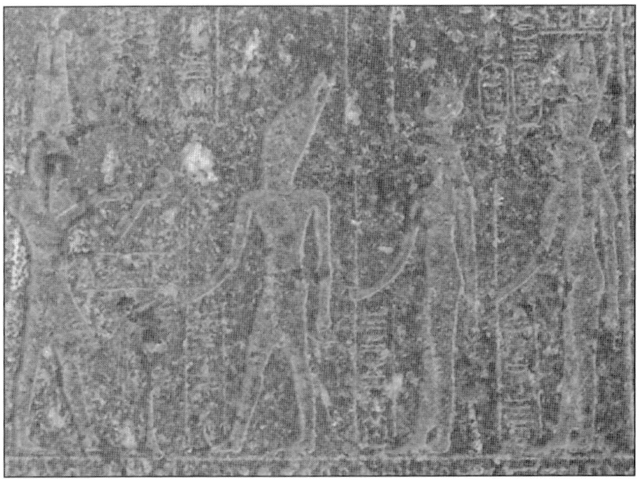

Figure 109. Detail of cat. no. 2L, showing (from the left) Ptolemy II with Atum, Hathor and Arsinoë.

Lands, Ptolemy (I), the divine Philadelphos. They arrived in the Eastern Nome of the Harpoon, it was the city of their father Atum [*cf.* Mueller's (2006, 195) translation 'her father']. The King discussed with his sister, the Wife and Sister of the King, to protect Kemet against enemies … .

This text describes Arsinoë as a living queen, actively participating in official affairs. Furthermore, it recounts that Ptolemy II discussed with Arsinoë how to protect Egypt against enemies. This proclamation reveals a great respect towards Arsinoë. There was no reason to document a discussion of civil affairs between the Ptolemaic siblings if such never took place. Such an affirmation in any other situation would have been seen as an indication of royal weakness. Ptolemy turned to Arsinoë for advice, but as a sole ruler discussing official concerns with his spouse he would not be able to claim his success in upholding universal order as illustrated in cat. no. 2R. The text, rather, seems to be a declaration of a socio-political equality between Ptolemy II and Arsinoë, expressing co-regency. Accordingly, cat. no. 2L is identified as referring to a period of time when Arsinoë was alive.

Any identification of the two additional divinities of cat. no. 2L depends on the determination of the two surrounding scenes. In terms of time, the scene on the far left relates to a period prior to the siblings' marriage. The right section has been established as post-dating Arsinoë, showing her as completely divine. Textually, cat. no. 2L refers to Arsinoë's lifetime, to her role as Ptolemy's co-regent. Atum is illustrated in all three sections. He has already been described in his aspect of the divine primeval father (cat. no. 2R), and the left-hand scene relates to Atum as the divine king, a status expressed primarily in the royal insignia. According to the artistic convention of practicality, there is no need to pictorially repeat any of these aspects. In order to establish a third aspect of Atum, his relationship with the goddess of cat. no. 2L needs to be clarified.

The main text refers to Hathor as the great mother ('Mother Hathor, Lady of Anet'). She has not so far, however, been identified among the depicted figures. As a consequence, and on the basis of her pictorial composition, her name being mentioned in the main text, and because she is the only remaining goddess for such a recognition, an identification of the goddess of cat. no. 2L as Hathor is suggested. Generally, Hathor is acknowledged in her relationship with Atum as the Hand of God/Atum (later dynastic periods: Amun). This Hathoric aspect is described in the creation myth, when Atum masturbates and creates Shu and Tefnut. The hand that performed the sexual act was given a feminine title, and she was identified with Hathor and venerated as a maternal fertility goddess. The two divine figures in cat. no. 2L can, thus, be identified as Atum and Hathor.

The scene illustrates Hathor in a pair with Atum, in a triad if incorporating Arsinoë. Arsinoë's cultural position, however, has been clarified as that of a living queen rather than a pure goddess, and this rules her role in the triad. As a living queen, she was regarded as an earthly manifestation of Hathor. Simultaneously, she was the divine daughter of Atum, also described in the main text. This scene, then, expresses both these aspects (and, thus, her religious role as high priestess: see pp.113–117). The active artistic temporal adjustments made in this section relate to Arsinoë's lifetime, even though cat. no. 2R refers to a period of time that post-dates her.

The discussion on pp. 142–148 demonstrates that high priestesses/queens were frequently associated with Tefnut, revealing yet another example of Egyptian religious complexity. Atum and Hathor, as mentioned above, created Shu and Tefnut. Hathor's role as the great mother is stressed in the main text. Therefore, Arsinoë's role in the triad may be interpreted primarily as an assimilated form of Tefnut, the daughter of Atum and Hathor. However, the complexity of Egyptian religion and the artistic adjustments of the scene allow Arsinoë to be shown, at the same time, as a living manifestation of Hathor. Cat. no. 2L places Arsinoë in one of the most fundamental Hathoric aspects, as it combines several characters in one persona. These can be summarised as follows: the Hathoric daughter role as Tefnut; the matrimonial aspect as the wife of Atum (high priestess); and, on the basis of the sexual union in the Holy Wedding, the maternal character providing the dynasty with a divine heir.

A further example of iconographic adjustment is revealed within this scene. Arsinoë, as the ruling queen, creates a cultural bridge through her position as the high priestess. She was considered divine, but simultaneously human. Her placement among the deities accentuates her divine legacy, but she is equal to her (living) husband-brother in the text. Her role enables Ptolemy to connect with the deities and, as the brother of Tefnut, Ptolemy manifests Shu. The iconography and textual record come full circle as the royal couple are textually described as children of Atum ('… of their father Atum') (*cf.* cat. nos 3–4). The text describes the couple as Atum's benefactors, this relating to their royal responsibilities as high priest and high priestess and confirming the suggested time period (during their lifetimes) for the scene.

Thus, the Pithom stele post-dates Arsinoë, but refers to her as still alive, an excellent illustration of the concept of temporal adjustment recorded above in cat. nos 1 and 36. Cat. no. 2 demonstrates, furthermore, the individuality of each illustrated section. Every section has been linked to a different time period, following a chronological order from left to right. Each individual scene relates to a textual section. The Pithom stele firstly describes Ptolemy as a sole ruler prior to his marriage with Arsinoë. Secondly, it refers to a time period when Arsinoë and Ptolemy ruled Egypt together as co-regents, attaining their religious responsibilities as high priest and high priestess. Thirdly, it records the period following the death of Arsinoë, explaining Ptolemy's first Sed festival. Arsinoë's importance is emphasised further by her midpoint position in the scene. Her personal register of text stresses her dualistic nature as human and divine, since she is described as the image of Isis and Hathor. The title reflects Arsinoë's role as co-founder of the dynasty through the connection with Isis and also describes her in her cultic role, as the earthly manifestation of Hathor and as high priestess.

In religious terms, each section of the Pithom stele emphasises Atum. The overall scene simultaneously displays the myth of Atum and events from Ptolemaic history. It describes Atum as the divine ruling master, as the father of all gods and humans and as the divine husband of an earthly wife manifested in the high priestess. In essense, cat. no. 2 is an excellent example of active artistic adjustment and pictorial relativity, incorporating rearrangements of size, position and time to further its message.

Combining the concepts of size, position and time

Cat. no. 26, located on the lintel of the so-called Gate of Nectanebo in Karnak, is analysed here as an example of an active and deliberate artistic adjustment in order to summarise all the topics presented above: it incorporates the (re)adjustment of size, position and time in order to emphasise a theme or character expressed in the scene. These adjustments will be discussed further in the overall interpretation of the crown of Arsinoë (below).

In its present state cat. no. 26 lacks the outer stone blocks that previously would have completed the scene's iconographic setting. The scene was never finished and it is the only Ptolemaic relief on the eastern gate of Karnak. The few additional decorated registers of relief date to Pharaoh Nectanebo II. Most of the gate, however, has remained undecorated. In terms of an overall pictorial setting, cat. no. 26 is divided in two halves, here cat. nos 26L–R. Ptolemy stands facing inward in both sections. Cat. no. 26R illustrates King Ptolemy II wearing the red crown of Lower Egypt, presenting the figure of Ma'at to a divine triad consisting of Amun, Khonsu and Arsinoë. In cat. no. 26L Ptolemy II is illustrated wearing the white crown of Upper Egypt and dedicating the figure of Ma'at to Amun, Mut and Arsinoë. All figures are identified in the hieroglyphic personal registers of text.

All the male figures are incomplete. The upper parts of Ptolemy, Khonsu and (right-side) Amun are complete down to the minor details. The upper part of Amun on the left side, however, shows only his crown – a double feather plume, which is complete in its details and carved in a deep sunken relief. The rest of his upper body has been neglected, the stone surface remaining untouched. There are no visible indications of an artistic attempt to attach this crown element to a body. Consequently, Amun lacks a torso, arms and head. This left figure of Amun is the only male figure illustrated with lower extremities: the legs of a male figure seated on a throne. The upper edge of Amun's leg(s) has a clear and finished relief cut, but there are no marks which might join his legs to a torso, arms and head to complete the figure.[18]

As documented in Figure 110, two thin outlines mark the beginning of a kilt on the left-side figure of Ptolemy II, suggesting that the artist began working on the lower extremities. These outlines, however, are only shallowly etched and do not join at a lower point. This abnormality seems to be an indication of artistic work that was unexpectedly interrupted. Such an hypothesis is supported by the artistic quality of Ptolemy's hand, as it is only partially outlined.

All female figures, in contrast, have their full bodily outlines, although they are still unfinished in terms of details. The right-side Arsinoë is carved in a much deeper relief than the two females of the left section. The sceptre and the text of Arsinoë's lower hieroglyphic register (26R) are also cut deeper than those of the left figures. A discrepancy in the depth of the hieroglyphs here indicates a working process started from below. Similarly, her sceptre is well defined on its lower end, whereas it is shallower above.

Another female figure is located in a standing position behind Ptolemy II in cat. no. 26L. A front outline shows the lower part of a female dress and the front part of feet. In front of her are listed her spoken words. The rest of her image is missing, as the stone blocks have been removed or have fallen down, thus fragmentising the scene.[19] A sharp vertical line behind Ptolemy's head indicates an original personal register of hieroglyphs once identifying the female figure. The identification of this female figure is a topic that relates to the encoded principles of position and time equally. King Ptolemy, who is associated with this female, stands as an active benefactor, a position that indicates a living ruler. Owing to the strict conventions of Egyptian art, the female figure standing behind the king must have had an active position corresponding to Ptolemy's. Thus, the scene showed a female figure in a protective stance, or performing a religious ritual. As mentioned above, the principles of Egyptian art placed only one female figure in this position: a living queen.

If we accept that the female figure behind Ptolemy II is his spouse, this raises further questions, primarily about the date of the scene. In order to answer this question it is necessary to establish the queen's identity.[20] In accordance with the conclusions reached above regarding cat. no. 36, combined with the depiction of two divine images of Arsinoë Philadelphos in cat. no. 26, the royal woman behind Ptolemy II in cat. no. 26L must be Arsinoë II. Her position as an active benefactor thus places the scene in Arsinoë's lifetime.[21] Such an identification is very important, since it establishes a use of the crown of Arsinoë prior to Arsinoë's complete deification.

Arsinoë's seemingly sudden death could possibly explain the unfinished relief: if she was alive when the artist began his work, he followed the ancient conventions in placing a queen as a benefactor behind the king. Her death, however, would have put the artist and priest in an awkward position if they had chosen to proceed in their work. It would be unconventional for an artist to continue engraving a relief of a queen positioned behind the living ruler if she was no longer alive, as the queen's soul was believed to ascend and join the Egyptian pantheon immediately after her death. Furthermore, the Egyptians believed that any form of artistic representation symbolised an actual event, regardless of whether the event did in fact take place in a physical sense. The souls of the figures depicted in a scene were thus captured or embedded in the illustration. It seems unlikely that a deceased queen could have been represented as alive if no additional information is provided in the scene to suggest an active temporal adjustment.

Cat. no. 26 conveys the upholding universal order (expressed by the figure of Ma'at) by the royal couple, Ptolemy and Arsinoë. The titles of Arsinoë, when she stands with the deities, place her in a socio-religious position as the wife of Amun: thus, as high priestess. Arsinoë's dual position as benefactor and beneficiary is represented also elsewhere. Cat. no. 1 illustrates Arsinoë as a queen and goddess, and, prior to her, Ramses II was depicted in this manner. Arsinoë positions are defined here, as reflecting her twofold cultural nature as a divine queen. Pictorially, Arsinoë functioned as a cultural bridge between the humans and gods. Culturally, she acted as such in her role as high priestess and could therefore be accepted on the same side as the divinities.

Cat. no. 26 relates to the concept of relative placement, as it places Arsinoë as benefactor and beneficiary equally. At the same time, these positions identify two different time periods and, therefore, stand also as an example of temporal adjustment.[22] It evidences also the concept of relative scaling, in this case primarily communicated by the figure of Amun, who is identified as the main subject in the scene based on his tall feather plume. The figural composition of

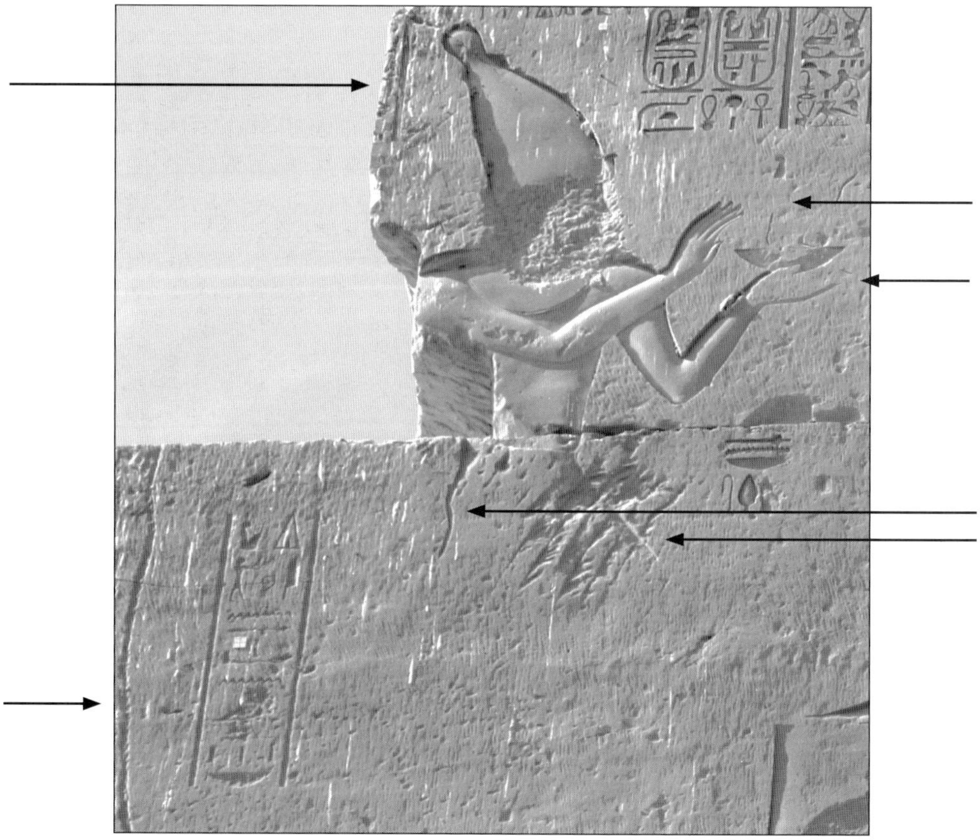

Figure 110. Detail of cat. no. 26L, showing the lower part of a female body. The left arrows point to the relief line of the personal register of text (top) and the lower part of the female body, including the lower hieroglyphic register (bottom). The right arrows show the unfinished outlines of Ptolemy and Ma'at.

Amun is unique, as he is depicted without an upper body (torso, arms, and head) but with a crown, and can thus still claim his hierarchic position.

Based on the discussion thus far, Table 18 shows the reassessment of the material as regards dating. Most scenes concur with a traditional dating; those scenes that have been revaluated as dating to Arsinoë's lifetime are shown in bold in the Table. Cat. no. 26 is dated to both Arsinoë's lifetime and to the reign of Ptolemy II.

Conclusion

Three aspects of message-conveying artistic adjustments have been examined here: size, (directional) position and time. The grids and horizontal lines anciently used to ensure correct proportions and placement according to mathematical and geometric rules have been co-opted here as instruments to measure and evaluate the structure of a scene, as explained above. A horizontal head line has previously been used in order to measure the height of the main characters of a scene: this method, in which all the heads of major figures are at the same level, is commonly referred to as isocephaly. The head line is recognised here, but is used only as a supplementary or complementary line. The importance of the crown as an integral part of any figural representation and its individuality as an essential part of the message of the relief are recognised here, although the ancient divisions and geometry of the grid do not take it into account: thus, an additional horizontal line, referred to as a crown line, has been introduced here. This clearly indicates the tallest figure of a scene and is the only indication of social order that adequately ranks the figures hierarchically. Variations in size do not indicate artistic freedom, as some earlier scholars believed, but rather emphasise specific aspects of a certain figure according to the message to be communicated to the viewer, as later scholars have accepted.

The crown line illustrates well the topic of relative scaling, which refers to an adjustment of scale/size of any given image or individual element in order to accentuate hierarchic order. In the material examined here Arsinoë's prominent role can be elucidated by the use of the crown line. Similarly, Hathor and the later Ptolemaic queens are frequently illustrated as the tallest figure (based on the crown line). The relative scaling of smaller items is regulated by similar criteria, as the figures and their associations are placed with the help of traditional horizontal lines below the crown line.

The second aspect of active adjustment, relative placement, describes the positional variations of figures and elements in a scene. It refers to the overall pictorial arrangement and encompasses directional variations. The main figures are distinguished according to an active or inactive position, establishing them as benefactors or beneficiaries. A traditional scene generally illustrates a pharaoh presenting offerings to the deities, classifying the ruler as an active benefactor and the deities as inactive beneficiaries. As with all artistic conventions, scenes occur with reversed positions in which the pharaoh receives the attention of the deities. Such scenes are associated with the topics of rebirth, rejuvenation and crowning, and frequently include Thoth and Seshat writing and handing over the official royal name to the king. These scenes often include inactive deities, who monitor the event.

The final type of artistic adjustment, temporal adjustment, deals with time. Most Egyptian scenes illustrate the pharaoh with a deity (scenes without a deity being rare). Scenes incorporating a pharaoh were believed to commemorate an actual event regardless of the ruler's actual physical participation, and each element in an artistic composition represented an aspect of the soul of the object of depiction. Accordingly, Egyptian art was limited to a contemporary time or to the past: future events were never portrayed (or were part of a person's soul). Thus, through the use of temporal adjustment a person could occur in the same scene twice: once when he/she was alive and once when he/she was dead or at another time of his/her life.

The scenes chosen to demonstrate the concept of temporal adjustment (cat. nos 1–2, 36) vary greatly in their individual compositions, but share a common theme. They describe more than one time period simultaneously, each one both describing Arsinoë as a living queen, co-ruling Egypt with Ptolemy II, and referring to the period following her

DATE ACCORDING TO RULER	SCENES	TOTAL NO. SCENES
Arsinoë's lifetime	8–9, 12?, 15, 26	4 (5?)
Ptolemy II	1–2, 5–7, 10–11, 13–14, 23, 26–33, 36	19
Ptolemy III	4, 24–25	3
Ptolemy IV	17–20, 22	5
Ptolemy V	3	1
Ptolemy VIII	16, 21, 34–35	4

Table 18. Dating of the scenes.

death, when Ptolemy II ruled Egypt alone. All three scenes relate to the topic of rejuvenation, directly or indirectly mentioning Ptolemy's Sed festival; it is likely that Arsinoë's death caused Ptolemy to celebrate a Sed festival in order to proclaim and demonstrate his capability to maintaining a continuous rule in the absence of his co-regent.

Alternatives to the traditional scholarly approach to art have been put forward here, and the importance of understanding each element in its complete structure has been demonstrated. A relief scene can be appreciated by a layman according to its immediate visual effects: its fundamental cultic value, the splendour of its colours and the skills of the artist. But a closer, scientific, approach to the material, involving an analysis of each aesthetic detail and an appreciation of the use of artistic adjustments, leads to a fuller understanding of the overall message of the scene as well as its place in the social and chronological development of society.

Notes

1 The renowned study of Groenewegen-Frankfort (1951) concentrates primarily on the change of time as it appears when illustrating the transfer to the Underworld after physical death. An art historian may use an interdisciplinary approach and incorporate concepts and ideas provided and discussed within the discipline of philosophy. Olson (2000, Chapter 7) summarises and discusses traditional philosophical works, including those by scholars such as Kant, Hegel, Nietzsche, Heidegger, Derrida and Husserl, in regard to concepts of time (*cf.* Gombrich 2000). For the ancient Egyptian terminology of time (linear and connected with the solar disc – Ra – *Neheh*; eternal and connected with the Underworld – Osiris – *Djed*), see Brecklinghaus (2002, 221f.).

2 'Temporal adjustment' is used here in agreement with the acknowledged terminology within postmodern theory (*e.g.* Murphy 2005, *passim*, esp. 126).

3 This is an artistic convention which was applied frequently in Egyptian art. Relative scaling was introduced together with other iconographical settings during the early dynastic period and developed during the Old Kingdom, where it was represented mainly in funerary art. The use of relative scaling is documented clearly in the famous sculpture of a male dwarf who is equalised in size with his wife through the adjustment of the elements. In this case, the dwarf is placed on a podium, which enables him to reach up to the level of his spouse (*e.g.* Russmann 1989, 40f., fig. 14; Schäfer 1974 [1919], 234; *cf.* Robins 2008, 21f.).

4 It is important to document such correlations in order to understand the complexity and entirety of any given scene. Bodily associated lines that do not correspond with another may indicate the lack of an original grid, a poor state of artistry, or a scene carried out in haste. It could, furthermore, identify a relief as a workman's draft never meant to be shown to the public.

5 Her shoulder line corresponds with Ptolemy II's chin and the back part of his wig. The other two lines do not adequately connect with any other pictorial element.

6 The temple cartouches of Arsinoë (cat. nos 16–18, 21–22, 24 and 34–35) are mainly on the same level as those of Ptolemy II, while being smaller compared to the cartouches of the ruling monarch in the same scene. However, some scenes (cat. nos 19 and 25) illustrate the cartouches of Arsinoë and Ptolemy II on an equal level and size to those of the ruling pharaoh. In scenes where Ptolemy II sacrifices to Arsinoë the cartouches are placed on either an equal level (cat. nos 23, 26, 30 and 33) or on a totally different level (cat. nos 27–29 and 31–32). In the latter position, the cartouche of Arsinoë is located on a higher horizontal level (cat. nos 27–28 and 31), next to the knees (cat. no. 29) or on a higher vertical level in the main personal register (cat. no. 32).

7 According to the traditional principles of hierarchy, a left-side position represents individual superiority (*e.g.* Bianchi 1988, cat. 14).

8 As the ruler, the pharaoh was considered to manifest Horus on earth. Similarly, he was regarded as the earthly, living son of Ra. Correspondingly, the queen represented the earthly form of Hathor, the daughter of Ra. It would be unacceptable to portrait a deceased pharaoh as the living Horus offering to the deities (*cf.* Troy 1986, chapter II.2.4).

9 The term 'objective' refers to (absolute) spatial time as it is measured by clocks: thus a (2-dimensional) linear development; while 'phenomenal, subjective' describes (relative) time which is based on individual experiences that go beyond the common perception (thus, 3-dimensional) (*e.g.* Havel 1994; Murphy 2005, 122).

10 Conceptions of time is a topic which is frequently discussed within the discipline of philosophy, but more rarely in art history – especially in regard to Egyptian reliefs. A general idea is presented by Freedman (2003, 48), stating that 'time is represented as a multidimensional space, rather than a straight line, which various cultural groups inhabit and influence as their ideas coexist and collide.'

11 The front figure is described as 'the living King, Lord of the Two Lands, Lord of the sacrifices (or of actions) (Strong is the soul of Ra, beloved of Amun) Son of Ra, like him, loved by him, the Lord of the crowns (Ptolemy)| may he live forever, beloved by Ba, the great god, the living Ra'. The back figure holds the titles 'Lord of the Two Lands (Strong is the soul of Ra, beloved of Amun)| the son of Ra, Lord of the crowns (Ptolemy)|'. As stated in the introduction, all translations are the present author's unless stated otherwise.

12 This interpretation negates the need for further discussion of date, other than to acknowledge a date for the stele that post-dates the death of Arsinoë.

13 This translation is one of the options presented by Sambin and Carlotti (1995, 407). The block is fragmentary and the text could be disrupted. Another option presented by Sambin and Carlotti suggests a translation reading '[servant] or [priestess] of the royalty/queen'. They dismiss an association between the large hieroglyphs and the figure venerating the couple. They do not dismiss a possibility that the text places the queen equal with the king.

14 Sambin and Carlotti (1995, 408, 412) propose that Ptolemy III's dedication to his parents should be seen as part of the ancestor cult, thus correlating with the Osirian theme expressed elsewhere on the gate. Arsinoë Philadelphos' name is textually mentioned several times in contextual scenes.

15 Among many things, she upheld the divine dualism of the royal couple, which is comparable with the ceremony of Amenhotep III and the roles of Tiye. In such context, Tiye is occasionally described only as the great royal wife, without a following name (*cf.* Sambin and Carlotti 1995, 407–10, 412).

16 Cat. no. 14 post-dates Arsinoë's lifetime, but provides further evidence to support the identification of Arsinoë's death as the cultural background for Ptolemy II's first Sed festival. The pictorial theme calls attention to fertility, with a depiction of Amun-Min with an erect penis and the field of reeds presented by Ptolemy on both sides. As noted above (pp. 74–75), fertility is associated with rebirth and rejuvenation. Such themes relate to Arsinoë's cultic rebirth as she entered her father's divine sphere after her death. In terms of comparison, the Alexandrian sculptured triad expresses Arsinoë's transformation from a ruling queen ('The One who sees Horus and Seth, Her appearance is more beautiful than the sun and the moon, Mistress of Upper and Lower Egypt, the Greatly feared/respected throughout Egypt, Great of prestige, She who care for her brother and keeps him safe') to an indefectible goddess (Amun states that he makes her into a goddess among the already existing deities, and that she is given life through his nostrils in order for her *ba*/soul to receive eternal life and for her body to be forever rejuvenated). The right section of cat. no. 14 relates to the statements expressed in the Alexandrian triad and, therefore, communicates a message similar to cat. nos 1R and 5. Moreover, 'She who sees Horus and Seth' associates Arsinoë directly with the religious position as a priestess. It is worth also drawing attention to the left side of cat. no. 14 in order to consider its association with the theme expressed in cat. nos 1–2, 26L–R and 36. The symbolism of the field of reeds held by Ptolemy combined with the figural setting, showing Harpocrates and Wadjet, conveys an indirect association with Ptolemy's rejuvenation ceremonies that took place during his first Sed festival. He stands before Wadjet, who symbolises the power of Lower Egypt. Harpocrates, as noted above (p. 79), occasionally expresses a rejuvenated aspect of the royal *persona*. Ptolemy wears the white crown and sacrifices the field of reeds in a pictorial section that is interpreted as emphasising his need to rejuvenate himself as a ruler of Lower Egypt. In addition to the already analysed scenes, cat. no. 14 is interpreted as an iconographic example of Ptolemy's requirement for a Sed festival in order to assume the complete conventional royal responsibilities after the death of Arsinoë, including the rule of Lower Egypt. His obligation to claim his right is strengthened by Arsinoë's kingship title and her state of transformation as she reunites with her divine father, Amun-Min.

17 The present author's (somewhat free) translations listed below generally agree with Roeder (1998, 108–28), if not otherwise stated.

18 The offering figure of Ma'at in cat. no. 26L looks almost identical to the left figure of Amun. Only the lower part of the body, combined with her individual crown attribute, the feather, was completed.

19 None of the stone blocks on the ground relate to this structural part.

20 As is generally known, Ptolemy II married twice in his life: with Lysimachus' daughter Arsinoë I, and with Arsinoë II, daughter of Ptolemy I and Berenice I and, thus, sister of Ptolemy II. Although Ptolemy II was renowned for having many mistresses, especially Bilistiche, he did not take another wife after the death of Arsinoë II.

21 The missing stone blocks behind Ptolemy in cat. no. 26R would have provided space for another figure. This suggests the illustration of another queen. The Egyptians always structured the figural settings symmetrically, indicating that Ptolemy was initially accompanied by a female figure.

22 Arsinoë's sudden death might have prevented the artist from finishing the relief, but it does not explain the overall bizarre relief work. Arguably, the artist began his work from the top blocks and continued downward, as demonstrated by the left figure of Ptolemy. The images of Arsinoë, however, immediately question this working method, since the lower parts of these images are carved much deeper than the upper ones, indicating that he started at the bottom and worked up. Arsinoë's death cannot provide any reason for the presence of three, arguably four, fully outlined female figures when all males are incomplete. Neither can her death explain the unfinished state of the remaining gate. Normally, an undressed gate would have been reused, or redressed if already decorated. Certainly, Arsinoë's death cannot account for Nectanebo II having only the gate's lower registers decorated. This scene has no counterparts in traditional Egyptian art. There are other reliefs that are unfinished, but these are generally preserved with a painted grid system, and the drafted figures reveal that they still await finishing relief work. Such unfinished scenes are documented in the Tomb of Ramose (18th Dynasty) in the Valley of the Nobles in Thebes, or in the small incomplete Chapel of Nitocris at Medinet Habu. The relief work of the tomb of Ramose is preserved with painted grids and drawings still awaiting its final relief scene. There is a clear workman's schedule and developing progress visible, which is very different to cat. no. 26. The scenes of the chapel of Nitocris follow the same artistic pattern as the Tomb of Ramose, with a clear step-by-step development. Other unfinished relief scenes demonstrate various indications of a work in progress. Cat. no. 26, however, does not follow any traditional artistic conventions of development at all.

Chapter 8

Hieroglyphic titles of Arsinoë

Arsinoë's hieroglyphic titles together provide a textual clarification of Arsinoë's socio-political and religious roles, which can be compared with the symbolic message communicated in the crowns.

Children received birth names immediately after birth to ensure the safety of their souls if something should go wrong in an early stage of life (*LÄ* III, 540–42). In the case of female royalty, titles could be given to a queen or princess through their dynastic and divine legacy, but also as a merit. Queens were also provided with designations based on religious positions, such as Arsinoë's epithet Philadelphos – the brother-loving. Traditionally, a queen received a name that was connected with the pharaoh's title when they were united in marriage (Tyldesley 2006, 155).

The symbolic value of the individual titles of a queen was equivalent to that of the king's designations throughout all pharaonic periods. The most important title for a royal woman was 'Great wife of the king'. This designation separated her from concubines, officially illuminating her position as a sole queen. Similarly, the title 'Mother of the king' was greatly valued: it indicated status, pure royal blood and legitimacy. Together with the previous title, 'Mother of the king' placed a royal woman at the top of the social hierarchy. Equally, it was an honour to be called 'Sister of the king'. Further examples of titles expressing a royal woman's connections with the pharaoh, including 'Daughter of the king' and 'Wife of the king' (among others purposes, these titles regulated and established the dualistic harmony of male and female: *cf.* Troy 1986), are listed below.

The titles of Arsinoë are numerous – in total, forty-one – and they appear in many variants. Some of her designations (as listed in the material), however, occur more frequently than others, and, owing to the great variety, the analysis concentrates here on the most frequently recurring designations of Arsinoë. However, less frequently occurring designations are also briefly studied for the purposes of comparison, as they appear in relation to one or several of the chief designations.[1]

King's daughter, king's sister, king's wife

Arsinoë is described as 'King's daughter, sister and wife' (=Royal daughter, sister and wife) thirteen times (Table 19). The full title also occurs with the following alternations: 'King's daughter, sister, his greatly beloved wife' (cat. no. 1R), 'Sister, daughter of the King of Upper Egypt, greatly beloved wife of the King of Upper Egypt' (cat. no. 1M), 'Daughter, sister of the King of Upper Egypt, king's great wife' (cat. no. 23), 'King's daughter, sister of the King of Upper Egypt, king's great wife' (cat. nos 26L–R), and 'King's wife, sister [and daughter]' (cat. no. 28). These titles can also be compared to the designations listed in cat. no. 13 (possibly also cat. no. 14): 'She who is in the heart of the king' (alternatively 'The one who is united with the heart of the king', Troy 1986, 183, A3/10).

The first title, 'King's daughter' (cat. nos 1L, 1R, 2L, 2R, 2M, 8, 26L–27, 29, 31–32),[2] was frequently used among royal women throughout the pharaonic periods. The royal position indicated by it could make possible, given a temporary lack of male heirs, a queen's accession to the throne based on her bloodline (*e.g.* Grimal 1992, 171; Ryholt 1997, 213f.; Troy 2003, 95f.). The social position indicated by the title could, however, also constitute a risk during the Ptolemaic period. As Ptolemaic descendants, the princesses were often caught up in political affairs as they sealed alliances through marriage.

'Sister of the king' (cat. nos 1L, 2R, 2L, 2R, 8, 27–29, 31–32)[3] was introduced at a far later date (12th Dynasty) than 'King's daughter' (Troy 1986, 194). The title strengthened a queen's dynastic bonds, but it was not necessarily connected with queenship. Interestingly, this title was also used by wives outside the royal house during the New Kingdom (Tyldesley 2006, 155).

The third title, 'Wife of the king' (cat. nos 1L, 2L, 2R, 2M, 8, 27–29, 31–32),[4] separated the main spouse from any mistresses or harem women (Tyldesley 2006, 26–35; Troy 1986, 193). It was eventually strengthened by an additional prefix, 'great', which indicated that the position of the main spouse was no longer in question and that the children of a main spouse were always regarded as the legitimate heirs of the throne.

The amalgamated title, 'King's daughter, king's sister and king's wife', was applied as an epithet of queens between the 17th and the 25th Dynasties, and was reintroduced *c.*750 years later as an epithet of Queen Arsinoë (Tyldesley 2006, 82–5; Grajetzki 2005). The merged title connects a queen with at least two male generations of the royal house, as it associates her with her father and her brother. By combining the three titles the queen enters a mythological role as Hathor in her relationship with Ra and Horus.[5]

All scenes that designate Arsinoë as 'King's daughter, sister and wife' date to the reign of Ptolemy II; these include two scenes also dated to Arsinoë's lifetime (cat. nos 1–2 and 26, while cat. no. 8 pictorially places her as a living queen). Those remaining – cat. nos 23, 27–29 and 31–32 – probably date to a period immediately following her death; in these Arsinoë is primarily illustrated as a beneficiary, standing opposite her husband-brother, thus indicating a divine role. 'Daughter, sister and wife' places Arsinoë in a direct royal lineage, explaining her royal ancestry and her relation to the ruling king (*cf. PM* III:2, 444; Troy 1986, 152; Tyldesley 2006, 38–40), and refers to a living queen, with or without the aid of an active temporal adjustment. The use of this title when describing Arsinoë after her death is a powerful political statement in which the queen functions as a binding link between the pharaoh, the deities and the royal dynastic ancestors.

This title is given to Arsinoë in cat. no. 8, a scene which establishes her pictorially in an active position as a benefactor (a position, as noted above, which indicates a living queen), where it supports this interpretation of the pictorial position. In cat. no. 26 (L–R) Arsinoë is described as 'King's daughter, sister of the King of Upper Egypt,

DESIGNATION	TRANSLITERATION	HIEROGLYPHS	CAT. NOS	TOTAL NO. EXAMPLES
King's daughter, sister, wife (Royal daughter, sister, wife)	*sꜣt nsw, snt nsw, ḥmt nsw*	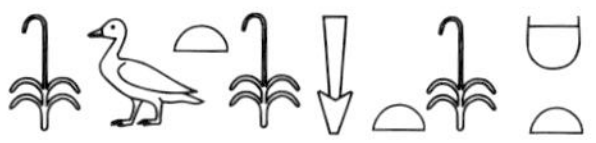	1R, 1M, 2L, 2R, 8, 23, 26L–29, 31–32	13
King of Upper and Lower Egypt or King of Lower Egypt	*nsw-bit; bit (tꜣwy)*	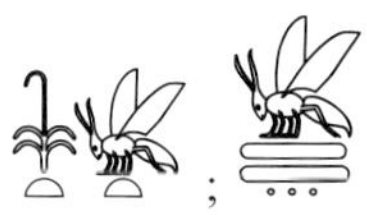	5, 7–8, 13–15R	7
Lady of the Two Lands	*nbt tꜣwy*	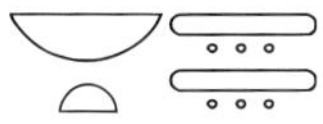	2L, 2R, 5, 11, 23, 26L–28, 30–33	13
Mistress of the Two Lands	*ḥnwt tꜣwy*	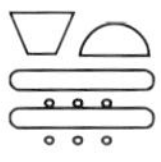	1L, 1M, 2M	3
Mistress of Upper and Lower Egypt	*ḥnwt rsy mḥw*	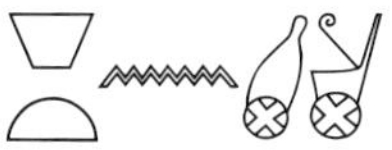	28, 31–32	3
Daughter of Amun[1]	*sꜣt Ỉmn*	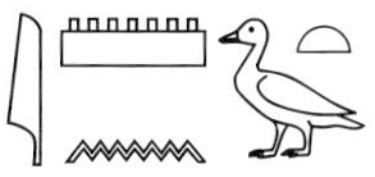	12–14, 23–29, 31–32	13
Theoi Adelphoi	*nṯr w-sn w*	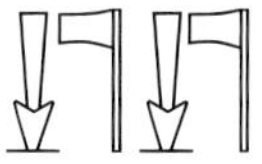	3–4, 16–19, 21–22, 24–25	10
Divine mother, royal mother, divine mother of his mothers	*mwt nṯr*	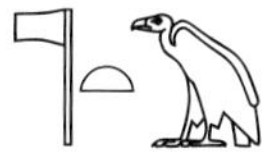	16–20, 22, 34–35	8
Image of Isis and Hathor[2]	*Ỉš.t tj t ḥ.t-ḥr (tj t Ỉš.t ḥ.t-ḥr)*	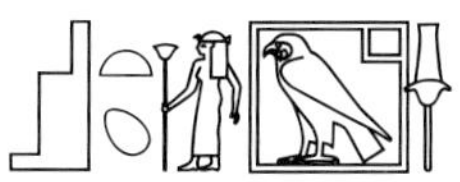	2, (26R)	2

Notes
1. *Cf.* cat. no. 1M 'Beloved of the ram'.
2. *Cf.* cat. nos 2L, 2R, 12–13 'Beloved of (all) the Gods'; cat. nos 2L, 2R, 12 (possibly cat. no. 14) 'She who is in the heart of Shu'.

Table 19. The most frequently applied designations of Arsinoë.

king's great wife', corresponding to the traditional queenly title. The title does, however, also provide further evidence to support the hypothesis, presented above, relating to Arsinoë's socio-political position as Ptolemy II's co-regent. The basis of this statement is found in the description of the king: the pictorial scene presents Ptolemy II as the King of Upper Egypt, as indicated by the white crown (cat. no. 26L). The title 'Sister of the King of Upper Egypt' could thus relate to Ptolemy's figural position in this left section, as he represents this role there. It is, however, crucial to recognise the pictorial structure of the full scene. In cat. no. 26R Ptolemy II wears the red crown, symbolising his regency of Lower Egypt. The full scene consequently illustrates Ptolemy II as the ruler of Upper and Lower Egypt simultaneously. The titles of Arsinoë are identical on both sides of the lintel: neither one describes Arsinoë as the sister of the King of Lower Egypt and therefore a clear association with Ptolemy II on any given side is excluded. Egyptian concepts of symmetric harmony and the symbolic arrangement of the figures in the full scene do not allow Arsinoë's title to refer to only one of the two figures of Ptolemy II. Instead, this scene seems to be connected with previous examples of scenes indicating co-regency between Ptolemy II and Arsinoë: the queen's socio-political position is, as suggested above, that of a pharaoh of Lower Egypt. The title is, furthermore, connected with her figural position as a ruling queen behind Ptolemy II in cat. no. 26L.

A fragment of a sculptured crown provides a comparative example from another artistic medium.[6] The fragment dates to the Ptolemaic period and includes the title 'King's daughter, sister, wife, great royal wife, she who satisfies the heart of Horus' (*e.g.* Albersmeier 2002, 113 (no. 88); *cf.* Troy 1986, C3/4). The full title is equivalent to Arsinoë's designations, especially in cat. nos 8 and 1M (*cf.* Troy 1986, 185). In addition to its royal symbolism, the sculpture text is associated with Hathor and her relationships with Ra and Horus. This elaborated title portrays Arsinoë in a complete Hathoric role, indirectly placing Ptolemy II as the earthly manifestation of Horus.[7]

King of Upper and Lower Egypt

Arsinoë is described as 'King of Upper and Lower Egypt' or 'King of Lower Egypt' seven times (six scenes) in the material (cat. nos 5, 7–8, 13–15R). Such (male) royal titles have previously been dismissed on the basis of the traditional dating of the reliefs to the period following Arsinoë's death. For many years, Quaegebeur (1971a; 1971b; 1988; 1989) unsuccessfully argued for Arsinoë's kingly position, basing his arguments mainly on textual references. His work will be continued here by the shedding of some new light on the dating quandary via an investigation of the scenes according also to their pictorial context, including the correlation between pictorial and textual frameworks, in order to evaluate the possibility that the scenes where Arsinoë is designated as the King of Egypt could belong to her lifetime instead.

Cat. no. 5 is a smaller copy of the more renowned Mendes stele (cat. no. 1). It depicts Arsinoë as a goddess and places her on the divine side exclusively (*cf.* the main Mendes stele, which places her also on the royal side). As with cat. no. 1, the main theme is the celebration of the newly incarnated ram god, combined with the deification of Arsinoë. The minor Mendes stele dates to the reign of Ptolemy II. It has been demonstrated above that the main Mendes stele manipulates size, position and time in order to capture the full written context also in the pictorial setting. Supposedly, the communicated message of cat. no. 5 concurs with the original stele. Arsinoë's complete individual designation in cat. no. 5 reads: 'King of Upper and Lower Egypt (Banebdjedet)| Lady of the Two Lands (Arsinoë Philadelphos)|'. The titles 'King of Upper and Lower Egypt' and 'Lord of the Two Lands' (here translated 'Lady') traditionally describe male pharaohs, and it is significant that they are listed in Arsinoë's personal register of text. Cat. no. 5 does conform to the Egyptian conventions that structured and regulated the registers of text, personal designations and epithets attached directly to figures, however, since it lists Arsinoë's name and personal epithet.

The overall title associates Arsinoë with the local ram god, Banebdjedet. According to Egyptian traditions, male names were incorporated in female titles to emphasise a family-orientated relationship, such as father–daughter or brother–sister (*e.g.* Troy 1986, 192–5, C Kinship). Cat. no. 5 lacks such a family-orientated connection; rather, the text placed in her personal register of text seems to refer exclusively to Arsinoë. Banebdjedet's name was possibly incorporated in Arsinoë's title in order to stress an intended aspect of Arsinoë, such as her lifetime role as the high priestess of Banebdjedet, and can as such be compared with 'Beloved of the ram', which describes her elsewhere (*e.g.* cat. no. 1). This religious role emphasises Arsinoë's royal position, places her as a living queen and links her with the ruling power, not only as a female royal spouse but as a King of Egypt.

In terms of the overall scene, cat. no. 5 differs pictorially from cat. no. 1. The former illustrates Ptolemy II presenting offerings to Banebdjedet, Isis and Arsinoë. As noted above, Egyptian conventions placed deities according to family relationships, generally illustrating a father, mother and child of a local triad; here Arsinoë is depicted as the triad's (adult) child, parented by Banebdjedet and Isis. Arsinoë is indirectly also represented in a Hathoric position as the daughter of Ra, as Banebdjedet is textually described as the 'Living soul of Ra'. Arsinoë is the tallest figure of the scene according to the crown line, which emphasises and indicates her thematic role in the scene. The central theme is rebirth, which is also indicated by the offering of a field of reeds brought forward by Ptolemy II. The theme of rejuvenation/rebirth relates to the newly incarnated ram god, but simultaneously also to the deification of Arsinoë as she enters the Underworld as a completely developed goddess. This message/theme is correlated with that of cat. no. 1. The simultaneous divine rebirths of Banebdjedet and Arsinoë are stressed in Arsinoë's title, which synchronises them. However, cat. no. 5 provides no information that conclusively suggests a date of creation, and therefore it cannot assist in the debate over the dating of the scenes and Arsinoë's assumption of the kingly titles.

Cat. no. 7 illustrates Arsinoë in a standing position on the left side of the scene, as a beneficiary receiving offerings from Ptolemy II. A horned altar is placed between them. Arsinoë is the tallest figure of the scene based on the crown line. She is designated 'King of Upper and Lower Egypt (Arsinoë Philadelphos)|'. Her eminent position on the left side, opposite Ptolemy II, and the illustrated altar between them, suggests that Arsinoë is shown here as a fully developed goddess. Given this, cat. no. 7, too, is unable to contribute to the debate at hand.

Cat. no. 8, however, can possibly shed some light on this issue. Arsinoë alone is depicted in a benefactor's position: that is, she is shown as a living queen. She is dressed in an elaborated sheat and wears sandals, also indicating that she is alive. The very fragmentary image of the deity to which she presents offerings is crowned with a crescent and a lunar disc, which, according to previous scholars, links the figure to Thoth or Khonsu (*e.g. LÄ* IV, 192–6; *cf.* Albersmeier and Minas 1998, 22–7). This crown could also connect with the Apis bull, which is generally depicted with shorter bovine horns, smoothly following the outlines of a solar disc. Cat. no. 12 supports such an identification and places Arsinoë in a Hathoric maternal role, as she is textually described as 'Mother of Hep (Hep = Apis)'. Furthermore, the prominent scale of the cow horns and solar disc in Arsinoë's crown in cat. no. 8 may indicate an association with Hathor as the mother of Apis. Arsinoë's full title (Figure 111) in cat. no. 8 reads: 'Great of Sweetness, Great of Praise, King's daughter, King's wife, Great daughter, King's sister (the king) who loves her and she loves him, King's great wife, King of Upper and Lower Egypt (Arsinoë Philadelphos)|, the Rightful'. Here, Arsinoë is described with royal titles ranking her higher than any other contemporary royal woman. The title 'Great daughter' marks her as the firstborn daughter in a legitimate royal marriage (compare 'Great wife', above (*cf.* Troy 1986, 195)). This title places Arsinoë socially above her younger sister, Philotera, who received a posthumous cult similar to Arsinoë's. Furthermore, 'Great daughter' allowed Arsinoë to claim her legitimate royal ancestry and her own right to descend the throne, indicated also by her last title as 'the Rightful'. Arsinoë was raised as the future ruler of Egypt during her first eight years, prior to the birth of Ptolemy II. Returning to Egypt as an adult, she could thus claim power through her legacy. As the 'Great wife', Arsinoë underlined her social position mainly in opposition to the former wife of Ptolemy II, Arsinoë I, the daughter of Lysimachus, who was expelled from the Alexandrian court at an unknown date for a reason connected with the return of Arsinoë (II). In terms of social status, the titles listed in cat. no. 8 are more suitable for a living queen than for a posthumous goddess, and, consequently, they suggest a date for the relief sometime during Arsinoë's lifetime.[8]

Cat. no. 13 describes Arsinoë as 'King of Lower Egypt, the Two Lands (she who is in the heart of the king, Beloved of (all) the gods)| Daughter of Amun, Lady of the crowns (Arsinoë Philadelphos)|'. The scene also shows Ptolemy II, who is textually referred to as 'King of (?) Egypt (Powerful is the soul of Ra, Beloved of Amun)| Son of Ra, Lord of the Two Lands (Ptolemy)|'. Structurally and symbolically, these titles agree. Ptolemy's title, however, is damaged and in parts indistinguishable. It is possible that he is described as 'King of Upper and Lower Egypt', but, given Arsinoë's title, his own may read, correspondingly, 'King of Upper Egypt'.[9] Both employ full royal titles equally, including Birth names and Throne names. Arsinoë's 'she who is in the heart of the king, Beloved of (all) the gods)|' is equivalent to Ptolemy's 'Powerful is the soul of Ra, Beloved of Amun)|'. There is a gender-orientated distinction: Arsinoë is 'Daughter of Amun' and 'Lady of the crowns', compared with Ptolemy's 'Son of Ra' and 'Lord of the Two Lands'. Thus far, the hieroglyphic titles listed in cat. no. 13 have provided fully comparable hierarchic ranks for Arsinoë and Ptolemy II. Both are regarded as rulers of Egypt. The pictorial context places Arsinoë, the tallest figure of the scene, on the left side, in an inactive position as a beneficiary. Cat. no. 13 cannot,

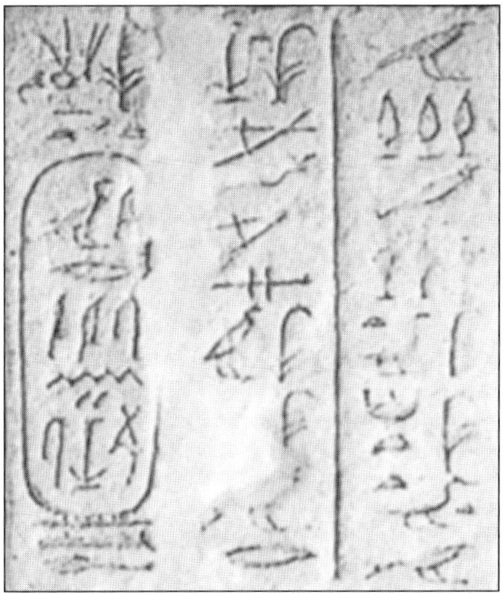

Figure 111. Detail of cat. no. 8: hieroglyphic text.

therefore, date to her lifetime, unless it is considered that her individual deification took place during her lifetime.

Corresponding with cat. no. 13, Arsinoë's full title in cat. no. 14 reads 'Daughter of Amun, Lady of the crowns (Arsinoë Philadelphos)| King of Upper and Lower Egypt, the Two Lands, [(she who is in the heart of the king/Shu] Beloved of [(all) the gods)|]'. Although it is partially damaged, the title once more describes Arsinoë in a hierarchic position equivalent to her brother-husband.[10] Her association with Amun-Min is noticeably emphasised in the pictorial scene as well as the text. Cat. no. 14, like cat. no. 13, cannot provide substantiating evidence to connect Arsinoë's kingship title with her lifetime.

The figural arrangement in cat. no. 15 has been analysed above, and the scene has been redated to Arsinoë's lifetime based on her active role as a benefactor. This iconographic interpretation proves its importance once more, as Arsinoë is textually described as 'King of Upper and Lower Egypt, Arsinoë'. Ptolemy's title is different from this conventional kingship title, and reads 'Lord of the Two Lands ('Powerful is the soul of Ra, Beloved of Amun)| Lord of the crowns (Ptolemy)|'. Arsinoë's designation stresses a direct superiority, while Ptolemy's more elaborated complete title emphasises his broad register of divine associations. Both titles describe kingship, thus assigning equal social ranks.

The title 'King of Upper and Lower Egypt' is hotly debated also in regard to queens other than Arsinoë (*e.g.* see Quaegebeur 1971a; Albersmeier and Minas 1998, 6f.; *cf.* Hazzard 2000). Six scenes in the material examined here, exclusively on stelai, designate Arsinoë as a King of Egypt. All date to the reign of Ptolemy II, and arguably include two scenes dated, on the basis of her active position, to Arsinoë's lifetime. All scenes illustrate Arsinoë as the tallest figure in the scene apart from cat. no. 14, which places her as the second tallest figure after Amun-Min.

A statue of Arsinoë now located in the Vatican Museum holds another key to understanding Arsinoë's political position during her lifetime.[11] Its hieroglyphic text describes the queen as 'Princess, Daughter of Geb, Governess, Daughter of the Merhu bull, Great of Completion, Great of Praise, Daughter of the King of Lower Egypt, the Sister and Wife, Queen of Upper and Lower Egypt, Image of Isis, Beloved of Hathor, Lady of the Two Lands, Arsinoë Philadelphos, Beloved of Atum, the Lord of the Two Lands'. The symbolic value of the titles listed on the statue obviously varies, but, most importantly, Ptolemy I is described as the King of Lower Egypt ('Daughter of the King of Lower Egypt). This geographical limitation of rule could relate to the last stage of Ptolemy's regency, when he co-ruled with Ptolemy II, suggesting that they divided their responsibilities accordingly. As was argued above, such a co-regency was practised later, between Arsinoë and Ptolemy II, and it seems likely that Arsinoë acted here as Ptolemy I's successor, taking over his responsibility for Lower Egypt.

'Ruler'

Arsinoë's title 'Ruler of (Upper and Lower) Egypt' obviously relates to 'King of Egypt'. Two or possibly four scenes (cat. nos 31–32, and possibly cat. nos 27–28), all located in the Temple of Philae, describe Arsinoë with this title. The full titles of cat. nos 31–32 describe Arsinoë as 'King's wife, daughter, his sister, Daughter of Amun, Lady of the Two Lands (Arsinoë)| the divine Philadelphos, Princess, Great of Praise, Lady of Sweet Love, Mistress of Upper and Lower Egypt, Ruler of Egypt, Lady of the Two Lands (Arsinoë)|' (cat. no. 32 includes: 'may she live forever'). Arsinoë was the only royal person ever to be described with the combination of hieroglyphs 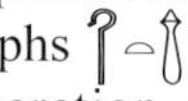 – *ḥḳ3t ꜥ3t Kmt*, 'Ruler of Egypt'.[12]

The discretion exercised here in only provisionally including the titles listed in cat. nos 27–28 is based on their contextual composition and current state of preservation. The text is fragmentary and only partially readable, and the signs are placed asymmetrically and outside the traditional registers. They are not as elaborated as those in cat. nos 31–32, as they individually read 'King's wife, daughter, and his sister, Daughter of Amun [...brother/sibling][...], ruler [...], Lady of the Two Lands (Arsinoë)| Philadelphos' (cat. no. 27) and 'Princess, Great of praise, Lady of (all) the people, Sweet of Love, Mistress of Upper and Lower Egypt, King's wife, sister [...], Daughter of Amun, Lady of the Two Lands (Arsinoë)| the divine Philadelphos' (cat. no. 28).

The partial title 'King's wife, daughter (his) sister, Daughter of Amun, Arsinoë' is identified in all four scenes. However, if the text that is presented individually in cat. nos 27–28 is combined it corresponds with the designations in cat. nos 31–32. This combination is plausible when taking into account the structural location of these scenes and the themes of surrounding scenes: cat. nos 27–28 are situated on the Gate of Philadelphos, and show Ptolemy II wearing the red crown on one side and the white crown on the other side, each side thus independently corresponding to Ptolemy's socio-political position as King of Upper Egypt and King of Lower Egypt. Consequently, the scenes have to be combined in order to understand the overall message, which relates to Ptolemy's rule of a united Egypt.

All the Philae scenes connote rulership and power. The titles in cat. nos 27–28 and 31–32 express Arsinoë's royal position rather than a purely divine role, regardless of the fact that they post-date Arsinoë's lifetime. They communicate a message of Arsinoë's individual royal power which was subsequently handed over to Ptolemy II.

To conclude, eight scenes (nine figures) describe Arsinoë with male royal titles, including 'King' and 'Ruler of Egypt'. The titles of Ptolemy II and Arsinoë are frequently comparable. The two reassessed scenes, here dated to Arsinoë's lifetime, indicate co-regency, shared between Arsinoë and Ptolemy respectively as the King of Lower Egypt and the King of Upper Egypt.

Lady of the Two Lands

This section joins three individual, but very comparable, titles under one thematic umbrella, where they function as female equivalents to male kingship titles, thus expressing queenship. These three female titles individually translate as 'Lady of the Two Lands', 'Mistress of the Two Lands' and 'Mistress of Upper and Lower Egypt'. As all three designations relate to a queen's hierarchic authority, they are differentiated mainly by the choice of wording.

The female determiners – *nb* (*t.*) *tꜣwy* and – *ḥnwt* are inconsistently translated by scholars, both being rendered as the English words 'Lady' and/or 'Mistress' (*cf.* Troy 1986, D1/4 and D2/12–13; *LGG* translates both words, *nb.t.* and *ḥnwt*, as 'Herrin'). The translation adopted here is based on an established translation of the male equivalent of the most frequent title; thus – *nb* (*t.*) *tꜣwy* is translated as 'Lady', corresponding to 'Lord' (*WB* II, 227, 232). Consistently, but without any corresponding male title, the alternative designation – *ḥnwt* is translated as 'Mistress'.

'Lady of the Two Lands' is listed in thirteen scenes, both in stelai and in temple reliefs, all dating to the reign of Ptolemy II, and is Arsinoë's most frequently occurring queenship title. Its use parallels that of 'Lord of the Two Lands' for a pharaoh, and together these refer to a ruling couple (Grajetzki 2005; Tyldesley 2006; *cf.* Troy 1986, 134).

'Mistress of the Two Lands' describes Arsinoë in two stelai (cat. nos 1–2), and occurs as a title three times. The stelai date to the reign of Ptolemy II. Textually and pictorially, cat. no. 1 refers to Arsinoë directly as a living queen. Cat. no. 2 textually describes her as a queen, and her pictorial representation agrees indirectly, in that she is placed among the deities but her titles and the combination of surrounding gods lead to an interpretion of her role as high priestess and thus queen. 'Mistress of the Two Lands' is considered here to be an indication of temporal adjustment, as it refers to a living queen. In the material, this title designates Arsinoë exclusively.

Similarly, 'Mistress of Upper and Lower Egypt' is a designation that describes Arsinoë alone. Three of the scenes containing this title (cat. nos 28, 31–32) are located in the Temple of Philae and date to the reign of Ptolemy II. There, the title is combined with other royal titles, including 'Lady of the Two Lands'. As noted above, the Philae scenes post-date Arsinoë's lifetime, although, via a temporal adjustment, they refer to her royal position.[13] Arsinoë's three individual queenship titles date to the reign of Ptolemy II and describe a living queen in a manner similar to 'King's daughter, sister and wife' (above). This interpretation is supported by the use of the titles by later Ptolemaic queens (as well as all previous queens) in scenes that show them in active positions. Any pharaoh's right to ascend the throne was provided via a female bloodline, either through the royal mother or through a royal sister whom the pharaoh married (*cf.* Roberts 1997, 3). Queens thus had an important role as an all-connecting royal force, which was established through her associations with Isis and Hathor (*e.g.* Macurdy 1932; Pomeroy 1984; Carney 2000).

Daughter of Amun

Thirteen scenes designate Arsinoë as 'Daughter of Amun' (cat. nos 12–14, 23–29, 31–32), a title always placed as a prefix to the name 'Arsinoë'. As such, it is placed above or in front of Arsinoë's Birth name cartouche. In cat. no. 12, however, Daughter of Amun is designated as a throne name by its placement within a second cartouche.[14] All the scenes illustrate Arsinoë as a beneficiary, although cat. no. 26L shows her also as a benefactor, standing behind Ptolemy II. 'Daughter of Amun' is represented in both stelai and temple scenes that date to the reigns of Ptolemy II and Ptolemy III. The assumption of the title 'daughter' in connection with Amun was a clear political and religious statement which connected Arsinoë with older Egyptian traditions and with Alexander the great, who was appointed as the son of Zeus-Amun.

The title does not appear to be recorded in pictorial temple reliefs prior to Arsinoë. It does, however, occur in other artistic media, where it describing a few previous queens, such as Hatshepsut and the Divine Adoratrices of the 25th and 26th Dynasties (*e.g.* Sander-Hansen 1940, 21f.). Prior to the Ptolemaic period, 'Daughter of Amun' occurred in variations such as 'Daughter of Amun whom he loves' and 'Daughter of Amun who is on his throne' (Troy 1986, 177f., 181).

A combination of the current title and Arsinoë's figural position in cat. no. 23 (paired with Khonsu) directly associates her with the most important (local) deity, Amun. The scene and the title together place Arsinoë and Khonsu as siblings, fathered by Amun. Through his dynastic kinship with Arsinoë, which is communicated by additional epithets in Arsinoë's designation, the scene also expresses Ptolemy II's divinity. Through an active artistic adjustment and the figural arrangement, Ptolemy II becomes an earthly manifestation of Khonsu.

Cat. no. 23, accompanied by cat. nos 24–26R, is located within the Temple complex of Karnak, the main cult centre of Amun (-Ra). This official designation, 'Daughter of Amun', thus places Arsinoë in a most prominent socio-religious position, that of both a queen and goddess (*cf.* Figure 112). The two scenes that date to the reign of Ptolemy III, cat. nos 24–25, are located in proximity to the other scenes that describe Arsinoë with this title (cat. nos 23, 26L–R). It is probable that the artist copied already listed designations of Arsinoë when he created the scenes of cat.

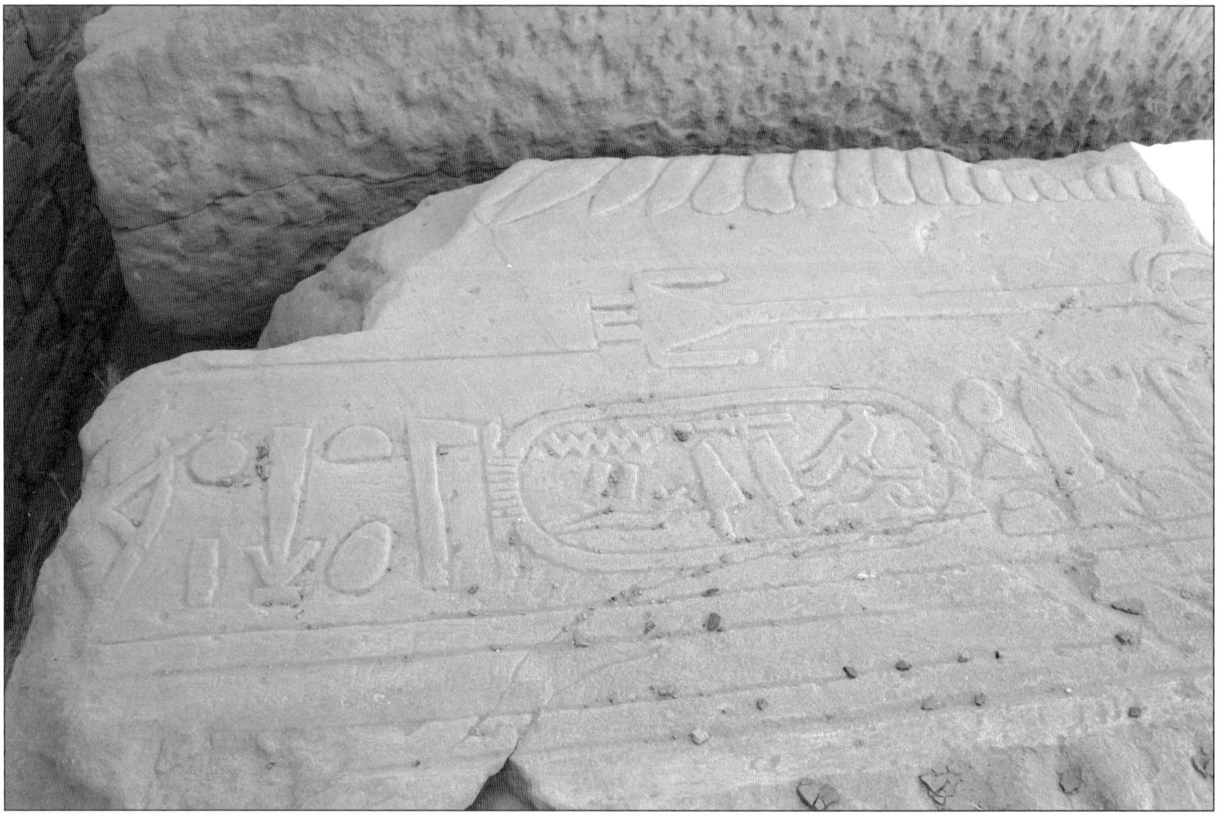

Figure 112. This block from Karnak (found in relation to the Opet Temple) designates Arsinoë as 'King's wife, Daughter of Amun, Arsinoë, the divine Philadelphos'. Notice the male suffix (-f) in Arsinoë's cartouche.

nos 24–25, nearby. Cat. no. 24 expresses the transit of royal power from one generation to the next, and surrounding scenes describe Ptolemy III and Berenice II as the royal heirs. The *theoi Adelphoi* are placed on the opposite side from the ruling pharaoh, but they are described with royal titles appropriate for a living couple. The scene expresses a socio-religious sphere where divine and human meet, an interpretation supported by the pictorial structure of cat. no. 25, which shows the *theoi Adelphoi* standing on the very left side behind a long line of deities and the *theoi Euergetai* on the right side in an equal, but mirrored, position. The left section is separated from the right by a large solar disc, to which the scene's forty-six figures express their praise. The scene is located on the southern face of the southern gate of Karnak, the Gate of Euergetes, opening up in full alignment with the Khonsu Temple. The royal couple on the right has been named elsewhere as the *theoi Soteres* (Winter 1978), but such an identification seems unlikely owing to surrounding pictorial scenes, all of which depict Ptolemy III (occasionally including Berenice II). The socio-religious situation during Ptolemy III must also be considered: the first Ptolemaic couple was excluded from the official eponymous cult and dynastic ancestral worship until the reign of Ptolemy IV (*P. Grad.* 10 (= *SB* 6283(b)); Oates 1964, 55; Fraser 1972, II, 369, n. 237), and the overall theme of the Gate of Euergetes visualises the transfer of dynastic power from Ptolemy II and Arsinoë to Ptolemy III and Berenice II. The right-side royal couple in cat. no. 25 lack official cultic titles, in contrast with the *theoi Adelphoi* on the left side, which alludes to the period during which the ruling couple attended official crowning ceremonies and received access to the dynastic power from their divine ancestors and traditional Egyptian deities in order to become the *theoi Euergetai*. It seems, therefore, that Ptolemy III and Berenice II chose to be illustrated in person rather than to be excluded in favour of their deceased grandparents. Given the general theme of the gate, cat. no. 25 is interpreted as a part of the commemoration of Ptolemy III's and Berenice II's official deification. Arsinoë's title, 'Daughter of Amun', verifies a royal divine connection, enabling the ruling couple to link themselves with Arsinoë as her dynastic divine children.

For the purposes of comparison, a statue base provides further information about this title (*cf. LdR* IV, 241; *Urk.*

II, 73; cat. no. 166 in Walker and Higgs 2001, 166f.).[15] The front section of the base reads ΑΡΣΙΝΟΗΣ ΦΙΛΑΔΕΛΦΟΥ, while an hieroglyphic inscription translates as follows (titles that describe Ptolemy (I and II) are placed within []):

> Great Bat, Daughter of Amun, God's wife, Sister of the King of Upper and Lower Egypt [Lord of the Two Lands, Powerful is the soul of Ra, Beloved of Amun,] Daughter of Amun, Arsinoë. Great splendid One, Beloved of Ra, Wife of the king [son of Ra, Lord of the Crowns, Ptolemy,] Daughter of Amun, Arsinoë. The respected, Beloved of Ptah, Sister of the King of Upper and Lower Egypt [Lord of the Two Lands, Powerful is the soul of Ra, Beloved of Amun,] Daughter of Amun, Arsinoë. The intelligent, Beloved of Thoth, Daughter of the king [Lord of the Two Lands, Chosen by Ra, Beloved of Amun, Lord of the Crowns, Ptolemy,] Daughter of Amun, Arsinoë. Beloved of Amun-Ra, the Lord of the Throne of the Two Lands, who is on the top of Karnak (?) [Beloved of] Mut, the great Lady of Asheru [Beloved of] Khonsu-in Thebes-Neferhotep'.

Arsinoë is described as Amun's daughter five times, combined with 'Beloved of Amun-Ra'. Her connection with other deities, including Thoth, Ptah, Ra, Mut and Khonsu, places her on an equal footing with all gods. She is, furthermore, described as the Great Bat, which associates her with the most ancient cow goddess, who eventually merged with Hathor. This syncretism between Arsinoë and Hathor (Bat) has traditional values and parallels with a designation translating 'God's wife' (Albersmeier 2002, no. 45, taf. 2a.; *cf.* Quaegebeur 1989, no. 1).

The religious position of God's wife

The titles 'Beloved of Amun', 'Beloved of the ram' (cat. nos 1R, 1M) and 'Beloved of (all) the gods' (cat. nos 2L–R, 13–14) are associated with 'Daughter of Amun'. They allude to a Hathoric role encompassing the daughter, sister, wife and mother of the God, and thus correspond to a religious position traditionally referred to as 'God's wife (of Amun)'. As such, they stress the cultic responsibilities held by a high priestess. Designations of this sort were given to living queens, simultaneously linking her with the pharaoh and god, establishing a dynastic legacy (*cf.* Blackman 1921, 13).

'God's Wife' has its cultural roots in a female cultic role dating to the 4th Dynasty that was initially described as 'musician priestess' (Blackman 1921, 9f.). Female priestesses were regarded as earthly manifestations of Hathor. In almost every case the queen held the office as high priestess, which associated her with the main deity of the temple. She was appointed personally by the king. As high priestess, the queen unified with the king in his role as high priest, symbolising the unification of the divine essence of dualism. Any given male god could reach out to a priestess, connecting himself with the human world in order to receive daily offerings and perform his tasks. This unification indirectly symbolised the coming together of the earth and sky (Blackman 1921, 10–13).

The queen, as high priestess, became the God's earthly wife when she assumed the religious position as high priestess (*cf.* Blackman 1921, 12, n. 5; Troy 1986, chapter II.4; 161, 188). She then used titles such as 'Wife', 'Protectress' and 'Mother of the God/Divine mother', these initially being epithets and descriptions of Hathor (Blackman 1921, 11, nn. 4–10). Arsinoë is described with these titles both during and after her lifetime. The queen was synchronised with Hathor as the eye of Ra, as the mother, daughter, wife and sister of the solar deity. As God's wife, she was also regarded as a political representative of royal authority, thereby becoming as powerful as the king (Troy 2003, 103). Priestesses worshipped and aroused the god using instruments, chants and dance. They vibrated the *menit* collar and rattled the sistra in order to invoke the divine spirit (Figure 113). From the New Kingdom the titles of high priestess increased to also include 'God's Hand',[16] 'God's wife of Amun', 'Divine Adoratrice' and 'Daughter of Amun', the latter being, as we have seen, one of the most common epithets of Arsinoë (*cf.* Troy 1986, chapter II.2.4).

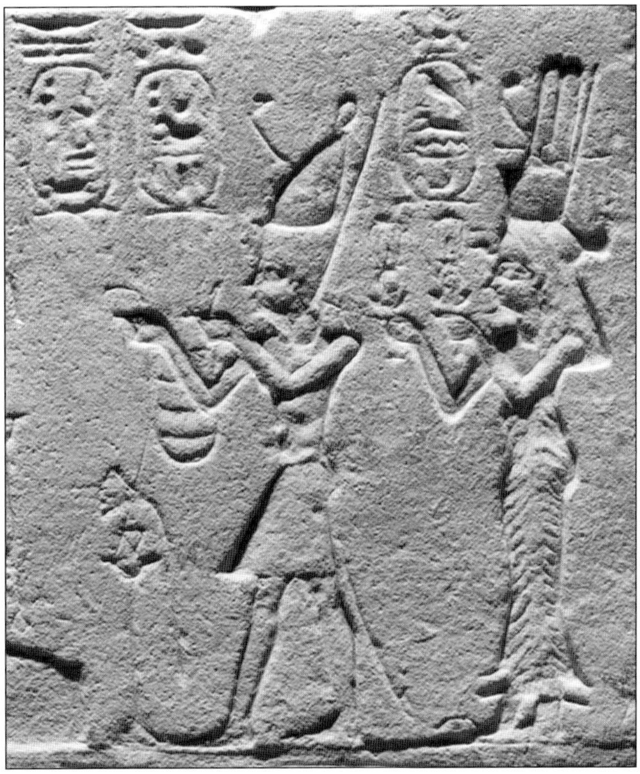

Figure 113. Detail of cat. no. 15R, showing the ruling couple, Ptolemy II and Arsinoë, in a religious act. Arsinoë is depicted as high priestess and rattles two sistra as part of the ceremony.

A comparable title translates as 'Mistress of Eternity, Lady of the solar disc (=Aten)' or, alternatively, 'Lady of all that the sun disc encircles' (Blackman 1921, 28f.; van Oppen 2007, 5), or 'Mistress of the whole circuit of the solar disc' (Troy 1986, 196).[17] This title describes Arsinoë in cat. nos 26L–R. It has previously been documented as a title of only three queens, all from the 25th–26th Dynasties: Amenirdis I, Shepenwepet II and Ankhnesneferibre (*cf.* Troy 1986, 196), who were inducted as 'God's wives'. The correlation between Arsinoë and the God's wives of the Third Intermediate Period/Late Period has been observed elsewhere, but it does not appear to have been investigated properly by modern scholars. Interestingly, in the list of titles compiled by Troy (1986), Arsinoë shares nine (identical) official titles with Ankhnesneferibre (Troy 1986, A1/7, A1/9, A2/1, B3/10, B4/11, D1/10, D2/1, D2/3, D2/15) and thirteen with Amenirdis I (Troy 1986, A2/1, B3/9, B3/10, B4/11, C3/1, C4/1, D1/4, D1/10, D2/1, D2/13), to which can be added various additional titles of a similar nature.

An older Egyptian text describes the initiation of a God's wife, directly connecting Arsinoë's title in cat. no. 26 with such a traditional religious role:

> … went into the house of Amun-Ra-Sonther, the prophets, *weᶜeb*-priests, lectors – the temple staff of Amun – following her, the great courtiers in front. She did all that was customary at the induction in the Temple of a God's Adorer of Amun. The scribe of the God's book and nine *weᶜeb*-priests of this temple helped her fastened the amulets and all the ornaments of a God's wife, the God's Adorer of Amun. (She was crowned with the double-plumed diadem and) was appointed *Mistress of Eternity, Lady of the solar disc* (after which her titular was enunciated.) All the customary were done for her as they were initially done for Tefnut. (Blackman 1921, 28f.).

The epithet applied to Arsinoë in cat. nos 26L–R, which is identical to the text emphasised in the quotation above, identifies her with previous queens known as 'God's wife' and 'Adorer of the God/Divine Adoratrice'. This text explains the inclusion of the double feather plume in the crown of Arsinoë (*cf.* Troy 1986, D3/4–7), while 'Mistress of Eternity, Lady of the solar disc' may, equally, explain the presence of the solar disc in her crown. The solar disc was mainly an attribute of Ra, thus placing a Hathoric personification of a protectress on the 'Lady of the solar disc' and drawing an association with the priestess (including Arsinoë) as an earthly manifestation of Hathor.

Another association with the religious position of God's wife is demonstrated in an additional title of Arsinoë in cat. no. 1: 'High priestess of Banebdjedet'.[18] This title places Arsinoë in the position of an earthly wife of the local ram god of Mendes – that is, a God's wife (*cf.* Troy 1986, 187). Arsinoë's induction to this role certainly made a strong socio-religious claim: both king and queen gained a stronger and more respectable socio-religious position as they assumed the most important roles of Egyptian culture. With Arsinoë in this position they were able to jointly rule Egypt, since the high priestess was considered a representative of the royal power in the absence of the pharaoh.[19]

Cat. no. 1(M) describes Arsinoë as 'She who belongs to the Lord'. Traditionally, 'Lord' has been interpreted as referring to Ptolemy II. However, on the basis of Arsinoë's additional titles and the theme of the scene, throughout associating Arsinoë with the ram God, 'Lord' is identified here with Banebdjedet, as the Lord of Mendes. The sentence 'She who belongs to the Lord' is placed in the first section of the main text. This initial part describes the marriage of Ptolemy and Arsinoë, and their time together while Arsinoë was alive, so it seems likely that this title refers to Arsinoë as a living queen. Thus, the designation 'She who belongs to the Lord' places Arsinoë as God's wife during her lifetime. Arsinoë's role as high priestess, an earthly manifestation of Hathor, is further emphasised in her lower hieroglyphic register in cat. no. 1L, as she states 'I protect you in (= wearing) your crown …'. This statement does not appear to be addressed to King Ptolemy II, but rather seems to be a direct promise to Banebdjedet. With these words, Arsinoë usurped the Hathoric role as protector of her father, brother, son and husband, all manifested in Banebdjedet.

Arsinoë is furthermore described in cat. no. 1L as 'Beloved of the ram', a title comparable to those mentioned above. This title strengthens the bonds between the god and his human protectress and wife. It has been concluded elsewhere that when a royal figure is described as beloved of a god, he or she becomes a form of that deity (Bell 1985, 290, n. 222). An example is found in cat. no. 5, which describes Arsinoë with a royal title, a personal name and the name of Banebdjedet. It appears, therefore, that her full assumption of his designation assimilates them as a divine couple with similar characteristics, as a couple, to those of Hathor and Ra/Horus/Amun.

Arsinoë's Hathoric role as God's wife is underlined also by additional titles listed in the material, such as 'Sweet of love' (cat. nos 1M, 2M, 28), 'Lady of sweet love' (cat. nos 31–32), 'Lady of loveliness' (cat. no. 2M), 'Great of sweetness' (cat. no. 8), 'Beautiful in appearance' (cat. no. 1M) and 'She who fills the palace with her beauty' (cat. no. 1M).[20] All these titles are valuable to this study, as they place Arsinoë in a traditional mythological position which emphasises the relationship between a king and his wife, which is comparable with that of Horus and Hathor. The listed titles have a rather erotic nature, since 'sweetness', 'beauty', 'love' and 'fragrance' symbolise the female scent. These titles connect Arsinoë with the Holy Wedding, in which the god impregnates the God's wife to bring forth the next pharaoh (Troy 1986, chapter II. 4). Female scent, the queen's sweetness and the priestess' beauty are all connected with a religious position that was associated with Hathor as the divine eye, the eye of Ra (*cf.* Žabkar 1988, hymn 3, for similar titles of Isis).

Each designation listed above establishes a righteous and respectable position for Arsinoë within a conventional Egyptian society. The divine lineage indicated by the titles strengthened the social position of any given queen employing them (*cf.* Troy 1986, 181). The role of Arsinoë as a God's wife (of Amun) can be summarised by the words of Sander-Hansen (1940, 21): '... "die Gotteshand", d.i. Hathor, allgemein als Gemahlin wie als Tochter des Allherrn angesehen wird' ('the Hand of God', that is Hathor, was generally regarded as the wife and daughter of the [main] God).

Theoi Adelphoi

The Egyptian form of the title 'Sibling gods', *ntr.w sn.w*, is a direct translation of the original Greek form, ΘΕΟΙ ΑΔΕΛΦΟΙ. The form of the title chosen here is '*theoi Adelphoi*', a transliteration of its original form, which is the most commonly recognised form describing the divine couple Arsinoë and Ptolemy II. The material examined here uses this title only when the couple are depicted together.[21] It is recorded in ten scenes: all post-date the couple and date instead to the reigns of Ptolemy III, Ptolemy IV, Ptolemy V and Ptolemy VIII. Two scenes, cat. nos 3–4, are illustrated on stelai, while the remaining ones are situated in the Temple of Edfu (cat. nos 16–19) and on the Gate of Euergetes at Karnak (cat. nos 24–25). Additional titles that surround '*theoi Adelphoi*' generally connect them with one of the main gods of the temple (or local shrines) as temple-sharing deities (*e.g.* Nock 1930, reprinted with additions and comments 1972). They are described as 'Lords of the house of Hathor' (cat. no. 16), 'Lords of the house of Ra' (cat. nos 18, 22) and 'Lords of Mesen (= Edfu)' (cat. no. 17), or as 'Dwellers of Mesen' (cat. no. 21), 'Dwellers of Karnak' (cat. no. 24) and 'Dwellers in the Temple of Horus' (cat. no. 19).

Cat. no. 3 textually describes Ptolemy II and Arsinoë as '*theoi Adelphoi*'. The title is listed in the main text below the figural scene as a part of the official dating protocol, listing the appointed eponymous priests and priestesses. The active benefactors, Ptolemy V and Cleopatra I, present a captured enemy in front of the divine couple Shu and Tefnut, followed by the Ptolemaic dynastic ancestors, *theoi Philopatores*, *theoi Euergetai* and *theoi Adelphoi*. The last of these couples is pictorially distinguished from the other dynastic ancestral couples, mainly by their crowns and also by Arsinoë's Hathoric position. The scene exemplifies dynastic propaganda, showing a ruling couple reconnecting with their ancestors in order to gain their power. The ruling couple associate themselves also with the mythological children of Ra, Shu and Tefnut, in an act where Shu hands over a khepesh sceptre of Horus to the pharaoh (*cf.* Vassilika 1989, 99).

A comparison between the main text and the pictorial scene shows an inadequacy. The text lists names of the priest of Alexander, the *theoi Soteres*, the *theoi Adelphoi*, the *theoi Euergetai*, the *theoi Philopatores* and the *theoi Epiphanes*, and also documents the official priestesses of Berenice II and Arsinoë, the *athlophoros* and *canephoros* (*Urk.* II, 171 (l. 6–8)). The text, therefore, refers to the official Alexandrian eponymous ruler cult, while the pictorial scene excludes Alexander and the *theoi Soteres*. The scene, furthermore, follows Egyptian conventions exclusively. Cat. no. 3 thus indicates an assimilation between the Alexandrian eponymous cult and the native Egyptian ruler cult through a combination of text and imagery. The figural arrangement of the *theoi Adelphoi* (as the last couple of the scene) suggests that Ptolemy II and Arsinoë retained their official role as the founders of the dynasty, regardless of the textual information. The official religious position of the *theoi Soteres* as the founders of the dynasty is limited to the reign of Ptolemy IV, and cat. no. 3 dates to the reign of Ptolemy V, which emphasises Ptolemy II and Arsinoë as the founders (*P. L. Bat.* 24 = Clarysse and Van der Veken 1983).[22]

Cat. no. 4, also dating to the reign of Ptolemy III, describes Ptolemy II and Arsinoë as '*theoi Adelphoi*'. The hieroglyphic designation, *ntr. w sn. w*, is placed above the head of Ptolemy II, between the individual cartouches of the couple. The title also occurs in the main text, where it is used to describe Ptolemy II and Arsinoë as Ptolemy III's parents. The following textual section states their cultic title in connection with the eponymous priesthood, as in cat. no. 3, and includes also the name of Arsinoë's *canephoros* (*Urk.* II, 126 (l. 5)). The text in cat. no. 4 indicates an assimilation of the Alexandrian eponymous cult with the native Egyptian worship of ancestors, although it is, again, separated from the pictorial scene. The scene focuses on the deification of Ptolemy III and Berenice II and their induction to the traditional Egyptian royal cult. The main event described in the pictorial scene is the writing of the annuals, performed by Thoth and Seshat.

Cat. nos 16–19 and 21–22, which date to the reigns of Ptolemy IV and Ptolemy VIII, are located in the Temple of Edfu. As demonstrated above, all these scenes illustrate a ruling pharaoh who presents offerings to his dynastic ancestors. Arsinoë is depicted throughout in a standing position behind Ptolemy II. The couple are generally described by individual titles located in their personal registers of text, and by their shared title in the board-register that crowns the scene. Thus, they kept their individuality simultaneously with their divine royal positions as Hathor and Horus. Cat. no. 24 concurs with previous scenes, as Ptolemy II and Arsinoë are described with individual titles in the personal registers of text and as a couple in the top register. This scene dates to the reign of Ptolemy III. Cat. no. 25 also dates to Ptolemy III, but places the shared title above the head of Ptolemy II, between their individual cartouches.

The scenes in the material indicate that the *theoi Adelphoi* were regarded as the founders of the Ptolemaic Dynasty. The pictorial material follows Egyptian conventions, and the scenes are located mainly in Upper Egypt. The combination of these two factors is important, since the native Egyptian ruler cult is traditionally differentiated from the Alexandrian ruler cult. Stelai with a dynastic setting seem to have functioned as a link between the two. All scenes that describe the couple with this title post-date their lifetimes, and are always in a conventional dynastic setting that expresses the transfer of power from one generation to the next.[23] In terms of iconographic arrangement, the *theoi Adelphoi* are separated from other ancestral couples. Arsinoë is frequently illustrated as the tallest figure of the scene on the basis of an item which also distinguishes this couple from the others – the crown. Arsinoë wears the crown of Arsinoë (other than in cat. no. 21), and Ptolemy II either an Osirian *atef* or an *anedjti* crown. All other females, without any exceptions, wear a traditional female crown. All other males wear one of the above-mentioned crowns, the *atef* or *anedjti*, in opposition to the one worn by Ptolemy II. These scenes (cat. nos 3, 16–17, 19–22) show Arsinoë standing behind Ptolemy II, raising her hand in a protective manner. Her hand's pose, combined with her position as the last figure of the left side, suggests a socio-religious position as the protectress of the entire dynasty, including the ruling royal couple.

All scenes mentioned above are classified as dynastic regardless of their figural arrangement, as mentioned above (*cf.* Winter 1978). The main symbolic theme of these scenes is a ruling pharaoh who claims his right to the throne and demonstrates his pure dynastic legacy and royal blood. The Gate of Euergetes presents a contrast, as it provides Queen Berenice II with a title that places her as the heiress of the *theoi Adelphoi* (*e.g.* Quaegebeur 1989, 97). This title underlines the importance of not only an individual scene but also the full setting or composition of scenes under one associated theme. It has been argued elsewhere (Winter 1978) that the link between a ruling pharaoh and his ancestors is unclear if they were placed on opposite sides of a scene. However, such a separation was necessary in order for the king to claim his right to the throne, as this claim could be made only as a result of the death of the previous ruler(s).

Exceptions include scenes that express crowning or rejuvenation themes, such as cat. no. 4, which provides further examples of pictorial adjustment and emphasises that time is not a main subject, but instead the ceremony itself. All figures in cat. no. 4 are equally illustrated as sons and daughters of Ra. The scene is unique because of its dualistic arrangement, in which all figures are depicted in pairs/couples, including the gods on the right side. The first Hathoric goddess on the right is coupled with Amun-Ra; Hathor with Horus; Tefnut with Shu, and the fourth female figure with a male counterpart now missing. The scene clarifies the divine legacy and places the Ptolemaic couples in a direct line with the primeval constitution of Egyptian religion.[24] Ptolemy III and Berenice II illuminate their dynastic legacy through the association with the deceased ancestors and emphasise their right to rule as they connect themselves with the divine rulers, Horus and Hathor, as husband and wife. Here the ruling monarch gains strength and emphasises his divine royal heritage as he claims his true right to the throne.[25]

Divine mother/mother of the god

Seven scenes describe Arsinoë as 'Divine mother/mother of the god'. This title primarily indicates a divine cultic position rather than a royal/queenly one. It is associated with the titles 'God's wife' and 'Daughter of Amun', once more portraying Arsinoë in a Hathoric role. As a comparison, 'Royal mother (= mother of the king)' clearly describes a queen in a different social position, but one still similar to the previous title because the pharaoh was regarded as divine (*e.g.* Troy 1986, 192). Cat. no. 16, which post-dates her lifetime, describes Arsinoë as 'Royal mother', while cat. nos 34–35 use 'Divine mother of his mothers'. Both titles are associated with Hathor's dynastic aspects, including her roles as the mother, daughter, sister, and wife of Ra/Horus/Amun. All dynastic ideas are based on this mythological structure.

As 'Divine mother' Arsinoë is always paired with Ptolemy II, with later Ptolemaic couples occasionally included. On the basis of the figural arrangement, 'Divine mother' is interpreted here as a purely dynastic title. A living queen would be more likely to receive titles such as 'King's daughter, sister, and wife'. 'Divine mother' describes Arsinoë in a socio-religious position from which her descendants could claim their royal ancestry and true bloodline. It explains her individual role, but more importantly serves as a female equivalent of the divine father, a title frequently used to describe Ptolemy II in these scenes.[26] The material indicates that 'Divine mother' was applied as a designation of Arsinoë long after her death.

Moving away from the dynastic theme associated with this title, cat. no. 12. describes Arsinoë as 'Mother of Hep' (the Apis bull). Once again, the title connects Arsinoë with Hathor and divine motherhood. The title is directly connected with the personal cult of Arsinoë at Memphis, where she had her own temple and priesthood, and was closely associated with Ptah. The crown of Arsinoë in cat. no. 12 shows enlarged cow horns and solar disc, also pictorially suggesting an assimilation with Hathor. 'Mother of Hep' places Arsinoë with Sekhmet/Hathor as the Memphite divine mother of the Apis bull, while the scenes documented above focus mainly on the dynastic ruler cult (*e.g.* Crawford 1980).

Image of Isis and Hathor

The title 'Image of Isis and Hathor' describes Arsinoë in cat. no. 2 (L–R). This epithet has a twofold meaning, as it communicates both the socio-political role and the religious role of the queen. It connects Arsinoë with two of the most essential Egyptian goddesses, who together rule and determine the arrangement and identification of each section of the whole scene. In this way, by reflecting Arsinoë's roles as a ruling queen and high priestess, as deified as part of the dynastic myth (with Ptolemy together manifesting Horus and Hathor – the divine rulers) and as an individual goddess posthumously, the title 'Image of Isis and Hathor' summarises the complete concept of Egyptian temporal adjustment (pp. 93–103). As the Pithom stele has been analysed already according to its pictorial setting, here the focus will be on a comparison with similar titles held by Arsinoë elsewhere.

The lintel-scene of cat. no. 26 (Figure 114) contains a section of a hieroglyphic text which deserves reassessment. Earlier publications (*LdR* IV, 240 F) dismiss this section as damaged or no longer visible, although more recent scholars have translated it in agreement with Sauneron (1960) 'la mere divine d'Apis-réplique-de-Ptah, la souveraine de tous les animaux sacres' (the divine mother of Apis, image of Ptah, the ruler (/Lord) of all sacred animals) (*Mwt – nṯrjt – njt – ḥp – ʿnḫ – whm– nj – Ptḥ – njšwt – nj – ʿwt – nbt – nṯrjt*; *cf.* Quaegebeur 1978, 262). The hieroglyphic signs are represented as follows:

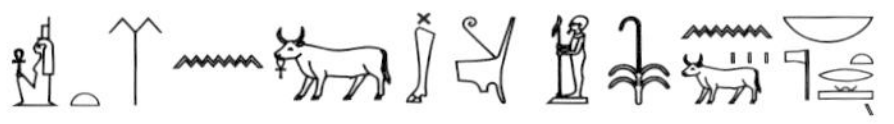

Firstly, the manifold symbolism expressed in the sign of Isis, which relates to the goddess simultaneously as aspects of maternity (LGG I, 61–5), should be stressed. Moreover, the latter sign of the bull (and its plural ending) should be translated as 'souls' rather than 'animals' (thus, transcribing the signs as *kȝ.w*). Consequently, the transliteration suggested here is as follows: *ȝst – (mwt) – m – n – ḥp – ʿnḫ – wḥm – n – Ptḥ – nsw – n – kȝ.w – nbt ntryt.*[27] The symbolic association with the goddess Isis is retained and the translation is as follows: 'Divine mother (Isis) of the living bull (=Hep/Apis), the manifestation of Ptah, the King of all souls, Lord of sacredness'. A complete translation of the designation of Arsinoë thus reads: 'Daughter of the king, sister of the King of Upper Egypt, King's great wife, Lady of the Two Lands, Mistress of Eternity, Lady of the sun disc (Aten), Daughter of Amun, Arsinoë, the divine Philadelphos, Divine mother (Isis) of the living bull, the manifestation of Ptah, the King of all souls, Lord of sacredness'.

On the basis of the analysed signs, the complete text describes Arsinoë as a living image of Isis, the mother of Apis. The subsequent passage stresses an association with Ptah, who was responsible for the opening of the mouth ceremony: as he blew life, reborn in divine form, into the deceased physical body, he allowed the soul to become immortal and join the celestial sphere. This theme is also described in cat. no. 1, which dates cat. no. 26R to immediately following the death of Arsinoë (*cf.* Graeco-Roman Museum, Alexandria, inv. no. 11261; Callim. *Apoth. Ars.* (= F 228); Macurdy 1932, 127–8; van Oppen 2007, 311). This title demonstrates yet another example of temporal adjustment, as the scene represents a ruling queen who stands in an active position behind Ptolemy. It further supports the suggestion presented on p.104 that it was the death of Arsinoë that prevented the artists from completing the scene. Finally, the link with Apis is associated with cat. no. 12, which describes Arsinoë as the mother of Hep (=Apis).

The reassessed section of Arsinoë's designation, therefore, places the queen in a religious position associated not only with Isis but also with Ptah and Apis. The translation of the text provides supporting material for the concept of temporal adjustment, suggesting that the creation of cat. no. 26, which began during the lifetime of Arsinoë, wass interrupted by her sudden death. The artist may have engraved the hieroglyphic text as his last task, after outlining the essential attributes of the deities in order not to disrespect them.

As mentioned above (p. 112), Arsinoë is also described in connection with Isis and Hathor on the 'Vatican statue' (Inv. no. 22681). The designation reads 'Image of Isis, Beloved of Hathor', again associating the queen with the two goddesses. In addition, a now-lost relief scene, once recorded and copied in the quarries of Masara, names Arsinoë as 'King of Upper and Lower Egypt, Isis-Arsinoë' (Howard-Vyse and Perring 1842, 100f., no. 9; see Quaegebeur 1978, 251). The copy of the relief shows two individual sections of one general scene. Ptolemy II presents offerings to an unknown deity, Khonsu-Ra-Harakhte and Isis-Arsinoë in the left section, and to Ra, Shu and Tefnut in the right.[28] The scene

Figure 114. Detail of cat. no. 26R, showing the hieroglyphic text.

is crowned with two sets of winged solar discs and is further decorated with papyrus and lotus clusters on each side. The figures are depicted within the outlines of a stylised *naos*. The figure of Khonsu-Ra-Harakhte is described as a child who comes forth from the eye of Ra, and is documented wearing a triple crown. His title is important because Arsinoë is included in the triad in a position of a divine mother and, thereby, the pictorial arrangement once again links her with Hathor as the eye of Ra. As in cat. no. 2, Arsinoë is associated equally with Isis and Hathor: textually with Isis and pictorially with Hathor. The figure missing from the copied scene could possibly be identified as Amun, based on the characterised aspect of Khonsu. Certainly, such an identification would support Arsinoë's religious role as a God's wife during her lifetime, and could also, given the use of relative placement in the scene, date the scene to Arsinoë's lifetime:[29] the right section illustrates the primeval family, including Ra and his two children, Shu and Tefnut. It is probable that, as in cat. no. 2, the two scenes interconnect, showing two facets of the same descriptive palette.[30]

Royal titles

The divine legacy was made unquestionable and comprehensible by the application of royal names, traditionally including five individual designations: the Horus name, the Two Ladies name, the Golden Horus name, the Throne name (*praenomen*), and the Birth name (*nomen*) (Beckerath 1984, 2–36; *LÄ* III, 540–56). As described above, each child was given a personal name immediately after birth in order to protect his or her soul in case of an early accident or sudden demise (the soul, in other words, was connected to the name). However, in order to separate royalty from commoners, the royal names were created and developed with the intention of strengthening and highlighting the true divine nature of the pharaoh; he was, therefore, given designations validating this legacy.

The Horus name

The Horus name presented and legitimated the pharaoh as a divine ruler. Regularly (but not always), the name was placed within a rectangle crowned by a falcon (Figure 115), denoting the royal palace and divine kingship (*e.g.* Manchip White 1970, 10; *cf.* Budge 2004 [1908], xiii). Originally, the Horus name was the only official royal name of the pharaoh and, as it dates to the first dynasties, it is the oldest recorded royal designation (Brier and Hobbs 1999, 61). Its fundamental significance was its use to describe the pharaoh as an earthly manifestation and incarnation of the sun-god Ra, materialised in his kingship role as the falcon (= Horus) (*LÄ* III, 540). Given Horus' earthly manifestation in the pharaoh, and the royal spirit, it is not surprising that the Horus name is occasionally referred to as a *ka* (= soul) name (Gardiner 1957, 72).

Among the examples of Horus names as provided by J. von Beckerath (1984, 11f.) are 'Powerful heart', 'Divine being', 'He who satisfies the Two Lands', 'He who upholds Ma'at', 'He who lives in the heart of the Two Lands', 'Lord of Ma'at', 'Strong bull arising in Thebes' and 'Image of the gods' (*cf.* Gardiner 1957, 72). Ptolemy II is one of only a few rulers having all five royal names listed in one document. This document, the Pithom stele (here listed as cat. no. 2) describes him as 'Strong Youth', relating him to the youngster Harpocrates. Previously, Ptolemy I assumed the Horus title 'Whose might is great, the valiant ruler' (Beckerath 1984, 118). Some of the male Horus titles listed by von Beckerath correspond to official designations of Arsinoë, and Arsinoë's title 'Image of Isis and Hathor' is particularly interesting as it is associated, in a feminine form, with 'Image of the gods'.

Beckerath includes in his list queens who are described as pharaohs, incorporating the Divine Adoratrices of the Third Intermediate Period.[31] Prior to the Ptolemaic queens at least four female rulers were given a Horus name. Sobeknefru was the first of these, with a name translated as 'Beloved of Ra' (Beckerath 1984, 67). This title, which connects the female ruler directly with the original solar deity, is documented as one of Arsinoë's, although it is not included in the material studied here. As noted above, titles that describe royals as 'Beloved of' communicate a message of belonging and identify the king/queen with the divine essence that is encapsulated in the god or goddess with whom he/she is associated.[32]

Several of Arsinoë's titles agree with previous male and female rulers' Horus names, as demonstrated below. However, at no point was Arsinoë provided with a name placed within the rectangular structure that conventionally formed a Horus name in texts. It is important, nonetheless, to recognise the complexity of the Ptolemaic development of the Middle (/Late) Egyptian language: the Graeco-Roman period offers various examples of adjustment of text and iconography. It is reasonable to question whether Arsinoë needed the conventional structure of an official Horus name, or whether a Horus name listed freely in the text would be equally accepted by the native Egyptians.

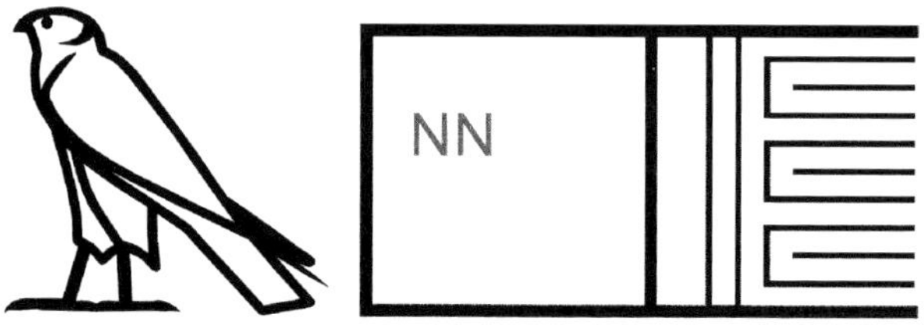

Figure 115. Horus name. Signs after JSesh.

Excluding the rectangular cartouche, there are three possibilities for a Horus name for Arsinoë in the main titles: 'Beloved of the ram', 'Image of Isis and Hathor' and 'Banebdjedet'. The first two titles have already been classified as valid Horus names, as they are recorded for Sobeknefru ('Beloved of the ram')[33] and as the male form 'Image of the gods'. The third, however, needs to be reassessed in order to understand its importance here.

Arsinoë's complete designation in cat. no. 5, 'King of Upper and Lower Egypt (Banebdjedet)| Lady of the Two Lands (Arsinoë)| Philadelphos', has caused a multi-generational debate. This full title is presented with two cartouches, one of which lists 'Banebdjedet'. It is traditional for a *praenomen* or *nomen* (Throne/Birth name) to be contained within a cartouche, but such a convention may be disregarded, since Arsinoë's official Throne name was '(She who is in the heart of Shu, beloved of all the gods)|' (cat. nos 2L–R, 12; *cf.* Troy 1986, A1/30), with 'King' occasionally substituted in the place of 'Shu' (cat. nos 13–14). The modern debate concerns 'Banebdjedet' and, to some degree, 'Lady (Lord) of the Two Lands'. These were interpreted above as personal titles of Arsinoë on the basis of their location in her personal register of text. 'Banebdjedet' places Arsinoë as an immediate female incarnation/manifestation of the local ram god, emphasising her direct lineage as a descendant of Ra, and reconnects her with the original applications of a Horus name, such as were documented during the very first Egyptian pharaohs, in which the ruler was described with the name of a god.

An identification of 'Banebdjedet' as Arsinoë's Horus title validates the iconographic interpretation given here of cat. nos 1 and 5 as reflecting not only the rebirth of the physical ram but also the incarnation of Arsinoë. The two stelai pictorially identify Arsinoë as Banebdjedet's daughter and, in cat. no. 1, his high priestess. The text in cat. no. 5 is comparable to the title assumed by the mother of the deified vizier Imhotep (3rd Dynasty), which describes her as 'Daughter of Banebdjedet' (Warner and Fernández-Armesto 2003, 296). It appears that no other preserved ancient records provide a list of high priestesses of Banebdjedet prior to Arsinoë. As Banebdjedet was a local form of Amun, however, his high priestess is equivalent to the God's Wives of Amun in Karnak, as will be discussed in more detail below. It can be concluded, on the basis of the material, that the official designation 'Banebdjedet' functioned as an intentional and legitimate official Horus name of Arsinoë. The ancient convention of connecting a Horus name with the primeval divine solar force, Ra, is adequately followed in the main text of cat. no. 1, where Banebdjedet, and therefore Arsinoë, is described as the soul of Ra.

Arsinoë is not described as 'Banebdjedet' elsewhere, but her connection with the ram god is textually and pictorially emphasised also in cat. no. 1, as noted above. In order to establish the actual existence of a Horus name in cat. no. 1 we must return to the unique insignia located behind the back figure of Ptolemy II. It is structurally compiled of a standard base (usually connected with geographical nomes), hieroglyphic signs symbolising rulership of the Two Lands, and a set of large cow horns holding two empty Horus names crowned by falcons, who in their turn wear the white crown and the red crown respectively (Figures

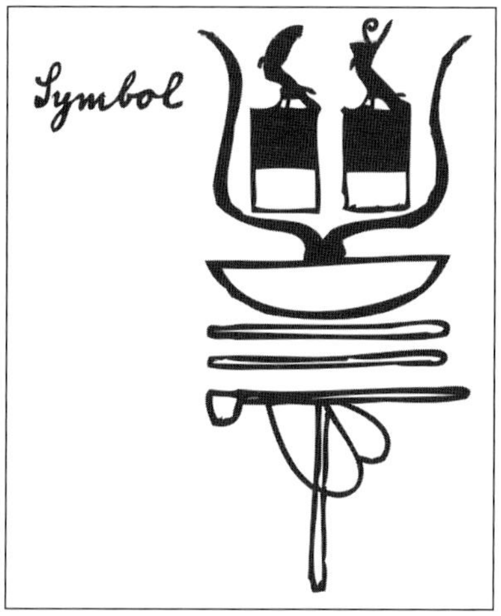

Figure 116. Insignia in cat. no. 1: copy from Sethe 1904 (=Urk. II), II.30.

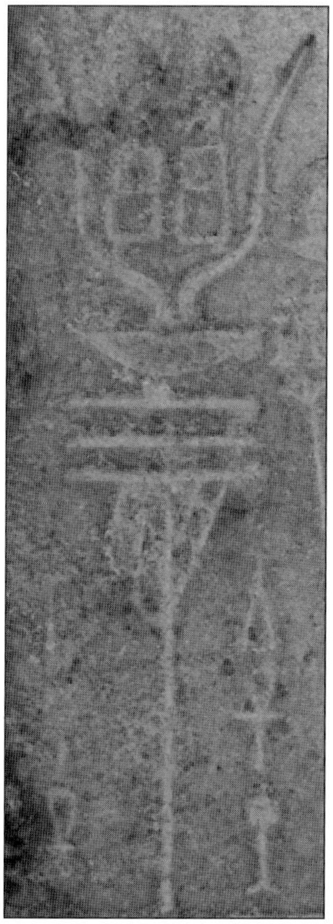

Figure 117. Detail of the insignia in cat. no. 1. Note how this photograph is a mirror opposite of Sethe's illustration.

116–117). The contextual hieroglyphic text states *sn.sn* (*sn.w*), identified here as 'siblings' rather than 'brothers' and thus identifying the insignia as a determiner of Ptolemy II and Arsinoë (*cf.* Revez 2003). The insignia, consequently, indicates the existence of two individual Horus names, describing Ptolemy II as the King of Upper Egypt and Arsinoë as King of Lower Egypt. This identification agrees with the figural arrangement and contextual setting of the scene, which pictorially emphasises a socio-political state of co-regency. The empty Horus name combined with the theme of cat. no. 1 emphasises Arsinoë's assimilation with Banebdjedet, and presents Arsinoë not only as his daughter and high priestess, but also as the one who maintains his incarnated soul. It was concluded on pp. 93–96, concerning the active temporal adjustment used in cat. no. 1, that the image of Arsinoë in cat. no. 1L is that of a living and ruling queen, which would agree with the use of a Horus name.

The Nebty name

The second royal designation related to conventional Egyptian kingship is the Nebty name, the designation of the Two Ladies (Figure 118) (*e.g.* Frankfort 1978, 46). In terms of visual identification, the vulture and serpent are primarily placed as individual signs in front of the personal name, although they occasionally (frequently during the Old Kingdom) occur indirectly within the main title itself, incorporated in titles such as 'He of the Two Ladies' (Beckerath 1984, 18). Although not as ancient as the Horus name, the Nebty title dates back to the Early Old Kingdom (Petrie 1900, pl. XI, no. 1 (CG 31773); Beckerath 1984, 13–18). It follows the conventions of Egyptian dualism, as it incorporates a feminine feature of male power (*cf.* Troy 1986, II.6). It symbolises the pharaoh's rule of the Two Lands, Upper and Lower Egypt, denoting his political position as a unifier of north and south (Brier and Hobbs 1999, 61). Scholars frequently regard this dualistic significance of the Nebty name as parallel with the *nsw-bit* title – 'King of Upper and Lower Egypt' (Gardiner 1957, 72). It corresponds to the presence of the vulture and risen cobra on the king's forehead, hence also signifying divine protection (*e.g.* Morkot 2005, 153f.; *cf.* Troy 1986, 115).

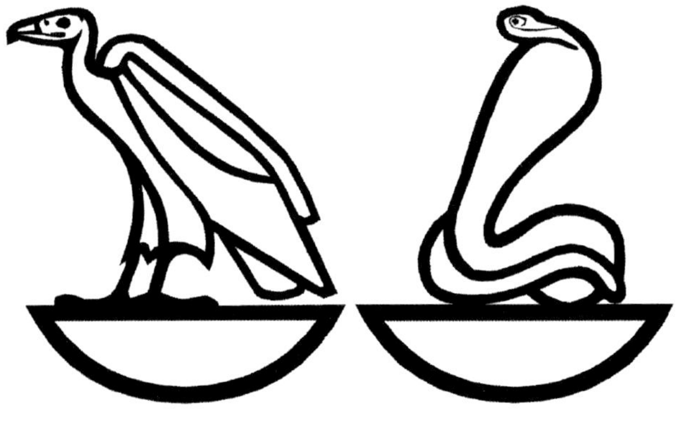

Figure 118. Nebty, the Two Ladies. Hieroglyph after JSesh G16.

In his compilation of pharaonic titles, Beckerath (1984, 16–18) provides examples of Nebty titles such as 'The Two Ladies are the dwellers of the two chapels', 'Companion of the Two Ladies' and 'He of the Two Ladies'. The Pithom stele presents Ptolemy II as '(He of the Two Ladies) Whose might is great'; his father before him was designated 'Who possesses the Two Lands with power as ruler' (*LdR* IV, 218 (XI)).

The female pharaoh Sobeknefru assumed a Nebty name corresponding to the traditional feminine title of Egyptian dualism, reading 'Daughter of the gracious One, Lady of the Two Lands' (Beckerath 1984, 67). Hatshepsut's Nebty name reads 'Flourishing of years', and is explained by G. Robins (1999, 104) as an unusual variation of a Two Ladies designation, as it neglects a direct association with the dualistic character of the vulture and cobra. The female king Tawosret was described as 'The one who establishes Egypt (the founder or organiser), the vanquisher of foreign lands'. No other queen was given an official Nebty name that accorded with the strict conventions that identify the Two Ladies in front of the personal name. However, as noted above, personal names occasionally refer to the vulture and cobra indirectly in the main designation, and it is, therefore, not uncommon to find this alternative type in official records during later periods, corresponding to the fashion of the Old Kingdom.[34]

As with the Horus name, indications of a Nebty name are located in cat. no. 1 among Arsinoë's official titles in the main text and following the words 'she was given the divine titles ...'. One of these epithets reads 'she who received the two forehead *uraei*', a title which refers, reasonably enough, to the double *uraeus* placed at Arsinoë's forehead in royal sculptures, which is associated with the Two Ladies. Arsinoë is portrayed as a ruling queen in cat. no. 1, as noted above, which indicates that she may have received a Nebty title during her lifetime. A comparison may be made with Arsinoë's title in the Mendes stele – 'Holder of the sacred insignia'. An interpretation of this title could be twofold, or even tripartite, but in fact the words 'sacred insignia', rather than being associated with any hand-held objects or the unique insignia placed behind the couple, may symbolise the crown of Arsinoë as a compilation of various sacred attributes.[35] During the Ptolemaic Period, the Nebty title was identified with the Greek title κύριος βασιλειῶυ ('Lord of the Crowns') (Gardiner 1957, 73). A female equivalent, 'Lady of the crowns', designates Arsinoë twice in the material (cat. nos 13–14). Previously, this title had been used for three queens only: Karomama II Merymut (22th Dynasty) and the two Divine Adoratrices Shepenwepet I and Ankhnesneferibre (Troy 1986, D2/15). An identification of 'Lady of the crowns' as an official Nebty name in cat.

nos 13–14 is possible on the basis of its textual location outside a cartouche, thus never replacing the prefix of the Throne name ('Son of Ra', here 'Daughter of Amun'), as discussed below. On the basis of the pictorial context, the arrangement of figures and the textual reference to Arsinoë's official designations, therefore, the title presented in cat. no. 1 seems most credible as an official Nebty title.

The Golden Horus name

The third official royal title, the Golden Horus title, is described less adequately in ancient sources. In terms of textual arrangement it is located in front of the Birth name, though occasionally in front of the Throne name, but it rarely followed any obvious regulations (compared with the two previous titles) (*LÄ* II. 740; *LÄ* III, 541). In pictorial terms it is shown as a falcon sitting on the hieroglyphic sign for gold () (Figure 119), signifying a pharaoh's association with the pure light, Ra, and Horus's victory over Seth (Frankfort 1978, 46). Egyptologists frequently relate the Golden Horus name to a heavenly aspect of kingship, seen in titles such as 'He who belongs in the solar heaven', 'The falcon of the solar sky' or 'Heir of the solar sky' (Beckerath 1984, 24). Pharaohs generally used a designation that related to the shining, golden character of the sun god, expressed in titles such as 'The golden falcon (or Falcon of gold)', 'Powerful is the golden falcon', or 'He (Amun) modelled me as a falcon of gold' (Beckerath 1984, 24f.; Gardiner 1957, 73). The secondary connection, Horus' triumph over Seth, is emphasised in the titles 'He who is above his enemy' and 'Superior to his enemies' (Beckerath 1984, 22). Interestingly, Ptolemy II assumed an official Golden Horus name reading 'Who his father has raised to the throne', which appears to be comparable to Arsinoë's title 'Rightful' (cat. no. 8). The same text places Arsinoë as the firstborn (and hereditary) daughter by naming her 'Great Daughter'.

The golden Horus name occurs less frequently among female pharaohs than the two previously discussed ones. Sobeknefru and Hatshepsut were the only queens who used

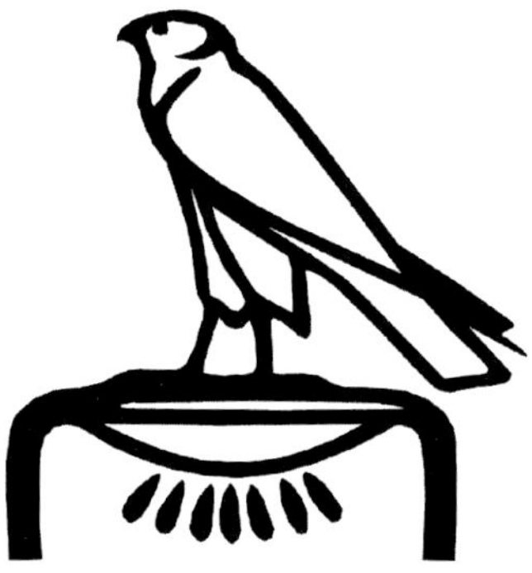

Figure 119. The Golden Horus name. Hieroglyph after JSesh.

one in a complete and conventional sense (Beckerath 1984, 24–6, 67, 84). Sobeknefru's official golden title translates as 'The Golden Falcon, Stable of Appearance', whereas Hatshepsut's is documented in two versions: 'Divine of appearances/crowns' (Robins 1999, 85f.) and 'The female Horus of fine gold' (Gardiner 1957, 73). The complexity of Hatshepsut's Golden Horus names is described by Robins (1999, 105), who concludes that both alternatives had been used previously as Nebty or Horus names.

Once more, it seems that the Mendes stele provides a plausible candidate here. Arsinoë is described in the main text as 'Beautiful of appearance', thus recalling the designations of Sobeknefru and Hatshepsut. Although their titles are not identical, the two Divine Adoratrices Amenirdis I and Ankhnesneferibre are also described with elaborated designations beginning with the words 'Beautiful of appearance ...' (Troy 1986, A2/16).

The Throne name

The fourth royal designation is generally referred to as a Throne name, coronation name or *praenomen* (Gardiner 1957, 72f.; Frankfort 1978, 46f.; Beckerath 1984, 27). After the Middle Kingdom it became the most important official designation of a pharaoh, establishing his socio-political power as ruler (Beckerath 1984, 27). It was bestowed upon the pharaoh on the day of his coronation, as he ascended the throne. The *praenomen* primarily follows the textual prefix *nsw-bitj*, which translates literally as 'He who belongs to the sedge and the bee', and places the pharaoh as the King of Upper and Lower Egypt (Gardiner 1957, 73; compare the Greek translation of the prefix as βασιλεὺς τῶν τε ἄνω καὶ τῶν κάτω χωρῶν [King of the Upper and Lower countries]). Occasionally, the sedge and bee were replaced by 'Lord of the Two Lands', which is comparable to Arsinoë's title in cat. no. 5 (p. 113). The personal name following this prefix is generally placed within a cartouche. Pharaonic coronation names principally reveal an association with Ra,[36] incorporated in titles such as 'Eternal is the Justice of Re', 'The manifestation of Ra remains', 'The soul of Ra comes into being' and 'Lord of truth is Ra' (Gardiner 1957, 72–5; Beckerath 1984, 27–32), or the early Ptolemaic example 'The heir of the Sibling-loving Gods (*theoi Adelphoi*), who is the chosen of Ra, the living image of Amun' (Ptolemy III) (*LdR* IV, 254, pl. XXXVIII). The latter title also emphasises the king's royal legitimacy as the heir of Ptolemy II and Arsinoë.

Female pharaohs, including the majority of the Divine Adoratrices of the Third Intermediate Period, received a Throne name during their lifetimes. The New Kingdom's female king Sobeknefru is described as 'Sobek is the soul of Ra'; Hatshepsut assumed the title 'The true one of the soul of Ra' (Ma'at-ka-Ra), possibly placing her in a socio-religious position as an earthly manifestation of the goddess Ma'at (Robins 1999, 106).[37] Queen Tawosret used the name 'Daughter of Ra, Beloved of Amun', a title equivalent to two individual epithets of Arsinoë (Beckerath 1984, 92). The Divine Adoratrice Shepenwepet I assumed a Throne name reading 'She who is in the heart of Amun' (alternatively 'United with the heart of Amun') (Beckerath 1984, 106), whereas her descendants associated themselves with Mut in various literary forms (Beckerath 1984, 109, 112f.; *LÄ* I, 197).

Three scenes in the material include a generally accepted Throne name of Arsinoë, translating as 'She who is in the heart of Shu, Beloved of all the Gods'. This title identifies her with Tefnut, pairing her with Shu in a manner reminiscent of the Divine Adoratrices centuries earlier (*cf.* Troy 1986, A1/28). Arsinoë's association with Tefnut has already been mentioned above, and is especially noticeable in cat. nos 2–3. The Pithom stele describes Arsinoë as 'Daughter of Atum', and the royal couple as the children of Atum. Furthermore, cat. no. 2L places Arsinoë in a physical setting in which she is related to the Hathorian sexual aspect as the Hand of God – the Hand of Atum. According to the myth, it was the Hand of Atum that gave birth to Shu and Tefnut. Cat. no. 3 places the divine sibling couple (*theoi Adelphoi*) in a dynastic scene revealing their claimed hereditary lineage from Shu and Tefnut. Pictorially, Arsinoë's figural position and the details of her image correspond to the figure of Shu, again demonstrating an association between the queen and Tefnut (*cf.* Howard-Vyse and Perring 1842, 100f., no. 9; Quaegebeur 1978, 251).

The second part of Arsinoë's coronation name, 'Beloved of all the Gods', is a designation conventional to both males and females. Examples of male pharaonic titles that incorporate 'Beloved of …' include (to mention just a few) 'Beloved of Hathor' (Thutmosis III: Gardiner 1957, 72), 'Beloved of Amun' (Seti I: Beckerath 1984, 236, E3), 'Beloved of Ma'at' (Ramses II: Beckerath 1984, 236, H1a) and 'Beloved of Ptah' (Seti II: Beckerath 1984, 241, E). 'Beloved of Amun' was favoured by Alexander the Great, followed by Ptolemy I and II (*LdR* IV, 216; Beckerath 1984, 285, 287). Among the female kings, Sobeknefru is described as 'Beloved of Ra', Hatshepsut as 'Beloved of Amun who created her beauty' (Troy 1986, A1/19) and Tawosret as 'Beloved of Amun' (Beckerath 1984, 92). The Divine Adoratrices also received Throne names similar to Arsinoë's, such as Amenirdis' title as 'Daughter of Amun of his body whom he loves', and Shepenwepet II's 'Beloved of Amun, the daughter who is created by Atum' (Troy 1986, A1/13, A1/15, A1/16). Cat. no. 1 describes Arsinoë as 'Beloved of the ram', a designation which chimes with titles in other artistic media that describe her in a plethora of associations, including 'Beloved of Amun', 'Beloved of Ra', 'Beloved of Atum', 'Beloved of Ptah', 'Beloved of Thoth', 'Beloved of Amun-Ra', 'Beloved of Khonsu' and 'Beloved of Mut'.[38] The last of these once more associates Arsinoë with the Divine Adoratrices.

Arsinoë's Throne name follows the conventions of Middle Egyptian designations, emphasising her relation with the divine sphere and her responsibilities as their heir and female manifestation. The fact that she is recorded with an official and recognisable Throne name and, more importantly, a male prefix has caused a heated debate regarding her political role while alive. Arsinoë's *nsw-bitj* – 'King of Upper and Lower Egypt' – title has been discussed by a number of scholars throughout the years (*e.g.* Pestman 1967; van Oppen 2007, 463). Quaegebeur (1971a, 204) lists the titles 'Lady of the Two Lands', 'Mistress of the Two Lands' and '(great) sovereign (here: ruler) of Egypt' as equivalent to the Greek form βασίλισσα (queen). However, all these titles demonstrate a female aspect and can be interpreted purely as queenship determiners (Troy 1986, II.6–7). *Nsw-bitj*, on the other hand, is identical with the male title βασιλεύς (king), although cat. no. 13 limits her sovereignty to Lower Egypt rather than the Two Lands. Meritneith, Nitocris, Hatshepsut and Tawosret were described with this official prefix *nsw-bitj* prior to Arsinoë, for whom it is documented here in six scenes (seven figures: cat. nos 5, 7–8, 13–15R; *cf.* Quaegebeur 1971a, 204f.; Robins 1999, 105f.).

Some previous scholars have concluded, on the basis of the lack of material pre-dating Arsinoë's death, that the description 'King of Upper and Lower Egypt' is an honorary title that was given to Arsinoë by Ptolemy II in connection with her posthumous deification (*e.g.* Otto 1960, 143–52; Burstein 1982, 197–212; Carney 1991, 154–72; 2000, 225–8; *cf.* van Oppen 2007). For example, Quaegebeur (1971a, 206) refers to the Chremonidean War and the Mendes stele, and how Arsinoë is described as influential although the documents post-date her lifetime (Hazzard 2000, 96, n. 90, denies that Arsinoë had any political power and dismisses the three Egyptian documents that describe Arsinoë as king). The material, however, argues against the traditional dating of at least two documents that describe Arsinoë as 'King of Upper and Lower Egypt', and instead, on the basis of her figural position as an active benefactor (cat. nos 8, 15), suggests a date in Arsinoë's lifetime. The title 'the Rightful' in cat. no. 8 agrees with this conclusion, as it emphasises Arsinoë's inherent right to rule.

The Birth name

The fifth official royal designation was the Birth name, or *nomen*, which was generally, as mentioned above, contained within a cartouche. This name was not limited to the pharaoh, but was always given also to royal women (including princesses). The Birth names of the king and queen (and princes and princesses) were differentiated primarily by gender, describing them according to the divine titles 'Son/Daughter of Ra', occasionally replaced by 'Beloved of Amun' or, as during later periods, 'Lord/

Lady of the crowns' (Frankfort 1978, 47; Beckerath 1984, 33; *LÄ* III, 540f.). The functions of the royal Birth name were to establish and control a genealogy and to declare a divine dynastic lineage between the ruling pharaoh and the primeval divine ruler, Ra.

Sobeknefru's, Hatshepsut's and Tawosret's Birth names had, in contrast with the male coronation prefix *nsw-bitj*, a female prefix reading *s3t Rꜥ*, 'Daughter of Ra' (*LdR* I, 341–3; *LdR* II, 236–50; *LdR* III, 145–8). They simultaneously used alternative prefixes, such as 'Lady of the Two Lands' and 'Mistress of the Two Lands', as did Arsinoë, who is never described in the material as the son or daughter of Ra, but as 'Daughter of Amun', which corresponds to the alternative prefix (Daughter of Ra) mentioned above (cat. nos 12–14, 23–29, 31–32). Two of these scenes date to Arsinoë's lifetime and are in this way comparable to those scenes containing the prefixes of the previous female kings (*cf.* Troy 1986, A1/12).

Conventional Birth names placed a pharaoh/queen in a precise and well-chosen association with one or several deities. Consequently, each individual *nomen* had a religious significance. The name Amenhotep, for example, translates as 'Amun is pleased', and Thutmosis as 'Born of the god Thoth' (Clayton 2006, 100). Whereas traditional pharaonic personal names thus structurally describe an association with any given deity, the Ptolemaic rulers, however, retained their original Greek name, directly transcribed to Egyptian hieroglyphs. The name of Ptolemy was written in a structured combination of signs, whereas Arsinoë's Birth name is recorded in various hieroglyphic arrangements, as the material demonstrates.

Conclusion

Many of the titles studied in this chapter relate to the pictorial units and elements included in the crown of Arsinoë. 'Daughter of Amun', 'Beloved of the ram', 'Banebdjedet' and 'She who is the high-priestess of Banebdjedet' are all designations associating Arsinoë with the ram and explaining the presence of the ram horns (*cf.* Dils 1998, 1308f.; van Oppen 2007, 82).

Along with titles from other artistic media, 'She who is the high priestess of Banebdjedet' and 'Daughter of Amun' demonstrate Arsinoë's socio-religious position as a God's wife. Traditional Egyptian texts have shown that the double feather plume was included in the sacred regalia of a God's wife and, therefore, these designations also explain the presence of the plume in the crown of Arsinoë.

The titles '(the living) image of Isis and Hathor', 'Divine mother' and 'Mother of Hep', and those with a sexual connotation – 'Sweet of Love' and 'She who fills the palace with her beauty' – as well as the unique 'Mistress of Eternity, Lady of the solar disc', correspond to Arsinoë's religious position as an earthly manifestation of Hathor, and the Hathoric maternal aspect related to the nurturing of the dynasty. These titles thus explain the application of the cow horns and solar disc as a joint pictorial element in the crown of Arsinoë.

To explain the presence of the red crown in the crown of Arsinoë, previous scholars have stressed a divine association between Arsinoë and Geb which is documented through the title 'Daughter of Geb' (Troy 1986, A1/7; Sauneron 1960, 107, n. 6; Quaegebeur 1978, 258; Quaegebeur 1988, 45, 47; Dils 1998, 1305, 1307; van Oppen 2007, 82). However, there may be a stronger link relating to the red crown's political symbolism, thus expressing a ruler of Lower Egypt. This interpretation is supported by Arsinoë's title 'King of Lower Egypt' and the reference to Ptolemy II as the 'King of Upper Egypt' in other scenes. Previous scholars' connection between Arsinoë and Geb is not invalidated by this interpretation, but it seems more likely that her crown is associated with the royal, religious and divine spheres, including a connection with her political position as the King of Lower Egypt.

Arsinoë's titles as listed in the material demonstrate a continuation of native Egyptian traditions. Various designations correspond to prominent queens of the pharaonic era, including Hatshepsut and Tiye. Most interesting, however, is the clear continuation of the official designations applied to queens of the Third Intermediate Period/Late Period. Chiefly, Arsinoë's epithets correspond with titles that describe Amenirdis I and Ankhnesneferibre in their religious positions as god's wives. One obvious example is 'Mistress of Eternity, Lady of the solar disc', which is documented as a title of only four queens, including Arsinoë and the god's wives.

This chapter has analysed the most frequent titles used by and/or for Arsinoë. Official designations were given to royal women at the time of their birth and later by marriage – as a merit – or in connection with a religious position as a priestess. In addition to her most renowned epithet – Philadelphos, the sibling/brother-lover, three designations occur more often than the others, including 'King's daughter, sister, and wife', 'Lady of the Two Lands' and 'Daughter of Amun'. The first title places Arsinoë in a royal socio-political position, providing her with an official recognition of her true royal bloodline. All scenes presenting this title date to the reign of Ptolemy II, including two scenes (re)dated here to Arsinoë's lifetime.

'Lady of the Two Lands' appears in the material as frequently as 'King's daughter, sister, and wife'. It places Arsinoë (and the later Ptolemaic queens) in a distinct socio-political role as a queen and an official feminine counterpart of the king. 'Lady of the Two Lands' is accompanied by two additional titles, 'Mistress of the Two Lands' and 'Mistress of Upper and Lower Egypt', together communicating a symbolic message providing the queen with an outstanding socio-political position.

'Daughter of Amun' designates thirteen images of Arsinoë. The title can be compared to the pharaoh's designation 'Son of Ra', and has a very similar socio-religious value. 'Daughter of Amun' places Arsinoë as God's wife, and her role as the high priestess is demonstrated in additional titles such as 'Beloved of the ram' and 'High priestess of Banebdjedet (= local form of Amun)'. Arsinoë, as the high priestess, entered the sacred role as the earthly manifestation of Hathor, including the sexual aspect of the goddess as the hand of Atum/Amun/god. In addition, the title 'Mistress of Eternity, Lady of the solar disc' connects Arsinoë with the traditional high priestesses. The title describes only a few previous queens, all of whom served as 'God's wives', 'Divine Adoratrices' or 'Hand(s) of God'.

The title 'King of Upper and Lower Egypt' represents a debatable issue in regard to queens. Six scenes, exclusively on stelai, describe Arsinoë with this title. All date to the reign of Ptolemy II and two of these, on the basis of her active position in the scene, also date to Arsinoë's lifetime. Arsinoë marks the tallest figure of all the scenes except for cat. no. 14. The title 'Ruler' may be regarded as related to 'King of Upper and Lower Egypt'. 'Ruler of Egypt (=Kemet)' is documented in a few Philae scenes and is applied exclusively to Arsinoë throughout all of Egyptian history. Succeeding Ptolemaic queens retained the title, though listing only 'Ruler'.

Arsinoë and Ptolemy II are described together by their venerating descendants as '*theoi Adelphoi*'. The title does not occur in any scene where Arsinoë is illustrated alone. All scenes listing this title are interpreted as having a dynastic setting or theme, and express the worship by a descendant of his deceased ancestors in order to reconnect with his royal–divine legacy and to validate his right to the throne.

Arsinoë's titles 'Divine mother' and 'Royal mother' again associate her with the dynastic ancestor cult. The designation is recorded in scenes post-dating Arsinoë's lifetime, and frequently also describes succeeding queens placed in an equal position to Arsinoë.

The final example of Arsinoë's titles relates to her socio-political position as a queen and her purely divine role as a goddess. 'Image of Isis and Hathor' associates Arsinoë with the divine representatives of the celestial dynastic mother (Isis) and the divine ruling queen (Hathor).

Notes

1 The stelai frequently include a main text located below the relief scene. Any reference to this main text is abbreviated as M. For the comprehensive list of titles see Appendix II.

2 Compare cat. nos 1M, 2M, 23 'Daughter of the king of Upper Egypt'; cat. no. 3 'Daughter of Ptolemy'; cat. no. 8 'Great daughter'. Also compare cat. nos 1M, 28, 31–32 'Princess'.

3 Include also cat. nos 1M, 23, 26L–R, 29 'Sister of the king of Upper Egypt'; cat. no. 16 'Sister-wife of Ptolemy'; cat. no. 21 'Divine sister of Ptolemy'.

4 Also include cat. no. 1R 'His greatly beloved wife'; cat. no. 1M 'Greatly beloved wife of the king of Upper Egypt'; cat. nos 8, 23, 26L–R 'King's great wife'; cat. no. 16 'Sister-wife of Ptolemy'.

5 *Cf.* a statue in New York, Metropolitan Museum of Art, inv. no. 20.2.21 (Albersmeier 2002, cat. no. 106; *cf. LdR* IV, 239–45; Quaegebeur 1998). Cat. nos 1M, 2M, 23, 26L–R and 29 list Arsinoë in a family-orientated relationship with her father and brother respectively as the 'King of Upper Egypt'.

6 A fragment of a statue crown of Arsinoë from the temple of Isis in ancient Koptos, modern Qift, now located in the Petrie Museum of Egyptian Archaeology, University College, London, inv. no. 14521.

7 The textual connection between the queen and Horus may be regarded as symbolising the pharaoh as an earthly manifestation of Horus. Now at an unknown location, the stele of Saft el-Henneh describes Arsinoë with the triple title. Arsinoë is depicted as the last figure of seven deities to whom Ptolemy II presents offerings. All deities are illustrated in a standardised squatting position. This position is associated mainly with the figure of Ma'at (who is the second deity of the scene). Here, Arsinoë is connected with Horus, Hathor and Harsomtus. Again, the item dates to the reign of Ptolemy II. It supports the dynastic association described above. The title also describes Arsinoë on a priest stele from Saqqara, now BM 1029. It designates her 'King's daughter, sister and wife, the Daughter of Amun, Lady of the Two Lands, Arsinoë the divine Philadelphos' (*e.g.* Quaegebeur 1989, 246, no. 1; *PM* III, 23, 743; Troy 1986, 178; *cf. LdR* IV, 241; *Thes. Inscr.* IV).

8 Compare the title of Arsinoë on the 'Vatican statue' (p. 112) as 'Inherent princess', and later as 'First' (see 'Great').

9 Compare cat. nos 1M, 2M, 23, 26L–R, 29 describing Ptolemy I and II respectively as 'King of Upper Egypt'.

10 Ptolemy II's title reads 'King of Upper and Lower Egypt, Lord of the Two Lands (powerful is the soul of Ra)| son of Ra, Lord of the Two Lands (Ptolemy)|'.

11 Vatican, inv. no. 22681. The statue of Ptolemy = Vatican, inv. no. 22682. Compare also the Saqqara stela, BM, inv. no. 1029, that describing Arsinoë's sister Philotera as 'Sister of the King of Upper Egypt, Daughter of the King of Lower Egypt' (*e.g. LdR* IV, 221; *PM* III, 23, 743).

12 However, later Ptolemaic queens held similar titles, documented in Nilsson (2010, cat. nos 142, 156, 158 as 'Great ruler'). Compare the title documented by Champollion (1844, 214) on the ancient road/route between Aswan and Philae, which describes Arsinoë as 'King's wife, daughter, and sister, Daughter of Amun [...], Lady of the Two Lands (Arsinoë)|, [...] the divine Philadelphos, Great of praise, Lady of Sweet Love, Mistress of Upper and Lower Egypt, Ruler of Egypt, Lady of the Two Lands (Arsinoë)| may she live forever/the eternally living'. The crook was introduced as a sign of kingship during the Middle Kingdom, but Arsinoë was the first queen to receive this title (*cf.* Troy 1986, 196).

13 Relating to her queenship role, cat. no. 28 describes Arsinoë as 'Lady of (all) the people'.

14 Cat. nos 23–26R situate 'Daughter of Amun' immediately before Arsinoë's Birth name, whereas cat. nos 13–14, 27–29 and 31–32 separate it by another epithet. Thus, cat. nos 13–14 read 'Daughter of Amun, Lady of the crowns (Arsinoë)|...',

while cat. nos 27–29 and 31–32 state 'Daughter of Amun, Lady of the Two Lands (Arsinoë)| …'.

15 Oriental Institute of Chicago, inv. no. 10518.

16 The title referred to the hand of Atum, who by masturbation gave birth to Shu and Tefnut. The myth describes the hand as a feminine element, Hathor. The title is associated with the sexual role of Hathor, which in turn played an important role in the life of the queens, in securing true heirs to the throne.

17 Troy (1986, 196) translates the word *ḥnw.t* as 'lady' (here translated as 'mistress') and *nb* as 'all' (which in this study is translated as 'lady' owing to its placement within the sentence). Troy (among others) further translates *šnw* as 'encircles', while here it is given as *šn* 'eternity'. The sign *šn* can be translated 'eternity' or 'protection', and is depicted sometimes held in the claws of a falcon/vulture stretching out its wings protecting the pharaoh. It is also depicted in connection with the 'reckoning of time-symbolism'. The sign *šnw* has the circular form of a cartouche, and can be translated as 'everything that the sun encircles'. Given this, there seems no need to add the *nb*-sign in the present sentence, especially not when written directly in front of *itn* – Aton, or the solar disc. There are thus two female epithets in the full sentence, 'Mistress of Eternity' (or Eternal Mistress) and 'Lady of the solar disc'. The general symbolism of these titles, however, remains similar.

18 Compare Khereduankh's (mother of the more renowned Old Kingdom architect Imhotep) claim to be Banebdjedet's daughter (*e.g.* Warner and Fernández-Armesto 2003, 296).

19 Compare the political situation during the 25th Dynasty when Amenirdis I 'ruled' Upper Egypt in her role as the God's wife of Amun, centered in Karnak, while her brother, Shabaka, ruled Lower Egypt with his centre in Memphis (*e.g.* Blackman 1921, 16).

20 Compare the title of Arsinoë in the Alexandrian triad, Graeco-Roman Museum, Alexandria, inv. no. 11261: 'An appearance more beautiful than the sun and the moon'.

21 The form *Philadelphos*, *mr-sn*, is of course related to the same position, though in itself not indicating divinity.

22 See cat. nos 16–17, 19–22, 34–35, dating to Ptolemy IV–VIII, where the *theoi Soteres* are excluded from the official dynastic ancestors.

23 The couple are never described as '*theoi Adelphoi*' when they actively perform a religious ceremony, such as is demonstrated in cat. nos 1L, 15L–R and 26L–R. Compare, however, the Greek-styled Ptolemaic coinage, which designates the couple with such a title during their lifetime.

24 The *theoi Adelphoi* may be interpreted as manifestations of Shu and Tefnut, the divine siblings. Such an association is demonstrated in esp. cat. no. 2, where Ptolemy II and Arsinoë are described as the children of Atum.

25 The dynastic relationship was stressed also through the introduction of the couples as temple-sharing deities long after their initial deification. Isis Arsinoë Philadelphos, the *theoi Adelphoi* and the *theoi Euergetai* were introduced as temple-sharing gods in the temple of Hermonthis in 149/148 BC. Although of an unknown origin, *P. Yale* 46 describes a priest who was active in a temple of Amun and Arsinoë, including also the *theoi Adelphoi* and the *theoi Euergetai*. The text underlines a clear separation between the official dynastic cult – *i.e.*, that of the *theoi Adelphoi* – and the individual cult of Arsinoë. Here, yet again, Arsinoë is associated with Amun, possibly as his divine wife. An inscription documented on a small sandstone altar found in the precinct of the Sarapis temple at Hermopolis Magna further describes the *theoi Adelphoi* as sharing a temple with the *theoi Euergetai*, to whom statues and shrines were dedicated by the cavalry located in the area. (*e.g. P. Yale* 46; Quaegebeur 1971, 243 n. 19; Wace *et al.* 1959; Fraser 1972, 234; II, 384 n. 256).

26 Dynastic scenes describe all deceased females with similar titles, including 'Divine mother' and 'Royal mother'. Similarly, the male deceased ancestors are described with identical titles, including 'Divine royal father'.

27 *Wḥm- n -Ptḥ* was used also as a title of Apis (*e.g. WB* I, 344). *LGG* (VIII, 188f.) document the title 'Der das Leben des Ptah wiederholt', though it does not list the signs of cat. no. 26. The following description, *nsw- n- kꜣ.w- nbt -ntryt*, can be compared with *nsw-n-ꜥwt -nbt- ntryt*, listed in *LGG* (IV, 323), again as a title of Apis.

28 Compare the notes of Howard-Vyse and Perring (1842, 100f. with no. 9) as they state: 'In the centre is the name of the 'Queen Ese-Arsinoe', the sister, and the wife of the king; and she appears to offer incense to "Amoun-ra" and to "Khons" …'. The position of the queen cannot be that of a benefactor, as she is as the last figure of the left scene, facing in the same direction as the other deities – toward the king.

29 As the queen, the high priestess and God's wife, Arsinoë was regarded as divine and could therefore be placed on the same side as the traditional gods through figural adjustment/relative placement.

30 The textual association of Arsinoë and Isis is also documented in a priest stele from Saqqara = BM inv. no. 124: 'King's daughter, sister, and wife, Daughter of Amun, Lady of the Two Lands, Arsinoë the divine Philadelphos, Isis'. Compare Arsinoë's title listed in *OGIS* 30. For examples of Greek material, see the faience vases (*oinochoai*) in D. B. Thompson (1973). Compare also Arsinoë's position as a temple-sharing goddess in the temple of Hermonthis (modern Armant) = *P. Lond.* 590; *P. Petrie* I 25, 2 Z. 1; II 46 Z. 9. Documents outside the material that describe Arsinoë's association with Isis originate chiefly in the area of Alexandria or Fayyum. Interestingly, it is in the 'Greek areas' where Arsinoë is assimilated almost completely with Aphrodite. It is generally accepted that Aphrodite was the Greek equivalent of Hathor (*e.g.* Quaegebeur 1971b).

31 He lists Nitocris (6th dynasty), Sobeknefru (12th dynasty), Hatshepsut (18th dynasty), Taworset (19th dynasty), Shepenwepet I, Amenirdis I, Shepenwepet II, Amenirdis II, Nitocris I, Ankhnesneferibre, Nitocris II (all belonging to the Third Intermediate Period). Included in his list are also the majority of the Ptolemaic queens who at any point were given a royal designation.

32 Compare the textual records that describe Ptolemy IV as beloved of the native gods as well as of the *theoi Adelphoi*, *theoi Euergetai*, and *theoi Philopatores*, thus including himself and Arsinoë III (*e.g.* Quaegebeur 1989, 101, n. 48). As the second female king described with a Horus name, Hatshepsut assumed the title 'Powerful of souls', *Wsrt-kꜣw*, which is a female formula unique to the queen (*e.g.* Beckerath 1984, 84; Robins 1999, 103f.)

33 Cat. no. 1. also includes the various titles listed in the 'Vatican sculpture' (p.112) – 'Beloved of Hathor', 'Beloved of Atum' – and the Chicago statue base (p.127, n. 15) – 'Beloved of Ra', 'Beloved of Ptah', 'Beloved of Thoth', 'Beloved of Amun-Ra', 'Beloved of Mut', 'Beloved of Khonsu'.

34 It could be asked why Arsinoë concerned herself with the very ancient traditions of royal names when the Graeco-Roman period is renowned for its development of, and decadent approach to, the hieroglyphs of the conventional Middle Egyptian. However, Arsinoë utilised various designations that had not been in continuous use since the Old Kingdom, or possibly the Middle Kingdom. In the material, Arsinoë is described as the mother of Hep (Apis), which is associated (pp.111–118f.) with the designation 'Daughter of the Merhu bull', listed on the 'Vatican statue'. The latter name describes only two previous queens, dating to the Old Kingdom and to the Third Intermediate Period with the God's wife Ankhnesneferibre. Although described in another artistic medium, Arsinoë's designation 'Beloved of Thoth' can be compared to the Old Kingdom descriptions of the queens as priestesses of Thoth. These aspects are naturally interesting, as they indicate a close connection between the royal house and the priesthood. There are no indications to suggest that Arsinoë had any personal knowledge of the ancient Egyptian language (*cf.* Quaegebeur 1971b, 247f. with n. 54; Troy 1986, A1/9 and B2/14; van Oppen 2007, 99–101).

35 Sculptures of Arsinoë are often recognised and identified by the double *uraei*, which was unique to her among the Ptolemaic queens (*e.g.* Ashton 2000; Albersmeier 2002, 43; Maehler 2006, 217–19; *cf.* Maehler 2003).

36 However, the pharaohs of the Old Kingdom did not necessarily include the name of Ra (*e.g.* Gardiner 1957, 74; Robins 1999, 105).

37 Compare the alternative reading as 'Ma'at is the soul of Ra', similar to 'Sobek is the soul of Ra' (Robins 1999, 106).

38 Quaegebeur (1971b, 245, n. 41) noted the association between 'Beloved of Ptah' and the coronation rites (and the *sꜣ Rꜥ*-title) in Memphis during the later Ptolemaic period. It cannot be seen as a pure coincidence that Arsinoë was worshipped alongside Ptah (as his consort and therefore assimilated with Tefnut) in Memphis.

Chapter 9

The eradication of visual representations

Even though the issue and symbolic consequences of the (later) eradication of Egyptian reliefs have been acknowledged among art historians, it has been in a matter of generalisation without any detailed technical overview.[1] This is an issue which has been overlooked or neglected as an element of Egyptian reliefs, which is understandable given that the damage was not a part of the original scene.[2] However, as C. Hedrick notes (2000, xii), 'it must be recognized that silence and erasures are themselves signs'. This topic will be briefly studied here because of its direct impact on the scenes as they are preserved for modern viewers. Possibly of greater importance here, as will become evident below, is that the crowns are almost always preserved. This is a point that may be an important key to enabling scholars of today to read art in a new light and to better understand the concepts of ancient Egyptian symbolism as it was approached by (contemporary and) later cultural groups. The topic will be approached like any other element of the scenes in order to see if there are any relevant connections with the crowns and if there are any differences between the crowns and other pictorial elements in terms of destructive adjustments.

'Eradication of visual representation' means the deliberately damage and mutilation of figures of the original scene. This feature must be acknowledged in order to understand Egyptian art and its value during the last ancient centuries. While an art historian would view the consequences of these marks on the basis of their character as an destructive agent, and as such categorise them within the recognised concepts of iconoclasm or *damnatio memoriae* – condemnation of memory – a more technical and methodical approach will be taken here to establish the physical impact made by the marks on the scenes and to demonstrate the need for a new terminology for damage to art that includes Egyptian art, prior to a general summary of their effects. The term used here, 'cut marks', refers to small scratched, etched, hacked and/or dotted cuts that were made by a chisel or any other sharp object (*e.g.* Clark and Engelbach 1990, Appendix I). These are recorded solely in temple reliefs, and cat. nos 1L–15R (the stelai) are thereby excluded from the analysis here. In terms of location within the temple, these deliberate, destructive marks are focused mainly on the area within the figural outlines, while the flat, undecorated background has been left undamaged. The marks are characterised primarily by one deep cut where the chisel has hit the surface, occasionally followed by a shallower 'tail', as Figure 120 shows. The material shows cut marks that were caused by chisels that were rectangular and narrow-headed, square and even circular.

Table 20 shows the most frequent placement of cut marks within the scenes. There is an obvious concentration of cut marks in the 'skin' area. An enhanced photograph of Arsinoë from cat. no. 16 (Figure 121), for example, shows cut marks that have damaged her uncovered facial areas, although her crown, wig and vulture cap are preserved. Figure 122, showing cat. no. 26L, displays two types of cut marks that have damaged Arsinoë's face, wig and vulture cap, but her crown is preserved in full detail. A first series of devastating marks is located in the area around Arsinoë's crown, including the flat background and the lower part of the (back) hieroglyphic text. These marks have been made by a large rectangular chisel: they are placed in a linear sequence creating a diagonal pattern. Such a pattern is frequently seen on non-dressed stone blocks and block-faces that were never intended for relief work. A brief overview of

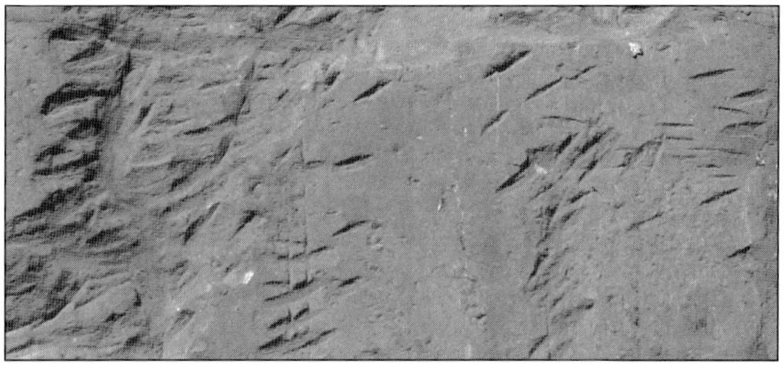

Figure 120. Detail of scene from Edfu. Narrow elongated singular cuts to the right and broader cuts with a short 'tail' to the left, all of which have been caused by a rather large, wide chisel.

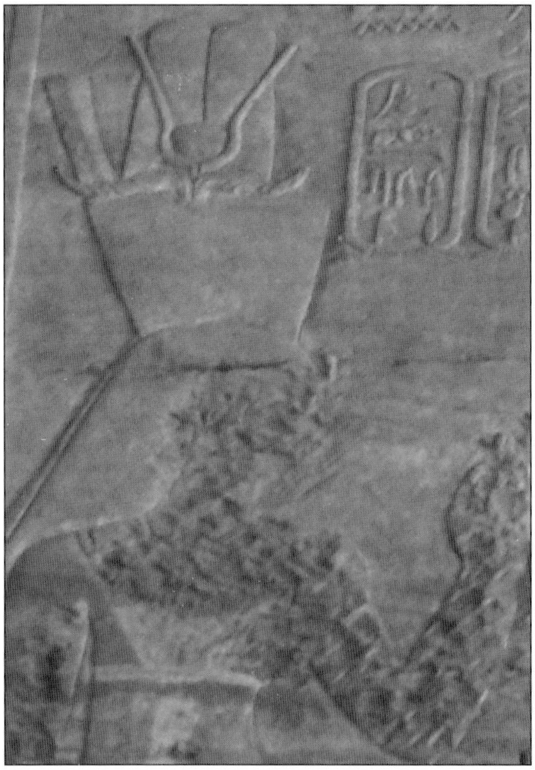

Figure 121. This detail of cat. no. 16 shows cut marks that have been intentionally placed to damage the face, neck and arms, while the wig, crown and dress remain intact and unharmed.

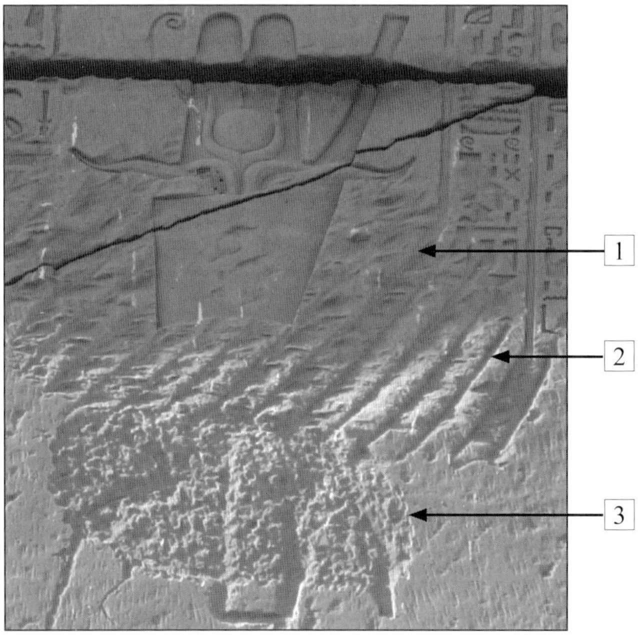

Figure 122. Detail of cat. no. 26L. The arrows point to the hieroglyphic text (1) and the two types of cut mark (2–3).

any Egyptian temple, as they are preserved today, will show that blocks with this type of undressed face were normally placed in concealed architectural parts and were never intended to be viewed (Figure 123). Identical or similar series of elongated linear (vertical or diagonal) marks often cover entire quarry-faces/walls throughout Egypt.

The first series of marks in cat. no. 26L can thus be compared to quarry marks that were created at the time when the stone was quarried. This could explain why the marks are overlapped by the relief of Arsinoë's crown, which must have been carved subsequently. The surface of the crown is smooth but was never finished, as a few previous cut marks illuminate its centre. In contrast to their relationship with the crown, these marks have damaged and interrupted the hieroglyphic text located behind Arsinoë. The hieroglyphs are carved deeper, and have been overlapped by the marks: the former must thus pre-date the latter. The obvious discrepancy between the three elements (the two series of marks and the crown of Arsinoë) indicates three different working stages: the 'quarry marks' pre-date Arsinoë's crown but post-date the hieroglyphic signs. Arsinoë's crown, being engraved over the marks, has to be considered as a final addition to or alteration of the relief. The three phases of workmanship suggests not that the marks were made at the time of quarrying, but rather that they correspond to a stage of dressing – or rather redressing – of the stone (thus, they are identified as dressing marks) (*e.g.* Clark and Engelbach 1990, chapter IX).

These hieroglyphs, in terms of their depth and combination of signs, are comparable in quality and style to Arsinoë's personal register of text. They are, however, different in scale: the signs used in Arsinoë's text are somewhat larger. The hieroglyphic text located behind the crown refers to Amun-Ra and his lordship in Karnak, and does not mention Arsinoë (or any other royalty) at all. Owing to the lack of historical names, an absolute date cannot be established. The three phases of workmanship, the 'style' of the marks and a textual discrepancy indicate that this first series of cuts, the dressing marks, is related to the removal of an original

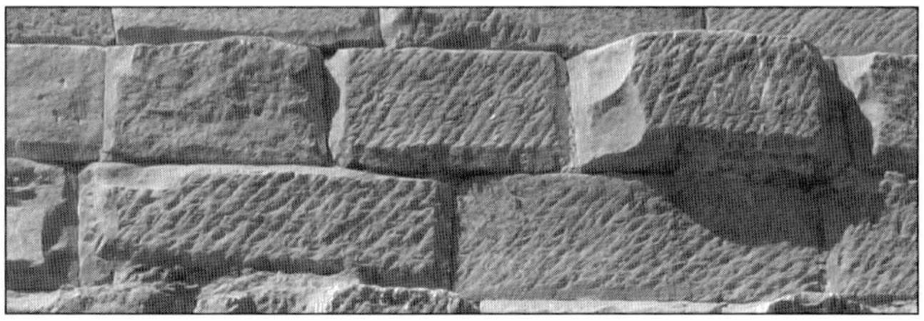

Figure 123. Detail of the undressed section of the northern gate at Karnak. The rough faces of the stone blocks show diagonal elongated chisel marks that are identical to the pattern surrounding the crown of Arsinoë in cat. no. 26L. The relief of the decorated faces (N–S) dates to the reign of Ptolemy III.

crown (and head) in order to replace it with the (head and) crown of Arsinoë; therefore, the original relief of the lintel scene is likely to pre-date the Ptolemaic Period.

A second series of cut marks is concentrated within an oval area below the first: it consists of many small, narrowly placed dots, created by a much smaller chisel than the first, and has devastated face, wig and shoulders. The original outlines of Arsinoë's shoulders and tripartite wig still illuminate the marked surface, while all other details have been erased completely. These marks are placed over Arsinoë's relief and are therefore later, suggesting that the cut marks were placed deliberately in this area to erase the head. However, all items physically attached to the head, such as the crown, are unharmed.

Table 20 shows that cut marks have disfigured sixteen figures in the unclothed area of the arms/hands, and fifteen on the legs/feet. Another ten figures have been mutilated in the breast area. Together with the face, these unclothed areas of the body record the highest concentrations of cut marks, while additional pictorial elements that are attached physically to the body are better preserved. The crown of Arsinoë has never been mutilated (*cf.* Nilsson 2010, 455, table 27, with 19% of mutilated crowns worn by Hathor of Dendera). Similarly, most hand-held objects and thrones are preserved. None of the scenes and/or full figures is erased in its entirety.

As an important element of the overall scene, the hieroglyphic texts have been included in this discussion. Hieroglyphic script has been damaged, but never entirely obliterated, in twenty-one scenes. For example, in cat. no. 26 a few individual signs have been deliberately and precisely damaged: all erased signs in the personal registers of Arsinoë originally related to divine names and individuals, incorporating the names of Amun, Ptah, Apis and Isis (Figure 124), while Arsinoë's personal name remains intact. In the main scene, most hieroglyphs that illustrate birds, including owls, falcons, ducks and vultures, are erased.[3]

In the material examined here cut marks are documented on all heights, levels, registers and architectural elements. For example, cat. no. 25, which forms a minor board that runs above the main lintel scene on the Gate of Euergetes, Karnak, is far above normal reach (the gate is 21m high: Arnold 1999, 167), but almost all its figures have been mutilated. A deep deposit of alluvial mud could have created the access required to reach this height, if one assumes that these marks were made at a far later date.[4] However, such a suggestion is instantly disproven by cat. no. 24, a scene located on the second register (measured from below) on the same gate: the figures here are defaced exactly like those in cat. no. 25, suggesting that both scenes were damaged at the same time and that, therefore, the person responsible for the marks had used some form of ladder in order to reach the highest lintel scene and was clearly prepared to go to some effort to do so.

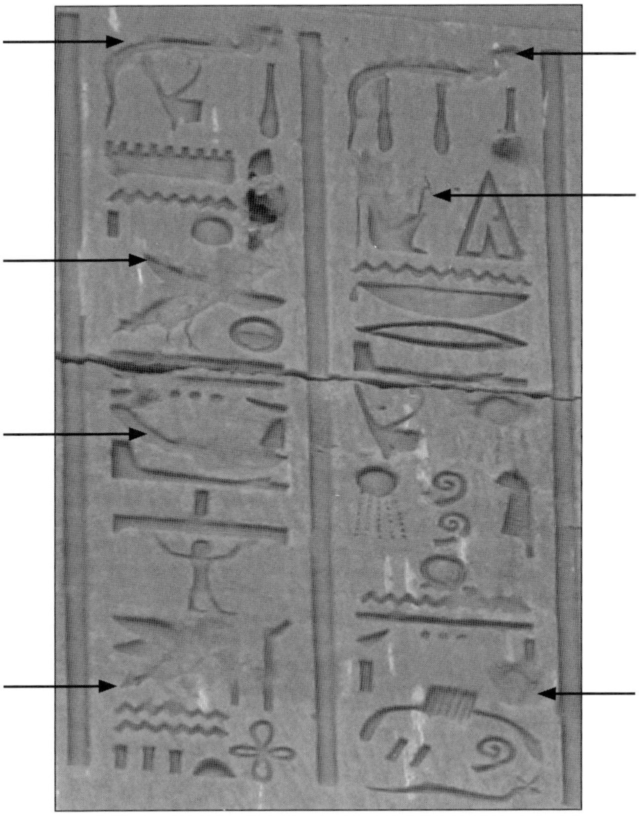

Figure 124. Section of Amun's title in cat. no. 26R. The arrows points to the damaged/erased signs.

DAMAGED AREA	SCENES	TOTAL NO. FIGURES
Crown	–	0
Head/face	16–17, 19–27, 29, 31, 34	15
Breast	16–17, 19–23, 25, 29, 34	10
Arms/hands	16–17, 19–29, 31, 34	16
Legs/feet	16–17, 19–22, 24–29, 31, 34	15
Handheld objects	17, 21, 29	3
Hieroglyphic titles	24, 26L–R, 29, 31	5
Full scene	–	0

Table 20. Placement of cut marks on Arsinoë.

The cut marks seen in the material do not always follow an easily understood 'destructive pattern'. The hands, feet and faces of all the figures in cat. no. 24 have been mutilated, but legs, arms, breasts and necks remain unharmed. As Figures 125–126 shows, the image of Arsinoë in cat. no. 19 is damaged by cut marks, but her facial features are still legible. Her left arm and both feet are mainly undamaged, but her right arm, hand and both legs have been eradicated. A good example of the apparently random nature of the damage is provided by cat. nos 31–32, in the inner sanctuary of the Temple of Philae (Figures 127–128). Cat. no. 31 is situated on the left side on entering the room, and cat. no. 32 on the right. Both scenes illustrate Ptolemy II as an active benefactor who presents offerings to Isis and Arsinoë. Cat. no. 32 includes also the smaller figure of Harpocrates, who is breast-fed by Isis. All figures in cat. no. 31 have been damaged by cut marks. Their headdresses and crowns, however, are unharmed. In contrast, Arsinoë in cat. no. 32 is preserved in full detail, without any later adjustments. In the same scene, the face, legs and arms of Ptolemy are erased. Isis' face has been eradicated in its entirety, which is most plausibly interpreted as an act following from the religious programme of iconoclasm, since the entire stone block has been removed. These two scenes differ only in minor details and present no obvious pictorial or textual information that can explain the choices made by those carrying out the iconoclasm.

Scenes that show a completely eradicated individual figure in an undamaged context may, at first, be compared to scenes of Hatshepsut or Akhenaten: their images and names were erased (/damaged) by later generations owing to changes in the socio-religious situation. This kind of mutilation is, as mentioned above, generally referred to as *damnatio memoriae*, a term originating with the Roman practice of (physically) erasing from memory those of whom the regime disapproved (*e.g.* Varner 2004, 13f.). The fundamentals of the expression are based on the shared ancient belief that the soul was immortal and that each individual could be remembered through representation and name, and that a magician could bring back life to the person depicted in an iconic image (Varner 2004, 8f.). However, the Egyptian religion and ideology are different from the Roman, and thus, in this context, the term *damnatio memoriae* needs to be expanded, reconsidered or completely abandoned in favour of a more general terminology that is applicable also to other ancient ideological concepts.

As mentioned above, an image was considered to hold the essence of the soul or the reality of an event (even if the person depicted never executed that event in actuality). Therefore, any form of physical eradication would harm the purity and perfection of the (divine) soul and prevent the deceased from entering the Underworld. Erased figures, however, also include deities, indicating

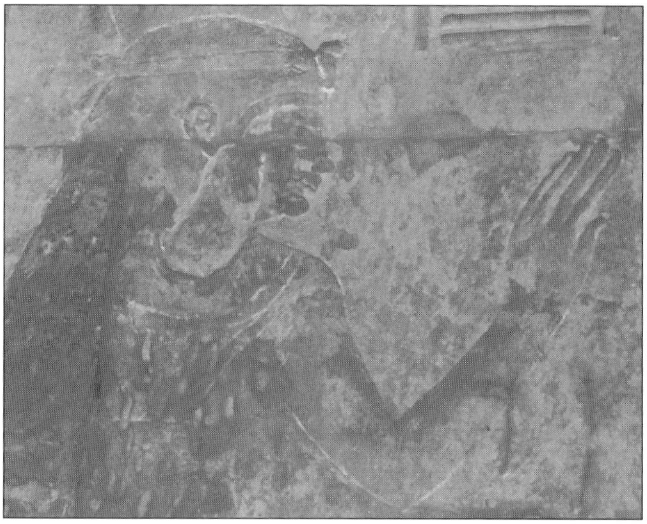

Figure 125. Detail of cut marks in cat. no. 19. The upper body of Arsinoë has been damaged by cut marks, but the left arm and hand are preserved.

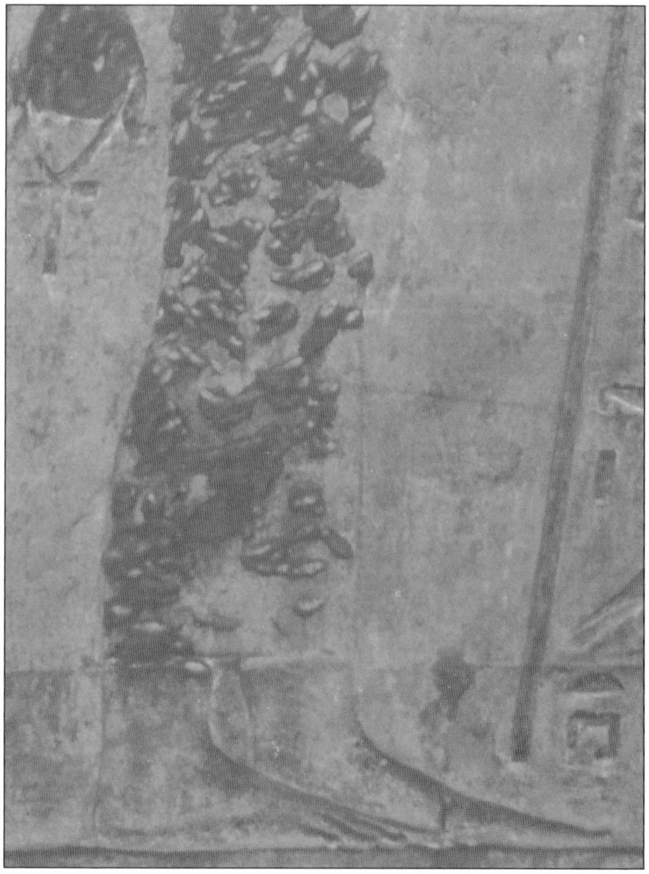

Figure 126. Detail of cut marks in cat. no. 19. The enhancement of the lower part demonstrates how the feet are preserved, whereas the legs are damaged.

that there were other fundamental cultural intentions behind such damage. Another scholarly term that may be useful here is 'iconoclasm', which refers to an aspect of religion that has existed since the introduction of Platonism and philosophy (*cf.* Besançon 2000, 1. Lib. 30.8–9): any form of religious objection to or adjustments to art that expresses a non-orthodox message. Iconoclasm was not necessarily intended to erase the past, but to adapt it into a new cultural setting (*cf.* Meskell 2004, 8). Initially, it was associated with the contradiction between the material and the divine, but from the time of Emperors Leo III and Constantine V (7th–8th century AD), iconoclasm was called upon also in the hunt for and prosecution of pagans, when thousands of pagan religious artefacts were destroyed (Louth 2007, 55). Modern scholars seem to generally agree that cut marks were caused by early Christians or Muslims; however, this brief investigation suggests that other groups should also be considered as perpetrators.

The person, or more probably persons, who negatively adjusted a scene clearly concentrated on precise parts. Most scenes in the material show cuts primarily in the uncovered areas of the body, such as the face, neck, breast, hands and feet. In contrast, the dress, headdress, crown, hand-held objects and throne are generally preserved in full detail. This might indicate an iconoclastic programme at work, but the presence of scenes that show an opposing pattern, in which the mutilation has focused on the dressed sections while leaving unclothed areas unharmed (see Figures 125–126), indicates that the principles behind these acts of devastation were not straightforward.[5] The placement of marks suggests that the person was aware of the value of each pictorial element – that he/she understood their meaning – which indicates some form of respect towards and knowledge of conventional Egyptian symbolism: in a clear majority of the scenes the crowns and other attributes of authority are undamaged (*cf.* Frankfurter 1998, 277–9).

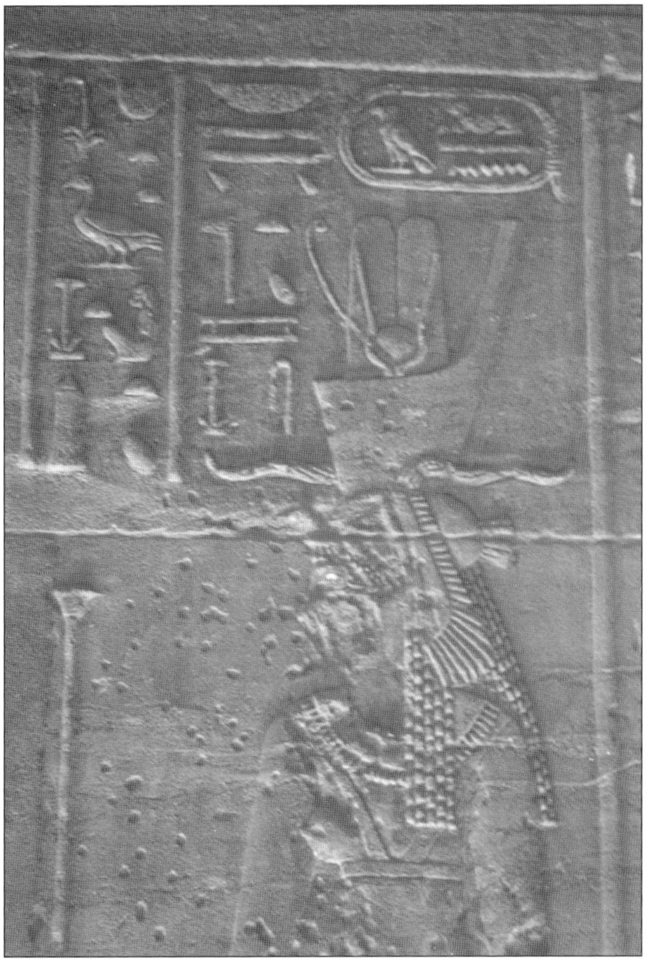

Figure 127. Detail of cut marks in cat. no. 31. A damaged image of Arsinoë.

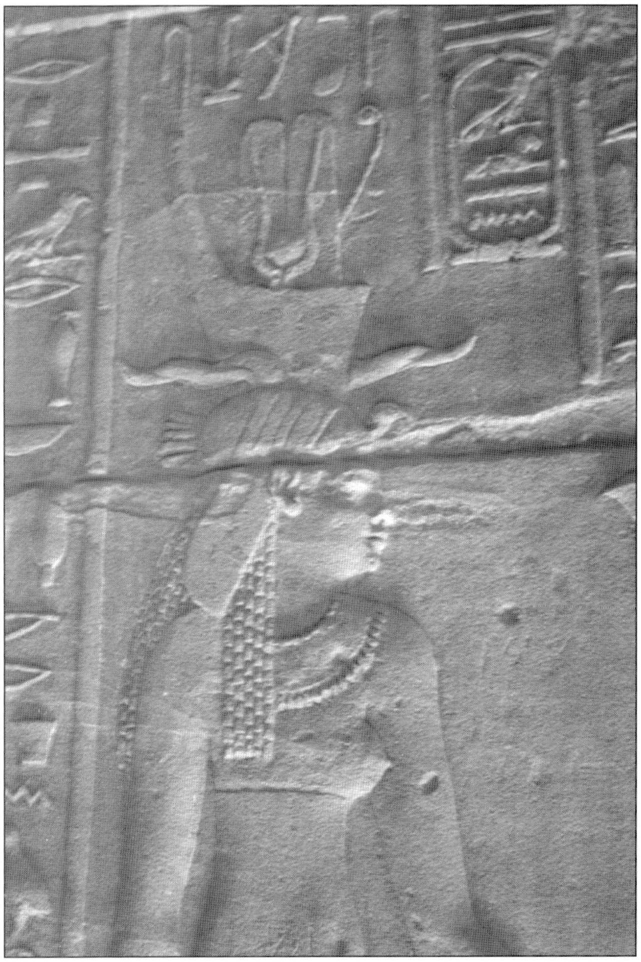

Figure 128. Detail of cat. no. 32. An intact image of Arsinoë.

The destructive agent does not separate styles but elements: a crown was a crown regardless of its pictorial composition. It may be assumed that the crown itself was considered a holder of symbolic value, which consequently spared it from an otherwise eradicating chisel. Similarly, staves and sceptres are primarily preserved, but the *cucupha* head of the *was* stave is often damaged, which suggests a personal recognition of the message communicated by this detail.

The same is true of the hieroglyphic texts as well, since only specific signs have been erased (*cf.* Young 1981, 353f.; Frankfurter 1998, 265). Although in general O. Goldwasser's (1995, 79) theory that the hieroglyphs represent metaphors in numerous incarnations seems sound, his belief that birds were erased because their spirit could fly away seems less so: according to the ancient beliefs, each creature in nature had a soul, which was not always limited by physical appearance. Moreover, the material has demonstrated a lack of continuity in this regard even within one particular register or complete scene: thus, as noted above, not all birds are erased from cat. no. 26. The person or group behind these marks, it may be argued, was inducted in the (sacred) knowledge of the ancient tradition of writing: otherwise, they would not focus specifically on only a few signs. They were aware of the message communicated by each pictorial element, including the crowns, thrones and hand-held objects: all express an immediate association with divine power, represented by both deities and royalties. The deliberate selection of elements implies a deeper knowledge also of general Egyptian symbolism and iconography, and, therefore, the traditional viewpoint that all cut marks are related to iconoclasm appears flawed. However, the present study deals only with the cut marks in the material, and it is clear that some later adjustments, such as the removal of Isis' head in cat. no. 32 and Min's erected penis and other pictorial elements that have a sexual symbolism (mainly outside the material studied here), *are* connected with iconoclasm. Many Egyptian temples were reused and restructured in order to become Christian places of worship, and were later used also by the Muslims. Numerous temple walls demonstrate the presence of devoted pilgrims in the form of religious graffiti. On the basis of this evidence it would be difficult to argue against the existence of iconoclasm in Egypt, but the evidence of the material examined here mean that other possibilities, too, cannot be dismissed.

However, the evidence contained within the reliefs does not allow the identification of a specific group of people responsible for these cut marks (which would provide an argument for, or against, iconoclasm). However, several questions have been raised here which open up avenues for further research. It is important to extend the concepts of iconoclasm and *damnatio memoriae*, and perhaps even to include new aspects or use a different terminology, a need which the material demonstrates. It may be the case that the group or socio-religious movement responsible does not necessarily succeed the ancients by far: such a faction might be found in a very close relation, in time and religious beliefs, to the people who originally carved the relief. It would not be the first time in history, after all, that a people has destroyed its secrets rather than handing them over in the dawn of a new era.

Conclusion

This brief analysis has dealt with 'cut marks' made with the deliberate intention of damaging the original scene. They have been included in order that no aspect of the scenes, as they are preserved for modern viewers, should go unanalysed. Various examples show that certain aspects of a scene have been deliberately erased, and that the cut marks were carefully placed to preserve surrounding elements. The crowns, hand-held objects and thrones are generally untouched by cut marks, as are the hieroglyphic texts, but distinctive signs are erased on occasions in the latter, which may be read as an indication of an understanding of the symbolism, including the words and the language itself. Today, and during ancient times, an erased face is associated with dishonour and shame: in art history, the removal of certain elements of a figure is connected with iconoclasm, *damnatio memoriae* or even the concept of the palimpsest. However, if the cut marks that are documented in the material are related only to these concepts and their ideological connotations, why did they not erase all the symbolic elements that were associated with paganism, superiority and control? There is no information in the present study that can identify the group responsible for the cut marks, be that a specific later ruler, or later religious groups – perhaps Christians and Muslims. Rather, the material indicates that the responsible person or group was educated in the symbolism and culture of the ancient Egyptians, and scholarly attention should perhaps be turned towards the last priests of the ancient Egyptian society, who in the age of Christianity's introduction tried to protect the divine spirits of paganism depicted on the temple walls.

Notes

1 However, descriptions of the acts of destruction are often found in early Christian written records, such as those of Libanius of the late 300s (*e.g.* Frankfurter 1998, Chapter 7, esp. 277–84).

2 Art historians, however, frequently mention the erasure of the imagery of Hatshepsut and Akhenaton as general examples of *damnatio memoriae* (*e.g.* Meskell 2004, 8; Varner 2004, 13f.).

3 Interestingly, none of the hieroglyphs in the personal registers of Amun or Ptolemy II is damaged in cat. no. 26L, while the bird-signs and a few others are erased in the nearby register of

Mut and in the lower hieroglyphic register of Arsinoë at the far left of the scene. Goldwasser (1995, 79) argued that birds have been erased because their earthly manifestation could fly away (*cf.* Meskell 2004, 8f.)

4 It is commonly known that the East Bank of ancient Thebes, after the fall of paganism, was gradually covered by layers of mud from the annual inundation of the Nile. Luxor Temple, to take an example, was not liberated from its mud until 1885 (*e.g.* Frank 2007, 271).

5 Thus, the face is the most common area of destruction, but there are examples of scenes where other elements are damaged and the face is untouched.

Chapter 10

Arsinoë and royalty – a female pharaoh?

The iconographical analysis presented above aimed to establish Arsinoë's various cultural roles as they are communicated firstly in her crown and secondly in the contextual setting of the scene. In the following chapters, all artistic aspects come together and form a foundation for an iconological interpretation, with the aim of understanding how the artistic representations correlate with Arsinoë's three individual but connected socio-political roles – female pharaoh, high priestess and goddess. It will be argued that the living Arsinoë received her personal crown as a result of her prominent social role, which made her politically equal to her husband-brother, her religious devotion to the native Egyptian cults, and her respect of ancient traditions, before a final assessment of the significance of her crown and its pictorial incorporation of all cultural aspects.

Kingship and queenship

Arsinoë's socio-political role as one of the most important Ptolemaic queens is indisputable. The reliefs demonstrate that Ptolemaic queens (Cleopatra III and VII) after her reused her personal crown and usurped designations created exclusively for this second Macedonian Queen of Egypt. In addition to the reliefs, sculptures and coins also bear witness of a continuation of the double cornucopia and the double cobra. The present material reveals that Arsinoë was regarded (by a majority of the Ptolemaic descendants) as the female founder of the Ptolemaic dynasty, and dynastic relief scenes show her descendants venerating her in this role together with Ptolemy II.

Traditionally, a queen was regarded as the pharaoh's female counterpart, and as a couple they articulated the concept of divine androgyny (*e.g.* Troy 1986, 2–4). The analysis above demonstrated how everything in life that is encompassed by the earthly and divine spheres was arranged according to two protagonists. The relationship between male and female royals – the king and queen – manifested such cultural conventions universally, representing humans and gods equally. An example of their inseparable unification is the importance of a queen's presence during the celebrations and ceremonies of the king's Sed festival: she was considered a Hathoric source of his rejuvenation and eternal incarnation, enabling him to proceed as a youthful ruler. Any given queen was regarded as a crucial counterpart in all cultural aspects and was responsible for the survival of kingship. Here the concepts of queenship are acknowledged, but the focus is on (female) kingship, and how the artistic material expresses Arsinoë's hierarchic position as equivalent to the role of Ptolemy II.

Throughout ancient and modern narration alike, historians have endeavoured to establish as accurate a list of Egyptian pharaohs as possible, including or excluding female kings such as Hatshepsut and Tawosret. Modern scholars base their records on four main ancient sources – the Palermo Stone, the Turin Royal Canon, Abydos' King list and Manetho's *Aegyptiaca* – combined with a variety of additional fragmentary descriptions (Gardiner 1988; Breasted 1906, I, 76–167; *cf.* the Karnak Tablet, South Saqqara Stone, Saqqara Tablet; Hdt. 2; Diod. Sic. 1, 70–72; Eratosth. *FGrH* 241 F 1a = Clem. Al. *Strom.* 1.138.1–3). The problems of creating an accurate pharaonic king list are immense, due mainly to the individual dating formulas of each individual pharaoh, but also to the differentiation between the Gregorian calendar and the ancient Egyptian time reckoning. Those dealing with the Ptolemaic and Roman periods face even further challenges resulting from the introduction of additional calendar systems. Since the majority of the Graeco-Egyptian ancient sources that record a king list pre-date the Ptolemaic period, they are of little help in regard to Ptolemaic rulers, especially Arsinoë. Nor can Manetho shed any light on this issue, since he (supposedly) wrote his *Histories* during the reign of either Ptolemy I or II. There are apparently no ancient records post-dating Ptolemy II that list Ptolemaic kings and include female rulers in addition to Cleopatra VII (*cf.* the 'Canon of Ptolemy': *e.g.* Stahlman 2000). Instead, we must turn to modern scholars and narration subsequent to the ancient period.

Most modern scholars follow A. Samuel's (1962) work listing each male Ptolemy, I–XII (sometimes through to

Ptolemy XV), and ending with Cleopatra VII, occasionally including in their discussions the political positions of Cleopatra II–III and Berenice IV (*cf.* Neuffer 1979; Stanwick 2002; Bagnall and Derow 2004, table I). Arsinoë is excluded from modern scholars' king lists, although her political involvement remains a topic of discussion. Few scholars include any records of Ptolemaic co-regencies in their chronological lists, although a few briefly discuss the co-regency of Ptolemy I and II following W. Murnane's 'Ancient Egyptian coregencies' (1977). Generally, modern publications completely disregard the shared rule between Ptolemy II and Ptolemy the son (here identified with Ptolemy Nios). Whereas the co-regency between father and son (Ptolemy I and II) lasted for around two years, the later joint rule lasted longer, *c.* 267–259 BC, according to ancient sources, but the identification of Ptolemy the son remains ambiguous (*P. Sorb.* inv. 2440; *P. Louvre* 2424; *Gr. dem Medinet Habu* 77; *P. Hib.* 1.100; *cf.* Cadell 1998, 1; http://www.tyndalehouse.com/egypt/ptolemies/nios_i_fr.htm). The shared regency between Ptolemy II and Arsinoë has been consistently overlooked in modern sources, and, although reference to it does occur, conclusions tend to be stated without comprehensive investigations. Therefore, the aim here is to bridge this insufficiency by discussing the prospect of co-regency between Ptolemy and Arsinoë, considering all aspects of kingship according to the sources that structure the material as well as the socio-political roles of Arsinoë and their relationship to the principles of kingship. While an argument cannot be made for sole rule by Arsinoë, co-regency between her and Ptolemy II seems very likely given the results gleaned from the material.

Within the modern disciplines of Egyptology and classicism, most scholars agree that the concepts and perceptions of Egyptian kingship are very complex (*e.g.* Frankfort 1978). To the modern scholar's disappointment, there is a distinct lack of ancient sources that sufficiently describe kingship (Bierbrier 1980, 100; Troy 1986, 104). The roles of the pharaoh can be approached from various directions, and one ancient medium does not necessarily correspond to another. The definition within textual records is also divergent, describing the qualities and conceptions of the king according to any given topic of discussion. However, regardless of the medium, most ancient sources agree on a few socio-religious fundamentals that together structure the role of a pharaoh and what was expected of him.

Fundamental concepts of kingship

Every pharaoh was considered divine from the time of the royal proclamation (divine birth), in which he was traditionally identified as an heir of the previous pharaoh. The godly character of the pharaoh was emphasised in his genealogy, which claimed a divine kinship while at the same time dismissing an actual mortal father: he was regarded the son of Amun-Ra, mothered by an earthly representation of Hathor (= the queen). The direct lineage between the ruling pharaoh and the almighty solar deity was emphasised in the Turin King list and Manetho's *Aegyptiaca*, both of which begin with a list of the primeval gods. From the time of his coronation the pharaoh became an earthly manifestation of Horus, the son of Ra, the eternal ruler. The complexity of Egyptian rulership has already been analysed in various forms, and the chapters above show how Ra assumed different forms throughout the day, most prominently the midday sun, the aspect of full kingship. This, the third level of transfiguration, reveals Ra as the all-powerful light, manifested as a strong falcon, described as Horus and corresponding to the eternal royal rule and triumph over evil (Assmann 2001, 108).

The pharaoh was considered a mediator between the human and the divine spheres, as he represented the gods and humans equally. These theological concepts placed the pharaoh in a cultural position out of the reach of humans, and his rule was based on divine criteria rather than human ones (Najovits 2003, 153). As a consequence, his divinity created his absolute power over the people: as soon as he completed the royal ceremonies of coronation he became their high priest, magician or sorcerer, and it was he alone who could control the concepts of Ma'at on earth.

Pictorial regalia and representation

The principles of royal iconography are as complex as the concepts of kingship, and the modern understanding of the symbolism embedded in ancient Egyptian regalia remains fragmentary. The analysis above presented various royal attributes that denote kingship: one of the most important was the crown, primarily the double crown, symbolising the unification of Upper and Lower Egypt. As described, the double crown could be separated into the red and white crowns, and the pharaoh is documented wearing the respective crown in temple structures individually corresponding to Upper and Lower Egypt, and at the same time symbolising Nekhbet and Wadjet as the Two Ladies of North and South. The red and the white crowns, individually and combined, belong to the most ancient royal attributes in Egyptian iconography: very much based on the Narmer palette, they are interpreted as signifying royal power (CG 32169; Morenz 2004). In addition to the more traditional interpretations of these crowns, an association has been suggested here with the Hathoric nest and the egg, signifying the eternal and unbreakable bond between Hathor and Ra.

The analysis above of the pictorial units/elements included in the headdresses and crowns described the *uraeus* as the element most obviously related to kingship. The risen cobra was placed in the forehead of the pharaoh primarily as a sign of divine (Hathoric) protection, but it also emphasised the pharaoh's protective role towards his subjects (Stanwick 2002, 34). The ram horns were interpreted as denoting Egyptian kingship and connecting the pharaoh with prominent deities such as Amun and Horus. They appear primarily (in addition to the divine crowns) in the *anedjti* crown, which, in various locations throughout Egypt, is associated with war and the triumph over evil. The ram horns formed an integral part of the crown of Arsinoë, making the royal crown unique among the headgear of queens: no other females wear the ram horns as a fundamental part of a crown composition.

In addition to the crowns, the royal attributes included various sceptres, staves and maces, the most prominent signs being the crook and flail.[1] Arsinoë holds a lotus-shaped flail in four scenes which date to her lifetime (cat. no. 12) and to the reign of Ptolemy II (cat. nos 27, 29, 36) (see Table 18). Cat. no. 36, which depicts Arsinoë with a lotus-flail, relates to the theme of Ptolemy II's Sed festival. He is depicted as a ruling pharaoh in accordance with all Egyptian artistic conventions, and the festival pavilion encircles him. Although Ptolemy is the direct subject of the scene (and, indeed, the entire gate), Arsinoë is of fundamental importance as she functions as the key for comprehending the communicated message of the gate. The complete Sed festival Gate of Ptolemy (Medamoud), which includes various degrees of royal propaganda and traditional celebrations of rejuvenation, illustrates Arsinoë only in this one scene. Her physical position behind Ptolemy, her iconographic attribute (the flail) and her designation as a female king indicate a living and ruling queen. However, her presence in this form as Ptolemy II's equal and his co-regent is limited, as noted, to this one scene, and such may be interpreted as indicating the reason for Ptolemy's early rejuvenation ceremony: Arsinoë's death. The conventional regalia held by Ptolemy in this scene demonstrate a rejuvenated and powerful sole ruler of Egypt who managed the tasks of the ceremonies with the support and guidance of his deified sister-wife, thus following the principles of the Hathoric mode.

Aside from the pictorial attributes immediately connected with the main image, the theme of smiting an enemy (enemies) was a frequently occurring indication of kingship. None of the scenes shows Ptolemy II and Arsinoë in this role. However, the textual material depicts Arsinoë in a socio-political role as defending her country against the enemy, which agrees with this fundamental concept of kingship: cat. no. 2, the Pithom stele, describes how Arsinoë accompanied Ptolemy to the eastern border of Egypt in order to secure the boundaries against threatening invasion (*cf.* Assmann 1970). Correspondingly, her political role was sufficiently important to the Greeks for them to acknowledge her influence in the Chremonidean War, a commemoration post-dating her lifetime (*SIG*[3] I.434/5, l. 17; *e.g.* Austin 2006, 94f.; *cf.* Hazzard 2000, 94f.). Additional ancient sources describe Arsinoë's political involvement in the Ptolemaic navy and refer to her as a person in charge (*e.g.* Hauben 1970). One describes Arsinoë's chariot victories, which can be compared with the pharaoh's official demonstration of power expressed in the illustrations of him in the chariot (*P. Mil. Vogl.* VIII 309, AB 12.20–33). Together with cat. no. 2, the textual sources present a female royal actively participating in Egypt's national and foreign affairs during her lifetime.

Official documents commemorating kings' participation in royal actions and events are associated with the topic of the pharaoh as a war lord and cultic leader. Such tributes include the documentation of campaigns, royal proclamations and ritual ceremonies. Cat. nos 1–15 demonstrate such royal proclamations, although they vary greatly in their communicated messages. Cat. no. 1 describes Arsinoë's participation in the cult of Banebdjedet during her lifetime. Cat. no. 8 illustrates Arsinoë, figurally, as unaccompanied (without Ptolemy II) and facing an unidentified deity. These scenes show Arsinoë fulfilling her cultic responsibilities: one of the fundamental conventional concepts of kingship (*CAH*[2] II, 649). The latter scene is unique in its structural composition, as it not only illustrates Arsinoë alone as an active benefactor but also textually describes her as King of Egypt. Most importantly, cat. no. 8 (along with cat. no. 15) has been(re)dated here, placing it in Arsinoë's lifetime on the basis of the figural setting.

It was argued above that Arsinoë was provided with all five official royal titles, each one equally represented in a textual and iconographic form. The suggested designations do not always follow the conventional textual structure of each royal name, and the identification is based on epithets rather than determined by traditional prefixes, but such an application of titles was common during the Old Kingdom, a period from which several of Arsinoë's titles date (some were used only during the Old Kingdom). An analysis of the iconographic structure in the relief material studied here demonstrates that pictorial elements can communicate a message more clearly than textual records: a combination of both makes a very valid foundation for interpretation. The combination of textual and iconographic records presented above suggests a conclusion that Arsinoë was recognised as a female king in accordance with each official royal title during her lifetime (*cf.* Beckerath 1984, 2; Shaw 2003, 179): she held an equal position to Ptolemy II.

When Alexander the Great was crowned as the new Egyptian pharaoh he accepted the ancient Egyptian conventions of a divine legacy that made him an earthly manifestation of Horus, the celestial King. Thus, Alexander became the son of Ra and was expected to uphold universal order through his judgements and actions.[2] In the spirit of Alexander, the early Ptolemies were crowned and ruled Egypt in agreement with ancient Egyptian conventions, primarily demonstrated in their official designations 'Son of Ra' and 'King of Upper and Lower Egypt': titles that are used also to describe Arsinoë.

Arsinoë is recorded with the hieroglyphic title (coronation prefix) 'King of ...' in cat. nos 5, 7–8 and 13–15R, which unquestionably places her as a ruler in Egypt. Several of these scenes emphasise her prominent position also in the pictorial structure: in accordance with the crown line and her left-side position, she is identified as the most important figure in all scenes (except for cat. no. 14, where she is second, after Amun-Min), and she is repeatedly described as 'Daughter of Amun/Banebdjedet', which is comparable to the male royal title 'Son of Ra'. Except for cat. no. 8, these scenes emphasise her relation with her brother-husband and demonstrate a couple of equal hierarchic ranks (cat. no. 15, however, places both rulers as benefactors). Cat. nos 8 and 15 date to Arsinoë's lifetime, but those scenes that post-date her life retain a pictorial recognition of her as a pharaoh which is supported by textual records of a living ruler: thus, the majority of these scenes agree with the concepts of artistic adjustment as noted above. Thus cat. no. 5 concurs with the theme of the main Mendes stele (cat. no. 1), although the pictorial setting is different.

Cat. nos 1–2, 26L–R and 36 indicate Arsinoë's kingly position in the figurative arrangement and the contextual structure of the scenes rather than the textual records. Cat. no. 1, one of the most important scenes in the material, provides pictorial and textual records of Arsinoë's kingship: it relates to Arsinoë as living queen, high priestess and (posthumously deified) goddess simultaneously. In cat. no. 1L Arsinoë is identified as King of Lower Egypt and Ptolemy as King of Upper Egypt, high priestess and high priest, on the basis of the contextual details that individually symbolise these geographic areas. The identification of Ptolemy II as the King of Upper Egypt is supported by Arsinoë's designation as 'Sister/Wife of the King of Upper Egypt', which concurs with Arsinoë's title in cat. no. 13: 'King of Lower Egypt'.[3] Furthermore, symbolically speaking, the co-regency is stressed in the main text of cat. no. 2, which refers to year 12 of Ptolemy's rule, when the king travelled through Egypt with his sister-wife in order to inspect Egypt's borders and decide how to protect their country against enemies. Arsinoë was viewed not only as a female counterpart to the king, a queen, but as his co-regent in charge of Lower Egypt.

A combination of figural arrangements and textual records reveals a political cause for Ptolemy's need for a symbolic rebirth and rejuvenation through the celebration of a Sed festival. Arsinoë's presence in cat. no. 36 stresses her importance in the ceremony, not least because in this case she was the reason for it, and is comparable to her prayers in cat. no. 1R: 'I pray for you to the master of the Gods, so that he gives you numerous years as a king (*i.e.*, of rule)', relating to the jubilee. She communicates a similar message in cat. no. 2: 'I pray for your life to your father Atum; that he will give you numerous years of Sed festivals' (cat. no. 2L) and 'I wish for you to celebrate numerous Sed festivals (with the blessings) of the gods' (cat. no. 2R). Both apply an active artistic adjustment which correlates with Arsinoë's lifetime as well as the period following her death.

In addition to the immediate signs of Arsinoë's kingship, various scenes convey an impression of a powerful and politically important queen. She is frequently established as the most important figure in a scene based on the crown line. Furthermore, the material depicts a (divine) queen described with royal titles that places her as a ruler of Egypt: as the rightful, hereditary firstborn daughter of the king. Arsinoë's political importance is also stressed in scenes post-dating Ptolemy II, such as Ptolemy III's official designation that describes him as the heir of the sibling gods. Even during later Ptolemaic periods, Ptolemy VIII, Cleopatra III and Cleopatra VII found Arsinoë's political position so important that they felt obligated to commemorate her in forms of active veneration, and the queens were depicted wearing her regalia in Egyptian temples made to last for thousands of years (*cf.* Arnold 1999).

Reassessing the Ramesside crown as a male alternative to the crown of Arsinoë

A relief located in the vicinity of cat. no. 30 (Figures 129–130) that shows Ptolemy II with a Ramesside crown precipitates a reconsideration here of the crown presented in Chapter 4 as the Ramesside crown. This Philae scene is the only depiction of Ptolemy II wearing a Ramesside crown. In Chapter 4 a gender-orientated labelling of this crown was rejected in favour of a designation in agreement with its most frequent previous wearer, and it was concluded that the crown of Arsinoë and the Ramesside crown are differentiated only by the cow horns, which have a Hathoric symbolism. However, the Ramesside crown was never worn by a queen or goddess (except for Arsinoë's types AC 19–20), and, given that the relief shows Ptolemy II wearing a Ramesside crown, a hypothesis relating to gender-orientated crowns may in fact be valid.

The scene in question shows Ptolemy II as an active benefactor standing on the left side (*cf.* Berlin photos 1066; Bénédite 1893, 43, pls XIV–XV). He presents, as offerings, papyrus plants to the local divine triad: Osiris, Isis and Harpocrates. The scene embraces Ptolemy's veneration of the local triad, but suggestively, also declares a political message. The family of veneration is the divine royal family, from which the living king received his lineage of divine kingship, and by whom he was blessed with guidance and protection.[4] The papyrus plants held by Ptolemy symbolise Lower Egypt. The offerings combined with the divine family may indirectly describe Ptolemy II's symbolic declaration of his new political role as ruler of Lower Egypt following the death of Arsinoë.

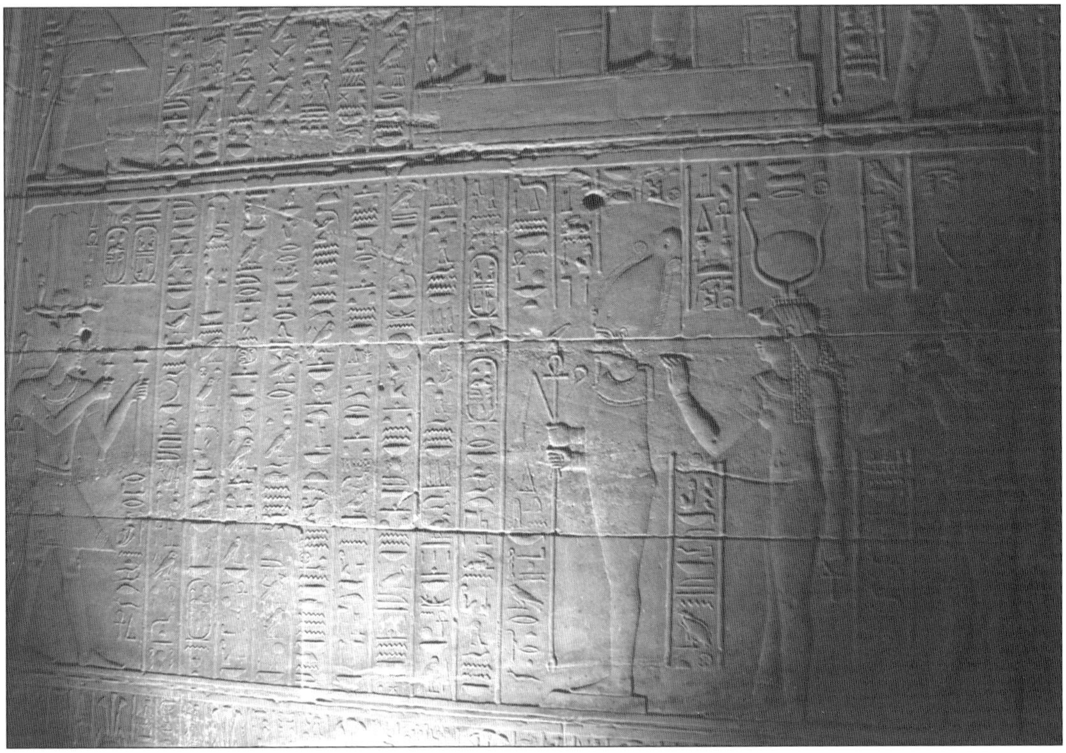

Figure 129. Detail of Ptolemy II (far left) sacrificing to the royal divine triad (left to right), Osiris, Isis and Harpocrates, Temple of Philae.

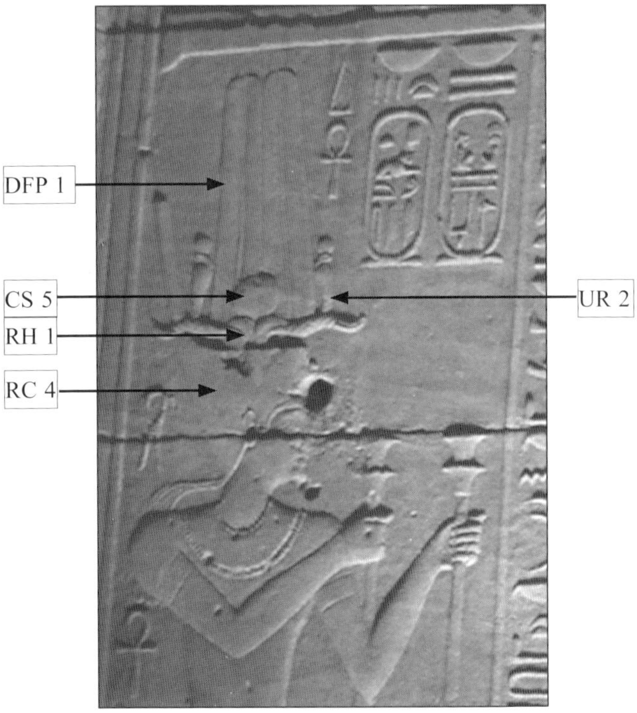

Figure 130. Detail of the Philae scene illustrating Ptolemy II. The arrows point to the individual pictorial units according to the abbreviations given in Chapter 4.

The material has demonstrated above various indications of co-regency between Arsinoë and Ptolemy II. The Temple of Philae records seven individual scenes illustrating Arsinoë in which Ptolemy II noticeably expressed piety and a socio-religious association with her. All post-date Arsinoë, being relating to a period of time when Ptolemy was a sole ruler of Egypt. This Philae scene is interpreted here as expressing Ptolemy's usurpation of a full royal position incorporating the designation 'King of Lower Egypt'. This theme is associated with the Sed festival celebrated by Ptolemy II after Arsinoë's death (*cf.* cat. nos 1, 2, 5, 26), and with Ptolemy II's reassurance to Egypt's inhabitants that he was capable of ruling alone after two periods of co-regency.[5] By depicting himself with the Ramesside crown, Ptolemy II appeared to the people in a head attribute identical to the crown of Arsinoë other than the lack of female cow horns associated with Hathor. He became Arsinoë's male equivalent, suggesting that these crowns can, consequently, be categorised according to the gender of its wearers.

Documenting a male and a female variant of the crown composition enables an association with the socio-religious dualistic structure that is fundamentally incorporated in all aspects of Egyptian culture, relating male and female, king and queen, brother and sister, husband and wife. As such, Ptolemy II and Arsinoë manifested as the son and daughter of Amun-Ra.

Notes

1 The material includes only one scene of Ptolemy II holding these items (cat. no. 36), otherwise presenting the pharaohs in a position of active veneration. Scenes that post-date Ptolemy II depict him mainly with the conventional *ankh* and *was* stave.

2 The complexity of a Macedonian ruler becoming a pharaoh of Egypt is embedded and expressed in the Alexander Romance, describing his kinship with Nectanebo II. Nectanebo was said to have entered the Macedonian court as an Egyptian priest, spending the night with Olympias and together conceiving the son of Zeus-Amun, Alexander. Similar stories place Ptolemy I as the half-brother of Alexander and the heir of Philip II, rather than of Lagus (ps.-Callisth. I.1–8).

3 'King of Lower Egypt' is documented also in other artistic media: a fragmentary *naos* that originates in Sais states 'The prophets and the godfathers of the Temple of Neith reached the place where the king was and they said to his Majesty: Sovereign our Lord, let the effigy appear of the King of Lower Egypt, Heiress of the Two Lands, Isis Arsinoë Philadelphos' (Quaegebeur 1989, 109). This text describes Arsinoë as a divine daughter, demonstrates a correlation between the court and the priesthood of Sais, determines Arsinoë as the King of Lower Egypt and describes her as the rightful heir of the throne. It must be emphasised that the prophets and priests came to Ptolemy rather than *vice versa*, an event which indicates Arsinoë's individual importance.

4 Here, the reader can also include previous scholars' assumptions that the crown of Arsinoë expresses a relation with Lower Egypt, based on a symbolism which is present also in the Ramesside crown (*e.g.* Abubakr 1937, 42).

5 Ptolemy initially co-ruled Egypt with his father, and probably thereafter with Arsinoë. After the death of Arsinoë, Ptolemy co-ruled Egypt with Ptolemy the son. A co-regency with Arsinoë would place Ptolemy II as a sole ruler for only thirteen years.

Chapter 11

Arsinoë and piety – priestess and goddess

Whereas Arsinoë's socio-political role as queen/king has been a topic of debate over the years, her religious position as a (living) high priestess has been neglected. Cat. no. 1 textually entitles Arsinoë 'She who is the high priestess of Banebdjedet' and, although most scholars acknowledge this title, they conclude that it was an honorary title given to her after her death (based on the date of the stela). Similarly, it has been suggested above, on the basis of their pictorial representation, that the Mendes stele depicts Ptolemy II and Arsinoë as high priest and high priestess. However, this cultic aspect remains unexplored in terms of its associations and function. Arsinoë's religious aspect as a goddess, in contrast, has been a topic of debate for quite some time. However, the discussion rarely engages with the actual divine aspects, but instead focuses on the date of deification. This chapter will deal with both these issues.

The high priestess

Arsinoë's role as the priestess of Banebdjedet is occasionally mentioned in connection with the Mendes stele, but always without any proper analytical reassessment (*e.g.* Hölbl 2001, 101). Quaegebeur (1971a; 1971b) proposed an association between Arsinoë's title 'Daughter of Amun' and the Divine Adoratrices, but such a possible connection has been generally dismissed and left unexplored since then (*cf.* van Oppen 2007). Quaegebeur's discussion will be continued here with an examination of the evidence in the material for the active religious role of Arsinoë as high priestess according to ancient Egyptian principles and an argument that she resumed the respected office as God's Wife of Amun.

The role of priestess is a religious office that could be practised by any given queen during her lifetime. Possibly, previous scholars have kept their distance from such a discussion in regard to Arsinoë because of the problems surrounding the dating of her images and scenes. However, it was argued on pp.90–93 that three (possibly four) scenes depict Arsinoë in an indisputable position as an active benefactor: she is depicted as a royal person, standing in a position opposite the traditional deities, and she presents offerings or participates in a religious ceremony in order to invoke the divine spirit. Such an active role (as in cat. nos 8 (and possibly 9), 15 and 26L) belongs to a royal person who must be alive: therefore, Arsinoë must be considered high priestess during her lifetime (*cf.* cat. no. 36).[1] With this conclusion as a starting point, the present section will focus on the practicality of the office and the ways in which the material shows Arsinoë as a God's wife of Amun. In deference to the concept of temporal adjustment, all scenes that relate to Arsinoë's royal position as a high priestess will be included here regardless of their actual date; the analysis will be based on the message communicated in the scene and the religious position that it reflects.[2]

As discussed in the previous section, one of the most important concepts of kingship was embedded in the pharaoh's cultic position as high priest (Brewer and Teeter 2007, 47). Traditionally, the queen had an equally important corresponding religious position, and as high priestess she performed ceremonies associated with music and dance in order to invoke and arouse the main god (Blackman 1921, 20). The importance of the Theban high priests during the New Kingdom is well documented in ancient and modern sources. The male Theban priests retained their socio-religious power throughout the centuries, encompassing more or less political influence, but they were surpassed by their female equivalents during the latter half of the Third Intermediate Period (Dodson 2002, 179 with n. 1; *cf.* Assmann 2003, 296–300). The high priestesses of this period reassumed the royal titles that had been officially introduced during the early New Kingdom, and they associated themselves with a religious position that dates back to Early Dynastic times (Blackman 1921). They referred to themselves with official designations that expressed their position of piety, including the most recognised titles 'God's wife', 'God's Hand' and 'Divine Adoratrice'. Additional applied designations include 'Daughter of Amun', 'God's Daughter' and 'Daughter of Ra', combined with a spectrum of optional structural combinations referring to an association/assimilation with the goddess Tefnut (as a Hathoric aspect), all of which expressed kinship with the solar deity Ra (Sander-Hansen 1940).

Divine Adoratrices also occupied a political position as representatives of royal power in the king's absence (Sander-Hansen 1940, 24). In this respect, they can be considered as female co-regents. When the male pharaoh performed his duties as a war lord, defending the boundaries of Egypt and, therefore, being absent from internal affairs, the female pharaoh was in command. Consequently, it is not surprising to find reference to the Divine Adoratrices as also practising a political and financial authority (*e.g.* Sander-Hansen 1940, 28).

The queenly role of priestess has been investigated and summarised by Troy (1986) in her doctoral thesis concerning patterns of queenship (*cf.* Blackman 1921; Sander-Hansen 1940). The fundamentals include an identification with the goddess Hathor: the queen usurps the position as the goddess's earthly manifestation (Troy 1986, 53). Such assimilation is represented in, for example, images of queens shaking Hathor's sistrum. The sistrum was used together with other sacred instruments, as well as with singing and dancing, in order to honour the goddess during religious ceremonies. Therefore, the shaking of a sistrum expresses an active position, a benefactor's role, performed by a person who is alive (*cf.* Blackman 1921, 20; Troy 1986, 86f.). In the material, Arsinoë is depicted shaking the sistrum/sistra in two main scenes (cat. nos 9, 15L–R) incorporating three individual figures; these scenes, therefore, provide the evidence required in order to identify Arsinoë as a living priestess. The ceremonial shaking of the sistrum was one of the most important tasks of a high priestess, but records show that even priestesses of a lower rank did so: it was not limited to the main queen (Blackman 1921, 8f., 22f.). Accordingly, the sistrum alone does not indicate Arsinoë's official position as the high priestess (and God's wife), as it was used also by priestesses of lower rank.

Whereas the sistrum was an item connected with priestesses in general, the double feather plume (occasionally accompanied by cow horns and a solar disc) was a cultic attribute exclusive to the high priestess (queens and goddesses) (Blackman 1921, 28f.; Troy 1986, II.6.3.1.). The feathers symbolise the dualism of Egyptian religious conventions, and are associated with the eyes of Horus/Ra, the divine siblings Shu and Tefnut, masculinity and femininity: all reflecting the concept of androgyny. The double feather plume was an essential element in the crown of Arsinoë and its symbolism will be discussed further below.

Previous high priestesses, especially the Divine Adoratrices during the Late Period, were referred to as manifestations of Tefnut (*e.g.* Blackman 1921, 29; Troy 1986, A1/28; Pereyra de Fidanza 2003, 362). Lesko (1999, 150) suggests that such an association was based on the queen's royal legacy as pharaoh's daughter, comparable to Tefnut's divine kinship with the king of the gods. In the material, cat. nos 2–4 and 26 associates/identifies Arsinoë with Tefnut. Cat. no. 2L was interpreted above as describing Arsinoë as the daughter of Atum and Hathor, the latter in her sexual aspect as the Hand of God, identifying Arsinoë with Tefnut (and Ptolemy II with Shu). Cat. no. 3 depicts Arsinoë in an symbolic correspondence with Shu with the use of comparable pictorial details, consequently associating her with Tefnut. A symbolic association between the couples Arsinoë–Ptolemy and Shu–Tefnut is seen in the arrangement of figures in cat. no. 4. The stele refers to an official ceremony in which the royal deceased and deified ancestors support the ruling couple (*cf.* the now-missing stele from Masara: Howard-Vyse and Perring 1842). Arsinoë's Throne name, as listed in cat. nos 2(L–R), 12 and possibly 14, designates her as 'She who is in (/united with) the heart of Shu'. The name of Tefnut is obviously not included, but the identification is implicit, as she was his sister and wife.[3]

An identification of a high priestess with the Hathoric Tefnut reflects another theological complexity, since she is simultaneously described in her maternal role, as God's Hand, together with Atum (or the main god), creating Tefnut (thus, herself). The amalgamation of these two aspects, the mother and daughter, forms the religious platform for the complex concept of a God's wife (these were regarded as Amun's daughters, while at the same time being his wives in order to bring forward a legitimate heir to the royal throne). An identification of the high priestess with Tefnut demonstrates the Hathoric mother–wife–daughter complex manifested in royal women.

Owing to the complexity of divine kinship and the identification with Tefnut, it is not surprising to find direct reference to God's wives as divine daughters, principally daughters of Amun, again emphasising a kinship based on the solar cult (Pereyra de Fidanza 2003, 361). 'Daughter of Amun', as noted above, was one of Arsinoë's most common official designations during her lifetime and immediately following her death, but none of the later reliefs describe her with such a title. Chapter 8 (pp. 108–128) provided additional designations that identify Arsinoë as a Hathoric manifestation and God's wife, primarily 'Beloved of the ram' and 'Beloved of all the gods'. The material also reveals indirect associations with Arsinoë's position as God's wife. In cat. no. 1, for example, Arsinoë is addressed as 'She who fills the palace with her beauty', 'Sweet of love' (cat. nos 1M, 2M, 28, 31–32) and 'Great of Sweetness' (cat. no. 8) (*cf.* Troy 1986, A1/12–18, A1/19; *cf.* Frankfort 1978, 105).[4] Cat. no. 1, moreover, designates Arsinoë as 'She who belongs to the Lord', a title that is interpreted here as placing her as the wife of Banebdjedet, in contrast to the more traditional view that associates her with Ptolemy II.

As noted on p. 116, Arsinoë's documented titles are connected with the ceremonies of the Holy Wedding, and are believed to symbolise the erotic female scent, arousing the god. The ceremonial Holy Wedding between the god and his earthly wife culminated in the birth of the royal heir, who is the incarnated divine soul. The Mendes stele describes the reincarnated soul of the ram, commemorating this event in image and text alike. However, cat. no. 1 also refers to the incarnated soul of Arsinoë and, based on her identification with Banebdjedet, the stele also signifies their matrimonial unification.

In addition to the reliefs, the most important support for the argument is in a hieroglyphic text written on the above mentioned statue bases. Arsinoë's initial three epithets read 'Great Bat, Daughter of Amun, God's wife ...', thus identifying her with the primeval Hathoric goddess Bat, possibly the most powerful mother-goddess in the Egyptian pantheon, and combining this with the Hathoric positions as daughter and wife. The text provides evidence of a continuation of the office of Amun's high priestess, otherwise recognised as Divine Adoratrice, God's Hand and God's wife (of Amun).

Royal adoptions – the continuation of the religious office

The office of high priestess was continued through a series of royal female adoptions, especially during the Late Period (*e.g.* Dodson 2002). The adopted descendant claimed her socio-religious position through an assumed divine lineage. Arsinoë's title 'Daughter of Amun', as it is presented in cat. nos 24–25, located on the Gate of Euergetes, may connect with such a continuation of the religious office. These two scenes are the only ones with this title that post-date Ptolemy II: dating to the reign of Ptolemy III, they are related to the gate's general coronation theme. Concurring with Ptolemy III's declaration of descent in cat. no. 24, Berenice II claims her divine ancestry from Arsinoë in a nearby scene. Neither Arsinoë nor Ptolemy II was the biological parent of Berenice, but she retained conventional references to a direct dynastic lineage on the same level as Ptolemy III. Her claim as Arsinoë's heir indicates that Berenice II regarded herself the political heir of the Ptolemaic dynasty, but it also shows that she declared herself the religious successor of Arsinoë in her role of high priestess. Arsinoë's title in cat. nos 24–25, 'Daughter of Amun', which otherwise belongs to a living queen, makes a statement about a continuation of the religious position of high priestess, which was transferred from Arsinoë to Berenice II through the adoption.[5] In line with the hereditary nature of the Divine Adoratrices, Arsinoë's adoption of Ptolemy II's children, including Ptolemy III's spouse, awarded them equal status with blood children, automatically placing Berenice II as a subsequent God's wife. The identification of such a religious (dynastic) adoption furthermore supports the interpretation of cat. no. 25 reached here, in which the right-side couple are identified as Ptolemy III and Berenice II (rather than Ptolemy I and Berenice I); this correlates in terms of time with their individual deification (coronation?) as the *theoi Euergetai*.

The goddess

Arsinoë's role as a goddess has received much scholarly attention. Her divine aspect is generally acknowledged in accordance with the divinity of conventional Egyptian kingship, but conclusions and interpretations differ in terms of the date of deification.[6] Chapter 1 has already presented the various cultic roles of Arsinoë: she was placed in the official Alexandrian eponymous cult together with Ptolemy II, as the *theoi Adelphoi*, and individually as *thea Philadelphos*, and in the Egyptian forum according to the ancient principles of the royal cult, with a main centre in Memphis side by side with Ptah, and as the divine ancestor and founder of the dynasty (together with Ptolemy II as the divine siblings – *nṯrw snw*). The present section will discuss Arsinoë's divinity in more detail.[7]

Two main individual cults are revealed in the material aside from the ruler cult of the living Pharaoh Arsinoë (a religious position which is based on her active role as a benefactor): the individual cult of Arsinoë Philadelphos and the ancestor cult of the *theoi Adelphoi*. The ancestor cult was examined in Chapter 6 and this section will, therefore, concentrate on the individual cult of Arsinoë as it is represented in cat. nos 1–2, 5–7, 10–11, 13–14, 23 and 26–33. All these scenes date to the reign of Ptolemy II and depict the king in a figural position of active veneration.[8]

Scenes that show Arsinoë being venerated as an individual goddess have been used by modern scholars as an argument for determining her divinity and cult as posthumous, and, in general, that is the view taken here. However, there is evidence that such veneration occurred also within Arsinoë's lifetime, based on her physical position as an active benefactor, which has been related above to the ruler cult of a living monarch. Cat. no. 26 is the primary evidence against the mainstream conclusion, as it portrays Arsinoë as a benefactor (26L) and, simultaneously, as a deified queen (26L–R). In accordance with her divinity, she is depicted as a daughter of Amun: the left half identifies her as the daughter role of Amun and Mut, whereas the right emphasises her kinship with Khonsu, interpreted here as her brother. Arsinoë's designations accentuate her divine position, and as mentioned on pp. 113–117, place her as a God's wife of Amun, thus incorporating another step of the Hathoric daughter-wife-mother concept.[9] The significance of these scenes' dating is that they were begun during Arsinoë's lifetime but interrupted by her death. Arsinoë is illustrated as a living queen who performs religious duties placed upon her according to Egyptian principles, while at the same time being venerated as a goddess among the local deities.

Arsinoë's twofold figural setting echoes that in a scene of Ramses II that dates to his lifetime: on the basis of this similarity and the overall figural arrangement, cat. no. 26 can thus be shown to disagree with the generally accepted conclusion of an exclusively posthumous veneration of Arsinoë.

The Mendes stele describes Arsinoë's physical death and the transformation of her royal soul during the traditional Egyptian ceremony of opening the mouth; it explains her apotheosis and how this followed ancient Egyptian conventions. The words that are spoken by the back figure of Ptolemy II may be associated with this event, as he says 'I unite your limbs and put together your body in the chapel of Tenenet.' Such a proclamation is traditionally identified with words spoken by Isis and Nephthys (connected with the Osirian myth) rather than a royal person. However, the arrangement of figures and the textual records demonstrate a theme of rejuvenation and incarnation, thereby adapting the words for an alternative theme, one aimed at Arsinoë. Once the ceremony of opening the mouth was accomplished, her soul was free to join the primeval celestial soul who had originally created her.[10] Previous scholars have identified the incarnated soul (the main theme of the stela) with the *ba* of the ram, a theory supported here, but, in addition to this, it may be related to Arsinoë's reincarnated soul: the main text states

> In the year 15, of the month Pachons [2nd month of the summer] this goddess ascended to the sky, where she/her soul was unified with their souls (those who created her beauty). After the four days ritual of the Opening of the mouth ceremony, this goddess ascended as a soul. They sang for her in the city of Anpet and they celebrated her [funerary] festival, and they released her soul to live close to the living Ba, who became the support (strength) for her, and for all the gods and goddesses from the primeval times until today.

Following her deification, Ptolemy instructed the priests to place images of Arsinoë in all Egyptian temples, an event in which the priests rejoiced because of her admirable way towards the Egyptian people:

> His majesty instructed (ordered) that her image was as placed in all the gods houses (*i.e.*, temples). It was beautiful on the heart (*i.e.*, pleased) of the priests that she had been recognised as divine [based on her excellent way towards all the people] and would be with all the deities.

The reliefs place Arsinoë as a goddess primarily in a daughter aspect. Pictorially and textually, she is identified as the daughter of Amun in all his local forms and variations (Banebdjedet, Amun-Min, etc.).[11] Maternal figures are less accentuated: the pictorial variation of mother-goddesses shows that the concept itself is more important than a specific identification by name. Arsinoë's daughter role automatically places her as the daughter of Ra and Hathor.

In a few scenes, Arsinoë's kinship with Amun is not explicit, but is instead indicated by her associated figures. Cat. no. 23, for example, describes Arsinoë textually as daughter of Amun, but her divine father is not physically depicted: rather, Ptolemy II is shown presenting offerings to Khonsu and Arsinoë. Based on Arsinoë's title and the character of Khonsu (as the son of Amun), the figural arrangement in cat. no. 23 identifies them as siblings, the children of Amun (and Mut), while an iconographic adjustment emphasises Ptolemy II's divine kinship.

A majority of the Philae scenes, cat. nos 27–29 and 31–32, designate Arsinoë as Amun's daughter while pictorially associating her with Isis (Nephthys in cat. no. 28): thus, the theme is that of Arsinoë as a divine daughter with her mother accentuated pictorially and her father textually. The maternal role of Isis emphasised here naturally agrees with the main theme of the temple.

Cat. no. 11 serves as an example of the complexity of Egyptian religion in portraying Ptolemy II as an active benefactor presenting offerings to Harsomtus, Horus, Hathor, Sarapis and Arsinoë. This scene has a unique pictorial value, providing an identification of not only a divine triad but also a complex contextual organisation that places Arsinoë in a complete Hathoric character. The kinship between Horus, Hathor and Harsomtus is generally accepted. However, the combination of Sarapis and Arsinoë is of greater interest in terms of the current debate, and brings to mind Arsinoë's maternal association with Apis as mentioned in cat. nos 12 and 26 ('Mother of Hep'). Sarapis is generally acknowledged as an amalgamated Hellenistic form of (primarily) Apis, Osiris and Zeus, including aspects of Amun, Ra and Asclepius. Here, Sarapis assumes a position as Arsinoë's divine spouse, implicitly linked with Arsinoë's religious role as high priestess during her lifetime. In addition to the matrimonial role, Arsinoë's position may be interpreted as a divine daughter: she is linked with Sarapis and the dynastic triad in order to emphasise the continuation of the Ptolemaic dynasty. Her maternal connection with Apis (thus, Sarapis) results in a tripartite identity reflecting all three Hathoric roles (wife, daughter and mother). Moreover, cat. no. 11 stresses the royal kinship between Ptolemy II and Arsinoë, above all in Arsinoë's royal designations, placing her husband-brother in a divine association with all depicted deities. The message of cat. no. 11 is thus similar to that of cat. no. 2, with a fundamental association with the primeval solar deity, here represented by Sarapis.

Arsinoë's divine position is thus that of an individually venerated goddess equivalent to Hathor's daughter role, the eye of Ra. She received a divine status equal to the majority of the traditional Egyptian deities and was, as a consequence, associated with many of them.[12] She was considered a child of the main solar forces, the result of a unification of male and female, of the primeval mother and father. Her daughter role reflects her divine responsibility to secure the dynasty's continuation, which explains her (symbolic) adoption of Berenice II (p. 144). The material shows that Arsinoë was accepted in the Egyptian pantheon on the basis of qualifications and fundamentals equal to those of previous pharaohs and her religious position during her lifetime. She was a royal woman who respected and acknowledged the ancient traditions of Egyptian society, and her complete deification was accepted (partially) on the basis of her position as God's wife.

Notes

1 It has been suggested on pp. 93–103 that scenes dating to Ptolemy II express ancient Egyptian conventions of temporal adjustment, and, in terms of time, incorporate reference of a twofold nature. These scenes relate to more than one time period and describe at least two historical events. Whereas cat. nos 8 and 15 (L–R) (possibly also cat. no. 9) depict Arsinoë in a benefactor's position exclusively (depicting her as a living queen), cat. nos 1 and 26 illustrate her also as a beneficiary (and a goddess). Thereby, these scenes apply a pictorial concept that was practised during the time of Ramses II.

2 All scenes that place Arsinoë in a dynastic setting are excluded here, since these show her together with her husband-brother as the *theoi Adelphoi*, and as such they are the objects of veneration (beneficiaries) in the ancestor cult.

3 Related to the topic is Arsinoë's designation in cat. no. 26 (L–R), 'Mistress of Eternity, Lady of the Solar disc (/Mistress of all that the sun disc encircles)'. Prior to Arsinoë, this epithet described only three queens: Amenirdis I, Shepenwepet II and Ankhnesneferibre, all having been ritually initiated in order to become God's wives of Amun, Divine Adoratrices. Troy overlooked the title of Shepenwepet II in Medinet Habu that is documented here. The analysis quoted ancient records that describe the initiation of God's wives of Amun in Karnak. An initiation text describes how priestly attributes were placed on a queen as she was appointed Mistress of eternity, Lady of the solar disc, and the finishing line in the text identifies the initiated high priestess as a direct descendant from Tefnut. Describing Arsinoë with an identical title, the geographic location of cat. no. 26 in Karnak must be considered, as it is separated from the Osirian Chapel of Amenirdis by only a few metres. It is unlikely to have been pure coincidence that Arsinoë is described with a title indistinguishable from some of the most important Divine Adoratrices, one of whom is located nearby.

4 Textually, Arsinoë's designations can be compared with the most eminent of God's wives, including Hatshepsut, Tawosret, Amenirdis I, Shepenwepet II, Nitocris I and Ankhnesneferibre. The titles of Arsinoë in general can be compared with titles of the above-mentioned high priestesses listed by Troy (1986). A brief comparison shows that Arsinoë shared sixteen titles with Hatshepsut (corresponding to Troy's list: A1/12, A1/19, A2/7, A2/16, B2/25, B3/9, B4/11, C2/2, C2/5–6, C3/1, C4/1, C4/14, D1/4, D2/1, D2/13); eight with Tawosret (Troy 1986, A1/11, A2/1, B2/25, B3/10, C2/5, D1/4, D2/1, D2/13); eighteen with Amenirdis I (Troy 1986, A1/1, A1/13, A1/16, A2/1, A2/7, A2/16, A4/5, B2/25, B2/29, B3/9–10, B4/10, C3/1, C4/1, D1/4, D1/10, D2/1, D2/13); eleven with Shepenwepet II (Troy 1986, A/1/5, A1/15, A2/1, A2/4, B2/25, B3/10, B4/11, C4/1, D1/4, D2/1, D2/13); seven with Nitocris I (Troy 1986, A1/14, B2/25, B2/29, B2/37, C3/1, C4/1, C4/7); and sixteen with Ankhnesneferibre (Troy 1986, A1/7, A1/8, A1/9, A2/1, A2/16, B2/25, B2/25, B2/37, B3/10, B4/10–11, C4/8, D1/10, D2/1, D2/3, D2/15). To a Greek audience, the Holy Wedding between a queen/high priestess and a god was compared with the *hieros gamos* between Zeus and Hera. When Ptolemy II and Arsinoë performed their official duties as a high priest and high priestess they simultaneously fulfilled the ceremonial coming together of the divine force in the Holy Wedding. This is recorded for the Greek population in the words of Theocritus' *Idyll* XVII, comparing the marriage of the royal couple with the Greek Olympian sibling couple. Similarly, Arsinoë supported the cult of Adonis and Aphrodite, and compared her mother with the Greek goddess of love (*cf.* van Oppen 2007, II).

5 Greek sources could also reflect the continuation of the office of high priestess from Arsinoë to Berenice II. For example, Callimachus (*Com. Ber.* (=F. 110), lines 57–58) describes how Berenice II went to the Temple of Arsinoë (Aphrodite) Zephyritis, where she dedicated a lock of hair for the safe return of her husband. The direct identification of Hathor as Aphrodite has been generally accepted by scholars, and the assimilation of Arsinoë and Aphrodite can, therefore, be approached as an indication of Arsinoë's role as an earthly manifestation of the goddess. In her role as the high priestess Berenice reconnected with her deceased ancestor for support and guidance (*cf.* Catull. 66, 57–58; van Oppen 2007, II). Arsinoë's connection with her adopted children is revealed also in cat. no. 1, when it is stated that statues of the royal children were carried in the procession when honouring Arsinoë after her death. This is a textual reference, but, regardless, it is possible to compare this statement with the high priestess/queen's maternal role expressed in the title 'she of the carrying-chair'. The chair was associated also with the Sed festival, which has been mentioned many times above (*cf.* Troy 1986, II.3.2.1).

6 The ancient Egyptians believed that the royal soul, the *kꜣ*, carried and represented divine kingship, and that each pharaoh was its possessor from the time of coronation. The royal soul was considered as anchored in divine primeval times, in the main solar force (Ra/Atum/Amun). Most modern scholars agree that the divine aspect of kingship exists, but their perspectives on royal divinity are varied. The most accepted opinion is that a king had a divine lineage bestowed upon him on the day of his coronation, that he was a living incarnation or manifestation of divine kingship (=Horus), but that he himself did not become a complete deity until the day he died. For the royal soul, see Assmann 2001, 119; Morkot 2005, 156. Compare the *ba* (p. 63, n. 4). For a discussion on the dating, see Cadell 1998.

7 The Alexandrian cult is excluded based on the Egyptian character of the material, but it is examined for the purposes of comparison.

8 Cat. nos 3–4, 16–22, 24 and 34–35 pair Arsinoë with her husband-brother in scenes that express dynastic propaganda. These date to the reigns of Ptolemaic successors, from Ptolemy III to Ptolemy VIII, and illustrate the couple as beneficiaries or, as in cat. no. 20, as inactive spectators participating in official ceremonies providing Ptolemy IV with his Throne name.

9 Any given pharaoh was placed on the throne in order to uphold divine justice, Ma'at, and to keep Egypt safe from her enemies. He was considered as an earthly manifestation of Horus, just as the queen held the incarnated soul of Hathor. The current scholarly interpretation of a pharaoh's divinity is that it was incomplete until his death. However, he claimed his divine legacy and was regarded a true heir of the primeval solar force; he was the son of Ra, and stood in a cultural position much higher than any other living being in his contemporary society. Inscriptions and illustrations throughout Egypt demonstrate the divine kinship of the ruling pharaoh, and his socio-religious aspect as God's son is undeniable. The material reveals that Arsinoë received an official cultural position equivalent to a pharaoh's, and her socio-political role may be interpreted as King of Lower Egypt, Ptolemy II's co-regent: Arsinoë was considered divine already during her lifetime based on her hierarchic position as a pharaoh.

10 A similar description of Arsinoë's death, funerary ceremonies and return to the primeval divine soul is found in the Alexandrian triad (p.107, n. 16). Like the Mendes stela, the text of the sculpture firstly portrays Arsinoë as a living and ruling queen. The same passage describes a festival celebrated in her honour, most probably referring to the public *Arsinoeia*. Since the passage is interpreted here as referring to Arsinoë's lifetime, the *Arsinoeia* was celebrated while the queen was still alive. In a second textual passage, located on the side of the statue, Amun states to Arsinoë that he makes her into a goddess among the already existing deities, as he blows eternal life through her nostrils to rejuvenate her body (*cf.* Sauneron 1960; Quaegebeur 1988, 43f.).

11 Cat. no. 6 is used here as an example of a different male character. Their poor state of preservation makes it impossible to establish absolutely the identities of the deities that accompany Arsinoë in cat. no. 6. However, on the basis of the poorly preserved textual records, combined with the figural outlines, an identification with Horus and Hathor is suggested. The combination of these two deities primarily communicates a message of divine dynastic power, but their matrimonial relationship is not to be suppressed: Horus represented a ruling solar king and his sexual unification with Hathor secured the continuation of the monarchy and the royal heir. On the basis of this union, Arsinoë's association with Horus and Hathor is interpreted as a divine daughter ensuring the Ptolemies a dynastic continuance. Cat. no. 6 demonstrates that a father-figure (as contrasting Amun) occasionally shows different divine aspects, but retains the fundamental principles and family-orientated value behind the concept.

12 For example, Arsinoë is recorded in association with Ptah, Montu, Ra, Thoth, Amun-Ra, Horus, Seth, Bat, Hathor, Tefnut, Sekhmet, the Merhu bull, Geb and so on (*e.g.* Quaegebeur 1998).

Chapter 12

The crown of Arsinoë as a symbol of authority

The crown of Arsinoë as a symbol of kingship

Arsinoë's socio-political role as king has been discussed above in relation to the fundamental conventions of kingship, its pictorial representation in royal attributes and the official royal designations. These come together here as they are embedded in the symbolism of the crown of Arsinoë. The five official royal names are used as a basis for discussion because they represent a tangible aspect of kingship. As mentioned above, previous scholars have argued that Arsinoë's royal titles were given to her posthumously as a part of an honorary programme instituted by Ptolemy II. However, the material examined here has offered the possibility of reassessment, and two, possibly three, scenes have been identified as belonging to Arsinoë's lifetime (four if incorporating also cat. no. 26L, initiated during her lifetime and interrupted by her death). Consequently, all the titles listed below concur with a living queen/female king.

Chapter 8 identified Arsinoë's epithet 'Banebdjedet' (the ram god) with the first and oldest conventional royal title, the Horus name. As a local form of Amun, Banebdjedet is depicted with horns identical to those of Arsinoë, and since both aspects of the ram god are described as Arsinoë's father they are interpreted here as being pictorially associated with the ram horns in the crown of Arsinoë. The horns symbolise eternal kingship and are incorporated in crowns that were worn as a reflection of the rejuvenated sun disc – the main solar force and divine king, Ra. Alternatively, the horns were worn by kings in their role of war lords and signified their responsibility to protect Egypt. The ram horns in the crown of Arsinoë thus symbolise her Horus name, her socio-political position as a (living) co-regent of Egypt (King of Lower Egypt) and her general associations with the ram god.

The second royal title, the Nebty name, signifies the Two Ladies, the vulture and cobra, Nekhbet and Wadjet, and their divine protection of the pharaoh. Except for the most obvious pictorial representation as the vulture and cobra in her headdress (cat. nos 8 and 23–24 and the double *uraeus* in sculpture), the double nature of the Nebty name is associated primarily with Arsinoë's double feather plume. This interpretation is based on two plausible Nebty names – 'She who received the two forehead *uraei*' and 'Lady of the crowns' – both of which are associated with the dualism traditionally expressed by a Nebty title.

Thirdly, a Golden Horus name may be identified in Arsinoë's title 'Beautiful of appearance'; its pictorial counterpart appears in the solar disc. Arsinoë's title may be interpreted as relating to the shining element of the Golden Horus which manifested in the crown of Arsinoë as a solar disc positioned within the protecting cow horns. The latter express Arsinoë's protective role in her Hathoric position, and relate to the responsibilities of any given pharaoh to protect his or her people from enemies.

Arsinoë's Throne name is generally identified with the designation 'She who is in the heart of Shu/King, Beloved of all the Gods'. However, the symbolic correlation with the crown of Arsinoë is provided not by the title itself but by her coronation prefix 'King of Lower Egypt'. The geographical area of Lower Egypt is traditionally symbolised by the red crown, which is a fundamental component of the crown of Arsinoë.

All individual details incorporated in the crown of Arsinoë have a direct or indirect association with Amun. Therefore, Arsinoë's Birth name prefix 'Daughter of Amun' is associated not with one pictorial unit exclusively but instead with the complete composition. Her socio-political role is reflected in each part of the crown, and her cultural position as the King of Egypt – the legitimate daughter of Amun – is communicated by the complete structure of the crown. Arsinoë was recognised, therefore, as a female king in accordance with each official royal title during her lifetime, and they were all embedded in the complex symbolic structure of her crown, which belongs to her lifetime.[1]

The crown of Arsinoë as a symbol of her religious position as God's wife

Arsinoë's cultic position as high priestess, a God's wife, has been established above as an office held by the queen during her lifetime. This position has been documented in the pictorial composition of the reliefs, but the evidence is presented primarily in Arsinoë's textual designations: these connect with the previous Divine Adoratrices, especially Hatshepsut, Tawosret, Amenirdis I and Ankhnesneferibre, and portray a ruling queen who was initiated in the most sacred religious mysteries of the traditional pharaonic period.

Arsinoë's religious role as high priestess is reflected both in the individual details and in the overall composition of her crown. A new perspective may be added here to the more general interpretation of the red crown: as it is structurally incorporated in the crown of Arsinoë, it is interpreted as expressing Hathoric maternal protection, as indicating a mother's womb or nest, always holding the double feather plume – the children Shu and Tefnut. Such an association links the red crown and double feather plume with Arsinoë's Hathoric role as the eye of Ra, as she was sent out to the primeval darkness in order to light it up and find the two missing children, Shu and Tefnut.

As noted on pp. 91–92, the crown of Arsinoë is divided into two main stylistic types on the basis of the location of the ram horns (on top of or at the base of the red crown). When the ram horns are placed on top of (read: within) the red crown, and are accompanied by the physically attached cow horns and solar disc, the Hathoric maternal symbolism encompasses these items also. The crown of Arsinoë thus symbolises also the maternal protection of the divine royal soul. It describes, moreover, the Hathoric protection of the primeval light as the source of all life, as Ra is identified with the solar disc. In the overall constellation, Arsinoë's Hathoric assimilation comes full circle, as it expresses the eternally entwined dualistic relation between the fundamentals of nature (androgyny). On the basis of the association between the red crown and the items placed 'within' it, the crown of Arsinoë is interpreted as symbolising Hathor's roles as the mother of Shu and Tefnut and as the wife and female equivalent of Ra-Horus. The third Hathoric aspect (as the daughter) is communicated in the persona of Arsinoë herself, being the daughter of Amun-Ra: this is textually documented in her individual *nomen* prefix, which describes her as 'Daughter of Amun'.

In addition to the interpretation given above, this symbolism emphasises also the sexual Hathoric role as God's Hand, since it was in this aspect that she mothered Atum's children. Such an association agrees with the fundamental concept of a high priestess as the wife of God (documented as an individual title 'Hand of God'). Thus, the double feather plume corresponds with the dualism of Egyptian religion, and is assimilated primarily with the Hathoric form as Tefnut (together with Shu).

As all other things interconnect, so do the ram horns, as they are related to her title 'Daughter of Amun'. The cow horns and solar disc reveal a symbolism principally connected with Arsinoë's Hathoric role as a divine wife, the sexual element that ensures the safety of the divine continuation of the dynastic lineage. The symbolism of the crown of Arsinoë is, thus, as anchored in her cultic aspect as it is in her political role as a co-regent of Ptolemy. The two are inseparable and reflect one of the most fundamental principles of the ancient Egyptian belief system: that is, duality.

As an example of this principle, the marriage of Ptolemy II and Arsinoë will be briefly considered. Most scholars identify the cultural background for this marriage with ancient Egyptian traditions of sibling marriage or as a part of an active propaganda emphasising their divinity. However, another aspect of similar cultural value to those mentioned above may be added here. Arsinoë spent her initial eight years as the great (firstborn) daughter of the first Ptolemaic couple, presumably being brought up according to the customs of a crown heir. The possibility that Arsinoë was raised to ascend the throne cannot be disregarded.[2] However, regardless of any intended political positions during childhood, the ancient sources provide evidence that Arsinoë was involved in the state religion, incorporating the Egyptian *chora*. When she returned to Egypt and became the great wife and co-regent of the king, it was expected that she would assume the religious role as high priestess, as Ptolemy was already the high priest (cat. no. 1L). Their marriage was based (in addition to other things) on the conventional religious concepts of Egyptian kingship, and their unification symbolised, primarily, the Holy Wedding between the high priest and the high priestess, being the manifestations of Horus/Ra/Amun and Hathor. According to Egyptian conventions, the couple were considered as earthly manifestations of divine rulers, consequently being divine already by royal birth (= throne ascension). The unification of Hathor and Ra is incorporated in the symbolism of the cow horns and solar disc, both of which are included in the crown of Arsinoë. A direct consequence of the sexual meeting between a god and his earthly wife placed the high priestess as a royal/divine mother.[3] Therefore, Arsinoë as God's wife assumed also the third and final family-orientated Hathoric position.

The crown of Arsinoë as a symbol of *thea Philadelphos*

Evidently, Arsinoë's divine daughter role is closely associated with, if not assimilated into, her socio-political and religious positions during her lifetime. Therefore, the iconological interpretation reached here will be based on very similar criteria. The ram horns are interpreted as reflecting Arsinoë's identification with the local ram god Banebdjedet and, similarly, with Amun, from whom she received the divine breath of eternal life. Her daughter role is emphasised in the double feather plume, which, according to the discussion above, associates her with Tefnut. In addition to her individual role, the double feather plume corresponds also with her relationship to Ptolemy II, as it reflects the divine position of the *theoi Adelphoi*: it commemorates the identification of Ptolemy II and Arsinoë with Shu and Tefnut as the children of Atum, Horus and Hathor as the divine rulers, and was essentially a symbol of a completely conventional Egyptian dualism.

Naturally, the cow horns represent Arsinoë's Hathoric persona, here expressing a complete tripartite role as daughter, mother and wife. The solar disc situated within the horns denotes a kinship with the primeval solar force, from which the divine Philadelphos originated. Finally, the red crown retains its association with Arsinoë's royal position and links her with the divine daughter Wadjet, symbolising the power of Lower Egypt.

Each and every element of her crown can be related to Arsinoë's distinct cultural roles as (female) king, high priestess (God's wife) and goddess, and encompasses also her three royal positions as the king's daughter, sister and wife. Through the royal adoption of Berenice II, she finally became the traditionally powerful king's mother.

Notes

1 Naturally, it belongs also to her posthumous period.

2 Similarly, it is possible that Ptolemy I at one point wished for the siblings to rule Egypt together, in a way comparable to the will of their Ptolemaic descendant generations later (Ptolemy XII regarding Cleopatra VII and Ptolemy XIII) (*e.g.* Caes., *B. Civ.* 3, 108.4–6; *B. Afr.* 33; Peek 2008, 105).

3 In cat. nos 16–20, 22 and 34–35 Arsinoë is referred to as 'Divine mother/mother of the God' as well as 'Royal mother/Mother of the king', fundamentally relating to the same divine concept. Arsinoë's Hathoric maternal role is emphasised also in her association with Apis, through her designation 'Mother of Hep' (cat. nos 12 and 26L–R). Pictorially, the religious Hathoric role as 'God's mother' is communicated in dynastic scenes that show Arsinoë holding her hands in a protective manner and guarding her dynastic descendants just as Hathor protected the pharaoh as a manifestation of Horus (symbolising the entire dynasty).

Chapter 13

Conclusion

In this thematic study of thirty-six Ptolemaic reliefs, documented on stelai and in native Egyptian temples and incorporating textual evidence, the ideological, socio-political and religious significance and the symbolic meaning of the crown of Arsinoë have been examined with the help of Ptolemaic cultural principles and ideas that have thus far been overlooked. In order to answer the main question – what significance and cultural expressions did the crown of Arsinoë have? – each detail of the individual crowns, the complete figure of the crown, the entire scene, and the associated hieroglyphic designations has been analysed. Following this, socio-political and religious aspects have been discussed in accordance with three main positions: the royal (female pharaoh), the religious (high priestess/God's wife) and the cultic (goddess). Many of the cultural complexities that surround the historical person of Arsinoë have been taken into consideration. In terms of time, the material incorporates scenes from Arsinoë's lifetime to the reign of Ptolemy VIII, a span of *c.* 150 years.

Arsinoë's cultural positions – female pharaoh, high priestess and goddess, both living and deceased – have formed the focal points of the study. Despite previous attempts to distinguish Arsinoë's true political position, scholars have not been successful so far in confirming or denying her position as a female pharaoh. Her cultic role as high priestess has been more or less neglected until now by modern scholars. Her role as goddess – *thea Philadelphos* – has been acknowledged throughout academic circles, where the scholarly focus has been aimed at when, rather than whether, she was deified. The ongoing debate demonstrates that certain aspects of Arsinoë still need to be reconsidered.

This study has painted a very diverse and somewhat complex picture. The scenes commemorate a multifaceted cultural panorama in which all socio-religious and political aspects merge. The discussion on pp. 136–141 concerning Arsinoë's function in the state has demonstrated that she was considered a female pharaoh by the Egyptians, fundamentally equal to Ptolemy II. In particular, cat. nos 1–2, 5, 7–8, 13–15R, 23, 26 and 36 emphasise Arsinoë's position as King of Lower Egypt and the equality between her and Ptolemy as co-rulers. More importantly, cat. nos 8, 15 and 26 indicate that Arsinoë received her official royal designations during her lifetime. Finally, a combination of iconography and textual records demonstrates that Arsinoë was the female pharaoh of Lower Egypt, co-ruling with Ptolemy II, the pharaoh of Upper Egypt. Her kingship of Lower Egypt is expressed chiefly in the red crown as one of the individual elements of the crown of Arsinoë.

Arsinoë's religious position as high priestess of the ram god Banebdjedet in Mendes is traditionally recognised, but too often neglected. The material has demonstrated Arsinoë's close association with the god in both his local, Mendesian form and his more nationally renowned character as Amun. The crown of Arsinoë is composed of a combination of pictorial units, each feature fundamentally connected with Amun. The investigation suggests that the conventionally male ram horns in the crown identify Arsinoë with Banebdjedet, a conclusion which, moreover, agrees with the textual records. Various scenes illustrate Arsinoë as an active benefactor, shaking the sistrum in a Hathoric sexual role to invoke the divine spirit. This role as active benefactor, someone giving something to or doing something for the gods, can be undertaken only by a living being. Thus, these scenes have been redated here to Arsinoë's lifetime, thereby making Arsinoë Egypt's high priestess, a God's wife. She is described with designations equivalent to previous Divine Adoratrices of Amun, and the material supports such identification elsewhere as well. Her equivalence with the Divine Adoratrices is also suggested by her designation as Amun's daughter, a kinship which was emphasised pictorially, too.

The evidence provided here suggests that Arsinoë's divinity as the goddess Philadelphos manifests itself in a pluralistic cultic arrangement. Firstly, she was venerated as the living and ruling pharaoh according to the ancient Egyptian traditions of ruler cult, and was thus considered divine during her lifetime. Secondly, she was venerated as an individual goddess by her brother when she was placed in a figural setting as a divine daughter of (primarily) Amun.

Modern scholars traditionally identify this individual cult of Arsinoë as Ptolemy II's invention immediately following Arsinoë's death, but the material has provided evidence that the queen was indeed proclaimed divine during her lifetime on the basis of her role as pharaoh. Thirdly, later Ptolemies worshipped Arsinoë alongside with Ptolemy II as the founders of the dynasty, described textually as the sibling gods (*theoi Adelphoi*), the divine mother and father. This last cult corresponds with the native Egyptian conventions of ancestor cult. In this position Arsinoë is associated with the maternal Hathor and, as such, provides continuous safety and rejuvenation for the dynasty. Thus, Arsinoë's divine role is an excellent example of Egyptian plurality (rather than duality), incorporating the royal cult of her as a pharaoh, her individual cult as the divine Philadelphos and her shared divinity with Ptolemy II as the *theoi Adelphoi*. The last two cults relate to the Egyptian Osirian conventions, demonstrating a pharaoh firstly assuming complete divinity after death and secondly being venerated as a divine ancestor by descendant rulers.

The study shows, primarily, that the crown of Arsinoë communicates Arsinoë's pluralistic cultural positions, all of which are associated with aspects of Hathor. The two come together as divine royal mothers, daughter, sisters and wives, and their assimilation is documented in pictorial and textual sources equally. The symbolism expressed in the crown validates Arsinoë's royal as well as her divine legacy, and was eventually further utilised to emphasise her kinship with Ptolemaic descendants.

When creating a visible and recognisable hierarchic system, crowns were utilised for each figure in a deliberate strategy. In the discussion of artistic adjustment, existing theories relating to the concepts of size and position have been further developed here. Relative placement has been reassessed to show that an association of figural positions and size could be used as an indicator of time. The Ptolemaic rulers and their artists could show different time periods in one and the same scene, as in cat. no. 26, where Arsinoë is living on one side and the divine (deceased) Arsinoë on the other, thus becoming narrative iconography.

As one of the more important factors in reading Egyptian reliefs, the crown has also been presented, through the creation and implementation of a crown line, as an element that visually establishes hierarchy. The scholarly approach adopted to, and subsequent conclusions about, this crown line are based on a combination of iconographic theory of relative scaling and ancient geometry. Consequently, the material has been examined on the basis of modern and ancient methods, and a wide spectrum of cultural connotations and denotations has been elucidated. While all other pictorial elements in a scene were regulated by ancient Egyptian artistic conventions, the crown stands out as a 'free agent', following its own logic. The artist was able to arrange this autonomous element according to the message to be communicated by the scene. The material has revealed that this ultimately resulted in the introduction of a vast number of new composition crowns during the Ptolemaic Period. The crown became an ideal tool for communicating individuality and status when all the other elements were fundamentally strictly regulated within artistic tradition. The material shows that the crown of Arsinoë placed the queen as the most important figure in a clear majority of the scenes, though her status was secondary in scenes that emphasised her kinship with Amun.

The topic of 'eradication of visual representations' in the scenes was briefly approached here. This subject is too often ignored, and this study has revealed the necessity of further research in order to properly understand and read the reliefs as they are preserved today. Later cut marks have occasionally damaged entire scenes, but they are more frequently centred on the uncovered areas of the body, such as the face, arms/hands and legs/feet. Importantly, the crown is one of the pictorial elements that is undamaged, alongside hand-held objects and thrones. It does not appear that these marks should necessarily be classified as religious iconoclasm (Christian or Muslim) or *damnatio memoriae*: rather, it seems more likely that the person or group responsible for the damage was initiated in the ancient Egyptian sacred traditions, as the erasure of hieroglyphs and pictorial elements is deliberate, delicate and specific. Although these marks belong to a later time period, a date is still in question: pp. 129–135, and especially cat. no. 26L, has shown that there are various ways to establish a relative date of cut marks through a comparison with contextual and physically attached pictorial elements, and these methods can be applied to any given relief. Further research of cut marks will give the modern scholar an opportunity to understand the continuation of certain ancient belief systems and the acknowledgment of sacred insignia.

In summary, a new approach has been presented here to a limited ancient iconographic material in which one main cultural female figure has been reassessed. On the basis of the symbolism embedded in her individual crown, Arsinoë is portrayed as a female ruler equal in status and power to her husband; as a royal daughter claiming her divine ancestry from the main solar force, Amun-Ra; and as a divine mother who protects and ensures the continuation of the divine dynasty. Via an interdisciplinary approach, a bridge has been provided over the gap that separates the modern scholarly institutions of classical studies and Egyptology. The Graeco-Roman period marked the end of the ancient Egyptian era and therefore holds a very important key to the understanding of pharaonic traditions in their assimilated forms.

This study of the crown of Arsinoë has revealed essential socio-political and religious elements of Ptolemaic ideology hitherto unexposed. Even though the historical figure of Arsinoë has been a scholarly topic of discussion for generations, this study shows that there are still aspects that could be further considered and explored. An aim here has been to clarify the (early) Ptolemies' active participation in the traditional Egyptian religious cults, which ultimately developed into new religious and artistic forms that lasted throughout the Roman period. Another goal has been to emphasise the interaction of religious, political and social concepts, as they are all incorporated in an imagery that expresses female kingship, power, piety and divinity. Despite the unwillingness among some scholars to accept female Ptolemaic authority, Arsinoë's royal position as a ruling pharaoh, governing Lower Egypt while Ptolemy II was in charge over Upper Egypt, has been demonstrated convincingly: she ruled as an individual on her own terms rather than as a part of a propagandistic agenda, and in cooperation with the powerful priesthood when establishing a functioning and recognisable symbol of authority. On the basis of her defined politico-religious positions during her lifetime, to which later Ptolemaic female rulers reconnected, it is argued here that Arsinoë should be included in the official pharaonic king list as Ptolemy II's co-regent: her royal authority should be considered equivalent to that of Hatshepsut, Tawosret and Amenirdis II, as one of the most important royal women in Egyptian history. This study has argued that all aspects of Arsinoë's complex persona (female pharaoh, high priestess/God's wife, and goddess) were embedded in a unique attribute – her crown – and that this remained a symbol of authority throughout the last centuries of the ancient Egyptian period. In accordance with her spoken words in the Mendes stele, 'I protect you in (=wearing) your crown', Arsinoë personified the royal and divine: she became the 'Lady of the crowns'.

Catalogue of material

The subject of the present study is thirty-six religious reliefs illustrating Arsinoë, thirty-four of which show her wearing her personal crown. The reliefs date to a period of time extending from Arsinoë's lifetime to the reign of Ptolemy VIII Euergetes, a period of just under 200 years. All images derive from within the precincts of ancient Egypt. The first fifteen scenes listed in the Catalogue (below) are depicted on the upper part of decrees and stelai and incorporate also a few fragmentary reliefs, all of which are reasonably well preserved. The latter part of the catalogue consists of temple reliefs which are still *in situ* and in a generally good state of preservation. A few scenes are preserved with original colours. The material consists primarily of sandstone, but there are also items made of limestone and granite.

All the scenes in which the crowns are illustrated have a religious character that follows ancient Egyptian pictorial conventions, always representing at least one deity. The scenes are further distinguished in agreement with the main theme of the scene, *i.e.*, the religious act performed by the pharaoh (or royal couple) in either an 'active' or 'inactive' position (placement and role) in regard to the deities.

All scenes have been investigated by the author, who photographed the scenes, which are still located in the temples, and some of the stelai. The remaining objects shown here, which are now located in international museums, were professionally photographed by museum personnel.[1] The plates presented in the Catalogue demonstrate the full relief scene. When possible, the crown is shown in a separate picture in order to demonstrate each pictorial unit and to stress the correlation between them. (A few scenes are located in dark rooms, in a problematic architectural position, or are only partially preserved; therefore, the original photograph is sometimes of insufficient quality to allow this enhancement.) Each crown is presented by a drawn, detailed illustration in the Catalogue description (see also Appendix I).

Organisation

The images of Arsinoë are divided as objects located in museums and temple scenes which are *in situ*. The reliefs of the stelai and decrees are listed acccording to their respective museum and inventory number. Descriptions of temple reliefs include their present location and position within the structure.[2] When a scene includes more than one section, each will be presented individually. For example, cat. no. 2 is presented as 2L (L=left) and 2R (R=right). Each catalogue number has a subsequent plate, which consists of a main photograph of the full relief scene and an enlarged detail of the crown if possible. A few scenes are represented as drawings based on photographs made by the author or J. Ward if not otherwise stated. Each relief is classified in accordance with the following directory:

- Type of relief[3]
- Material
- Measurements[4]
- Provenance
- Date
- Previous publications[5]
- Crown in the scene
- Hand-held objects
- State of preservation
- Iconographical description[6]
- Remarks[7]

Catalogue description

Stelai

1. Egyptian Museum, Cairo, CG 22181 (Mendes stele)

Sunken relief
Limestone
1.47m high
Provenance: Tell el-Rub'a, Tell el-Timai – Greek Mendes-Thmuis
Date: Ptolemy II Philadelphos
Published: *PM* IV, 36; *LÄ* IV, 45f.; Mariette 1879, 43–5 (a, b); *Thes. Inscr.* IV, 629–31, 658–69, 739f.; *Urk.* II, 28–54; Kamal 1905, 159–68, pls LIV, no. 22181; Meulenaere 1965, 53–65; Quaegebeur 1971a, no. 8; Quaegebeur 1971b, 242; Meulenaere and MacKay 1976, 173–77, pls 1 and 31, no. 111; Quaegebeur 1978, 253; Derchain 1985, 35f.; Quaegebeur 1985, 76; Quaegebeur 1988, 43–5; Grzybek 1990, 103, 107; Roeder 1998, 168–88; Quaegebeur 1998, no. 7; van Oppen 2007, *passim*
Left scene
Crown of the scene: AC 1

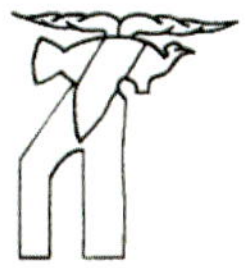

Hand-held objects: *Ankh* and bearded emmer wheat
State of preservation: This section is preserved in a generally good condition, but the area around Arsinoë is discoloured. The lower part of the figure is well preserved, whereas the top part has been damaged by natural processes. The crown is almost entirely erased/faded. Only vague outlines of the facial features are preserved. The personal register of text is mainly preserved with only minor damage, while the lower hieroglyphic register has a couple of damaged signs.
Right scene
Crown of the scene: AC 2

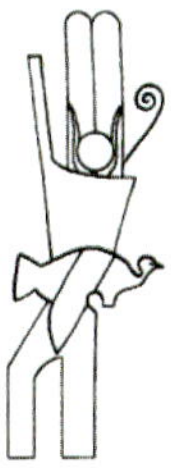

Hand-held objects: *Ankh* and a papyrus sceptre
State of preservation: This section and the image of Arsinoë are well preserved in general, with only minor damage. The crown is well preserved except for the very back, where a small fracture cuts into the stone. However, none of the details are fully clear. The personal register of text is well preserved, though the text above the figure's head is slightly damaged in connection with the fracture. The lower hieroglyphic register of text is well preserved.
Iconographical description: The full scene depicts eight main figures and four minor ones.

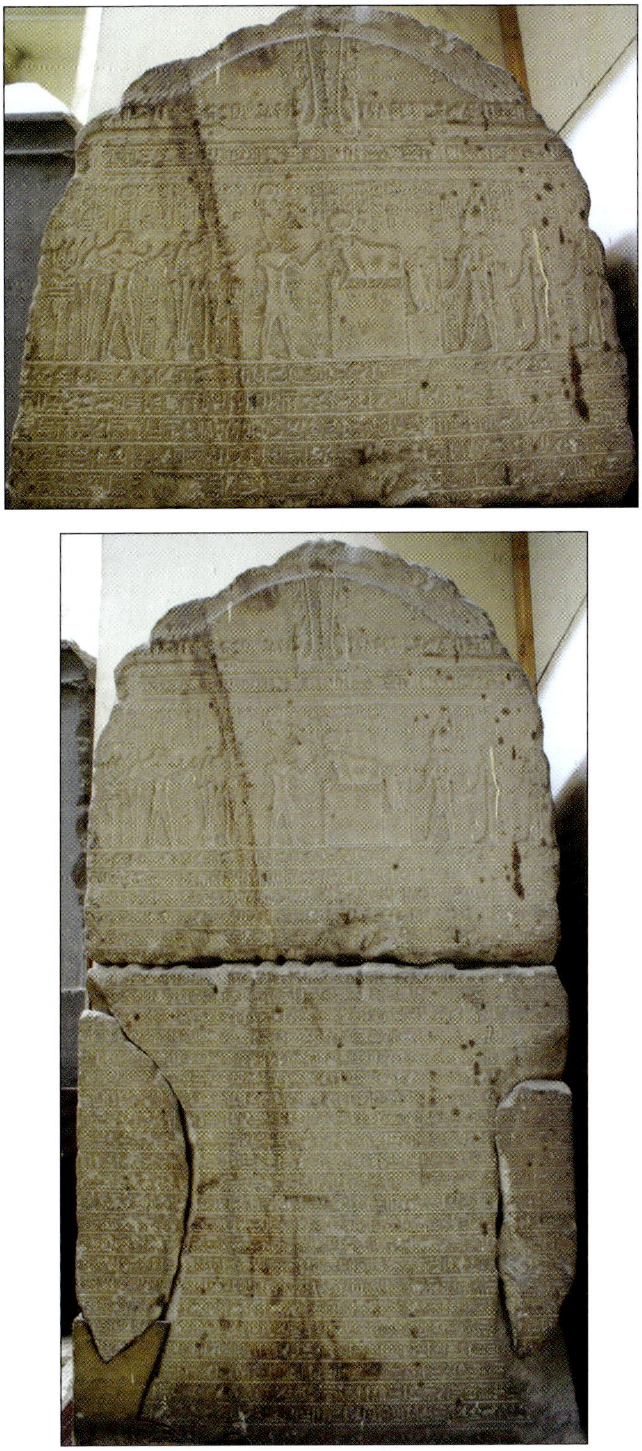

1. Egyptian Museum, Cairo, CG 22181 (Mendes stele) Photo: The author.

On the left side, starting from the centre, the king wears a double crown, a single forehead *uraeus* and a royal diadem. A smaller solar disc is located above his head, surrounded by two serpents holding *ankh*s. The king wears the traditional kilt with the bull's tail. He holds a small cup of ointment in one hand and has a small amount of incense/perfume in the other. He is described in the text as 'Living King, Lord of the Two Lands, Lord of the sacrifices (/of actions) (Strong is the soul of Ra, beloved of Amun)|, Son of Ra: like him, loved by him, Lord of the crowns (Ptolemy)|, may he live forever, Beloved by Ba, Great God, the living Ra'. He says to the new Ram: 'I bring you, the father, incense of flowers and I place myrrh on the nose of the god'. The figure of Ptolemy is well preserved. A plant is depicted in front of King Ptolemy.

Arsinoë stands behind Ptolemy: she wears a tripartite wig and the crown of Arsinoë. She is dressed in the traditional sheat dress and wears a necklace. She holds an *ankh* in her resting hand and bearded emmer wheat in the other. Textually, she is described as 'Holder of the sacred insignia, the divine Philadelphos, Beloved of the ram, Mistress of the Two Lands (Arsinoë)|'. She says: 'I protect you in (*i.e.*, wearing) your crown, you who are larger and greater than all other gods'.

Behind her, placed above a cluster of papyrus, is a falcon that wears a solar disc: it is surrounded by two signs of eternity. He is described in the text as 'Horus of Behutet, he who spreads his wings, he who gives protection to his mother'. The figure is fairly well preserved.

Behind the small falcon is a male figure who wears a *khepresh* crown, a single forehead *uraeus* and a royal diadem. He wears the traditional kilt and the bull's tail. He presents a small cup of ointment and a looped textile band. He is described in the text as 'Lord of the Two Lands (Strong is the soul of Ra, beloved of Amun)|, the son of Ra, Lord of the crowns (Ptolemy)|'. He states 'I unite your limbs and put together your body in the Chapel of Tenenet'. The figure is well preserved.

The next figure shows a vulture that sits above a cluster of lotus. It is surrounded by the signs of eternity and the Sed festival. The vulture wears an *atef* crown and is described in the text as 'Nekhbet, the White One from Nekhen, the great vulture, she who will protect her son with her wings'. The small figure of Nekhbet is well preserved.

Behind Nekhbet is a standard which is composed by two empty Horus cartouches, above which two small Horus figures are depicted; one wears the red crown and the other the white crown. The standard also includes the *nb-t3*-signs (*i.e.*, Lord/Lady of the Two Lands). The text that is connected with the standard states 'King of Upper Egypt and King of Lower Egypt, the two Horuses, the siblings are united [...] Lands', and the text in front states 'Giving life, stability and prosperity like Ra'.

The first figure of the right side, starting from the centre, is a ram which stands on a podium. It wears a large solar disc that rests on top of ram horns. A small cup with burning incense is placed in front of the ram (on the podium). He is described in the text as 'King of Upper and Lower Egypt, the living soul (Ba) of Ra, the living soul of Ma'at, the living soul of Geb, the living soul of Osiris, the living soul of all the rams, the Lord of the Lords, the soul and heir of the Gods in the Chapel of Tenenet'. The figure of the ram is well preserved.

Behind the ram stands a smaller figure of Harpocrates on a low podium. He is illustrated with a prince (side) lock and is dressed in a thin shawl that hangs from his shoulders. He

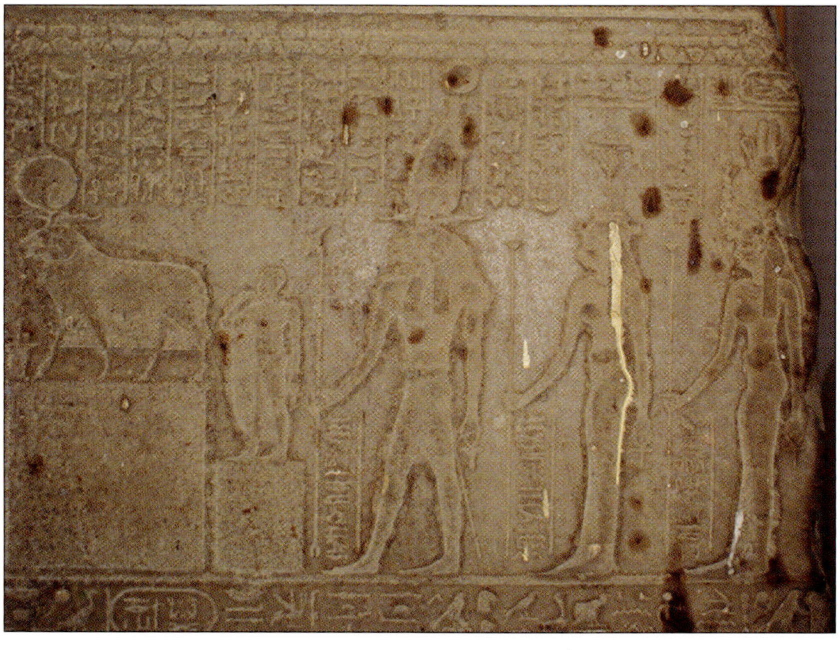

1. Egyptian Museum, Cairo, CG 22181 (Mendes stele). Photo: J. Ward.

holds an *ankh* in his resting hand. He is described in the text as 'Harpocrates, Great God, he who dwells in Dedet (*i.e.*, Mendes), he who comes forth of Isis' (?) (normally translated as 'he who sits on his throne next to Isis), who has the Two Lands under his protection'. The figure is well preserved.

Behind Harpocrates stands Banebdjedet, who wears an *atef* crown that rests on ram horns, to which is added two *uraei* that wear a solar disc as crowns. He is depicted as a ram-headed anthropomorphic figure, wears a *nemes* wig and has ram horns curled behind his ears. He is dressed in a traditional kilt and the bull's tail. Banebdjedet holds an *ankh* and a *was* stave in his hands. He is described in the text as 'the Ram (Banebdjedet), Lord of Dedet, Great God, the living Ra, the bull, the creator, the male ruler of the women, Lord of Heaven, King of the gods, he who gives life like Ra'. He states 'I give (secure) you that the people of the great foreign countries will bow to your will'. The figure is well preserved.

Behind the ram-god is the female figure of Hat-Mehit, who wears the standard of the nome (with a local fish) as a crown, which rests on a tripartite wig and a vulture cap. She holds an *ankh* and a papyrus sceptre in her hands. She is described in the text as 'Hat-Mehit, the strong, who dwells in the city of Dedet, the divine wife (normally translated as the goddess of Gods), who lives in the house of the ram (*i.e.*, Banebdjedet), the eye of Ra, the Lady of the Sky, the Mistress of all the gods'. In the lower hieroglyphic register she states 'I place love for you in the hearts of the gods and I place misery in the heart of all your enemies'. The figure of Hat-Mehit is well preserved, but has been damaged by modern yellow paint and dark dots of chemicals.

Behind the female figure stands a second image of Arsinoë. She wears a tripartite wig, a vulture cap and the crown of Arsinoë. She is dressed in a traditional sheat dress. She holds an *ankh* and a papyrus sceptre in her hands. She is described in the text as 'King's daughter, sister, his greatly beloved wife, the divine Philadelphos, Arsinoë'. She says: 'I pray for you to the master of the Gods, so that he gives you numerous years as a king (*i.e.*, of rule)'.

The symbol of Behutet stretches out its wings above the scene, accompanied by two pendant serpents that wear the white crown and the red crown respectively. The winged solar disc is described in the text on the right side as 'Behutet, Great God, Lord of Heaven, the light-giver who comes forth of the horizon, first among the gods of Upper Egypt, he who gives life and prosperity'. On the left side he is described as 'Behutet, the great god, Lord of Heaven, the light-giver who comes forth of the horizon, first among the gods of Lower Egypt, he who gives life and prosperity'. The two *uraei* are described as 'Nekhbet, the White One of Nekhen' (right) and 'Wadjet of Pe and Dep (=Buto)' (left). A text between the two serpents says 'Giving life, stability and prosperity like Ra'.

The following text from the main register of text is connected with Arsinoë (*cf.* Roeder 1998):

> Then the king united himself (through marriage) with his sister [under the protection of] the gods, who is of … theirs, beloved by the god Osiris (in one form) and by the gods of the east. She was given the divine title Princess, Great of Praise, She who belongs to the Lord, Sweet of Love, Beautiful in appearance (she) who received the two forehead *uraei* (=Upper and Lower Egypt), She who fills the palace with her beauty, She who is the high priestess of Banebdjedet, Beloved of the ram, Sister of the King of Upper Egypt, Daughter of the King of Upper Egypt, Greatly beloved wife of the King of Upper Egypt, Mistress of the Two Lands, Arsinoë. […] In the year 15, of the month Pachons (2nd month of the summer) this goddess ascended to the sky, where she/her soul was unified with their souls [those who created her beauty]. After the four days ritual of the Opening of the mouth ceremony, this goddess ascended as a soul. They sang for her in the city of Anpet and they celebrated her (funerary) festival, and they released her soul to live close to the living Ba, who became the support (strength) for her, and for all the gods and goddesses from the primeval times until today. Then the city became a place of rejoicing for the Kingdom of all the gods and it is again a city of youth on which she is breathing (blowing) fresh air. It is a place of joy for all the goddesses in which the life is maintained, in which every 10th day the god is offered myrrh, flowers and incense. His majesty instructed (ordered) that her image was as placed in all the gods houses (*i.e.*, temples). It was beautiful on the heart (*i.e.*, pleased) of the priests that she had been recognised as divine [based on her excellent way towards all the people] and would be with all the deities. They carried her image in a procession through the fish nome together with the living soul of the ram and also statues of the royal children. Her image was as placed in every nome by the priestesses, and was as placed together with the other statues of the gods. Her name was established as She who is beloved by the ram, the divine Philadelphos Arsinoë.

Remarks: The figure of Banebdjedet is the tallest figure of the main scene.

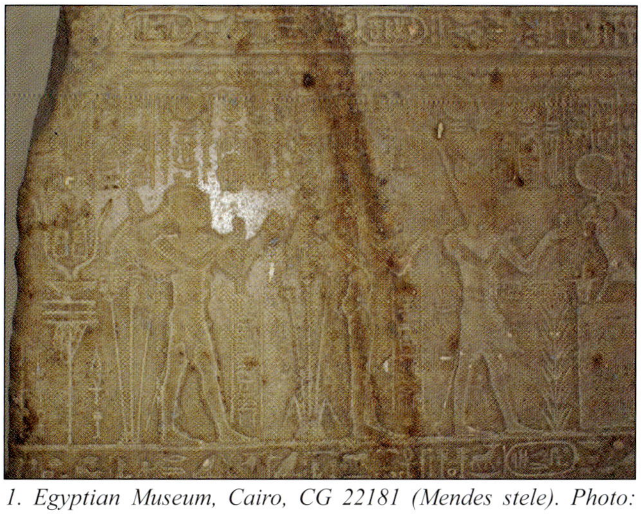

1. Egyptian Museum, Cairo, CG 22181 (Mendes stele). Photo: J. Ward.

2. Egyptian Museum, Cairo, CG 22183 (the Pithom stele)

Sunken relief
Grey granite
1.28m high
Provenance: Tell el-Maskhuta – ancient Temple of Atum in Pithom
Date: Ptolemy II Philadelphos (264 BC)
Published: *PM* IV, 54; *LÄ* IV, 1055f.; *Thes. Inscr.* IV, 855; Naville 1885, pls 8–10; Naville 1902, xl, pls iii–v, 66–75, pls 3–5; Andersson and Sjöberg 1904, 223–36; Kamal 1904, 171–7, no. 22183, pl. lvii; *Urk.* II, 81–105; Quaegebeur 1971a, no. 9; Lorton 1971, 160–64; Quaegebeur 1971b, 242; Fraser 1972, II, chapter 5, nn 346, 348, 350, 356, 359; Quaegebeur 1978, 253; Quaegebeur 1988, 47; Grzybek 1990, 67–112; Winnicki 1990, 157–67; Minas 1994, 203–12; Quaegebeur 1998, no. 8; Roeder 1998, 108–28; Mueller 2006, 152f., appendix II; van Oppen 2007, *passim*; 2010, *passim*
Left scene
Crown of the scene: AC 3

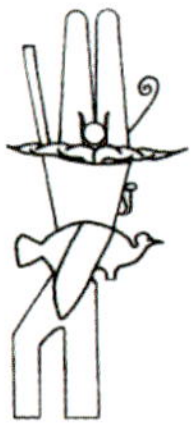

Hand-held objects: *Ankh* and a papyrus sceptre
State of preservation: The figure is in a good state of preservation and damaged only by natural processes. All main details are preserved.
Right scene
Crown of the scene: AC 3

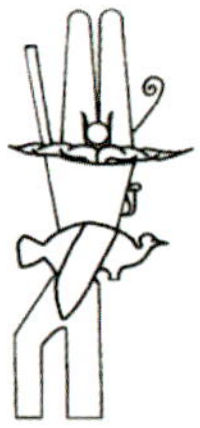

Hand-held objects: *Ankh* and a papyrus sceptre
State of preservation: The figure is well preserved and damaged only by natural processes.
Iconographical description: Twelve figures are illustrated in the main scene, above which a large solar disc spreads its wings. Two *uraei* rise up on the sides of the solar disc. On the left side the inscription says 'Behutet, Great God, Lord of Heaven, he who comes forth of the Horizon'. On the right side it says 'Lord of Mesen, Great God, Lord of Heaven, he who comes forth of the Horizon'.

The stele is divided in three minor sections: two depict Arsinoë and are catalogued as cat. nos 2L–R. The third scene is not catalogued individually, and is referred to as the third scene. This third scene is located at the extreme

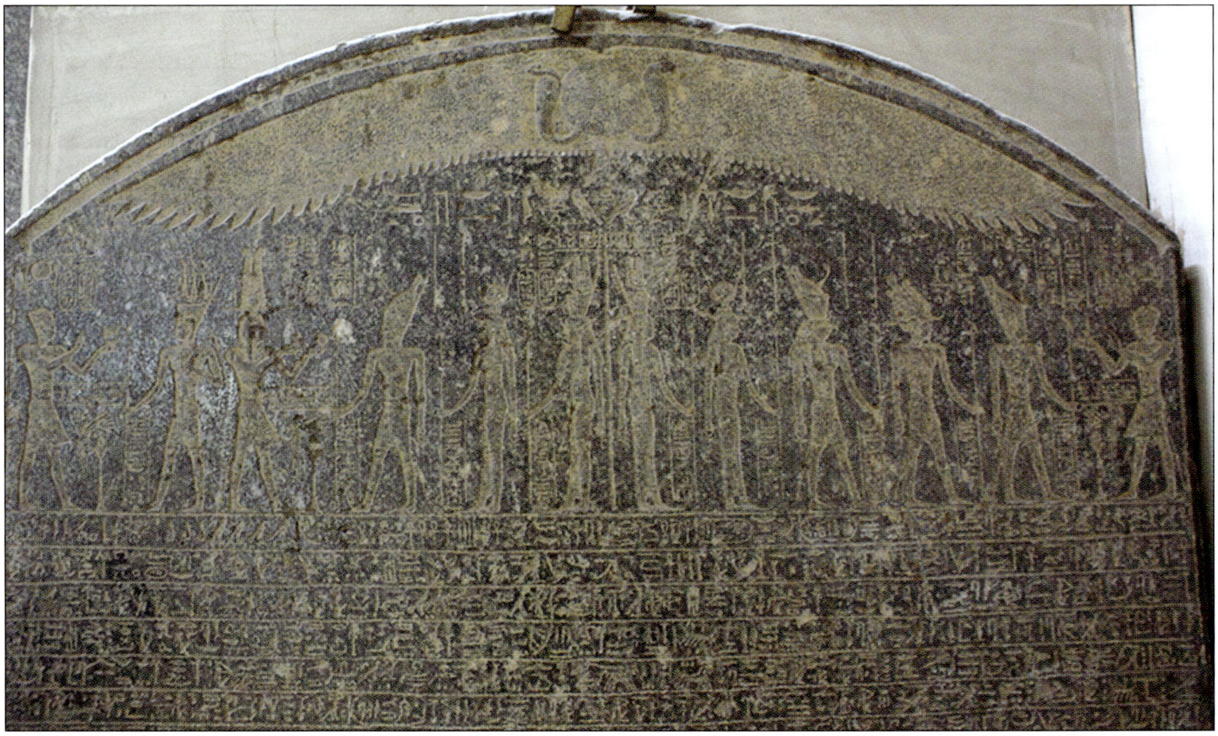

2. Egyptian Museum, Cairo, CG 22183 (the Pithom stele). Photo: J. Ward.

left. At the far left stands Ptolemy. He wears a *khepresh* crown with a single forehead *uraeus*. He is depicted with the pharaonic beard. Above his head is a small solar disc accompanied by two *uraei* that hold *ankh*s. The king is dressed in a traditional kilt and a bull's tail. He presents the Eye of Ra (Wadjet) as an offering. He is described in the text as 'Lord of the Two Lands (Strong is the soul of Ra, beloved of Amun)| Son of Ra, Lord of the crowns (Ptolemy)|'. In the lower hieroglyphic register he says 'I present to you the offering of the divine eye which was made (*i.e.*, born) and given life by him (*i.e.*, Ra)'. The figure of the king is well preserved and damaged only by natural erosion. A small incense stand with a cluster of lotuses is located in front of the king.

In front of the king stands a male figure. He wears the *hemhem* (= triple crown) which sits on top of ram horns and a red crown. He is dressed in a traditional kilt and the bull's tail and holds a flail and a *was* stave in his hands. The personal register of text is uninscribed. He says: 'I wish you to rule the Two Lands and also to rule the foreign countries (/desert areas) like Ra, may he live forever'. The figure is well preserved.

In cat. no. 2L, still on the left side of the main scene, stands King Ptolemy. He wears an *anedjti* crown with two *uraei*. He wears a *nemes* wig, a single forehead *uraeus* and pharaonic beard. He is dressed in a traditional kilt and a bull's tail, and he presents two small rounded vessels. He is described as 'Lord of the Two Lands (Strong is the soul of Ra, beloved of Amun)| Son of Ra, Lord of the crowns (Ptolemy)|'. In front of him is a small censer stand with a cluster of lotuses. The figure is well preserved.

In front of the king stands Atum. He wears a double crown and pharaonic beard. He is dressed in a traditional kilt and a bull's tail. He holds an *ankh* and a *was* stave in his hands. He is described in the text as 'Atum, Great God who dwells in the city of Teku...'. He says in the lower hieroglyphic register 'I wish you joy (happiness/ pleasure) in this kingship just like Ra'. The figure is well preserved.

The figure behind Atum is a female deity who wears a tripartite wig, vulture cap, low modus, large cow horns and a solar disc. She holds an *ankh* and a papyrus sceptre. The personal register of text is blank. The lower hieroglyphic register says 'I wish that you will rule the Two Lands in peace and that the souls (of the people?) will be united'. The figure is in a good state of preservation.

The figure behind the unnamed female figure is Arsinoë. She wears a tripartite wig, a vulture cap, the crown of Arsinoë, and is dressed in a traditional sheat dress. She holds an *ankh* and a papyrus sceptre in her hands. She is described in the text as 'King's daughter, sister, and wife (She who is in the heart of Shu, Beloved of the gods)| Great Lady of

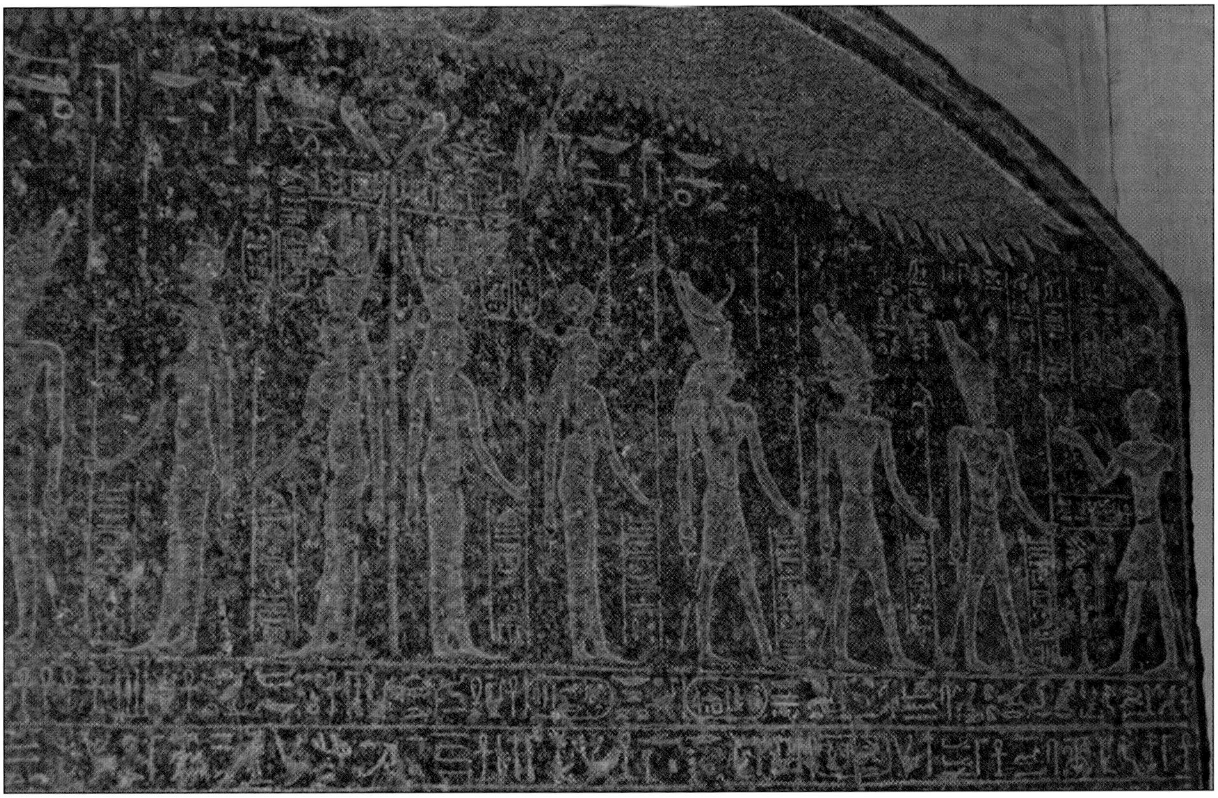

2. Egyptian Museum, Cairo, CG 22183 (the Pithom stele). Photo: J. Ward.

the Two Lands (Arsinoë)| Living image of Isis and Hathor'. In her lower hieroglyphic register she says 'I pray for your life to your father Atum; that he will give you numerous years of Sed festivals'.

Cat. no. 2R shows, at the very right the king who wears a *khepresh* crown with a single forehead *uraeus*, and a pharaonic beard. A solar disc is depicted above his head, accompanied by two serpents, each one holding an *ankh*. The king is dressed in a traditional kilt and a bull's tail, and he presents the figure of Ma'at. The king is described as 'Lord of the Two Lands (Strong is the soul of Ra, beloved of Amun)| Son of Ra, Lord of the crowns (Ptolemy)|'. In front of him is a small incense stand with a small jug and a cluster of lotus flowers. The figure is well preserved.

In front of King Ptolemy stands Atum. He wears a double crown, and has a pharaonic beard. He is dressed in a traditional kilt and a bull's tail. He holds an *ankh* and a *was* stave in his hands. He is described in the text as 'Atum, Great God of Teku, overseer of the divine (gods) for eternity, Lord of Heaven, King of the Gods'. In the lower hieroglyphic register he says 'I wish you to spend your lifetime as King in all eternity'. The figure is in a good state of preservation.

Behind Atum is the figure of Osiris. He wears an *atef* crown that rests on top of ram horns. He has a pharaonic beard. He is dressed in a traditional kilt and a bull's tail. He holds an *ankh* and a *was* stave in his hands. He is described in the text as 'Osiris, Lord of Ro-jabet (*i.e.*, the door to the East), the first of the house of Per-kerhet (*i.e.*, Teku)'. He says 'I wish that you rise to the throne like Ra in Heaven'. The figure is well preserved.

The figure behind Osiris wears a double crown. He is depicted anthropomorphically with a falcon's head. He is identified in the main text as Horus of Behutet (= Edfu). Horus is dressed in a traditional kilt and a bull's tail, and holds an *ankh* and a *was* stave in his hands. He says 'I wish you as the strong master of the Two Lands'. The figure is well preserved.

The female figure behind Horus wears a tripartite wig, a vulture cap, a low modus, large cow horns and a solar disc. She holds an *ankh* and a papyrus sceptre in her hands. The personal register of text is empty. She says 'I wish that you will rule the Two Lands in peace as well as Ra does'. The figure is well preserved.

The figure behind the Hathorian figure is identified as Arsinoë. She wears a tripartite wig, vulture cap and the crown of Arsinoë. She is dressed in a traditional sheat dress. She holds an *ankh* and a papyrus sceptre in her hands. She is described in the text as 'King's daughter, sister, and wife (She who is in the heart of Shu, Beloved of the gods)| Great Lady of the Two Lands (Arsinoë)| Living image of Isis and Hathor'. In the lower hieroglyphic register she says 'I wish for you to celebrate numerous Sed festivals (with the blessings) of the gods'.

The following sections from the main register of text are connected to Arsinoë (*cf.* Roeder 1998):

> Year 12, the first month of the flood, day three of His Majesty's rule, the king pronounced his wish and he travelled through Egypt together with the queen who is Great of Praise, a Lady of Loveliness, Sweet of Love, King's wife, Mistress of the Two Lands, Arsinoë, Daughter of the king (of Upper Egypt), Lord of the Two Lands, Ptolemy, the divine Philadelphos. They arrived in the Eastern Nome of the Harpoon; it was the city of their father Atum. The king discussed with his sister, the wife and sister of the king, to protect Kemet against enemies. [...] he founded a large royal city and gave it the great name of the daughter of King Ptolemy. A temple was built in honour of Queen Arsinoë Philadelphos. He placed images (*i.e.*, statues) of his divine sister in the temple. All the ceremonies were practised by the priests in connection with the building of the Temple of their father Atum, the Great God, who dwells in the city of Teku, like it is made in all the Temples of Upper and Lower Egypt...

Remarks: Arsinoë is depicted as the tallest figure in cat. no. 2R, but Ptolemy the tallest figure in the main scene.

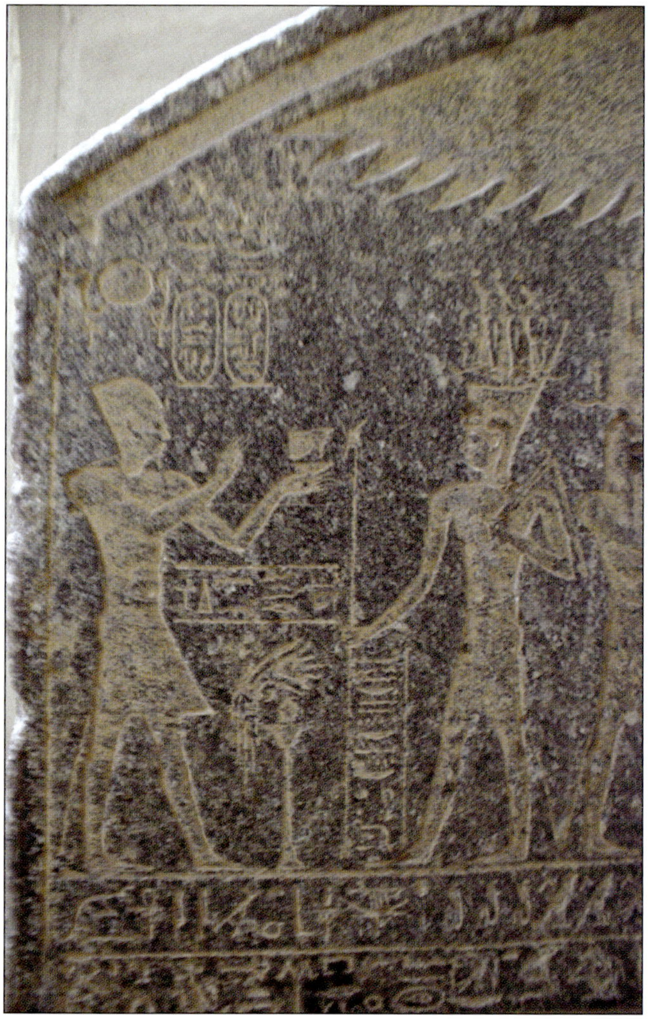

2. Egyptian Museum, Cairo, CG 22183 (the Pithom stele) Photo: J. Ward.

3. Egyptian Museum, Cairo, CG 22188 (Damanhûr stele)

Sunken relief
Limestone
1.28m high
Provenance: el Nibeira – Greek Naukratis
Date: Ptolemy V Epiphanes.
Published: *PM* IV, 50; Kamal 1904, pls lxii, lxiii, 183–7, no. 22188; II, 166–98; *LdR* IV, 244 n. 1; Quaegebeur 1971a, no. 12; Winter 1978, 152 n. 6; Quaegebeur 1978, 252, 255; Crawford 1980, 34 n. 6; Quaegebeur 1998, no. 69
Crown of the scene: AC 4

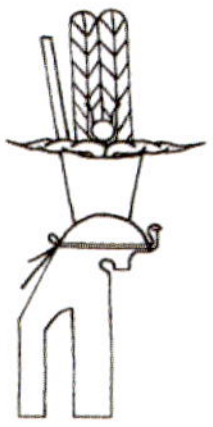

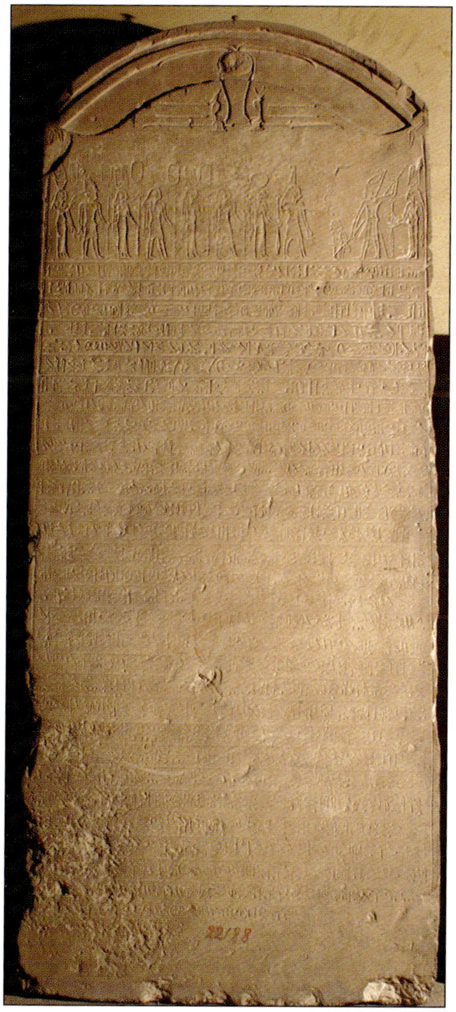

3. Egyptian Museum, Cairo, CG 22188 (Damanhûr stele). Photo: Egyptian Museum, Cairo.

Hand-held objects: *Ankh*
State of preservation: The figure is in a good state of preservation, though slightly damaged on the top part of the crown owing to a fracture in the stone surface. Otherwise the figure is damaged only by natural processes.
Iconographical description: Ten main figures are depicted in the scene (eleven including the prisoner), above which a winged solar disc is illustrated, accompanied by two pendant *uraei* that hold eternity signs and the feather flabella. The hieroglyphic sign for the sky crowns the scene.

The ruling couple stands at the far right slaying a captured enemy in front of their ancestors. Cleopatra (I) stands to the far right: she wears a tripartite wig, a low modus and a traditional female crown. She holds an *ankh* and a papyrus sceptre in her hands. She is not described with a traditional cartouche in the main scene, but the text below the figures establishes her as Cleopatra I. The figure is well preserved, without any major damage.

In front of and facing the deities stands Ptolemy V. He wears a double crown. He is dressed in a traditional kilt and a bull's tail. He holds a long spear in his hands, pointing to a captured enemy who kneels and has his hands tied together behind his back. The king is described in the main scene as King Ptolemy V Epiphanes. The figure is well preserved, without any major damage.

In front of the king and the captured enemy stands Shu. He wears a *nemes* wig, a single forehead *uraeus* and a royal diadem. He also wears a single *atef* feather. He is dressed in a traditional kilt. He holds an *ankh* in his resting hand and a small sceptre with the head of Horus (traditionally designated *ḫpš*) in his outstretched hand. The figure has no personal registers and is well preserved.

Behind Shu is a female figure who wears a solar disc on her head. The facial area has been damaged but it probably depicts a lioness. The figure is identified as Tefnut. She holds an *ankh* and a papyrus sceptre in her hands. The figure has no personal registers.

Behind the female figure is a male figure, identified as King Ptolemy IV, the father of the ruling king. He wears an unrecognisable crown (if any at all) on top of a *nemes* wig. He holds an *ankh* and a *was* stave in his hands. He is dressed in a traditional kilt. He has a (now) empty cartouche, but is identified in the main text. The figure is slightly damaged by natural erosion, especially in the upper part of the body.

The figure behind King Ptolemy IV is Arsinoë III, the mother of the ruling king. She wears a tripartite wig, a low modus and a traditional female crown. She holds an *ankh* and a papyrus sceptre in her hands. An empty cartouche is depicted in her personal register: she is identified in the main text. The figure is, in general, in a good state of preservation, though slightly damaged by natural processes.

Behind Arsinoë III stands Ptolemy III. He wears a *nemes* wig and a single forehead *uraeus*. The area above his head is slightly damaged and there are no signs of any crown. He holds an *ankh* and a *was* stave in his hands. King Ptolemy III is dressed in a traditional kilt. The cartouche has been left uninscribed, but he is identified in the main text.

The figure of Berenice II is depicted behind Ptolemy III. She wears a tripartite wig, a low modus, and a traditional female crown. She holds an *ankh* and a papyrus sceptre in her hands. The cartouche is left uninscribed, but she is identified in the main text. The figure is well preserved and only slightly damaged by natural processes.

Ptolemy II stands behind Berenice II. He is depicted with an *atef* crown that sits on top of ram horns. He wears a *khat* cap that covers his head and neck. He holds an *ankh* and a *was* stave in his hands. He is dressed in the traditional kilt. His cartouche is left uninscribed, but is identified in the main text.

Behind Ptolemy II stands the last figure of the scene, Arsinoë II. She wears a tripartite wig, a single forehead *uraeus*, a royal diadem and the crown of Arsinoë. She is dressed in a traditional sheat dress. She holds an *ankh* in one hand while holding the other in a protecting manner. The cartouche has been left uninscribed, but she is identified in the main text as Arsinoë.

A winged solar disc is depicted above the main scene. He is described as Behutet, and is accompanied by two *uraei*, one that wears the crown of Upper Egypt and the other the crown of Lower Egypt: both hold the *šnw*-sign of eternity and royalty. Two large *was* staves enclose the main scene. No hieroglyphic inscription follows any of the figures.

Remarks: The stele is textually comparable to the Rosetta stone. Arsinoë is depicted as the tallest figure of the scene.

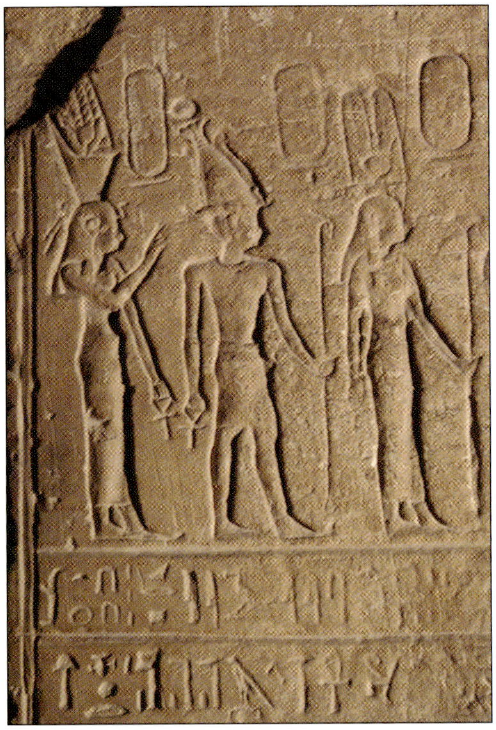

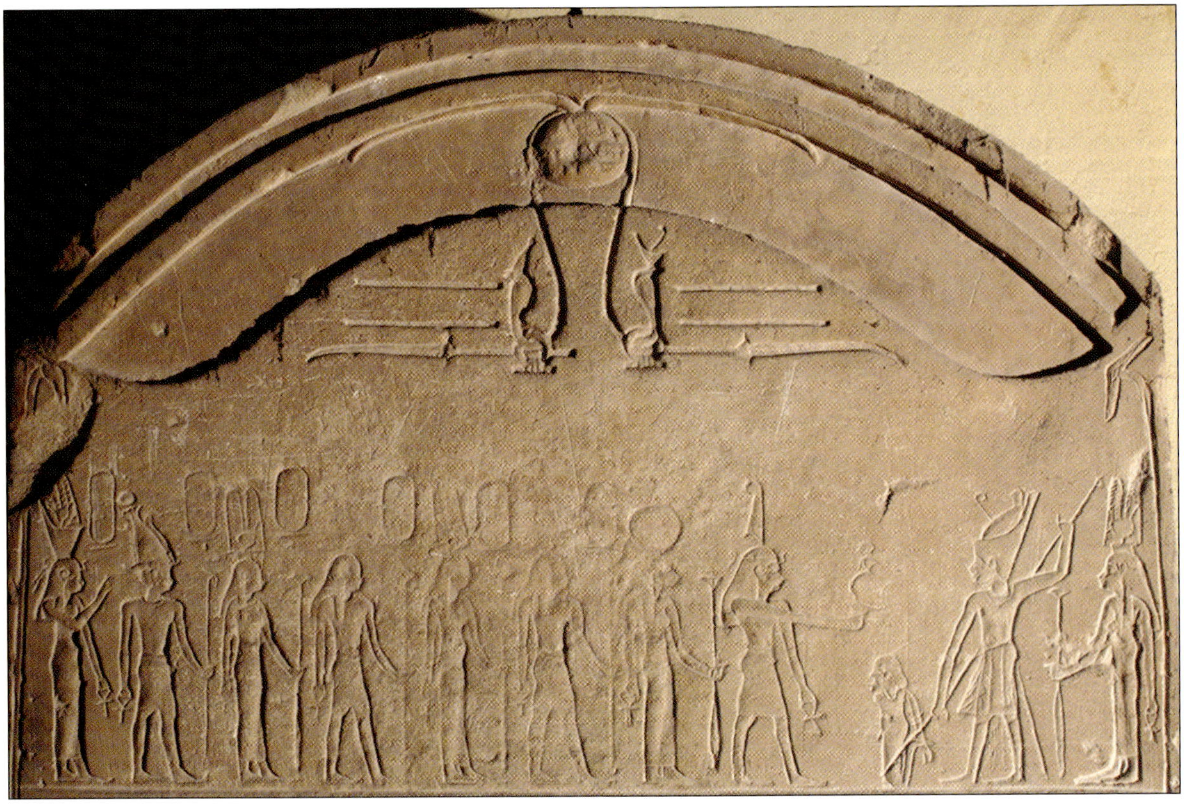

3. *Egyptian Museum, Cairo, CG 22188 (Damanhûr stele). Photos: Egyptian Museum, Cairo.*

4. Egyptian Museum, Cairo, CG 22186 (Kanopus decree of Kom el-Hisn)

Sunken relief
White limestone
2.22 × 0.78m
Provenance: Kom el-Hisn – ancient Imu
Date: Ptolemy III Euergetes
Published: *LÄ* III, 321; *Thes. Inscr.* IV, 1554–78; Birch 1876, 81–90; Kamal 1904, 182f., pls lix–lxi; *Urk.* II, 124–54, 156; Budge 1904, vol. III; Chabas 1909, 488–95; Roeder 1998, 142–66; Bernand 1970, 989–1036; Quaegebeur 1971a, no. 10; Quaegebeur 1971b, 243f.; Quaegebeur 1978, 247f. with fig. C; Winter 1978, 152 n. 6; Quaegebeur 1988, 48 with fig. 23, 52; Clagett 1995, 330, 338, 574; Simpson 1996, 224–41; Quaegebeur 1998, no. 9; van Oppen 2007, *passim*
Crown of the scene: AC 5

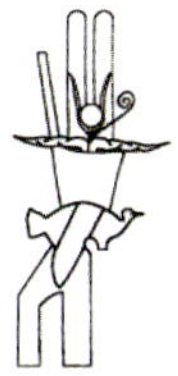

Hand-held objects: *Ankh* and a papyrus sceptre
State of preservation: The figure is well preserved including the minor relief details, although the figure is slightly damaged in the face by natural processes.
Iconographical description: Fifteen figures (originally sixteen) are depicted in the relief scene, which has been damaged by a fracture on its right side. The winged solar disc and two pendant *uraei* that hold the signs of eternity are depicted above the main scene. The hieroglyphic sign for sky crowns the scene.

The figures in the scene are divided in the centre as the figures of the left side face those of the right. The ruling couple is depicted as the first couple on the left side, thus in its centre. Ptolemy III wears a double crown, a single forehead *uraeus* and a royal diadem. He holds an *ankh* and a *was* stave in his hands. He is dressed in a special cloak that stretches down to his feet and folds in several layers. He is described in the text as 'King Ptolemy Euergetes'. His figure is well preserved.

Behind the king is the figure of Berenice II. She wears a traditional female crown, a tripartite wig, a single forehead *uraeus* and a royal diadem. She holds an *ankh* and a papyrus sceptre in her hands. She is described in the text as 'Lady of the Two Lands, Berenice', and is, together with her husband, designated the '*theoi Euergetai*'. Her figure is well preserved.

Behind Berenice II stands the figure of Thoth. He is depicted anthropomorphically with an ibis-head. He wears an *atef* crown, which sits on top of ram horns, and has two *uraei* that wear solar crowns. He holds a notched palm branch and a writing reed in his hands. He is dressed in a traditional kilt and a bull's tail. He is described in the text as Thoth. The figure is well preserved.

Behind Thoth is the figure of Seshat. She wears her traditional headdress, the symbol  of her name *sšꜣt sšt*. She wears a tripartite wig, a single forehead *uraeus* and a royal diadem. She is dressed in her typical panther-skin garment, though not a full dress but rather a kilt, with her upper part of the body left naked. She holds the same attributes in her hands as Thoth does, underlining her role as a recording chronographer. She is described in the text as Seshat. The figure is well preserved.

Behind Seshat is the figure of King Ptolemy II. He wears an *atef* crown that rests on top of ram horns. The crown also includes a centred solar disc. He is dressed in a traditional kilt and a bull's tail. He holds an *ankh* and a *was* stave in his hands. He is described in the hieroglyphic text as King Ptolemy. *Theoi Adelphoi* is written above his head.

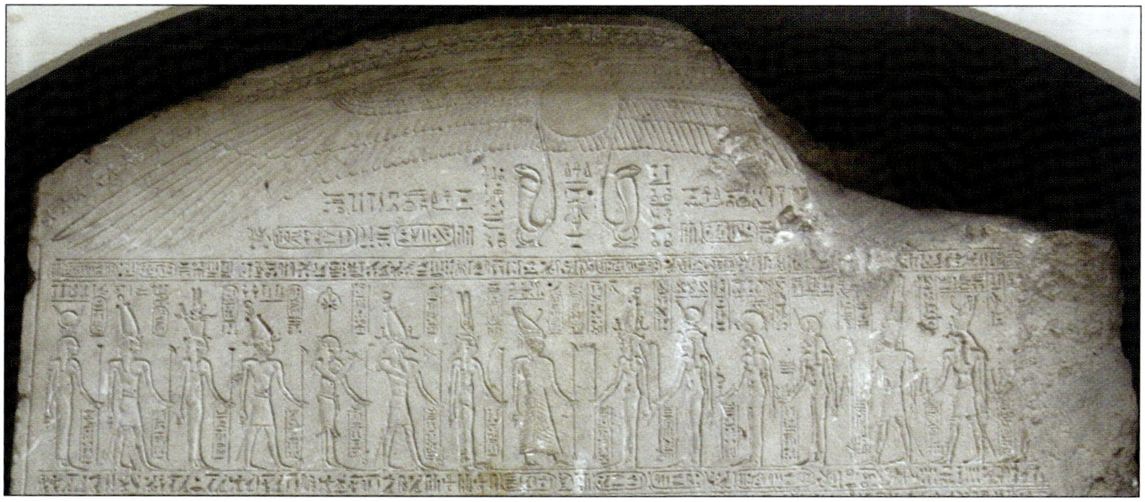

4. Egyptian Museum, Cairo, CG 22186 (Kanopus decree of Kom el-Hisn)

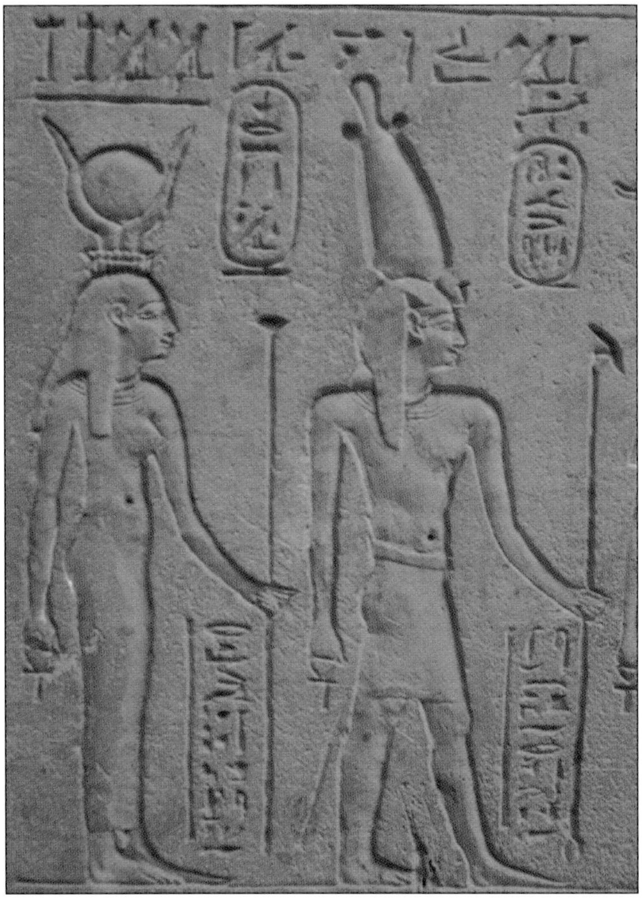

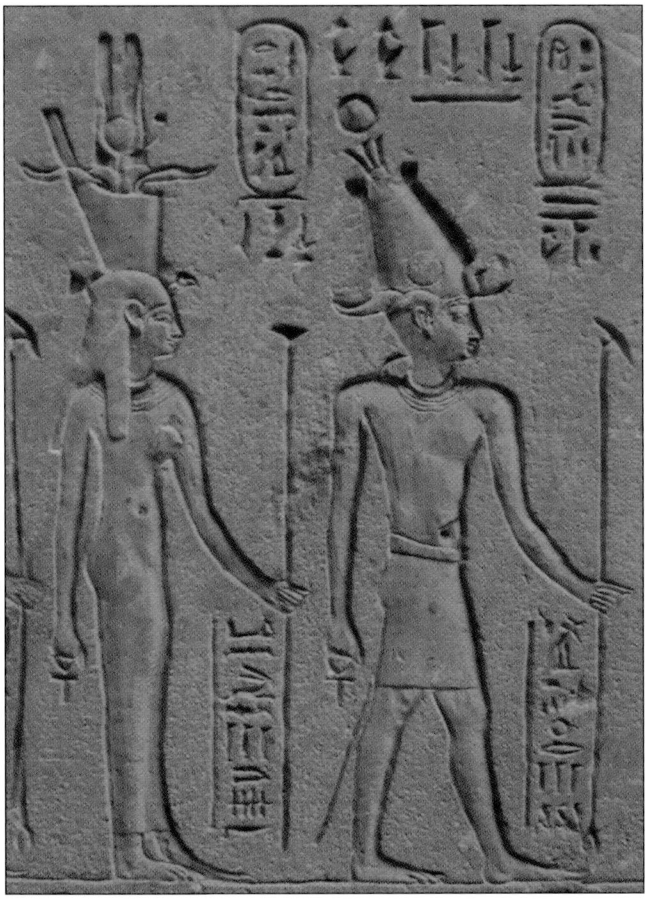

Arsinoë stands behind the king. She wears a tripartite wig, a vulture cap and the crown of Arsinoë. She is dressed in a traditional sheat dress. She holds an *ankh* and a papyrus sceptre in her hands. She is described in the text as 'Arsinoë Philadelphos'.

Behind Arsinoë is Ptolemy I. He wears a traditional *nemes* wig and a single forehead *uraeus* and a plain *atef* crown. He is dressed in a traditional kilt and a bull's tail. He holds an *ankh* and a *was* stave in his hands. He is described in the text as Divine King Ptolemy.

Behind him, as the last figure of the left side, is Berenice I. She wears a tripartite wig, a tiara of *uraei*, large cow horns and a large solar disc. She holds an *ankh* and a papyrus sceptre in her hands. She is described in the text as Berenice, and the register above her head states *theoi Soteres*.

Seven visible deities are depicted on the right side of the scene, at one time most certainly including one more figure in the right corner where the stone has been damaged by a fracture.

Starting from the centre, the first figure wears a tripartite wig, a vulture cap and an *atef* crown that rests on ram horns, with two *uraei* rising up on the sides, each one wearing solar discs. She is dressed in a traditional sheat dress. She holds an *ankh* and a *was* stave: a horizontal *ankh* comes out of the *cucupha* head. She is described in the text as a local goddess of the third nome of Lower Egypt, a form of Hathor. The figure is well preserved.

The second figure (from the centre) wears a tripartite wig, a vulture cap, a low tiara of *uraei* and a crown composed of large cow horns and solar disc. She is dressed in a traditional sheat dress. She holds an *ankh* and a notched palm branch, normally connected with the reckoning of time. She is described in the text as Hathor. The figure is well preserved.

Behind Hathor is a female anthropomorphic figure with a lioness head. She wears a large solar disc and a single *uraeus*. She is dressed in a traditional sheat dress and holds an *ankh* and a low papyrus sceptre with a semi-circular additional figure, from which an *ankh* arises (the latter item is unclear). She is described as Sekhmet. The figure is well preserved.

The fourth figure is an anthropomorphic deity depicted with the face of a cow. She wears large cow horns and solar disc. A large serpent is depicted in the centre of the solar disc. She is dressed in a traditional sheat dress and holds an *ankh* and the -sign. She is described in the text as Sekhat-Heru. The figure is, in general, in a good state of preservation.

Behind the last female figure stands a male one. He wears an elongated double feather plume and a centred solar disc that rests upon a low crown-cap. He is dressed in a traditional kilt and bull's tail. He holds an *ankh*, a *was*

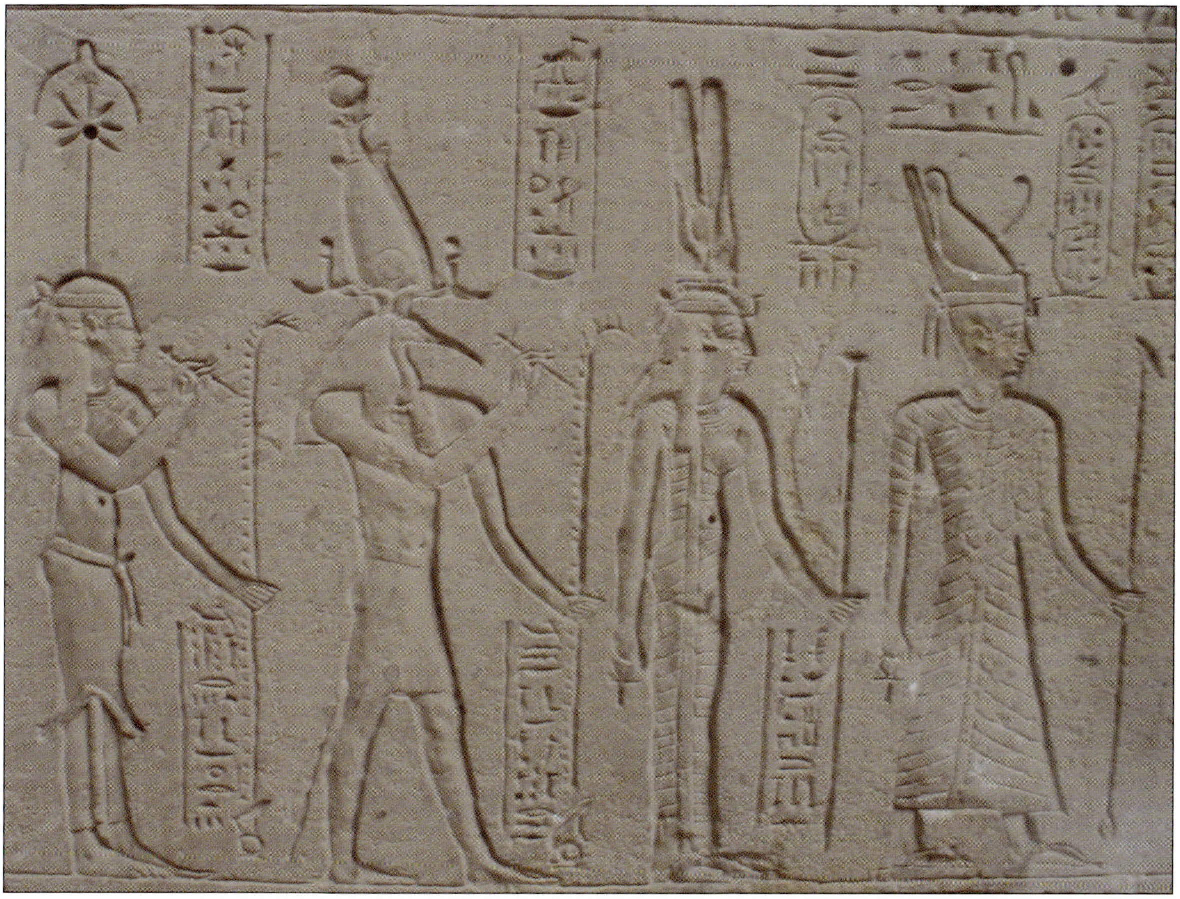

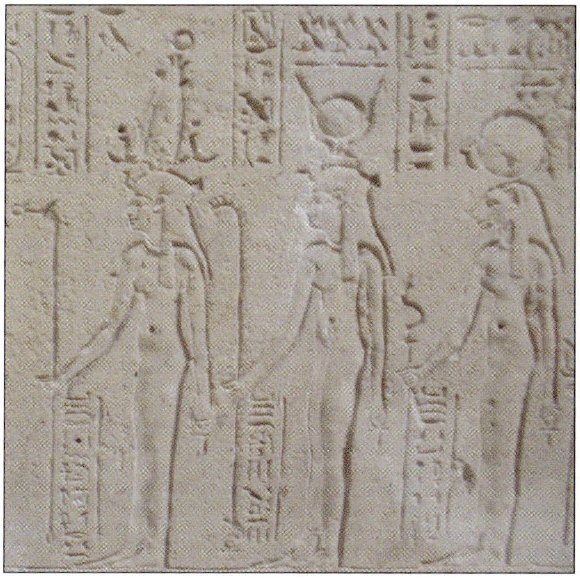

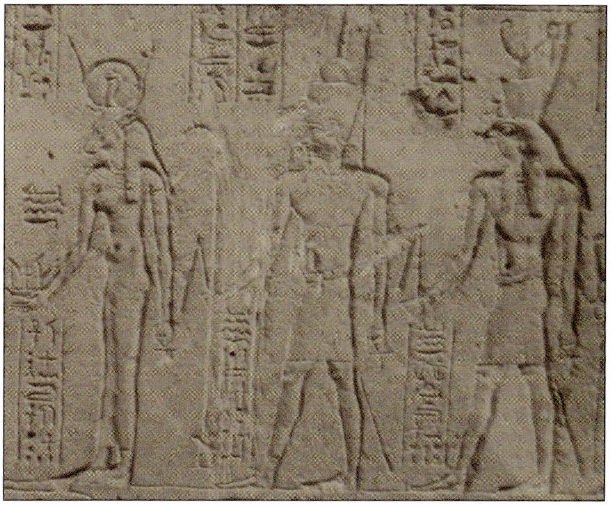

4. Egyptian Museum, Cairo, CG 22186 (Kanopus decree of Kom el-Hisn). Photos: J. Ward.

stave and a flail. The personal register of text, which has been damaged, describes him as Amun-Ra.

Behind Amun-Ra stands the figure of Horus. He wears a double crown and a single forehead *uraeus*. He is dressed in a traditional kilt and bull's tail. He holds an *ankh* and a flail in his hands. He is described as Horus in the personal register of text. The figure is in a good state of preservation.

The last figure of the scene is preserved only in fragments, leaving only the arm and front leg visible. The figure holds an *atef* feather and a crook in his hands. The text has been damaged.

Remarks: Arsinoë and Amun are depicted as the tallest figures of the scene.

5. Zagazig 228 = Herriat Raznah Museum Nr. H 854 (miniature copy of the Mendes stele)

Sunken relief
Limestone
41.8 × 38.5cm
Provenance: Mendes
Date: Ptolemy II Philadelphos
Published: Quaegebeur 1971a, no. 13; Quaegebeur 1978, 250f., fig. G; Meulenaere and MacKay 1976, no. 112; Yoyotte 1996, photo on p. 30; Quaegebeur 1998, no. 15
Crown of the scene: AC 5

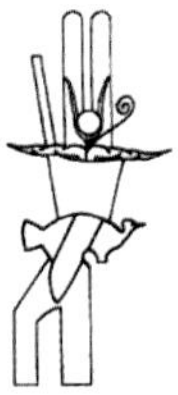

Hand-held objects: *Ankh* and a papyrus sceptre
State of preservation: The figure is well preserved, including the major relief details. The crown, the wig and the cap are well preserved in general. Only the main outlines of the facial features are preserved. The *ankh* and the sceptre are well preserved. The hieroglyphic text has faded in many sections.
Iconographical description: Five main figures are depicted in this scene. The king stands at the far right, wearing a double crown. He is dressed in a traditional kilt and a bull's tail. He presents a *sḫt* sign of the growing fields. He is described in the text as 'King Ptolemy, may he live forever like Ra'. In front of the king is a small censer stand with a lotus flower. The figure is preserved without any major damage.

Banebdjedet stands on a podium in front of the king. He wears a large solar disc that sits on top of ram horns. He is described as 'the Ram (Ba) of Mendes'. The figure is, in general, well preserved.

Behind the ram is a male ram-headed anthropomorphic figure. He wears an *atef* crown that rests on top of ram horns. He also wears a *nemes* wig. He is dressed in a traditional kilt and a bull's tail. He holds an *ankh* and a *was* stave in his hands. He is described in the text as the 'Living ram'. The figure is, in general, preserved, though slightly damaged in the facial area.

Behind him stands Isis. She wears a tripartite wig, a vulture cap, large cow horns and a solar disc. She holds an *ankh* and a papyrus sceptre in her hands. She is described in the hieroglyphic text as 'Great Isis'. The figure is in a generally good state of preservation.

Behind Isis, the last figure of the scene is Arsinoë. She wears a tripartite wig, vulture cap and the crown of Arsinoë. She is decorated with a necklace and is dressed in a traditional sheat dress. She holds an *ankh* and a papyrus sceptre in her hands. She is described as the 'King of Upper and Lower Egypt (Banebdjedet)| Lady of the Two Lands (Arsinoë)| Philadelphos'.

A winged solar disc and two pendant *uraei* (holding *ankh*s) are depicted above the main scene. The disc is described as 'Behutet, Great God, Lord of Heaven'. A hieroglyphic sign for heaven stretches out over the main scene.
Remarks: Arsinoë is depicted as the tallest figure of the entire scene.

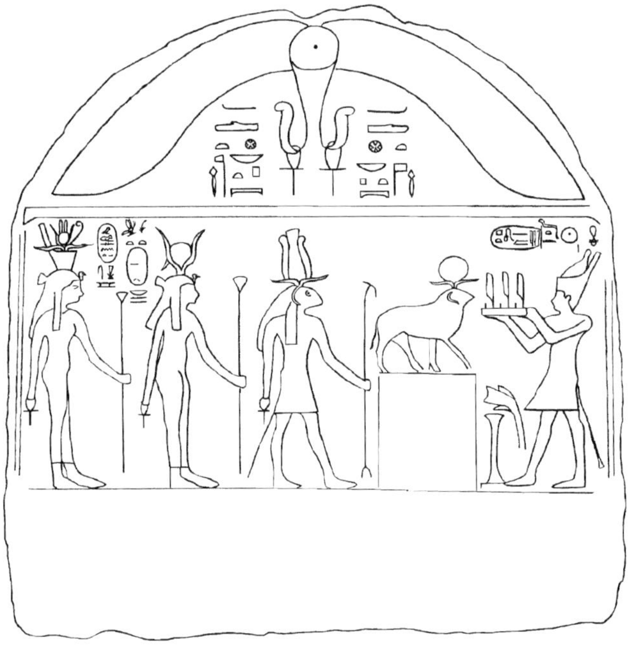

5. Zagazig 228 = Herriat Raznah Museum Nr. H 854 (miniature copy of the Mendes stele) Drawing: The author.

6. Brussels MRAH E. 8387

Sunken relief
Limestone
61.5 × 36.5cm
Provenance: Hû/Hiw – Greek Diospolis Parva
Date: Ptolemy II Philadelphos (255/254 BC)
Published: Quaegebeur 1978, 250f.; Meulenaere 1978, no. 1310; Cheshire 1982, 109, n. 39; Quaegebeur 1998, no. 6
Crown of the scene: AC 6

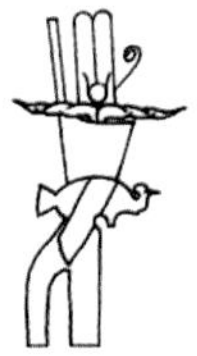

Hand-held objects: *Ankh* and a papyrus sceptre
State of preservation: The figure has been badly damaged by natural processes, especially the upper part of the body.

The crown is mainly damaged in the area of the ram horns, though leaving the main outlines visible. The head, including the wig and the cap, has been damaged, though some outlines are still visible. The lower part of the body is better preserved than the upper part, though some minor fractures have damaged various areas. The hand-held objects have been damaged but are still visible. The text has been badly damaged.

Iconographical description: Four main figures are depicted in this scene.

The king stands at the very left of the stele and wears the red crown. He is dressed in the traditional kilt and bull's tail. His arms are both raised as in an offering position but the objects held in his hands are no longer visible because of the condition of the stone surface. The text has been badly damaged and almost totally erased. The figure has been badly damaged by natural processes and a large fracture in the stone surface.

In front of the king stands two deities plus Arsinoë. The two deities have been badly damaged and almost entirely erased. The first figure is a male deity wearing the red crown. He is dressed in the traditional kilt and bull's tail. He holds an *ankh* and a *was* stave in his hands. No further information is visible owing to the bad state of preservation. The personal register of text is likewise damaged and no longer visible, though one of the signs could be the *ḥr* sign of Horus.

The second figure is a female deity wearing the traditional sheat dress. She most probably wears the large cow horns and solar disc, generally indicating either Hathor or Isis. She holds an *ankh* in her resting hand while the other hand is held in a protective position. The figure has been badly damaged and no further information is visible. The text is equally damaged.

The last figure of the scene is Arsinoë, who is dressed in an elaborated sheat dress and an additional shawl. She wears the crown of Arsinoë, the tripartite wig and the vulture cap. She holds an *ankh* and a papyrus sceptre in her hands. She is described in the text as Arsinoë.

Above the main scene is the winged solar disc depicted together with two pendant *uraei* possibly holding *ankh*s. The figure is described in the damaged text as 'Behutet, the great god, the Lord of Heaven…' (the last signs are no longer clear). Above the figure of Behutet is the sky depicted in its hieroglyphic form.

Remarks: Arsinoë is the tallest figure of the scene.

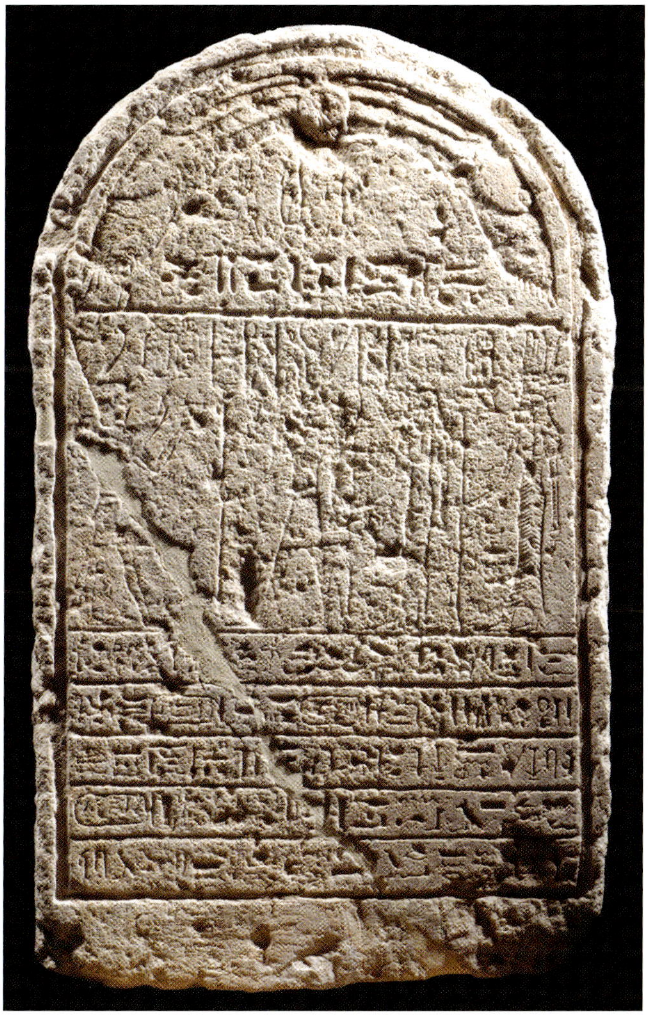

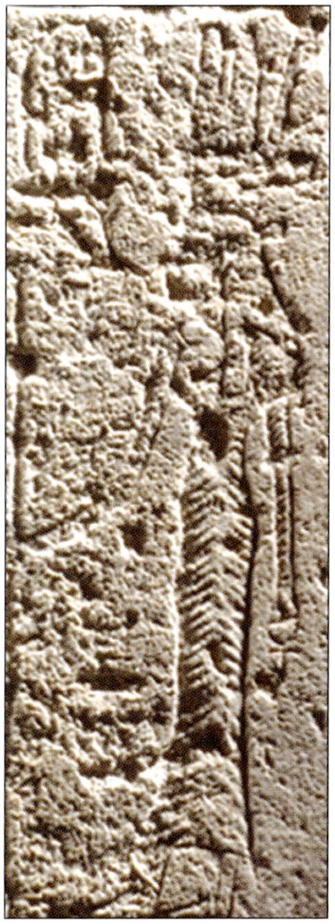

6. Brussels MRAH E. 8387. Photos: Raymond Monnaerts © Musées Royaux d'Art et d'Historie, Brussels.

7. Moscow I.i 5375

Sunken relief
Limestone
27 × 21cm
Provenance: Abu Sir – Greek Taposiris Magna (found in 1889)
Date: After 270 BC
Published: Quaegebeur 1971a, 191–3, pl. XXIX; Quaegebeur 1978, 251; Hodjash and Berlev 1982, 184–6, fig. 127; Quaegebeur 1988, 53, n. 26; Quaegebeur 1998, no. 14
Crown of the scene: AC 7

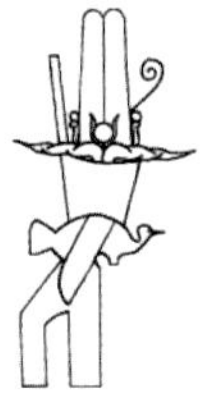

Hand-held objects: *Ankh* and a papyrus sceptre
State of preservation: The figure is, in general, in a good state of preservation, including the relief details. The personal register of text is well preserved with only minor damage resulting from natural processes. There are some traces of red colouring in the solar disc and black colouring in the king's crown and hieroglyphs.

Iconographical description: Two main figures are depicted in this scene.

King Ptolemy II is depicted at the right side of the scene wearing the double crown, a single forehead *uraeus* and the royal diadem. He is dressed in the traditional kilt and the bull's tail. He presents a trey with bread and cakes. He is described in the text as the 'Ling of Upper and Lower Egypt (Strong is the soul of Ra, beloved of Amun)| Son of Ra, Lord of the crowns (Ptolemy)|'. In front of the figure of Ptolemy is a small horned altar with burning incense. The figure is well preserved with only minor damage owing to natural erosion.

On the other side of the altar and standing at the left side of the scene is Arsinoë. She wears a tripartite wig and a vulture cap above which is placed the crown of Arsinoë with two *uraei* rising up on the sides. She is dressed in the traditional sheat dress and holds an *ankh* and a papyrus sceptre in her hands. She is described in the text as the 'King of Upper and Lower Egypt (Arsinoë Philadelphos)|'.

Above the couple is the winged solar disc, Behutet, depicted with two *uraei* hanging down on its side. No hieroglyphic text belonging to the Behutet figure is visible.
Remarks: The two figures are depicted with exaggerated eyes and facial features in a rather non-classical fashion. Arsinoë is depicted higher than Ptolemy.

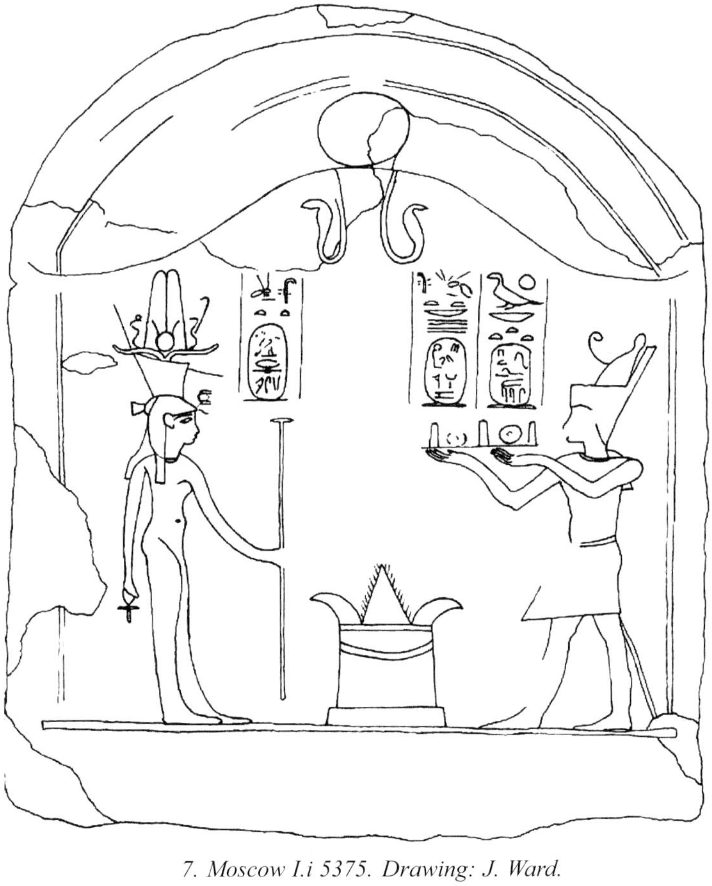

7. Moscow I.i 5375. Drawing: J. Ward.

8. Relief of Arsinoë, University of Trier (Archäologisches Institut der Universität Trier)

Sunken relief
Limestone
37.0 × 26.5cm
Provenance: Unknown
Date: Arsinoë's lifetime
Published: Albersmeier and Minas 1998; Quaegebeur 1998, no. 64
Crown of the scene: AC 8

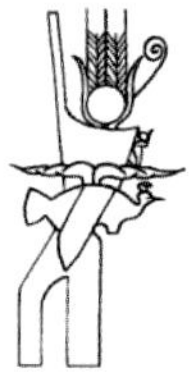

Hand-held objects: Unknown object with two ends, and possibly a sceptre
State of preservation: The relief is divided in four different fragments and the image of Arsinoë is divided into three fragments. The top block divides the figure on top in the central area of the double feather plume and the back part of the top part of the red crown; the lower cut is just under the eyes of the figure. The middle block includes only the arm holding the unknown object and the front part of the belly. The lower block includes the lower part of the legs and the entire feet. Except for the fragmented state of preservation the figure is well preserved, including all the relief details. The crown is well preserved with all the main relief details, including a *uraeus* wearing the cow horns and solar disc. The wig is mainly missing from the relief, though the minor part which is preserved is well decorated and well preserved. The vulture cap is highly decorated with all the minor details and includes not only the vulture head but also the head of a serpent, the sign of Upper and Lower Egypt. Of the facial features only the eye and the upper part of the ear are preserved. The bracelet is well preserved with a broad main row, and two small rows of beads. The objects held in the hand are very fragmentary and it is only clear that one object is the shaft of a sceptre. The two other details are too fragmented to make a clear interpretation; possibly they are the lower parts of the same object, or they may be two different objects probably being connected to the royal regalia. The dress is well preserved in its lower part with a clear middle section and a diagonal striped pattern leading down from the centre part, ending in two layers of flounce. The feet, with an ankle bracelet on each foot, and the sandals are well preserved.

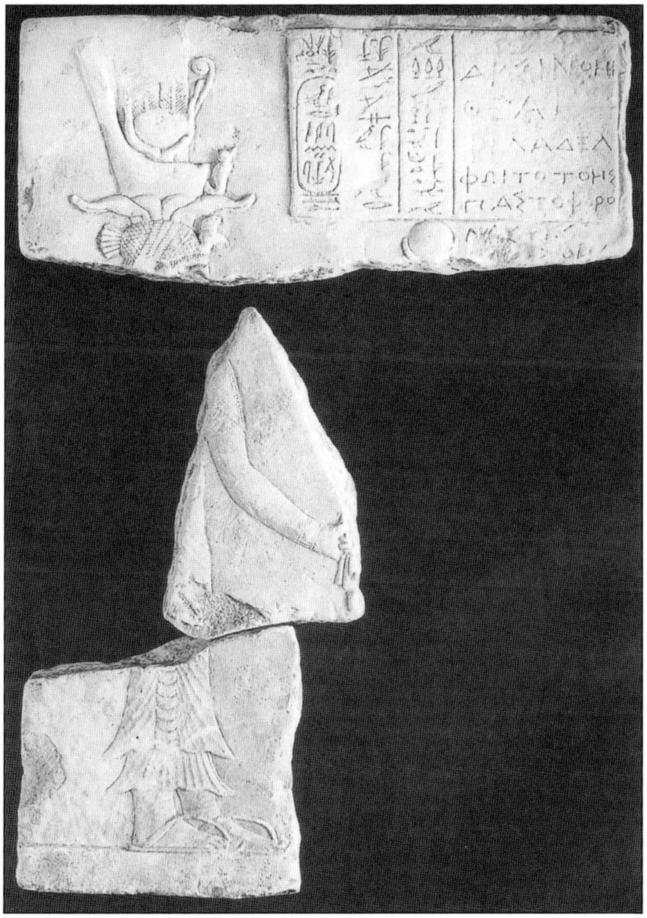

8. Relief of Arsinoë, University of Trier (Archäologisches Institut der Universität Trier) Photo: Archäologisches Institut der Universität Trier, Deutschland.

Iconographical description: Two figures are depicted on this stele. Arsinoë stands at the far left and faces the second figure (which is visible only through its crown). She wears the tripartite wig and a vulture cap with the heads of both vulture and *uraeus*. The crown of Arsinoë is accompanied by a single *uraeus* attached to the front of the red crown, which wears cow horns and a solar disc. She is dressed in an elaborated sheat dress with an additional shawl. She wears a bracelet, an ankle bracelet and sandals. The relief is broken in the area of the hand-held objects, though the remaining fragments indicate a sceptre and an unknown object with two ends, possibly a textile ribbon. She is described in the hieroglyphic text as 'Great of Sweetness, Great of Praise, King's daughter, King's wife, Great daughter, King's sister, who loves her and she loves him, King's great wife, King of Upper and Lower Egypt, Arsinoë Philadelphos, the Rightful'. She is further described in the Greek text as 'Arsinoë the divine Philadelphos'. The following Greek text is somewhat unclear, though, saying '*Totoes Pastophoros*, sailor of Arsinoë…'.

The second figure is preserved by its crown exclusively, illustrating a crescent and a disc or horns and a disc.
Remarks: Arsinoë is the tallest figure of the scene.

9. Relief of Arsinoë, Hildesheim 1025 (Pelizaeus-Museum)

Sunken relief
Limestone
29.5 × 26.5 × 6.5cm
Provenance: Unknown, possibly Memphis
Date: Arsinoë's lifetime – Ptolemy II Philadelphos
Published: Ippel and Roeder 1921, 86; Quaegebeur 1971a, 73–8; Bianchi 1988, 76 with fig. 43, 169f.; Quaegebeur 1998, no. 71
Crown of the scene: AC 9

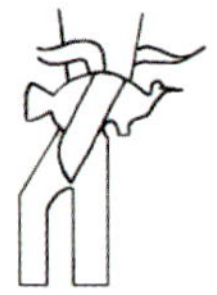

Hand-held objects: Sistrum
State of preservation: The fracture of the relief has cut the figure above the lower part of the red crown on the upper part; behind the vulture's tail at the left side; below the breast at the bottom; behind the sistrum on the right side. The preserved part of the crown is in a good state, though the left ram horn has been cut off at its centre. The horns are depicted on each side of the crown, not put together but separated by the red crown. The wig is well preserved, including its relief details, though damaged at the lower left end by a fracture in the stone. The vulture cap is well preserved except for the vulture-head, which has been damaged, most probably by natural processes. The face has been damaged above the ear and the lips, while the rest of the facial features are preserved, including the details of 'natural' hair. The upper part of the body is well preserved, though the shoulder and upper arm of the hand holding the sistrum have been damaged by a fracture in the stone block. The sistrum is well preserved (except for the right side of the item, which is slightly damaged by a fracture), including the head of Hathor. Only the top part of a cartouche is preserved, without any indications of a title or name.
Iconographical description: This fragmentary relief depicts the upper part of the image of Arsinoë. She wears a tripartite wig, the vulture cap and the crown of Arsinoë. She wears a necklace with one main row and she holds a sistrum in her hand. The figure on this relief is in a good state of preservation with clear outlines and relief details.
Remarks: Vague lines of the right-side ram horn are visible on the lower part of the red crown, exposing the artist's geometric measurements.

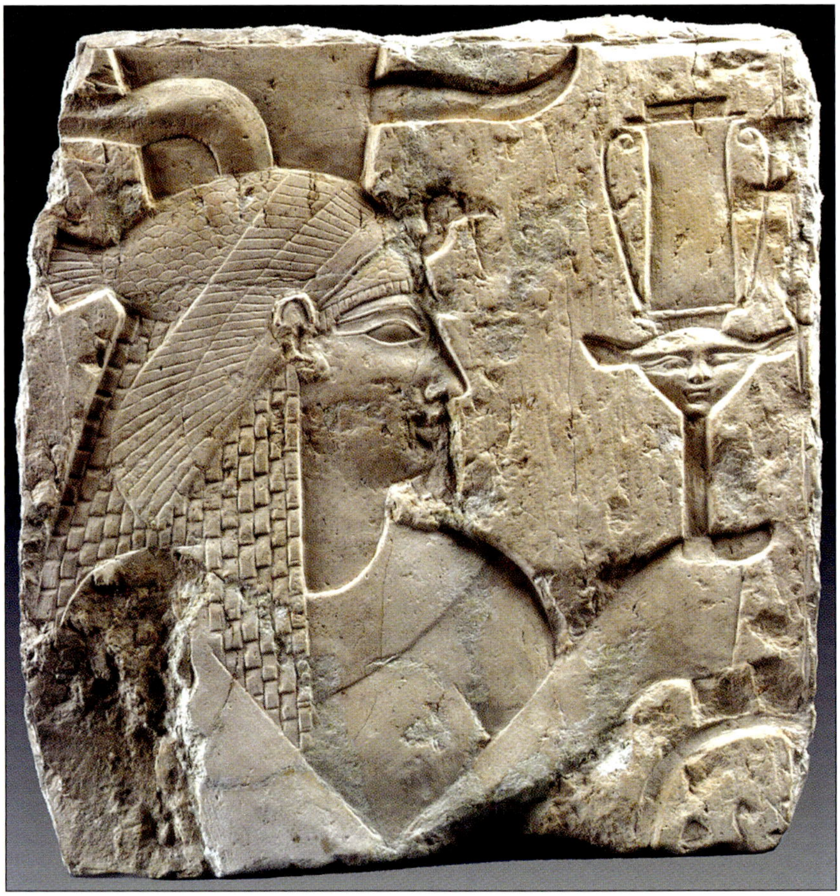

9. Relief of Arsinoë, Hildesheim 1025 (Pelizaeus-Museum). Photo: J. Ward.

10. Stele Toronto 979.63 (Royal Ontario Museum)

Sunken relief
Limestone
0.27 × 0.16m
Provenance: Unknown
Date: Ptolemy II Philadelphos
Published: Bianchi 1988, 44, 46, fig. 16, 74f.; Quaegebeur 1989, 112; Quaegebeur 1998, no. 73
Crown of the scene: AC 4

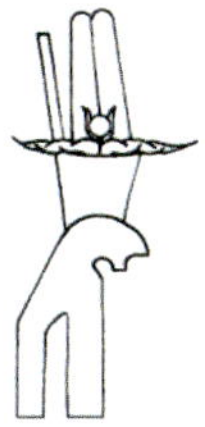

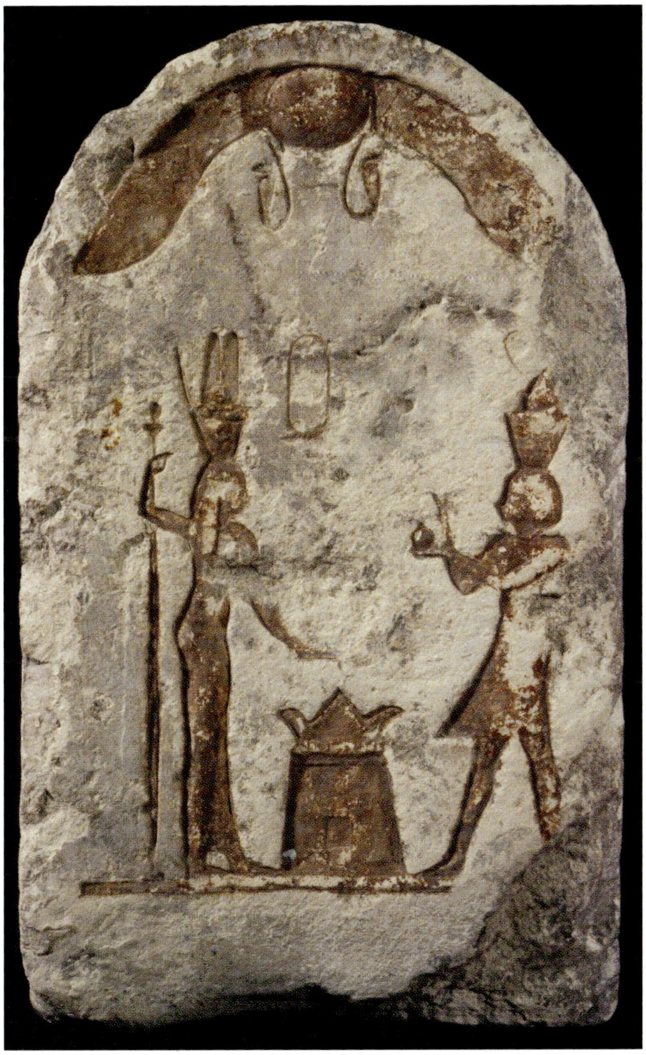

10. Stele Toronto 979.63 (Royal Ontario Museum) Photo: By permission of the Royal Ontario Museum © ROM.

Hand-held objects/connected objects: *Ankh* and a sceptre
State of preservation: The figure is preserved with minor damage as a result of natural processes. The crown is well preserved, including all its details. The ram horns are placed on top of the base of the red crown. The red crown is slightly damaged on its lower part by natural processes. The wig and the face are well preserved, the face with only minor damage resulting from natural erosion, though the outlines of the lips and nose are still revealed. The main figure is well preserved in general, though damaged in the area of the breast. The figure is mainly well preserved, including colour traces.
Iconographical description: This stele includes two main figures.

The king stands at the right side wearing the double crown on top of a *khat* cap covering the head and neck. He is dressed in the traditional kilt without the attached bull's tail. He presents a small circular vessel in one hand while holding the other hand in a blessing manner. There is no personal register of text or cartouche of this figure. The king is mainly well preserved, with only minor damage caused by natural erosion and minor fractures in the stone block. Traces of colour are still preserved on the figure. In front of the figure is a small horned altar.

Arsinoë stands at the left side of the altar. She wears the tripartite wig above which is placed the crown of Arsinoë. She is dressed in a traditional sheat dress and she holds an *ankh* and a sceptre in one hand while holding the other hand over the altar. The figure is depicted with an uninscribed cartouche. The figure is mainly well preserved though some parts have been badly damaged by small fractures in the stone block as well as natural fading of the colour.

Above the two figures is the winged solar disc depicted with two pendant *uraei*. No inscription is visible.
Remarks: Arsinoë is the tallest figure.

11. Egyptian Museum, Cairo, CG 31104

Sunken relief
Limestone
0.55 × 0.345m
Provenance: Krokodilopolis? Horbeit – Pharbaithos according to Quaegebeur 1971a
Date: Ptolemy II Philadelphos
Published: Spiegelberg 1904, I, 38, pl. VII; Otto 1905, 268, n. 5; Quaegebeur 1971a, no. 15bis; Quaegebeur 1998, no. 10
Crown of the scene: AC 6

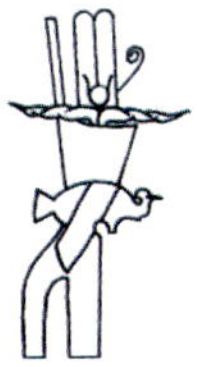

Hand-held objects: *Ankh* and a papyrus sceptre
State of preservation: The figure has been damaged by natural processes, though the main outlines of the figure are generally preserved. The crown is preserved with minor damage, though the back upper part of the red crown has been damaged in connection with the fractures of the outer stone surface and the area of the cow horns and solar disc is also slightly damaged. The facial features, as well as the breast area, are no longer preserved as a result of natural erosion. The arm holding the *ankh* is slightly damaged, including the hand-held object. The personal register of text is slightly damaged by natural processes.
Iconographical description: Six main figures are depicted in this stele.

King Ptolemy stands at the very right wearing a *khat* cap and a single forehead *uraeus*. He also wears the *anedjti* crown. He wears the traditional kilt, which is decorated in the normal ray-striped manner in the relief. He presents a small rounded vessel to the five deities standing in front of him. He is described in the text as 'Lord of the Two Lands (Ptolemy)| may he live forever like Ra'. The figure is, in general, preserved, though the facial features and the back part of the figure are slightly damaged by natural processes.

In front of the king stands the smaller figure of Harsomtus on a podium. He wears the double crown, a prince lock and a single forehead *uraeus* (possibly also the royal diadem). He is dressed in a thin shawl which hangs from his shoulders. He holds an *ankh* in his resting hand while putting a finger of his other hand in his mouth. He is described in the text as 'Harsomtus the youth, Great God, Lord of Shetit' (*shet*, possibly followed by *njwt i.e.*, the city sign, see below under Hathor). The figure is, in general, in a good state of preservation, though the upper part of the figure is slightly damaged by natural erosion.

Horus stands behind Harsomtus. He wears the double crown and a single forehead *uraeus*. He is dressed in the traditional kilt and the bull's tail. He holds an *ankh* and a sceptre (probably a *was* stave, though the head of the sceptre has been damaged by natural processes). He is described in the personal register of text as 'Horus, great of love (*mr? r r*), Great God, Lord of Shetit' (*shet*, possibly followed by *njwt*). The figure is, in general, in a good state of preservation, though divided into two fragments by a fracture in the stele.

Following the figure of Horus is Hathor, wearing a tripartite wig, the vulture cap, the large cow horns and solar disc. She holds an *ankh* and a papyrus sceptre in her hands. She is described as 'Hathor, the great Lady of Shetit' (*i.e.*, Krokodilopolis, the capital of the Arsinoïtes Nome in Fayyum). The figure is, in general, in a good state of preservation, though slightly damaged all over by natural erosion. The personal register of text is written horizontally instead of, as is the case of the other figures, vertically.

Behind the figure of Hathor is the figure of Sarapis. He wears a large solar disc surrounded by a single *uraeus*. The face of the figure has been damaged and its form is not clear, though it is obvious that it is a face of an animal, most probably the bull's face in his connection with Apis. He also wears the *nemes* wig. The figure of Sarapis is dressed in the traditional kilt and the bull's tail. He holds an *ankh* and a *was* stave in his hands. He is described in the text as 'Sarapis, the great god, Lord of Shetit'. The figure of Sarapis is mainly preserved, though damaged by natural processes.

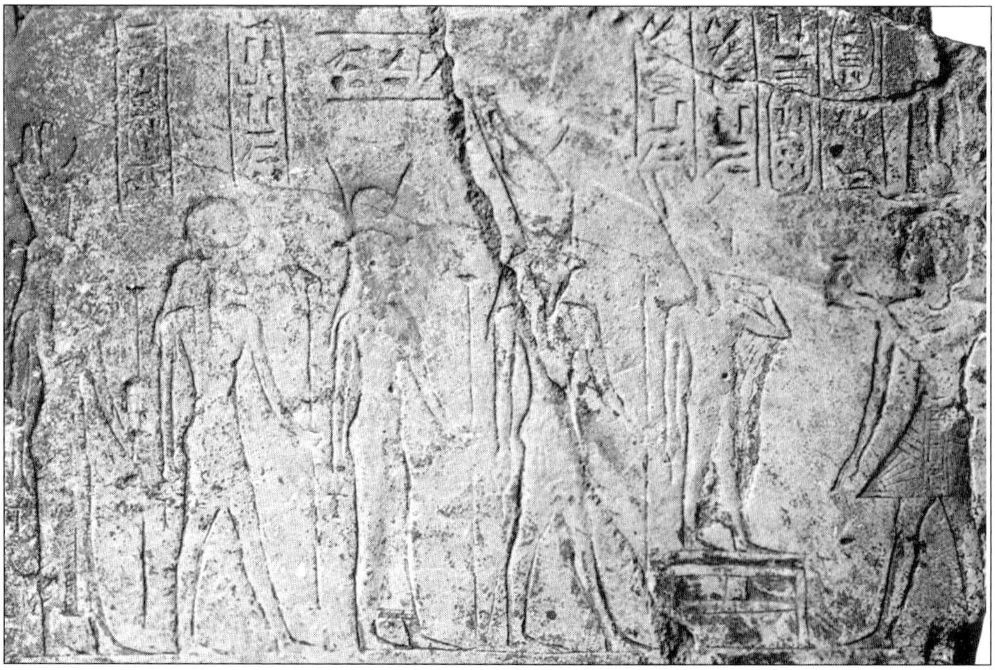

11. Egyptian Museum, Cairo, CG 31104. Photo: After Spiegelberg 1904, I, 38, pl VII.

Arsinoë stands behind Sarapis. She wears a tripartite wig and a vulture cap, above which is placed the crown of Arsinoë. She is dressed in the traditional sheat dress and she holds an *ankh* and a papyrus sceptre in her hands. She is described in the personal register of text as 'Lady of the Two Lands (Arsinoë)| may she live forever'.

The winged solar disc, Behutet, is depicted above the main scene with two pendant *uraei*. The figure has been damaged by a fracture at the top, especially to the right side of the stele. No inscription has been preserved.

Under the main scene is a small fragmented demotic inscription states 'Sarapis, Great God, Harsomtus, the great divine son, who gives life …'.

Remarks: The king is depicted as the tallest figure.

12. Relief of Queen Arsinoë II as Hathor, Harvard Art Museum (Arthur M. Sackler Museum, Gift of Mr. and Mrs. Samuel H. Lindenbaum, 1983.96)

Sunken relief
Limestone
42.5 × 57.7cm
Date: Most probably Ptolemy II Philadelphos
Provenance: Probably Memphis
Published: Quaegebeur 1978, 259; Bianchi 1988, cat. 65; Quaegebeur 1998, no. 40; Chauveau 1998, 81 (cat. 42), Wolohojian 2008
Crown of the scene: AC 10

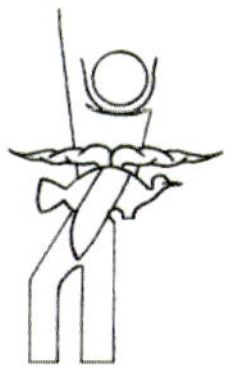

Hand-held objects: Lotus-shafted flail
State of preservation: The figure is well preserved, though the relief is a fragment cutting the upper part of the crown and the lower part of the breast. The upper cartouche has been badly damaged and only the lowest part is preserved. The relief is preserved with white and red colour fragments. The figure is preserved with all its relief detail.

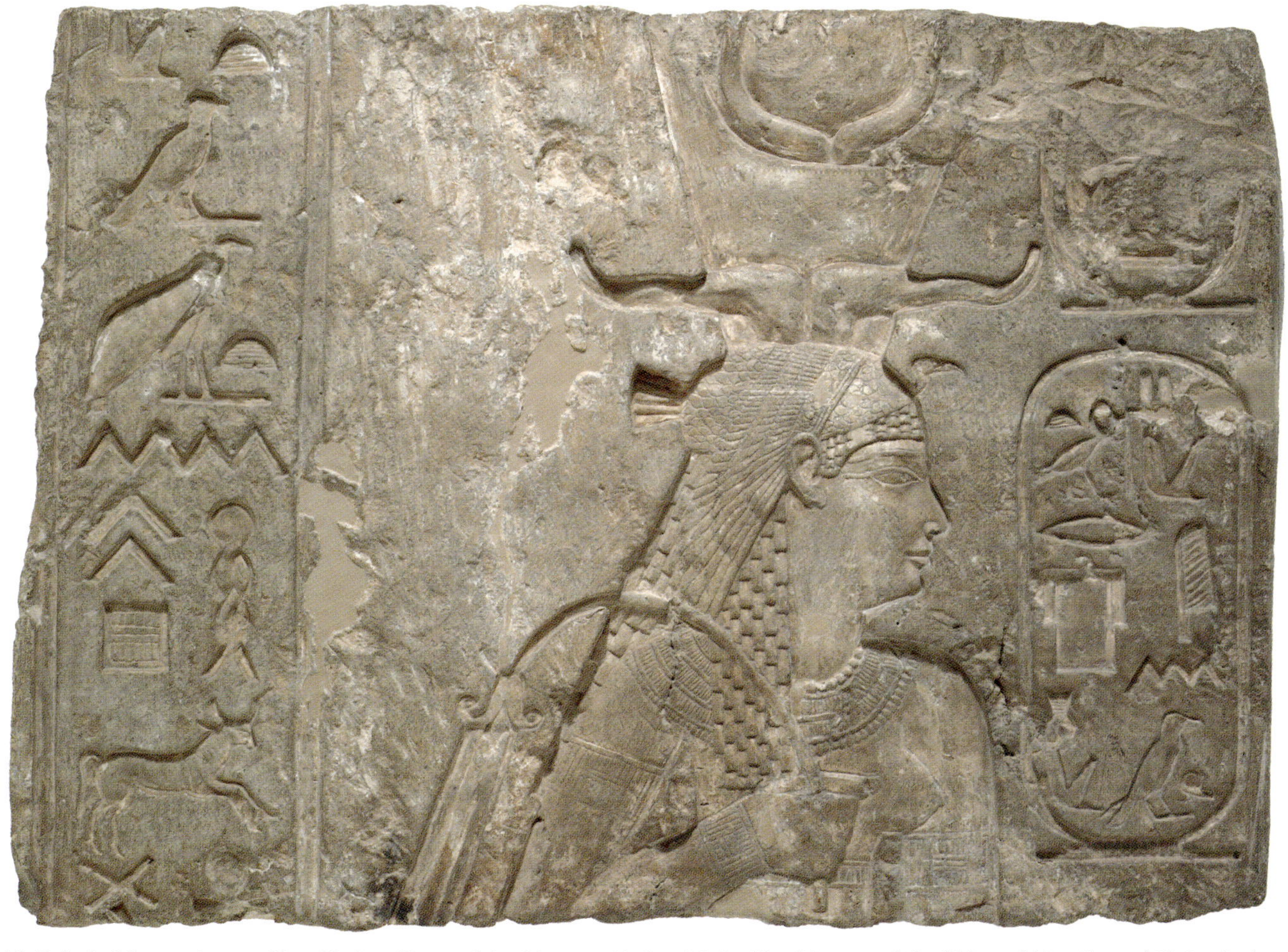

12. Relief of Queen Arsinoë II as Hathor, Harvard Art Museum (Arthur M. Sackler Museum, Gift of Mr. and Mrs. Samuel H. Lindenbaum, 1983.96). Photo: Katya Kallsen © President and Fellows of Harvard College.

Iconographical description: In this fragmentary relief it is only the upper part of the image of Arsinoë that is preserved. She wears the tripartite wig and the vulture cap, above which her crow is placed. The crown is broken off just above the top of the large solar disc. She is dressed in the traditional sheat dress and wears a necklace with four rows of beads, upper arm bracelets and a normal bracelet. She holds a lotus-shafted flail in her hand. The figure is described in the text as 'Daughter of Amun, Arsinoë ([She who is in the heart of Shu] Loved [by (all) the gods])|, mother of Hep, repeating life'.

13. British Museum EA 1056

Sunken relief
Limestone
42.0 × 34.3cm
Date: Ptolemy II Philadelphos (dated 200–190 BC in Quaegebeur 1988)
Provenance: San el-Hagar– ancient Dja'net, Greek Tanis
Published: *PM* IV, 24; Petrie 1883–4, II, 36 with pl. X; Budge 1909, 269, pl. xlviii; Sauneron 1960, 107f., n. 6; Quaegebeur 1971a, 194, no. 25; Quaegebeur 1978, 251; Bowman 1986, 23, fig. 12; Quaegebeur 1988, cat. 14, pl. 14; Mysliwiec 1988, 85; Brissaud and Zivie-Coche 1998, 170 and pl. 24; Quaegebeur 1998, no. 12; Stanwick 2002, 22; Albersmeier 2002, 112, n. 633

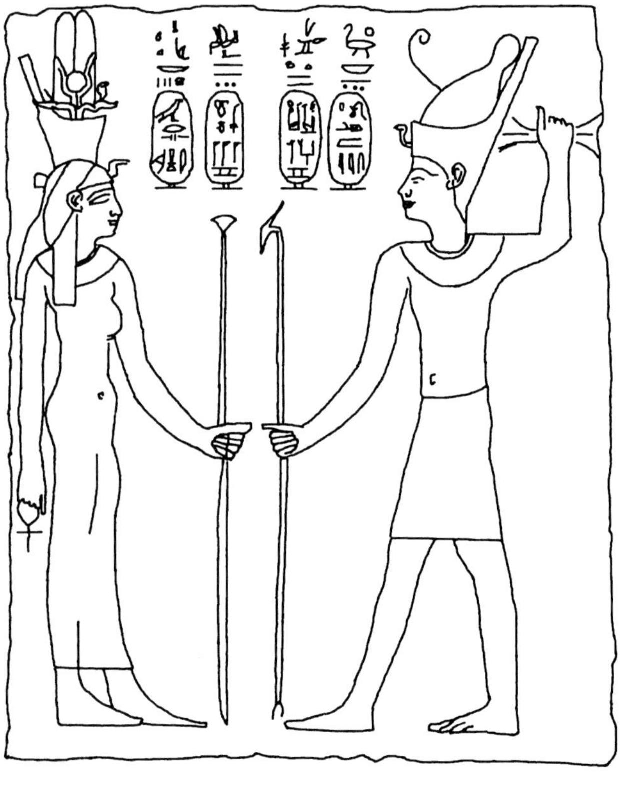

13. British Museum EA 1056. Drawing: The author.

Crown of the scene: AC 12

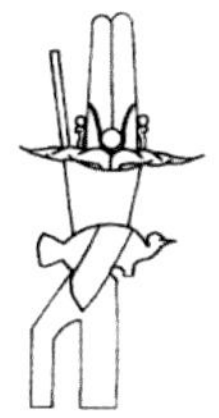

Hand-held objects: *Ankh* and a papyrus sceptre
State of preservation: The figure is well preserved, including the relief details. The crown is well preserved, though with lines suggesting that this is a sketched practice piece, a draft, a theory also supported by the vague outlines of the *uraeus*. The ram horns are placed on top of the base of the red crown. The wig is well preserved and so is the cap, though the artist who created the piece has not connected the tail to the main body of the vulture. The facial features are well preserved, including small details as, for example, of the ear, and the features are in the right proportions. The main body is well preserved with only minor damage owing to some scratches, especially on the lower part. The *ankh* and the sceptre are both well preserved, though the shaft of the sceptre is not symmetrical above and under the hand holding it.
Iconographical description: Two figures are depicted in this scene.

King Ptolemy stands on the right side of the scene wearing the double crown and a single forehead *uraeus*. He is dressed in the traditional kilt and is decorated with a single lined necklace. He holds a *was* stave in his front hand and an unknown object of three sticks in the other, which is held up in a brandished position behind his body. There are traces of red colour of the main body of the king. He is described in the text as 'King of Upper and Lower Egypt (Strong is the soul of Ra, beloved of Amun)| Son of Ra, Lord of the Two Lands (Ptolemy)|'. The figure is well preserved, including facial features and the main relief details. There are thin lines and patterns surrounding the figure of the king and the shaft of the sceptre is not symmetrical above and below his hand.

Arsinoë stands at the left side of the relief. She wears the tripartite wig, a vulture cap and the crown of Arsinoë, with two rising *uraei* attached to the ram horn. She is dressed in the traditional sheat dress and is decorated with a necklace with one main row. She holds an *ankh* and a papyrus sceptre in her hands. She is described in the text as 'King of Lower Egypt, the Two Lands (She who is in the heart of the king, Beloved of (all) the gods)| daughter of Amun, Lady of the crowns (Arsinoë Philadelphos)|'.
Remarks: Arsinoë is depicted as the tallest figure of the scene.

14. British Museum EA 1057

Sunken relief
Limestone
50 × 48cm
Date: Ptolemy II Philadelphos
Provenance: San el-Hagar– ancient Dja'net, Greek Tanis
Published: *PM* IV, 26; Petrie 1885, I, 31 with pl. XV, II, pl. X; Budge 1909, p. 269; Quaegebeur 1971a, 201 (no. 15); Bianchi 1988, 105 (cat. 15); Mysliwiec 1988, 85; Favard-Meeks 1998, 110; Quaegebeur 1998, no. 13; Albersmeier 2002, 112, n. 633
Crown of the scene: AC 11

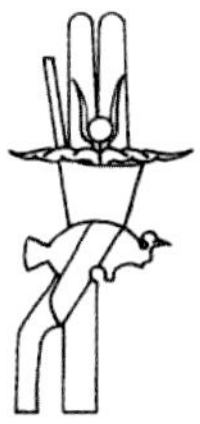

Hand-held objects: *Ankh* and a papyrus sceptre
State of preservation: The figure has been badly damaged in various areas by natural erosion. The crown is slightly damaged, though all the main outlines are visible and clear. The wig, cap and facial features have been damaged in the same fashion as the crown, leaving only the main outlines and vague outlines of the enlarged eyes visible. The main body is preserved with only the main outlines still visible and without any further details. The *ankh* and the sceptre are slightly damaged by natural erosion. The personal register of text has been badly damaged in one of the cartouches and some of the other signs are slightly damaged.
Iconographical description: Six figures are depicted in this scene.

The general scene is divided into two sections. In the right scene the king is depicted at the very right wearing the red crown. No further details of any headdress are visible owing to the poor preservation of the figure. He is dressed in the traditional kilt. The offering object has been badly damaged by natural erosion but it is possibly the *sht* sign of the growing fields. The personal register of text has been badly damaged, almost completely erased, by a large fracture in the stone block. The figure has been badly damaged in various areas and only the main outlines are visible.

In front of the king stands Amun-Min. He wears his traditional high double feather plume. He raises his arm and holds a flail. The personal register of text has been badly damaged and the only signs visible state 'Lord of the Two Lands'. The figure has been badly damaged by natural processes and some minor fractures in the stone block.

Behind the figure of Amun-Min stands Arsinoë as the last figure of the right section of the scene. She wears the tripartite wig, a vulture cap and the crown of Arsinoë. She is dressed in the traditional sheat dress and holds an *ankh* and a papyrus sceptre in her hands. She is described in the text as the 'Daughter of Amun, Lady of the crowns (Arsinoë Philadelphos)| King of Upper and Lower Egypt, the Two Lands ([She who is in the heart of the king/Shu] Beloved of [(all) the gods])|'.

At the very left of the left scene is the king depicted once again. This time he wears the white crown and the royal diadem. He is dressed in the traditional kilt and the bull's tail. He presents the same object as in the right scene, the field of reeds, and a small censer stand with a now almost destroyed flower above it is placed in front of him. The personal register of text has been badly damaged by natural erosion plus small fractures in the stone block, though stating him as 'King and Lord of the Two Lands ([Strong is the soul of Ra, beloved of Amun])|, son of Ra, Lord of the Two Lands ([Ptolemy])|'. The figure is in a bad state of preservation.

In front of the king stands the smaller figure of Harsomtus on a low podium. He wears the double crown and is illustrated with a prince lock. No further details concerning the headdress are visible owing to the bad state of the figure. He is dressed in a thin shawl which hangs from his shoulders; otherwise he is depicted naked. He holds an *ankh* in his resting hand while suckling on a finger of the other hand. He is described as Harsomtus.

Behind Harsomtus is a female figure wearing the red crown. She holds an *ankh* and a papyrus sceptre in her hands. There are no further personal attributes of this figure and the personal register of text has been badly damaged by natural erosion, only mentioning the figure as being the 'Lady of the Two Lands'. She is here identified as Wadjet.

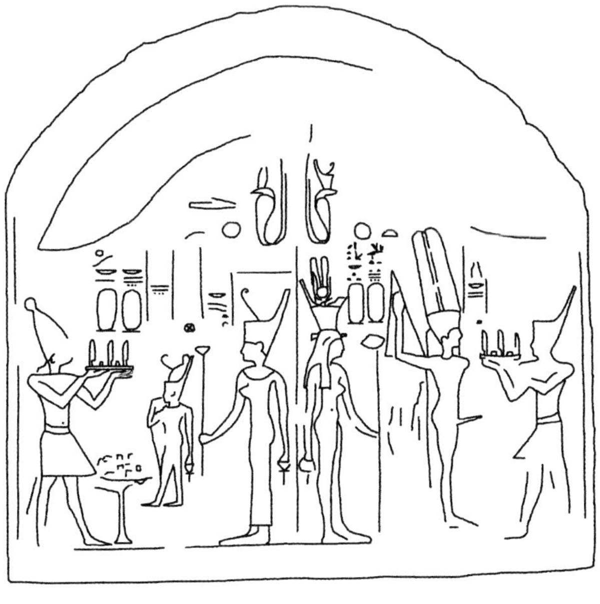

14. British Museum EA 1057. Drawing: The author.

Above the full scene is the winged solar disc depicted with two pendant *uraei*. The attached hieroglyphic text has been badly damaged by fractures in the stone block together with natural erosion, though the three visible signs state Behutet.

Remarks: The stele is in a bad state of preservation mainly as a result of natural processes but also because of smaller fractures in the stone block. The figure of Amun is the tallest figure of the scene.

15. Architrave Stockholm MM 10026 (Medelhavsmuseet)

Sunken relief
Limestone
38cm W
Date: Arsinoë's lifetime
Provenance: Tell Atrib – ancient Hut-Heryib; Greek Athribis
Published: George and Peterson 1982; Quaegebeur 1988, 45; Albersmeier and Minas 1998, 7
Left scene
Crown of the scene: AC 6

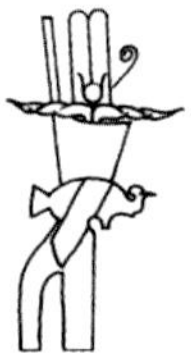

Hand-held objects: Two sistra
State of preservation: The figure is mainly well preserved, though it has been badly damaged in various areas by natural erosion. The red crown and the double feather plume are in general preserved, while the ram horns are preserved only in fragments and there is only a vague outline of a solar disc and possible cow horns resting on the lower top of the red crown. The wig and the vulture cap are mainly preserved with some relief details. The facial features have been damaged by natural erosion but still show exaggerated eyes, nose and lips. The dress is well preserved with a linear pattern linked together in its centre. The feet are mainly preserved, with minor damage resulting from a small fracture in the stone block, with a line indicating that the figure was depicted wearing sandals. The offering objects have been badly damaged and are only vague in appearance, though still visible. The cartouche is mainly preserved with only minor damage on the signs inside the cartouche, though these are still clear and readable.
Iconographical description: Four figures are depicted in this scene.

Arsinoë stands at the very left, wearing a tripartite wig, a vulture cap and the crown of Arsinoë. She is dressed in the elaborated sheat dress and wears sandals on her feet. She holds two sistra in her hands. She is described in the text as 'King of Upper and Lower Egypt (Arsinoë)|'.

King Ptolemy stands in front of Arsinoë facing the deities of the scene. He wears the double crown, a single forehead *uraeus* and the royal diadem. He is dressed in the traditional kilt and the bull's tail. He holds a ceremonial collar (*bb*) in his hands. He is described in the text as 'Lord of the Two Lands (Strong is the soul of Ra, beloved of Amun)| Lord of the crowns (Ptolemy)|'. The figure is preserved with some damage caused by natural erosion. The face, the *uraeus* and the royal diadem are only vaguely preserved. The main figure is, in general, well preserved. The offering and the personal register of text are well preserved with only minor damage resulting from natural processes. In front of Ptolemy is a small offering table/censer stand depicted above which is placed a jug and a lotus flower.

Horus is depicted seated on his throne in front of Ptolemy. He wears a large solar disc encircled by a single *uraeus*. The crown is detached from the head and gives the impression that it hangs in the air. He holds an *ankh*, though it is only vaguely visible, and a *was* stave in his hands. The figure is preserved with only minor damage, though it is made in a rather sloppy way and without any clear details except for the face. The *ankh* is almost completely missing and the sceptre is preserved only with shallow outlines. The personal register of text describes the figure as 'Horus Chentechtai, Lord of Athribis'. The second register of text, above his head, describes him as 'Great God, Lord of Heaven'.

The figure behind Horus is a lion-headed anthropomorphic female deity. She wears the same crown as Horus. She holds an *ankh* in her resting hand while keeping her other hand in a protective manner behind Horus. The hieroglyphic text of the personal register has been badly damaged and only a few signs are still clearly visible; these say 'Sekhmet, the great goddess who dwells in the city of Athribis, eye of Ra, Lady of the Sky, Mistress of all the Gods'. The figure has been badly damaged in various areas by natural erosion, though some details, such as the facial features are still well preserved.
Right scene
Crown of the scene: AC 6

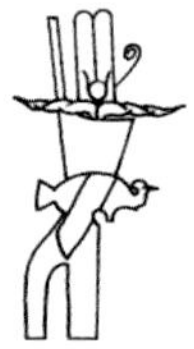

Hand-held objects: Two nao-form sistra
State of preservation: The figure is well preserved, including the majority of the relief details. The crown is better preserved than that of the left scene, including all the details of the composition. The ram horns are depicted simply as two curled lines. The wig and the cap are preserved without any further details. The facial features

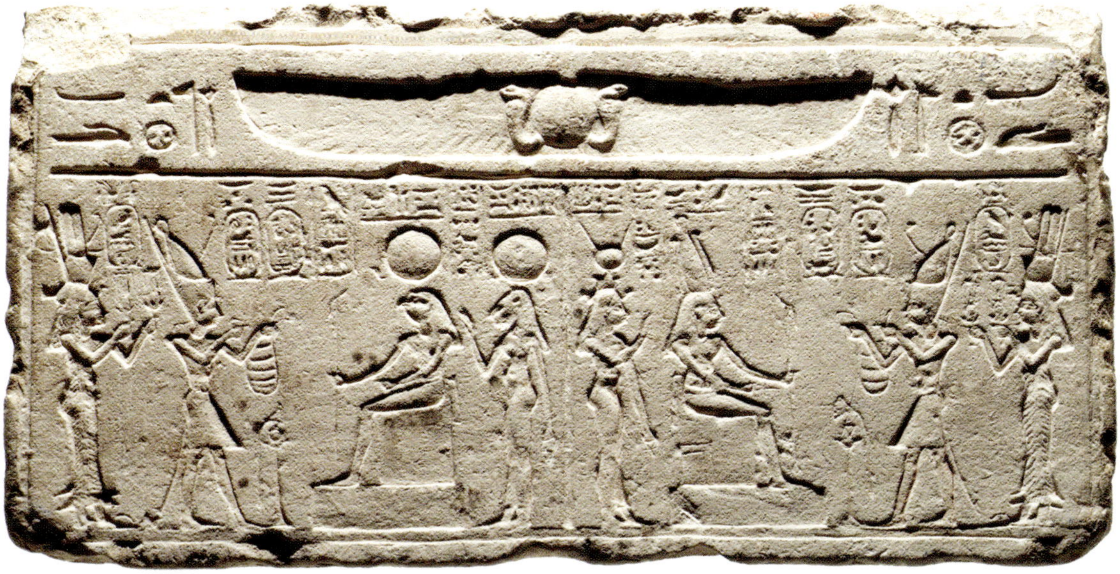

are all preserved, with exaggerated eyes. The dress consists of a draped *chiton* depicted in a very similar way to the traditional sheat dress, though with a different lower part. She wears sandals on her feet. The figure holds two *naos*-formed sistra in her hands. The figure is, in general, well preserved, with only minor damage resulting from natural erosion. The hieroglyphic text is preserved with only minor damage on some of the signs.

Iconographical description: Four figures are depicted in this right scene.

Arsinoë stands at the very right wearing a tripartite wig, a vulture cap and the crown of Arsinoë. She is dressed in an elaborated sheat dress and wears sandals on her feet. She holds two nao-formed sistra in her hands. She is described in the text as 'King of Upper and Lower Egypt (Arsinoë)|'.

King Ptolemy stands in front of Arsinoë and faces the deities. He wears the double crown, a single forehead *uraeus* and the royal diadem. He is dressed in the traditional kilt with the bull's tail. He holds a ceremonial necklace (bb) in his hands. He is described in the text as 'Lord of the Two Lands (Strong is the soul of Ra, beloved of Amun) Lord of the crowns (Ptolemy)|'. The figure is mainly well preserved with only minor damage, especially in the face, resulting from natural processes. In front of the king is a small offering table/censer stand with a small jug and a lotus flower bent over it.

In front of and facing the king is a male deity who is seated on a throne. He is depicted in an anthropomorphic form and wears a single forehead *uraeus* and the *atef* crown resting upon the *nemes* wig. He holds an *ankh* and a *was* stave in his hands. The personal register of text has been badly damaged and only a few signs are still clearly visible. He is described as 'Osiris Chentechtai, Horus who dwells in the city of Athribis'. The figure is mainly preserved with only minor damage resulting from natural erosion. The *was* stave and the *ankh* have been depicted only as thin lines and are therefore less clear than the rest of the figure. The throne is mainly well preserved.

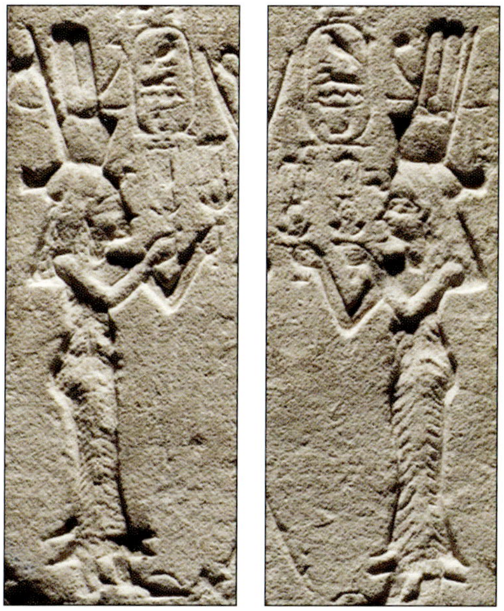

15. Architrave Stockholm MM 10026 (Medelhavsmuseet) Photos: Ove Kaneberg, © Medelhavsmuseet.

Behind the seated figure of Horus stands a female figure. She wears a tripartite wig, a vulture cap and a modus in a triangular form, on top of which the large cow horns and solar disc are resting. She is dressed in the traditional sheat dress. The figure holds an *ankh* in her resting arm while holding the other hand in a protective manner behind the figure of Horus. The personal register of text has been badly damaged by natural erosion and only a few signs are clearly visible. She is described as 'Chuit [...?] the God, the foremost Lady of the city of Athribis, the Mistress of all the gods'. The figure is mainly preserved with only minor damage resulting from natural processes.

The full scene is divided in the middle by a shallow line. The winged solar disc with two pendant *uraei* is depicted above the scene still preserved with details of the feathers. The figure is described in the text on both sides as 'great god Behutet'. There are some vague colour traces preserved on the architrave of yellow, blue and red pigments.

Remarks of the full scene: The two images of Arsinoë are depicted as the tallest figures.

Temple reliefs

16. Edfu, outer hypostyle hall (C), eastern partition, top register

Raised relief

Sandstone

Date: Ptolemy VIII Euergetes II

Published: *PM* VI, 132 (90); *Edfou* III, 190–92, pl. 63; Quaegebeur 1971a, 214, no. 32; Quaegebeur 1978, 252f.; Winter 1978, 150; Cauville 1987, 134–7, fig. 42; Quaegebeur 1998, 91, no. 23; SERAT 900212

Crown of the scene: AC 11

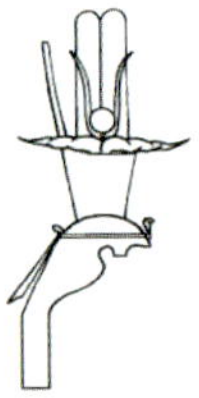

Hand-held objects: *Ankh*

State of preservation: The figure is mainly well preserved, including some colour of the dress, though damaged in the facial area and on the arms. The crown composition is in good condition, as is most of the wig and the royal band. Only the outlines of the cut marks informs us of a previous *uraeus*. The face is completely destroyed by cut marks. As with the *uraeus*, the outlines of the cut marks reveal a previous necklace. Both arms and hands have been badly damaged by cut marks, leaving only the outlines. The left foot of the figure has been badly damaged by cut marks while the right foot is left untouched, still with traces of red colour forming a spiral pattern. The dress is well preserved, with traces of white, red and blue colours. The navel and the hips have been damaged by chisel marks. Only the top outlines of the breast are preserved but the area has not been destroyed by cut marks.

Iconographical description: Three main figures are depicted in this scene.

The king presents an offering to Ptolemy II and Arsinoë. The king, standing at the left side, wears a corkscrew wig, the royal diadem and a single forehead *uraeus* above which is a crown composed by the ram horns, the double feather plume, the solar disc and two *uraei* each wearing the solar disc on its head. He wears the pharaonic kilt and is decorated with the bull's tail. He presents a small cup of ointment and the looped textile band. He is described in the text as Ptolemy VIII Euergetes II. Behind his back is the following written 'may he live his life in serenity as the Lord of abundance forever like Ra'. The figure has been badly damaged in the 'skin area', *i.e.*, the face, hands and legs, by

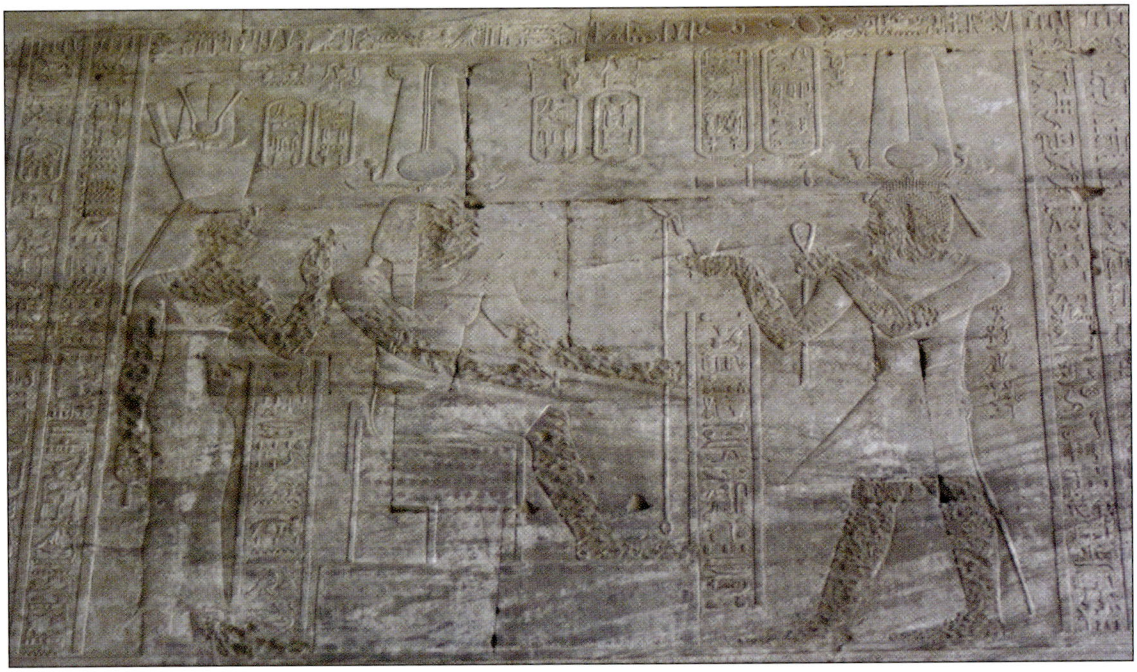

16. Edfu, outer hypostyle hall (C), eastern partition, top register. Photo: The author.

cut marks. The crown, the kilt and the offering objects are well preserved, in places with colour fragments.

Sitting on a throne in front of the ruling king, the figure of Ptolemy II wears the *nemes* wig and the *anedjti* crown with one serpent on each side of the feather plume. White and red colouring is still preserved on his clothes as well as on his throne. He holds an *ankh* and a *was* stave. Face, arms and legs are destroyed by cut marks, leaving the clothes, throne, hand-held objects and crown untouched. He is described in the text as 'The divine king (Strong is the soul of Ra, beloved of Amun)| the divine ruler (Ptolemy)|'.

Arsinoë stands behind Ptolemy II. She wears a wig, a single forehead *uraeus* and the royal diadem. She also wears her traditional crown, the crown of Arsinoë. She is dressed in the traditional sheat dress and is decorated with a necklace. She holds an *ankh* in her resting hand while holding the other hand in a protective manner. The text describes the figure as 'Royal mother (Arsinoë)| the sister-wife of (Ptolemy)|.' The text above them describes the couple as '*theoi Adelphoi*, Lords of the house of Hathor'.

Remarks: The ruling king is depicted as the tallest figure of the scene.

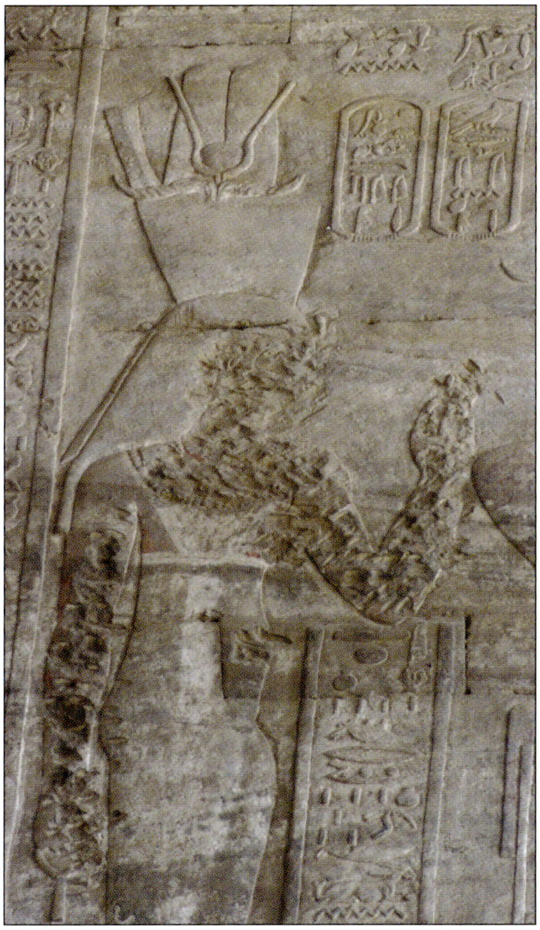

16. Edfu, outer hypostyle hall (C), eastern partition, top register. Photos: The author.

17. Edfu, offering hall (outer vestibule, R), northern partition, middle register (3rd from below)

Raised relief

Sandstone

Date: Ptolemy IV Philopator

Published: *PM* VI, 141 (157 though the figures are not described); *Edfou* I, 479f., taf. 35a; Quaegebeur 1971a, 214, no. 34; Quaegebeur 1978, 252f. n. 42; Winter 1978, 149; Quaegebeur 1998, 90, no. 19; SERAT 901707

Crown of the scene: AC 11

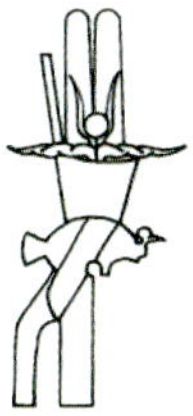

Hand-held objects: *Ankh*

State of preservation: The figure is, in general, preserved, including colours on the dress, though with damage caused by cut marks. The crown, the wig and the cap are well preserved, with damage caused only by cut marks. The back part of the wig still shows details of the corkscrews. The face, necklace, arms and feet have been damaged by cut marks. The dress is well preserved with fragments of colour, including the patterns of the dress. The colours include red, blue and white. The pattern is preserved on the lower part of the dress, forming a blue cross net pattern with a red background. The *ankh* has been damaged and is

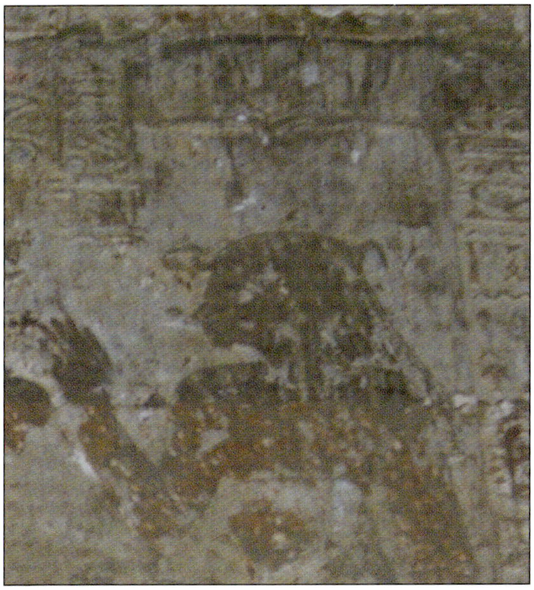

17. Edfu, offering hall (outer vestibule, R), northern partition, middle register (3rd from below). Photos: The author.

visible only through its outlines. The hieroglyphic text is well preserved but the few signs above the cartouche are not fully visible except for the *ntr* sign.

Iconographical description: Three main figures are depicted in this scene.

The king, standing at the left side, wears the double crown, with a single forehead *uraeus* and the royal diadem. His face is completely preserved, with the colours of the eye still visible. He wears the traditional kilt and is decorated with the bull's tail. The king makes an incense offering and in his other hand he holds a libation jar out of which he pours liquid onto the offering table in front of him. He is described in the text as Ptolemy IV Philopator. Behind his back it is written 'may he live in serenity as the Lord of abundance forever like Ra'. The figure of the king is well preserved in general, including the facial features, which are preserved in clear relief detail. Only the king's legs and feet have been damaged by cut marks; otherwise the figure is preserved with only minor damage resulting from natural processes.

In front of the king is the figure of Ptolemy II seated on a throne. He wears the Osirian *atef* crown resting on the ram horns. He is dressed in the traditional kilt. He holds an *ankh* and a *was* stave in his hands. He is described in the hieroglyphic text as Ptolemy II. The body and face have been badly damaged by cut marks, leaving no traces of the outlines. The crown is well preserved including some colour fragments showing red, blue and white traces. Fragments of the same colours are also preserved on some areas of the main body.

Arsinoë stands at the very right. She wears a tripartite wig, a vulture cap and the crown of Arsinoë. She is dressed in the traditional sheat dress and wears a necklace. She holds an *ankh* in her resting hand while holding her other hand in a protective manner. The text describes the female figure as 'Divine mother (Arsinoë)| the divine Philadelphos'.

The royal couple is described in the text above their head as 'the *theoi Adelphoi*, the Lords of Edfu (Mesen)'.

Remarks: Arsinoë is the tallest figure and her cartouche is placed slightly above the other cartouches of the scene.

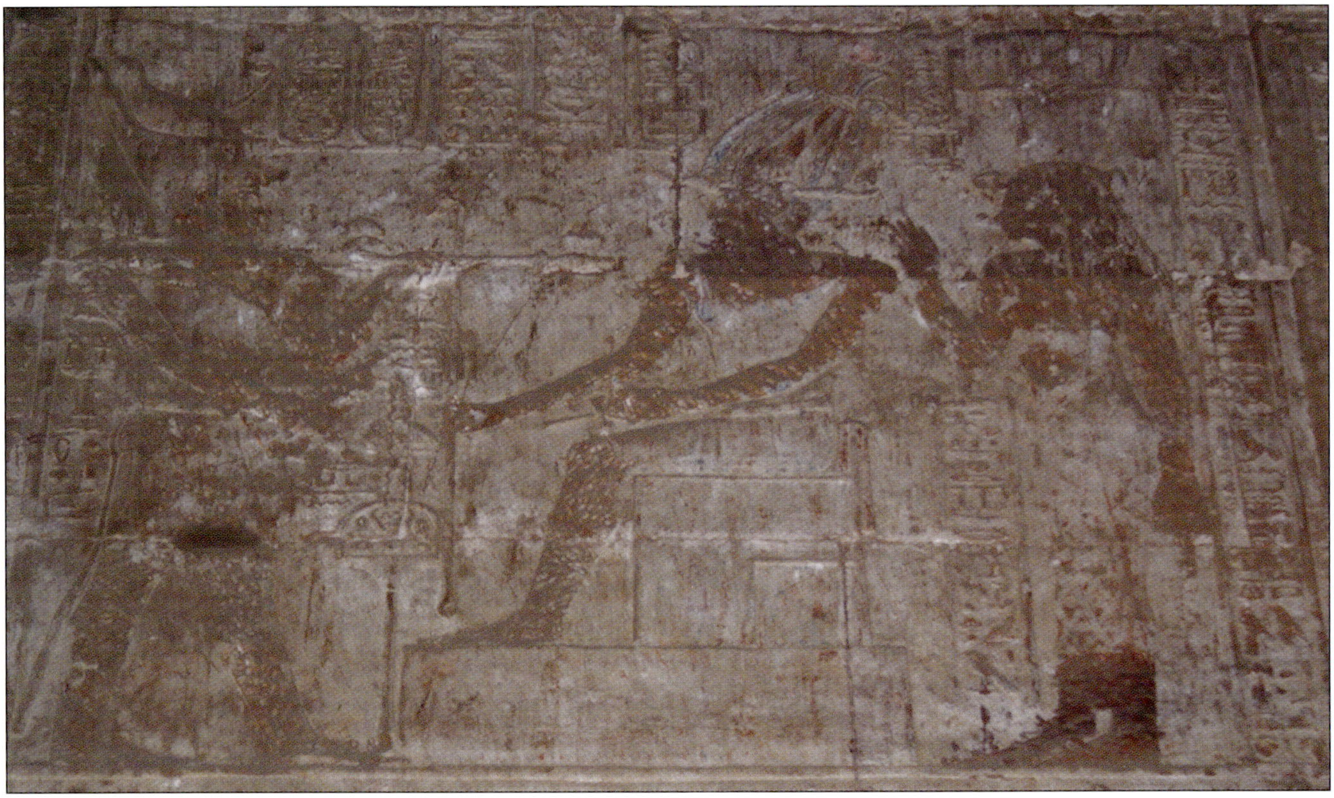

17. Edfu, offering hall (outer vestibule, R), northern partition, middle register (3rd from below). Photos: The author.

18. Edfu, stairway chamber, northern partition, lower register

Raised relief

Sandstone

Date: Ptolemy IV Philopator

Published: *PM* VI, 142 (165); *Edfou* I, 526f., Taf. 36a; Winter 1978, 152; Quaegebeur 1971a, 214, no. 33; Quaegebeur 1978, 252f., n. 42; Quaegebeur 1998, 90, no. 20; SERAT 901731

Crown of the scene: AC 12

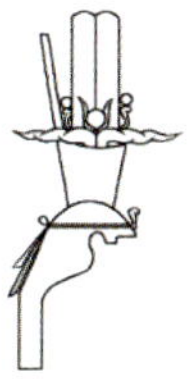

Hand-held attributes: *Ankh* and a papyrus sceptre

State of preservation: In general, the figure is very well preserved with traces of colour and pattern. The crown is divided into three fragments by the joint of the stone blocks. Another joint has split the face into two fragments. Yet another two joints split the body in three parts just under the necklace and by the knees. The hieroglyphic text is well preserved.

Iconographical description: Ten figures are depicted in this scene.

The king, standing in the right hand corner, wears the red crown, the Osirian *atef* crown, the ram horns, a solar disc and two *uraei* wearing the solar discs on their head. He also has the royal diadem and a single forehead *uraeus* and is depicted with the pharaonic beard. Behind his head is a small *s3* sign depicted for protection and further down there is a text saying 'may he live in serenity as the Lord of abundance forever like Ra'. He wears the traditional kilt and is decorated with the bull's tail. In his hands, the king holds a *sekhem* sceptre and a *sqer* mace. The figure of the king is well preserved, including the minor relief details. He is described in the text as Ptolemy IV Philopator. The king consecrates offerings to the deities and his ancestors. This table of offering includes birds, vessels etc.

In front of the king stands the figure of Horus. He wears the double crown. He holds an *ankh* and a *was* stave in his hands. He wears the traditional kilt and the bull's tail. He is described as 'Horus of Edfu, the Great God, Lord of Heaven, he who dwells in the temple' etc. The figure is well preserved, including all the minor relief details.

Behind him stands the female figure of Hathor, wearing a tripartite wig and a vulture cap upon which has been placed a small modus, large and high cow horns and the solar disc. She holds an *ankh* and a papyrus sceptre in her hands. Traces of blue colouring are still preserved on the necklace that she wears. The figure of Hathor also wears arm bracelets on the upper arms as well as normal bracelets. Some black colouring is preserved on the wig. In her face the colour is well preserved, showing the details of the eye. Only minor fragments of colour are preserved on her dress. She is described in the text as 'Hathor the Great Lady of Dendera, she who dwells in Edfu' etc.

Behind Hathor stands Harsomtus, who wears the double crown, the prince lock and a single forehead *uraeus*. He holds an *ankh* and the *was* stave. He is dressed in the traditional kilt and is decorated with the bull's tail. The figure is well preserved, including the minor relief details. He is described in the text as the 'Harsomtus, the divine son of Hathor'.

Behind this group of traditional deities stand the Ptolemaic dynastic ancestors with the latest couple (*i.e.*, Ptolemy III and Berenice II) closest to the ruling couple. Ptolemy III

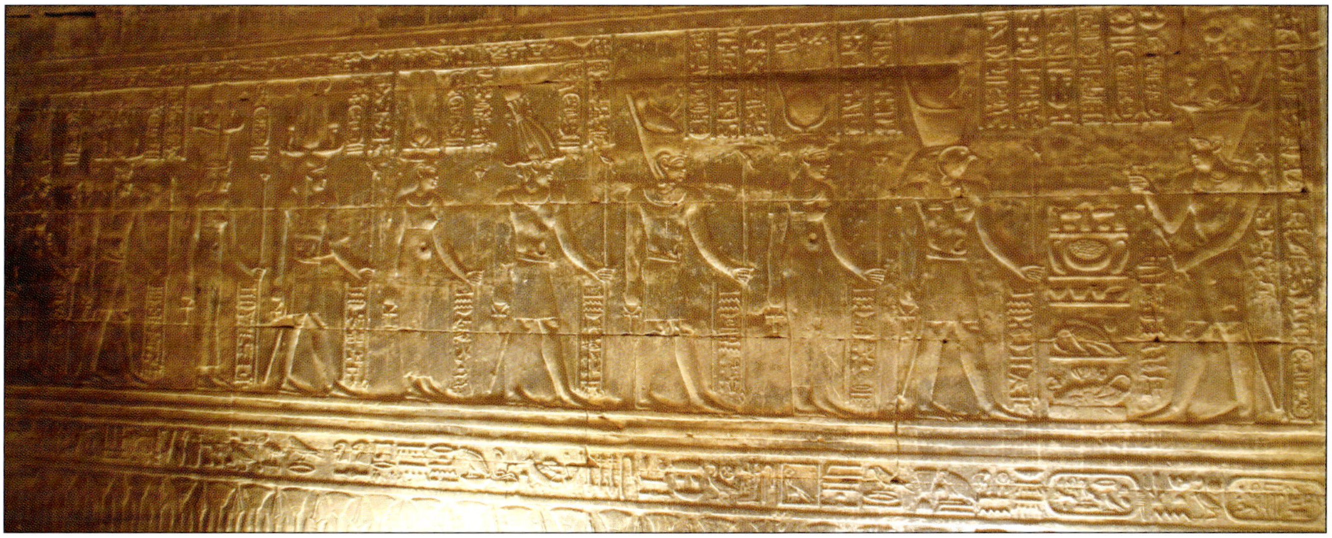

18. Edfu, stairway chamber, northern partition, lower register. Photo: The author.

wears the Osirian *atef* crown with the ram horns and the solar disc. He is depicted with the pharaonic beard. He holds an *ankh* and a *was* stave in his hands. Traces of colour are preserved on his kilt and crown. He also wears a single lined necklace, the traditional kilt and the bull's tail. He is described in the text as Ptolemy. The figure is in a good state of preservation.

Behind Ptolemy III stands Berenice II, who wears a wig, the royal diadem and a single forehead *uraeus*. The crown is the traditional female crown resting upon a low modus. Berenice II wears a single lined necklace. In her hands she holds an *ankh* and a papyrus sceptre. She is described in the text as Berenice. The figure is well preserved including the minor relief details, though no colours are preserved.

Behind Berenice II is the figure of Ptolemy II. He wears the *nemes* wig with a single forehead *uraeus*, above which is placed the *anedjti* crown with two serpents wearing the solar disc on their heads. He holds an *ankh* and a *was* stave in his hands. He is dressed in the traditional kilt and decorated with the bull's tail. He is described in the text as Ptolemy. The figure is well preserved, though no colours remain.

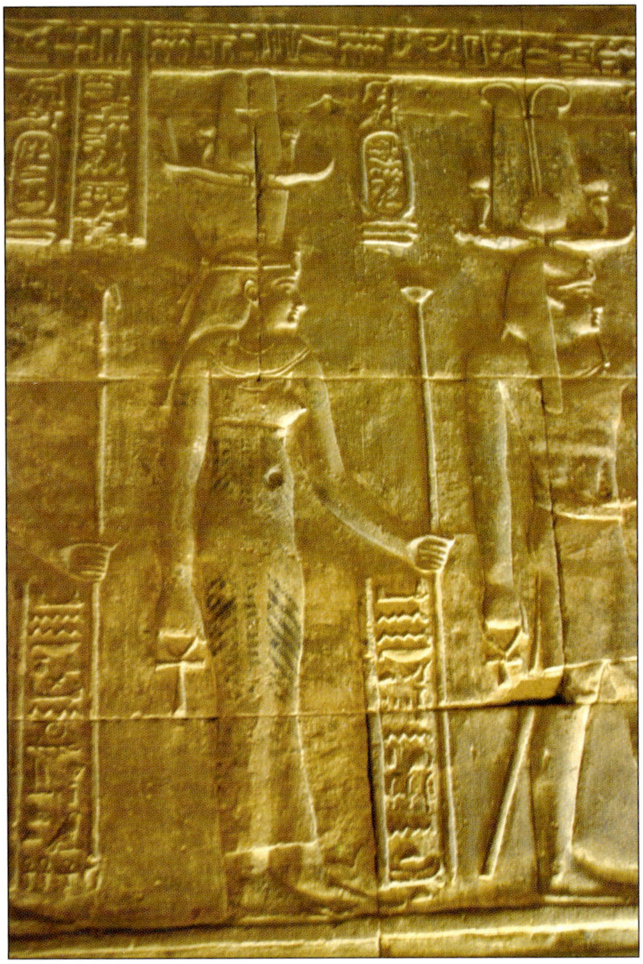

18. Edfu, stairway chamber, northern partition, lower register. Photo: The author.

Behind Ptolemy II stands Arsinoë. She wears a wig, a single forehead *uraeus* and the royal diadem. She wears her traditional crown of Arsinoë incorporating two *uraei* wearing a solar disc on their heads. She is dressed in an elaborated sheat dress and is decorated with a necklace, arm bracelets on both upper arms and a bracelet on the hand holding the *ankh*. She holds an *ankh* and a papyrus sceptre. The text describes the figure as 'Divine mother (Arsinoë)|'. Together they are described in the text above them as the '*theoi Adelphoi*, the Lords of the house of Ra'.

Behind Arsinoë II stands the figure of Ptolemy I wearing the *nemes* wig and a single forehead *uraeus*, above which is placed the Osirian *atef* crown, the ram horns, the solar disc and the two *uraei* with solar discs placed on their heads. He holds an *ankh* and a *was* stave in his hands. He is dressed in the traditional kilt and decorated with the bull's tail. He is described in the text as Ptolemy. The figure is well preserved.

The last figure of this dynastic scene is the female figure of Berenice I. She wears a wig, the royal diadem and a single forehead *uraeus*. The crown is composed of a low modus on which rests the traditional female crown. Berenice I wears a single lined necklace. She holds an *ankh* and a papyrus sceptre in her hands. She is described in the text as Berenice. The figure is well preserved, including the minor relief details.

According to the text, the first couple standing behind the divine trinity is the '*theoi Euergetis*, Lords of Mesen', Ptolemy III and Berenice II. After this couple stands '*theoi Adelphoi*, Lords of the house of Ra', Ptolemy II and Arsinoë II. The last couple in line is Ptolemy I and Berenice I, described as the '*theoi Soteres*'.

Remarks: One of the most obvious things is Queen Arsinoë III's absence in the scene. The dynastic ancestors are mainly equal in size as the tallest figures of the scene.

19. Edfu, inner sanctuary (A), eastern partition, middle register

Raised relief
Sandstone
Date: Ptolemy IV Philopator
Published: *PM* VI, 146 (216–17); *Edfou* I, 46, taf. 12, 227; Winter 1978, 149; Quaegebeur 1971a, 214, no. 36; Quaegebeur 1978, 252f., n. 42; Cauville 1987, 1, fig. 1 (p. 2); Quaegebeur 1998, 90, no. 17; SERAT 900045
Crown of the scene: AC 5

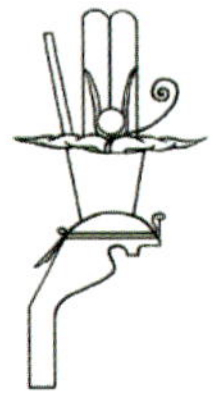

Hand-held objects: *Ankh*
State of preservation: The crown is in a good state of preservation. The wig and parts of the face have been partly preserved while the rest of the body has been badly damaged by cut marks. Some details are still visible in the face, such as the ear. The arm that is raised in a blessing manner has been left untouched by cut marks, as have the feet. The hieroglyphic text is well preserved, without any major damage.
Iconographical description: Three main figures are depicted in this scene.

King Ptolemy, who stands at the very right, wears the double crown, a single forehead *uraeus* and the royal diadem. Behind his head is a small *s3* sign depicted for protection. Further down, behind his back, is a hieroglyphic text saying 'may he live in serenity as the Lord of abundance forever like Ra'. The king wears the traditional kilt and the bull's tail. The upper part of the figure has been badly damaged by cut marks, though the abdomen and kilt are preserved mainly untouched. The cartouches describe him as Ptolemy IV Philopator. He presents the looped textile band and a cup of ointment.

In front of the ruling king is the figure of Ptolemy II seated on a throne. He wears the *anedjti* crown. He also wears the *nemes* wig, the royal diadem and a single forehead *uraeus*. He holds an *ankh* and a *was* stave in his hands. He is dressed in the traditional kilt and is decorated with the bull's tail. He is described as 'Divine royal father (Ptolemy)|' in the text. The figure has been badly damaged by cut marks, leaving only the kilt, the crown, the throne and the hand-held objects untouched.

Arsinoë stands behind Ptolemy II. She wears a tripartite wig, a single forehead *uraeus*, the royal diadem and the crown of Arsinoë. She is dressed in the traditional sheat dress and is decorated with a necklace. She holds an *ankh* in her resting hand while holding her other hand in a blessing manner. The cartouche describes the figure as 'Divine mother (Arsinoë)|'.

In the personal text of Ptolemy the couple is described as '*theoi Adelphoi*, dwellers in the Temple of Horus'.
Remarks: Arsinoë is the tallest figure of the scene.

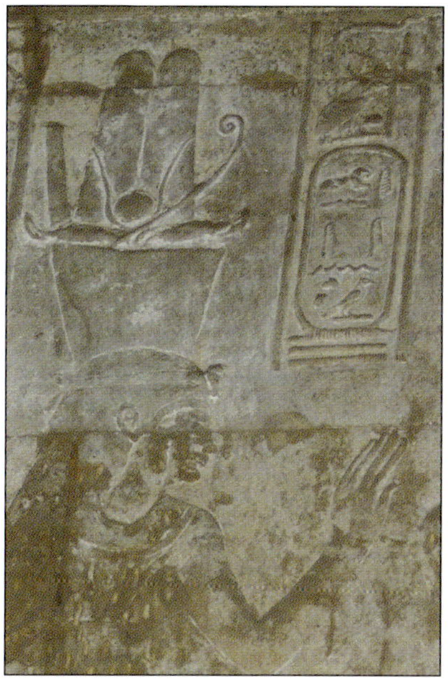

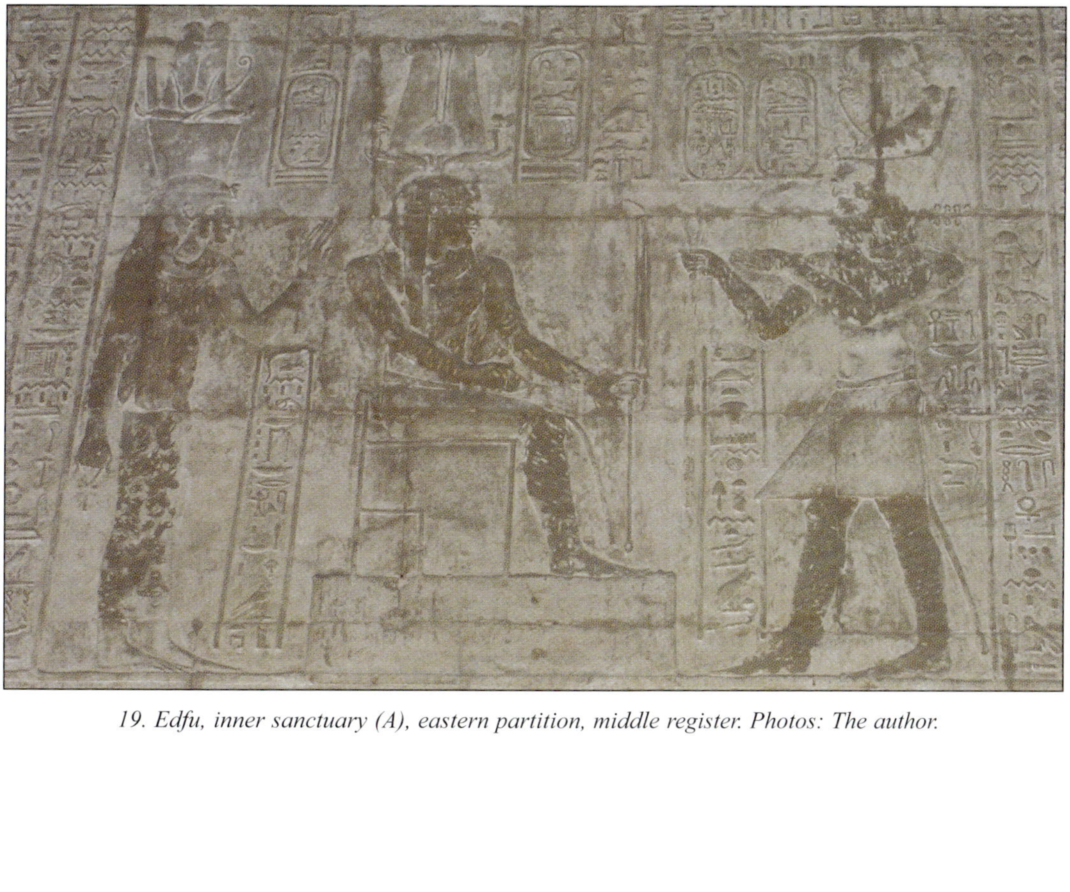

19. Edfu, inner sanctuary (A), eastern partition, middle register. Photos: The author.

20. Edfu, mysterious corridor, eastern partition, top register

Raised relief

Sandstone

Date: Ptolemy IV Philopator

Published: *PM* VI, 148 (235); *Edfou* I, 112 (Arsinoë's name is wrongly written as Khonsu but corrected in the new publication); Quaegebeur 1971a, 214, no. 37; Winter 1978, 149; Quaegebeur 1978, 252; Cauville 1987, 17, fig. 6 (p. 15); Quaegebeur 1998, 90, no. 18; SERAT 900402

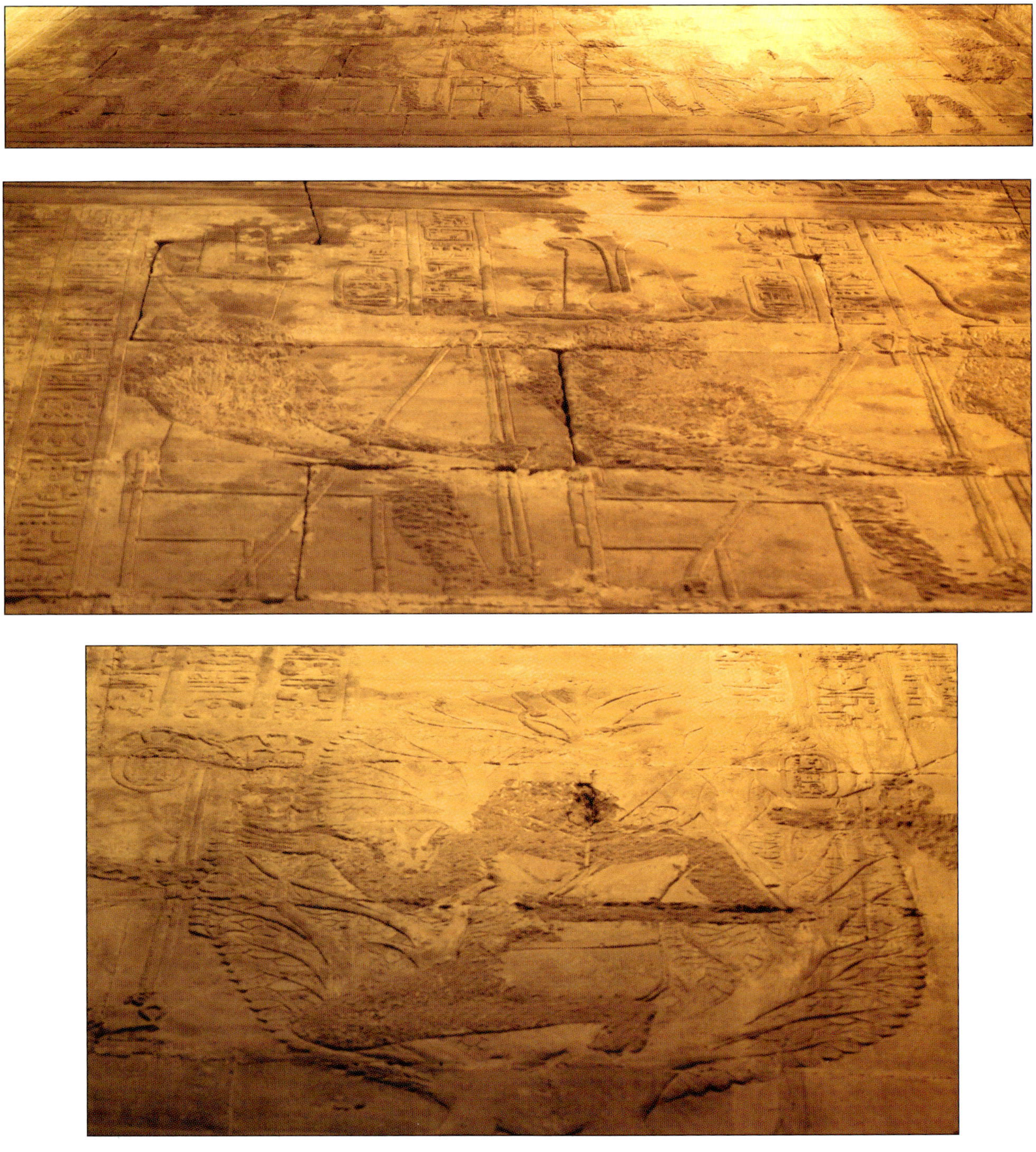

20. Edfu, mysterious corridor, eastern partition, top register. Photos: The author.

Crown of the scene: AC 12

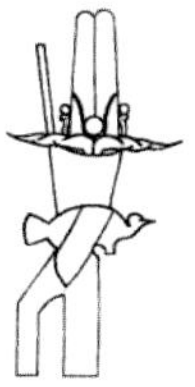

Hand-held objects: *Ankh*-giving notched palm branch
State of preservation: The figure has been badly damaged in the 'skin' area by cut marks. No facial features are preserved. The crown, the back part of the dress, the hand-held objects and the throne have all been left untouched.
Iconographical description: Six figures are depicted in this scene.

On the far left Arsinoë is depicted wearing a tripartite wig, a vulture cap and the crown of Arsinoë with two *uraei* rising up on each side of the plume, wearing solar discs on their heads. She is dressed in a traditional sheat dress and is depicted seated on a throne. She holds three notched palm branches with *ankh*s. She is described in the text as the 'Divine mother, the eye of Horus (Arsinoë)|'. The second register of text connects Arsinoë directly with Hathor.

In front of Arsinoë is the figure of Ptolemy II seated on a throne. He wears a *khat* cap and a single forehead *uraeus* above which is placed the *anedjti* crown with two *uraei* rising up wearing solar discs on their heads. He is seated on a throne. He holds the same objects in his hands as Arsinoë: notched palm branches with *ankh*s. The figure has been badly damaged by cut marks centred on the uncovered areas of the body. The crown and the throne have been left untouched. He is described in the text as Ptolemy II.

Hathor is seated on a throne in front of Ptolemy II. She wears a tripartite wig and a vulture cap above which is placed a low modus and the traditional Hathorian crown. She holds the same objects in her hands as the two above-mentioned figures. The figure has been badly damaged by cut marks, though the crown and the throne have been left untouched and are still preserved with a pattern. She is described in the text as 'Hathor, the Great Lady of Dendera, Eye of Ra' etc.

In front of Hathor is the figure of Horus seated on a throne. He wears the double crown and holds notched palm branches incorporating the Sed festival-sign as well as the egg with the cartouche of the king. The figure has been badly damaged by cut marks, leaving only the crown and the throne untouched. The figure is described as 'Horus of Edfu, the Great God, Lord of Heaven'.

In front of the figure of Horus is the king crouching down inside the tree of rejuvenation, receiving the Sed festival-sign as well as his cartouches from the deities. He wears the double crown. The cartouches name him as Ptolemy IV.

Behind the figure of Ptolemy IV stands the figure of Khonsu-Thoth. He is depicted with a falcon head and he wears the moon disc and crescent together with a single *uraeus* centred in the disc. He is dressed in the traditional kilt and the bull's tail. He holds the writing tools in his hands. The figure has been badly damaged by cut marks, though leaving the crown, kilt and hand-held objects untouched. He is described in the text as 'Khonsu-Thoth, the great god who dwells in the city of Edfu'.

Behind the figure of Khonsu-Thoth stands the figure of Seshat. She wears a wig above which is placed her own sign (*sš3t*) as a crown. She holds the year-sign in her hands. The figure, excluding the crown, the sheat dress and the hand-held objects, has been badly damaged by cut marks. She is described in the text as 'Seshat, the great Lady of the scribes'.
Remarks: Arsinoë is depicted as the tallest figure of the scene.

21. Edfu, corridor, western partition, top register

Sunken relief
Sandstone
Date: Ptolemy VIII Euergetes II
Published: *PM* VI, 156 (294); Champollion 1844, Taf. Cxxxix ter 4; *Edfou* IV, 148f., Taf. 87; Quaegebeur 1971a, 214, no. 38; Winter 1978, 150f.; Quaegebeur 1978, 252f., n. 42; Cauville 1987, 142f. fig. 44; Quaegebeur 1998, 91, no. 22; SERAT 900638
Crown of the scene: TFC

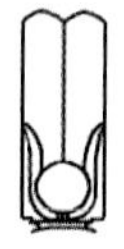

Hand-held objects: *Ankh*
State of preservation: The figure has been badly damaged by cut marks which are focused on the uncovered areas of the body. The crown has been left untouched.

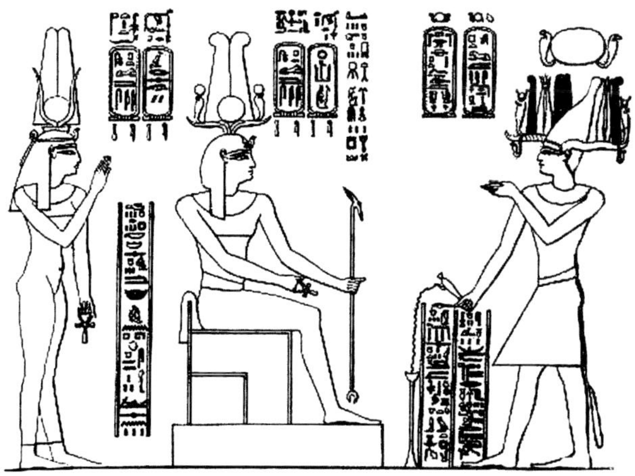

21. Edfu, corridor, western partition, top register Drawing: Champollion 1844. cxxxix ter No. 4.

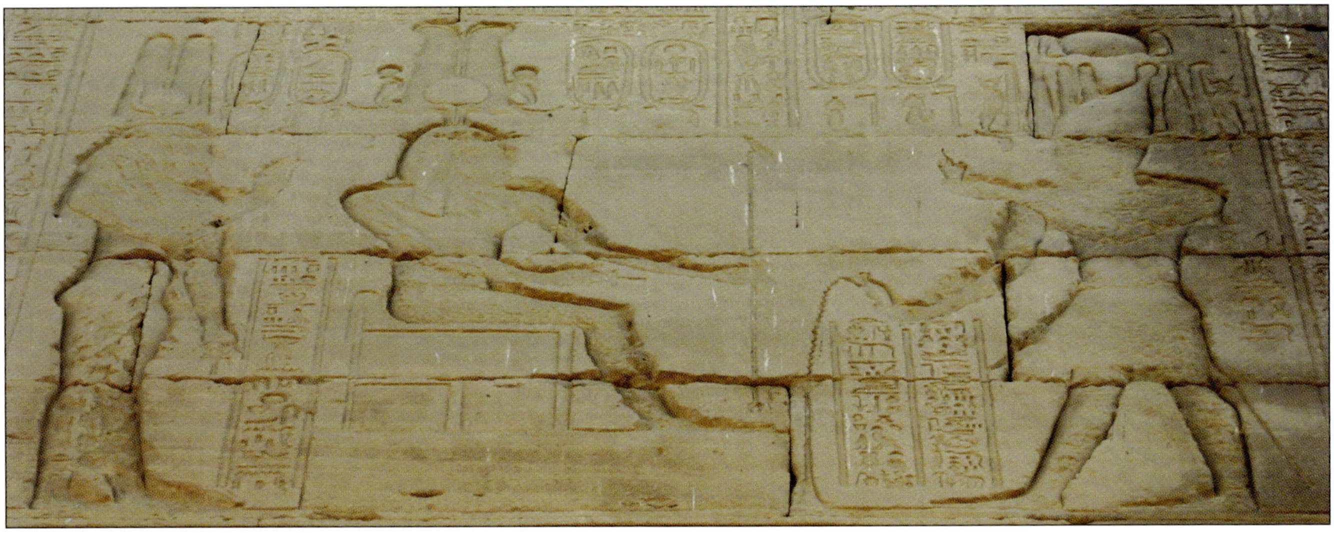

21. Edfu, corridor, western partition, top register. Photo: The author.

Iconographical description: Three figures are depicted in this scene.

The king, standing at the very right, wears the white crown with ram horns coming out of it with two additional *atef* feathers, one on each side, two *atef* 'tops', the double feather plume and two pendant *uraei*. Above his head is a solar disc depicted with two *uraei*. The king is dressed in the traditional kilt and the bull's tail. He presents a cup of incense and performs a libation. He is described as Ptolemy VIII Euergetes II. The figure has been badly damaged by cut marks, though leaving the crown untouched.

Ptolemy II is seated on a throne in front of the king. He wears the *anedjti* crown, the *nemes* wig and a single forehead *uraeus*. He is dressed in the traditional kilt and holds an *ankh* and a *was* stave in his hands. He is described as '(Ptolemy)| (Strong is the soul of Ra, beloved of Amun)|'. The figure has been badly damaged by cut marks, leaving only the crown and the throne untouched.

Behind the figure of Ptolemy II stands Arsinoë. She wears a tripartite wig, a single forehead *uraeus*, the royal diadem and the traditional female crown resting on a low modus. She is decorated with a necklace and is dressed in the sheat dress. She holds an *ankh* in her resting hand while holding the other hand in a protective manner. She is described in the text as 'The mistress of her brother (?) (Arsinoë)| (Ptolemy's)| (his) divine sister'. The couple are together described as the '*theoi Adelphoi*, who dwells in Edfu (Mesen)'.

Remarks: Arsinoë is depicted as the tallest figure of the scene.

22. Edfu, Inner hypostyle hall, western partition, top register

Raised relief
Sandstone
Date: Ptolemy IV Philopator
Published: *PM* IV, 136 (113f. incorrectly placed as no. 110); *Edfou* II, 55, I pl. XL; Quaegebeur 1971a, 214 no. 33; Quaegebeur 1978, 252f. with n. 42; Winter 1978, 149; Cauville 1987, 115, fig. 37 (p. 118); SERAT 901850
Crown of the scene: AC 11

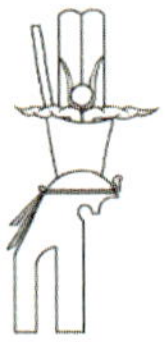

Hand-held objects: *Ankh*
State of preservation: The figure is in a bad state of preservation owing to cut marks, which damage all the uncovered areas of the body and totally erase the facial features. The crown is well preserved.
Iconographical description: Three figures are depicted in this scene.

The king, standing at the left side, wears the double crown, the royal diadem and the pharaonic beard. He is dressed in the traditional kilt and bull's tail and holds a mace and a papyrus stem in his hands. The figure has been badly damaged by cut marks, though some red paint is left on the feet. He is identified in the text as Ptolemy IV Philopator.

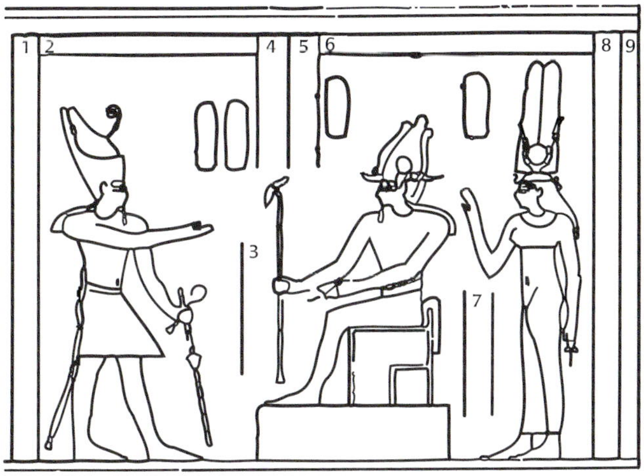

Drawing: Chassinat Edfou, *II pl. XL (The crown is incorrectly drawn – Compare below).*

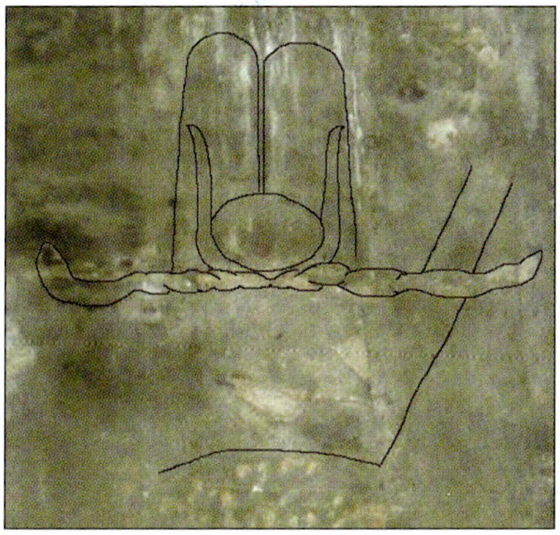

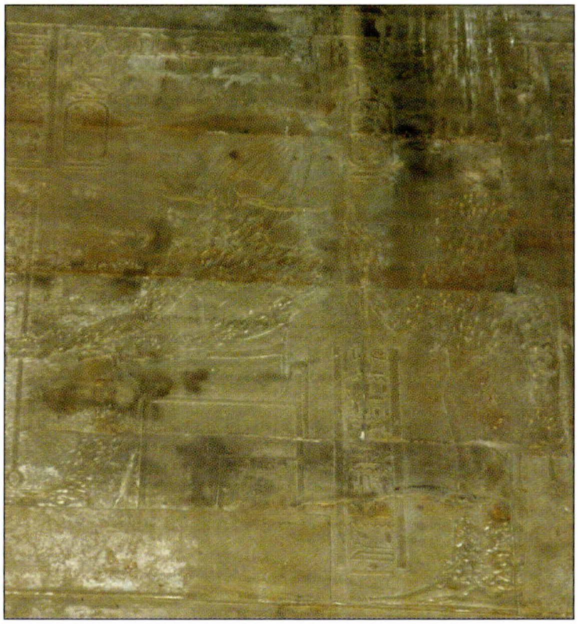

22. Edfu, Inner hypostyle hall, western partition, top register. Photos and editing: The author.

In front of the king is Ptolemy II seated on a throne. He wears the *atef* crown with ram horns, the royal diadem and the pharaonic beard. He is dressed in the traditional kilt and holds an *ankh* and a *was* stave in his hands. He is described in the text as Ptolemy II.

Behind the figure of Ptolemy II stands Arsinoë. She wears a tripartite wig, a single forehead *uraeus* and the crown of Arsinoë. She holds an *ankh* in her resting hand while holding the other hand in a protective position. She is described in the text as the 'Divine mother (Arsinoë)|'. Together they are identified as '*Theoi Adelphoi* who dwells in Edfu (Mesen)'.

Remarks: This scene (room) is heavily damaged by soot and the lightning is poor, resulting in very poor photographs. The previously published drawing of this scene illustrates the crowns of both Arsinoë and Ptolemy II wrongly. The crown of Arsinoë is not the traditional female crown but the crown of Arsinoë and the crown of Ptolemy II is far more elaborate than the first drawing shows. Arsinoë is depicted as the tallest figure.

23. Karnak, Khonsu temple, pylon, northern partition (peristyle court), lintel scene

Raised relief

Sandstone

Date: Ptolemy II Philadelphos

Published: *PM* II, 229 (12e–f); Schwaller de Lubicz 1998, II, pl. 254; Quaegebeur 1971a, 213, no. 27; Quaegebeur 1998, 91 no. 25; *Khonsu II*, 5 with pl. 116a; Quaegebeur 1983, 133 n. 22; SERAT 402261

Crown of the scene: AC 13

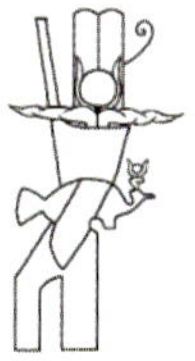

Hand-held objects: *Ankh* and a papyrus sceptre

State of preservation: The crown is in a good state of preservation. The upper part of the body from the belly up to the crown has been badly damaged by cut marks, leaving no outlines or details of the figure or face. The middle section of the body is preserved without any major damage. The feet have been badly damaged by cut marks. The arms and hands have been left untouched. The text is in a good state of preservation.

Iconographical description: King Ptolemy presents offerings to two deities. The king, standing at the very right, wears the *khepresh* crown and a single forehead *uraeus*. A small *s3* sign is depicted behind his head. He wears an elaborated kilt, with elongated fabric stretching down to his feet, and a bull's tail. He holds a flail and an oar. The upper part of the body, from

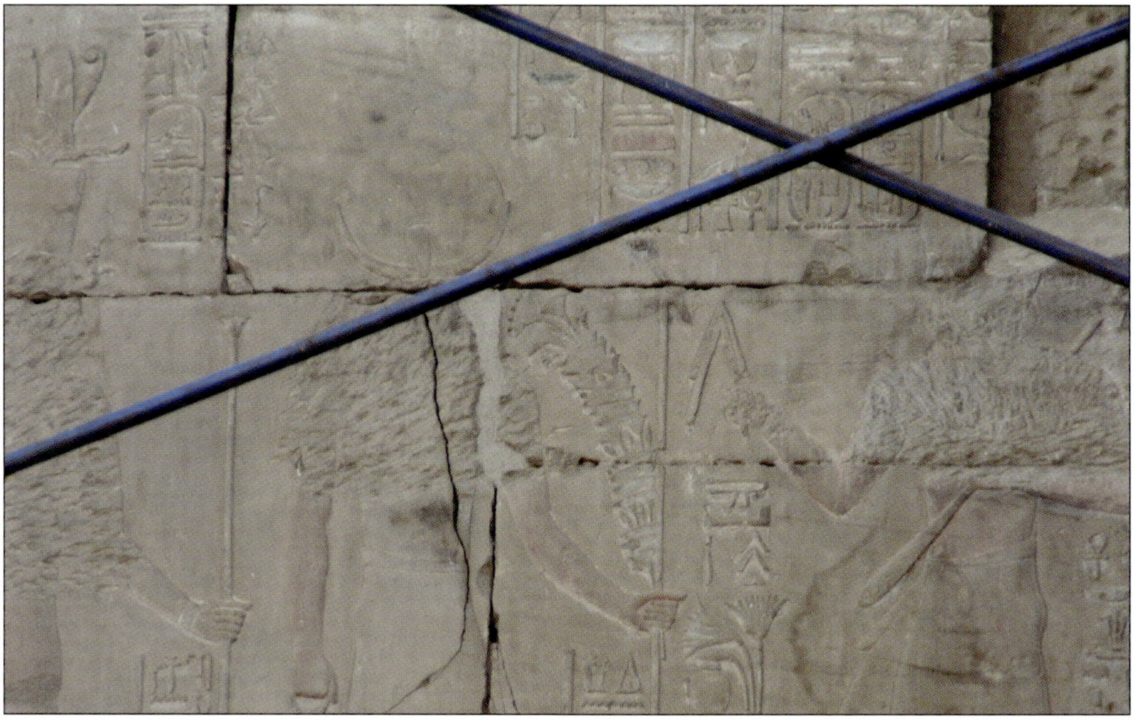

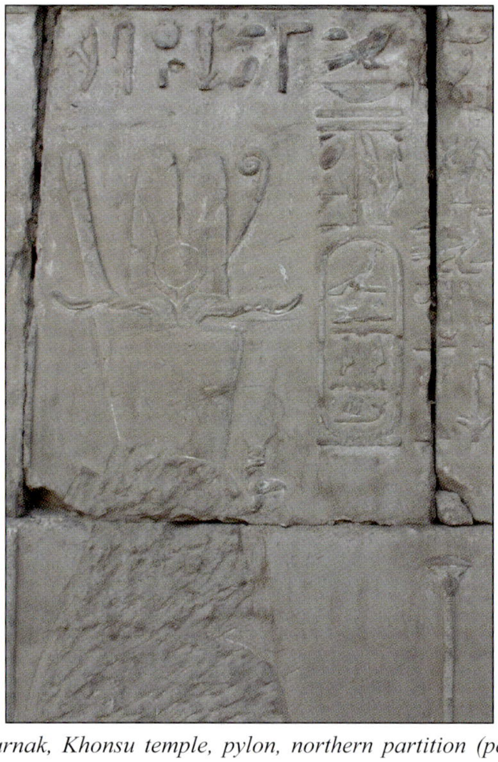

23. Karnak, Khonsu temple, pylon, northern partition (peristyle court), lintel scene. Photos: The author.

the breast and including the upper part of the arms, has been badly damaged by cut marks, not even leaving the outlines of the face. The legs, from the knees down to the feet, are also badly damaged by cut marks. The figure is preserved, with traces of red and blue colouring. He is identified in the text as the 'King of Upper and Lower Egypt, Lord of the Two Lands (Strong is the soul of Ra, beloved of Amun)| Son of Ra, Lord of the crowns (Ptolemy)|'. In front of the king is an altar/censer stand with a vessel and lotus plants.

The male figure standing in front of Ptolemy wears a crown of the crescent and the moon disc and a single centred *uraeus*. His head, which is erased by cut marks, was most probably in the shape of the falcon, based on a thin part of the back wig. He is dressed in the traditional kilt and the bull's tail. He holds a *was* stave and a branch of lotus flowers in one hand while holding an *ankh* in the other. The figure has been badly damaged by cut marks, though the crown, clothing and hand-held objects are left untouched. The figure is preserved with traces of red colouring, mainly on the uncovered areas of the body. He is described by the hieroglyphic text as 'Khonsu-Ra the Lord of Thebes'.

Behind Khonsu-Ra stands Arsinoë. She wears a tripartite wig and a vulture cap with an additional serpent's head wearing cow horns and a solar disc. Her crown is her individual crown of Arsinoë. She is dressed in the traditional sheat dress and is decorated with bracelets. She holds an *ankh* and a papyrus sceptre in her hands. The hieroglyphic text describes her as 'Daughter of the King of Upper Egypt, sister of the King of Upper Egypt, King's great wife, Lady of the Two Lands, Daughter of Amun, Arsinoë, the divine Philadelphos'. The name Arsinoë is ended in a male suffix (*-f*).

Remarks: All the crowns as well as the hand-held objects are untouched by cut marks. Traces of white paint are spread all over the scene. Arsinoë is depicted as the tallest figure of the scene.

24. Karnak, gate of Euergetes, inner side of the eastern partition, second register from below

Sunken relief
Sandstone
Date: Ptolemy III Euergetes
Published: *PM* II, 226 (3f); Quaegebeur 1971b, 213, no. 28; Quaegebeur 1978, 525, 257, ill. J.; Winter 1978, 149; Schwaller de Lubicz 1998, pl. 276; Quaegebeur 1988, 48, 50 fig. 21; *Denkmäler* III, 55; Quaegebeur 1998, 91 no. 26; SERAT 410041
Crown of the scene: AC 13

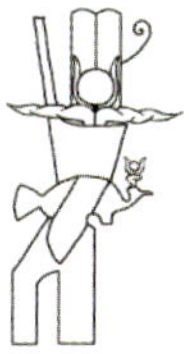

Hand-held objects: *Ankh* and a papyrus sceptre
State of preservation: The crown is in a good state of preservation, though with a small fracture due to the joint of the stone blocks. The face has been totally erased by cut marks but the wig and vulture cap have been left untouched. The main body has been left untouched by cut marks with

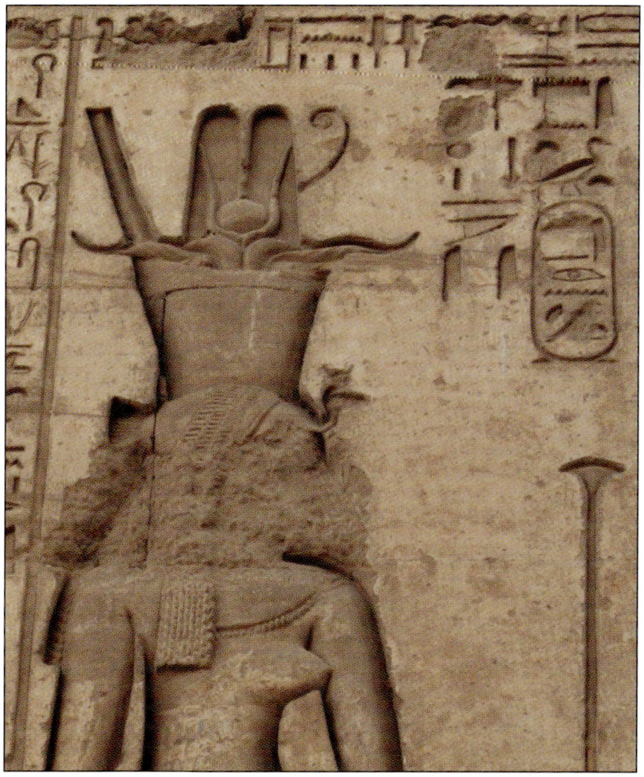

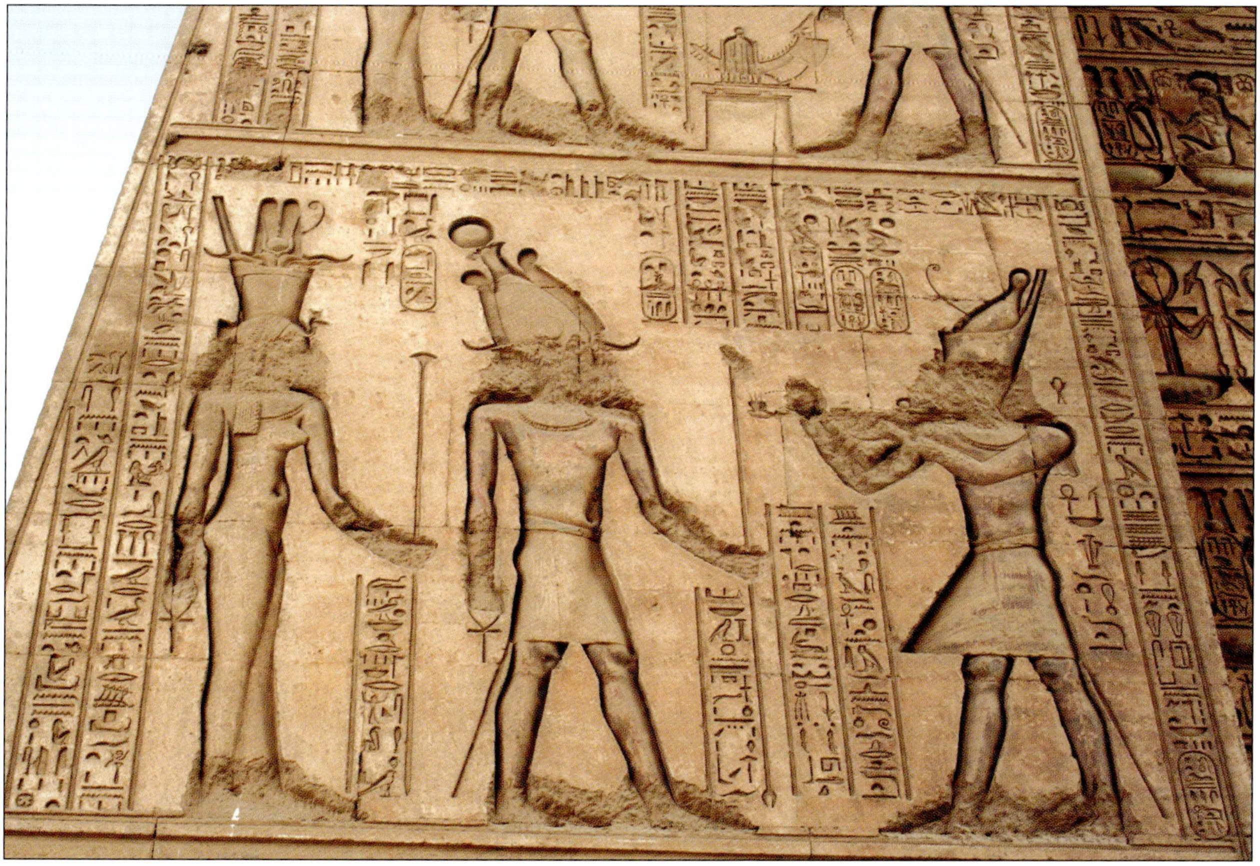

24. Karnak, gate of Euergetes, inner side of the eastern partition, second register from below. Photos: The author.

the exception of the lower parts of the arms and the feet, which have been badly damaged. The top part of the dress of the figure is still showing traces of colour and a pattern. The colours preserved are turquoise, red and white. The lower part has no traces of colour preserved. The necklace shows one main broad row and one line of beads; no colours are preserved. No colour is preserved on the hand-held objects. The personal register of text is mainly well preserved, with only minor damage on the female *ntr* sign (*i.e.*, goddess).
Iconographical description: Three figures are depicted in this scene.

In the scene King Ptolemy (III) presents offerings to his parents, Ptolemy II and Arsinoë, as the *theoi Adelphoi*. He stands at the very right of the scene. The king wears the double crown, a single forehead *uraeus* and the royal diadem. Behind his head is a small *sꜣ* sign depicted for protection. Further down, a hieroglyphic text states 'may he live in serenity as the Lord of abundance forever like Ra'. He wears a two-rowed necklace and is dressed in the traditional kilt and the bull's tail. He presents incense. Traces of colour and pattern are still visible on his abdomen, kilt and legs. His face, hands and feet have been badly damaged by cut marks, leaving no traces of the outlines of the facial features. He is identified in the text as Ptolemy III. The text is well preserved.

The figure in front of him, the late King Ptolemy II, wears the Osirian *atef* crown with additional ram horns. He holds an *ankh* and a *was* stave. The face, the hands and the feet have been badly damaged by cut marks and, just as on the figure of Ptolemy III, no outlines or facial features are preserved. The head of the *cucupha* has been badly damaged by cut marks. He is dressed in the traditional kilt and the bull's tail. Fragmentary traces of colour are preserved in various areas of the figure, especially on the kilt. He is described as the 'Divine King (Ptolemy)|'.

Behind the king stands Arsinoë, who wears a tripartite wig and a vulture cap with an additional *uraeus* wearing cow horns and solar disc, and, above the vulture cap, the crown of Arsinoë. She is dressed in the traditional sheat dress and is decorated with a necklace. She holds an *ankh* and a papyrus sceptre in her hands. The text describes her as 'Daughter of Amun, Arsinoë, the divine Philadelphos'. Above the scene the royal couple is described as the '*theoi Adelphoi* (who dwells in) Apet – Karnak'.
Remarks: Arsinoë is the tallest figure of the scene.

25. Karnak, gate of Euergetes, southern partition, lintel scene, small board of figures above the main scene

Sunken relief
Sandstone
Date: Ptolemy III Euergetes.
Published: *PM* II, 225, 1; *Denkmäler* IV, 10; Clere 1961, taf. 17f.; Quaegebeur 1971a, 213 no. 29; Quaegebeur 1978, 242, 252 and ill. D on p. 248; Winter 1978, 152; Quaegebeur 1998, 92 no. 27
Crown of the scene: AC 6

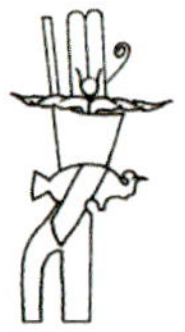

Hand-held object: Praising manner
State of preservation: The full figure has been badly damaged by cut marks with the exception of the crown.
Iconographical description: The main scene is a long board of forty-six figures, split in the middle by the solar disc. Arsinoë stands at the very left end holding her hands in a praising manner behind her brother-husband, Ptolemy II. Arsinoë wears a tripartite wig and a vulture cap, above which is placed the crown of Arsinoë. She wears the traditional sheat dress and is decorated with a necklace. Both hands are held in a praising manner. The text describes the figure as 'Arsinoë, Daughter of Amun'.

In front of Arsinoë stands Ptolemy. He wears the *atef* crown and is dressed in the traditional kilt and bull's tail. The figure has been badly damaged by cut marks. He is described as Ptolemy and above his head the text states '*theoi Adelphoi*'.

Between Ptolemy II and Ptolemy III on the opposite side there are forty-two figures depicted. The figures are placed symmetrically on each side of the solar disc. Starting from the solar disc and moving outwards are the following deities: Montu, Atum, Shu, Tefnut, Geb, Nut, Osiris, Isis, Thoth, Nephthys, Horus, Hathor, Sobek, Tenenit and Iunit. The following six (twelve in total, including both sides) male figures are all depicted equally, wearing the *nemes* wig and

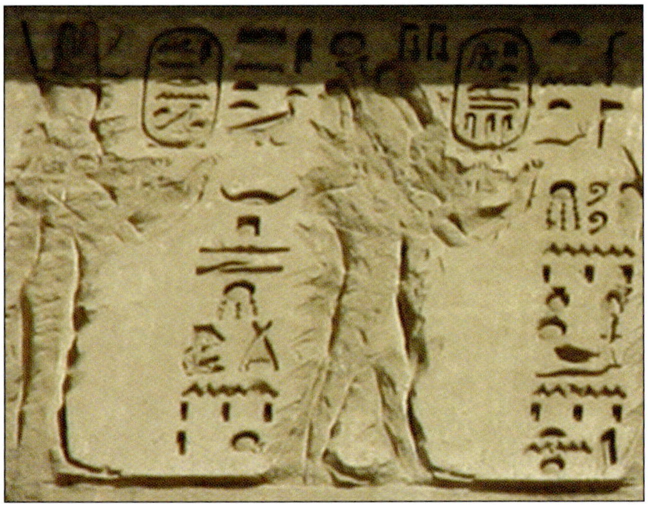

25. Karnak, gate of Euergetes, southern partition, lintel scene, small board of figures above the main scene

dressed in the traditional kilt and bull's tail. All figures hold their hands in a praising manner. Iunit, Hathor, Isis and Nut wear the traditional Hathorian crown. The other deities all wear their traditional crowns/attributes. All deities have been badly damaged by cut marks, though leaving the crowns and attributes untouched.

At the very right stands another Ptolemaic couple. The queen, standing far right, wears the traditional female crown. She wears a tripartite wig and a single forehead *uraeus* and is dressed in the traditional sheat dress. She is described in the text as 'Berenice, Divine Mother'. This figure is well preserved without any damage resulting from cut marks.

In front of Berenice stands Ptolemy. He wears the *atef* crown and is dressed in the traditional kilt and bull's tail. He is described in the text as 'Ptolemy, Divine King'. The figure has been badly damaged by cut marks.

Remarks: The right-hand Ptolemaic couple is here interpreted as the *theoi Euergetai* rather than *Soteres*. Arsinoë is depicted equal in size with the tallest figures of the scene.

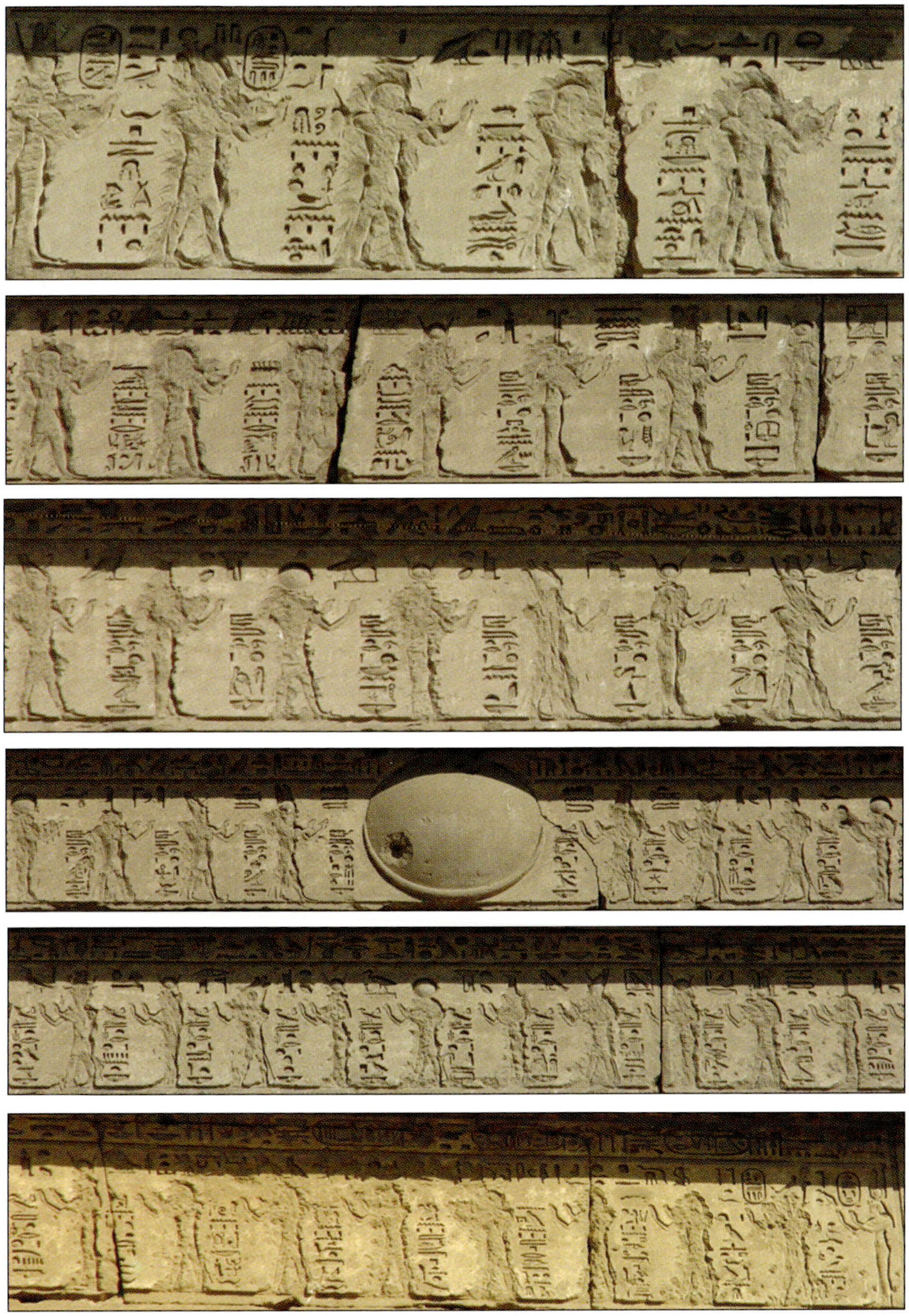

25. Karnak, gate of Euergetes, southern partition, lintel scene, small board of figures above the main scene. Photos: The author.

26. Karnak, East Gate (so called Gate of Nectanebo or Bab el-Melacha), eastern partition, lintel scene

Sunken relief
Sandstone
Date: Arsinoë's lifetime and Ptolemy II Philadelphos
Published: *PM* II, 208 (3); *Urk.* II, 106f; *LdR* IV, 240 F (text); Schwaller de Lubicz 1998, II, pl. 241–3; Quaegebeur 1971a, 213, no. 26; Troy 1986, 179; Quaegebeur 1998, 91, no. 24; *Denkmäler* IV, 8a, 8bis, text III, 38; SERAT 453001–2
Right scene
Crown of the scene: AC 13

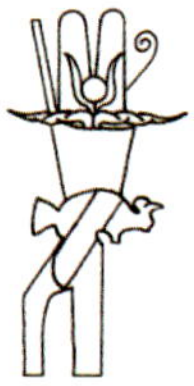

Hand-held objects: *Ankh* and a papyrus sceptre
State of preservation: The head, the shoulders and the neck have been badly damaged by cut marks, leaving only the outlines of the tripartite wig and a necklace visible. The crown is well preserved except for the fracture in the stone work due to the joint. The relief of the main body, excluding the arms, is cut or carved in the traditional manner but the arms are much shallower than the rest of the body. The hands are detailed but the arms are just chiselled out. The lowest part of the sceptre is much deeper than the top. Three deep cut marks damage the area between the thigh and the sceptre. The lower part of the hieroglyphic inscription next to the legs is much deeper than the upper part. Cut marks have also damaged the legs and feet. The personal register of text is mainly preserved, though some signs have been deliberately erased.

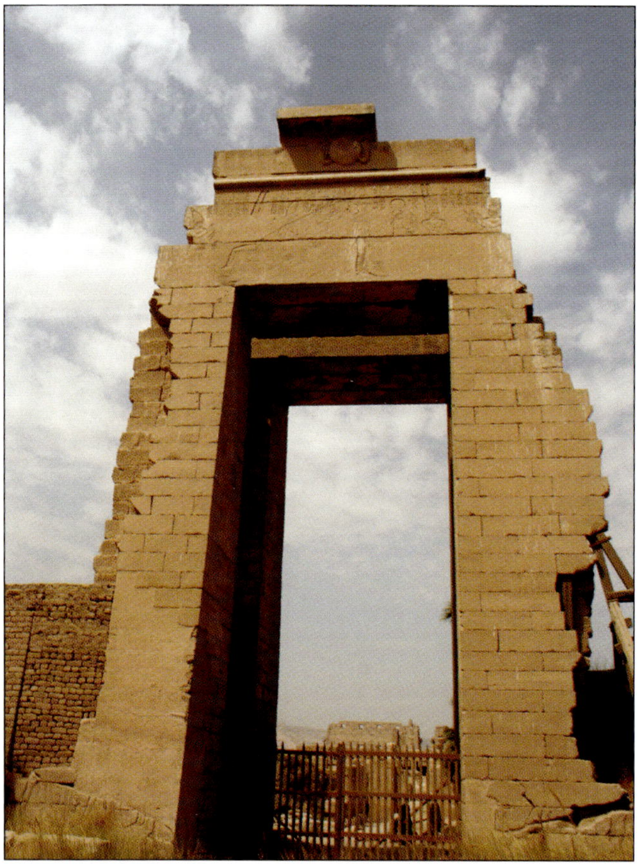

26. Karnak, East Gate (so called Gate of Nectanebo or Bab el-Melacha), eastern partition, lintel scene.

Iconographical description: In the right scene King Ptolemy (II) presents the figure of Ma'at to three deities.

The king wears the red crown, a single forehead *uraeus* and the royal diadem. He wears a single lined necklace (there may be more than one row but the state of preservation does not allow certainty here). The king presents the seated figure of Ma'at. Only the top part of the figure has been finished, leaving the figure totally without the lower part, from the abdomen downwards. The right side of the figure has been damaged because stone blocks are missing. The face has been badly damaged by cut marks, though leaving the outlines of the face, and the crown has been damaged, though because of the fracture in the stone blocks. The figure of Ma'at has been damaged by cut marks. The figure is described in the text as 'King of Upper and Lower Egypt (Strong is the soul of Ra, beloved of Amun)| Son of Ra, Lord of the Two Lands (Ptolemy)|'. Under the personal register of text another inscription says 'may he live forever like Ra'.

In front of and facing the king is the figure of Amun-Ra depicted wearing his double feather plume and crown. He holds a *was* stave in his hand. The face has been badly damaged by cut marks, though the outlines are still visible. He wears a necklace with an amulet and a bracelet on each upper arm. The lower part of the body is missing in the similar manner to that of the figure of Ptolemy II.

The figure behind Amun is identified as Khonsu in his form of 'Neferhotep' (of Karnak), wearing the moon disc and the horns. He holds the three royal standards, the crook, the flail and the special *was* stave with the *djed* pillars. He also wears the *menit* collar of Hathor. The inscription above Khonsu says '…in the city of Karnak'. The head of the *cucupha* has been damaged by cut marks. The head of Khonsu has also been damaged badly by cut marks, though leaving the outlines of the head, showing the figure with a human head. The figure lacks the lower part of the body.

The last figure in the scene is identified as Arsinoë. She wears a tripartite wig, a vulture cap and the crown of Arsinoë. She is dressed in the traditional sheat dress and wears a necklace. She holds an *ankh* and a papyrus sceptre in her hands. The text describes her as 'Daughter of the king, sister of the King of Upper Egypt, King's great wife, Lady of the Two Lands, Mistress of Eternity, Lady of the sun disk (Aten), Daughter of Amun, Arsinoë, the divine Philadelphos, Divine mother (Isis) of the living bull, the manifestation of Ptah, the King of all souls, Lord of sacredness'.

Left scene

Crown of the scene: AC 13

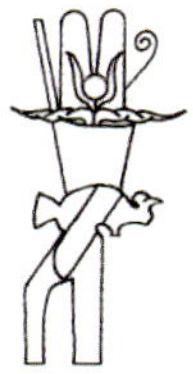

Hand-held objects: *Ankh* and a papyrus sceptre

State of preservation: The crown is in a good state of preservation with only minor damage in the centre of the red crown caused by cut marks. The face and neck has been badly damaged by cut marks, as have the legs, including the feet and the area between the middle section of the body and the arm. The *ankh* and the sceptre are preserved. The relief outlines of the main body including the *ankh* and the sceptre plus the hieroglyphic line next to the figures' legs are much shallower than that of the crown. The personal registers of text are mainly well preserved except for some signs which have been erased intentionally.

Iconographical description: In the left scene, King Ptolemy and a female figure present offerings to three deities. The female figure is preserved in a fragmentary state, showing the front, lower extremities, *i.e.*, from the hips and down, including the feet and the lower hieroglyphic register. The upper part of the stone block is missing totally, though it is clear that the figure was described with a personal register the border line of which is preserved on the next block.

The king wears the crown of Upper Egypt, a single forehead *uraeus* and the royal diadem. He wears the traditional kilt. He presents the offering of the figure of Ma'at. The figure of Ma'at is unfinished, showing only the lower extremities of the body and the feather. Similarly, only the upper extremities of the figure of Ptolemy are finished, with only two main outer lines marking the back and front of a skirt. The area in front of the back line has been damaged by cut marks. He is described as Ptolemy II. Only a fragmentary hieroglyphic text, clearly not finished, is preserved in front of that damaged area. The figure has been damaged by the loss of the stone blocks both above it and to its left.

The figure in front of the king depicts Amun-Ra. The only iconographical details visible are the double feather plume, the throne he sits on, and his lower extremities, *i.e.*, the legs and feet. His upper extremities of the body have not been carved. The inscription above the figure is finished and of the same dept as the surrounding script. The double feather plume is deeper and bolder than the rest. The throne is well preserved, while the lower part of the legs, including the feet, has been damaged by cut marks. The figure's relief ends abruptly above the hips

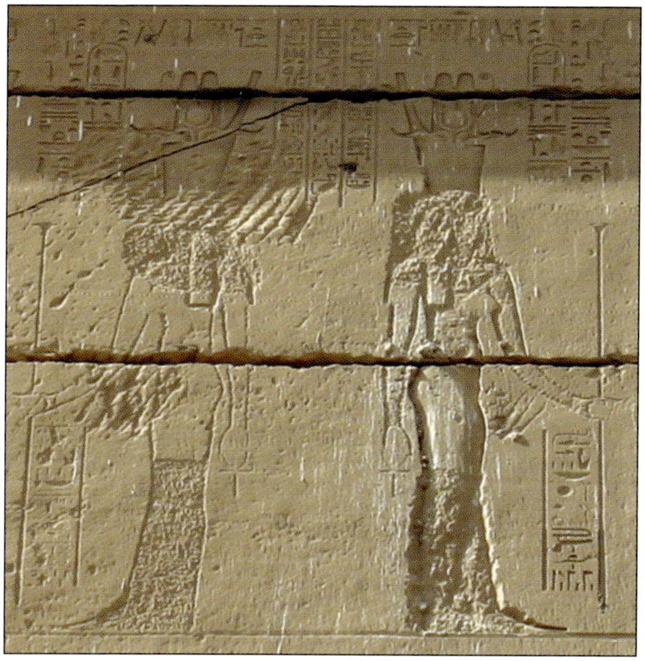

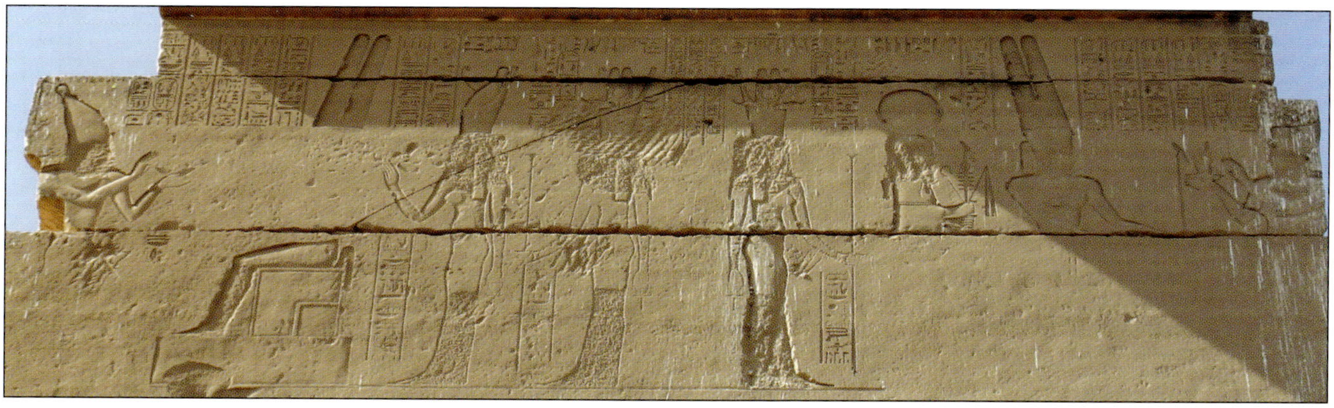

26. *Karnak, East Gate (so called Gate of Nectanebo or Bab el-Melacha), eastern partition, lintel scene. Photos: The author.*

with a clear cut. He is described in the text as 'Amun-Ra, the great Lord of the thrones of Karnak, Lord of Heaven, King of all the Gods'.

Behind Amun-Ra stands the figure of Mut, who wears the double crown. She is described as 'Mut … the Mistress of the Gods, the Lady of the Sky … of the Mut Temple of Karnak, eye of Ra'. She stands in a protecting manner and holds an *ankh* in her stretched arm. The relief of the upper extremities are finished, while the lower ones have only shallowly chiselled outlines. The face has been badly damaged by cut marks but the outlines are still preserved and show that she wears a tripartite wig. The lower part of the legs, including the feet, has been damaged by cut marks. The area under the *ankh* has been damaged by cut marks.

Behind the figure of Mut stands Arsinoë. She wears a tripartite wig, a vulture cap and the crown of Arsinoë. She is dressed in the traditional sheat dress and is decorated with a necklace. She holds an *ankh* and a papyrus sceptre in her hands. The text describes the figure as 'King's Daughter, sister of the King of Upper Egypt, King's great wife, Lady of the Two Lands, Mistress of Eternity, Lady of the solar disc, Daughter of Amun, Arsinoë the divine Philadelphos…' 'the manifestation of Ptah, the King of all souls, Lord of sacredness'. The hieroglyphs of this figure are more damaged than those of the other figure.

Remarks: The figures of Amun are the tallest figures of the complete scene.

27. Philae, gate of Ptolemy II Philadelphos, southern partition, facing east, bottom register

Raised relief

Sandstone

Date: Ptolemy II Philadelphos

Published: *PM* VI, plan 212; text 214 (69); Quaegebeur 1971a, 214, no. 39; Quaegebeur 1988, 45, fig. 17 on p. 47; Hölbl 2001, 96, fig. B; Ashton 2000, 8 fig. 8; Vassilika 1989, 37f. (not mentioning Arsinoë); SERAT 343301

Crown of the scene: AC 14

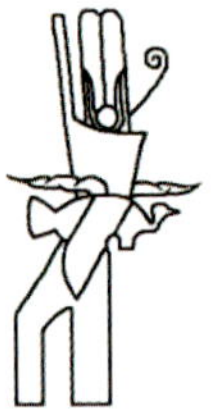

Hand-held objects: *Ankh* and a lotus-topped flail

State of preservation: The figure has been badly damaged by sporadic cut marks as well as by natural wear. Minor circular and cylindrical marks have damaged the crown, though most of it is intact. The wig and vulture cap are more or less preserved, though with some damage in their central area. The face has been badly damaged by cut marks, leaving only the outlines of the ear visible. Only vague traces indicate that the figure was decorated with a necklace. The main body of the figure has been badly damaged, in some places only with the outlines preserved. The feet are totally erased, without any outlines to suggest their form. The *ankh* is mainly preserved, though with damage in the circular area and the lower part. The flail is also mainly preserved, being damaged only on the shaft. The personal register of text and the randomly placed sign surrounding the figure are in a bad state of preservation, though the majority is still readable.

Iconographical description: In the main scene King Ptolemy presents offerings to two female figures.

The king wears the white crown, the royal diadem and a single forehead *uraeus*. Above his head is a solar disc depicted with two pendant *uraei*. Behind his head is a small *s3* sign depicted for protection. Below are signs placed more or less sporadically, saying 'life, serenity, abundance, Lord…' He wears a traditional kilt with a relief decoration that has been damaged by cut marks and the bull's tail. He presents the field of reeds. The hieroglyphic text surrounding the king has been badly damaged; some signs have totally been erased, though through the ones that

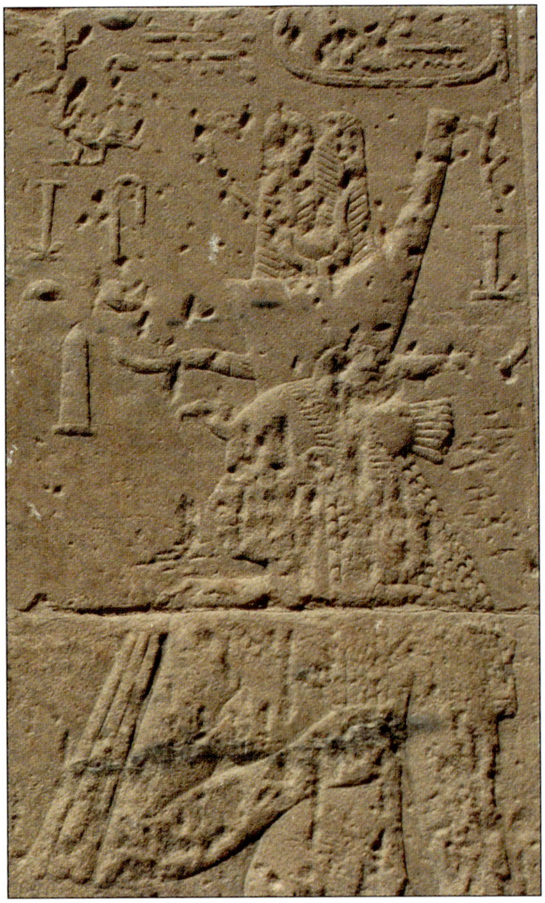

27. Philae, gate of Ptolemy II Philadelphos, southern partition, facing east, bottom register. Photo: The author.

are still visible he is identified as '[*nfr nṯr*? *i.e.*, Good God] Lord of the Two Lands (Strong is the soul of Ra, beloved of Amun)| son of Ra, Lord of the crowns (Ptolemy)|'. Next to his cartouches reads 'given life'. In front of the king is a vessel and lotus flowers (one in bloom and two buds). Minor outlines indicate a censer stand underneath the vessel.

The figure in front of the king wears the tripartite wig, the vulture cap and the traditional Hathorian crown. A single pendant *uraeus* comes down from the cow horns. The crown rests on a tiara of *uraei*. She holds an *ankh* and a papyrus sceptre. The dress shows details of a relief pattern and the figure also wears arm bracelets. The lower part of the legs has been badly damaged; the feet are no longer visible. The hieroglyphic text surrounding the female figure has been badly damaged and only minor parts are still visible. She is described as 'Isis, the great divine mother (or, as usually translated, mother of the god), the Lady of [Philae]'.

Behind this figure stands Arsinoë. She wears a tripartite wig, a vulture cap and the crown of Arsinoë. She is dressed in the traditional sheat dress and is decorated with a necklace. She holds an *ankh* and a flail in her hands. The hieroglyphic text surrounding the female figure of the present investigating has been badly damaged and left with only sporadic signs. The signs have also been placed in a non-traditional manner, in a random order. The figure is described as 'King's wife, daughter, and his sister, Daughter of Amun [...brother/sibling][...], ruler [...], Lady of the Two Lands (Arsinoë)| Philadelphos'.

Remarks: The hieroglyphic text of the scene is very simple and randomly placed in various areas. The top part of the scene is disconnected from the lower scene owing to a fracture in connection with the joint of the stone blocks. There is a clear difference in colours between the lower and upper stone blocks. The artist made a mistake when carving the cow horns on the crown of Arsinoë, since they go below the upper outline of the red crown. The figures are mainly equal in size.

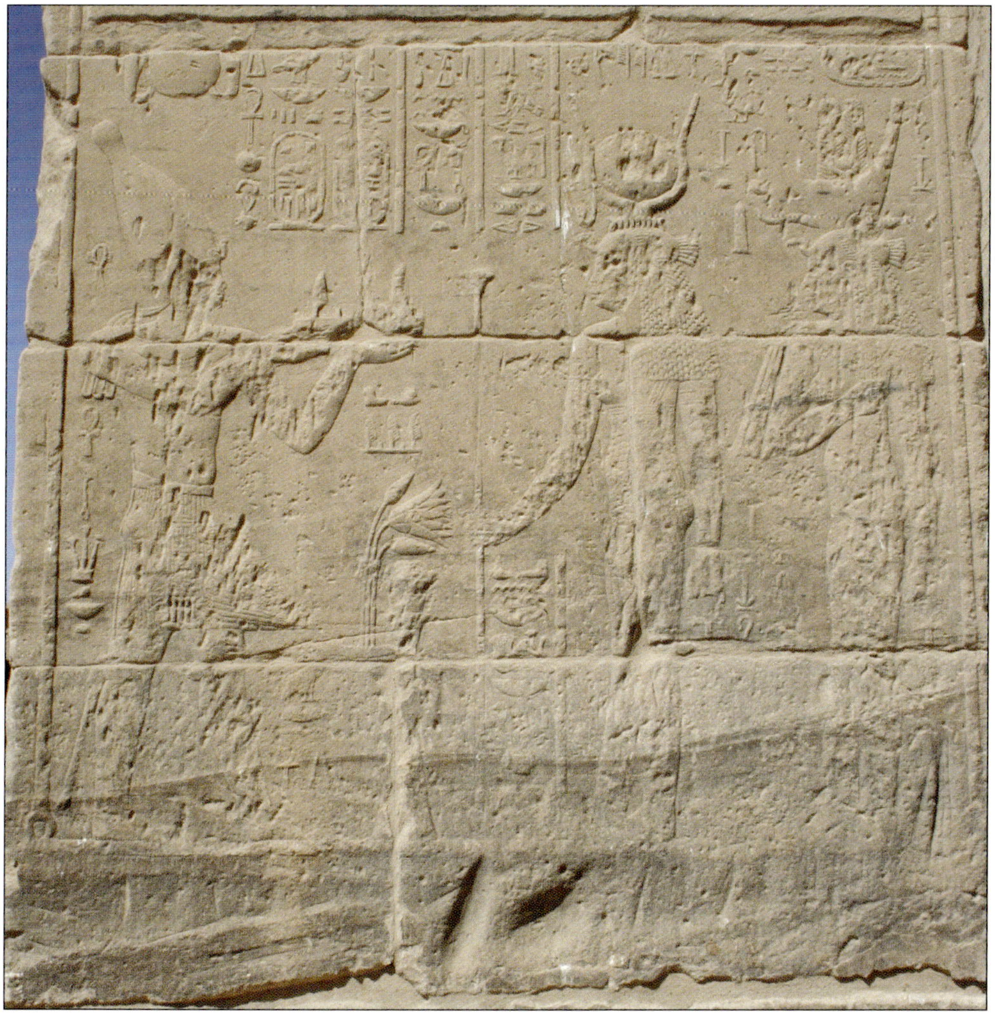

27. Philae, gate of Ptolemy II Philadelphos, southern partition, facing east, bottom register. Photo: The author.

28. Philae, gate of Ptolemy II, northern partition, facing east, first register

Raised relief

Sandstone

Date: Ptolemy II Philadelphos

Published: *PM* VI, 214 (70); Quaegebeur 1971a, 214, no. 39; Quaegebeur 1988, 45, fig. 17 on p. 47; Vassilika 1989, 37f. (not mentioning Arsinoë); Hölbl 2001, 96, fig. B; SERAT 343306

Crown of the scene: AC 15

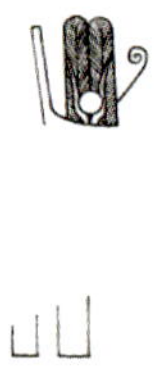

Hand-held objects: Papyrus sceptre and traces of an *ankh*

State of preservation: The figure is in a bad state of preservation, in particular the area surrounding the head and lower part of the crown. The stone has been badly damaged by a big fracture splitting it into two fragments. This fracture leaves no traces of the facial structure or the lower part of the crown. The main body is also badly damaged, especially the lower part of the legs and the feet, but also the hand that held the *ankh*, which is formed in the holding position but lacks the *ankh* and parts of the lower part of the arm. The majority of the surrounding hieroglyphic text has been damaged.

Iconographical description: In the main scene King Ptolemy presents offerings to two female figures. He wears the red crown, a single forehead *uraeus* and the royal diadem. Above his head is a solar disc depicted with two pendant *uraei*. Behind his head is a small *sꜣ* sign depicted for protection. Further down is written 'life, serenity, abundance, Lord…'. He wears the traditional kilt, which is elaborately decorated in relief, and the bull's tail. He presents two blooming lotus flowers, with an additional set of the double lotus buds, in each hand. Next to his legs is a censer stand placed with a lotus resting on top of it. The king is described in the hieroglyphic text as '[*nfr ntr i.e.*, the good god] Lord of the Two Lands (Strong is the soul of Ra, beloved of Amun)| son of Ra, Lord of the crowns (Ptolemy)|'. Next to the cartouches is written 'given

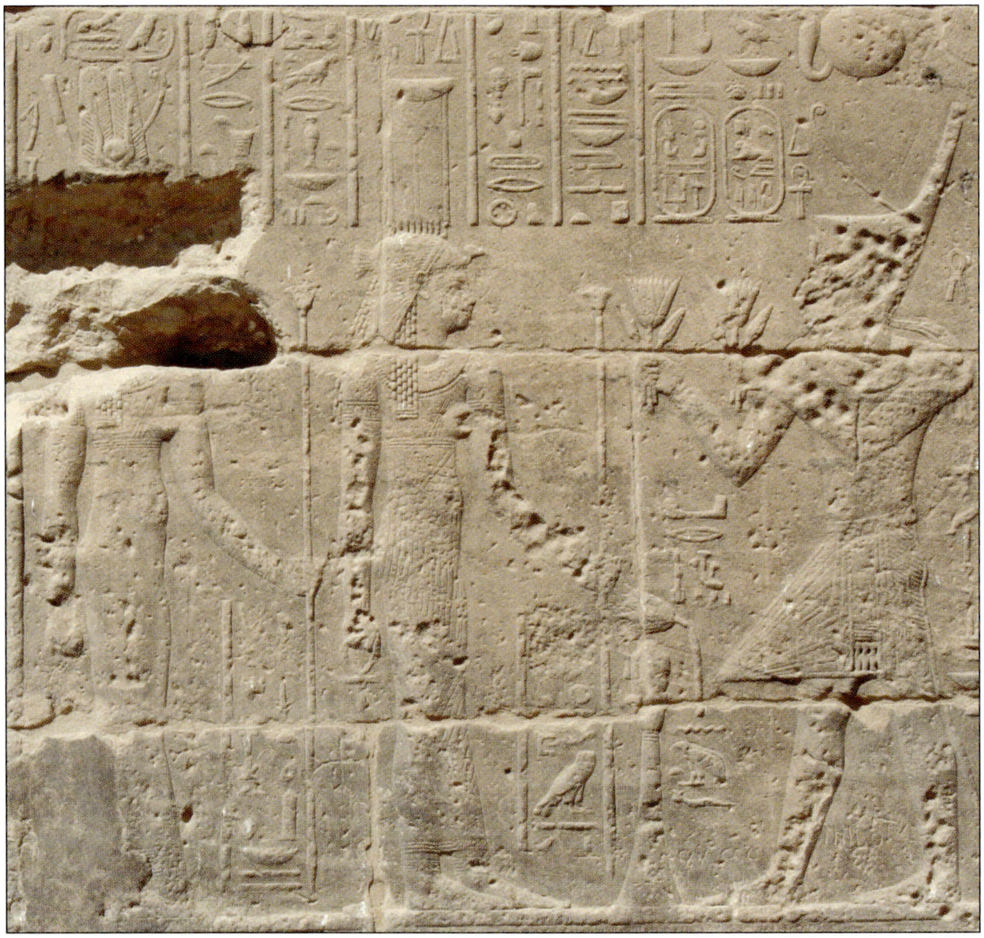

28. Philae, gate of Ptolemy II, northern partition, facing east, first register. Photo: The author.

life'. The lower hieroglyphic register of text describes the figure in front of him as his mother. The figure of the king has been badly damaged by cut marks, which also have damaged the red crown. There is later graffiti, written in Greek, between the legs of the king, though this will not be discussed here.

The female figure in front of the king wears the tripartite wig, the vulture cap, a tiara of *uraei* and Nephthys' traditional crown. She wears a decorated dress, arm, ankle and hand bracelets and a necklace, and holds the *ankh* and a papyrus sceptre in her hands. The figure is, in general, in a bad state of preservation because of cut marks. The crown has been left untouched, as have the feet, though the face and the main body, especially the arms, have been badly damaged. The speaking register in front of the figure has been badly damaged and in places erased. The personal register of text above the figure is damaged by the fracture in connection with the joint of the stone blocks. The still-visible inscription surrounding the figure states that she was: 'the one who is in the heart of all the gods; she of Aa-lek (*i.e.*, Philae)'. A small cross is etched behind the legs of the deity.

The figure behind her is identified as Arsinoë. She wears a tripartite wig above which the crown of Arsinoë has been placed. She is dressed in the traditional sheat dress and is decorated with a necklace, arm bracelets and a normal bracelet. She holds a papyrus sceptre in her hand and there are traces of an *ankh*. The maintained text (though extensively damaged) describes her as 'Princess, Great of praise, Lady of (all) the people, Sweet of Love, Mistress of Upper and Lower Egypt, King's wife, sister [...], Daughter of Amun, Lady of the Two Lands (Arsinoë)| the divine Philadelphos'.

Remarks: Arsinoë is the tallest figure of the scene, though only slightly taller than the other female goddess. Deep cut marks have damaged the lower part of the scene.

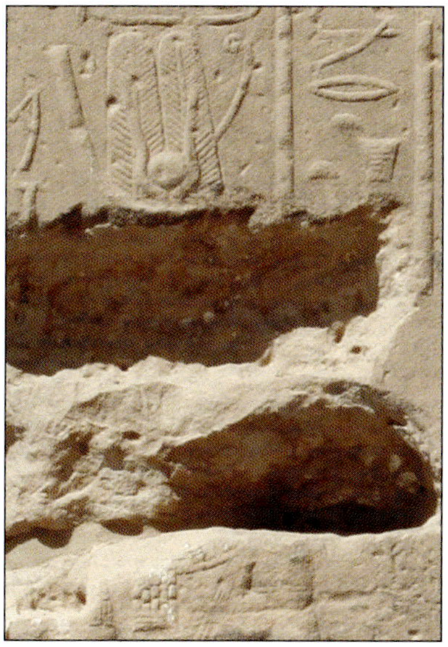

28. Philae, gate of Ptolemy II, northern partition, facing east, first register. Photo: The author.

29. Philae, antechamber (chamber I), northern partition, eastern side, bottom register

Raised relief
Sandstone
Date: Ptolemy II Philadelphos
Published: *PM* VI, 238 (295); Bénédite 1893–5, 7f., pl. II; Berlin photos 1125, 692f.; Quaegebeur 1971a, 214, no. 40; Quaegebeur 1998, 93, no. 36; SERAT 310021
Crown of the scene: AC 14

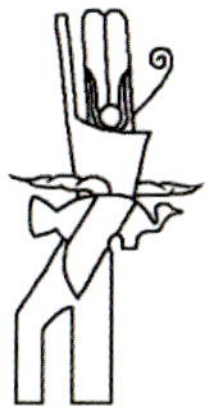

Hand-held objects: *Ankh* and a lotus-topped flail
State of preservation: The figure has been badly damaged in general by cut marks. The crown has in the main been left without any damage but the fracture in the stone by the joint cuts away the ram horns and splits the crown in two fragments. There are no facial features or outlines preserved, except for the outline of the top part of the head. Some

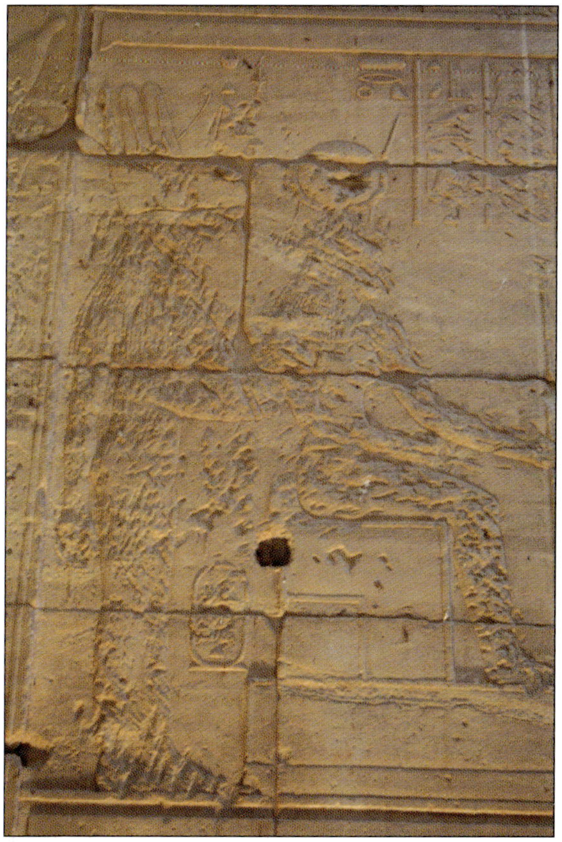

29. Philae, antechamber (chamber I), northern partition, eastern side, bottom register. Photo: The author.

of the outlines of the vulture cap are still visible, just like those of the wig. The main body has been badly damaged by later, sporadically placed, cut marks. The *ankh* and the flail have been badly damaged. The hieroglyphic text is also badly damaged by cut marks, though leaving some details and outlines.

Iconographical description: Three figures are depicted in this scene.

The main scene is broken and is now displayed in a fragmentary state. The section where the king is supposed to stand has been removed, leaving an image of the two beneficiaries. Details of the text describing the king states '(Ptolemy)| (Strong is the soul of Ra, beloved of Amun)|'.

The female in front of the king is seated on a throne. She wears a tripartite wig, a vulture cap, a tiara of *uraei* and the traditional Hathorian crown with a *uraeus* coming down from the horns. She holds an *ankh* and a papyrus sceptre. The text describes the figure as 'Isis, the great Mother goddess of Philae'.

The standing figure behind her is identified as Arsinoë. She wears a tripartite wig, a vulture cap and the crown of Arsinoë. She is dressed in the traditional sheat dress and wears a necklace. She holds an *ankh* and a flail in her hands. The text and the cartouche describe the figure as 'King's wife, daughter, sister, Daughter of Amun, sister of the King of Upper Egypt (Arsinoë)|'. The hieroglyphs have been badly damaged and are only partly visible.

Remarks: The scene has been broken in order to reuse and restructure the space of the room, making it bigger and opening up to a larger area. Arsinoë is the tallest figure.

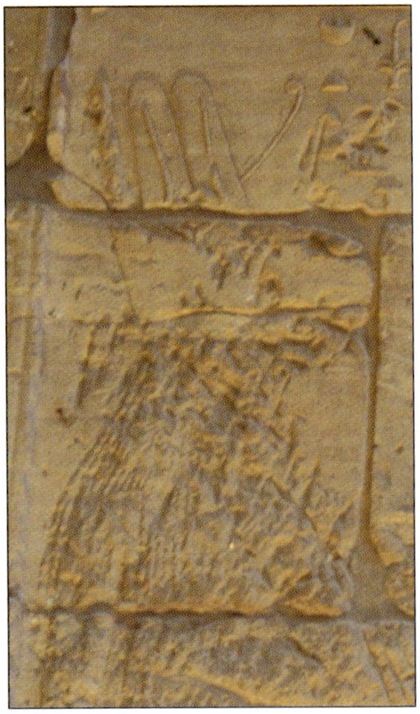

29. Philae, antechamber (chamber I), northern partition, eastern side, bottom register. Photo: The author.

30. Philae, inner part (outer wall of the sanctuary)(chamber VII), northern partition, eastern side of the door, lower main register

Raised relief

Sandstone

Date: Ptolemy II Philadelphos

Published: *PM* VI, 241 (340); Bénédite 1893–5, 48f., pls xviii.; Berlin photos 1073; Champollion 1844, lxxxv (3); Quaegebeur 1971a, 214, no. 42; Quaegebeur 1998, no. 34; SERAT 310118

Crown of the scene: AC 16

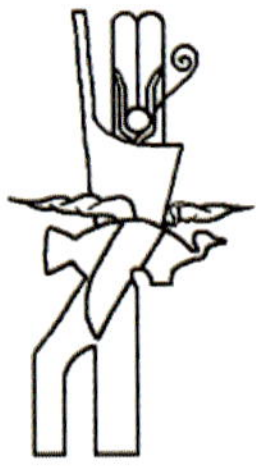

Hand-held objects: *Ankh* and a papyrus sceptre

State of preservation: The figure is in a good state of preservation except for the area where the stone blocks meet at the joints, which is unfortunately where the ear of the figure is depicted, and it is therefore badly damaged.

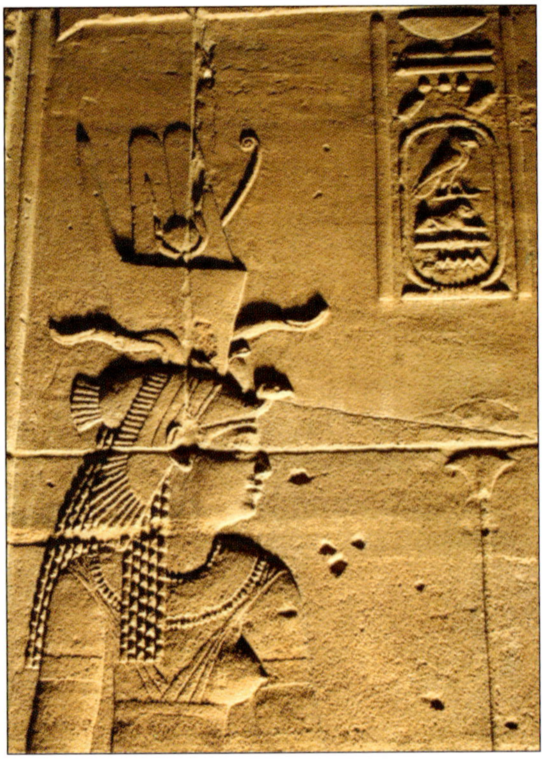

30. Philae, inner part (outer wall of the sanctuary)(chamber VII), northern partition, eastern side of the door, lower main register.

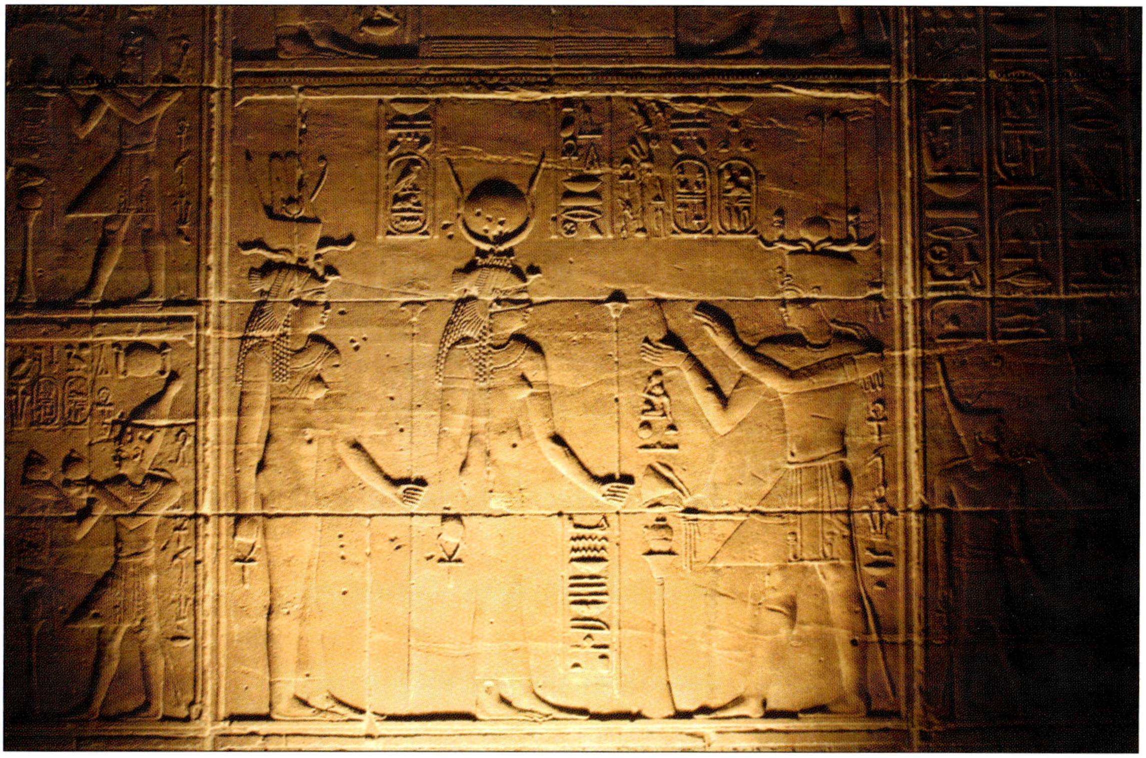

30. Philae, inner part (outer wall of the sanctuary)(chamber VII), northern partition, eastern side of the door, lower main register. Photos: The author.

Iconographical description: In the main scene the king presents offerings to two female figures.

The king wears the *khepresh* crown, the royal diadem and a single forehead *uraeus*; the double feather plume, the solar disc, ram horns and two *uraei* with solar discs on their heads coming up from the horns. Behind his head is a small *s3* sign depicted for protection. Further down the text says 'may he live forever in serenity and abundance'. He wears the traditional kilt and the bull's tail. In front of him stands a papyrus pillar holding a small vessel with a stylised bloomed lotus and two buds bending over it. He presents lettuce to the deities in front of him. He is described in the text as 'Lord of the Two Lands (Strong is the soul of Ra, beloved of Amun)| Lord of the crowns (Ptolemy)|'. The figure is well preserved except for the damage caused by the joints of the stone blocks. The hieroglyphic text is also well preserved.

The figure in front of the king is a standing female figure, described in the text as 'Isis, she who gives life, prosperity and serenity, Isis, the life giving Lady of Philae'. She wears the tripartite wig, the vulture cap, a tiara of *uraei* and the traditional Hathorian crown, and in her hands she holds an *ankh* and a papyrus sceptre. The figure is well preserved and damaged only by fractures related to the joints of the stone blocks.

Behind the figure of Isis stands Arsinoë. She wears the tripartite wig, a vulture cap and the crown of Arsinoë. She wears the traditional sheat dress and wears a necklace. She holds an *ankh* and a papyrus sceptre in her hands. The hieroglyphic text describes the figure as 'Lady of the Two Lands (Arsinoë)|'.

Remarks: The hieroglyphic text in the scene is minimised. The lower hieroglyphic register of Arsinoë is not inscribed and reveals no indication of any attempt to finish it. Ptolemy is the tallest figure.

31. Philae, inner sanctuary (chamber X), western partition, lower register

Raised relief

Sandstone

Date: Ptolemy II Philadelphos

Published: *PM* VI, 243 (355); Bénédite 1893–5, pl. XXIV; Žabkar 1988, 89; Berlin photos 1028; Quaegebeur 1971b, no. 44; Quaegebeur 1998, no. 33; SERAT 310162

Crown of the scene: AC 17

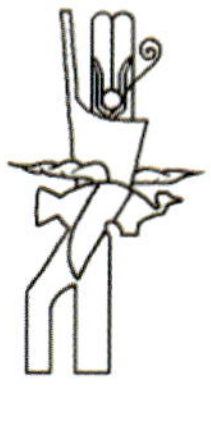

Hand-held objects: *Ankh* and a papyrus sceptre

State of preservation: The figure has been damaged by cut marks, especially the face, but the crown is well preserved. The face has been badly damaged and there is no trace of features; only the outlines of the nose are still visible. The damaging cut marks are sporadically placed on the main body, mainly centring on the lower parts of the arms, the doughnut belly and the legs. The upper extremities, *i.e.*, the shoulders, the breast and the abdomen surrounding the belly button, are left mainly without cut marks. The personal register of text is well preserved.

Iconographical description: In the general scene the king presents offerings to two female figures.

The king wears the *khat* cap covering the head and neck, a single forehead *uraeus* and the royal diadem. Behind his head is a small *s3* sign depicted for protection. Further down it is written 'may he live forever in serenity and abundance'. In the corner above his head is a vulture depicted handing the *ankh* to the king with the text 'given life like Ra'. He wears the traditional kilt with additional elongated fabric and the bull's tail. The shaft of a knife is visible on his belt of the kilt. He presents a tray of four vessels (of water). He is also supported and guided by the vulture holding an *ankh* in the top corner. The king is described as 'Lord of the crowns (Strong is the soul of Ra, beloved of Amun)| Lord of the Two Lands (Ptolemy)|'. The figure has been damaged by cut marks centred on the face.

The standing female figure in front of the king is described in the text as 'Isis, the life giver of the site of Philae, the divine loving Mother'. She wears the tripartite wig, the vulture cap, a tiara of *uraei* and the traditional Hathorian crown. She holds an *ankh* and a papyrus sceptre. This figure has been badly damaged in the face and on the feet but is otherwise mainly in a good state of preservation. The personal text is well preserved.

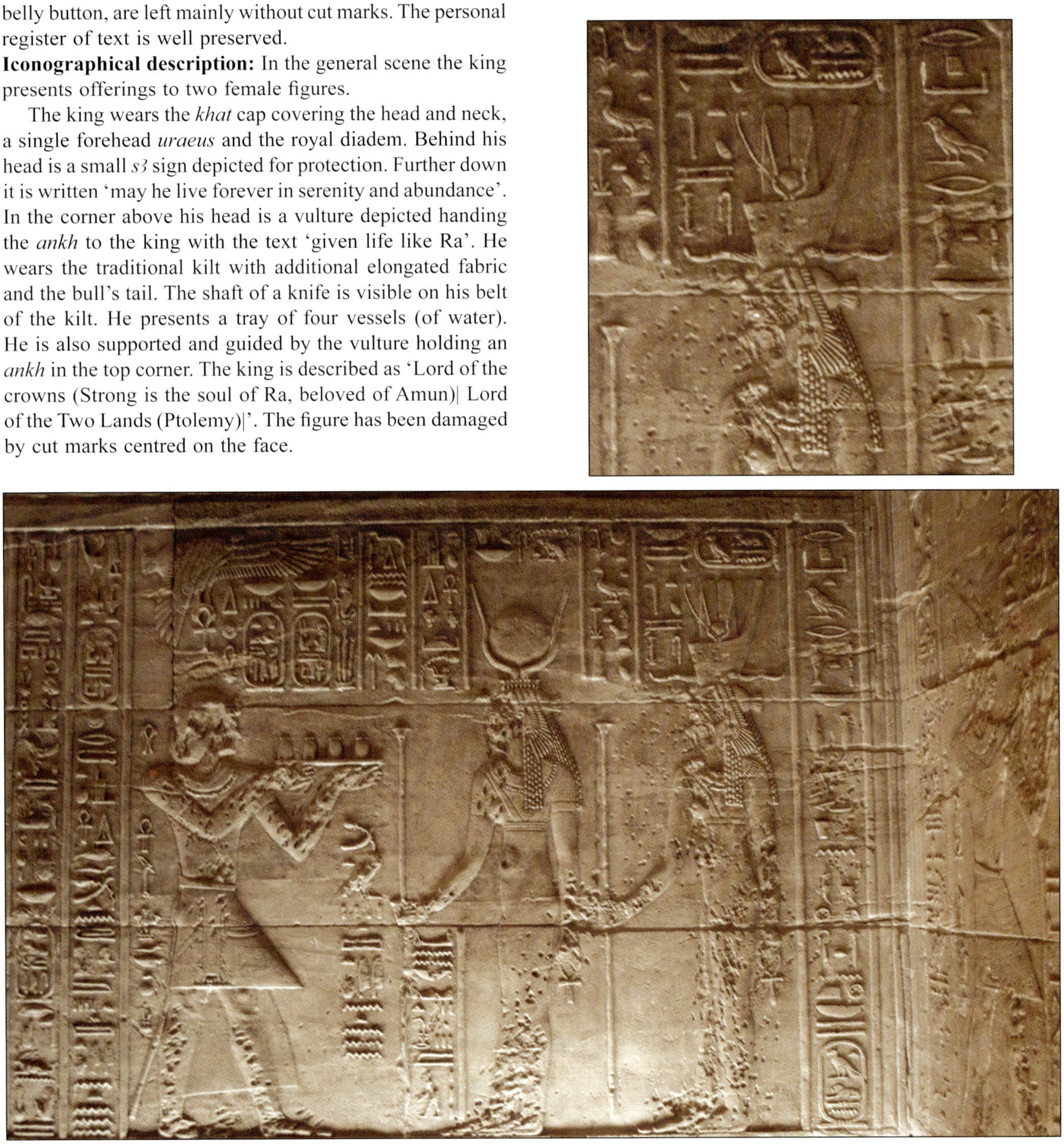

31. Philae, inner sanctuary (chamber X), western partition, lower register. Photos: The author.

Behind the figure of Isis stands Arsinoë. She wears a tripartite wig, a vulture cap and the crown of Arsinoë. She is dressed in the traditional sheat dress and she holds an *ankh* and a papyrus sceptre in her hands. The text describes her as 'King's wife, daughter, sister, Daughter of Amun, Lady of the Two Lands, the divine Philadelphos, Arsinoë, Princess, Great of Praise, Lady of Sweet Love, Mistress of Upper and Lower Egypt, Ruler of Egypt, Lady of the Two Lands (Arsinoë)|'.
Remarks: Arsinoë has not received any lower hieroglyphic register of text, even though the scene has been finished. The two female figures depicted are the tallest in the scene.

32. Philae, inner sanctuary (chamber X), eastern partition, lower register

Raised relief
Sandstone
Date: Ptolemy II Philadelphos
Published: *PM* VI, 243 (357); Bénédite 1893–5, pl. xxiii; Žabkar 1988, 89; Berlin photos 1023; Quaegebeur 1971b, no. 43; Quaegebeur 1998, no. 33; SERAT 310151
Crown of the scene: AC 14

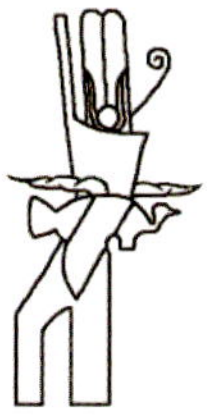

Hand-held objects: *Ankh* and a papyrus sceptre
State of preservation: The figure is in a good state of preservation and damaged only by the fracture caused by the joints of the stone blocks.
Iconographical description: Four figures are depicted in this scene.

The king wears a single forehead *uraeus* and the royal diadem, and it otherwise depicted with a shaved head or possibly a priest cap. Behind his head is a small *s3* sign depicted for protection. Further down it is written 'may he live forever in serenity and abundance like Ra'. In the corner above his head is a vulture depicted handing the *ankh* to the king with the text 'given life like Ra'. He wears the traditional kilt, which is decorated in the relief, and the bull's tail. He presents a tray of four small vessels (water). This

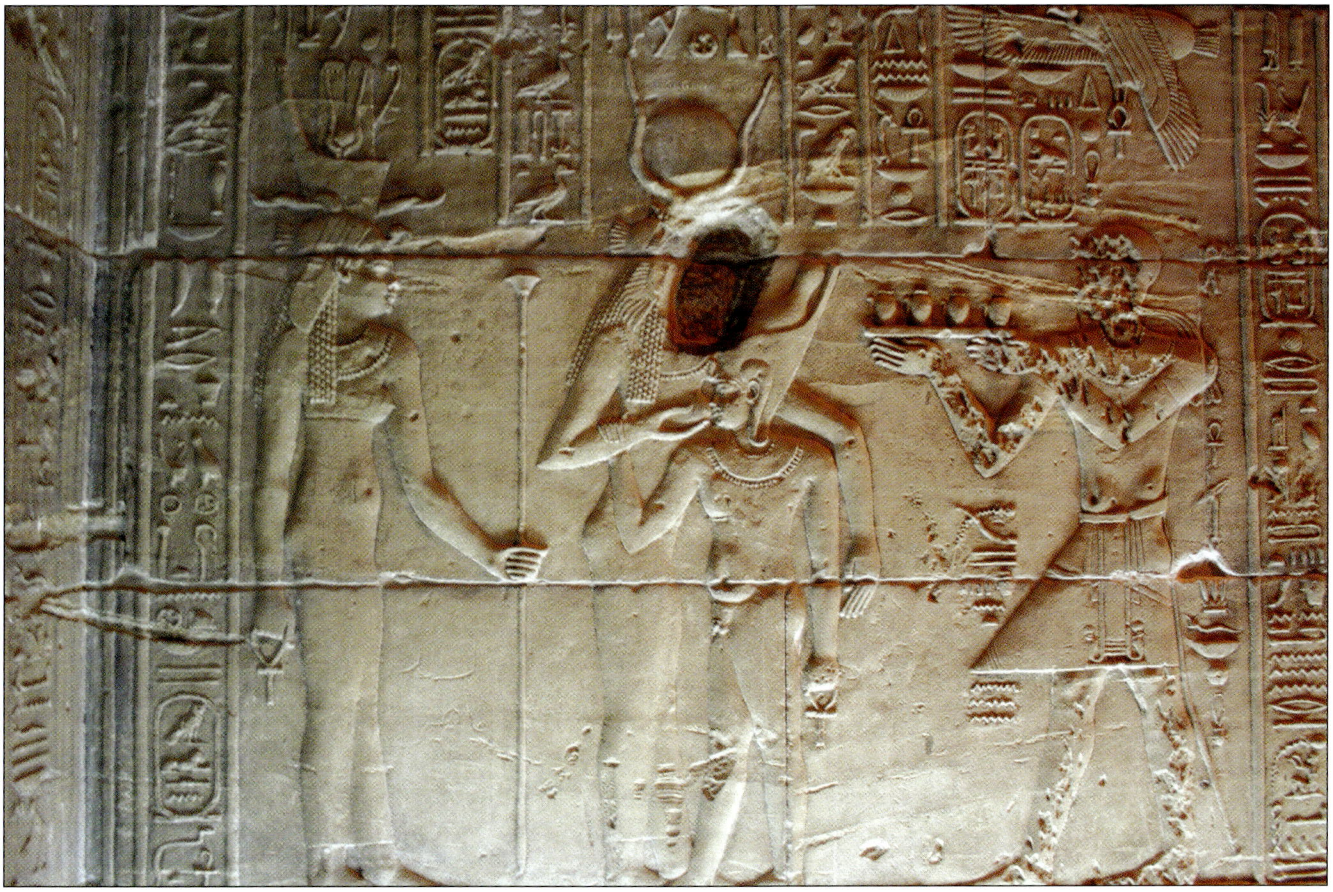

32. Philae, inner sanctuary (chamber X), eastern partition, lower register. Photo: The author.

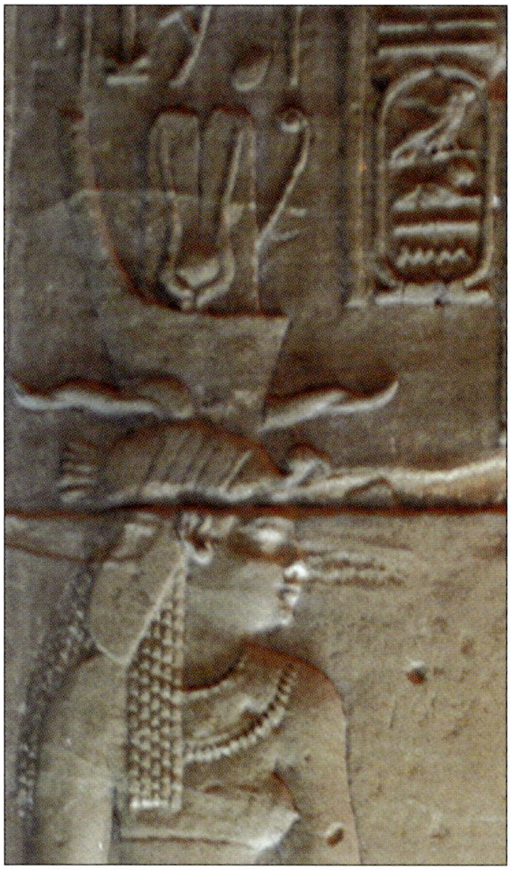

32. Philae, inner sanctuary (chamber X), eastern partition, lower register. Photo: The author.

figure has been badly damaged by cut marks, especially in the face, the arms and the legs. He is identified in the text as 'Lord of the Two Lands (Strong is the soul of Ra, beloved of Amun)| Lord of the crowns (Ptolemy)|'.

The figure in front of him is a female deity described as 'Lady Isis, the great divine Mother'. She wears the tripartite wig, the vulture cap and the traditional Hathorian crown. The main body is well preserved but the entire head has been cut out deeply, leaving no outlines whatsoever. She is breast-feeding the figure of Harpocrates, who wears the double crown, the prince lock and a single forehead *uraeus*. He holds an *ankh* in his hand. He is left without any personal text or direct description.

Standing behind them is Arsinoë. She wears a tripartite wig and a vulture cap, above which is placed the crown of Arsinoë. She is dressed in the traditional sheat dress and wears a necklace. She holds an *ankh* and a papyrus sceptre in her hands. According to the text the figure depicts 'King's wife, daughter, his sister, Daughter of Amun, Lady of the Two Lands, Arsinoë the divine Philadelphos, Princess, Great of Praise, Lady of Sweet Love, Mistress of Upper and Lower Egypt, Ruler of Egypt, Lady of the Two Lands (Arsinoë)|, may she live forever'.

Remarks: Arsinoë is equal to the figure of Isis in height.

33. Philae, chamber V, southern partition, west side of the door jamb

Raised relief

Sandstone

Date: Ptolemy II Philadelphos

Published: *PM* VI, 240 (317); Bénédite 1893–5, 25f., pl. IX; Žabkar 1988, pl. 9 on p. 13; Berlin photos 1104; Quaegebeur 1971a, no. 41; Quaegebeur 1998, no. 35; SERAT 310060

Crown of the scene: AC 18

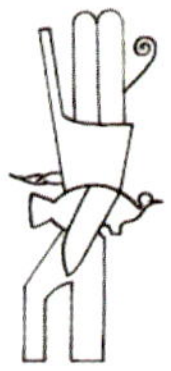

Hand-held objects: *Ankh* and papyrus sceptre

State of preservation: The figure is well preserved, though slightly damaged owing to fractures in the stone blocks. The crown has been damaged over the lower part of the

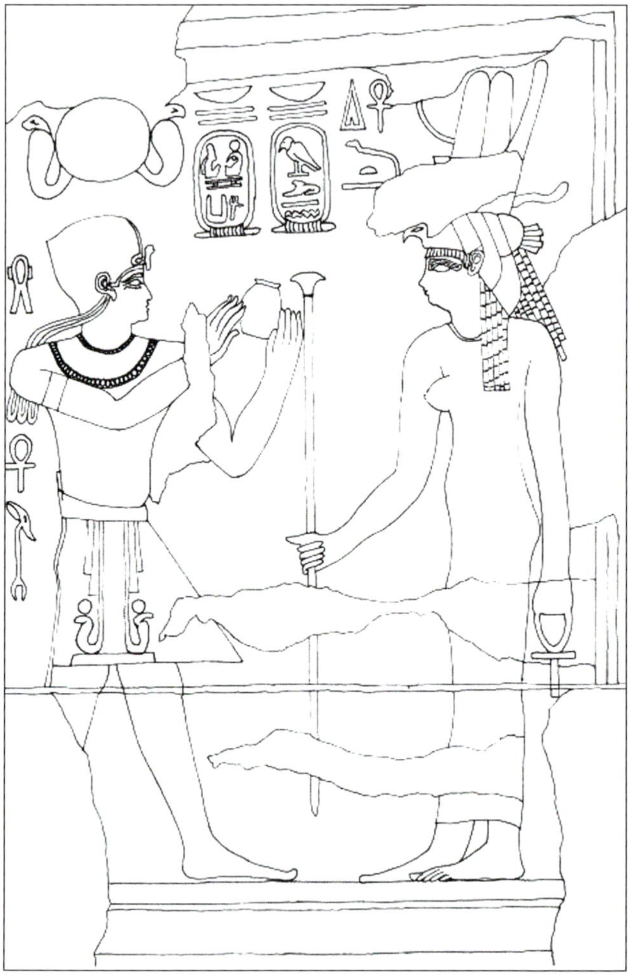

33. Philae, chamber V, southern partition, west side of the door jamb Drawing: J. Ward.

red crown, normally showing the cow horns and solar disc, leaving the front ram horn only vaguely visible. The horns are divided by the red crown. The lower part of the body, the hand holding the *ankh* and the lower part of the sceptre are also damaged by fractures.

Iconographical description: Two main figures are depicted in this scene.

The king stands at the very right wearing the blue *khepresh* crown, a single forehead *uraeus* and the royal diadem. Above his head is a solar disc depicted with two pendant *uraei*. The area above the minor figure has been damaged and is no longer visible. A small *s3* sign is depicted behind the head of the king. He wears a necklace and is dressed in a traditional kilt decorated with two pendant *uraei* and hanging textile bands. The kilt is also decorated with the traditional bull's tail. He presents a *nemset* vase. The figure is well preserved, including all the relief details, and damaged slightly only by fractures in the stone blocks. The right leg is mainly missing owing to a fracture. He is described as 'Lord of the Two Lands (Strong is the soul of Ra, beloved of Amun)|'.

In front of the king stands Arsinoë. She wears a tripartite wig, a vulture cap and the crown of Arsinoë. She is dressed in the traditional sheat dress and holds an *ankh* and a papyrus sceptre in her hands. She is described in the text as 'Lady of the Two Lands (Arsinoë)| given eternal life'.

Remarks: This is the only scene on Philae where Arsinoë is depicted on her own as receiving an offering. Arsinoë is depicted as the tallest figure of the scene, with her crown reaching up to the top level of the solar disc.

34. Qasr el-Aguz, inner sanctuary, east wall, top register

Raised relief
Sandstone
Date: Ptolemy VIII Euergetes II
Published: *PM* II, 529 (9); *LÄ* V, 40f.; Mallet 1909, 68f., fig. 30; Winter 1978, 151; Quaegebeur 1971a, no. 30; Quaegebeur 1998, no. 38; Quaegebeur 1978, 252; SERAT 420022
Crown of the scene: AC 19

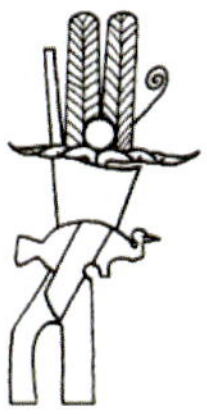

Hand-held objects: *Ankh* and a papyrus sceptre
State of preservation: The figure has been badly damaged by cut marks, leaving only a few outlines and details untouched. The crown has been left mostly untouched and thus still shows colours and painted details. The crown seems to have been coloured mainly in red paint, with outline traces on the crown of Lower Egypt as well as on the ram horns. The solar disc and the crown spiral are painted completely in red. The double feather plume shows painted details, with two middle vertical lines on each feather and smaller diagonal lines pointing upwards from the middle lines, thus depicting the typical feather. The hieroglyphic text above the head of the figure is also painted red while

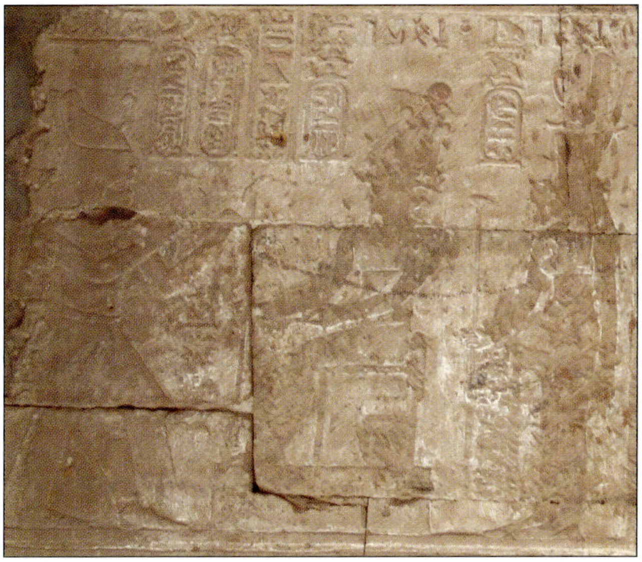

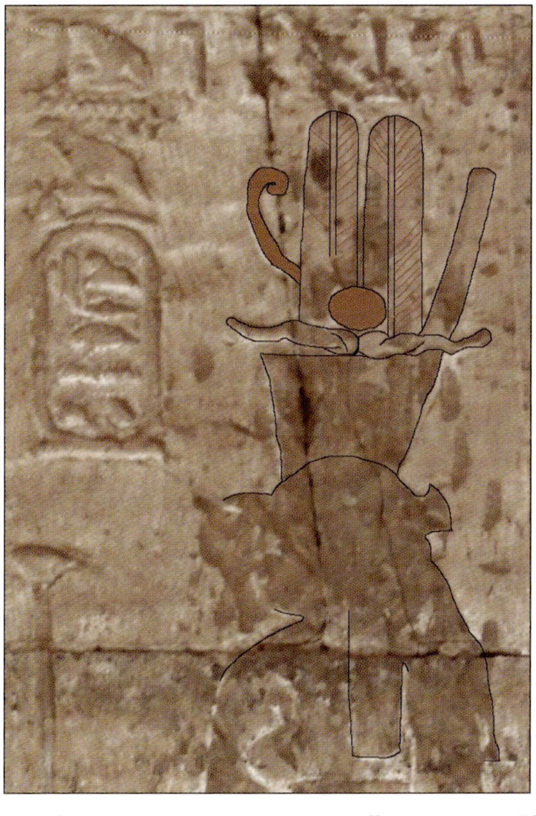

34. Qasr el-Aguz, inner sanctuary, east wall, top register. Photos and editing: The author.

the background of the cartouche shows white pigment with the hieroglyphs outlined in red. White and red colours are preserved on parts of the dress. The shaft of a papyrus sceptre has been coloured turquoise. White colour pigments are spread over various areas of the figure and are more an indication of later plaster work than of actual contemporary paint. The personal register of text is well preserved, though the lower hieroglyphic register has been badly damaged by later interference.
Iconographical description: Three figures are depicted in the scene.

The king, standing at the left side, wears the double crown with a single forehead *uraeus* and the royal diadem. He is dressed in the traditional kilt and the bull's tail. He adores the deities in front of him. The king is described as Ptolemy VIII Euergetes II.

The male figure in front of him is seated on a throne. He wears the *atef* crown resting on the ram horns. Some colours are still visible on the crown, showing blue/turquoise, red and white details. He also wears the pharaonic beard. He holds an *ankh* and a *was* stave in his hands. Minor traces of red, turquoise and white colouring are still visible on his chest. The majority of the figure has been badly damaged by cut marks, in particular the face. This figure is described as 'Divine father (Ptolemy)| the divine Philadelphos'.

Behind the figure of Ptolemy stands Arsinoë. She wears a tripartite wig, a vulture cap and the crown of Arsinoë. She is dressed in the traditional sheat dress and wears a necklace. She holds an *ankh* and a papyrus sceptre in her hands. According to the hieroglyphic text the female figure depicts 'Divine mother of his mothers, Arsinoë the divine Philadelphos'.
Remarks: The scene is surrounded by additional scenes of ancestor cult. Arsinoë is the tallest figure of the scene.

35. Tod

Raised relief
Sandstone
Date: Ptolemy VIII Euergetes II
Published: *PM* V, 168f. (without a description of the scene) – see plan on p. 165; Bisson de la Roque 1937, 22–33; Quaegebeur 1971a, no. 31; Winter 1978, 151; Grenier 1983, 33, fig. 1; Minas 2000, taf. 17; Quaegebeur 1998, no. 39; Thiers 2003, no. 318; SERAT 500057.
Crown of the scene: AC 20

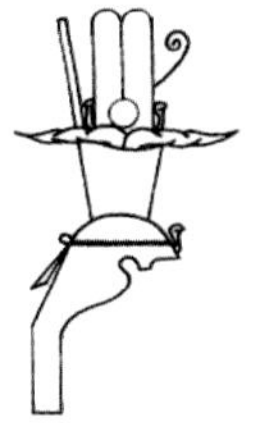

Hand-held objects: Hand held in protecting manner
State of preservation: The figure has been badly damaged in various areas and the lower part of the body is totally erased because the relief surface of the stone blocks is missing/destroyed. The body is cut just under the abdomen and there is a deep fracture in connection with the joint of the stone blocks, which divides the figure into two fragments. The crown is well preserved, including the minor relief details. The wig, the cap, the *uraeus* and the royal diadem are all well preserved except for the vulture head. The face is well preserved except for the very front area, which has been damaged in connection with the fracture of the joint of the stone blocks. The necklace and the dress are well preserved. The object of the other hand is no longer visible because of the above-mentioned damage of the lower part of the main body. The hieroglyphic text is preserved with only minor damage caused by natural processes. The figure is surrounded by deep cut marks.
Iconographical description: In the main scene the ruling couple stands at the very right making an offering to their ancestors, who are divided between two horizontal lines on top of each other. Each scene includes five figures, making a total of twelve figures including the ruling couple. At the very right the queen is depicted wearing a tripartite wig, a vulture cap, a single forehead *uraeus* and the royal diadem. She wears the traditional female crown resting on a low modus and is dressed in the traditional sheat dress. She holds two elongated flower compositions of papyrus and lotus. She is described in the text as '(Cleopatra)| the Lady of the Two Lands'. The figure has been badly damaged by large fractures in the stone blocks but also by cut marks damaging especially the face and the hands.

In front of the queen, facing in the same direction, stands the king. He wears the double crown, a single forehead *uraeus* and the royal diadem, and is decorated with the pharaonic beard. He is dressed in the traditional kilt and the bull's tail. He presents four censer offerings, while performing a libation from a jar held in his other hand. The libation is poured at a small censer stand placed in front of the king. He is identified in the badly damaged text as Ptolemy VIII Euergetes II. The figure has been badly damaged by large fractures in the stone blocks as well as by cut marks, mainly centred on the facial area.

In front of the ruling king are two scenes. The first figure of the upper scene is a male depicted with the *atef* crown resting upon the ram horns. He is dressed in the traditional kilt and the bull's tail. He holds an *ankh* and a *was* stave in his hands. The hieroglyphic text has been badly damaged, but states the name to be Ptolemy. According to the latest research the figure is described in the text as Ptolemy VI Philometor (SERAT 500057). The figure has been badly damaged by cut marks, erasing the entire figure except the sceptre, though leaving the main outlines visible.

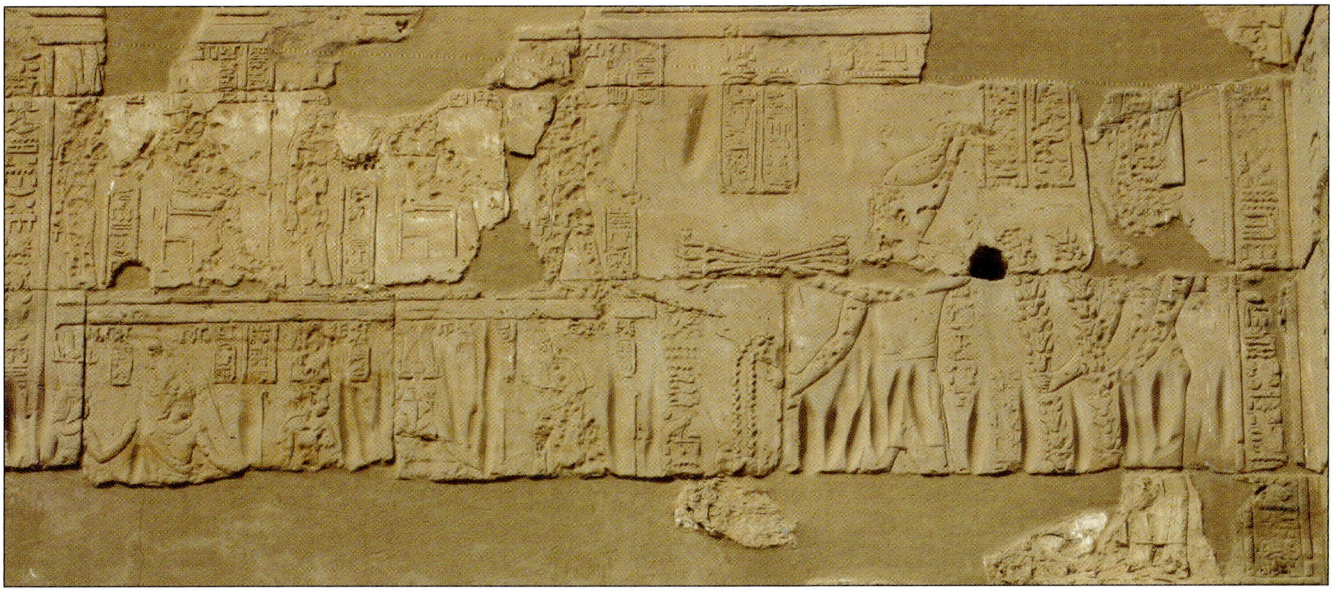

Behind the first male figure is another male figure seated on a throne. He is depicted wearing a now almost entirely destroyed *atef* crown resting upon the ram horns, of which only a minor front piece is preserved. He also wears the royal diadem, a single forehead *uraeus* and the pharaonic beard. He is dressed in the traditional kilt. He holds an *ankh* and a now almost destroyed *was* stave. Only the very bottom of the cartouche is preserved, leaving only the ending of the name Ptolemy visible. The figure is, in general, badly damaged by large fractures in the relief surface and cut marks mainly centred on the facial area. Only the throne and the lower part of the legs are still preserved.

Behind the seated male figure stands a female figure. She wears a tripartite wig, a single forehead *uraeus* and the royal band. Her crown is composed of a tiara of *uraei* and the traditional female crown. She is dressed in the traditional sheat dress and stands in a position of blessing the figure in front. She holds an *ankh* in her resting hand. The figure has been badly damaged by large fractures in the stone blocks but also by cut marks, leaving only the mid section of the legs untouched. The cartouche is not preserved.

Behind the female figure is a male figure seated on a throne. He wears an *atef* crown resting upon the ram horns and also wears the royal diadem, a single forehead *uraeus* and the royal beard. He holds a *was* stave in his hand, while the object held in the other hand is no longer visible owing to cut marks. He is described in the cartouche as Ptolemy. The figure has been badly damaged by large fractures in the stone blocks but mainly by cut marks, especially in the facial area and the abdomen. The crown has been left untouched by cut marks but is slightly damaged on the top by a fracture. The throne has been left untouched by cut marks.

Behind the male figure stands another female figure in a protective position. She wears a tripartite wig, the royal diadem and a single forehead *uraeus*. She wears the traditional female crown. She holds an *ankh* in her resting hand. The figure has been badly damaged mainly by cut marks which focus on the facial area but also include the main body. The cartouche is erased by a fracture in the stone block.

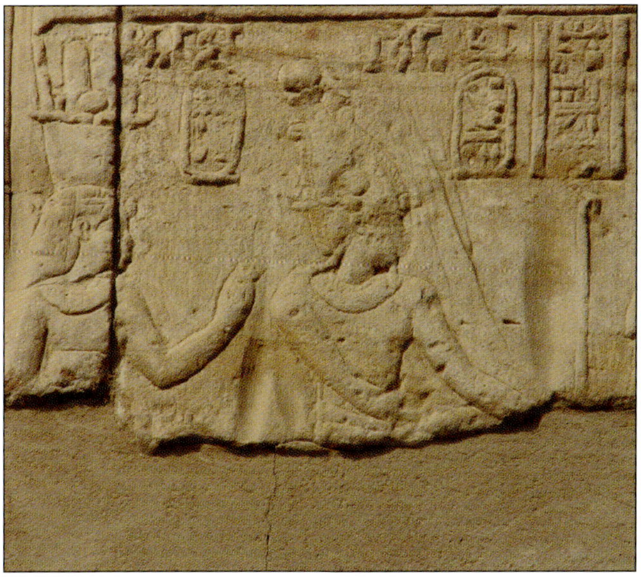

35. Tod. Photos: The author.

Another set of five figures is depicted in the lower section. The first figure is a male wearing the *atef* crown resting on the ram horns. He also wears the royal diadem and the pharaonic beard. He holds a *was* stave in his hand. The figure has been badly damaged by large fractures in the stone blocks but also by cut marks focusing on the facial area. The lower part of the body is totally erased by the fractures. The hieroglyphic text has been badly damaged by later interference, but states the name Ptolemy.

The figure behind the male figure is another male. He wears the *nemes* wig, a single forehead *uraeus*, the royal diadem and the pharaonic beard. He wears the *anedjti* crown and is decorated with a necklace. The figure has been badly damaged by large fractures in the stone block and later cut marks. The crown and the majority of the facial features are preserved without any major damage. Only the left side of the upper part of the cartouche is preserved, though the following text describes him as Ptolemy III Euergetes.

Behind the male figure is a female figure wearing the tripartite wig, a single forehead *uraeus* and the royal diadem. She wears the traditional female crown resting on a low modus. She is also decorated with a necklace and is dressed in the traditional sheat dress. She holds her hand in a protective manner. The other hand is no longer visible owing to a large fracture in the stone block. The text in the cartouche has been badly damaged by later interference. She is described as the 'Divine mother (Berenice)| *thea Euergetis*'. The lower part of the figure is erased by a large fracture in the stone block while the rest of the figure has been badly damaged by cut marks.

The figure behind the female figure is a male who wears the *atef* crown resting upon the ram horns. He also wears the royal diadem, a single forehead *uraeus*, the royal diadem and a necklace. He holds a *was* stave in his hand. He is described in the text as Ptolemy Philadelphos. The lower part of the figure is erased by the large fracture in the stone surface while the upper part of the figure has been badly damaged by cut marks, especially in the facial area.

Behind Ptolemy Philadelphos stands Arsinoë. She wears a tripartite wig, a single forehead *uraeus*, a royal diadem and the crown of Arsinoë. She is dressed in the traditional sheat dress and wears a necklace. Arsinoë holds her preserved hand in a protective manner. She is described in the text as 'Divine mother of his mothers, Arsinoë the divine Philadelphos'.

Both scenes of ancestors are crowned by the hieroglyphic sky-sign.

Remarks: The female figures are all equal in size and are all depicted higher than the male figures.

36. Medamoud, Sed festival Gate of Ptolemy II

Sunken relief
Sandstone
Date: Ptolemy II Philadelphos
Published: Sambin and Carlotti 1995, 383–457; Quaegebeur 1998, no. 31
Crown of the scene: TFC

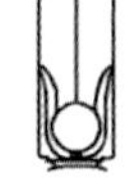

Hand-held objects: Lotus flail
State of preservation: The figure is divided by the fracture of the stone block. The fracture cuts off the back part of the figure, *i.e.*, the back part of the head and headdress, the left arm and the hips, and the lower end cuts the figure just under the hips. The relief is, in general, in a good state of preservation, including the main details.
Iconographical description: Two main figures are depicted on this fragmentary relief.

The queen, standing at the right, wears a tripartite wig, a single forehead *uraeus* and the traditional female crown resting on a low modus. She is dressed in the traditional sheat dress and holds the lotus flail in her hands. The figure is preserved only in a fragment, leaving only the front part of the queen visible, with the fracture dividing the figure at the back of the head as well as at the lower end just below the hip area. Except for the fragmented condition of the relief, the figure is in a good state of preservation.

In front of Arsinoë is Ptolemy II. He is dressed in the red crown, a single forehead *uraeus* and the pharaonic beard. He wears the traditional kilt and holds the royal regalia. He is depicted inside the Sed festival pavilion, including his cartouche, which states 'Lord of the crowns (Ptolemy)|'.

A third figure is only vaguely visible because of a fracture in the stone block as well as its position. Only the back part of a head is preserved, showing a figure wearing either a *khat* cap or a short wig. The figure is either in a position of *proskynesis* or of offering.

A hieroglyphic inscription located opposite the royal couple states 'Female Pharaoh'.

Remarks: Quaegebeur has documented another fragmentary block from Medamoud which was found among the debris of the foundation of the pylon, in which Arsinoë wears her traditional personal crown. Unfortunately neither Quaegebeur nor Sambin published a photograph of the item and the IFAO has not been able to relocate this block. Arsinoë is the tallest figure of the scene.

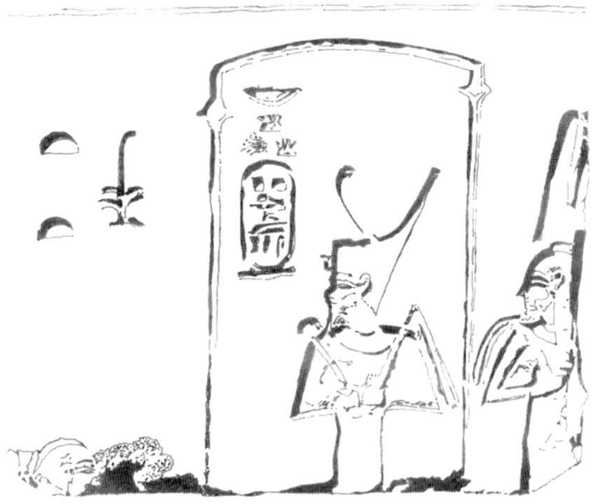

36. Medamoud, Sed festival Gate of Ptolemy II. Drawing: J. Ward.

Notes

1 The compiled scenes of Arsinoë include all existing reliefs of the queen except for four scenes. The first two excluded scenes depict Arsinoë in a pure Egyptian style in which she is placed among the local deities. These two reliefs exist only as drawings made during the 19th century, and their present state of preservation or precise location is unknown. Early drawings of relief scenes are sometimes inaccurate, hence the exclusion of these two scenes. However, they will be discussed as external references. The first relief scene was documented on a stele found in the modern city of Saft el-Henneh and is documented in E. Naville's publication of 1888, but since then has been lost. Recently it was briefly mentioned in connection with the Sais stele and the introduction of the cult of Arsinoë in the *chora* (*e.g.* Collombert 2008, 93, and fig. 2 on p. 101). The second relief was found in 1837 in the Masara quarries, in connection with work carried out in the Giza area. A drawing was published of the relief in 1837 by R. W. Howard-Vyse and J. S. Perring (1842), and has not been relocated since. J. Quaegebeur (*e.g.* 1978, 251, fig. H) refers several times to this relief. The other two scenes are documented by Quaegebeur (1998) as fragmentary blocks illustrating the crown of Arsinoë. He places the origin of the objects in Medamoud and Mut (Karnak) temples respectively. However, the objects have not been published and their current location is unknown. Consequently, these objects have not been studied.

2 Capital letters within brackets correspond to the official designations given in the Edfu (*Edfou*) and Dendera (*Dendara*) publications.

3 These are divided here as raised or sunken relief (relating to the conventional terms relief and intaglio).

4 This is documented only in cat. nos 1–15 owing to the medium (*i.e.*, stelai or decrees).

5 Cat. nos 37–154 are published previously mainly in a general introduction or in connection with the publication of the hieroglyphic text of the scene (only rarely translated).

6 With reference to previous publications describing the full scene rather than the crown itself.

7 Including the tallest figure of the scene.

Appendix I
Summary of the contextual structure of the material

SCENE	ILLUSTRATION	CROWN TYPE	HANDHELD UNITS	OFFERING	TYPE OF SCENE	ARSINOË IS TALLEST FIGURE	FIGURAL POSITIONS	LOCATION	DATE	IDENTIFICATION	DEITIES IN THE SCENE	CUT MARKS/ RECUT
1L	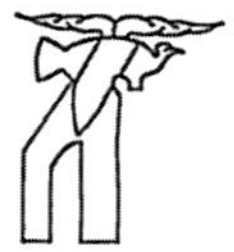	AC 1		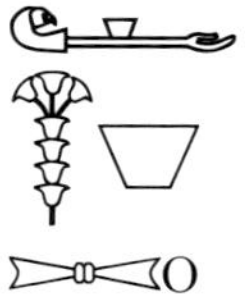 O	A		B **L** *S*	MEN	PT II	Arsinoë	–	
1R	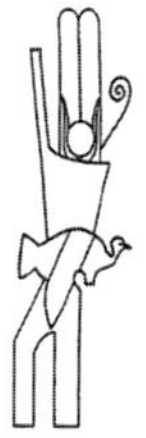	AC 2			O		R **R** *S*	MEN	PT II	Arsinoë	Banebdjedet x 2, Harpocrates, Hat-Mehit, Arsinoë	
2L	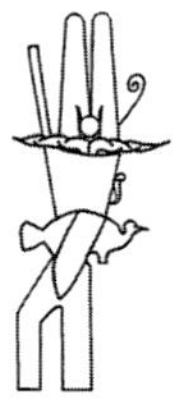	AC 3		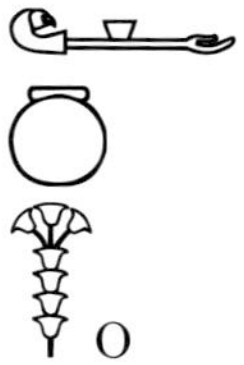 O	A		R **R** *S*	PIT	PT II	Arsinoë	Atum, Hathor, Arsinoë	
2R	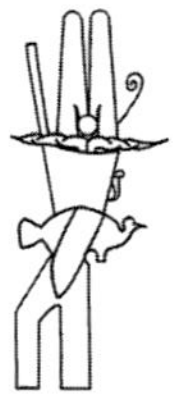	AC 3		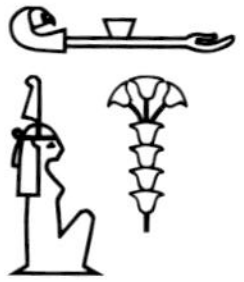	A	•	R **L** *S*	PIT	PT II	Arsinoë	Atum, Osiris, Horus, Isis, Arsinoë	
3	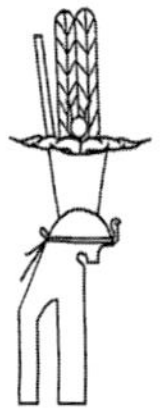	AC 4	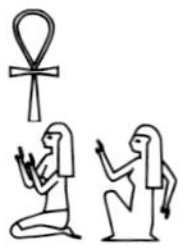	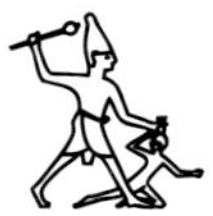	S+D	•	R **L** *S*	NAU	PT V	Arsinoë	Shu, Tefnut, ADE, EUE, PAT	

SCENE	ILLUSTRATION	CROWN TYPE	HANDHELD UNITS	OFFERING	TYPE OF SCENE	ARSINOË IS TALLEST FIGURE	FIGURAL POSITIONS	LOCATION	DATE	IDENTIFICATION	DEITIES IN THE SCENE	CUT MARKS/ RECUT
4	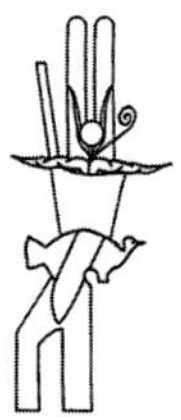	AC 5			R+D		R **L** *S*	KOM	PT III	Arsinoë	Hathor x 2, Horus, Amun-Ra, Atum, Tefnut, Shu, Thoth, Seshat, ADE, SOT	
5	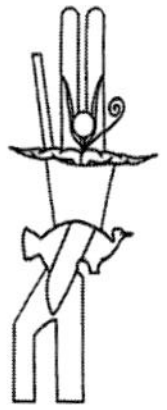	AC 5		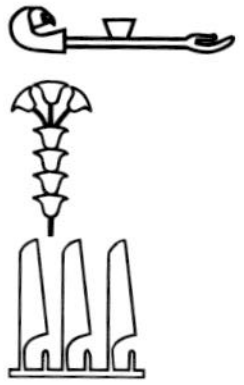	A	•	R **L** *S*	MEN	PT II	Arsinoë	Banebdjedet, Isis, Arsinoë	
6	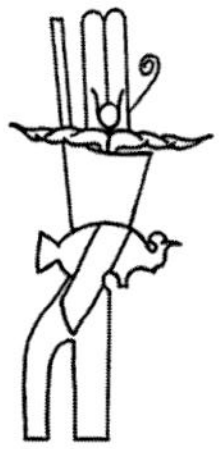	AC 6		O	A	•	R **R** *S*	DIO	PT II	Arsinoë	Horus(?), Hathor(?), Arsinoë	
7	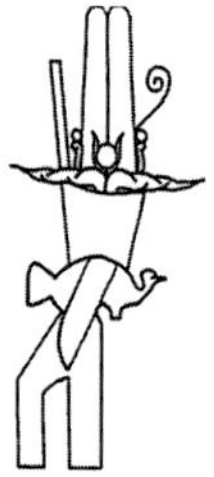	AC 7		O	A	•	R **L** *S*	TAP	PT II	Arsinoë	Arsinoë	
8	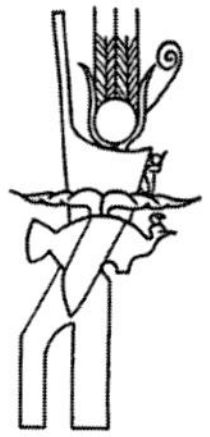	AC 8		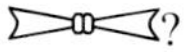?	A	•	B **L** *S*	?	AL	Arsinoë	Thoth or Khonsu or Apis ?	

SCENE	ILLUSTRATION	CROWN TYPE	HANDHELD UNITS	OFFERING	TYPE OF SCENE	ARSINOË IS TALLEST FIGURE	FIGURAL POSITIONS	LOCATION	DATE	IDENTIFICATION	DEITIES IN THE SCENE	CUT MARKS/ RECUT
9	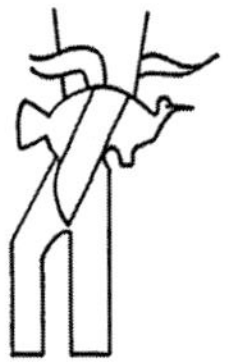	AC 9	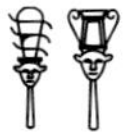		A+E		B **L** *S*	MEM?	AL	Arsinoë	–	
10	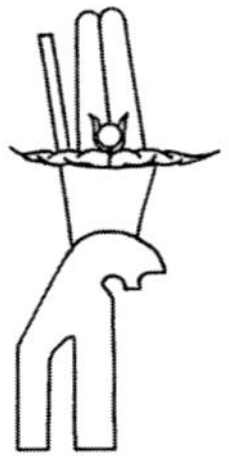	AC 4	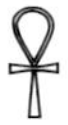	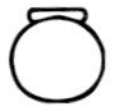	A	•	R **L** *S*	?	PT II	Arsinoë	Arsinoë	
11	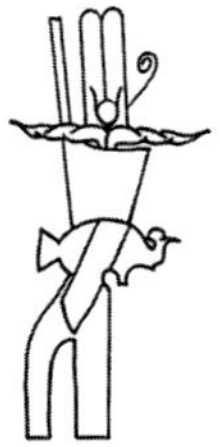	AC 6		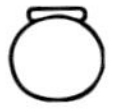	A		R **L** *S*	CRO?	PT II	Arsinoë	Harsomtus, Horus, Hathor, Sarapis, Arsinoë	
12	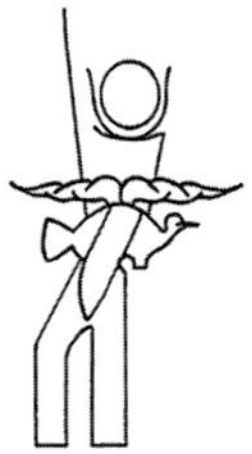	AC 10	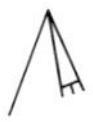		O		B? **L** *S*	MEM?	AL	Arsinoë	–	
13	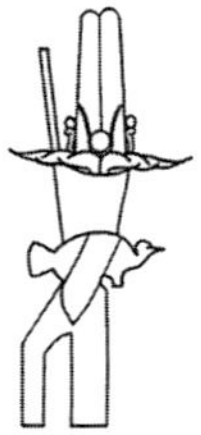	AC 12		O	A	•	R **L** *S*	TAN	PT II	Arsinoë	Arsinoë	

SCENE	ILLUSTRATION	TYPE	UNITS	OFFERING	OF SCENE	IS TALLEST FIGURE	POSITIONS	LOCATION	DATE	IDENTIFICATION	SCENE	RECUT
14	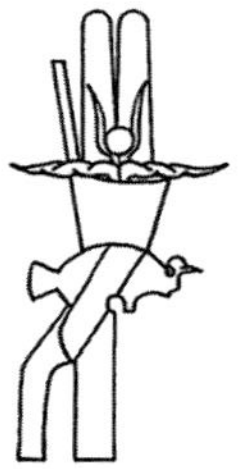	AC 11		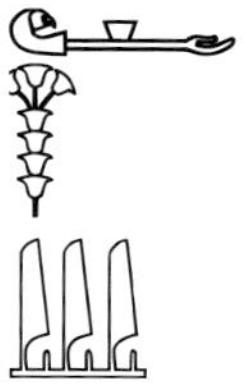	A		R **L** *S*	TAN	PT II	Arsinoë	Amun-Min, Arsinoë; Harsomtus, Wadjet	
15L	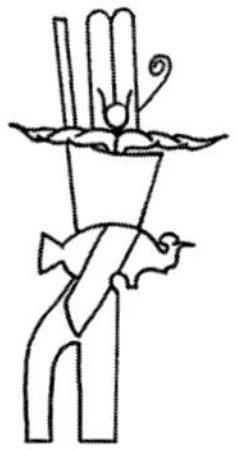	AC 6	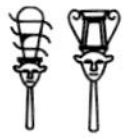	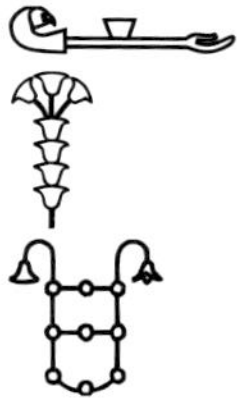	A+E	•	B **L** *S*	ATH	AL	Arsinoë	Horus, Sekhmet	
15R	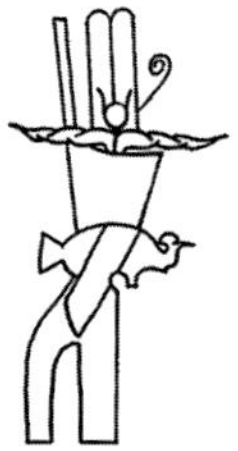	AC 6	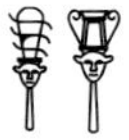	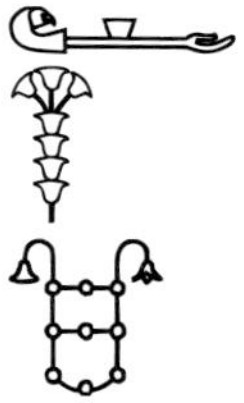	A+E	•	B **R** *S*	ATH	AL	Arsinoë	Osiris, Khuit	
16	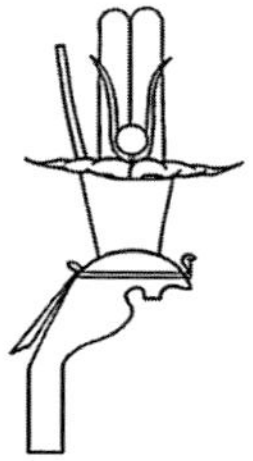	AC 11	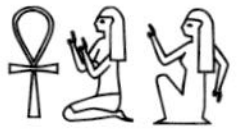	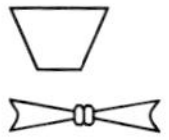	A+D		R **L** *S*	EDF	PT VIII	Arsinoë	ADE	•
17	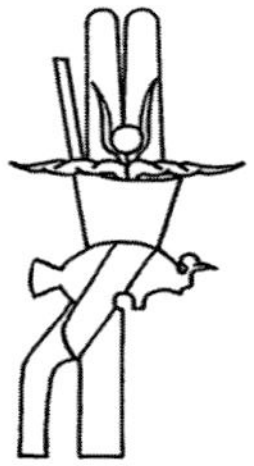	AC 11	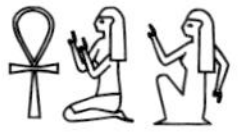	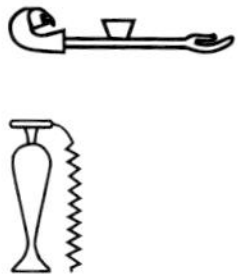	A+D	•	R **R** *S*	EDF	PT IV	Arsinoë	ADE	•

SCENE	ILLUSTRATION	CROWN TYPE	HANDHELD UNITS	OFFERING	TYPE OF SCENE	ARSINOË IS TALLEST FIGURE	FIGURAL POSITIONS	LOCATION	DATE	IDENTIFICATION	DEITIES IN THE SCENE	CUT MARKS/ RECUT
18	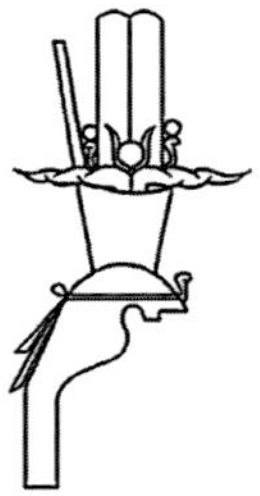	AC 12	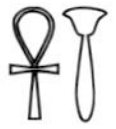		A+D		R **L** *S*	EDF	PT IV	Arsinoë	Horus, Hathor, Harsomtus, ADE, EUE, SOT	
19	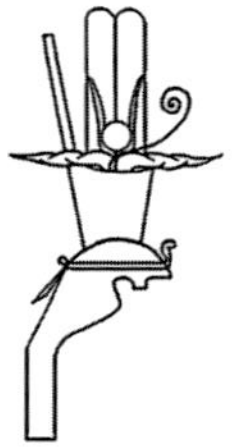	AC 5	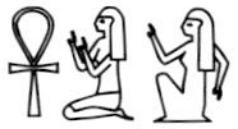	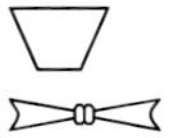	A+D	•	R **L** *S*	EDF	PT IV	Arsinoë	ADE	•
20	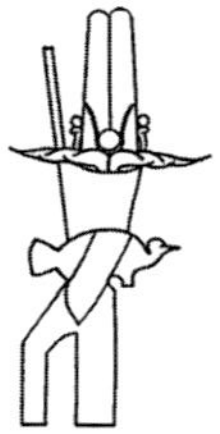	AC 12			R+D	•	**L** *T*	EDF	PT IV	Arsinoë	Thoth, Seshat, Horus, Hathor, ADE	•
21	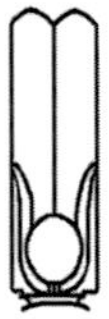	TFC	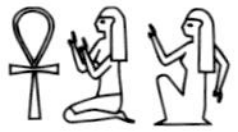	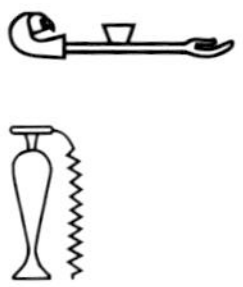	A+D		R **L** *S*	EDF	PT VIII	Arsinoë	ADE	•
22	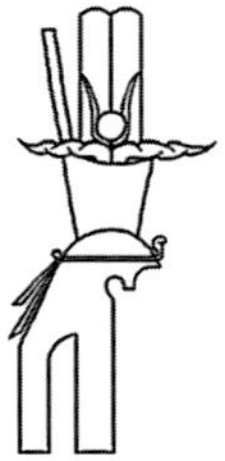	AC 11	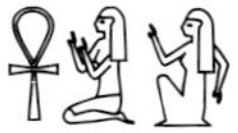	O	A+D	•	R **R** *S*	EDF	PT IV	Arsinoë	ADE	•
23	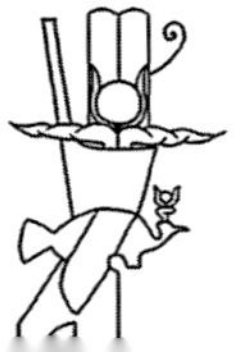	AC 13		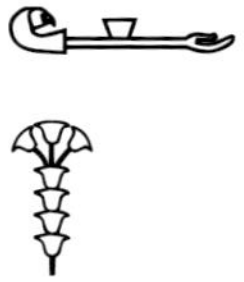	A	•	R **L** *S*	KAR	PT II	Arsinoë	Khonsu, Arsinoë	•

SCENE	ILLUSTRATION	CROWN TYPE	HANDHELD UNITS	OFFERING	TYPE OF SCENE	ARSINOË IS TALLEST FIGURE	FIGURAL POSITIONS	LOCATION	DATE	IDENTIFICATION	DEITIES IN THE SCENE	CUT MARKS/ RECUT
24	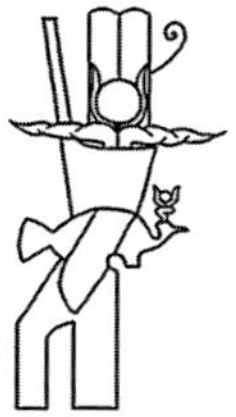	AC 13		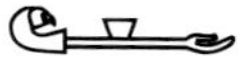	A+D	•	R **L** *S*	KAR	PT III	Arsinoë	ADE	•
25	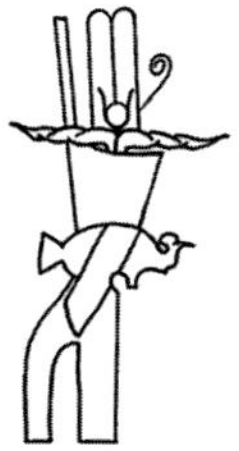	AC 6	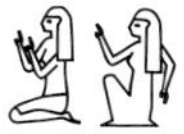		AD	•	– **L** *S*	KAR	PT III	Arsinoë	Pantheon, ADE, EUE	•
26L	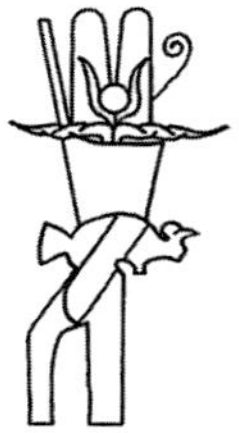	AC 13		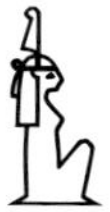	A		B+R **L+R** *S*	KAR	AL+ PT II	Arsinoë	Amun, Mut, Arsinoë	•
26R	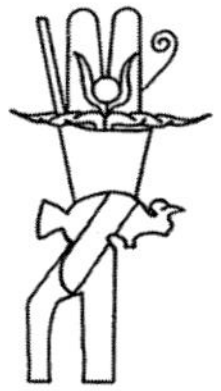	AC 13		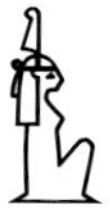	A		R **L** *S*	KAR	AL+ PT II	Arsinoë	Amun, Khonsu, Arsinoë	•
27	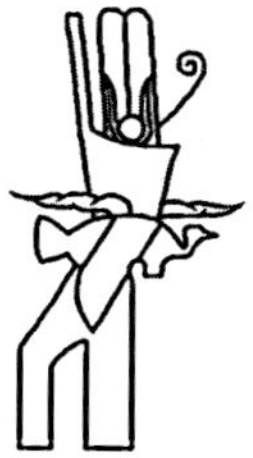	AC 14	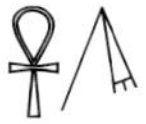	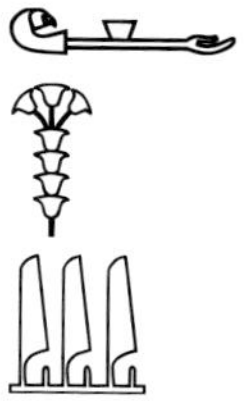	A		R **R** *S*	PHI	PT II	Arsinoë	Isis, Arsinoë	•

SCENE	ILLUSTRATION	CROWN TYPE	HANDHELD UNITS	OFFERING	TYPE OF SCENE	ARSINOË IS TALLEST FIGURE	FIGURAL POSITIONS	LOCATION	DATE	IDENTIFICATION	DEITIES IN THE SCENE	CUT MARKS/ RECUT
28	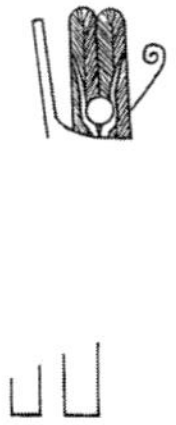	AC 15		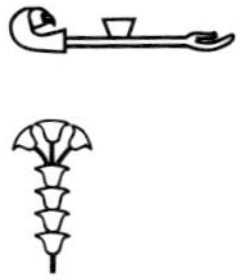	A	•	R **L** *S*	PHI	PT II	Arsinoë	Nephtys, Arsinoë	•
29	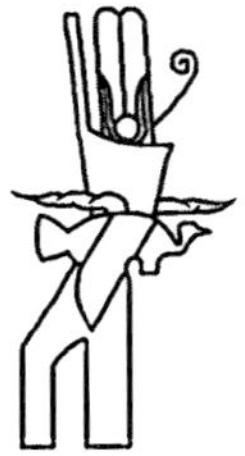	AC 14	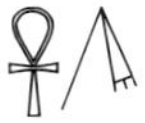	O	A	•	R **L** *S*	PHI	PT II	Arsinoë	Isis, Arsinoë	•
30	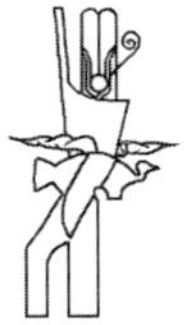	AC 16		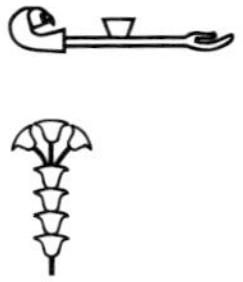	A		R **L** *S*	PHI	PT II	Arsinoë	Isis, Arsinoë	
31	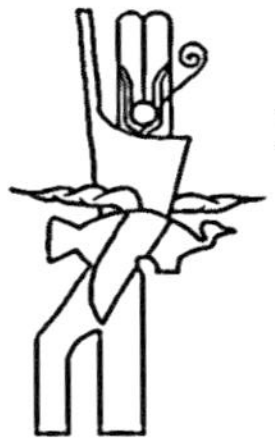	AC 17	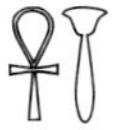	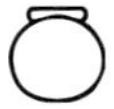	A	•	R **R** *S*	PHI	PT II	Arsinoë	Isis, Arsinoë	•
32	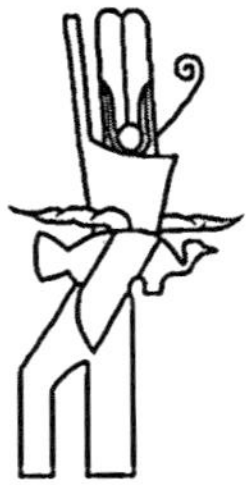	AC 14		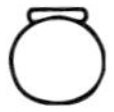	A		R **L** *S*	PHI	PT II	Arsinoë	Isis, Arsinoë	

SCENE	ILLUSTRATION	CROWN TYPE	HANDHELD UNITS	OFFERING	TYPE OF SCENE	ARSINOË IS TALLEST FIGURE	FIGURAL POSITIONS	LOCATION	DATE	IDENTIFICATION	DEITIES IN THE SCENE	CUT MARKS/ RECUT
33	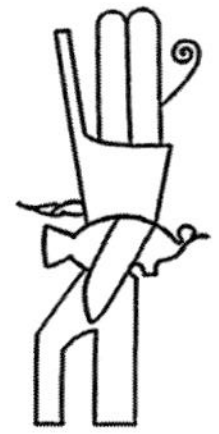	AC 18	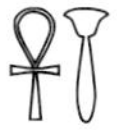	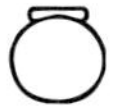	A	•	R **R** *S*	PHI	PT II	Arsinoë	Arsinoë	
34	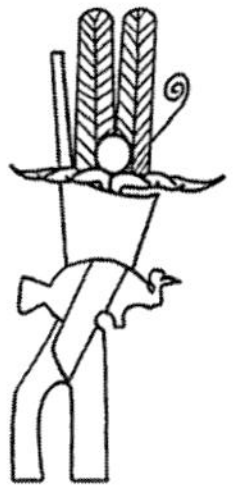	AC 19			AD+D	•	R **R** *S*	QAS	PT VIII	Arsinoë	ADE	•
35	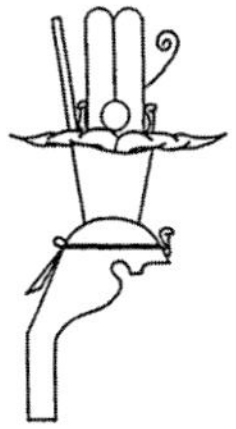	AC 20	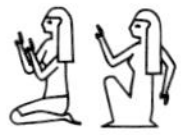	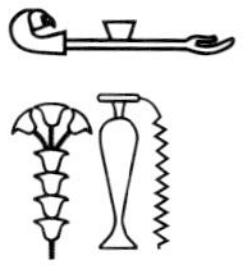	A+D		R **L** *S*	TOD	PT VIII	Arsinoë	ADE, EUE, PAT, EPI, MET, EUP	
36	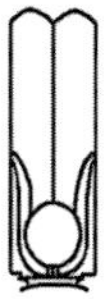	TFC	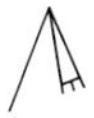		R	•	R **R** *S*	MED	PT II	Arsinoë	–	

Key:

Crown type: AC = Crown of Arsinoë; TFC = Traditional female crown

Handheld objects:

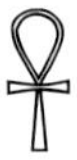 = *ankh*

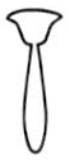 = papyrus sceptre

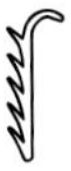 = notched palm branch

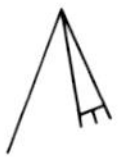 = flail

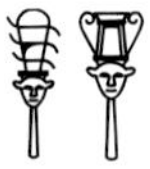 = sistrum

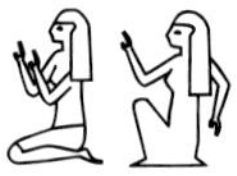 = hand held in protective manner

Offerings:

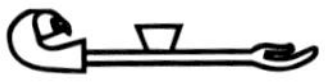 = all incense

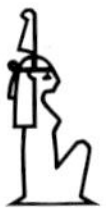 = figure of Maat

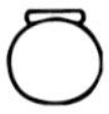 = wine and water

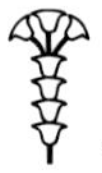 = Flowers

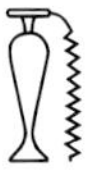 = libation and *hes* vessel

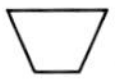 = ointment

 = offering table or tray

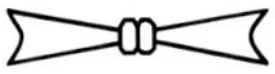 = textile band/cloth

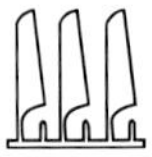 = field of reeds

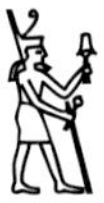 =*sekhem* stave

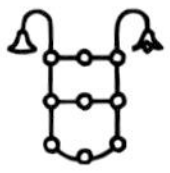 = ceremonial collar

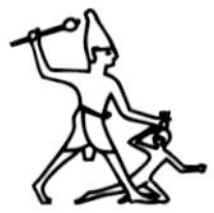 = spearing enemies; O = other or unrecognised

Type of scene: A = Active offering; AD = Adoration; I = Inactively standing before the deity; S = Smiting scenes; R = Rejuvenation/sed/crowning ceremonies; D = Dynastic scenes; E = Evoking/arousing the god; O = Other

Figural positions: Top line: B = Benefactor or R = Recipient; middle line (bold): **L** = Left side position or **R** = Right side position; Bottom line (italic): *S* = Standing or *T* = Throne (sitting)

Location/place of origin: EDF = Edfu; PHI = Philae; KAR = Karnak; QAS = Qasr el Aguz; MED = Medamoud; TOD = el Tod; MEN = Mendes; MEM = Memphis; PIT = Pithom; TAN = Tanis; ATH = Athribis; NAU = Naukratis; KOM = Kom el Hisn

Date: AL = Arsinoë's lifetime; PT = Ptolemy (II–XII)

Deities: SOT = *theoi Soteres*; ADE = *theoi Adelphoi*; EUE = *theoi Euergetai*; PAT = *theoi Philopatores*; EPI = *theoi Epiphanes*; MET = Ptolemy VI Philometor; EUP = Ptolemy VII Eupator

Appendix II
Translated designations

1L 'Holder of the sacred insignia, the divine Philadelphos, Beloved of the ram, Mistress of the Two Lands, Arsinoë'

1R 'King's daughter, sister, his greatly beloved wife, the divine Philadelphos, Arsinoë'

1M Above the scene: 'King's Daughter, sister, wife, Mistress of the Two Lands, Arsinoë, may she live forever'
'Princess, Great of Praise, she who belongs to the Lord, Sweet of Love, Beautiful in appearance, who received the two forehead *uraei* (= Upper and Lower Egypt), she who fills the palace with her beauty, she who is the high-priestess of Banebdjedet, Beloved of the ram, sister of the king (of Upper Egypt), daughter of the king (of Upper Egypt), greatly beloved wife of the king (of Upper Egypt), Mistress of the Two Lands, Arsinoë'

2L 'King's daughter, sister, and wife, She who is in the heart of Shu, Beloved of the gods, Great Lady of the Two Lands, Arsinoë, the living image of Isis and Hathor'

2R 'King's daughter, sister, and wife, She who is in the heart of Shu, Beloved of the gods, Great Lady of the Two Lands, Arsinoë, the living image of Isis and Hathor' [*cf.* Troy 1986, 182: the one who is united with the heart of Shu]

2M 'King's wife, daughter, Mistress of the Two Lands, Arsinoë, Daughter of the king (of Upper Egypt), Lord of the Two Lands, Ptolemy, the divine Philadelphos' ... 'Queen who is great of praise, a Lady of Loveliness, sweet of love, King's wife, the Mistress of the Two Lands, Arsinoë, Daughter of the king (of Upper Egypt), Lord of the Two Lands, Ptolemy, the divine (goddess) Philadelphos'

3 'Arsinoë the divine Philadelphos, *theoi Adelphoi*'

4 'Arsinoë Philadelphos, *theoi Adelphoi*'

5 'King of Upper and Lower Egypt, Banebdjedet, Lady of the Two Lands, Arsinoë Philadelphos'

6 'Arsinoë'

7 'King of Upper and Lower Egypt, Arsinoë Philadelphos'

8 'Great of Sweetness, Great of Praise, King's daughter, King's wife, Great daughter, King's sister, who loves her and she loves him, King's great wife, King of Upper and Lower Egypt, Arsinoë Philadelphos, the Rightful'

9 –

10 empty cartouche

11 'Lady of the Two Lands, Arsinoë, may she live forever'

12 'Daughter of Amun, Arsinoë, [She who is in the heart of Shu] Loved [by (all) the gods], mother of Hep, repeating life'

13 'King of Lower Egypt, the Two Lands, she who is in the heart of the king, Beloved of (all) the gods, daughter of Amun, Lady of the crowns, Arsinoë Philadelphos'

14 'Daughter of Amun, Lady of the crowns, Arsinoë Philadelphos, King of Upper and Lower Egypt, the Two Lands, [she who is in the heart of the king/Shu] Beloved of [(all) the gods]'

15L–R 'King of Upper and Lower Egypt, Arsinoë'

16 'Royal mother, Arsinoë, the sister-wife of Ptolemy' '*Theoi Adelphoi*, Lords of the house of Hathor'

17 'Divine mother, Arsinoë the divine Philadelphos' '*Theoi Adelphoi*, Lords of Edfu (Mesen)'

18 'Divine mother Arsinoë' '*Theoi Adelphoi*, the Lords of the house of Ra'

19 'Divine Mother Arsinoë' '*Theoi Adelphoi*, who dwells in the temple of Horus'

20 'Divine mother, the eye of Horus (his great eye?), Arsinoë'

21 'The mistress of her brother (?) Arsinoë, Ptolemy's (his) divine sister' '*Theoi Adelphoi* who dwells in Edfu (Mesen)'

22 'Divine mother, Arsinoë, *Theoi Adelphoi*, Lords of the house of Ra'

23 'Daughter of the King of Upper Egypt, sister of the king of Upper Egypt, King's great wife, Lady of the Two Lands, Daughter of Amun, Arsinoë, the divine Philadelphos'

24 'Daughter of Amun, Arsinoë, the divine Philadelphos' '*Theoi Adelphoi* (who dwells in) Apet – Karnak'

25 'Arsinoë, daughter of Amun' '*Theoi Adelphoi*'

26L 'King's Daughter, sister of the king of Upper Egypt, King's great wife, Lady of the Two Lands, Mistress of Eternity, Lady of the solar disc, Daughter of Amun, Arsinoë the divine Philadelphos ...' 'the manifestation of Ptah, the king of all souls, Lord of sacredness'

26R	'Daughter of the king, sister of the king of Upper Egypt, King's great wife, Lady of the Two Lands, Mistress of Eternity, Lady of the sun disk (Aten), Daughter of Amun, Arsinoë, the divine Philadelphos, Divine mother (Isis) of the living bull, the manifestation of Ptah, the king of all souls, Lord of sacredness'
27	'King's wife, daughter, and his sister, Daughter of Amun [... brother/sibling][...], ruler [...], Lady of the Two Lands, Arsinoë Philadelphos'
28	'Princess, Great of praise, Lady of (all) the people, Sweet of Love, Mistress of Upper and Lower Egypt, King's wife, sister [...], Daughter of Amun, Lady of the Two Lands, Arsinoë the divine Philadelphos'
29	'King's wife, daughter, sister, Daughter of Amun, sister of the king of Upper Egypt, Arsinoë'
30	'Lady of the Two Lands, Arsinoë'
31	'King's wife, daughter, sister, Daughter of Amun, Lady of the Two Lands, the divine Philadelphos, Arsinoë, Princess, Great of Praise, Lady of Sweet Love, Mistress of Upper and Lower Egypt, Ruler of Egypt, Lady of the Two Lands, Arsinoë'
32	'King's wife, daughter, his sister, Daughter of Amun, Lady of the Two Lands, Arsinoë the divine Philadelphos, Princess, Great of Praise, Lady of Sweet Love, Mistress of Upper and Lower Egypt, Ruler of Egypt, Lady of the Two Lands, Arsinoë, may she live forever'
33	'Lady of the Two Lands, Arsinoë, given eternal life'
34	'Divine Mother of his mothers, Arsinoë the divine Philadelphos'
35	'Divine Mother of his mothers, Arsinoë the divine Philadelphos'
36	'Female Pharaoh'

Appendix III
Arsinoë's cartouches

DESIGNATION	TRANSCRIPTION	HIEROGLYPHS	CAT. NOS.
Arsinoë	*Ỉ-r-s-n-ꜣ*	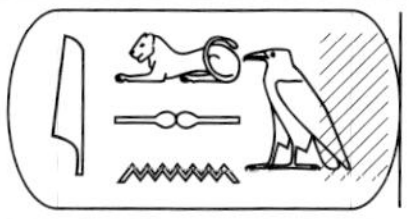	1L
	Ỉ-r-s-n-ꜣ-j-t	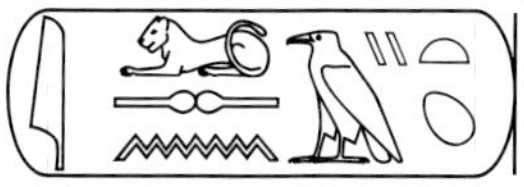	1M
	Ỉ-r-s-n-i-ꜣ	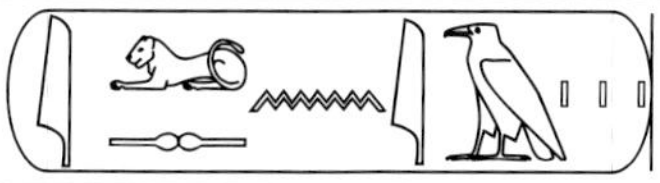	2L
	Ỉ-r-s-[n-]i-ꜣ	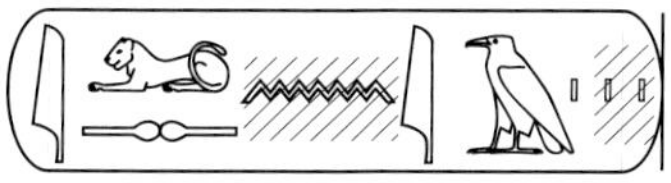	2R
	Ỉ-r-s-n-ꜣ-t	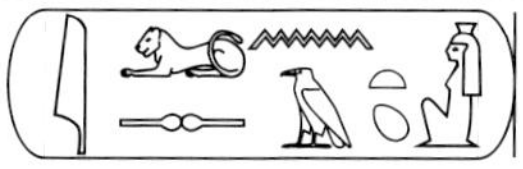	2M
	J-r-s-ꜣ-t	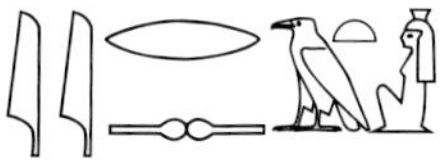	3
	ꜣ [...] [*j*]	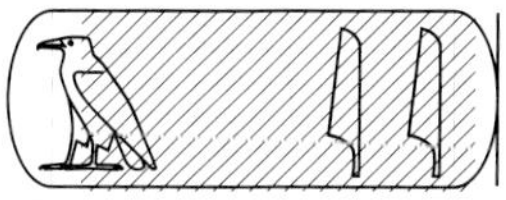	6
	Ỉ-r-s- [...] *n*	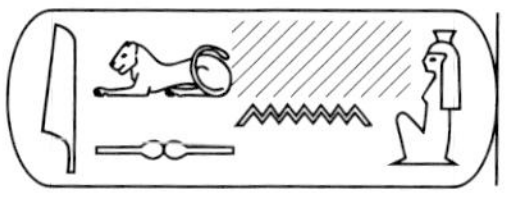	11
	sꜣt Ỉmn Ỉ-r-s-n-ꜣ	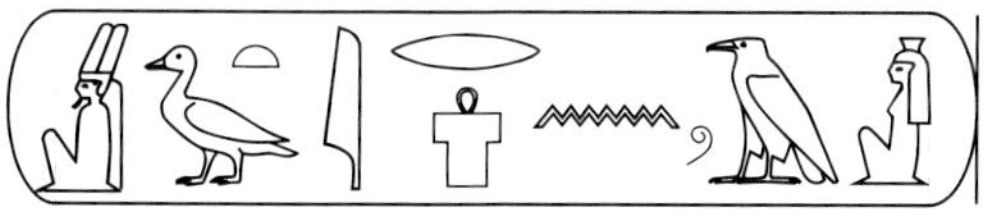	12
	ꜣ-r-n [...]	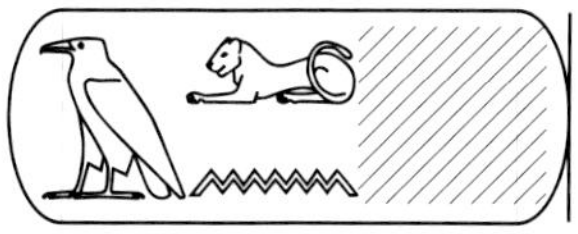	15L
	ꜣ-r-n-f [...]	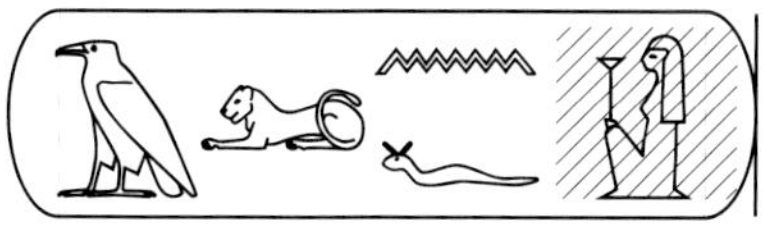	15R
	ꜣ-r-j-j-n-t	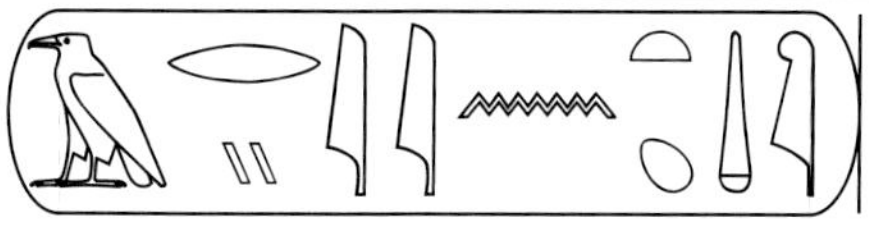	16
	Ỉ-r-s-sn-n-ꜣ-t	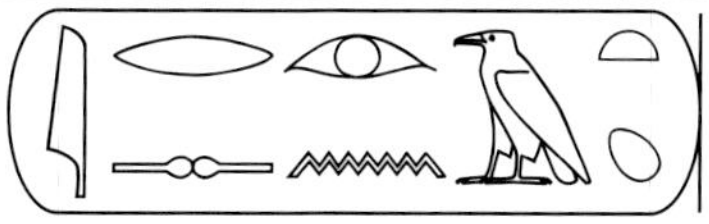	18
	Ỉ-r-s-j-n-ꜣ-t	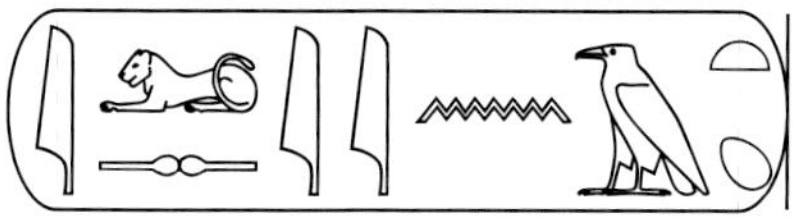	19

DESIGNATION	TRANSCRIPTION	HIEROGLYPHS	CAT. NOS.
	Ỉ-r-s-n-sn-ꜣ	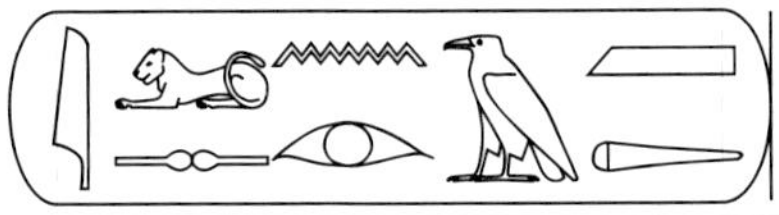	20
	ꜣ-r-s-sn-j	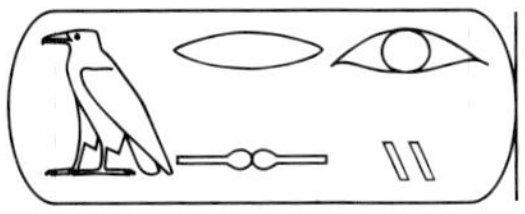	21
	ꜣ-r-s-sn-n-ꜣ-t	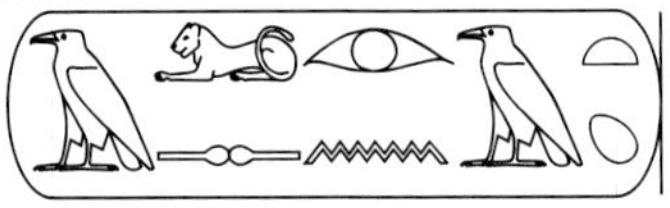	22
	Ỉ-r-s-sn-n-ꜣ-t	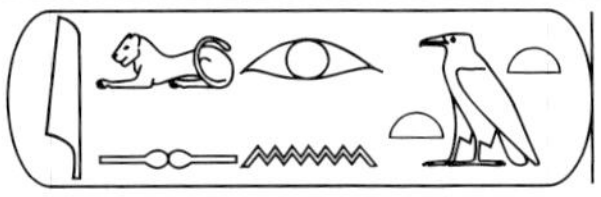	25
	ꜣ-r-s-n-t	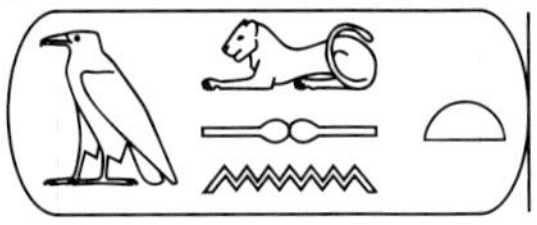	29
	ꜣ-r-s-n	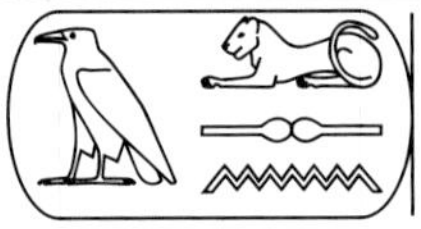	30–33
Arsinoë Philadelphos	*Ỉ-r-s-sn-t i-n-t-sn*	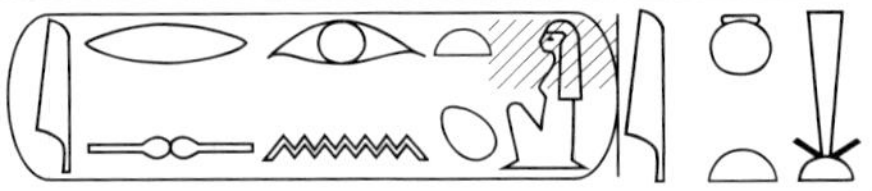	4
	ꜣ-r-s-n [...] [...] *mr-sn*	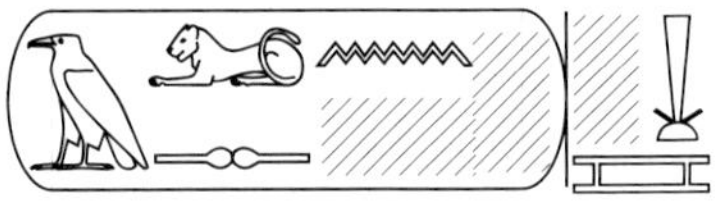	5
	ꜣ-r-s- [*n*] *mr-sn-s*	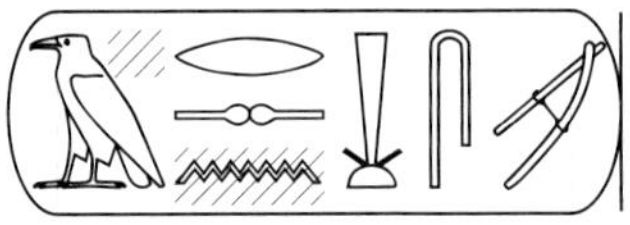	7
	Ỉ-ꜣ-r-s-j mr-sn-s	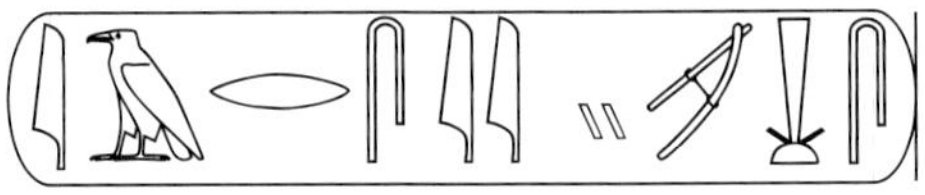	8
	ꜣ-r-s-ỉ mr-sn	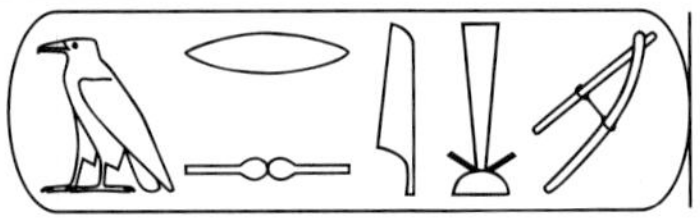	13
	ꜣ-r-s-j-n [*i*] [*mr-sn*]	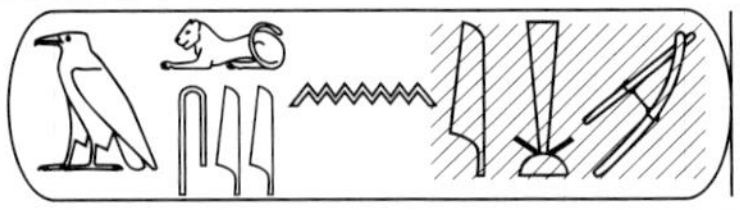	14
	ꜣ-r-s-n ḥt-sn	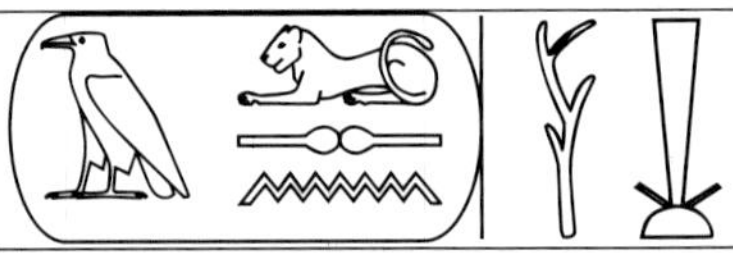	27
Arsinoë the divine Philadelphos	*Ỉ-r-s-n-ꜣ nṯrt mr-sn-s*	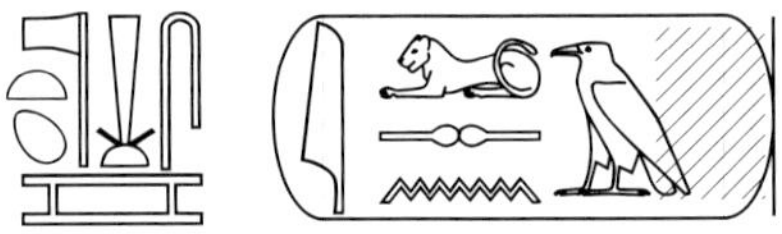	1R

DESIGNATION	TRANSCRIPTION	HIEROGLYPHS	CAT. NOS.
	Ỉ-r-s-n-ꜣ-t ntrt it mr-sn-s	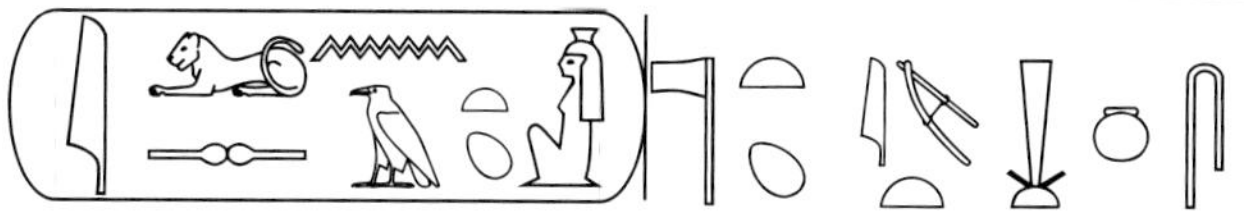	2M
	Ỉ-r-s-sn-n-ꜣ-t ntrt ꜣ mr-sn	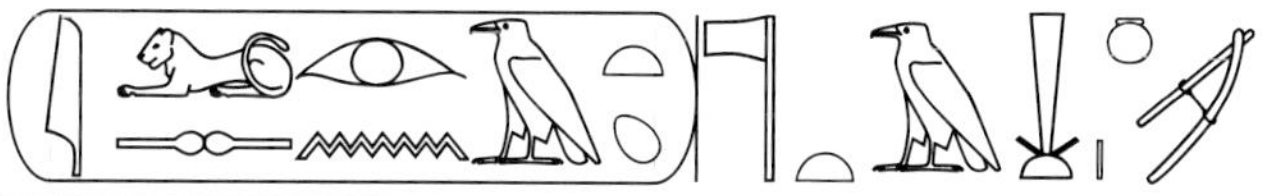	3
	ꜣ-r-s-sn-n-w-t ntrt mr-sn-s	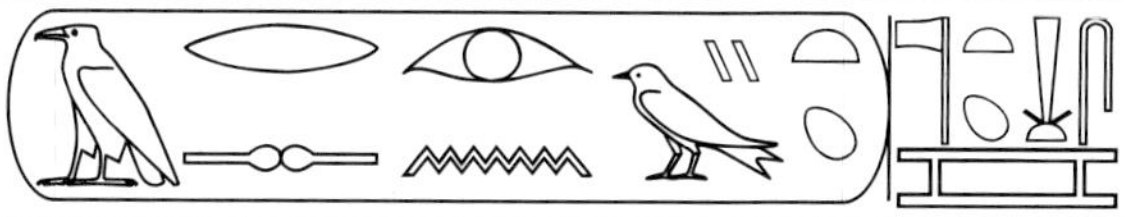	17
	ꜣ-r-s-j-n-j-f ntrt mr-sn-s	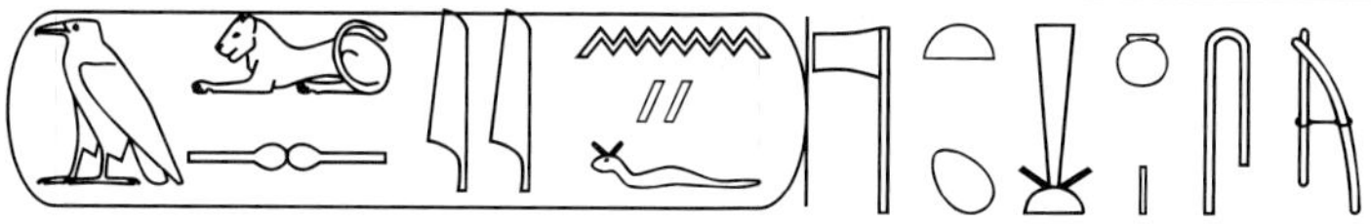	23
	ꜣ-r-s-sn-n-ꜣ-t ntrt mr-sn-s-j	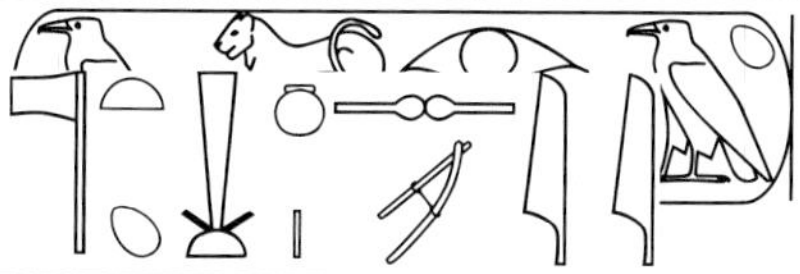	24
	Ỉ-r-s-j-n ntrt mr-sn-s	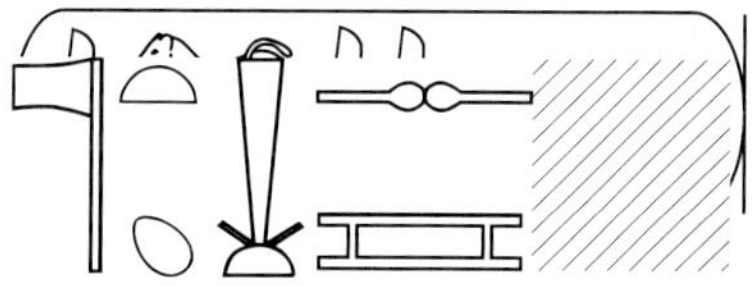	26L–R
	ꜣ-r-s-n ntrt mr-sn	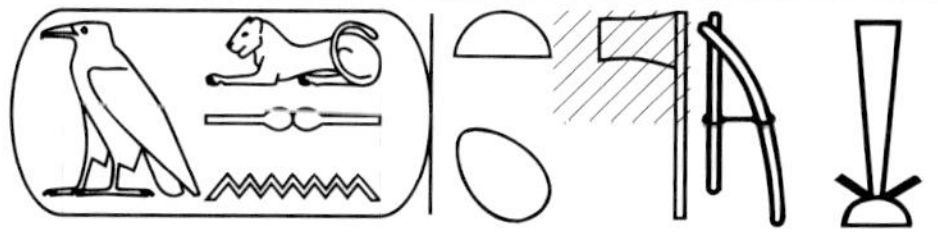	28
	ꜣ-r-s-n ntrt mr-sn-s	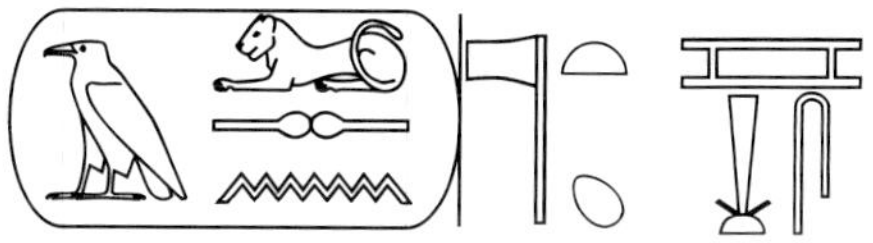	31
	ꜣ r s n ntrt mr-sn s	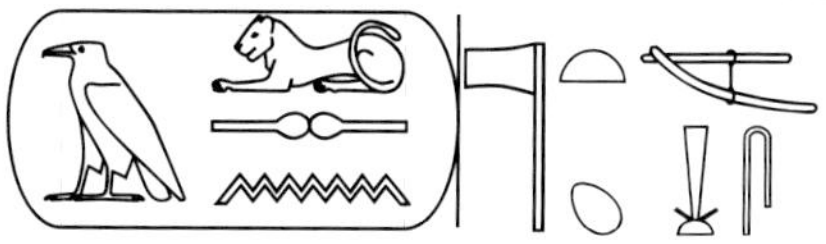	32
	Ỉ-r-s-sn-n-t ntrt mr-sn-s	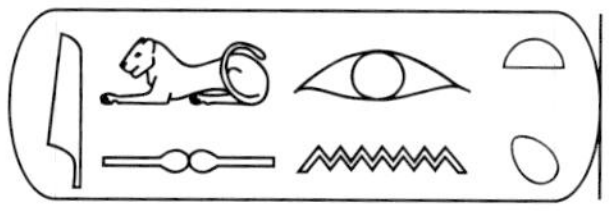	34
	[...]-*n-i-t ntrt* [*mr-*] *sn*	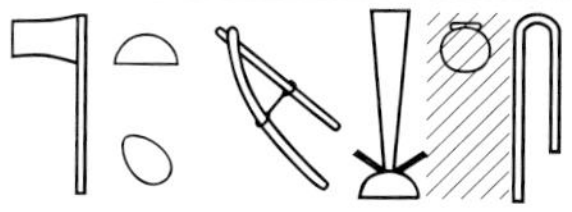	35
		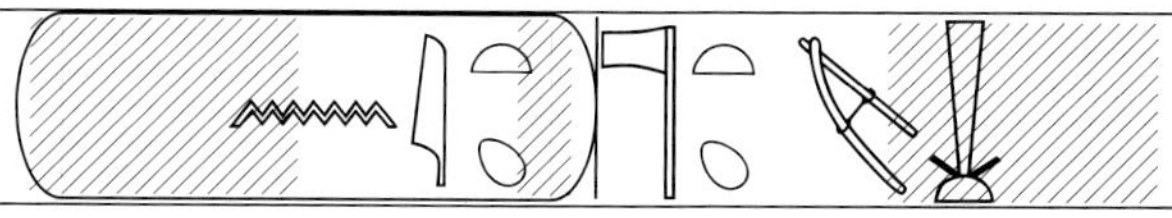	

Appendix IV
The Ptolemaic Dynasty

Rulers[1]

Ptolemy I Soter		304/305–282
	co-ruling with Ptolemy II	285/284–282
Ptolemy II Philadelphos		282–246
	co-ruling with Arsinoë II	27?–270/268
	with Ptolemy the son	267–259
Ptolemy III Euergetes		246–222
Ptolemy IV Philopator		222–204
	co-ruling with Ptolemy V	210–204
Ptolemy V Epiphanes		204–180
Ptolemy VI Philometor		180–145
	co-ruling with Cleopatra I	180–178/177
	with Ptolemy VIII Euergetes II and Cleopatra II Euergetis	170–164
	with Cleopatra II	163–145
	with Ptolemy Eupator	152
Ptolemy VIII and Cleopatra II		145–132
	co-ruling with Cleopatra III	132–130, 124–116
Cleopatra II		130–127
Cleopatra II, III and Ptolemy IX Soter II		116–115
Cleopatra III and Ptolemy IX		115–107
Cleopatra III and Ptolemy X Alexander I Philometor		107–101
Ptolemy X and Cleopatra Berenice Philopator		101–88
Ptolemy IX and Cleopatra Berenice		81
Cleopatra Berenice and Ptolemy XI Alexander II		80
Ptolemy XII Neos Dionysus Philopator Philadelphos		
	and Berenice V	80–69
Ptolemy XII		69–58
Berenice IV and Cleopatra Tryphaena		58–55
Ptolemy XII		55–51
Cleopatra VII Philopator and Ptolemy XIII Philopator		51–48
Ptolemy XIII and Arsinoë IV		48–47
Cleopatra VII and Ptolemy XIV		47–44
Cleopatra VII and Ptolemy XV Caesar Philopator Philometor ('Caesarion')		44–30

Note
1. The list is based on C. Bennett's *Ptolemaic Genealogy*, at http://www.tyndalehouse.com/Egypt/ptolemies/genealogy.htm.

Official names of the deified couples

Theoi Soteres	The saviour gods (Ptolemy I and Berenice I)
Theoi Adelphoi	The sibling gods (Ptolemy II and Arsinoë II)
Theoi Euergetai	The benefactor gods (Ptolemy III and Berenice II)
Theoi Philopatores	The father-loving gods (Ptolemy IV and Arsinoë III)
Theoi Epiphanes	The manifest gods (Ptolemy V and Cleopatra I)
Theoi Philometores	The mother-loving gods (Ptolemy VI and Cleopatra II)
Theoi Euergetai (II)	The benefactor gods (Ptolemy VIII, Cleopatra II and III)
Theoi Philometores Soteres	The mother-loving saviour Gods (Ptolemy IX, Cleopatra II and III)
Theoi Philometores Soteres	The mother-loving saviour gods (Ptolemy X and Cleopatra III)
Theoi Philopatores kai Philadelphoi	The father-loving and sibling-loving gods (Ptolemy XII and Cleopatra V)
Theoi Philopatores kai Philadelphoi	The father-loving and sibling-loving gods (Cleopatra VII and Ptolemy XIV)

Appendix V
Egyptian dynasties

Predynastic period

Ma'adi culture, northern Egypt, *c.* 4000–3300/3200 BC
Badarian culture, Middle Egypt, *c.* 4500–3800 BC
Naqada culture (I–III, Dynasty 0), Southern Egypt, *c.* 4000–3050

Early dynastic period

1st Dyn., c. *3050–2890 BC*

Aha
Djer
Djet
Den
Anedjib
Smerkhet
Qa'a

2nd Dyn., c. *2890–2686 BC*

Hotepsekhemwy
Reneb
Nynetjer
Weneg
Peribsen
Khasekhemqy

Old Kingdom

3rd Dyn., c. *2686–2613 BC*

Nebka
Zoser
Sekhemkhet
Khaba
Huni

4th Dyn., c. *2613–2494 BC*

Sneferu
Khufu (Cheops)
Djedefre
Khafre (Chefren)
Nebka
Menkaure
Shepseskaf

5th Dyn., c. *2494–2345 BC*

Weserkaf
Sahure
Neferirkare
Shepseskare
Neferefre
Nyuserre
Menkauhor
Djdkare-Isesi
Unas

6th Dyn., c. *2345–2181 BC*

Teti
Weserkare
Pepi I
Merenre
Pepi II
Nitocris (Female Pharaoh?)

First Intermediate Period

7th–8th Dynasties, c. *2181–2125 BC*

c. 16 kings

9th–10th Dynasties (Heracleopolis), c. *2160–2025 BC*

11th Dyn., pre-unification Thebes, c. *2125–2055 BC*

Mentuhotep I
Intef I
Intef II
Intef III

Middle Kingdom

11th Dyn., unification, c. *2055–1985 BC*

Mentuhotep II
Mentuhotep III
Mentuhotep IV

12th Dyn., c. *1985–1795 BC*

Amenemhat I

Senusret I
Amenemhat II
Senusret II
Amenemhat III
Amenemhat IV
Female King Sobeknefru

Second Intermediate Period

13th Dyn., c. *17950–1650 BC*

c. 65 kings, including:
Amu-sa-hornedjherjotef
Chendjer
Sobekhotep III
Neferhotep I
Sihathor I
Sihathor II
Sobekhotep IV
Neferhotep III

14th Dyn., c. *1750–1650 BC*

Up to 76 kings ruling from Sais, overlapping the 13th and 15th Dynasties

15th Dyn. (Hyksos), c. *1650–1550 BC*

Salitis
Khayan
Apophis
Khamudi

16th Dyn. (Hyksos), c. *1650–1550 BC*

c. 17 minor kings/vassals, overlapping the 15th Dyn

17th Dyn. (Thebes), c. *1650–1550 BC*

c. 14 kings, including:
Intef IV
Ta'o I
Ta'o II
Khamose

New Kingdom

18th Dyn., c. *1550–1295 BC*

Ahmose
Amenhotep I
Tuthmosis I
Tuthmosis II
Female Pharaoh Hatshepsut
Tuthmosis III
Amenhotep II
Tuthmosis IV
Amenhotep III
Amenhotep IV/Akhenaten
Smenkhare
Tutankhamen
Ay
Horemheb

19th Dyn., c. *1295–1186 BC*

Ramses I
Seti I
Ramses II
Merenptah
Amenmesses
Seti II
Siptah
Female Pharaoh Tawosret

20th Dyn., c. *1186–1069 BC*

Sethnakht
Ramses III
Ramses IV
Ramses V
Ramses VI
Ramses VII
Ramses VIII
Ramses IX
Ramses X
Ramses XI

Third Intermediate Period

21st Dyn. (Tanis), c. *1069–945 BC*

Smendes
Amenemnisu
Psusennes I
Amenemope
Osorkon the Elder
Siamen
Psusennes II

22nd Dyn. (Libyan), c. *945–735 BC*

Sheshonk I
Osorkon I
Sheshonk II
Takelot I
Osorkon II
Takelot II
Sheshonk III
Pami
Sheshonk V

Theban kings*, c. *818–730 BC

Pedubast I
Input I
Sheshonk IV (?)
Osorkon III
Takelot III
Rudamen
Iny

23rd Dyn. (Libyan)*, c. *735–710 BC

Pedubast II
Osorkon IV
Psammous

Local dynasties*, c. *730 BC

Thotemhat and Nimlot (Hermopolis)
Peftjauawybast (Heracleopolis)
Input II (Leontopolis)

24th Dyn.*, c. *727–715 BC

Tefnakht
Bakenrenef

25th Dyn. (Kushite)*, c. *760–653 BC

Kashta
Piye
Shabaka
Shebitku
Taharka
Tanutameni

Late Period

26th Dyn. (Saite)*, c. *664–525 BC

Neko I
Psamtik (Psammetichos) I
Neko II
Psamtik II
Apries
Amasis
Psamtik III

27th Dyn. (Persian)*, c. *525–404 BC

Cambyses
Darius I
Xerxes I
Artaxerxes I
Darius II
Artaxerxes II

28th Dyn.*, c. *404–399 BC

Amyrtaeus

29th Dyn.*, c. *399–380 BC

Nephrites I
Hakor
Nephrites II

30th Dyn.*, c. *380–343 BC

Nectanebo I
Teos
Nectanebo II

31st Dyn. (Persian)*, c. *343–332 BC

Artaxerxes III
Arses
Darius III

Ptolemaic Dynasty (see Appendix IV)

Roman period (see Appendix V)

Note

Rulers and dates in accordance with EAAE, xxvii–xxx.

Appendix VI
Word list

Aha	Fighter of the demons, associated with Bes	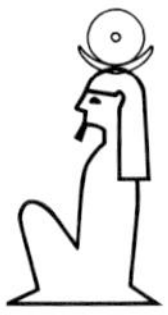
Amun	'The Hidden/Secret One', one of Egypt's most important male deities, primeval god in the Ogdoad of Hermopolis (paired with Amunet, representing air). Main cult centre in Karnak, Thebes, worshipped with the Theban triad (with Mut and Khonsu). Depicted as a ram, goose or in an anthropomorphic form	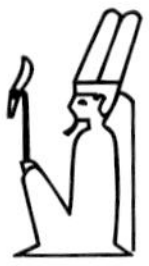
Amunet	Female divine equivalent to Amun in the primeval Ogdoad (representing air)	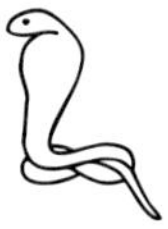
Anedjti	Crown composed of ram horns, a double feather plume and a solar disc (occasionally with additional elements)	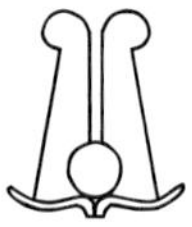
Ankh	A symbol of life	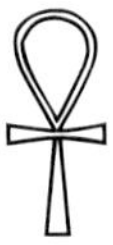
Anubis	Canine deity responsible for the mummification process and guarding the burial sites. Judged the dead	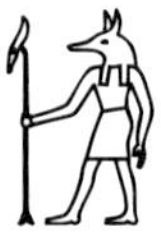 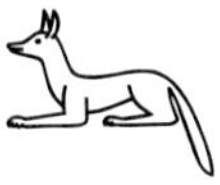
Apis	Sacred bull in Memphis. Physical form of Ptah	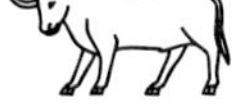
Apophis	Snake god of the Underworld	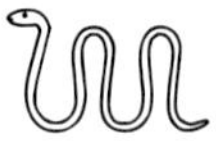
Arsinoeia	Festival in honour of Arsinoë II	
Atef	Ostrich feather	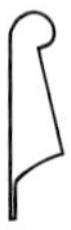
Atef crown	Crown composed of two ostrich feathers, a form of the original white crown, ram horns and a solar disc. Traditionally connected with Osiris	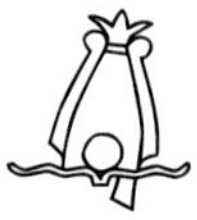

Aten	The solar disc (physical manifestation of Ra)	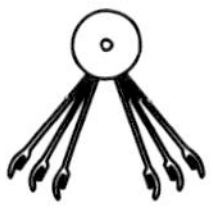
Atum	The primeval creator god, father figure in the Helipolitan Ennead. Represented the afternoon phase of the sun's cycle	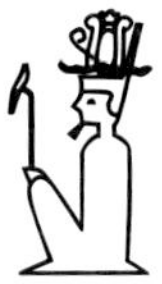
Ba	The human soul which could leave and return to the physical body	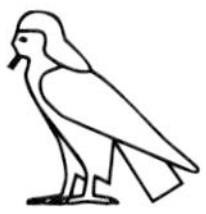
Banebdjedet	Local form of Amun, manifested as a ram, with a cult centre in Mendes (northern equivalent to Khnum)	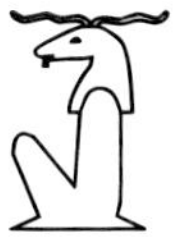
Bastet	Feline goddess closely associated with Hathor. Atum's spouse and daughter. Cult centre in Bubastis (Delta)	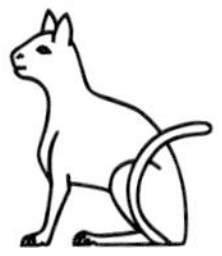
Bat	Predynastic cow goddess	
Bes	Dwarf deity who protected women during childbirth. Protector against demons through dancing and drumming	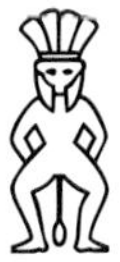
Canephoros	The basket-bearing, eponymous priestess of Arsinoë II	
Cucupha	Mythical, unidentified animal head on top of the *was* stave	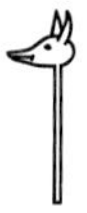
Dado	The lowest register of relief in a temple, usually in a smaller size than the main scenes. Traditionally showing processions	
Dikeras	The double cornucopia. Symbol of Arsinoë. Connected with the myth of Zeus, Amalthea and the birth of Dionysus	
Djed	'Stability'. Believed to represent the backbone of Osiris	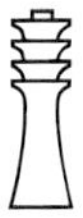
Four-feathered crown	Crown composed of four straight, tall feathers	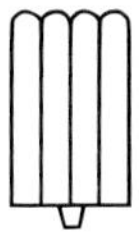

Geb	Earth/chthonic god, brother and spouse of Nut, together the children of Shu and Tefnut (thus, the third generation of the Ennead). Always shown in human form	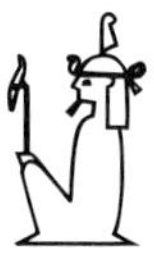
Harakhte	Horus-Ra, Horus the divine ruler, representing the midday sun	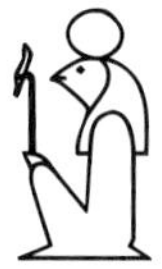
Haroeris	Horus the elder	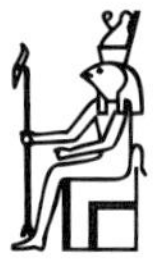
Harpocrates	Horus the child, son of Isis and Osiris, Hathor and Horus, or any local form of the mother/father-gods	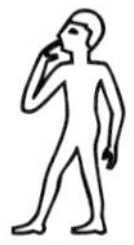
Harsomtus	Horus the uniter, was born and rose up from a lotus	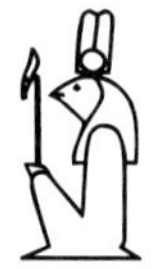 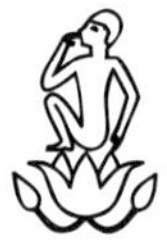
Hathor	Primeval solar-associated goddess, eternally counterpart to the primeval male form. Reversed aging. Mother-daughter-wife of Ra/Horus/Amon/Atum. Main cult centre in Dendera	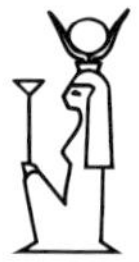 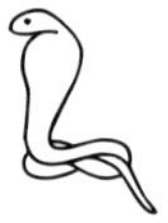
Hat-Mehit	Local form of Hathor. Spouse of Banebdjedet and mother of Harpocrates in Mendes	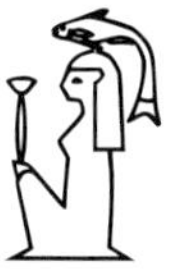
Hauhet	Infinity goddess. Female counterpart of Heh in the Ogdoad. Usually depicted with the head of a frog	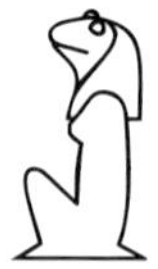
Heh	Infinity god. Male counterpart of Hauhet in the Ogdoad	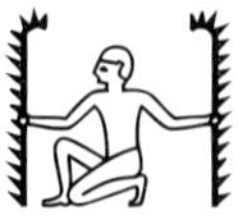
Hemhem	Complex crown composition. Usually referred to as the triple crown	

Hes	Libation vessel	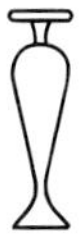
Horus	Divine king, ruler of heaven. Son of Isis and Osiris, husband of Hathor, brother of Seth. Depicted completely or partially as a falcon. Cult centre in Heliopolis and Edfu	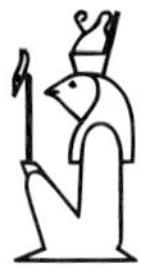 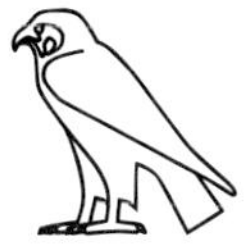
Iatdit	Temple of Isis in Dendera	
Ihy	The sistrum player. Son of Hathor and Horus	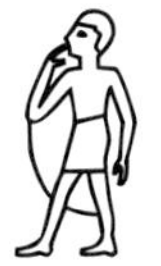
Isis	Mother goddess. Daughter of Geb and Nut, sister and wife of Osiris, sister of Nephthys, mother of Horus. Forth generation of the Ennead. Main cult centre in Philae	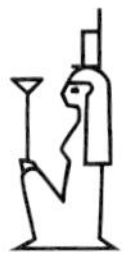 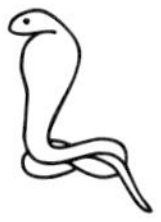
Ka	Human spirit which left the body at the time of death	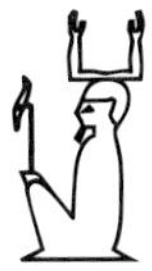
Khat	Wig	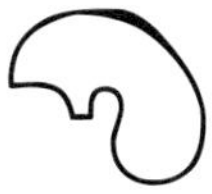
Khepri	Scarab/beetle deity representing the morning phase of the sun. Symbolises change and creation. No individual cult centre	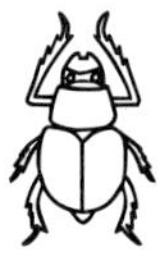
Khepresh	The blue war crown	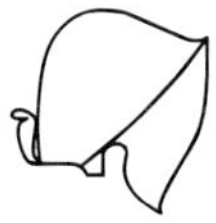
Khnum	Local form of Amun, controlled the Nile inundation. Creator deity. Southern form of Banebdjedet. Cult centre in Elephantine	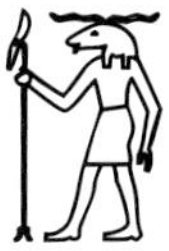
Khonsu	Moon god, son of Amun and Mut in Thebes (Ptah and Sekhmet in Memphis). Depicted with a crescent and moon disc	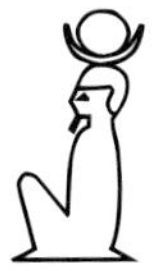

Ma'at	Personification of the fundamental concepts of Egyptian cosmology: truth, justice, balance, etc. Daughter of Ra. Depicted with an ostrich feather	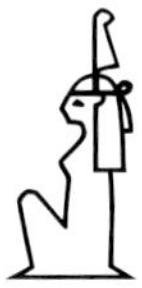
Mehnyt	The risen cobra. Form of Hathor	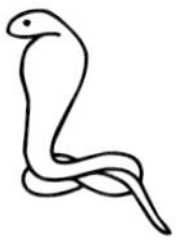
Menit	Necklace worn by Hathor and her worshippers. Sacred in rituals	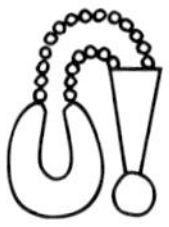
Min	Fertility god, always depicted with an erected penis. Often associated with Amun	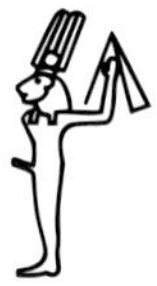
Montu	Falcon-headed war god. Depicted with the double feather plume and solar disc. Main cult centre in Armant	
Mut	Mother goddess included in the Theban triad with Amun and Khonsu. Represented the old wise woman. Depicted with the vulture cap and double crown. Cult centre in Karnak	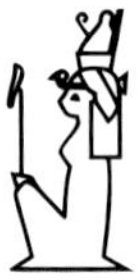
Naos	Holiest and most central room in a temple. Inner sanctuary	
Nebet Hetepet	Lady of the offerings. Aspect of Hathor	
Nefertem	Local form of Harpocrates/Harsomtus. Horus the youngster who rose from the lotus. Son of Ptah and Sekhmet	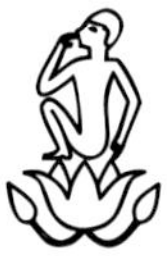
Neith	Creator and hunting goddess. Depicted with two crossed arrows or the red crown. Cult centre in Sais	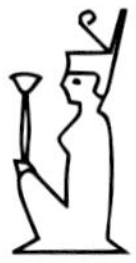
Nekhbet	Vulture goddess. Depicted with the white crown and as a vulture. Cult centre in Nekheb (el-Kab). Paired with Wadjet as the Two Ladies	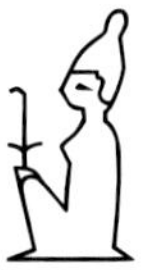 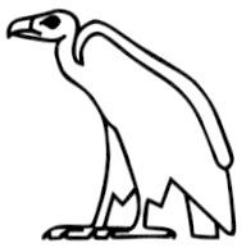
Nemset	Type of vessel	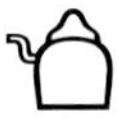

Nemes	Pharaoh's wig, often striped with blue and golden colours	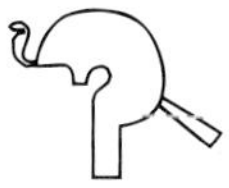
Nephthys	Protectress goddess. Daughter of Geb and Nut, sister of Isis and Osiris, sister and wife of Seth. Depicted with a personal hieroglyphic attribute signifying 'Lady of the House'	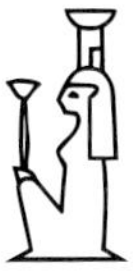
Nun	Personification of the primeval waters from which everything originated. Father figure in the Ogdoad, depicted with the face of a frog	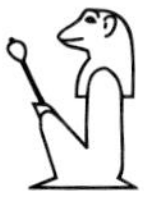
Nut	Sky and mother goddess. Daughter of Shu and Tefnut, sister and wife of Geb. Usually depicted as a woman stretching over the world	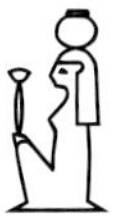 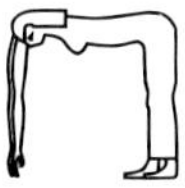
Oinochoai	Greek faience vessel	
Opet	Mother goddess who protected pregnant women and childbirth. Cult centre in Karnak	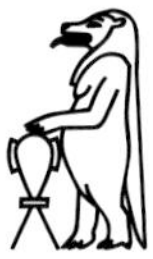
Osiris	Lord of the Underworld. Son of Nut and Geb, brother of Seth and Nephthys, brother and husband of Isis, father of Horus	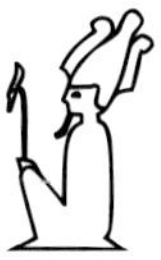
Procession deities	Usually personifications of geographical areas, Nile deities, *ka*-souls, etc. Depicted on the dadoes in processions carrying *hes* vessels, offering trays, plants, etc.	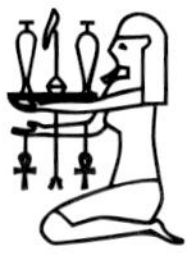 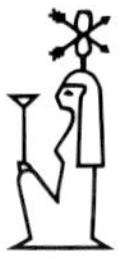 
Ptah	Creator god, main god in Memphis, paired with Sekhmet and Nefertem/Harpocrates. Associated with Apis	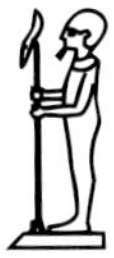
Ra	Male primeval solar god, source of all other deities	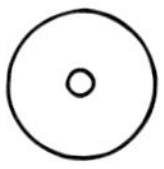 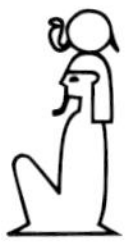
Ra'at	Female form of Ra. Aspect of Hathor	
Rekht	Egyptian bird often depicted with a star in specific temple locations	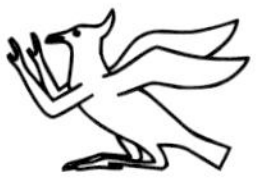
Sarapis	Hellenistic fusion of the most powerful Egyptian and Greek male deities, including Apis, Osiris, Zeus, Asclepius, etc.	

Sema	'Unification'. The sign appears frequently with Harsomtus, Horus the unifier	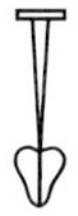
Sekhem	Magical sceptre of power	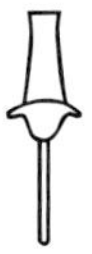
Sekhmet	Aggressive aspect of Hathor, represented as the wild lioness. Spouse of Ptah in Memphis	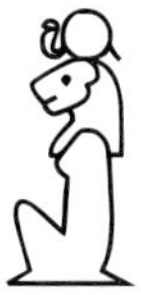
Seshat	Female counterpart of Thoth. Recorder of time and the world. Depicted with a personal flower and is usually dressed in a panther skin. Actively engaged in the reckoning of the time ceremony	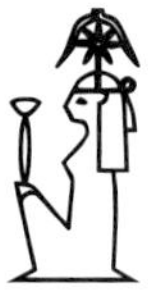
Seth	Chaotic dog-like deity. Son of Nut and Geb, brother of Isis, Osiris and Nephthys (the latter being his spouse). Cult centre in Kom Ombo	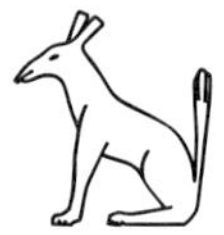
Shu	God of the life-giving air. Son of Atum, brother and husband of Tefnut. Second generation of the Ennead	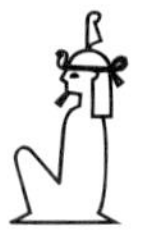
Sobek	Crocodile god, 'the Raging One'. Worshipped in the Delta as a creator god who rose from the dark waters. Main temples in Krokodilopolis and Kom Ombo	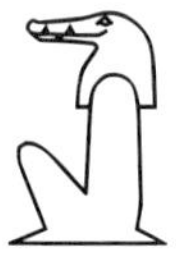
Sopt/Sobt	Male personification of the Sirius star	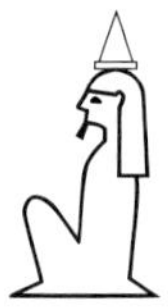
Tefnut	Goddess of moisture. Daughter of Atum, sister and wife of Shu. Second generation of the Ennead. Associated with Hathor. Often shown with a lioness head	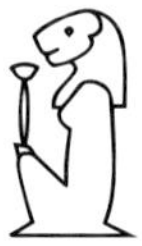
Thoth	Lunar god of wisdom and writing. Invented the script. Depicted as a baboon or ibis bird. Paired with Seshat, always present writing the annuals and handing over the cartouche in crowning ceremonies	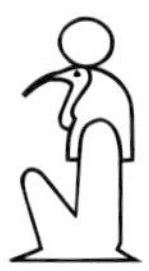

Uraeus	The risen cobra	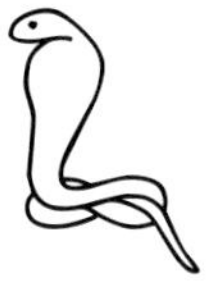
Wadjet	Serpent goddess. Daughter of Ra, associated with Hathor. Paired with Nekhbet as the Two Ladies. Depicted with the red crown, as a serpent, or as the eye of Ra. Cult centre in Buto	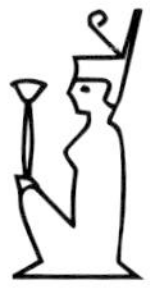 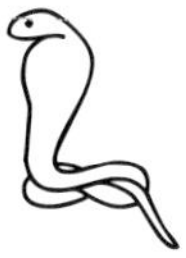 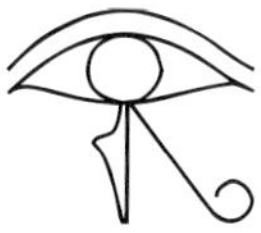
Was	Sacred stave	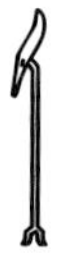

Bibliography

Abbreviations for ancient authors and work – including inscriptions, papyri, prosopographies and so on – follow those recommended in the *OCD*[3]. Abbreviations of journals and series, as used by classicists, follow those that are listed in the *American Journal of Archaeology* 104, 2000, 10–24 (also at www.ajaonline.org) and the online list of EEF version 37 (March 2010): http://www.egyptologyforum.org/EEFrefs.html. All used translations of ancient sources are Loeb editions unless otherwise stated.

Abbreviations

ÄA	Ägyptologische Abhandlungen
Berlin photos	*Berliner Photos der preussischen Expedition 1908–1910 nach Nubien*, eds H. Junker and H. Schäfer, Ägyptologisches Microfiche-Archiv 3, Wiesbaden, 1975
BIFAO	*Bulletin de l'Institut Français d'Archéologie Orientale*, Cairo
BM	British Museum, London
CAH[2] II and IV	I. Edwards, ed. *Cambridge Ancient History II, Part 2: the Middle East and the Aegean Region, c. 1380–1000 BC*, Cambridge, 2000 J. Boardman, ed. *Cambridge Ancient History IV, Persia, Greece, and the Western Mediterranean, c. 525–479 BC*, Cambridge, 2002
CG	Egyptian Museum, Cairo
Dendara	E. Chassinat, F. Daumas and S. Cauville, *Le temple de Dendara*, Cairo, 1934–2002
Denkmäler	R. Lepsius, *Denkmäler aus Aegypten und Aethiopien*, Leipzig, 1897–1913
EAAE	*Encyclopedia of the Archaeology of Ancient Egypt*, ed. K. Bard, London and New York, 1999
Edfou	Chassinat with Rochemonteix, *Le temple d'Edfou*, Paris, 1892–1985
Edfu	*Edfu*, vol. I–VIII, ed. D. Kurth, Wiesbaden, 1990–
EEF	Egyptologists' Electronic Forum
FGrH	*Fragmenten griechische Historiker*, ed. F. Jakoby, Berlin, 1923–
IFAO	Institut Français d'Archéologie Orientale, Cairo
Khonsu II	*The Temple of Khonsu*, vol. II, OIP 103, Chicago, 1981
LÄ	*Lexikon der Ägyptologie*, ed. W. Helck and E. Otto, Wiesbaden, 1975–92
LdR	H. Gauthier, *Le Livre des Rois d'Egypte*, 5 vols, MIFAO 16, 18–21, 40, Cairo, 1907–17
LGG	*Lexikon der ägyptischen Götter und Götterbezeichnungen*, OLA 110–16, vols I–VIII, ed. Ch. Leitz, Leuven, 2002–3
LOEB	Loeb Classical Library, Cambridge, MA, and London 1911–
Mariette, *Dendérah*	A. Mariette, *Dendérah: description générale du grand temple de cette ville*, vols I–V, Paris, 1869–80
MIFAO	Mémoires publiés par les membres de l'Institut français d'archéologie orientale du Caire, Cairo
MDAIK	*Mitteilungen des deutschen archäologischen Instituts, Abteilung Kairo*, Mainz am Rhein, 1945–
MM	Medelhavsmuseet, Stockholm
MMA	Metropolitan Museum of Art, New York
OCD[3]	*Oxford Classical Dictionary*, 3rd edn, Oxford, 1996
OEAE	*The Oxford Encyclopedia of Ancient Egypt*
OGIS	*Orientis Graeci Inscriptiones Selectae*, Supplementum Sylloges Inscriptionum Graecarum, ed. W. Dittenberger, 2 vols, Leipzig, 1903–5
OIP	Oriental Institute Publications

OLA	Orientalia Lovaniensia Analecta, Leuven
PM	B. Porter and R. L. B. Moss, *Topographical Bibliography of Ancient Egyptian Hieroglyphic Texts, Statues, Reliefs, and Paintings*, 8 vols, Oxford, 1927–
PT	Pyramid Texts
Pyr.	*Ancient Egyptian Pyramid Texts*, transl. R. O. Faulkner, Oxford, 1969
ROM	Royal Ontario Museum, Toronto
SIG[3]	*Sylloge inscriptionum graecarum*, 3rd edn
Syll.	*Sylloge Inscriptionum Graecarum*, ed. W. Dittengerg, Leipzig, 1883; 1898–1912; 1915
Thes. Inscr.	K. H. Brugsch, *Thesaurus Inscriptionum Aegyptiacarum*, Leipzig, 1883–91
Urk. II	*Urkunden des aegyptischen Altertums* II: *Hieroglyphische Urkunden der griechisch-römischen Zeit*, ed. K. Sethe, Leipzig, 1904
Utt.	Utterance
Vatican	Museo Gregoriano Egizio
WB	*Wörterbuch der Aegyptischen Sprache*, I–V, A. Erman and H. Grapow, Berlin, 1982 (1950, 1971)

Ancient sources

Ath.	Athenaeus, *Deipnosophistae*
Auson. *Mos.*	*The works of Ausonius*, ed. R. P. H. Green, Oxford, 1991
Caes.	Caesar
B. Afr.	*Bellum Africum*
B. Civ.	*Bellum Civile*
Callim.	Callimachus
Apoth. Ars.	*Apotheosis Arsinoes* (=F 228, *Diegesis*. X.10): ed. R. Pfeiffer, Oxford, 1949
Com. Ber.	*Coma Berenice* (=F 110): ed. R. Pfeiffer, Oxford, 1949
Catull.	Catullus
Clem. Al.	Clemens Alexandrinus
Strom.	*Stromateis*
Diod. Sic.	Diodorus Siculus
Eratosth.	Eratosthenes
Hdt.	Herodotus
Hes. *Theog.*	Hesiod, *Theogonia*
Horapollo	*Hieroglyphica: The Hieroglyphs of Horapollo*, transl. and ed. G. Boas, Princeton, 1993 (1950, 1978)
Just. *Epit.*	Justinus, *Epitome* (of Trogus)
Juv.	Juvenal
Lib.	Libanius
Manetho	Manetho
Paus.	Pausanias
Pliny *NH*	Pliny, *Naturalis historia*
Plut.	Plutarch
Alex.	*Life of Alexander*
Mor.	*Moralia*
Vit. Demetr.	*Vitae Parallelae Demetrius*
Posidip.	*The Greek Anthology: Hellenistic Epigrams*, I–II, ed. A. Gow and D. Page, Cambridge, 1965; *Supplementum Hellenisticum*, ed. H. Lloyd-Jones and P. Parson, Berlin, 1983–2005
ps.-Callisth.	Pseudo-Callisthenes, *Historia Alexandri Magni*, ed. W. Kroll, Berlin, 1926
Schol. Theocritus	C. Wendel, *Scholia in Theocritum Vetera*, Stuttgart, 1914
Theoc. *Id.*	Theocritus, *Idylls*

Collections of papyri

Gr. Dem. Medinet Habu 77	H. J. Thissen, *Die demotischen Graffiti von Medinet Habu*, Sommerhausen, 1989
P.Brit.Mus.	(*Catalogue of the Demotic Papyri in the British Museum*) *The Rhind Mathematical Papyrus, British Museum 10057 and 10058*, ed. T. Peet, London, 1923
P.Cair.Zen.	*Catalogue général des antiquités égyptiennes du musée du Caire. Zenon papyri*, vols I–IV, Cairo, 1925–34
P.Col.Zen.	*Columbia papyri* III, *Zenon Papyri: Business Papers of the Third Century BC Dealing with Palestine and Egypt* I, ed. W. L. Westermann and E. S. Hasenoehrl, New York, 1934
P.Chester Beatt	A. Gardiner, *Hieratic Papyri in the British Museum*, 3rd series, vols I–II, London, 1935
P.Eleph.Dem.	*Demotische Papyrus von der Insel Elephantine*, Dem.Stud. 2, ed. W. Spiegelberg, Leipzig, 1908
P. Grad. 10	G. Plaumann (ed.), *Griechische Papyri der Sammlung Gradenwitz*, Heidelberg, 1914
P.Hib.	*Hibeh papyri*, ed. E. Turner, London, 1955
P. L. Bat.	P. W. Pestman *et al.*, *A guide to the Zenon Archives*, P. L. Bat. 21, Leiden, 1981; W. Clarysse and G. Van der Veken, *The eponymous priests of Ptolemaic Egypt*, P. L. Bat. 24, Leiden, 1983
P. Lit. Goodsp.	E. J. Goodspeed, 'Alexandrian hexameter fragments', *JHS* 23, 1903, 237–47; R. W. Allison, 'Guide to the Edgar J. Goodspeed papyri', *ZPE* 16, 1975, 27–32
P.Lond.	*Greek Papyri in the British Museum*, III, ed. F. Kenyon and H. Bell, London, 1907
P. Louvre	T. Devéria, *Catalogue des manuscrits égyptiens écrits sur papyrus, toile, tablettes et ostraca en caractéres hiéroglyphiques, hiératiques, demotiques, grecs, coptes, arabes et latins qui sont conservés au Musée égyptien du Louvre*, Paris, 1872
P. Lugd. Bat.	*Chronologie Égyptienne d'après les textes démotiques (332 av. J.-C.-453 ap. J.-C.)* (P. Lugd. Bat. 15), ed. P. W. Pestman, Leiden, 1967
P. Mil. Vogl.	G. Bastianini and C. Gallazzi, eds, with C. Austin, *Posidippo di Pella: Epigrammi (P.Mil.Vogl.VIII 309)*, Papiri dell'Universita degli Studi di Milano, 8 (Milan, 2001), 24–6
P.Oxy.	*Oxyrhynchus papyri XXVII*, eds B. Grenfell and A. Hunt, ed. and transl. E. G. Turner *et al.*, London, 1962
PP	W. Peremans *et al.*, *Prosopographia Ptolemaica VI: La cour, les relations internationales et les possessions extérieures, la vie culturelle. Nos 14479-17250*, Louvain, 1968
P.Petrie I–II	*The Flinders Petrie Papyri*, I–II, ed. J. P. Mahaffy, Milano, 1975 (Dublin, 1891–3)
PSI	*Papiri Greci e Latini, Pubblicazioni ricerca dei papyri gregi e latini in Egitto*, 1912–
P.Sorb.	*Papyrus de la Sorbonne*, ed. H. Cadell, Paris, 1966; H. Cadell, in *Le culte du souverain dans l'Égypte ptolémaïque au IIIe siècle avant notre ére*, ed. H. Melaerts, Leuven, 1998, 1–4
PT Utt.	*Die altägyptischen Pyramidentexte*, vols I–IV, ed. K. Sethe, Leipzig, 1908–22
P.Yale	*Yale Papyri in the Beinecke Rare Book and Manuscript Library*, I, ed. J. Oates, A. Samuel and C. Welles, New Haven and Toronto, 1967
SB	*Sammelbuch Griechischer Urkunden aus Ägypten*, ed. F. Preisigke *et al.*, Wiesbaden, 1922–

Secondary sources

Abubakr, A. (1937) *Untersuchungen über die ägyptischen Kronen*, Glückstadt, Hamburg, New York.

Albersmeier, S. (2002) *Unterschungen zu den Frauenstatuen des ptolemäischen Ägypten*, Mainz am Rhein.

Albersmeier, S. and Minas, M. (1998) 'Ein Weihrelief für vergöttlichte Arsinoe II', in *Egyptian Religion: The Last Thousand Years. Studies Dedicated to the Memory of Jan Quaegebeur*, ed. W. Clarysse, A. Schoors and H. Willems, OLA 84, Leuven, 3–29.

Allen, J. (2001) *Middle Egyptian: An Introduction to the Language and Culture of Hieroglyphs*, Cambridge.

Allison, R. W. (1975) 'Guide to the Edgar J. Goodspeed papyri', *ZPE* 16, 27–32.

Andersson, E. and Sjöberg, N. (1904) 'E. Akmar, La stèle de Pithom et les estampages de M. Ed. Naville', *Sphinx* 8, 223–36.

Andrews, C. (1994) *Amulets in Ancient Egypt*, Bath.

Armour, R. (2001) *Gods and Myths in Ancient Egypt*, Cairo.

Arnold, D. (1999) *Temples of the Last Pharaohs*, Oxford.

Arnold, D. (2003) *The Encyclopaedia of Ancient Egyptian Architecture*, New York.

Artioli, G. (2010) *Scientific Methods and Cultural Heritage: An Introduction to the Application of Materials Science to Archeometry and Conservation Science*, Oxford and New York.

Ashton, S.-A. (2000) 'The Ptolemaic influence on Egyptian royal sculpture', in *Current Research in Egyptology*, BAR International Series 909, ed. A. McDonald and C. Riggs, Oxford.

Ashton, S.-A. (2001a) *Ptolemaic Royal Sculpture from Egypt*, Oxford.

Ashton, S.-A. (2001b) 'Identifying the Egyptian-style Ptolemaic queens', in *Cleopatra's Egypt: From History to Myth*, ed. S. Walker and P. Higgs, London, 148–55.

Ashton, S.-A. (2003) *The Last Queens of Egypt*, London.

Assmann, J. (1970) *Der Köning als Sonnenpriester: Ein kosmographischer Begleittext zur kultischen Sonnenhymnik in thebanischer Tempeln und Gräber*, ADAIK 7, Glückstadt.

Assmann, J. (2001) *The Search for God in Ancient Egypt*, transl. D. Lorton, New York (*Ägypten: Theologie und Frömmigkeit einer frühen Hochkultur*, Stuttgart, 1984).

Assmann, J. (2003) *The Mind of Egypt: History and Meaning in the Time of the Pharaohs*, transl. A. Jenkins, Cambridge, MA (*Ägypten: Ein Sinngeschichte*, Munich, 1996).

Austin, M. (2006) *The Hellenistic World from Alexander to the Roman Conquest: A Selection of Ancient Sources in Translation*, Cambridge.

Bagnall, R. and Derow, P. (eds) (2004) *The Hellenistic Period. Historical Sources in Translation*, Oxford.

Baines, J. (1976) 'Temple symbolism', *Royal Anthropological Institute News* 15, 10–15.

Baines, J. (1991) 'Society, morality, and religious practice', in *Religion in Ancient Egypt: Gods, Myths, and Personal Practice*, ed. B. Shafer, Cornell, 123–200.

Baines, J. and Málek, J. (2002) *Atlas of Ancient Egypt*, Oxford.

Barbantani, S. (2005) 'Goddess of love and mistress of the sea: notes on a Hellenistic hymn to Arsinoe-Aphrodite (P. Lit. Goodsp. 2, I–IV)', *Anc. Soc.* 35, 135–66.

Bastianini, G., Gallazzi C. and Austin, C. (eds) (2001) *Posidippo di Pella: Epigrammi (P.Mil.Vogl.VIII 309)*, Papiri dell'Universita degli Studi di Milano 8, Milan..

Beckerath, J. von (1984) *Handbuch der ägyptischen Königsnamen*, München.

Beinlich, H. (1978) 'Ein altägyptischer Räucherarm in Heidelberg', *MDAIK* 34, 15–31.

Bell, L. (1985) 'Luxor temple and the cult of the royal Ka', *JNES* 44, 251–94.

Bénédite, G. (1893–5) *Le temple de Philae*, I–II, Paris.

Bernand, A. (1970) *Le delta egyptien d'apres les texts grecs*, MIFAO 91, Cairo.

Besancon, A. (2000) *The forbidden image: an intellectual history of iconoclasm*, transl. J. M. Todd, Chicago.

Bianchi, R. S. (ed.) (1988) *Cleopatra's Egypt: Age of the Ptolemies*, Brooklyn Museum, Mainz am Rheine.

Bianchi, R. S. (2004) *Daily life of the Nubians*, Westport.

Bierbrier, M. (1980) 'Terms of relationship at Deir el-Medina', *JEA* 66, 100–107.

Bingen, J. (2002) 'La victoire pythique de Callicratès de Samos [*Posidippe, P. Mil. Vogl. VIII 309*, XI.33–XII.7]', *CE* 77, 185–90.

Birch, S. (1876) 'Decree of Canopus', in *Records of the past*, ed. S. Birch, vol. VIII, London, 81–90.

Bisson de la Roque, F. (1937) 'Tôd (1934 à 1936)', *FIFAO* 17, 22–33.

Blackman, A. M. (1912) 'The significance of incense and libations in funerary and temple ritual', *ZÄS* 50, 69–77.

Blackman, A. M. (1918–19) 'Sequence of the episodes in the Egyptian daily temple liturgy', *Journal of the Manchester Egyptian and Oriental Society*, 27–53.

Blackman, A. M. (1921) 'On the position of women in the Ancient Egyptian Hierarchy', *JEA* 7, 8–30.

Blackman, A. M. and Fairman, H. W. (1943) 'The myth of Horus at Edfu – II', *JEA* 29, 2–36.

Boardman, J. (ed.) (2002) *Cambridge Ancient History IV, Persia, Greece, and the Western Mediterranean, c. 525–479 BC*, Cambridge.

Borghouts, J. F. (1978) *Ancient Egyptian Magical Texts*, Leiden.

Bowman, A. (1986) *Egypt After the Pharaohs: 332 BC –AD 642: From Alexander to the Arab Conquest*, Berkeley.

Brass, M. (2003) 'Tracing the origins of the ancient Egyptian cattle cult', in *A Delta Man in Yebu*, ed. A. K. Eyma and C. J. Bennett, Boca Raton, FL, 101–9.

Breasted, J. H. (1906) *Ancient Records of Egypt*, vols I–V, Chicago.

Brecklinghaus, H. (2002) *The Human Beings are Awoken, You have Set them Upright: Body Structure and Conception of Man in Ancient Egyptian Art and the Present Day*, transl. N. Hanefeld and H. Brecklinghaus, Gundelfingen (*Die Menschen sind erwacht, du hast sie aufgerichtet. Körperstruktur und Menschenbild in der Kunst des alten Ägypten und heute*, 1997).

Brewer, D. and Teeter, E. (2007) *Egypt and the Egyptians*, Cambridge.

Bricault, L. (1999) 'Sarapis et Isis, sauveurs de Ptolémée IV à Raphia', *CE* 74, 334–43.

Brier, B. and Hobbs, H. (1999) *Daily Life of the Ancient Egyptians*, Westport.

Brissaud, P. and Zivie-Coche, C. (eds) (1998) *Mission Francaise des Fouilles de Tanis, 1987–1997*, Paris.

Brugsch, H. (1883–91) *Thesaurus inscriptionum Aegyptiacarum. Altaegyptische inschriften, gesammelt, verglichen, übertragen, erklärt und autographiert I–VI*, Leipzig.

Brunton, G. and Caton-Thompson, G. (1928) *The Badarian Civilisation and Predynastic Remains near Badari*, London.

Budge, E. A. (2003 [1904]) *The Decrees of Memphis and Canopus*, vols I–III, London/Whitefish.

Budge, E. A. (2004 [1908]) *The Book of the Kings of Egypt*, Part One, London/Whitefish.

Budge, E. A. (1909) *A Guide to the Egyptian Galleries (Sculpture)*, London.

Burstein, S. M. (1982) 'Arsinoe II Philadelphos: a revisionist view', in *Philip II, Alexander the Great and the Macedonian Heritage*, eds W. L. Adams and E. N. Borza, Washington, 197–212.

Cadell, H. (1998) 'À quelle date Arsinoé II Philadelphe est-elle décédée?' in *Le culte du souverain dans l'Égypte ptolémaïque au IIIe siècle avant notre ére*, ed. H. Melaerts, Leuven, 1–4.

Calverley, A. and Gardiner, A. (1933) *The Temple of Sethos I at Abydos: Volume I The Chapels of Osiris, Isis and Horus*, London and Chicago.

Cameron, A. (1995) *Callimachus and His Critics*, Princeton.

Carney, E. (1991) 'What's in a name? The emergence of a title for royal women in the Hellenistic period', in *Women's History and Ancient History*, ed. S. Pomeroy, Chapel Hill and London, 154–72.

Carney, E. (2000) 'The initiation of cult for royal Macedonian women', *CPh* 95, 21–43.

Cauville, S. (1987) *Essai sur la théologie du temple d'Horus à Edfou* I, BdE 102/1–2, Cairo.

Chabas, F. (1909) 'Le decret de Canope', in *Oeuvres diverses*, ed. F. Chabas, vol. 5, Paris, 488–95.

Chace, A. (1927–9) *The Rhind Mathematical Papyrus: Free Translation and Commentary with Selected Photographs, Translations, Transliterations and Literal Translations*, Classics in Mathematics Education 8, vols I–II, Berlin.

Champollion, J.-F. (1844) *Monuments de l'Égypte et de la Nubie: Notices Descriptives*, Paris.

Chandler, D. (2002) *Semiotics: The Basics*, London.

Chassinat, E. (with M. de Rochemonteix) (ed.) (1892–1933) *Le temple d'Édfou*, vols I–VIII, Cairo.

Chassinat, E., Daumas, F. and Cauville, S. (eds) (1934–2002) *Le temple de Dendara*, I–XI, Cairo.

Chauveau, M. (1998) *La Gloire d'Alexandrie*, exh. cat., Paris.

Cheshire, W. (1982) 'Zur Deutung eines Szepters der Arsinoe II. Philadelphos', *ZPE* 48, 105–11.

Clagett, M. (1995) *Ancient Egyptian Science: A Source Book*, vol. II, Philadelphia.

Clark, S. and Engelbach, R. (1990) *Ancient Egyptian Construction and Architecture*, New York.

Clarysse, W. (2007) 'A royal journey in the delta in 257 B.C., and the date of the Mendes Stele', *CE* 82, 201–6.

Clarysse, W. and Van der Veken, G. (1983) *The Eponymous Priests of Ptolemaic Egypt*, P. L. Bat. 24, Leiden.

Clarysse, W., Schoors, A. and Willems, H. (eds) (1998) *Egyptian Religion: The Last Thousand Years. Studies Dedicated to the Memory of Jan Quaegebeur*, I–II, OLA 84–85, Leuven.

Clayton, P. (2006) *Chronicle of the Pharaohs: The Reign-by-reign Record of the Rulers and Dynasties of Ancient Egypt*, London.

Clere, P. (1961) *La porte d'Evergete a Karnak*, Cairo.

Collombert, Ph. (2008) 'La "stèle de Saïs" et l'instauration du culte d'Arsinoé II dans la chora', *Anc. Soc.* 38, 83–102.

Crawford, D. (1980) 'Ptolemy, Ptah and Apis in Hellenistic Memphis', in *Studies on Ptolemaic Memphis*, ed. W. Peremans, Studia Hellenistica 24, Leuven, 5–42.

Crawford, D., Quaegebeur, J. and Clarysse, W. (1980) *Studies on Ptolemaic Memphis*, Studia Hellenistica 24, ed. W. Peremans, Leuven.

D'Alleva, A. (2009) *Methods and Theories of Art History*, London.

Darby, W. J., Ghalioungui, P. and Grivetti, L. (1977) *Food: The Gift of Osiris*, London.

Delia, D. (1998) 'Isis and the Moon', in *Egyptian Religion: The Last Thousand Years. Studies Dedicated to the Memory of Jan Quaegebeur*, ed. W. Clarysse, A. Schoors and H. Willems, part I, OLA 84, Leuven, 539–50.

Derchain, P. (1985) 'Une mention meconnue de Ptolemde "le Fils"', *ZPE* 61, 35–6.

Derchain-Urtel, M.-T. (1990) 'Die Krone … und ihre Nebenformen … in Edfu', *Edfu* I, 1–18.

Derchain-Urtel, M.-T. (1994) 'Die Hptj-Krone in Edfu und ihre Varianten', *Edfu* IV, 25–71.

Desroches-Noblecourt, C. (1968) *Le petit temple d'Abou Simbel*, I, Cairo.

Dils, P. (1998) 'La couronne d'*Arsinoe* II Philadelphe', in *Egyptian Religion: The Last Thousand Years. Studies Dedicated to the Memory of Jan Quaegebeur*, ed. W. Clarysse, A. Schoors and H. Willems, part II, OLA 85, Leuven, 1299–330.

Dittenberger, W. (ed.) (1903–5) *Orientis Graeci Inscriptiones Selectae*, Supplementum Sylloges Inscriptionum Graecarum, I–II, Leipzig.

Dittenberger, W. (ed.) (1915–24) *Sylloge inscriptionum graecarum*, 3rd edn, I–IV, Leipzig.

Dixon-Kennedy, M. (1998) *Encyclopedia of Greco-Roman Mythology*, Santa Barbara.

Dodson, A. (2002) 'The problem of Amenirdis II and the heirs to the office of God's wife of Amun during the twenty-sixth dynasty', *JEA* 88, 177–86.

Edgar, C. C. (1906) *Sculptors' Studies and Unfinished Works, Catalogue Generale du Musee du Caire*, Cairo.

Edwards, I. (ed.) (2000) *Cambridge Ancient History II, Part 2: the Middle East and the Aegean Region, c. 1380–1000 BC*, Cambridge.

Emery, W. (1961) *Archaic Egypt*, Harmondsworth.

Englund, G. (2001) 'Offerings: an overview', in *OEAE*, ed. D. Redford, vol. 2, Oxford, 564–9.

Erman, A. (1911) *Hymnen an des Diadem*, Berlin.

Erman, A. and Grapow, H. (1982) *Wörterbuch der Aegyptischen Sprache*, I–V, Berlin.

Fairman, H. W. (1958) 'A scene of the offering of truth in the temple of Edfu', *MDAIK* 16, 86–92.

Fakhry, A. (1954) 'The excavation of Snefru's Monuments at Dashur: second preliminary report', *ASAE* 52, 563–94.

Faulkner, R. (1958) *British Museum. Manuscript. Papyrus 10569. An Ancient Egyptian Book of hours*, Pap. Brit. Mus. 10569, Oxford.

Faulkner, R. (1962) *Concise Dictionary of Middle Egyptian*, Oxford.

Faulkner, R. (1969) *The Ancient Egyptian Pyramid Texts Translated into English*, and *Supplement of Hieroglyphic texts*, vols I–II, Oxford.

Favard-Meeks, C. (1998) 'Mise à jour des ouvrages de Flinders Petrie sur les fuilles de Tanis', in *Tanis: trauvaux récents sur le tell Sân el-Hagar. Mission français des fuilles de Tanis, 1987–1997*, ed. P. Brissaud and C. Zivie-Coche, Paris, 101–78.

Fischer, H. G. (1963) 'Varia Aegyptiaca: 4 The evolution of the armlike censer', *JARCE* 2, 28–34.

Fletcher, J. (1994) 'A tale of hair, wigs and lice', *Egyptian Archaeology: Bulletin of the Egypt Exploration Society* 5, 31–3.

Frank, K. (2007) *Lucie Duff Gordon: A Passage to Egypt*, New York.

Frankfort, H. (1949) 'Myth and Reality', in *Before Philosophy*, ed. J. Wilsen and T. Jacobsen, Harmondsworth, 11–36.

Frankfort, H. (1978) *Kingship and the Gods: A Study of Ancient Near Eastern Religion as the Integration of Society and Nature*, Chicago.

Frankfurter, D. (1998) *Religion in Roman Egypt: Assimilation and Resistance*, Princeton.

Fraser, P. (1972) *Ptolemaic Alexandria*, I–III, Oxford.

Freedman, K. (2003) *Teaching Visual Culture: Curriculum, Aesthetics, and the Social Life of Art*, New York.

Friis Johanses, K. (1953) *Weihinschriften aus dem Nymphenheiligtum des Kafizin Hügels*, Dan. Arkaeol. Kunsthist. Medd. 4.1, Copenhagen.

Gardiner, A. H. (1957) *Egyptian Grammar: Being an Introduction to the Study of Hieroglyphs*, Oxford.

Gardiner, A. H. (ed.) (1988) *Royal Canon of Turin*, Oxford.

Gardiner, A. H., Peet, T. and Černý, J. (1952–5) *The Inscriptions of Sinai*, I–II, London.

Gauthier, H. (1907–17) *Le Livre des Rois d'Egypte*, vols I–V, MIFAO 16, 18–21, 40, Cairo.

George, B. and Peterson, B. (1982) *Medelhavsmuseet: en introduction*, Stockholm.

Gilbert, G. (2004) *Weapons, Warriors and Warfare in Early Egypt*, Oxford.

Goebs, K. (2001) 'Crowns', in *OEAE*, ed. D. Redford, vol. 1, New York, 321–6.

Goebs, K. (2008) *Crowns in Egyptian Funerary Literature. Royalty, Rebirth, and Destruction*, Oxford.

Goldwasser, O. (1995) *From Icon to Metaphor: Studies in the Semiotics of the Hieroglyphs*, Friebourg.

Gombrich, E. H. (2000) *Art and Illusion: A Study in the Psychology of Pictorial Representation*, Princeton.

Goodspeed, E. J. (1903) 'Alexandrian hexameter fragments', *JHS* 23, 237–47.

Graham, G. (2001) 'Insignias', in *OEAE*, ed. D. Redford, vol. 2, Cairo, 163–7.

Grajetzki, W. (2005) *Ancient Egyptian Queens: A Hieroglyphic Dictionary*, London.

Green, L. (2001) 'Hairstyles', in *OEAE*, ed. D. Redford, vol. 2, Cairo, 73–6.

Grenier, J.-C. (1983) 'Ptolemee Evergete II et Cleopatra II d'apres les texts du temple de Tod', in *Alessandria el il Mondo ellenistico-romano: Studi in onori di A. Adriani I*, ed. A. Adriani, N. Bonacasa and A. Di Vita, Rome, 32–7.

Griffin, K., 'An analysis and interpretation of the iconography of the rekhyt on temple architecture in pharaonic Egypt', forthcoming dissertation, Swansea University.

Grimal, N. (1992) *A History of Ancient Queens*, Oxford.

Groenewegen-Frankfort, H. (1951) *Arrest and Movement: An Essay on Space and Time in the Representational Art of the Ancient Near East*, London.

Grzybek, E. (1990) *Du calendrier macédonien au calendrier ptolémaïque: problèmes de chronologie hellénistique*, Basel.

Gutzwiller, K. (2005) 'The literariness of the Milan Papyrus, or 'What difference a book?' in *The New Posidippus: A Hellenistic Poetry Book*, ed. K. Gutzwiller, New York, 287–319.

Hall, E. Swan (1986) *The Pharaoh Smites His Enemies: A Comparative Study*, MÄS 44, Munich.

Hanotte, O. *et al.* (2002) 'African pastoralism: genetic imprints of origins and migrations', *Science* 296 (5566), 336–9.

Hart, G. (2005) *The Routledge Dictionary of Egyptian Gods and Goddesses*, New York.

Hauben, H. (1970) *Callicrates of Samos. A Contribution to the Ptolemaic Admiralty*, Studia Hellenistica 18, Leuvense.

Havel, I. (1994) 'Scale dimension in nature', *International Journal of General System* 24, 295–324.

Hazzard, R. A. (2000) *Imagination of a Monarchy: Studies in Ptolemaic Propaganda*, Toronto.

Head, J. (2008) 'Introduction, a theory of changes', in *The Despotic Eye: An Illustration of Metabletic Phenomenology and its Implications*, ed. R. Romanyshyn, New York, 505–27.

Hedrick, Ch. (2000) *History and Silence: Purge and Rehabilitation of Memory in Late Antiquity*, Austin.

Heidegger, M. (1962) *Being and Time*, transl. J. Macquarrie and E. Robinson, London (*Sein und Zeit*, 1917).

Hodjash, S. and Berlev, O. (1982) *The Egyptian Reliefs and Stelae in the Pushkin Museum of Fine Arts, Moscow*, Leningrad.

Hoffman, M. (1984) *Egypt before the Pharaohs: The Prehistoric Foundations of Egyptian Civilization*, New York.

Hölbl, G. (2001) *A History of the Ptolemaic Empire*, London and New York (*Geschichte des Ptolemäerreiches*, Darmstadt, 1994).

Hornung, E. (1996) *Conceptions of God in Ancient Egypt: The One and the Many*, transl. J. Baines, New York (*Der Eine und die Vielen*, Darmstadt, 1971).

Houlihan, P. (1996) *The Animal World of the Pharaohs*, London.

Howard-Vise, R. W. and Perring, J. S. (1842) *Operations Carried on at the Pyramids of Gizeh in 1837: With an Account of a Voyage into Upper Egypt, and an Appendix*, London.

Hunter, R. (2003) *Encomium of Ptolemy Philadelphus*, Los Angeles and London.

Huss, W. (1998) 'Ptolemaios der Sohn', *ZPE* 121, 229–50.

Ippel, A. and Roeder, G. (1921) *Die Denkmäler des Pelizaeus-Museums zu Hildesheim*, Hildesheim.

Johnson, S. (1990) *The Cobra Goddess of Ancient Egypt: Predynastic, Early Dynastic, and Old Kingdom Periods*, London and New York.

Kamal, A. (1904–5) *Catalogue général des antiquités égyptiennes du muse du Caire*. Nos 22001–22208 – *steles ptolémaiques et romaines*, Cairo.

Karenga, M. (2004) *Maat, The Moral Ideal in Ancient Egypt: A Study in Classical African Ethics*, New York.

Kees, H. (1953) *Probleme der ägyptologie*, I: *Das Priestertum im ägyptischen Staat vom neuen Reich bis zur Spätzeit*, Leiden and Cologne.

Keightley, T. (1866) *The Mythology of Ancient Greece and Italy*, New York.

Kjelland, E. (1955) *Geometry in Egyptian Art*, London.

Kristeva, J. (1980) *Desire in Language: A Semiotic Approach to Literature and Art*, ed. L. S. Roudiez, transl. T. Gora, A. Jardine and L. S. Roudiez, New York.

Kurth, D. (ed.) (1990–) *Edfu*, vols I–VIII, Wiesbaden.

Kurth, D. (1996) 'Die Säulendekoration im Tempel von Edfu', *Studien zur Altägyptischen Kultur* 23, 255–80.

Kyrieleis, H. (1975) *Bildnisse der Ptolemäer*, Berlin.

Laufer, B. (1926) *Ostrich Egg-shell Cups of Mesopotamia and the Ostrich in Ancient and Modern Times*, Chicago.

Leclant, J. (1956) 'La "Mascerade" des boeufs gras et le triomphe de l'Égypte', *MDAIK* 14, 128–45.

Legon, J. (1992) 'A Kahun mathematical fragment', *Discussions in Egyptology* 24, 21–4.

Leprohon, R. (2001) 'Offerings: offering formulas and lists', in *OEAE*, ed. D. Redford, vol. 2, Oxford, 569–72.

Lesko, B. (1999) *The Great Goddesses of Egypt*, Norman.

Lesko, L. (1991) 'Ancient Egyptian cosmogonies and cosmology', in *Religion in Ancient Egypt: Gods, Myths, and Personal Practice*, ed. E. Shafer, Cornell, 88–122.

Liphocka, B. (1986) 'La statue d'Aphrodite sur les monnaies de Ptolémée III', in *Iconographie classique et identités régionales: [colloque international], Paris, 26 et 27 mai 1983*, ed. L. Kahil, C. Augé and P. Linant de Bellefond, Athens, 311–30.

Lorton, D. (1971) 'The supposed expedition of Ptolemy II to Persia', *JEA* 57, 160–64.

Louth, A. (2007) *Greek East and Latin West: The Church AD 681–1071*, New York.

Lucas, A. (2003) *Ancient Egyptian Materials and Industries*, Altrincham.

Lurker, M. (2002) *The Gods and Symbols of Ancient Egypt: An Illustrated Dictionary*, New York.

McKenzie, J. (2007) *The Architecture of Alexandria and Egypt c. 300 BC–A.D.700*, New Haven and London.

Macurdy, G. (1932) *Hellenistic Queens: A Study in Woman-Power in Macedon, Seleucid Syria and Ptolemaic Egypt*, Baltimore.

Maehler, H. (2003) 'Ptolemaic Queens with a triple uraeus', *CE* 78, 294–303.

Maehler, H. (2006) *Schrift, Text und Bild: kleine Schriften*, Munich and Leipzig.

Maehler, H. and Strocka, V. (eds) (1978) *Das ptolemäische Ägypten. Akten des internationalen Symposions 27.–29. September 1976 in Berlin*, Mainz am Rhein.

Mallet, D. (1909) *Le Kasr-el-Agouz*, MIFAO 11, Cairo.

Manchip White, J. E. (1970) *Ancient Egypt: Its Culture and History*, New York.

Mariette, A. (1869–80) *Dendérah: description générale du grand temple de cette ville*, vols I–V, Paris.

Mariette, A. (1879) *Monuments divers recueillis en Egypte et en Nubie*, Paris.

Massey, G. (2008 [1907]) *Ancient Egypt – The Light of the World: A Work of Reclamation and Restitution in Twelve Books*, London.

Matthews, R. and Roemer, C. (eds) (2003) *Ancient Perspectives of Egypt*, London.

Mattingly, H. (1950) 'Zephyritis', *AJA* 54, 126–8.

Meltzer, E. (2001) 'Horus', in *OEAE*, ed. D. Redford, vol. 2, Cairo, 119–22.

Meltzer, E. (2002) 'Horus', in *The Ancient Gods Speak: A Guide to Egyptian Religion*, ed. D. Redford, New York, 164–8.

Meskell, L. (2004) *Object Worlds in Ancient Egypt: Material Biographies Past and Present*, Oxford and New York.

Meulenaere, H. de (1965) 'De Stele van Mendes', *OG* 2, 53–65.

Meulenaere, H. de and MacKay, P. (1976) *Mendes*, II, Warminster.

Meyboom, P. (1994) *The Nile Mosaic of Palestrina: Early Evidence of Egyptian Religion in Italy*, Leiden, New York, Cologne, Brill.

Michaelidou-Nicolaou, I. (1976) *Prosopography of Ptolemaic Cyprus*, Göteborg.

Mikics, D. (2007) *A New Handbook of Literary Terms*, New Haven and London.

Milligan, G. (1927) *Selection from the Greek Papyri*, Cambridge.

Minas, M. (1994) 'Die Pithom-Stele. Chronologische Bemerkungen zur frühen Ptolemäerzeit', in *Aspekte Spätägyptische Kultur: Festschrift für Erich Winter zum 65. Geburtstag*, Aegyptiaca Treverensia 7, ed. M. Minas and J. Zeidler, Rhein am Meinz, 207–9.

Minas, M. (1995) 'Die Kanephoros: Aspekte des ptolemäischen Dynastiekults', in *Le culte du souverain dans l'Égypte ptolémaïque au IIIe siècle avant notre ère. Actes du colloque international, Bruxelles 10 mai 1995*, Studia Hellenistica 34, ed. H. Melaerts, Leuven.

Minas, M. (2000) *Die hieroglyphischen Ahnenreihen der ptolemäischen Könige: Ein Vergleich mit den Titeln der eponymen Priester in den demotischen und griechischen Papyri*, Aegyptiaca Treverensia: Trierer Studien zum griechischen-römischen Ägypten 9, Mainz am Rhein.

Mitford, T. (1950) *Opuscula Archaeologica IV*, Skrifter utgivna av svenska institutet i Rom XV, Rome.

Momigliano, A. (1993) *The Development of Greek Biography*, Cambridge, MA.

Mooren, L. (1975) *The Aulic Titulature in Ptolemaic Egypt: Introduction and Prosopography*, Verh. AWLSK 78, Brussels.

Morenz, L. (2004) *Bild-Buchstaben und symbolische Zeichen: Die Herausbildung der Schrift in der hohen Kultur Altägyptens*, Freiburg.

Moret, A. (1902) *Du Caractere Religieux de La Royaute Pharaonique*, Whitefish.

Morgan, L. (1985) 'Idea, idiom and iconography', in *L'iconographie minoenne. Actes de la table ronde d'Athenes, 21–22 avril 1983*, BCH, Suppl., 11, ed. P. Darcque and J.-P. Poursat, Athens, 5–19.

Mørkholm, O. (1991) *Early Hellenistic Coinage*, Cambridge.

Morkot, R. (2005) *The Egyptians: An Introduction*, New York.

Mueller, K. (2006) *Settlements of the Ptolemies: City Foundations and New Settlements in the Hellenistic World*, Leuven.

Murnane, W. J. (1977) *Ancient Egyptian Coregencies: An Aspect of the Transference of the Royal Power in Pharaonic Times*, Chicago.

Murphy, J. (2005) 'Beckett's Purgatories', in *Beckett, Joyce and the Art of the Negative*, ed. C. Jaurretche, New York, 109–24.

Murray, M. A. (with contributions by N. Boulton and C. Heron) (2000) 'Viticulture and wine production', in *Ancient Egyptian Materials and Technology*, ed. P. Nicholson and I. Shaw, Cambridge, 577–608.

Mysliwiec, K. (1988) *Royal Portraiture of the Dynasties XXI–XXX*, Mainz am Rhein.

Najovits, S. (2003) *Egypt, Trunk of the Tree: A Modern Survey of an Ancient Land*, vol. 1, New York.

Naville, E. (1885) *The Store-city of Pithom and the Route of Exodus*, London.

Naville, E. (1902) 'La stèle de Pithom', *ZÄS* 40, 66–75.

Neuffer, J. (1979) '"Ptolemy's Canon" debunked?' in *Andrews University Seminary Studies*, ed. K. A. Strand, XVII, No. 1, 39–46.

Nilsson, M. (2010) 'The crown of Arsinoë II. The creation and development of an imagery of authority', unpublished PhD thesis, Gothenburg University.

Nock, A. (1930) 'Synnaos Theos', *HSCPh* 41, 1–62.

Oates, J. (1964) 'Theoi Soteres', *EP* 8, 55.

Olson, C. (2000) *Zen and the Art of Postmodern Philosophy: Two Parts of Liberation from the Representational Mode of Thinking*, New York.

Olsson, V. (2006) *The Lenaia Vases Revistited: Image, Ritual and Dionysian Women*, Gothenburg.

O'Neill, J. (2003 [1897]) *Night of the Gods: An Inquiry into Cosmic and Cosmogonic Mythology and Symbolism*, part II, London.

Oppen, B. van (2007) 'The religious identification of Ptolemaic queens with Aphrodite, Demeter, Hathor and Isis', unpublished PhD thesis, New York.

Oppen, B. van (2010) 'The death of Arsinoe II Philadelphus: the evidence reconsidered', *Zeitschrift für Papyrologie und Epigraphik* 174, 139–50.

Osing, J. (1977) *Der Tempel Sethos' I. in Gurna. Die Reliefs und Inschriften*, I, AV 20, Mainz am Rhein.

Otto, E. (1960) *Das ägyptische Mundöffnungsritual*, ÄA 3, vols I–II, Wiesbaden.

Otto, E. (1964) *Gott und Mensch nach den ägyptischen Tempelinschriften der griechisch-römischen Zeit*, Heidelberg.

Otto, W. (1905–8) *Priester und Tempel im hellenistischen Ägypten*, I–II, Leipzig and Berlin.

Parente, A. (2002) 'Ritrattistica e simbologia sulle monete di Arsinoe II', *NumAntCl.* 31, 259–78.

Parisinou, E. (2005) 'Brightness personified, light and divine being in ancient Greece', in *Personification in the Greek World: From Antiquity to Byzantium*, ed. E. Stafford and J. Herrin, Aldershot, 29–44.

Peek, C. (2008) 'The expulsion of Cleopatra VII: context, causes, and chronology', *Anc. Soc.* 38, 103–36.

Peet, T. (1923) *The Rhind Mathematical Papyrus, British Museum 10057 and 10058*, London.

Peirce, C. S. (1870) *Description of a Notation for the Logic of Relatives, Resulting from an Amplification of the Conceptions of Boole's Calculus of Logic*, Cambridge, MA, 1870 (= *Memoirs of the American Academy of Arts and Sciences* 9, 317–78).

Peirce, C. S. (1883) *Studies in Logic by Members of the Johns Hopkins University* (SIL), Boston.

Peirce, C. S. (1983) *Foundations of Semiotics, Volume 1*, ed. A. Eschbach, Amsterdam.

Peirce, C. S. (1994) *Peirce on Signs: Writings on Semiotic*, ed. J. Hoopes, Chapel Hill.

Peirce, C. S. (1998) *Charles S. Peirce: The Essential Writings*, vol. 1–2, ed. E. Moore, New York.

Pereyra de Fidanza, M. V. (2003) 'The Amenirdis Stela in the Casa Padilla Museum', in *Egyptology at the Dawn of the Twenty-first Century*, Proceedings of the Eighth International Congress of Egyptologists, Cairo 2000, vol. 3, ed. Z. Hawass and L. Pinch Brock, Cairo, 360–67.

Perpillou-Thomas, F. (1993) *Fêtes d'Ègypte ptolémaïque et romaine d'après la documentation papyrologique grecque*, Studia Hellenistica 31, Leuven.

Perrot, G. and Chipiez, C. (1882) *De l'Art dans l'Antiquité*, I, Paris.

Pestman, P. W. (1967) *Chronologie égyptienne d'après les textes démotiques (332 av. J.-C.-453 ap. J.-C.)*, Leiden.

Petrie, F. (1883–4) *Tanis*, vols I–II, London.

Petrie, F. (1923) *Social Life in Ancient Egypt*, London.

Petrie, F. (1927) *Egyptian Hieroglyphs of the First and Second Dynasties*, London.

Petropoulou, M.-Z. (2008) *Animal Sacrifice in Ancient Greek Religion, Judaism, and Christianity, 100 BC to AD 200*, Oxford.

Phillips, J. (2009) 'Ostrich eggshell', in *UCLA Encyclopedia of Egyptology*, ed. W. Wendrich, Los Angeles.

Pinch, G. (2002) *Handbook of Egyptian Mythology*, Santa Barbara.

Pomeroy, S. B. (1984) *Women in Hellenistic Egypt from Alexander to Cleopatra*, New York.

Poo, M. (1995) *Wine and Wine Offering in the Religion of Ancient Egypt*, London.

Porter, B. and Moss, R. (1991–2009) *Topographical Bibliography of Ancient Egyptian Hieroglyphic Texts, Reliefs and Paintings*, ed. J. Malek, vols I–VII, Oxford.

Quaegebeur, J. (1971a) 'Ptolémée II en adoration devant Arsinoé II divinisée', *BIFAO* 69, 191–217.

Quaegebeur, J. (1971b) 'Documents concerning a cult of Arsinoe Philadelphos at Memphis', *JNES* 30, 239–70.

Quaegebeur, J. (1978) 'Reines ptolémaïques et traditions égyptiennes', in *Das ptolemäische Ägypten. Akten des internationalen Symposions 27.–29. September 1976 in Berlin*, ed. H. Maehler and V. Strocka, Mainz am Rhein, 245–62.

Quaegebeur, J. (1980) 'The genealogy of the Memphite high priest family in the Hellenistic period', in *Studies on Ptolemaic Memphis*, Studia Hellenistica 24, ed. W. Peremans, Leuven, 47–81.

Quaegebeur, J. (1985) 'Arsinoé Philadelphe, Reine, "Roi" et Déesse, a Hildesheim', *GM* 87, 73–8.

Quaegebeur, J. (1988) 'Cleopatra VII and the cult of the Ptolemaic queens', in *Cleopatra's Egypt: Age of the Ptolemies*, ed. R. Bianchi, Mainz am Rhein, 41–54.

Quaegebeur, J. (1989) 'Egyptian clergy and the Ptolemaic cult', *Anc. Soc.* 20, 93–113.

Quaegebeur, J. (1998) 'Documents égyptiens anciens et nouveaux relatifs à Arsinoé Philadelphe', in *Le culte du souverain dans l'Égypte ptolémaïque au IIIe siècle avant notre ère. Actes du colloque international, Bruxelles 10 mai 1995*, ed. H. Melaerts, Leuven.

Quibell, J. E. (1904) *Archaic Objects. Catalogue général des antiquités égyptiennes du Musée du Caire: nos. 11001–12000 et 14001–14754*, vol. II, Cairo.

Raven, M. (1983) 'Wax in Egyptian magic and symbolism', *OMRO* 64, 7–47.

Raven, M. (1998) 'A new type of Osiris burials', in *Egyptian Religion: The Last Thousand Years. Studies Dedicated to the Memory of Jan Quaegebeur*, ed. W. Clarysse, A. Schoors and H. Willems, part I, OLA 84, Leuven, 227–40.

Reden, S. von (2007) *Money in Ptolemaic Egypt: from the Macedonian Conquest to the end of the Third Century BC*, Cambridge.

Redford, D. (2002) *The Ancient Gods Speak: A Guide to Egyptian Religion*, Oxford.

Reed, J. (2000) 'Arsinoe's Adonis and the poetics of Ptolemaic imperialism', *Transactions of the American Philological Association* 130, 319–51.

Reisner, G. (1931) *Mycerinus: The Temples of the Third Pyramid at Giza*, Cambridge.

Revez, J. (2003) 'The metaphorical use of the kinship term sn "Brother"', *Journal of the American Research Centre in Egypt* 40, 123–31.

Robert, L. (1966) *Documents de l'Asie mineure méridionale. Inscriptions, monnaies et géographie*, Paris.

Roberts, A. (1997) *Hathor Rising: The Power of the Goddess in Ancient Egypt*, Rochester, Vermont.

Robins, G. (1993) *Women in Ancient Egypt*, Cambridge, MA.
Robins, G. (1999) 'The names of Hatshepsut as king', *JEA* 85, 103–12.
Robins, G. (2008) *The Art of Ancient Egypt*, Cambridge, MA.
Robins, G. and Fowler, A. S. (1994) *Proportion and Style in Ancient Egyptian Art*, Austin.
Robins, G. and Shute, C. (1987) *The Rhind Mathematical Papyrus: An Ancient Egyptian Text*. London.
Roeder, G. (1998) *Die ägyptische Götterwelt*, Düsseldorf and Zürich.
Rosenzweig, R. (2004) *Worshipping Aphrodite: Art and Cult in Classical Athens*, Ann Arbor, MI.
Rundle Clark, R. (1959) *Myth and Symbol in Ancient Egypt*, London.
Russmann, E. (1989) *Egyptian Sculpture: Cairo and Luxor*, Austin.
Ryholt, K. (1997) *The Political Situation in Egypt during the Second Intermediate Period c. 1800–1550 BC*, Copenhagen.
Sambin, C. and Carlotti, J.-F. (1995) 'Une porte de fete-sed de Ptolemee II remployee dans le temple de Medamoud', *BIFAO* 95, 383–457.
Samuel, A. (1962) *Ptolemaic Chronology*, Munich.
Sander-Hansen, C. E. (1940) *Das Gottesweib des Amun*, Copenhagen.
Sauneron, S. (1960) 'Un document égyptien relatif à la divinisation de la reine Arsinoé II', *BIFAO* 60, 83–110.
Sauneron, S. (2000) *The Priests of Ancient Egypt*, transl. D. Lorton, New York.
Saussure, F. de (1974) *Course in General Linguistics*, London (*Cours de linguistique générale*, 1916).
Saussure, F. de (2006) *Writings in General Linguistics*, transl. C. Sanders, Oxford (*Écrits de linguistique générale*, eds S. Bouquet and R. Engler, Paris, 2002).
Säve-Söderbergh, T. (1953) *On Egyptian Representations of Hippopotamus Hunting as a Religious Motive*, Horae Soederblomianae III, Uppsala.
Schäfer, H. (1974 [1919]) *Principles of Egyptian Art*, ed. E. Brunner-Traut and J. Baines, Oxford.
Schwaller de Lubicz, R. (1998) *The Temples of Karnak*, II, transl. D. Lawlor and R. Lawlor, Vermont (*Les temples de Karnak II*, Paris, 1982).
Serpico, M. and White, R. (2000) 'Oil, fat and wax', in *Ancient Egyptian Materials and Technology*, ed. P. Nicholson and I. Shaw, Cambridge, 390–429.
Sethe, K. (1904) *Hieroglyphische Urkunden der griechisch-römischen Zeit*, I–II, Leipzig.
Shaw, I. (2003) *Exploring Ancient Egypt*, Oxford and New York.
Silverman, D. (1991) 'Divinities and deities in ancient Egypt', in *Religion in Ancient Egypt: Gods, Myths, and Personal Practice*, ed. B. Shafer, Cornell, 7–87.
Simpson, S. (1996) *Demotic Grammar in the Ptolemaic Sacerdotal Decrees*, Oxford.
Smith, R. and Redford, D. (1976) *The Akhenaten Temple Project: Volume I Initial Discoveries*, Warminster.
Spalinger, A. (1998) 'The limitations of formal ancient egyptian religion', *JNES* 57, 241–60.
Spiegelberg, W. (1904) *Die Demotischen Inschriften*, Catalogue Général des Antiquités égyptiennes du Musée du Caire. *Die demotischen Denkmäler*, vol. I, Leipzig.
Stahlman, W. (2000) *Ptolemy's Handy Tables: The Astronomical Tables of Codex Vaticanus Graecus 1291*, New York.
Stanwick, P. (2002) *Portraits of the Ptolemies: Greek Kings as Egyptian Pharaohs*, Austin.
Stephens, S. (2004) 'For you Arsinoe...', in *Laboured in Papyrus Leaves: Perspectives on an Epigram Collection Attributed to Posidippus (P. Mil. Vogl. VIII 309)*, ed. B. Acosta-Hughes, M. Baumbach and E. Kosmetatou, Cambridge, MA, and London, 161–76.
Stephens, S. (2005) 'Battle of the books', in *The New Posidippus: A Hellenistic Poetry Book*, ed. K. Gutzwiller, Oxford and New York, 229–48.
Stockstad, E. (2002) 'Early cowboys herded cattle in Africa', *Science* 296, 236.
Struwe, W. (1930) *Mathematischer Papyrus des Staatlichen Museums der schönen Künste in Moskau*, Quellen und Studien zur Geschichte der Mathematik B. I.I, Berlin.
Sugi, A. (2000) 'Ankh: an archetype model for the semantics of iconography', in *Current Research in Egyptology*, BAR International Series 909, ed. A. McDonald and C. Riggs, Oxford, 103–10.
Sviatoslav, D. (2007) 'The last marriage and the death of Lysimachus', *GRBS* 47, 135–49.
Svoronos, J. N. (1904) *Ta Nomismata tou kratous ton Ptolemaion*, vol. 1, Athens.
Teeter, E. (1997) 'The life of ritual', in *Ancient Egypt*, ed. D. Silverman, London, 148–65.
Thiers, C. (2002–3) *Tôd: Les Inscriptions du temple ptolémaique et romain*, vols II–III, Cairo.
Thompson, D. Burr (1973) *Ptolemaic Oinochoai and Portraits in Faience: Aspects of the Ruler-Cult*, Oxford.
Thompson, D. J. (1988) *Memphis under the Ptolemies*, Princeton.
Tobin, V. (2002) 'Amun and Amun-Re', in *The Ancient Gods Speak: A Guide to Egyptian Religion*, ed. D. Redford, New York, 18–21.
Tomoum, N. (2005) *The Sculptors' Models of the Late and Ptolemaic Periods: A Study of the Type and Function of a Group of Ancient Egyptian Artefacts*, Cairo.
Török, L. (2009) *Between Two Worlds: The Frontier Region between Ancient Nubia and Egypt 3700 BC–500 AD*, Leiden.
Troxell, H. (1983) 'Arsinoë's non-era', *American Numismatic Society Museum Notes* 28, 60–62.
Troy, L. (1986) *Patterns of Queenship in Ancient Egyptian Myth and History*, BOREAS 14, Uppsala.
Troy, L. (2003) 'She for whom all that is said is done: the ancient Egyptian queen', in *Ancient Queens: Archaeological Explorations*, ed. S. M. Nelson, Walnut Creek and Oxford, 93–116.
Tyldesley, J. (2006) *Chronicle of the Queens of Egypt: From Early Dynastic Times to the Death of Cleopatra*, Cairo and London.
Uphill, E. (1965) 'The Egyptian Sed-festival rites', *JNES* 24, 365–83.
Vallois, R. (1929) 'Le temple d'Arsinoé Philadelphos ou d'Agathè Tyche', *CRAI*, 32–40.
Varner, E. (2004) *Mutilation and Transformation: Damnatio Memoria and Roman Imperial Portraiture*, Leiden.
Vassilika, E. (1989) *Ptolemaic Philae*, Leuven.

Vassilika, E. (1998) 'The pronaos decoration of the temple of Horus at Edfu', in *Egyptian Religion: The Last Thousand Years. Studies Dedicated to the Memory of Jan Quaegebeur*, ed. W. Clarysse, A. Schoors and H. Willems, part II, OLA 85, Leuven, 937–60.

Vischak, D. (2002) 'Hathor', in *Ancient Gods Speak: A Guide to Egyptian Religion*, ed. D. Redford, New York, 157–61.

Wace, A., Megaw, A. and Skeat, T. (1959) *Hermoupolis Magna, Ashmunein, the Ptolemaic Sanctuary and the Basilica*, Alexandria.

Walker, S. and Higgs, P. (eds) (2001) *Cleopatra's Egypt: From History to Myth*, London.

Walsem, R. van (2005) *Iconography of Old Kingdom Elite Tombs: Analysis and Interpretation, Theoretical and Methodological Aspects*, Leiden.

Warner, M. and Fernández-Armesto, F. (2003) *World of Myths*, Texas.

Westendorf, W. (1978) 'Uräus und Sonnenscheibe', *SAK* 6, 201–25.

Wilkinson, J. G. (1837) *Manners and Customs of the Ancient Egyptians*, vol. III, London.

Wilkinson, R. (1994) *Symbol and Magic in Egyptian Art*, London.

Winnicki, K. (1990) 'Bericht vom einem Eeldzug des Ptolemaios Philadelphos in der *Pithom*-Stele', *JJP* 20, 157–67.

Winter, E. (1978) 'Der Herrscherkult in den ägyptischen Ptolemäertempeln', in *Das ptolemäische Ägypten. Akten des internationalen Symposions 27.–29. September 1976 in Berlin*, ed. H. Maehler and V. Strocka, Mainz am Rhein, 147–60.

Witt, R. (1997) *Isis in the Ancient World*, London (*Isis in the Graeco-Roman World*, New York, 1971).

Witwowski, S. (1911) *Epistolae privatae Graecae, quae in papyri aetatis Lagidarum servantur*, Lipsiae.

Wolohojian, S. (ed.) (2008) *Harvard Art Museum/Handbook*, exh. cat., Cambridge, MA.

Young, D. (1981) 'A monastic invective against Egyptian hieroglyphs', in *Studies Presented to Hans Jakob Polotsky*, ed. D. Young, Beacon Hill, 348–60.

Yoyotte, J. (1996) *L'egypte du delta: les capitales du Nord*, Dossiers d'Archeologie 213, Dijon.

Žabkar, L. (1988) *Hymns to Isis in her Temple at Philae*, Hannover.

Digital sources

Hieroglyphica: Hieroglyphica Project, Hieroglyphic Database at http://www.hieroglyphica.com/ Accessed 30 December 2011.

http://www.continentalfeathers.com/images/ostrichwingblackbig.jpg Accessed 30 December 2011.

http://www.friendsofjamaicapond.org/images/EmeraldBird/GreatHornedOwls/GooseFeather5463s.jpg Accessed 30 December 2011.

http://www.metmuseum.org/learn/for%20educators/publications%20for%20educators/the%20art%20of%20ancient%20egypt Accessed 23 January 2012.

http://www.thefreedictionary.com/isocephaly Accessed 30 December 2011.

http://www.themodernapprentice.com/feathers.htm Accessed 30 December 2011.

http://www.tyndalehouse.com/egypt/index.htm Accessed 23 January 2012.

Jsesh: JSesh Hieroglyphic Database at http://jsesh.qenherkhopeshef.org/ Accessed 30 December 2011.

SERAT: Serat Datenbank at http://www.serat.aegyptologie.uni-wuerzburg.de/ Accessed 30 December 2011.

Index

In the index **bold** denotes discussion of the item indexed. Fig. refers to figure number.